W9-CRA-405

SIXTH EDITION

COLLEGE ENGLISH AND COMMUNICATION

KENNETH ZIMMER, Ed.D.
Professor Emeritus of
Business Education and
Office Administration
School of Business and Economics
California State University
Los Angeles, California

SUE C. CAMP, Ed.D.
Associate Professor of
Business Administration
Broyhill School of Management
Gardner-Webb College
Boiling Springs, North Carolina

GLENCOE

Macmillan/McGraw-Hill

New York, New York   Columbus, Ohio   Mission Hills, California   Peoria, Illinois

COLLEGE ENGLISH AND COMMUNICATION, SIXTH EDITION
Instructor's Annotated Edition

Send all inquiries to:
GLENCOE DIVISION
Macmillan/McGraw-Hill
936 Eastwind Drive
Westerville, OH 43081

ISBN 0–02–803016–8

Printed in the United States of America.

2 3 4 5 6 7 8 9   RRD-C   99 98 97 96 95 94 93 92

College English and Communication, Sixth Edition

College English and Communication is an educational program designed for college-level business communication courses. The nine-part program includes a student's text, a student's activities workbook, a student's case study booklet, an instructor's edition of the text, an instructor's edition of the workbook, a set of transparency masters, a printed test bank, a microcomputer test bank, and an English skills practice set on microcomputer disk.

- *College English and Communication, Sixth Edition,* is a 592-page text that provides students with the knowledge and skills that they will need for effective communication in business.
- *Activities for College English and Communication* offers an array of carefully planned activities to reinforce and enrich students' learning of the text principles.
- The *Instructor's Edition* of the text provides a complete student textbook with additional resources including:
  1. Short teaching suggestions in the margin of the student page to which they apply.
  2. Short answer keys in the margin of the student page adjacent to the exercises.
  3. Specific goals that students should achieve after completing each section.
  4. Brief chapter summaries and section overviews.
  5. Additional teaching suggestions and additional exercise keys.
  6. An explanation of the supplementary materials that accompany this program.
  7. Suggested time schedules.
- *Case Studies for Critical Thinking* simulates business situations in which the student assumes the role of a typical business worker.
- The *Instructor's Edition* of the activities workbook provides a complete facsimile key of the student activities.
- A set of transparency masters highlights communication principles and illustrates important concepts presented in the text.
- A microcomputer test bank for the IBM PC gives instructors the opportunity to make up their own

tests using preprogrammed questions or questions of their own.

Together, the *College English and Communication* text, the *Activities for College English and Communication* workbook, the instructor's editions of both text and workbook, the *Case Studies for Critical Thinking* booklet, the transparency masters, the English skills practice set, the printed test bank, and the microcomputer test bank provide a comprehensive course in business communication.

ESTABLISHING GOALS

Students do better when they know what is expected of them; therefore, the instructor should discuss course objectives with students. Goals, such as those that follow, should be given to the students at the first class session.

Students who complete this course should be able to:

1. Use words precisely and imaginatively.
2. Recognize spelling pitfalls.
3. Write letters that sell a good or service or that promote goodwill.
4. Prepare a résumé and a letter of application that will be effective in getting a job.
5. Write memorandums, reports, news releases, minutes, and telecommunications correctly, clearly, and concisely.
6. Arrange the parts of letters, memorandums, and other business communications in their proper order, so that the communications are visually appealing and easy to read.
7. Speak correctly, tactfully, and convincingly, whether addressing an audience or speaking to telephone callers, visitors, employers, coworkers, or others.
8. Listen attentively, comprehend oral communications fully, and participate effectively in oral discussion.

Program Overview

CEC TEXT, STUDENT EDITION

Chapter Opener
  • Chapter Outline
Section Opener
  • Performance Objectives
Instructional Material
  • Text
  • Memory Hooks
  • Checkups (answers at end of text)
Margin Features
  • Living Language
  • Language Lapse
  • World View
  • Language Tip
  • Study Tip
Section Review
  • Practical Application
  • Editing Practice
  • Critical Thinking Skills (selected chapters)
Appendix
Index

CEC TEXT, INSTRUCTOR'S ANNOTATED EDITION

Instructor's Manual
  • Introduction to the Program
  • Section-by-Section Guide
    —Chapter Introduction
    —Section Objectives
    —Section Teaching Suggestions
    —Section Answer Keys (if needed)
Annotated Text
  • Checkups (answers shown on text page)
  • Margin Annotations
    —Key Point
    —Suggestion
    —Reinforcement
    —Information
    —Cross-Reference
    —Critical Thinking
    —Global Note
  • Answer Keys
    —Short Answers (shown on text page)
    —Long Answers (shown in instructor's manual
      with page reference in text)

ACTIVITIES WORKBOOK (SE)

  • Section-by-Section Coverage:
    —Skill-Building Exercises
    —Reinforcement Exercises
    —Additional Practice Exercises
    —Challenge Exercises
    —Document Applications

ACTIVITIES WORKBOOK (IAE)

  • Reduced student pages with answers overprinted
    in a second color.

EVALUATION MATERIALS

Text Materials

  • Checkups
    —Immediate reinforcement
      within selected sections
  • Section Review
    —Practical Application
    —Editing Practice
    —Critical Thinking Skills
      (selected chapters)

Printed Test Bank

  • 1,000 test items grouped by
    section from which instructors
    may assemble quizzes, tests,
    and examinations.

Microcomputer Test Bank

  • Software version of the
    printed test bank.
  • Instructors can add their own
    items.
  • Instructors can select items or
    can request computer selec-
    tion and assembly.

ADDITIONAL RESOURCES

Case Studies Booklet

  • A series of 55 practical
    applications of communication
    skills in a variety of business
    settings.
  • Issues include personnel
    matters; interpersonal
    relationships; decision making
    and critical thinking skills;
    business ethics, and
    international applications.

Transparency Masters

  • A series of 50 masters includ-
    ing model documents, key
    points, content reviews.

**Microcomputer Data Disk:
English Skills Practice Set**

  • Sentence Items*
  • Paragraph Items*
  • Document Applications**
  *Skill coverage restricted to current
  section
  **Skill coverage cumulative

9. Read rapidly and comprehend what is read.
10. Apply psychological principles to written and oral communications.

Learning objectives appear at the beginning of each section of the text; more specific goals for each section are provided, along with an overview, teaching suggestions, and additional exercise keys, on pages I-6 through I-62.

MOTIVATING STUDENTS

The instructor must make sure that students understand the importance of developing effective communication skills. Students will be more highly motivated if they see how business communication is related to their future careers. The instructor should stress that *every* business employee must use his or her communication skills in the workplace, regardless of the specific job. When students understand that communication skills are required of *all* business employees, they have an incentive for applying themselves to this course. Invariably, the men and women who succeed in their business careers are those who excel in using the language arts.

THE ROLE OF THE TEXT

To attain the far-reaching goals of this course, students will need a comprehensive communication program that goes beyond the basics of letter writing. Students will also need a text that offers a total communication program. *College English and Communication* discusses the theory of communication and also offers practical business applications of the text principles.

Memory Hooks

Several sections include brief, easy-to-remember clues to help students analyze and memorize some of the points being taught. These are called "Memory Hooks."

Marginal Features

New to the sixth edition are 95 marginal features that reinforce, augment, or illustrate material presented in the text.

Language Tips. Language Tips present concise, often pithy advice from eminent grammarians, lexicographers, and other commentators.

Living Language. Living Language selections provide vivid illustrations of effective grammar, usage, and style. They include excerpts from nonfiction and literature and memorable quotations from authors, celebrities, and personalities in various professions.

Study Tips. As the name implies, Study Tips offer suggestions on how to remember various rules and how to apply learning principles to students' study patterns.

Language Lapses. Language Lapses give students an opportunity to hone their ability to detect and correct errors in written communications. A corrected version of each incorrect writing sample appears below the feature for immediate reinforcement.

World View: Global Notes address some of the international issues important in today's business and communication. They offer students tips on some of the special situations that arise in dealing with people around the world who may speak different languages and have business customs unlike our own.

Checkups

Brief sequences of exercises are interspersed throughout many sections to give students immediate practice in applying the principles just presented in the text. Checkups are especially appropriate for classroom use; answers appear beside the exercises in the margin of the instructor's edition. Answers to Checkups are also included at the back of the student text.

Section Reviews

The Section Reviews appear at the end of each section and provide students with essential practice. Only through such practice can students truly master the principles of communication taught in the text.

Practical Application. Practical Application exercises at the beginning of each Section Review may be assigned as homework or used as in-class practice or test materials. Each set of Practical Applications provides students with sufficient material to reinforce the principles they have learned in each section. Throughout most of Chapter 2 and all of Chapter 3, the material in Practical Application B is cumulative —

rather than applying only to the preceding section — to reinforce earlier learning.

Editing Practice. Editing and proofreading are skills that one must acquire in order to write masterful business communications. Although two sections of the text are devoted specifically to proofreading and editing, each Section Review includes one or more Editing Practice exercises to build students' proofreading and editing skills. These Editing Practice activities help students expand their vocabularies, reinforce their spelling knowledge, distinguish between confusing pairs of words, test their knowledge of plurals and possessives, eliminate redundancies, and rewrite paragraphs effectively.

Critical Thinking Skills. Critical Thinking Skills assignments conclude Section Reviews in Chapters 1, 10, and 11. These tasks, stated in terms of the Bloom taxonomy, help train students to comprehend, analyze, synthesize, and evaluate information and to apply their knowledge to problems and everyday work situations.

THE ROLE OF THE INSTRUCTOR'S EDITION

The *Instructor's Annotated Edition of College English and Communication, Sixth Edition*, offers the instructor an expanded package of varied resources. Its aim is to help the instructor ensure that students will be proficient and effective business communicators after they have completed this course.

The *Instructor's Annotated Edition* includes the complete student textbook. The text is amplified by marginal teaching suggestions on the student pages to which they apply and marginal short-answer keys adjacent to the exercises.

In addition, this special instructor's section includes many other valuable resources. It describes the nine components of the *College English and Communication* program, explains the supplementary materials that accompany this program, and offers suggested time schedules for covering the material in the student text, as well as selected references relevant to this communication course.

The instructor's section also presents a general overview of each text chapter followed by an extensive examination of the sections in the chapter. This section-by-section coverage begins with objectives, a list of goals more specific than those shown in the student text. Next, there is an overview of the specific topic of

the section. This is followed by teaching suggestions, which may reinforce and expand upon the suggestions in the margins of the student pages in the *Instructor's Annotated Edition* or offer additional ideas for stimulating student learning and performance. Finally, exercise keys for long-answer assignments are included for all appropriate sections of the text.

ADDITIONAL PRACTICE MATERIALS

Activities Workbook

Carefully planned exercises are provided in *Activities for College English and Communication, Sixth Edition.* Each section offers skill-building and reinforcement exercises that enable the instructor to provide additional practice for slower learners, to reinforce the skills of average students, and to challenge the expertise of brighter students.

CASE STUDIES BOOKLET

Case Studies for Critical Thinking augments the text by simulating 55 business situations in which the student assumes the role of a typical business worker. Most of the case studies deal with common but awkward human relations situations that all business employees encounter; for example, dealing with a supervisor's grammatical errors, being asked for confidential information, working for more than one supervisor, and so on.

TRANSPARENCY MASTERS

The transparency masters for *Business English and Communication, Sixth Edition*, have been designed to reinforce or supplement key principles and concepts presented in the text. By visually highlighting and reinforcing important communication precepts, the transparencies are yet one more aid to student learning.

TEST MATERIALS

Printed Test Bank

A separate printed test bank provides instructors with test items, grouped by section, that can be used for quizzes, tests, and examinations.

Microcomputer Test Bank

Additional tests are available on a microcomputer test bank for the IBM PC. Instructors can print pre-programmed tests, assemble unique tests from pre-programmed questions, and add questions of their own.

Using the Tests

Tests should, of course, measure students' growth, but tests should also provide a learning experience for students. Instruct students to analyze their incorrect answers by asking themselves the following questions:

1. *What is my error?* The student must first identify the error.
2. *Why did I make this error?* Whatever the reason for the error, understanding the reason should help the student to avoid repeating the error. For example, if the student misunderstood the test instructions, then he or she should review the text section on developing reading skills.
3. *What is the correct answer?* If the student merely forgot the correct answer, then this error analysis should reinforce his or her knowledge. If the student does not understand why it is the correct answer, then he or she should review the appropriate text section.
4. *How can I remember this principle in the future?* The student must make a concentrated effort to understand the principle by carefully reviewing it in the textbook. The student should memorize any rule or rules that apply to the principle or should create his or her own mnemonic device to ensure retention.

TIME SCHEDULES

College English and Communi... ...h Edition, is designed primarily for a two... ...se of 16 weeks each semester (3 day... ...quarter course of 12 weeks each... ...eek). A minimum of 96 hours i... ...cover the 55 sections of the text... ...e two class sessions; however, th... ...oility for the instructor who mus... ...o meet specific needs.

In a course th... ...r to 16 weeks, the instructor mus... ...ough all the topics presented in... ...to the success of the future busi... ...structor may have to omit certa... ...mple, if students are re-quired t... ...ech course, the instructor may de... ...apter on oral communica-tion... ...st shows that relatively few stud... ...nal instruction in grammar or if... ...course is communication, the in... ...e to cover language structure in... ...nents or to review language struc-... ...ions on writing techniques are pre-

...ne limitations may be, however, even ...course in communication should cover ...g chapters of the text:

...ter 1 Understanding Communication
...apter 5 Sharpening Writing Skill
...apter 7 Writing Memorandums
Chapter 8 Writing Business Letters
Chapter 9 Preparing Reports and Special Communications
Chapter 11 Communicating for Job Results

Goals, Additional Teaching Suggestions, and Exercise Keys by Section

CHAPTER 1
UNDERSTANDING COMMUNICATION

Communication — both verbal and nonverbal — is the exchange of messages. Ideally, the sender's intended message is identical to the actual message sent and to the receiver's interpretation of it. Succeeding in business, as in all other aspects of life, requires good communication skills. To the skills of listening, speaking, reading, and writing, business communicators must add interpersonal skill, or the willingness to consider the needs and feelings of others. All the chapters that follow this one help students better understand and sharpen their skills in these five areas.

Section 1.1   Effective Communication in Everday Living

Objectives

After completing Section 1.1, the student should be able to:

1. Define communication.
2. Contrast communication that informs and communication that attempts to persuade.
3. Distinguish between verbal and nonverbal information.
4. Describe the five components of communication.
5. Demonstrate how feedback can be used to avoid breakdowns in face-to-face communication.
6. Explain how an understanding of the factors that influence communication can lead to successful communication.
7. Describe the effect of interpersonal skills and human relations techniques on communication skills.

Overview

Effective communication — both verbal and nonverbal — can positively affect all human relationships. Miscommunication can have the opposite effect. This introductory section defines communication, describes the purposes and components of communication, and explains how interpersonal skills affect communication skills. Good communication skills, in turn, can be the key to a successful business future.

Teaching Suggestions

Make students aware that as business people, they will be expected to communicate facts, ideas, opinions, and instructions.

Role-playing situations of stress or conflict is a good way of showing students the importance of maintaining good interpersonal skills in a business setting. Understanding the needs of message receivers and practicing human relations techniques can improve students' communication skills.

Exercise Keys

Note: *Wherever possible, solutions to text exercises appear in the left margin of the text page where the exercises occur. Some exercises, however, require longer solutions. These include writing memos and letters as well as other exercises where the answers are too long to fit in the margin. The solutions to these exercises appear at the end of the instructor's notes for the particular section. The answers are clearly keyed to the exercise and page to which they refer.*

Practical Application (page 8)

A. Communication is the exchange of messages. Four main purposes: to inquire, to inform, to persuade, to develop goodwill.

B. Verbal communication uses words to exchange spoken and written messages; nonverbal communication is communication without words, such as gestures, facial expressions, and body movements. (Combining verbal and nonverbal makes communication more effective.)

C.

1. Background of the receiver — knowledge, personality, related experiences, plus interest and motivation.

2. Communicator or communication appearance — a neat appearance encourages a positive response. A poor appearance can do the opposite.
3. Communication skills of sender and receiver — the degree of speaking, writing, listening, and reading skills determines the effectiveness of the message exchange.
4. Distractions — physical or mental factors that draw the receiver's attention away from the message.

D. Determining the needs and circumstances of the person or group receiving your communication; deciding what would motivate the receiver to respond favorably; empathizing; demonstrating a positive attitude; being a good listener; being considerate of others.

Section 1.2 The Communication Skills: Listening, Speaking, Reading, and Writing

Objectives

After completing Section 1.2, the student should be able to:

1. Explain the concept of pairing in terms of communicators and of communication skills.
2. Describe how each of the four communication skills affects a person's personal life, education, and work.
3. Explain how listening is reinforced by speaking, reading, and writing.
4. Discuss how speaking is strengthened by listening, reading, and writing.
5. Give specific examples of how reading is affected by listening, speaking, and writing.
6. Describe a recent situation in which one's writing was improved by earlier listening, speaking, and reading.

Overview

This section reiterates the fact that communication is always a two-way process between sender and receiver; both sides are responsible for the success of that process. Listening, speaking, reading, and writing reinforce and strengthen one another. While these four communication skills are important in all aspects of life, including those involving family, friends, and school, communication skills are crucial to success in the business world.

Teaching Suggestions

Inform students that although two communication skills may seem to predominate in certain life situations, all four skills usually play a part. Have students recount a recent experience or conversation in which the four communication skills were used. To get students started, give them a simple example such as the following. One student (speaking) asked another (listening) whether she wanted to go to a certain movie. She said no because she had read a negative review of it written by her favorite movie critic.

Exercise Keys

Practical Application (page 13)

A. Communication is a two-way process with a sender and a receiver. Some communication skills involve sending messages and some involve receiving messages. Every speaker (sender) needs a listener (receiver); every writer (sender) needs a reader (receiver).

B.
1. Talking (to offer advice and understanding)
2. Reading (to research the subject), writing (notes to use in making the speech)
3. Reading (background information), talking (asking for opinions), listening (to hear answers)
4. Writing (taking notes)
5. Writing (taking notes)

Editing Practice (page 13)

Errors are underscored.

Conversation, sending, corrected, specifications, installation, communication system, thermostat, relocated, upstairs, revised, properly, stationery, later, than, October.

Section 1.3 Language and Communication Skills in Business

Objectives

After completing Section 1.3, the student should be able to:

1. Name three ways that good communication contributes to a company's success.
2. Discuss the differences and similarities between the business goals of external communication and internal communication.

3. Define tone as it applies to communication, and describe how tone is achieved.
4. Name several types of written communication used within a company and several types used for those outside the company.
5. Describe five ways to overcome listening blocks.
6. List five questions that sensitive communicators ask themselves about their communications.

Overview

No matter how superior a company's goods or services may be, that company may not be successful if its employees do not communicate well both with others in the company and with suppliers and customers outside the company. Good communication results in a company's efficient operation, team spirit, and shared goals.

Technological advances such as electronic mail, electronic storage, and sophisticated information systems have increased productivity and the speed and efficiency of information transmission. As a result, workers are communicating more information, and good language and communication skills in the workplace are more important than ever.

Teaching Suggestions

Point out to students that they will be taking the first step toward job success by understanding the role of good communication in business, the requirements of effective internal and external communications, and the importance of displaying sensitivity in their listening, speaking, reading, and writing. In succeeding chapters students will learn how to fulfill the role of good business communicators, how to satisfy the requirements of internal and external communications, and how to sharpen their language and communication skills.

Exercise Keys

Practical Application (page 19)

A. Internal communication is the transfer of information between persons on different levels and from different departments within a company. External communication is the transfer of information to people outside a company.

B. The four skills needed to communicate effectively in business are writing, speaking, listening, and reading. (Examples will vary.)

C. Sensitive writers and speakers always consider the concerns and needs of their audiences, and sensitive listeners and readers try to eliminate listening blocks and reading distractions.

Editing Practice (page 19)

Possible answers:

1. Your shirt (catalog #456-861) will be shipped just as soon as the enclosed postage-paid card is returned to us. On that card, please indicate what color shirt you want.
2. In our recent sales campaign, we sold 6,000 CD players. Because we want 6,000 — not 5,999 — satisfied customers, we have shipped you a new CD player.
3. The terms of our contract offered a discount if payment was received within 10 days. Because the discount was inadvertently taken after 30 days, we would appreciate your sending us the $50 balance.

CHAPTER 2
EXPANDING LANGUAGE SKILLS

The basis of all effective communication is a solid grounding in English grammar. The many thousands of words in our language can be divided into just eight parts of speech: nouns, pronouns, verbs, adjectives, adverbs, prepositions, conjunctions, and interjections. These constitute the building blocks of language. When correctly and skillfully combined, they permit us to transmit and receive virtually any message we can imagine.

Section 2.1   Language Structure

Objectives

After completing Section 2.1, the student should be able to:

1. Identify nouns, pronouns, verbs, adjectives, adverbs, prepositions, conjunctions, and interjections in sentences.
2. Identify subjects and predicates of sentences.
3. Identify clauses and label them as dependent or independent.
4. Identify prepositional, infinitive, and verb phrases.

5. Distinguish between complete sentences and sentence fragments.
6. Distinguish between singular and plural subjects.
7. Identify simple subjects and compound subjects.
8. Rewrite inverted sentences in normal sentence order.

Overview

This section establishes the broad framework of language that students must use to climb higher in their quest for mastery. Section 2.1 describes — briefly but clearly — the eight parts of speech and discusses subjects and predicates, phrases, clauses, and sentences. Although our goal here is *not* to master the terminology of grammar, we must understand some basic terms in order to understand language structure itself.

Teaching Suggestions

Stress that nouns and pronouns are interchangeable by asking students to substitute nouns for pronouns in text sentences — and vice versa. After students have completed Checkup 2, test their skills at identifying verbs by having them supply verbs after each pronoun in the following chart:

I _____   we _____

you _____   you _____

he _____ ⎫
she _____ ⎬   they _____
it _____   ⎭

Every correct choice will reinforce the use of verbs as action words. Emphasize that using this chart provides a nearly foolproof method of testing whether a word is really a verb.

Adjectives are generally easy for students to understand. Again, ask students to substitute adjectives for each example given in the text. Use sentence pairs such as the following to stress the difference between adjectives and adverbs.

Joel prepares _____ reports.
Joel prepares reports _____.

If writers cannot identify prepositions and prepositional phrases, they usually will have difficulty making subjects and verbs agree. Ask students to make up sentences with prepositional phrases to ensure that they do understand their use.

Understanding conjunction use will help students improve their writing skill. Ask students to develop sentences showing how conjunctions join words, phrases, and clauses. Interjections are not as important in business writing, but they are included in an effort to provide a thorough backdrop for students.

The text sentences provided enable students to easily identify subjects and predicates and clauses and phrases. Make sure that students understand the difference between clauses and phrases — and especially the difference between independent and dependent clauses.

Students' understanding of the sentence is critical to their writing ability. Stress the basic premise that *a sentence is a complete thought.* As they analyze sentences, students may ask why our standard one-word answers such as "No" and "Yes" are often accepted as complete sentences. Explain that such answers are really shortcuts. For example, let's look at the question "Do you want to go to the movies?" The answer "Yes" really is a short way of saying, "Yes, I do want to go to the movies." Because we understand the complete answer without having to repeat every word, the one-word answer "Yes" is indeed a complete sentence (it expresses a complete thought).

Use the text key to help students find complete subjects, unravel inverted sentences, identify simple and compound subjects, and so on.

Spend extra time reviewing students' answers to the end-of-section exercises so that they will feel comfortable with their skill in identifying the eight parts of speech, subjects and predicates, clauses, phrases, and sentences.

Exercise Keys

Practical Application (page 35)

C. Complete subjects are underscored, clearly showing which sentences are inverted and which are normal. For each sentence, the simple or compound subject is given below.

1. Mr. and Mrs. Messineo (compound)
2. agent (simple)
3. South Shore Bank (simple)
4. houses (simple)
5. cottage and pool (compound)
6. Jackie Messineo (simple)
7. assistants (simple)

8. suppliers and customers (compound)
9. Dom Messineo (simple)
10. children and pets (compound)

D. Complete subjects are underscored, clearly showing which sentences are inverted and which are normal. For each sentence, the simple or compound subject is given below. For each fragment, possible responses are given in parentheses.

1. decision (simple)
2. fragment (As soon as we receive the auditor's report, we will send you a copy.)
3. fragment (The two people in the accounting department who do that work are on vacation.)
4. vendors and buyers (compound)
5. you (simple)
6. drawings and photographs (compound)
7. fragment (Although this accounting system was in effect between 1962 and 1991, we do not have those records in our files.)
8. they (simple)
9. files (simple)
10. fragment (Until Mr. Nicholson agrees to the reorganization plan that you submitted last April, we cannot hire any new employees.)

Section 2.2 Verbs

Objectives

After completing Section 2.2, the student should be able to:

1. Identify verbs and verb phrases in sentences, including sentences in inverted order.
2. Distinguish between the helping verb and the main verb in a verb phrase.
3. Given the present tense of a regular verb, form the past tense, the past participle, and the present participle.
4. Given various tense forms of regular verbs, write sentences using the verbs correctly.
5. Given the present tense of 50 commonly used irregular verbs, form the past tense, the past participle, and the present participle.
6. Identify all forms of the verb *to be*.
7. Distinguish between transitive and intransitive verbs; identify the objects of transitive verbs.
8. Given the present tense, form the past tense, the past participle, and the present participle of *lie*, *lay*, *sit*, *set*, *rise*, and *raise*.

Overview

This section teaches students the standard pattern for forming the different tenses of most verbs — or what we call regular verbs. Unlike regular verbs, irregular verbs exhibit no one pattern that will solve the usage problems surrounding them. Therefore, Section 2.2 also presents students with a list of the principal parts of the most commonly used irregular verbs, which must be memorized. Special emphasis is given to "being" verbs and the significance of transitive and intransitive verbs.

Teaching Suggestions

The "regular verb pattern" is so strongly established at an early age that toddlers, for example, will say "broked" instead of "broken" or "eated" instead of "eaten" as they force these irregular verbs into the pattern for regular verbs. Stressing the simplicity of forming tenses for *most* verbs will create an incentive for students to master the pattern.

As suggested in the text, delay discussion of the verb *to be* until students have mastered the standard pattern for forming the different tenses of regular verbs. Then spend extra time on the "being" verbs to make sure that students can form all parts of the verb *to be* and use the verb correctly in their writing and speaking.

The verbs *lie*, *lay*, *sit*, *set*, *rise*, and *raise* also deserve extra attention — especially *lie* and *lay*. Certain forms of *lie* and *lay* are so seldom used correctly that the right choices will sound wrong to students! As suggested in the marginal annotation, be sure that students understand the logic behind the rule for identifying transitive verbs.

Emphasize correcting common illiteracies such as "I been," "she seen," and "he don't," which unfortunately are reinforced through television, movies, and popular songs to the extent that they, too, "sound right" to many students.

Use text examples to dramatize how verbs show us the time of action. Be careful, however, not to allow all the many different terms to trap students. It is their ability in *using* verbs correctly, not their skills at *labeling* verbs properly, that is important here.

Exercise Keys

Answers to all exercises in this section appear as marginal notes next to the exercises.

Section 2.3 Nouns: Plural Forms

Objectives

After completing Section 2.3, the student should be able to:

1. Form the correct plurals of common, proper, and compound nouns.
2. Form the correct plurals of courtesy titles used with proper names.
3. Form the correct plurals of some commonly used irregular nouns, such as *woman* and *child*.
4. Form the correct plurals of nouns ending in *o*, *f*, or *fe*.
5. Form the correct plurals of nouns of foreign origin (including both the English and the foreign form for those nouns that have two different plural forms).
6. Correct errors in the use of all the above plural forms.

Overview

For most students, this section should simply be a review. The rules here are rather easy and straightforward, except for the irregularly formed plurals such as *man*, *men*, which are familiar anyway.

Teaching Suggestions

Impress upon students that some irregularly formed plurals must be memorized and that even "good spellers" will routinely use a dictionary to check the plural forms of words ending in *o*, of foreign nouns, and of other troublesome words. Students, too, should develop the dictionary habit.

Many people err in forming the plural of proper names and of titles used with names. Check students' assignments carefully to determine whether you should spend extra time on these principles in class.

Explain to students that their ability to form plurals correctly will simplify their study of the next section.

Exercise Keys

Answers to all exercises in this section appear as marginal notes next to the exercises.

Section 2.4 Nouns and Pronouns: Possessive Forms

Objectives

After completing Section 2.4, the student should be able to:

1. Form the correct possessives of singular and plural nouns, including proper nouns and compound nouns.
2. Form the correct possessive to distinguish between joint ownership and separate ownership in compounds.
3. Use a possessive correctly before a gerund and in an appositive construction.
4. Use the possessive forms of personal pronouns correctly.
5. Distinguish correctly between homonym groups that include possessive pronouns.
6. Correct errors in the use of possessive nouns and pronouns.

Overview

In Section 2.4 students learn simple ways to master the correct uses of possessive nouns and pronouns. In particular, students are reminded that all possessive nouns must contain an apostrophe, and they are shown how they can avoid confusing the possessive forms of personal pronouns with similar words.

Teaching Suggestions

Practice is especially helpful in mastering the correct uses of possessive forms. Be sure to use *all* the text exercises and activities book exercises to reinforce correct use of possessives. Subsequent sections of the text offer occasional exercises specifically devoted to plurals and possessives.

As mentioned in the marginal note, emphasize the importance of pronouncing *all* singular nouns ending in *s* before deciding whether to add only an apostrophe or to add an apostrophe and an *s* to form the possessive of such nouns.

Direct students' attention to the chart of personal pronouns (page 67). Use examples to show students how each pronoun in the chart is used. Explain how each pronoun in the second column serves as an adjective: *my* pen, *your* card, *her* agency. Each pronoun in the third column can be used as a substitute for both the adjective and the word it modifies: *mine*, *yours, hers.* Note, too, that the illiteracy *mines* is formed in an effort to create a word that ends in an "s" sound, as all the other words in the third column do: *yours, his, hers,* and so on. If some of your students say "mines," you may take this opportunity to discuss this in a positive, rather than a negative, way.

Exercise Keys

Answers to all exercises in this section appear as marginal notes next to the exercises.

Section 2.5 Pronouns: Nominative and Objective Forms

Objectives

After completing Section 2.5, the student should be able to:

1. Form correctly the nominative and objective personal pronouns.
2. Use nominative pronouns as subjects of verbs and as complements of "being" verbs.
3. Use objective pronouns as objects of verbs and prepositions.
4. Use objective pronouns as both subjects and objects of infinitives.
5. Correct errors in the use of the nominative forms *who* and *whoever* and the objective forms *whom* and *whomever.*
6. Correct errors in the use of nominative and objective forms of pronouns in compound subjects and objects, in pronoun phrases, and in incomplete clauses.
7. Choose the correct case forms of pronouns in appositives.
8. Correct errors in the use of pronouns ending in *self.*

Overview

Leading naturally from the discussion of possessive forms of pronouns in Section 2.4, this section begins with a description of the nominative and objective forms of pronouns and ends with an explanation of the intensive and reflexive uses of pronouns ending in *self.* Throughout, students are given tips on how to choose the correct pronoun forms in a variety of contexts.

Teaching Suggestions

The chart used in Section 2.1 to help students identify verbs will, of course, be equally helpful in teaching students the uses of nominative pronouns:

I _____   we _____

you _____   you _____

he _____

she _____   they _____

it _____

Add *who* and *whoever* to this chart, stress that *who* and *whoever* are also nominative forms, and show how *who* and *whoever* serve as the subjects of verbs.

Make sure that students understand the need to use a nominative form as the complement of a "being" verb. Because many students have not heard "It is *I*," "This is *she*," and so on, on a regular basis, such usage will sound unfamiliar and therefore "sound wrong."

Use the following chart for objective pronouns:

_____ me   _____ us

_____ you   _____ you

_____ him

_____ her   _____ them

_____ it

To this chart, add the objective forms *whom* and *whomever.*

This chart is similar in construction to the chart used for nominative pronouns. The other chart shows that nominative forms *precede* verbs; this chart shows that objective forms *follow* prepositions and verbs. Here, ask students to suggest prepositions that might be used before these pronouns—*to, for, with,* and so on. Then repeat the exercise by asking students to suggest verbs that might be used before these objective forms—for example, *gave, hired, complimented,* and *promoted.*

The technique of substituting *him* or *her* to determine whether an objective form is correct is a simple yet foolproof method for choosing correctly between *who* and *whom*. Try to make this an "automatic" substitution for students.

Follow the suggestions in the text to make sure that students also understand the simple techniques for choosing the correct pronoun form in compound subjects and objects, in pronoun phrases, in incomplete clauses, and in appositives.

Be sure that students understand the two functions of pronouns ending in *self*. Emphasize that such pronouns must have an antecedent within the sentence, and provide additional examples of how misplaced pronouns ending in *self* cause confusing—sometimes ridiculous—sentences.

Exercise Keys

Answers to all exercises in this section appear as marginal notes next to the exercises.

Section 2.6   Predicate Agreement

Objectives

After completing Section 2.6, the student should be able to:

1. Correct errors in basic subject-verb agreement.
2. Correct errors in basic pronoun-antecedent agreement.
3. Correct errors in pronoun agreement with common-gender nouns and with indefinite-word subjects.
4. Correct errors in predicate agreement with collective-noun subjects and foreign-noun subjects.
5. Correct errors in predicate agreement with part, portion, or amount subjects and in sentences beginning with *a number* and *the number*.
6. Identify when compound subjects joined by *and* are really singular; correct agreement errors in such cases.
7. Correct errors in agreement when subjects are joined by *or* or *nor*.
8. Correct errors in agreement in clauses introduced by relative pronouns.

Overview

The ability to avoid agreement errors is as basic to good writing skills as spelling. Unfortunately, however, as the introduction to the first part of this sec-

tion points out, all too many of us have become accustomed to hearing popular songs and television shows reinforce *incorrect* grammar—especially agreement errors. Section 2.6 seeks to counteract this situation by providing students with information on how to avoid errors in predicate agreement with simple subjects, with special subjects such as collective nouns and foreign nouns, and with compound nouns. By avoiding such errors in their own writing, business writers are better able to spot and correct such errors when they are called upon to edit or revise other people's writing.

Teaching Suggestions

Ask students to name popular songs that illustrate agreement errors; they should have no difficulty finding many examples!

The skill of identifying inverted sentences, developed in Section 2.5, will now become more important as students search for the subject in an inverted sentence. Also, students' abilities to find intervening phrases and clauses will determine how successful they will be in making subjects and verbs agree. To help them, write on the chalkboard a simple sentence such as the following:

The man is Mr. Jones.

Then add phrases and clauses to describe the subject *man*, such as:

The man *with the cartons* is Mr. Jones.

The man *who is looking at the charts* is Mr. Jones.

The man *whom you saw earlier today* is Mr. Jones.

The man *walking toward the cars* is Mr. Jones.

With each example, stress that the subject and the verb have not changed. Use this technique to dramatize the fact that many different intervening phrases and clauses can possibly be added between a subject and its verb, but such interrupters have no effect on subject-verb agreement.

Dramatize the meaning of collective nouns by having class members act (1) as *one jury* delivering *its* verdict and then (2) as *individual members* of a jury arguing among *themselves*. Understanding the distinction will help students use collective nouns correctly.

Review the foreign nouns on page 60. As you do so, show students the patterns of forming plurals of some foreign nouns; for example, point out how singular nouns of Greek origin such as *analysis, basis,* and *parenthesis* all form their plurals by changing the *is* to *es*; how Latin feminine singulars (nouns ending in *a*) form their plurals by changing the *a* to *ae*; how Latin masculine singulars such as *alumnus* and *nucleus* form their plurals by changing the *us* to *i*; and so on.

Review with the class the different possibilities of predicate agreement when *or* or *nor* joins (1) two singular subjects, (2) two plural subjects, (3) a singular and a plural subject, and (4) a plural and a singular subject. In *all* cases, the predicate agrees with the subject that follows *or* or *nor*.

Spend extra time, if necessary, to help students make sure that they can always find the relative pronoun that begins a clause. As discussed in the Memory Hook, teach students to omit the relative pronoun in order to focus immediately on the correct agreement.

Compare sentences in which *who, which,* and *that* are relative pronouns with sentences in which they are *not* relative pronouns. Make sure that students understand the meaning of the word *antecedent*.

Exercise Keys

Answers to all exercises in this section appear as marginal notes next to the exercises.

Section 2.7   Adjectives

Objectives

After completing Section 2.7, the student should be able to:

1. Identify articles, possessive adjectives, limiting adjectives, proper adjectives, compound adjectives, descriptive adjectives, and demonstrative adjectives.
2. Given the positive degree of a descriptive adjective, form the comparative and superlative degrees.
3. Correct errors in the use of positive, comparative, and superlative degree forms in sentences.
4. Correct errors in "more than" comparisons.
5. Identify when articles and possessive pronouns should be repeated to show that two different people are intended; correct errors in such usage.
6. Correct usage errors involving *each other* and *one another*; *either* and *neither*; and *any, any one, no one, not any,* and *none.*
7. Hyphenate compound adjectives correctly.

Overview

Adjectives both enliven our communications and make them more precise. Section 2.7 shows students how to use the various kinds and forms of adjectives correctly and effectively in their own speaking and writing. Note that in Section 2.4 we identified *his, her, our,* and so on as possessive forms of personal pronouns; in this section we discuss the personal possessive pronouns under the heading "Possessive Adjectives" so that we might include them with possessive forms of proper nouns, which also serve adjectival functions.

Teaching Suggestions

On the chalkboard write sentences such as the following:

This is Audrey's memo.
This is her memo.
This is hers.
It is Ralph's calculator.
It is your calculator.
It is yours.

Use the first group of three sentences to point out that both *Audrey's* and *her* are adjectives (they modify the noun *memo*) but that *hers* is a pronoun that substitutes for (1) *Audrey's memo* or (2) *her memo.* Use the second group of three sentences to point out that *Ralph's* and *your* are adjectives (they modify the noun *calculator*) but that *yours* is a pronoun that substitutes for (1) *Ralph's calculator* or (2) *your calculator.* Develop other groups of sentences that continue this theme in an effort to show students precisely how adjectives function (whether they are formed from personal pronouns or from nouns—or from any other source, for that matter). At the same time, stress how pronouns function—as *substitutes* for nouns and their modifiers. This practice can be exceptionally effective.

Students should understand that our ability to use a proper noun as an adjective in, for example, "a San Francisco conference" provides us with a shortcut. We would otherwise have to say "a conference in San Francisco."

Most of the discussion on forming the comparative and superlative degrees of adjectives is rather simple and should cause little trouble. (The difficult comparisons will be those few irregular comparisons given in the text and, perhaps, absolute comparisons.) Throughout, be sure to stress that the comparative degree compares only *two* persons or things; the superlative degree, *three or more* persons or things.

Spend extra time on compound adjectives, because writers often use hyphens when they are not required—and omit hyphens when they are required. As suggested in the marginal note, emphasize the importance of using a dictionary to determine whether or not to use a hyphen in a compound adjective.

Exercise Keys

Answers to all exercises in this section appear as marginal notes next to the exercises.

Section 2.8   Adverbs

Objectives

After completing Section 2.8, the student should be able to:

1. Identify adverbs in sentences.
2. Given descriptive adjectives, form adverbs.
3. Given the positive degree, form the comparative and superlative degrees of adverbs.
4. Use conjunctive adverbs correctly to join two independent clauses.
5. Use subordinating conjunctions correctly to join a dependent clause to an independent clause.
6. Choose correctly between adverbs and adjectives, whichever 'are correct, in sentences; correct errors in such usage.

Overview

Section 2.8 highlights the similarities and differences between adverbs and adjectives, guiding students in the correct use of adverbs as modifiers of verbs, adjectives, and other adverbs. The section goes on to discuss conjunctive adverbs and adverbial clauses and then concludes by enumerating five principles of adverb use and explaining how students can avoid common adjective-adverb confusions.

Teaching Suggestions

Stress the obvious parallel between adverbs and adjectives—both are *modifiers*. Review with students some basic sentences that illustrate the role that adverbs play in modifying verbs, adjectives, and other adverbs. Then have students write sentences that illustrate the three functions of adverbs.

Although it is not important that students master such terminology as *conjunctive adverb* and *subordinating conjunction*, it certainly *is* important that they be

able to *use* these adverbs correctly in their writing. One good supplemental exercise, therefore, is to give students lists of conjunctive adverbs and of subordinating conjunctions (for example, the short lists on pages 104 and 105) and ask them to write sentences for each word in both lists. Read some of the student sentences in class, emphasizing the type of clauses (dependent or independent) and the punctuation required for the use of each type of adverb. Again, their ability to use these words correctly in sentences is an important writing skill.

Students will be able to avoid common adjective-adverb confusions (see pages 107 through 109) if they can identify no-action verbs. Using the text examples (as well as the exercise sentences in the text and in the workbook), emphasize how each adjective modifies a noun or a pronoun, while each adverb modifies a verb, an adjective, or another adverb.

Exercise Keys

Answers to all exercises in this section appear as marginal notes next to the exercises.

Section 2.9   Prepositions

Objectives

After completing Section 2.9, the student should be able to:

1. Identify prepositional phrases and label the preposition and its object or objects in each phrase.
2. Use correctly the specific prepositions required in 74 commonly used idiomatic expressions.

Overview

The ability to identify prepositional phrases helps students identify subjects and verbs and, consequently, helps them see whether subjects and predicates agree. For example, as discussed on page 113, in the sentence "The word processing operators *in this department* are reviewing the new rules carefully," the ability to spot the prepositional phrase simplifies the choice of *are* as the verb that must agree with the subject, *operators*. In many sentences, this ability will determine correct subject-predicate agreement. In addition to teaching students how to identify and use prepositions and prepositional phrases correctly, this section shows students how to avoid the most common preposition pitfalls.

Teaching Suggestions

Work with students to find prepositional phrases not only when reviewing this section but also when reviewing all sections of the text. As recommended in the text, also have students find the object of the preposition in each of the sample phrases.

To show students how versatile prepositional phrases are, use basic sentences such as "The woman is Jill" and have students suggest prepositional phrases that could possibly be added to the base sentence; for example, "The woman *on the platform* or *with the microphone* or *near Mark* or *by the table* is Jill." In each case, the prepositional phrase modifies the subject, *woman*, and is therefore an adjectival phrase.

As noted in the text, you may need to spend extra time on preposition pitfalls. The most troublesome for students is knowing when to use *between* and when to use *among*. You may find it helpful to give students additional examples of the use of *between* to express the relationship of one thing to each of several other things on a one-to-one basis.

Exercise Keys

Answers to all exercises in this section appear as marginal notes next to the exercises.

Section 2.10   Conjunctions

Objectives

After completing Section 2.10, the student should be able to:

1. Identify coordinating, correlative, and subordinating conjunctions in sentences.
2. Correct common errors in conjunction use.
3. Correct sentences (rewrite them, if necessary) to achieve parallel structure.

Overview

This section describes the three types of conjunctions — coordinating, correlative, and subordinating — and illustrates the use of each type. The section further explains how students can achieve parallel structure in their writing to produce effective business communications.

Teaching Suggestions

Again, the student's ability to *label* accurately each of the three different kinds of conjunctions (or conjunctions in general, for that matter) is not important; the student's ability to *use* conjunctions correctly in

sentences *is* important. However, the names of the three different kinds of conjunctions discussed in Section 2.10 provide clues to their uses, and these clues should be discussed with students. Read to the class the dictionary definitions of the adjectives *coordinate*, *correlative*, and *subordinate* and then show how each accurately describes the function of these three conjunctions. (Knowing these meanings will also improve each student's vocabulary.)

Spend adequate time to ensure that students understand what *parallelism* means. Review all of the examples in the text and discuss them with the class; in addition, review and discuss the sentences in Checkups 3 and 4 (pages 128 and 129, respectively), as well as those sentences in Practical Application A that illustrate parallel structure (or the lack of it).

Throughout, be sure to stress the most basic aspect of conjunction use: that conjunctions offer writers and speakers a variety of ways to combine phrases and clauses into interesting sentences and therefore avoid dull, routine sentences. To dramatize this for students, write on the board sentences such as the following: John left early. He had already finished his work. He was leaving for his vacation.

Then use conjunctions to join these routine, lifeless sentences into different combinations, such as:

Because he was leaving for his vacation, John left early, *but* he had already finished his work.

Exercise Keys

Answers to all exercises in this section appear as marginal notes next to the exercises.

CHAPTER 3
APPLYING THE MECHANICS OF STYLE

The mechanics of style — punctuation, capitalization, and so on — are the mortar that holds words together in phrases, clauses, and sentences and makes them understandable. One misplaced comma can change the intended meaning of an entire sentence; one carelessly omitted set of quotation marks can lead to serious legal problems. Correctly applying the mechanics of style, then, is a necessity in business communication.

Section 3.1   Sentence Enders

Objectives

After completing Section 3.1, the student should be able to:

1. Use periods correctly to end sentences, including indirect questions and sentences that end with abbreviations; correct errors in such usage.
2. Identify when periods are required to end items displayed on separate lines; correct errors in such usage.
3. Use periods correctly in headings; correct errors in such usage.
4. Correct errors in the use of periods with roman numerals and in even dollar amounts.
5. Correct period faults and comma-for-period faults.
6. Use question marks correctly after direct questions and in series of questions; correct errors in such usage.
7. Use exclamation points correctly; correct errors in such usage.

Overview

This first section on punctuation use begins with end punctuation, the three marks used to end sentences: the period, the question mark, and the exclamation point. Students should have few problems with these basic uses.

Teaching Suggestions

Be sure students understand the types of sentences that end in periods: declarative, imperative, requests phrased as questions, and indirect questions. If necessary, emphasize the difference between requests phrased as questions and true questions by giving paired examples such as these: Can you meet me at the bank in half an hour? Will you please meet me at the airport Tuesday at 3:30 p.m.

The period fault will cause trouble only for those students who do not yet understand the difference between independent and dependent clauses and are unable to distinguish between the two. Chapter 2 should help students who have this problem. Similarly, the comma-for-period fault illustrates an inability to identify two independent clauses (which, of course, should not usually be separated only by a comma). Begin the discussion of these two common pitfalls by reviewing dependent and independent clauses with the class.

As suggested in the marginal note, inform students that condensed answers to questions, such as "Yes" and "No," are considered complete sentences and therefore correctly end with periods.

Few problems arise with the use of question marks, probably because their use is so limited and so obvi-

ously restricted to interrogative sentences. Note that when a sentence contains a series of questions, the questions are usually joined by commas and a conjunction and the sentence ends with a question mark. However, when each item in the series is being individually questioned, the use of a question mark instead of a comma after each item makes that meaning more evident or precise. As suggested in the text, prepare students for Section 3.4 by pointing out why question marks are sometimes inside, sometimes outside, quotation marks.

Exercise Keys

Answers to all exercises in this section appear as marginal notes next to the exercises.

Section 3.2   Semicolons, Colons, and Dashes

Objectives

After completing Section 3.2, the student should be able to:

1. Use semicolons correctly to join independent clauses; correct errors in such usage.
2. Use semicolons and colons correctly before enumerations and explanations; correct errors in such usage.
3. Use colons correctly to introduce an independent clause and to emphasize; correct errors in such usage.
4. Capitalize correctly the first word following a colon; correct errors in such usage.
5. Use dashes correctly in sentences; correct errors in such usage.

Overview

Once again the student's ability to identify phrases and clauses is critical; without this skill, students will not be able to use semicolons, colons, and dashes correctly. Section 3.2 discusses how these three marks of punctuation are used within sentences and when each is most appropriate to the writer's purpose.

Teaching Suggestions

Review the text examples in detail, identifying each clause for the class. Then use Checkup 1 to test students' skills in identifying clauses. Show students that a period can be used instead of a semicolon to separate two independent clauses but that the period provides a stronger separation than the semicolon in each case (and this stronger separation is not always what the writer wants).

Stress the colon's ability to *point to* what follows and to provide special emphasis on what follows. Make sure students understand that a colon — unlike a semicolon — need not be followed by an independent clause or an introductory word or phrase. Use the Checkup 2 sentences to reinforce correct colon use for the class. Likewise, use the Checkup 3 sentences to review the uses of the dash.

As suggested in the text, point out that the colon provides a stronger pause than a semicolon and the dash provides a stronger pause than a colon. Also note that these three punctuation marks should not be used interchangeably.

Exercise Keys

Answers to all exercises in this section appear as marginal notes next to the exercises.

Section 3.3   Commas

Objectives

After completing Section 3.3, the student should be able to:

1. Use commas with conjunctions to separate independent clauses; correct errors in such usage.
2. Use commas to separate items in a series; correct errors in such usage, and substitute semicolons correctly for commas in series.
3. Use commas correctly with the abbreviation *etc.* and in company names; correct errors in such usage.
4. Use commas correctly following introductory words, phrases, and clauses; correct errors in such usage.
5. Use commas correctly after main clauses that are followed by subordinate clauses; correct errors in such usage.
6. Use commas correctly to set off interrupting, parenthetic, and explanatory elements; correct errors in such usage.
7. Use commas correctly to set off appositives, degrees and titles, calendar dates, and state names; correct errors in such usage.
8. Use commas correctly to separate nonessential clauses that begin with *which;* correct errors in such usage.

9. Determine when commas are needed between modifying adjectives; correct errors in such usage.
10. Use commas in omissions, in repeated expressions, and in direct address; correct errors in such usage.
11. Use commas correctly in numbers; correct errors in such usage.

Overview

The length of this section indicates the importance of the comma and its variety of uses in business writing. Section 3.3 begins with the basics: commas in compound sentences, in series, and following introductory words, phrases, and clauses. The section continues with discussion of comma use with subordinate clauses, interrupting elements, and appositives. Finally, Section 3.3 focuses on some of the finer points of comma usage — but these finer points, too, are needed by the business writer in routine business communications.

Teaching Suggestions

Although the use of commas in compound sentences, in series, and following introductory words, phrases, and clauses is rather easy, each case offers a potential trap for students:

1. In compound sentences, the most common error surrounds the confusion of compound sentences with sentences that have compound predicates. Spend extra time illustrating sentence pairs that point out this simple distinction. Use, for example, sentences 5, 6, and 8 in Checkup 1.
2. In series, one common error is to use a comma after the last item in the series. Another common error concerns the use of commas with *etc.* Review both with students.
3. After introductory words, phrases, and clauses, stress the natural pause that occurs when the sentences are said aloud. Ask students to read the text examples aloud; then ask them to make up similar example sentences.

Be sure students understand why semicolons must be used in place of commas when items in a series are long clauses or already contain commas: namely, to provide a stronger pause for the sake of clarity and ease of reading. As noted in the text, also emphasize that some of the words listed on page 156 are not always "introductory" words to be followed by a comma. Use sentences such as the following to make this point: "Finally finishing the report was a great relief to the staff."

Using commas correctly after main clauses that are followed by subordinate clauses requires more than the ability to identify main clauses and subordinate clauses. The writer must also be able to analyze whether the subordinate clause is essential or nonessential (also called "restrictive" and "nonrestrictive"). You may wish to spend extra time discussing this topic with the class.

Review the text examples, then change them as necessary to help students understand "essential" and "nonessential." For example, use this alternative to the sentence on page 158: "We will change the commission rate (?) as we agreed at our last directors meeting."

Depending on how one reads this sentence, a comma may or may not be necessary. One meaning can be "We will change the commission rate *precisely in the manner that we agreed at our last directors meeting*" — a restrictive interpretation. Another can be "We will change the commission rate, which, by the way, we agreed to do at our last directors meeting" — a nonrestrictive interpretation. Which is correct? The writer will always know what he or she intends.

Reading the text sentences aloud will help students see that commas provide for writing many of the natural pauses that we hear. In addition to the illustrative text sentences, read aloud the sentences in Checkup 4. In sentence 1, for example, exaggerate the incorrect pauses before and after the clause *who is interviewing applicants for this position*. On the other hand, in sentence 3 read rapidly over the clause *as we discussed yesterday* to point up the need for pauses before and after it. Such examples will help students grasp this concept.

Although the term *appositives* is certainly not an everyday word, appositive constructions are very commonly used in writing and speaking. Show the class how appositives provide us with another shortcut — a way of combining two sentences into one. For example, use this text sentence (see page 160): "The director of corporate communications, Andrea Patterson, is giving a seminar on desktop publishing." Show students how the appositive provides a way of combining two sentences ("The director of corporate communications is Andrea Patterson" *and* "Andrea Patterson is giving a seminar on desktop publishing") into one shorter sentence.

As suggested in the text, inform students that many people use *which* and *that* incorrectly. For this reason, students should be especially careful when using these words in their own writing and when proofreading or editing other people's writing.

When discussing commas with modifying adjectives, read aloud the examples in the text, exaggerating the pauses in each case. For instance, using the first example (page 164), lengthen the pause between the adjectives in "forceful, logical way." Tell students that the pauses between the adjectives that separately modify the noun serve as a substitute for the word *and*. Then change the sentence to "Carlotta voiced her opinion in an *effective* way," reading quickly through *effective* to dramatize that there is no pause.

Although students may not have realized, they have seen other examples where the comma substitutes for the word *and*. In an effort to save precious space, newspaper headlines will read, for example, "Becker, Sampras Vie for Title." From local newspapers, get current examples illustrating instances where a comma serves as a substitute for *and*. Examples from the sports pages might be especially welcome — and especially familiar.

When discussing commas for omissions and repeated expressions, again read the text examples aloud, exaggerating the pauses as you do so.

Exercise Keys

Answers to all exercises in this section appear as marginal notes next to the exercises.

Section 3.4 Quotation Marks, Parentheses, and Apostrophes

Objectives

After completing Section 3.4, the student should be able to:

1. Use quotation marks correctly for direct quotations, definitions, special expressions, unfamiliar terms, titles of articles, and so on; correct errors in such usage.
2. Combine other punctuation marks correctly with quotation marks in sentences; correct errors in such usage.
3. Use parentheses correctly to enclose words that give additional information and references; correct errors in such usage.
4. Combine other punctuation marks correctly with parentheses in sentences; correct errors in such usage.

5. Use apostrophes correctly to form possessive nouns and contractions; correct errors in such usage.

Overview

The basics of using quotation marks, parentheses, and apostrophes – discussed and illustrated in this section – are easily mastered. Nevertheless, students should develop the habit of supplementing the information presented here by using a good business reference handbook when they are not sure of the correct accepted practice.

Teaching Suggestions

If there is one "trick" to mastering the principles of using quotation marks, parentheses, and apostrophes, it is *practice*. Give students ample practice applying the rules presented in the text, and review all the completed exercises with them to ensure that they understand the accepted rules. Just by exposure to these rules, students who read a great deal should be more familiar with the accepted rules than students who do not read often. Although they may not understand why, for example, commas and periods are placed inside closing quotation marks (there is no logical reason, anyway), students who read a lot may have mental pictures that they consider "correct." (The British practice is the reverse of ours; the British place commas and periods *outside* quotation marks and colons and semicolons *inside*. Again, there is neither rhyme nor reason – just accepted usage – to dictate what is "right.")

Highlight for students the relationship of parentheses to commas and dashes when additional information is given. Note especially that parentheses de-emphasize additional information.

As suggested in the marginal note, review the use of apostrophes in contractions thoroughly so that students do not misuse them. Also inform students that whereas contractions are used frequently in speaking, they should be used sparingly in formal writing.

Exercise Keys

Answers to all exercises in this section appear as marginal notes next to the exercises.

Section 3.5 Capitalization

Objectives

After completing Section 3.5, the student should be able to:

1. Use capitals correctly for the first words of sentences, direct quotations, and items in outlines; correct errors in such usage.
2. Use capitals correctly in headings and in titles of publications; correct errors in such usage.
3. Capitalize correctly proper nouns, short forms used for proper nouns, personal and official titles used with proper names, and proper adjectives; correct errors in such usage.
4. Capitalize correctly the names of commercial products; correct errors in such usage.

Overview

Many of the rules presented here are familiar to students; they have read – and therefore have seen – proper nouns, proper adjectives, and so on, capitalized correctly many, many times. Other capitalization rules may be unfamiliar or confusing to students and are therefore discussed in detail in this section.

Teaching Suggestions

Stress the need to follow precisely (not merely guess at) the spelling of someone's name; stress, too, the many alternative spellings of names that students may not be familiar with. The point is certainly not to memorize these alternative spellings of proper names; doing so would be fruitless. The point is to make students aware that there are many variations in first names and surnames and that each should be respected.

Include in this discussion the use of capitals and lowercase letters for reference initials, inside addresses and envelope addresses, memo headings, letter notations, and so on (see Sections 7.2 and 8.1). Ask students to bring to class some typical "junk mail"; then ask them to point out in these letters and advertisements both the correct and the incorrect uses of capitals. Use examples of students' names and ask for the names of students' relatives and friends to illustrate "special" usage.

Exercise Keys

Answers to all exercises in this section appear as marginal notes next to the exercises.

Section 3.6 Abbreviations

Objectives

After completing Section 3.6, the student should be able to:

1. Use appropriate abbreviations correctly before and after personal names; correct errors in such usage.
2. Use abbreviations correctly in company and organization names; correct errors in such usage.
3. Use abbreviations correctly in addresses, units of measure, and expressions of time; correct errors in such usage.
4. Use miscellaneous business abbreviations correctly; correct errors in such usage.

Overview

Section 3.6 introduces students to some of the most commonly used business abbreviations and at the same time teaches them a consistent, accepted style for treating abbreviations in business communications.

Teaching Suggestions

Stress that accepted usage is what makes some abbreviations "correct" when lowercased and shown with periods (for example, *a.m.* and *p.m.*) and others correct in all-capital letters with no periods (for example, *OTC* for "over the counter"). As suggested in the marginal note, having students check a local phone directory for unusual spellings or treatments of organization names will reinforce this important point. For comprehensive, up-to-date coverage of business abbreviations, students should consult a business reference book.

Point out that words such as *lab* and *gym*, shortened forms of *laboratory* and *gymnasium*, are not considered abbreviations because they are now well established in our language as complete words.

Exercise Keys

Answers to all exercises in this section appear as marginal notes next to the exercises.

Section 3.7   Numbers

Objectives

After completing Section 3.7, the student should be able to:

1. Choose correctly when to express numbers in words and when to express them in figures in sentences; correct errors in such usage.
2. Use ordinal numbers correctly in business communications; correct errors in such usage.

3. Use correct punctuation and symbols, when appropriate, with numbers; correct errors in such usage.

Overview

There are two concerns when writing numbers in business correspondence: to choose correctly between words and figures and to write the words or the figures properly. Section 3.7 covers both these concerns in detail.

Teaching Suggestions

Review with the class the fact that figures tend to emphasize a number while words de-emphasize. Explain, moreover, that words tend to be more formal than figures. Then use the text examples to illustrate both the formal and the informal uses.

Once again, tell the class that accepted usage determines what is "correct" and what is not. Thus figures plus the word *percent* are considered "correct" for general business correspondence; figures plus the symbol % are "correct" in tables and charts.

Ask students to bring in examples of business letters and advertisements and discuss how numbers are expressed in those communications. As suggested in the text, also ask students what problems could result if the numbers in the advertisements were incorrect.

Exercise Keys

Answers to all exercises in this section appear as marginal notes next to the exercises.

CHAPTER 4
USING WORDS EFFECTIVELY

As Jonathan Swift wrote some 250 years ago, "Proper words in proper places make the true definition of a style." Finding the proper, or right, word often requires the use of reference materials: the dictionary, the thesaurus, the dictionary of synonyms. Simultaneously, these resources can also help us expand our vocabulary and help us spell words correctly. In turn, improving vocabulary power leads to greater reading comprehension, yet another vital skill of the successful businessperson.

Section 4.1 Using the Dictionary and Other Reference Materials

Objectives

After completing Section 4.1, the student should be able to:

1. Describe the types of information contained in dictionaries.
2. Use a dictionary to find the correct spelling, hyphenation, pronunciation, etymology, and meaning of a word.
3. Explain the benefits of using a thesaurus.
4. Use a thesaurus to find the precise words to achieve various communication purposes.
5. Discuss the capabilities and limitations of electronic reference tools.
6. Explain the difference between a dictionary of synonyms, a standard dictionary, and a thesaurus.
7. Use a dictionary of synonyms to add variety to communications.

Overview

Many good writers and speakers are "good" partly because they know when they need to check words in a reference source rather than guess about them. The three most important reference sources for words are the dictionary, the thesaurus, and the dictionary of synonyms. Section 4.1 describes the specific kinds of information these reference books contain and illustrates the ways they can be used to make communications accurate, precise, and vivid. The habit of looking up words will serve students well throughout their lives.

Teaching Suggestions

Urge students to form the habit of looking up words. As suggested in the text, keep a good selection of reference books in the classroom for students to consult.

Use the transparency suggested in the text, along with transparencies of a page from a thesaurus and a page from a dictionary of synonyms, to highlight how the three reference sources differ from and complement one another.

Emphasize that electronic reference tools have limitations. They cannot replace a dictionary, a thesaurus, and a dictionary of synonyms.

Exercise Keys

Practical Application (page 215)

B.

1. Chə-'lē-nē (Italian goldsmith and sculptor)
2. 'Pēps (English writer)
3. 'Lē-mən (American banker and politician)
4. Vä-'len-sə (Polish political leader)
5. 'Gə(r)-tə (German poet)

C.

1. 'Bā-'jin (capital of China)
2. 'Gläs-tər (city in Massachusetts)
3. Rē-'(y)ek-ə (city in Yugoslavia)
4. 'Lē-mən (lake on border between Switzerland and France; also called Lake Geneva)
5. ‚Sü-‚sānt-mə-'rē (city in Michigan and also in Canada)

D.

1. excise ('ek-,sīz) An internal tax levied on the manufacture, sale, or consumption of a commodity within a country. *We had to pay an excise tax on the American-made automobile we just purchased.*
2. lien ('lēn) A charge upon real or personal property for the satisfaction of a debt. *Because of the $10,000 owed by Mr. Jacobs, there was a lien on his house.*
3. bankruptcy ('baŋ-(,)krəp-(t)sē) The state of having done something that entitles one's creditors to have one's estate administered for the benefit of the creditors. *Because of the bankruptcy, all the store fixtures were sold at auction.*
4. ecology (i-'käl-ə-jē) A branch of science concerned with the interrelationship of organisms and their environments. *The waste from the burning fuel causes a problem in the ecology of our city.*
5. depreciation (di-prē-shī-'a-shən) The process of reducing the value of an object. *Every automobile has some depreciation from the moment it is purchased.*
6. franchise ('fran-,chīz) Freedom from some burden or restriction vested in a person or group; the right to vote. *We obtained a franchise to open an E-Z Kopy store.*
7. mortgage ('mor-gij) A conveyance of property on condition that it becomes void on payment. *After we made the last payment on our house, we burned the mortgage.*

8. accrual (ə-ˈkrü-əl) To come into existence as a legally enforceable claim. The interest we owed resulted in an accrual to our already existing debt.

9. incumbent (in-ˈkəm-bənt) The present holder of an office. Mr. Rolfe was the incumbent mayor, and Mrs. Lee was planning to run against him in the next election.

10. cartel (kär-ˈtel) A written agreement between belligerent nations. The oil-producing nations drew up a cartel.

Section 4.2   Improving Vocabulary Power

Objectives

After completing Section 4.2, the student should be able to:

1. Carefully choose the precise words that will best convey the meaning of a message.
2. Explain what homonyms and pseudohomonyms are.
3. Choose words appropriate to the interest and knowledge of the audience.
4. Use positive words and expressions.
5. Trim unnecessary and out-of-date words from his or her writing.
6. Avoid using overused words and expressions in writing and speaking.

Overview

Section 4.2 explains how students can improve their vocabularies and shows students the advantages of making those improvements. Effective communicators choose the specific words that are most appropriate to their message and the audience and avoid negative, unnecessary, and overused words.

Although this section will help all students broaden their vocabularies, extensive reading is the best way for students to increase the size and range of their vocabularies and to improve their understanding of words.

Teaching Suggestions

Stress the importance of choosing the precise words to convey the intended meaning of a message.

See whether students can come up with other sets of words that describe the same basic idea but have different shades of meaning — different connotations. For example, an extrovert might be described as a *showoff* or as someone *outgoing*, *warm*, or *friendly*.

If time permits, make and distribute to groups of four to six students photocopies of a crossword puzzle from a daily newspaper. Equip each group with a dictionary and allow them 15 minutes to work on the puzzle. Then have the groups compare their answers. Ask what new words they learned. Suggest that students try to use at least one of the new words during the coming week. You may also want to point out to students the calendars that offer a new word for each day of the year.

Exercise Keys

Practical Application (page 228)

C.   Students' answers will vary.

1. We received your letter today, but unfortunately our special offer ended last week.
2. Since the interruption prevented you from hearing my instructions, I will be happy to repeat them.
3. We will ship your filing cabinets as soon as you let us know whether you want legal- or letter-size.
4. Although I will be out of the office Tuesday, I will be happy to help you on Wednesday.
5. When sending a letter by an overnight delivery service, you must include a street address. The U.S. Postal Service is the only carrier that can deliver mail to post office boxes.

D.   Students' answers will vary. Some suggestions are listed here.

1. settle, determine, decide on
2. a productive, useful
3. an effective, an interesting, an educational
4. correct, revise, update, retype
5. disorganized, boring, ineffective
6. effective, experienced, likable
7. trustworthy, efficient, helpful
8. engrossing, entertaining, provocative
9. convenient, spacious, well-designed
10. correct, undo, rectify

E.   Students' answers will vary. Some possible answers are:

1. fails to do at least his or her share, disappoints you
2. being indecisive
3. no matter what, in any way possible, as best we can

4. finding and solving the problems in, correcting any errors or problems in
5. giving up, not continuing
6. is overproud or overbearing, pontificates, is haughty, boasts
7. tried very hard, spent great effort on
8. has little regard for, has a poor opinion of
9. completed it quickly, wasted no time in completing it
10. brag, boast, show off

F.

1. dangerous, insecure, unreliable, undependable
2. likely, certain, true, plausible
3. economical, reasonable, fair
4. shorten, decrease, contract
5. insensitive, crude, heartless, selfish
6. boring, dull, uninteresting
7. important, significant, major, essential
8. natural
9. secretly, furtively, surreptitiously
10. discourage, dishearten

Section 4.3 Mastering Spelling Techniques

Objectives

After completing Section 4.3, the student should be able to:

1. Apply the spelling principles for words ending in *y*, *ful*, *ous*, *ally*, and *illy*.
2. Apply the spelling rule for most *ei* and *ie* words.
3. Use the rule for doubling a final consonant to spell words correctly.
4. Recognize spelling pitfalls and use a dictionary to avoid them.
5. Analyze and memorize words commonly used in business that are troublesome because they follow no rules.

Overview

The rules presented in this section will help students see the spelling patterns that exist in English. Unfortunately, spelling rules in English are not simple, and there are many exceptions that simply must be memorized. Here again, the student who reads will be at an advantage because he or she will have mental images of what "looks" correct on the page.

Exercises throughout the section test students' ability to spell words used in business and difficult words that are often misspelled.

Teaching Suggestions

Ask students whether they have ever spotted misspellings in a newspaper or a set of printed instructions. If so, what was their reaction? Reinforce the fact that incorrect spelling gives a negative impression of the message and of the writer.

Emphasize that mastering spelling rules now will save students valuable time later because understanding and applying spelling rules reduces the number of words writers must verify each time they write.

Exercise Keys

Answers to all exercises in this section appear as marginal notes next to the exercises.

Section 4.4 Improving Reading Skill

Objectives

After completing Section 4.4, the student should be able to:

1. Explain the differences in reading for pleasure, for specific data, for retention or analysis, and for checking and copying.
2. Increase reading speed by adding to vocabulary, reading in thought units, keeping the eyes moving from left to right, not vocalizing, reading only word beginnings, and practicing rapid reading.
3. Improve reading comprehension by scanning, taking notes, and rereading and reviewing.

Overview

Reading skill is essential to job success. Section 4.4 explains how to read for different purposes and provides a plan for students who want to increase their reading speed and comprehension. As with the other communication skills, the key to reading improvement is practice.

Teaching Suggestion

An interesting way to point out the importance of reading is to have students imagine how they would get through a typical day if they were illiterate. Reading street signs and supermarket ads, filling out job application forms — these and many other activities would be difficult if not impossible. You may want to give students a copy or show a transparency of non-sense writing — letters grouped into word, phrase, and sentence combinations that do not spell English words. The frustration of trying to make sense of the nonsense can simulate the feelings of someone who cannot read.

Exercise Keys

Answers to all exercises in this section appear as marginal notes next to the exercises.

CHAPTER 5
SHARPENING WRITING SKILL

Like other facets of business, written communications require careful planning and organization. This means determining the purpose of the writing, gathering information, and presenting a message in an orderly, logical fashion. As mentioned in Chapter 2, joining words into appropriate thought units — or as Jonathan Swift would have it, putting them in "proper places" — eliminates reader confusion. Moving from words to phrases to clauses, the careful writer goes on to structure clear and lively sentences. Writing good sentences is a prerequisite to writing effective paragraphs. Such paragraphs join sentences into a series of thoughts that express one main idea. By reviewing and, where necessary, revising what has been written, the careful writer assures clarity of meaning and a graceful style.

Section 5.1   Planning for Effective Writing

Objectives

After completing Section 5.1, the student should be able to:

1. Establish the purpose of each business communication before starting to write.
2. Gather and organize needed information before beginning the actual writing process.
3. Demonstrate the importance of appearance and quality in all written communications.
4. Make business correspondence faster and easier by enclosing a reply copy, enclosing a card or return slip, or attaching a perforated form.

Overview

Planning is a vital part of business writing. As with other business activities, success depends on the quality and proper execution of plans. Business writing has a purpose. To achieve this purpose writers must plan, assemble information, and present the information in an orderly way. The communication must create a quality impression, and the information must be easy to understand. Business writers can try to facilitate action by using reply copies, enclosed cards or return slips, or attached perforated forms.

Teaching Suggestions

Point out to students that effective business writing requires much thought, study, practice, and experience. It is a skill that must be developed over time.

Read students the three questions noted on page 245 that business writers must consider before writing a letter, memo, or report. Then suggest some typical answers: for example, writing to a hotel to reserve a conference room. Finally, have students suggest other possible answers to the three questions.

When stressing the importance of logical order in presenting information, use the movie comparison suggested in the text to capture student attention. Ask students how they felt when they missed the first part of a movie, and compare their reactions to the reactions of readers of poorly organized letters, memos, and reports.

Exercise Keys

Answers to all exercises in this section appear as marginal notes next to the exercises.

Section 5.2   Structuring Phrases and Clauses

Objectives

After completing Section 5.2, the student should be able to:

1. Avoid errors in the placement of thought units composed of words, phrases, and clauses.
2. Make all pronoun references clear to the reader.
3. Use indefinite pronouns correctly and sparingly.
4. Correct *this* and *thus* faults.

Overview

In this section students will apply some of the rules of grammar they studied in Chapter 2 to improve their writing. Words, phrases, and clauses join to make sentences. Sentences, in turn, make paragraphs; and paragraphs combine to make letters, memorandums, and reports.

Thought units, made up of words, phrases, and clauses, are the thrust of this section. The section also includes practice in correcting errors in pronoun reference, a common problem in student writing.

Teaching Suggestions

Emphasize that even one word used incorrectly in a letter, memo, or report can negatively affect the impression made on the reader.

Remind students that the rules they learned in Chapter 2 will be applied in this section. Point out that the ability to write clear and accurate phrases and clauses is a skill, and like any other skill it requires practice—and more practice.

Exercise Keys

Practical Application (page 261)

A. Students' answers will vary.

1. Manuel took the computer, which everyone had been waiting to see, out of the box.
2. After the committee broke for lunch, the meeting reconvened.
3. Because of design defects, the Model Zoom lawnmowers were recalled by the manufacturer.
4. Men's exotic-looking ties are fashionable this season.
5. Glue the two pieces together while holding them in place with your fingers.
6. Walking on crutches, Rick found it difficult to climb stairs.
7. Having forgotten to save the document before turning off the computer, Susan had to reinput the report.
8. The skyscrapers were clearly visible while we were sitting close to the window.
9. People often buy things they don't need with credit cards.
10. Good keyboarders, with little or no training, can operate the new computers.
11. Ned finds that he spends less time in the kitchen since he began cooking food in the microwave oven.
12. Your rental agreement says that you may not have animals, unless they are caged, or children.
13. After much planning, we finally balanced the budget.
14. The mixer truck, only half full of cement, was wrecked by a substitute driver.
15. Upon request, we will give you a brochure that explains our diverse financial services.
16. The theater critic's acerbic review hurt ticket sales.
17. The printer noise was distracting to visitors when they were walking through the office.
18. Ms. Kantor sent the draft, covered with proofreader's marks, back for correction.
19. After working a 12-hour shift, he found that his head ached and his feet hurt.
20. To remove paint without scraping, soak the item two hours in solvent.

B. Students' answers will vary.

1. While she was in Chicago last week, Alice saw Katie.
2. Len and Judd researched the topic, but Judd actually wrote the report.
3. Dan's explanation was not clear, and he told Charlie that it wasn't.
4. Dr. Anne McCurry and Dr. Ben Lawson feel that more test trials are needed for the new arthritis treatment.
5. Although we interviewed 30 applicants, we hired only 3 laboratory technicians.
6. A positive attitude can make the difference between success and failure.
7. Don't move the computer terminal on my desk for any reason.
8. Rearranging the desks in this office may be a good idea.
9. Ms. Nichols was offered a 5-year lease or a 10-year lease. She will probably sign the 10-year lease next week.
10. As soon as Martha received the contract, she asked Caroline to review it.

C.

1. Because the meeting adjourned without our taking any action or making any decisions, we were dissatisfied.
2. It is not Dexter's fault that several folders were misplaced when we transferred the files.

3. We will have to work late because several computer files were damaged when the power was unexpectedly interrupted.
4. The company's top designer was not able to work with us because she was on vacation when we launched the project. Her absence affected the quality of our project.
5. By ignoring his father's good advice, Steven proved that he was stubborn.

Section 5.3 Writing Effective Sentences

Objectives

After completing Section 5.3, the student should be able to:

1. Recognize the advantages of using positive words in letters, memos, and reports.
2. Use repetition — of words or phrases — to emphasize important points.
3. Avoid using combinations of words that sound harsh or awkward.
4. Recognize and eliminate distracting words.
5. Demonstrate an understanding of proper coordination and subordination in writing letters, memos, and reports.
6. Use the active voice except to soften the blow of bad news by means of the passive voice.
7. Phrase comparisons so that they are parallel in structure.
8. Apply the principle of parallel structure to words, phrases, and clauses used in series.

Overview

When business communications flow smoothly, the reader understands the message the first time it is read. The reader is unaware of sentences, phrases, and clauses. This section emphasizes choosing the right combination of words that are balanced and effective in achieving the purpose of the message.

Teaching Suggestions

Emphasize the text suggestions that positive words and the active voice make messages upbeat and lively. As a result, responses to such messages tend to be positive and enthusiastic.

Write five or six pairs of related simple sentences on the chalkboard. Have students combine each pair into one sentence with a main clause and a subordinate clause. Then call on several students to read their sentences aloud and explain which thought is more important in each.

Exercise Keys

Practical Application (page 271)

A.

1. The lawyer summarized several of his comments.
2. The cashier's check ended the confusion.
3. Miss Pellettieri did not get Miss Carr's call.
4. The board became disinterested by noon.
5. Two paralegals studied law journals in the library.

B.

1. I will finish the report by 5 p.m.
2. We regret that we do not have a position for someone with your qualifications and experience.
3. Our 24-hour customer representatives will be happy to answer your questions about our cable TV service.
4. Installation instructions should be easy to understand.
5. Cashiers should be honest.

C.

1. Because the copier was broken, we could not distribute the report that was typed yesterday.
2. Because my train was late, I missed my first appointment.
3. You will get a bonus because you did a superb job on the project.
4. Because our sales figures were not accurate, we underestimated our losses.
5. We are going to employ you because you are the most qualified applicant.

D.

1. Because he was concerned about the rising cost of raw materials, the contractor added 5 percent to his estimated price.
2. He has applied for Workers' Compensation benefits because he injured his foot while operating the forklift.
3. Because my flight to Atlanta was canceled, I spent an extra night in Washington.
4. Since Dolores has been promoted, we wonder who will be named to fill her position.
5. I refused to accept the shipment because it was damaged in transit.

E.

1. Mrs. Bonney praised Gary when the committee accepted his design.
2. Your credit application cannot be accepted because of your short employment history.
3. The department managers discussed the new vacation policy.
4. Susan Sokolovsky outlined the new procedures, and Jim Conte filled in the details.
5. The proposed education budget was passed by the state legislature.

F.

1. Her business acumen is equal to, if not sharper than, theirs.
2. Did Jeanne or her assistant call the client?
3. I have tried, and will continue to try, to contact her.
4. The latest survey shows that women own more stock than men own.
5. In his briefcase were a calculator, a pen, a file folder, and an umbrella.
6. Sarah reminded me about the time that she had neither money nor employment.
7. I have much respect for and confidence in Ms. Nelson's decisions.
8. Armstrong Investment Specialists advertised for a mailroom assistant and an account executive.
9. We need temporary personnel to keyboard documents, to proofread correspondence, and to answer the phone.
10. Daria's communications skills are as good as, if not better than, those of her coworkers.

Section 5.4 Building Effective Paragraphs

Objectives

After completing Section 5.4, the student should be able to:

1. Establish one purpose for writing a letter, memo, or report.
2. Write paragraphs that focus on one main idea and are no more than six to eight lines long.
3. Limit each sentence in a paragraph to one main thought that supports the paragraph's main idea.
4. Use transitional words and expressions to provide continuity and ease of reading.
5. Make paragraphing decisions to ensure the attractive appearance and the readability of the communication.

6. Use variety in sentence length and sentence structure to make communications more interesting.
7. Avoid a series of short sentences that can cause the reader to lose interest.

Overview

Building effective paragraphs requires writing good sentences and combining them to get the message across to the reader. Each communication should have one message; each paragraph should have one main idea; and each sentence should have one main thought. Transitional words and phrases should provide continuity and ease of reading. Effective writers carefully control each of these factors to achieve the purpose of the communication.

Teaching Suggestions

Emphasize that paragraphs should be no longer than six to eight lines. Then ask students how short paragraphs can be. After allowing time for answers, refer students to the list of guidelines on page 276. As suggested in the note on this page, point out that these are not rules but general guidelines.

Inform students that they can vary the pace of their communications by writing sentences of from 10 to 20 words. Such variety tends to hold the reader's interest. A series of sentences all the same length can take on a sing-song quality that is boring or annoying.

Exercise Keys

Practical Application (page 278)

A. The operator's body should be erect; he or she should sit well back in the chair and lean forward slightly from the waist. Feet should be placed firmly on the floor. The body should be about a handspan from the front of the keyboard.

   Sitting too close to the machine can cause bottom-row errors, just as sitting too far away can cause top-row errors. Likewise, sitting too far to the left or right causes errors of the opposite hand.

B. Everyone is invited to attend a reception on Wednesday, September 26, in honor of Graham C. Dobbs, who is retiring as corporation counsel after 30 years. The reception will begin at 5:30 p.m. in the corporate dining room.

C.

Dear Mr. Grant:

Thank you for requesting information about Lakeview Family Campground. Our grounds, arranged to provide privacy, can comfortably accommodate tents, camping vehicles, and mobile homes.

Free activities include morning aerobic workouts, afternoon water games, and nightly movies. Each Saturday night, the camp recreation director arranges free entertainment such as puppet shows, folk singing, and short plays.

You may select various optional services, which are available at very low rates. Cable television, water connections, and electrical hookups are the most popular selections. Shuttle bus service to the village, panoramic boat tours, and water skiing — all reasonably priced — are offered daily. Baby-sitting services are available ($4 per hour) through the local teen club.

The enclosed brochure lists our rates. Please phone us soon to make sure that you get the reservations you want.

Sincerely yours,

Section 5.5   Revising for Effective Writing

Objectives

After completing Section 5.5, the student should be able to:

1. Identify and use two techniques for finding errors or other problems in a written communication.
2. Determine whether a letter, memo, or report has a clear purpose, matches the needs and knowledge of the intended audience, and displays the appropriate tone for that audience.
3. Assess the organizational structure of a letter, memo, or report in terms of logical order, unity of purpose, and effective transitional devices.
4. Decide whether a title is short, clear, and informative.
5. Review the language of a written communication to see whether the words precisely convey the intended meaning, whether the writing is colorful and specific, whether sentence structure is varied, and whether the active voice is used wherever possible.

Overview

The revision process involves checking purpose, audience, and tone; reviewing organizational structure; assessing the specific language; and then making any necessary changes and refinements.

Whenever possible, it is a good idea to put aside a piece of writing for a few hours or even a day or so. This allows the writer to return to the letter, memo, or report with a fresh perspective.

Section 5.5 provides two comprehensive revision checklists that students can use for revising any communications they write.

Teaching Suggestions

Stress the advantage of letting some time elapse between the writing and revising of one's own writing, whether it be a letter, memo, or report. When writers move directly from one process to the other, they are still too close to the writing to review it objectively; the tendency is to see what they intended rather than how the message will be received by the reader.

Remind students that two other ways to gain some perspective on what they have written are to read it aloud and to ask someone else to review it critically.

Too often students regard writing outlines as pointless drudgery. Point out to students that using an outline before they begin to write not only makes the writing easier and faster; it also reduces the number of changes necessary in the revision.

Exercise Keys

Practical Application (page 285)

A. *Revising* means looking over a work again in order to improve the writing.

B. Revising can improve all writing.

C. Transitions are words that serve as bridges between ideas and paragraphs. They should be used to connect thoughts and make the writing smoother.

D. Using the active voice makes writing more forceful. Examples will vary.

E. A thesaurus can help writers find precise words to substitute for dull and overused words.

Critical Thinking (page 286)

Students' answers and revisions will vary.

1. Create variety at the beginning of the sentences.
2. Use more colorful words. (*Replace such words as* spending *and* stopped.)

3. Check the order of the sentences. (*The third sentence is out of order.*)
4. Eliminate sentences that do not relate to the main idea (*the last sentence*).
5. Replace words that are used incorrectly (*the word accomplish*).

CHAPTER 6
DEVELOPING PROOFREADING AND EDITING SKILLS

Proofreading and editing skills are important for anyone involved in written communication. Proofreading is actually a part of the editing process. The goal of proofreading is to detect and correct errors, whereas the purpose of editing is to make a written communication as effective as possible.

Section 6.1   The Proofreading Process

Objectives

After completing Section 6.1, the student should be able to:

1. Name the kinds of errors to look for when proofreading.
2. Explain when proofreading should be done.
3. Discuss why proofreading is important.
4. Explain why it is easier to proofread someone else's work than one's own work.
5. Describe how technology can help in the proofreading process.
6. List and follow the five proofreading steps.
7. Recognize and correctly use proofreaders' marks.

Overview

Proofreading is a vital step in the writing process. Uncorrected errors not only create a bad impression, but also can cause misunderstanding and cost a business money. The final responsibility for errors rests with the document originator, but teamwork throughout document preparation is the key to a quality finished product.

Mastery of basic rules, appropriate use of reference sources, practice in finding errors, and awareness of frequently occurring errors will increase proofreading skill.

Teaching Suggestions

Give your students proofreading practice by asking them to bring in errors they find in newspapers, magazines, and books. After students have completed the section, have them use the proofreaders' marks given in the text to correct the errors.

Be sure that students are aware of the kinds of proofreading help that spell-checkers and certain software programs can provide. However, also emphasize the limitations of these devices. In addition, review the three techniques for proofreading on a computer screen.

Exercise Keys

Practical Application (page 293)

C.

1. Dr. Sam Martinez autographed copies of his latest book, *Healthy Eating for Busy Executives.*
2. His letter was misinterpreted by the newspaper editor.
3. Phil's Sandwich Shop opens daily at 10:30 a.m.
4. The camera and the film were shipped February 10.
5. Mrs. Anderson, I appreciate your willingness to participate in our charitable interests.
6. The shipment will arrive in three days.
7. Many business expenses are tax-deductible.
8. Tom and Mariel are looking forward to their summer vacation.
9. Alexandra went to Mexico and to South America.
10. We need a new ZIP Code directory.

Section 6.2   The Editing Process

Objectives

After completing Section 6.2, the student should be able to:

1. Describe the relationship between editing and proofreading.
2. Explain what a draft is and why most business communications require more than one draft.
3. Name and apply the six questions that editing seeks to answer.
4. Discuss how word processors and computers with word processing programs have made editing easier.

Overview

Editing is revising a document to improve it. The editing process ensures that the document is clear, complete, concise, consistent, correct, and courteous.

Technology has simplified the editing process. By simply pushing a few buttons, text can be added, changed, corrected, deleted, or rearranged. Button pushing is simple; the challenge is knowing *when* to push the buttons. This knowledge constitutes editing skill.

Teaching Suggestions

As suggested in the text notes, after each topic in this section is discussed, have students complete the related Practical Application.

Again, emphasize the limitations as well as the advantages of using word processing and computer technology in the editing process. Then go over the proofreaders' marks for editing on pages 291–292, making sure students know how to use these marks correctly.

Exercise Keys

Practical Application (page 298)

A. Underscored words should be replaced or deleted. Students' answers will vary.

1. use
2. I look forward to hearing from you soon. (delete "I remain")
3. As requested, I enclose a copy of your sales slip.
4. rather
5. get

D.

1. Use either solid capitals or underlining; do not mix styles.
2. . . . 2214, 2215, 2216.
3. . . . June, July, and August.
4. . . . Clary, Dixon, and White
5. . . . and Mr. Steven Horowitz

F. Students' answers will vary.

1. Your order will be shipped just as soon as we receive your shirt size. A preaddressed, postage-paid card is enclosed for your convenience in supplying the information.
2. Please call our toll-free number if we can make learning to operate your microwave oven quicker and easier.
3. Thank you, Ben, for the work you did on the Kansas project.
4. I can always depend on you, Ben, to find a solution to any public relations problem our company may have.
5. Our manager presented the award to John Torres.

Editing Practice (page 299)

Nancy Threlkeld will assume the position of Director of Employee Activities on Monday, July 1. In this position, she will be responsible for athletic teams, organizations, trips, and all other social events sponsored by our company. She will have a meeting Tuesday, July 2, at 2:30 p.m., in the Recreation Hall, to get your suggestions for August and September activities. On Wednesday, July 3, she will attend a conference to learn about activities offered by other companies.

CHAPTER 7
WRITING MEMORANDUMS

More than half of all written business communications are memorandums. Memos are used within a department, between departments, and between company divisions. Various types of these internal communications are used to inform, report, remind, transmit, and promote goodwill. A communication lifeline within an organization, memos are quick, inexpensive, and convenient and provide a written record of internal activities.

Section 7.1   Memo Purposes and Writing Techniques

Objectives

After completing Section 7.1, the student should be able to:

1. Indicate the advantages of using memorandums.
2. Distinguish among the six main uses of memos.
3. Demonstrate the ability to achieve appropriate tone in memos.
4. Organize memos according to statement of purpose, message, and statement of future action.
5. Identify and apply specific writing strategies to increase memo effectiveness.
6. Use special formatting and mechanical techniques appropriately and sparingly in memos.

Overview

Memorandums are the most frequently used written business communication. Thus two sections have been devoted to this topic.

Memorandums are quick, inexpensive, and convenient and provide an often-needed written record. They are used to inquire, inform, report, remind, transmit, and promote goodwill. They are used primarily within the organization, and they can be as important and as complex as any letter or as simple as an informal note.

This section discusses memo tone and organization—purpose, message, and future action. It also presents writing strategies to improve the effectiveness of memos, as well as special formatting and mechanical techniques to hold the reader's attention.

Teaching Suggestions

Because memos are internal communications, students may have a tendency to regard them as less important than communications to clients, suppliers, and others outside an organization. As suggested in the text, emphasize that memos are crucial to keeping an organization running smoothly and effectively.

Having students give an example for each memo use, as recommended in the text, will indicate whether you need to spend extra time on any of these uses.

Stress the three organizational elements of a memorandum, directing students' attention to the sample memo on page 305.

After students have illustrated various formatting and mechanical techniques, as suggested in the text, note whether the techniques were used appropriately and explain why such techniques must be used sparingly.

Exercise Keys

Practical Application (page 308)

A.

1. Memos are more appropriate when writing to people inside your organization.
2. Letters are more appropriate when writing to people outside your organization.

B.

1. Memos are quick.
2. Memos are inexpensive.
3. Memos are convenient.
4. Memos are a written record.

D. The three basic parts of the body of a memo are the statement of purpose, message, and future action.

Sample memo body:

I would like to request reimbursement for a course I am planning to take this fall.

The course is Data Processing 101 at Cranbury Community College. It starts on September 7 and meets every Monday for 12 weeks. I would earn three credit hours, and the tuition is $250.

Taking this data processing course will help me improve my productivity as a secretary and will, I believe, make me a more valuable employee.

Would you approve tuition reimbursement? I will call your office next week to learn of your decision.

Students' answers concerning the three parts of their memos will vary but should include these elements:
Statement of purpose: request for tuition reimbursement
Message: information about the course and its value to the company
Future action: will follow up about the approval

E. Special techniques in memos are (a) enumerations, (b) columns with headings, (c) all capitals and centering, (d) underlining and side headings, (e) bullets for emphasis, (f) boldface print and italics, and (g) color coding. Overuse of these techniques makes them commonplace.

Sample memo body:

As you requested, I have analyzed sales for April, May, and June by region. The results follow.

Region	April	May	June
1	$23,494	$22,577	$19,482
2	$33,458	$32,332	$25,854
3	$21,589	$21,887	$20,492

Please let me know if you need further information.

Section 7.2   Memo Types and Memo Style Style

Objectives

After completing Section 7.2, the student should be able to:

1. Describe and use the typical memo format.
2. Send informal notes—handwritten, typed, or on printed forms—when appropriate.
3. Identify and correctly use printed forms for standard memos, message memos, and routing information.

4. Correctly fill in the TO, FROM, DATE, and SUBJECT lines at the top of a memo.
5. Present the body of a memorandum in an appropriate style or the preferred "house" style of a particular organization.
6. Indicate any necessary notations (initials, enclosure, copy) at the end of a memo.

Overview

Section 7.2 describes and illustrates several types of memorandums, including typical memos, informal notes, and various printed forms. Also discussed here are typed or printed heading lines used in memos and how they should be completed.

Teaching Suggestion

Use the items students bring to class for the bulletin board display suggested in the text to augment the illustrations in the text. Point out differences, if any, to reinforce the fact that various organizations set their own memo style.

Exercise Keys

Practical Application (page 316)

A.

1. Phone messages from visitors are transmitted in message memos.
2. Routing slips are used to channel messages to specific people systematically.
3. Distribution lists are used when a memo goes to many people and a routing slip is not used.
4. The memo writer would include the addressee's job title if (a) the writer wishes to show deference, (b) the addressee has two or more job titles and the memo concerns only one title, and (c) the addressee has the same name as another employee or a similar name.
5. An enclosure notation and a copy notation might be needed below the initials of the typist of a memo.

D. Sample memo:

TO: Company Director
FROM: (Student's name), Administrative Assistant
DATE: (Current date)
SUBJECT: Fabric Choices of Designers for Fall Collections

I have completed the survey of designer-fabric choices for fall that you requested last Tuesday. The table below presents a summary of the preferences of the 20 leading designers of fall clothes last year. More extensive information is attached.

Designer Fabric Preferences
for Fall

Number of Designers / Fabric	0–5	6–10	11–15	16–20
Wool				X
Cashmere			X	
Mohair		X		
Flannel			X	
Corduroy		X		
Cotton		X		
Rayon	X			
Silk (mostly crepe de chine)		X		

Please let me know if you need further information.

Editing Practice (page 317)

Aaron Singer of Caralia Draperies will be here tomorrow morning at 10:30 to show us his line of window treatments. His best-selling draperies are bow and ribbon swags and eyelet tiebacks. Our competitors are doing quite well with these two styles of draperies, and we have lost some business because we do not have them.

CHAPTER 8
WRITING BUSINESS LETTERS

Just as memorandums are an organization's internal communication lifeline, business letters are one of an organization's vital links with the outside world of clients, suppliers, and the general public. Both content and appearance establish the effectiveness of business letters. Among their many uses, these letters make and answer requests, make claims and claim adjustments, sell an idea or a product, enhance the organization's image, and deliver social-business messages. Given the increasing volume of business correspondence and the available technology, business writers are turning to carefully crafted form letters and letters with form paragraphs to deliver many of their messages.

Section 8.1   Business Letter Style

Objectives

After completing Section 8.1, the student should be able to:

1. Explain the need for and use of each standard letter part.
2. Identify the optional parts of business letters.
3. List the order in which letter parts appear in business correspondence and use them correctly.
4. Use the letter formats considered acceptable in business, including the formats for personal-business letters and for social-business letters.
5. Avoid outdated expressions, redundancies, and fancy words in writing sentences.
6. Demonstrate conciseness, specificity, coherence, and completeness in writing business letters.

Overview

The first part of Section 8.1 is concerned primarily with the *style* — the *look*, the *appearance* — of the business letter and the importance of making a good first impression. The section presents students with the basic styles that are "acceptable" in business. Essentially, then, they learn the appropriate vehicles for delivering business messages. The section then moves on to a discussion of the content of the business letter, the lasting impression the letter writer leaves with the receiver. Included here is information on avoiding repetition and being up to date, concise, specific, coherent, and complete in business letter writing.

Teaching Suggestions

Explain why letter writing is critical to successful communication in today's business world. Discuss how letters convey an image of the writer, either a positive or a negative image. Furthermore, letters depict an image of the writer's company. Help students see that a neat, professional-looking letter does for the writer what neat, business-style clothes do for the job applicant.

Tell students that a practical approach for new employees is to select the letter format used by co-workers or preferred by the supervisor. You may want to discuss the use of an in-house style sheet to maintain consistency in communication style throughout a business or organization. In addition, emphasize the need for a comprehensive reference manual on the job.

Discuss, too, the need for and use of the personal-business letter format. Many students have already had opportunities to write letters of a personal-business nature and will surely write many more in the future. Unless a writer is using personal letterhead stationery, he or she will need to know this standard format.

Use the brief discussions under "The Lasting Impression: *Content*" to establish an awareness among students of the need to use current expressions, to avoid redundancy, and so on, in their business writing. (These topics are deliberately brief here because they are discussed in greater detail in the subsequent sections in Chapter 8.) Toward this end, review carefully the end-of-section text exercises, as well as the correlated activities workbook exercises, to develop these basic skills.

Exercise Keys

Practical Application (page 334)

A.   No key is required, but note these points: Many people who receive letters prepared in the simplified style dislike the style. The styles most frequently used and accepted are the block format and the modified-block format.

C.

1. Regarding your letter of June 27, . . .
2. As of August 4 we have still not received . . .
3. Your May 5 dividend will be $6,000.
4. If August 14 is inconvenient, please let us know when you would like the speakers delivered.
5. Since property sales are down because of a . . .

Editing Practice (page 335)

1. I would like to make an appointment to see you as soon as possible.
2. I hope to hear from you soon.
   Sincerely yours,
3. Please let us know your decision soon.
4. We are now revising the production schedule.
5. Since manufacturing costs are rising, we must increase prices accordingly.
6. Omit. (The time for thanks is after the task is done.)
7. Your order for a scanner is being shipped today.
8. Enclosed is our payment.
9. If you have a better suggestion, please tell me soon.

10. Research was not one of the director's responsibilities.

Section 8.2   Writing and Answering Requests

Objectives

After completing Section 8.2, the student should be able to:

1. Recognize that while writing and answering requests are routine matters in business, they should not be treated routinely.
2. Explain how to be complete, precise, reasonable, and courteous in writing request letters.
3. Write request letters that are complete, precise, reasonable, and courteous.
4. Discuss the advantages of being prompt, helpful, sales-minded, specific, complete, and positive in answering requests.
5. Demonstrate the qualities of promptness, helpfulness, sales-mindedness, specificity, completeness, and a positive approach in writing answers to business requests.

Overview

While adhering to the qualities of all business letters, requests must also be reasonable and courteous. Similarly, answers to requests should be prompt, sales-minded, and positive. Section 8.2 elaborates on all of these qualities and provides several illustrations of effective business requests and answers. Thirteen practical applications test students' ability to write effective request letters and answers to requests.

Teaching Suggestions

Review with students some of the many routine business tasks that involve requesting information or help of some kind — for example, making appointments, reserving conference rooms, obtaining brochures and pamphlets, inviting speakers to conferences, and scheduling meetings. Be sure that students understand that making requests is an ordinary part of the business day.

As noted in the text, business requests must be complete, precise, reasonable, and courteous. Write these four goals on the chalkboard; before continuing, ask students to explain in their own words why each is important. Then proceed to cover each goal in detail.

Stress that incomplete requests waste time — both the writer's time and the reader's time. In addition, the reader feels somewhat justified in rejecting an incomplete request. Note that writing a request that is complete — or writing any correspondence that is complete — requires careful thinking on the writer's part. For example, what additional information, if any, will help the reader grant this request promptly?

The need to be precise should be evident. Tell students that considering the request from the reader's point of view often prods the writer to provide the reader with *precise and complete* information.

Remind students that all of us have a tendency to view our own needs as critical needs. In an effort to do our jobs well, we sometimes fall into the trap of making unreasonable requests of others. Ask how many students have seen the popular cartoon of a man who is laughing uproariously while saying, "You want it WHEN?!" Tell them that in this cartoon, the request is so unreasonable that it is laughable — a reminder to business people who should consider the consequences of making unreasonable requests.

Emphasize to students that the need for courtesy is sometimes overlooked when people view their request as "strictly business." Use the example of a supervisor or manager who snaps an order to his or her assistant to "Stop whatever you're doing and get started on this right away." Note that this individual has forgotten the basic need for courtesy to coworkers — including subordinates. Likewise, point out that in request letters, basic courtesy is sometimes overlooked when the writer feels — or *knows* — the request is reasonable. Remind students that showing courtesy toward others is important in all aspects of interpersonal relations, including the writing of all letters.

In terms of answering requests, emphasize that every businessperson who receives a request letter — or any letter — has the responsibility to acknowledge that letter and to do so promptly. Not only does a prompt reply show courtesy, but it also is simply good business. Discuss this fact with the class, stressing that it applies to all letters.

List these six goals on the chalkboard: be prompt, be helpful, be sales-minded, be specific, be complete, and be positive. Then proceed to discuss each in detail. Point out to students the obvious repetition of some goals from the first part of this section; they will also be repeated in later sections. Stress that these are common objectives; they are not restricted to any one kind of letter. All letters must be complete, specific, courteous, and so on — thus the repetition.

Discuss the ways in which word processing equipment helps companies respond quickly to inquiries and still permits the writer to personalize a reply. In preparation for Section 8.7, ask students to bring in to the class any letters that illustrate how businesses use word processors to speed up the letter-writing process.

Review students' responses to the end-of-section exercises. Point out the specific ways in which their messages did and did not achieve the goals listed in the text.

Exercise Keys

Practical Application (page 351)

A.

Alvarez Office Furniture
1199 Memorial Boulevard
Des Plaines, Illinois 46043

Ladies and Gentlemen:

Thank you for sending your catalog and price list. We have decided on the No. 42F walnut desk with double file drawers on each end and a locking drawer in the center.

We will be moving into our new offices at 66 Sycamore Street on July 27 and would appreciate delivery no later than one week from that date.

Please charge this purchase to our account.

Sincerely yours,

B. Check each letter of request for completeness, accuracy, reasonableness, and courtesy. Letters should be related to the advertisements students have selected. Ask students to attach the selected advertisements.

C.

Superintendent of Documents
U.S. Government Printing Office
Washington, D.C. 20402

Ladies and Gentlemen:

Please send me a list of U.S. government publications about waste management. I am especially interested in forecasts of the role of the mechanical engineer and the demand for mechanical engineering in the next decade.

Sincerely,

D.

Rainbow Images Copiers
999 South Chillicothe Road
Aurora, Ohio 44202

Ladies and Gentlemen:

Please send me the names and addresses of your dealers in my city. I would also appreciate your sending any available catalogs and price lists for your Galaxy color copier and related products.

Sincerely,

E.

Consumer Reports
Mount Vernon, New York, 10962
Attention: Subscription Manager

Ladies and Gentlemen:

Please send us information about your group subscription plan.

Specifically, how large must a group be in order for its members to qualify for the group rate? What is the group rate, and what saving does it afford in comparison with the individual-subscriber rate? Do group subscribers receive the *Annual Buying Guide* or any of your other publications?

We will appreciate hearing from you as soon as possible. If a special subscription form is used to enroll groups, will you please send one?

Sincerely,

F.

Old Prints Museum
853 Oakridge Road
Minneapolis, Minnesota 55401

Ladies and Gentlemen:

Please send us a copy of your booklet *Care and Preservation of Lithographs.*
Our check for $3.95 is enclosed.

Sincerely yours,

G.

1. How nice it would be if . . .
2. I would appreciate . . .

3. How happy you would make me if . . .
4. Your offer to send a free sample of _____ is generous.
5. I hope I can repay you for . . .
6. I treasure your gift.
7. What a generous offer!
8. I am grateful for the opportunity . . .

H. Sample reply:

Mr. Steven Crowell
23 Saltway Drive
Saltway, Florida 33596

Dear Mr. Crowell:

Thank you for your letter of October 1 asking for a copy of the first issue of our new magazine *Video Visions*.

I wish that we could send you one, but demand has exceeded all our expectations, and the first issue has sold out. The next issue will be coming off the presses in 10 days, and I will make certain that you get a copy.

I have enclosed a subscription form for *Video Visions* as well as information about some of our other publications on the home entertainment field. Please let me know if I can help you in any other way.

Sincerely yours,

I. Sample reply:

Mr. John Rosetti
Howard House and Garden Shop
853 Wallace Street
Dearfield, Illinois 62705

Dear Mr. Rosetti:

We were delighted to receive your order of March 1 and look upon it as the beginning of a long and mutually beneficial relationship between our firm and yours. We will ship the merchandise by freight on March 15, and you should receive the shipment before March 25.

Our terms of payment are standard. Like most other manufacturers of gardening equipment, we allow a 2 percent discount for payment within 10 days of the date of the invoice; complete payment is due within 30 days of that date.

We are pleased to have you as a customer and pledge that we will do everything we can to give you the best in products and in service.

Sincerely yours,

J. Sample reply:

Mr. Craig Curtis
Chief Advertising Consultant
New England Best Business Consulting
212 Crofts Street
Peterborough, New Hampshire 03484

Dear Mr. Curtis:

Thank you for consenting to make a presentation to the convention of the New England Advertising League. As we agreed during our telephone conversation, the topic is "Advertising in the Electronic Age."

I now have further details of the meeting and can pass them along to you. The convention will be held on June 24 at the Merrick Hotel in Cambridge, Massachusetts. Your presentation will take place in the Peerless Ballroom at 4:30 p.m. and should last approximately 40 minutes. Immediately following will be a 20-minute discussion period. The group should consist of about 50 people, all League members, and League members tend to be lively.

You are also cordially invited to be our guest at the dinner to be held afterward, starting at 5:30 p.m. I have enclosed a complimentary ticket.

I look forward to hearing your presentation. If I can assist you in any way before the convention, please let me know.

Cordially yours,

K. Sample reply:

Mrs. John Fletcher
2224 Humbolt Street
Akron, Ohio 44313

Dear Mrs. Fletcher:

I am very sorry to report that an unprecedented parts shortage will prevent us from repairing and returning your Infinite Video Computer Game System within our usual service period of one week.

Your unit requires simple replacement of a cracked integrated circuit, or "chip," and the repair will cost only $15. Unfortunately, the particular chip needed, quite common and usually plentiful, has disappeared from the inventories of all national suppliers. We have ordered chips from the manufacturer but do not expect them for two weeks.

We know how much you must enjoy playing the many games available for the Infinite system, and we regret the delay in returning it to you. We have enclosed a brochure on some new game cartridges to be released shortly. We hope that these may add to your enjoyment of the Infinite system when we return it to you in perfect working condition.

> Very sincerely yours,

L. Sample reply:

Ms. Marilyn Novack, Chairperson
Association of Office Managers
8788 North Filmore Street
Blacksburg, Virginia 24060

Dear Ms. Novack:

Thank you for inviting me to speak at the meeting of the Association of Office Managers on January 15. Since I have always admired the work of the Association, I am flattered by the invitation.

Unfortunately, however, I feel that between now and the fifteenth I will not have enough time to prepare a worthwhile presentation. Since I received the invitation this morning, I have one week for preparation — and this week happens to be one in which I have many previous commitments.

I would be happy to speak to the Association at a later date. But in order to do justice to the subject and to the membership, I would need at least three weeks' advance notice. Once again, thank you for your invitation.

> Very truly yours,

M. Sample revision:

Ms. Rita D'Amico
1100 Rosemont Drive
Indianapolis, Indiana 46226

Dear Ms. D'Amico:

Thank you for your letter requesting Zapamatic motion picture equipment. The Zapamatic projector is a reliable, lightweight projector of the highest optical quality, reflecting years of careful development. The complementary equipment meets the same high standards. We are only manufacturers, however, and we have made agreements with other firms to sell our products retail. Therefore, we ourselves cannot fill your order as requested.

However, we can recommend our retailer in your area: Hagen Camera Retailers, 668 Northpoint Street, Indianapolis, Indiana 46221. Hagen has a long record of courteous, reliable service to the public. We feel sure that Hagen will be able to supply all your motion-picture needs. If for any reason you should need more information, please contact us again, and we will be happy to assist you.

> Very sincerely yours,

cc: Hagen Camera Retailers

Editing Practice (page 354)

1. We have noted the information in your application.
2. Thank you for taking the time to complete the questionnaire.
3. I have received your letter of October 10.
4. We still have not received your payment for last month.
5. We will be sending the fax card to you by Express Mail.
6. I am enclosing an invoice for $210.98.
7. If you are unable to accept the offer, please let us know.
8. I am enclosing the prospectus for Oakgrove Condominiums, Ltd.

Section 8.3   Writing Claim and Adjustment Letters

Objectives

After completing Section 8.3, the student should be able to:

1. Get all the relevant facts before making a claim.
2. Describe any claim completely and accurately.
3. Avoid accusations, threats, and demands in claim letters.
4. Suggest reasonable solutions to a claim.
5. Evaluate each claim letter received and make adjustments based on company policy, the claimant's possible role in causing the claim, and the law.
6. Write effective adjustment letters for allowable and partially allowable claims.
7. Acknowledge a nonallowable claim courteously, diplomatically explain why the claim cannot be granted, use a positive tone, show appreciation for the claimant's business, and try to maintain goodwill.

Overview

Admittedly, writing claim and adjustment letters is a specialized skill. Most students will not write claim and adjustment letters on a routine basis.

However, claim and adjustment letters provide an excellent vehicle for students to learn and apply basic negotiating skills and to develop common business sense. For example, claim and adjustment situations introduce students to the real business world, where companies sometimes make mistakes and customers at times demand more than they deserve. Students, consequently, are introduced to realistic decision-making problems.

In this section students learn that facts form the basis of all effective claim and adjustment letters. Once again, students encounter the need to provide *complete* information and *accurate*, *precise* data — dates, sizes, order numbers, check amounts, quantities, discount rates.

Teaching Suggestions

Explain to students that there is seldom any necessity to threaten, accuse, or demand when making a claim (certainly not in the first letter, anyway) because most companies are honest and fair.

Emphasize that handling claim letters — that is, writing adjustments — often requires good business sense and highly developed negotiating skills. As suggested in the text, however, caution students about the necessity of getting the required approvals before making any claim adjustments.

Be sure to elicit from students and discuss with the class any personal experiences students may have had with claims and adjustments.

Convince the class that students who can write effective claim and adjustment letters have developed an enviable skill — one that they will be able to apply to all their business letters.

Exercise Keys

Practical Application (page 363)

A.   Sample letter:

Mr. Benjamin Davis
Customer Service Representative
City-Wide Newspaper Delivery Service
322 Oxford Street
Detroit, Michigan 48226

Dear Mr. Davis:

On my first monthly statement for newspaper delivery, you have billed me for both the daily and the Sunday newspaper. Charges for these services were $7.20 and $3.40, respectively. I wish to point out that I ordered only the daily newspaper and that only the daily newspaper was delivered.

Please find and examine the order form that I filled out. The form should confirm that I ordered the daily newspaper only. In addition, this morning I asked your delivery boy on this route, Joey Cornell, and he clearly recalls delivering only the daily newspapers to my house. In view of these facts, I am requesting that you adjust my monthly bill to show charges for the daily newspaper only.

Sincerely yours,

B.   Sample reply:

Thank you for calling our attention to the error in your monthly bill for newspaper delivery. A check of our records has confirmed that you requested and received delivery of the daily newspaper only. A simple clerical error in the billing process caused the mistake in your statement.

We have adjusted your bill, removing the incorrect charge of $3.40 for Sunday newspapers. We apologize for the inconvenience that our error caused.

Very truly yours,

C.   Sample letter:

Dear Ms. Solfano:

Thank you for your letter of _____. We will be happy to replace the defective fan in your SuperSpool Rapid Film Processor. We are confident that the processor will work perfectly after this repair.

In addition, we will send our claims adjuster, Gregory Barnes, to examine the wasted film. Mr. Barnes is a capable and experienced claims adjuster, and we are sure that he can bring this claim to a satisfactory conclusion.

Allow me to apologize again for the inconvenience caused by the fan malfunction. Believe me, you can now count on your SuperSpool processor to provide months of trouble-free service.

Sincerely yours,

D. *Note:* Individual responses will vary. Students may choose to grant Ms. Solfano's request for compensation for all wasted film, since the defective fan was responsible. Students taking this view could argue that Ms. Solfano has purchased a $9,000 film processor, and so a $250 adjustment is worth granting since she may purchase more equipment if her business expands. On the other hand, common sense should have told Ms. Solfano to call for service before wasting a full 500 feet of film. Students may cite this reason (in diplomatic terms) for denying her request for additional compensation.

Sample reply:

Dear Ms. Solfano:

We are delighted to learn that the replacement fan has fully repaired your SuperSpool Rapid Film Processor.

Our claims adjuster, Gregory Barnes, has also confirmed that the damaged fan was partially responsible for the wastage of $250 worth of film. Since you are a new customer and are unfamiliar with our policies, we have decided to compensate you fully for this wastage, and our check is enclosed.

Should a similar malfunction occur in the future, however, please call our service department at once, and wait until repairs are completed before using any additional film. Ordinarily we limit adjustments for film wastage to the cost of a single roll.

If your SuperSpool performs as we expect, neither of us will have to worry about this problem again for some time.

Cordially yours,

E. Sample letter:

Whirling Wonder Kitchen Co.
One Bluegrass Way
Lexington, Kentucky 40506

Gentlemen:

I regret to report that our new Whirling Wonder food processor does not work properly. Although we have had the processor for only a few hours, my chef has already demonstrated that the machine slices in a very inconsistent manner. Many fine foods, of course, require even slices for correct appearance.

Your advertisements claim that the processor slices vegetables perfectly at any desired thickness between $1/16$ inch and 1 inch. This claim was a major factor in our decision to purchase your processor.

We wish to exchange our defective processor for one that works properly. We would appreciate your sending a new processor as quickly as possible.

Sincerely yours,

F. Sample reply:

Mr. William Roland, Manager
Le Crepuscule
665 Darien Street
Omaha, Nebraska 68108

Dear Mr. Roland:

This morning we received your letter reporting that your new Whirling Wonder is slicing unevenly.

Although the problem of uneven slicing is rare for the Whirling Wonder, we have noticed that when the problem does occur, the cause is usually a damaged slicing disk. You can determine whether the slicing disk is at fault quite easily. Just test the Whirling Wonder's operation with other attachments. If the two-bladed knife and the shredding disk do a good job of dicing, chopping, grating, grinding, and shredding, then the problem is almost certainly a damaged slicing disk.

We would appreciate your asking your chef to test the Whirling Wonder in these other functions. If your Whirling Wonder performs properly during the tests, then we will be happy to send you a new slicing disk at no charge.

We would be quite surprised if the Whirling Wonder does not perform correctly with the other attachments. In that unlikely event, however, we will send you a complete new Whirling Wonder.

We are sorry that you are experiencing problems with your new Whirling Wonder. We assure you that the Whirling Wonder is a reliable machine. Once we have restored your Whirling Wonder to good working order or replaced yours with another, you should enjoy years of trouble-free operation.

Sincerely yours,

Editing Practice (page 364)

1. Because of the great demand for the item you

ordered, we will not be able to make delivery by July 15.

2. We are returning the form to you so that you can fill in your taxpayer's identification number.
3. Perhaps you have mislaid our letter of June 10.
4. Your letter of October 3 does not clearly explain the reason for your delay in paying.
5. We will send a computer technician to your office as soon as possible.
6. We will be glad to repair the cabinet that was damaged in transit.
7. We were sorry to hear that you were not pleased with our sunscreen product.
8. Please send us the sales receipt for your stolen watch so that we can verify your claim.
9. We are sorry that Order 977 arrived late.
10. We find a difference of $27 in the total on our March 15 invoice.

Section 8.4   Writing Persuasive Letters

Objectives

After completing Section 8.4, the student should be able to:

1. Explain the importance of sales letters to modern business.
2. Identify two advantages of sales letters over broadcast advertisements.
3. Discuss the function of marketing in targeting audiences for various goods and services.
4. Distinguish between people's wants and needs.
5. Identify and describe what the five objectives of an effective sales letter do for the reader.
6. Explain, with examples, how sales appeals stimulate readers' buying motives.
7. List four ways in which writers of sales letters can give readers the opportunity to act.
8. Describe a typical sales letter campaign.
9. Discuss three steps that writers of credit and collection letters can take to get customers to pay their bills.

Overview

Section 8.4 focuses on two types of persuasive letters: sales letters and credit and collection letters. The first task of writers of sales letters is to target their audience and then to convince that audience that their product can meet the audience's needs and wants.

Students next learn how to write effective sales letters that accomplish the goals of attracting the reader's attention, establishing a relationship with the reader, appealing to the reader's buying motives, persuading the reader to act, and giving the reader an opportunity to act.

The goal of credit and collection letters is to get customers to pay their bills while maintaining their goodwill. Writers of such letters usually accomplish this goal by making sure customers understand the company's credit terms, assuming that customers will pay, and — when necessary — sending customers additional reminders.

Teaching Suggestions

Because the attention of many students is geared to electronic media, it is especially wise to emphasize the continuing importance of sales letters to all kinds of businesses. Stressing the advantages of sales letters over radio and television advertisements can help reinforce this point.

After students have read articles on how companies target audiences, have them share their findings with the class. Then work with the class to draw up a list of effective targeting strategies.

Go over the illustrations in this section with students and have them identify the objectives that each illustration accomplishes. Compare text illustrations with sales letters students bring to class. Ask which are effective and why.

Exercise Keys

Practical Application (page 373)

A. (1) Recipients can hold letters and reread them, and letters can be more direct and personal. (2) A *target audience* is the select group of prospective buyers that a sales letter is aimed at.

B. (1) It attracts the reader's attention, sets up a close relationship with the reader, appeals to one or more specific buying motives, persuades the reader to act, and gives the reader an opportunity to act. (2) Answers include: reply cards, order forms, coupons, and toll-free telephone numbers.

C. The rules are as follows: be sure customers understand the credit terms, assume that customers will pay, and send additional reminders if necessary.

D. Answers will vary.

E. Answers will vary.

Editing Practice (page 374)

1. We are sorry that we did not test your VCR after it was repaired.
2. Unfortunately, we are obliged to add a charge for delivering your furniture.
3. As soon as we receive your warranty number, we will repair your CD player.
4. If you send us your coupons, we can apply a discount to your purchase.
5. Please remit payment immediately.

Section 8.5 Writing Public Relations Letters

Objectives

After completing Section 8.5, the student should be able to:

1. Explain the purpose of public relations and every business writer's role in fostering good public relations.
2. Describe several special public relations opportunities.
3. Discuss some everyday public relations opportunities.
4. Write public relations letters that capitalize on special and everyday public relations opportunities to generate positive feelings toward the organization.
5. Use public relations techniques in writing all business letters.

Overview

Section 8.5 presents, once again, a very specialized subject, public relations. Although students may never work in the public relations department of a major corporation, most students will have daily opportunities to influence their companies' public image. Every employee whose job requires communication with people outside the company has a potential effect on the company's public image and therefore can help improve public relations. Thus PR specialists are not the only people who influence public opinion. All business writers influence public relations.

This section makes students aware of the importance of good public relations and provides them with some general techniques for improving public relations.

Teaching Suggestions

As suggested in the marginal note, help students recognize that winning positive feelings toward the organization is not the only goal of public relations efforts. A more important but less obvious goal is to sell the organization's product. Also help students understand the difference between selling and promoting something.

Discuss with the class current examples of public relations campaigns. The examples may be the elaborate, nationally televised campaigns of multinational corporations or a simple sign in front of the local firehouse: "Fighting fires in Westwood for 75 years." In any case, the examples should underscore the fact that public relations campaigns are not direct sales-promotion campaigns. The goal of public relations campaigns is to boost the public's opinion of the company in general, not just the public's opinion of a particular product.

Discuss with the class consumers' preferences for products from "favored" companies, companies that are known not only for their excellent products and superior service but also for their charitable deeds and their stature in the community. Companies know that favorable public opinion is a huge financial asset.

Exercise Keys

Practical Application (page 384)

A. No key is necessary. The student should consult the pages of this section that are devoted to techniques of promoting a new business.

B. Sample letter:

Dear _____:

BECAUSE we value our charge customers *very* much . . .

and

BECAUSE we haven't seen you for a while . . .

We've entered your name in our special Prized Charge Customer Prize Drawing. Come to the store next Tuesday night at 7:00, and you may win a whole new winter wardrobe.

Only the names of charge-card customers are entered in this drawing, which means you have a good chance to win. We'll also be eager to remind you of the other benefits of having our charge card:

1. A special event each month *for charge customers only*.
2. Discounts of 2 percent for paying within 10 days.
3. Extra-attentive service from our sales staff.
4. A new telephone-order line reserved for charge customers.

So come in, win a prize, find bargains galore, and let us show you what a treat it can be to be one of our prized charge customers.

Sincerely yours,

C. Probably the most important point to be emphasized in this letter is the need to keep the customer's business even though you are introducing a fee that the customer cannot be expected to like. The letter should show reasons for customers not to take their business elsewhere. An example follows:

We at Vanguard's wish we didn't have to write this letter, but . . .

We know you must be aware of all the pressures and problems that come from inflation. Perhaps the worst of all is the dramatic and persistent rise in interest rates. Well, we are as aware of this problem as you are. That's why we have been forced to write this letter.

As of November 1, we must introduce a $15 annual fee for charge cards. We have put off this step as long as we could. As you know, when we issue you a charge card, we are lending you money. And we are glad to do it. But where do we get the money that we lend you? From our bankers. And we don't get it free. We felt that introducing this once-a-year fee was the best way to deal with this problem. This way you will know exactly how much extra you are paying each year, and you will know that it is going to happen only *once* a year.

We hope that we can compensate you by striving harder than ever to bring you the widest assortment of high-quality merchandise from around the world and by giving you the best prices in the city.

If you prefer to avoid the fee, then we will be happy to serve you on a cash basis.

We are sure that you will understand why we have to institute this fee. We pledge to eliminate the fee as soon as interest rates are under control.

D. Sample invitation:

Dear Ms. Olliver:

In a recent review, *Home Beautiful* called Newlook's Sierra line of furniture and decorations "the most attractive American furniture design in the past 50 years."

We are pleased to invite you to a special showing of Sierra furniture and decorations in the Sierra Room at the Newlook Showroom, 657 Woodside Avenue, on March 21, from six until nine in the evening. Admission is *by invitation only* and is restricted to our charge customers, their families, and their friends. Your ticket, which is enclosed, will admit you and your guests.

Our Sierra Room will be open to the general public on March 28, but why wait until then? Join us on March 21 for an evening of refreshments, beautiful music, and dazzling furniture and decorations — an evening you will be sure to remember for years to come.

Sincerely,

E. Sample letter:

Dear New Resident:

Welcome to the Lindemann's Hardware service area. We're so convinced that you will like the service at Lindemann's that we're willing to give you $5 to come in and have a look. Come and use your $5 New Customer Coupon anytime before June 30.

Lindemann's is the finest hardware store in the metropolitan area. Since we're located on the outskirts of the city, we're a convenient place to stop on your way to work or on your way home. And we've got a full line of merchandise for your electrical, plumbing, and houseware needs — everything you would expect from a big-city hardware store.

We also pride ourselves on personal service. If you don't see what you want, just ask. We'll find it, and we'll give you a good price. Come and give Lindemann's a chance to prove that we're the answer to all your hardware needs.

Editing Practice (page 385)

1. I asked the messenger, who had arrived to pick up the package, to wait while Ms. Drake signed the cover letter.
2. . . . submit their health insurance claims . . .
3. . . . that was . . .
4. After looking in the desk drawers, Judy said she couldn't find any stamps for the letters.
5. You can use any of these four . . .

6. In order to prepare the inventory report, you will need all the figures.
7. . . . request to Ms. Medina, I received a reply from her.
8. . . . careless about . . .
9. . . . sometimes for days.
10. Since our engineers . . . , we shall be . . .
11. . . . the assembling of facts, and the writing of the report. (or . . . assemble the facts, and write the report.)
12. The consistent use of unnecessarily big words makes Simon's communications ineffective.
13. Perry always has been . . .
14. Clifford is one of the brightest summer interns in the program, if not the brightest.
15. . . . felt that . . .

Section 8.6   Writing Social-Business Messages

Objectives

After completing Section 8.6, the student should be able to:

1. Describe and correctly use the social-business letter format.
2. Identify situations for which congratulatory letters are appropriate and demonstrate an ability to write such letters.
3. Write effective thank-you letters for gifts, hospitality, courtesies, and recommendations.
4. Explain how to personalize condolence letters.
5. Send correct and appropriate invitations and replies to invitations.

Overview

Common courtesy and tradition dictate the writing of social-business letters. Such letters also provide good public relations for businesses.

This section describes and illustrates the correct social-business letter format for both printed letterhead stationery and plain stationery. It discusses various types of social-business messages, including congratulations and thank-you letters, condolence letters, and formal invitations and replies.

Teaching Suggestions

Because few students have seen social-business letters, they may not appreciate the relevance of social-business messages to their future careers. Discuss with the class the fact that once students are on the job, they will develop friendships with business associates. They will *receive* congratulatory notes and thank-you letters when appropriate, and they must *send* such notes when appropriate. Thus they must develop the ability to write social-business messages.

Ask students to list the ways in which birthdays, wedding anniversaries, major job promotions or career changes, and other special occasions are acknowledged in their social circles. Students may list parties and celebrations of various kinds, as well as shaking hands or congratulating someone face to face, but they should also mention that they buy and send greeting cards on special occasions. Remind the class that the greeting card is a written social message. Ask students to name the various categories of greeting cards in a stationery store — specifically, those kinds of cards that business people might use to send to associates. Sample areas should include thank-you cards, sympathy cards, and congratulatory notes. Indeed, cards are often appropriate to send a business associate, but a letter is expected in many situations. As suggested in the text, point out that congratulatory letters can be an effective public relations tool in business.

Discuss with the class the three categories of social-business letters presented in the text: congratulations letters, thank-you letters, and condolence letters. These three broad areas cover many of the different reasons we write personal social-business letters. Then introduce formal invitations and replies. Although students may never have received formal invitations, they should know how to write them and how to answer them *properly*.

Exercise Keys

Practical Application (page 398)

A.   Sample letter to a veteran employee upon his retirement:

Dear Albert:

Your impending retirement both pleases and saddens me. I am pleased because you will now be able to devote your unfailing energy to the many things that you have not as yet had time for. I am saddened because I will miss seeing you when I arrive for work every morning. Your early arrival each day and your dependable work set the tone for the whole company. What thanks could be adequate for thirty years of such loyal and productive service? You will have your pension, of course, but you earned every penny of it. I would be grateful if you would also accept the check for $500 that I have enclosed. Think of it not as a gift but as a last bonus for a job well done.

My consolation for your departure will be the knowledge that you now have so much to enjoy. You can take those long fishing trips that you used to try to squeeze into your vacations. You can shut off your alarm clock and live according to your own internal time. With your good health and those charming grandchildren, every day is going to seem like a treat prepared especially for you.

My sincere thanks for all you have contributed to Meridien. May you enjoy a long retirement, blessed with good health, activity, and companionship.

Sincerely,

B. Sample letter of congratulations:

Dear Annette,

When I heard the news of your promotion, my first reaction was, "It couldn't happen to a nicer person." My second reaction was to think, "It *didn't* just happen—Annette deserves it."

Please accept my sincere good wishes and congratulations upon your promotion to Assistant Director of Financial Analysis. I was delighted, too, to learn that part of the reward for your achievement is a trip to the Far East—just where you always wanted to go.

I wish you continued success in your work, a pleasant and educational tour of the Far East, and a triumphant return. Let's get together for lunch when you are back in the city.

Cordially,

C. Sample thank-you letter of a personal nature:

Dear Barbara and Peter:

When I look back on my three-day stay at your home, I almost feel that you should bill my company for "extraordinary services rendered." As I have already told you, without your help my stay in Louisville would have been doubled in length because of the transportation problems. Thanks to you, Barbara, everything was taken care of in almost record time!

The family sends its best regards and hopes that you will give us the opportunity to repay your hospitality. Is there any chance of your visiting with us during the Christmas holidays? Thanks again for your gracious hospitality, and good luck to you at the chess tournament next week.

Cordially,

P.S. I hope you enjoy the small gift that is on its way to you from Lowry's!

D. This letter of sympathy can parallel, in most respects, the letter illustrated in the section entitled "Condolence Letters" on page 395.

Editing Practice (page 399)

Students answers will vary.

On April 18 and 19, Dr. Alice Burns will give a one-hour presentation entitled "Stress on the Job" in our company auditorium. Each speech will begin at 10 a.m. and will be followed by a question-and-answer session.

We invite you to hear this noted author and lecturer, but seating is limited. If you are interested, select the day that is most convenient for you and notify the Training Department. Seats will be assigned on a first-come, first-served basis.

Section 8.7 Using Form Paragraphs and Letters

Objectives

After completing Section 8.7, the student should be able to:

1. Define the terms *variables* and *boilerplate* when referring to form letters.
2. List five advantages of using form letters rather than completely original letters.
3. Name three disadvantages of using form letters.
4. Describe form letters and explain when they might be used.
5. Explain what form letters with variables are and when they should be used.
6. Describe letters with form or boilerplate paragraphs and situations in which their use is appropriate.
7. Discuss how computer word processing programs can make composing form letters easier.
8. Write effective form letters, form paragraphs and letters with form paragraphs, and form letters with variables.

Overview

Modern word processors now permit us to handle large volumes of correspondence with an ease and at a speed that was only dreamed of a few years ago. Students — no matter what their future jobs — will certainly need to know at least the basic ways in which automated equipment can be used to facilitate letter writing.

Section 8.7 concentrates on one major letter-writing application of automated equipment — form paragraphs and letters. Students are introduced to three types of form letters: the complete form letter, the form letter with variables, and the letter with form paragraphs. The advantages and disadvantages of using such letters are also presented.

Teaching Suggestions

Review with the class the advantages and disadvantages of using form letters (see text pages 400 and 403). If your students are not familiar with automated equipment, give them a brief overview of how word processing equipment facilitates producing correspondence.

Explain to students why documents are keyboarded only *once* and how they are then retrieved whenever needed. Describe how files are saved (either on diskettes or in the computer's central memory) for future retrieval; how files that are saved can be easily retrieved and reprinted (or retrieved and edited before reprinting); and so on. Compare these features of automated equipment with the features of the standard typewriter. Make sure students understand that to create two original copies of a letter using a standard typewriter, the writer would need to rekeyboard the entire letter, risking the possibility of making typographical errors. Using automated equipment, the same letter, once corrected, could be printed — without error! — over and over again.

Explain to the class that to produce form letters, the body of the letter is keyboarded once, the copy is proofread, and then any necessary corrections are made. The revised letter is saved for future use (that is, the letter is *stored* either on a disk or in the computer's memory). The body can then be retrieved as needed. The operator must then keyboard all the inside addresses of the people who will receive this form letter. Again, the inside addresses must be proofread, corrected, and stored in memory. The operator then instructs the equipment to merge one copy of the let-

ter with each of the inside addresses, including the salutation for each letter. Thus, although the body of the letter was keyboarded only once, an individually typed letter is created for dozens, hundreds, or thousands of people.

Discuss the meaning of *variables*; support the discussion with the illustration on page 401. Ask the class to compare this letter with the form letter on page 402. Point out to the class that for every tour Terrific Tours offers, the *number*, the *deposit*, and the *balance* will vary from customer to customer, making it impossible to create a form letter to cover all possibilities. Yet Terrific Tours must send each customer a confirmation letter. By creating one "skeleton," a basic letter to which some essential details must be added, Terrific Tours can save time in developing confirmation letters.

Explain to students that of the three categories of form letters discussed, letters with form paragraphs represent the greatest amount of flexibility in changing copy from letter to letter. By simply selecting appropriate form paragraphs, the "writer" can create several different letters. Emphasize that the paragraphs had to be carefully written to cover most possibilities and to ensure a smooth transition from one paragraph to another. To write an "original," individualized letter, therefore, the writer simply completes a request form indicating the paragraphs selected and their sequence (and the inside address information, of course).

Exercise Keys

Practical Application (page 406)

A.

1. Form letter (no changes within the body).
2. Form letter with variables (changes within the paragraphs).
3. Letter with form paragraphs (letter composed of paragraphs selected from a group of prewritten paragraphs).

C. Students' answers will vary. A suggested solution follows.

Request for Form Letter

Form letter requested:	See below*
Requested by:	Betty Weaver, Manager

Date requested:	February 28, 19—
Date needed:	March 1, 19—
Name:	Mr. Denis Prior
Address:	Post Office Box 2849
City, State, ZIP:	Birmingham, AL 35238
Salutation:	Dear Mr. Prior:
*Paragraph No.	1
Paragraph No.	3
Paragraph No.	5
Paragraph No.	6
Special instructions:	None
Completed by:	
Date:	

Request for Form Letter

Form letter requested:	See below*
Requested by:	Betty Weaver, Manager
Date requested:	February 28, 19—
Date needed:	March 1, 19—
Name:	Ms. Ellen DePaula
Address:	Post Office Box 2619
City, State, ZIP:	Tampa, FL 33613
Salutation:	Dear Ms. DePaula:
*Paragraph No.	1
Paragraph No.	4
Paragraph No.	5
Paragraph No.	6
Special instructions:	None
Completed by:	
Date:	

CHAPTER 9
PREPARING REPORTS AND SPECIAL COMMUNICATIONS

Both informal and formal reports are used to convey information within and outside of organizations. The memorandum format, introduced in Chapter 7, is also used for informal reports, which may be written in paragraph, outline, or table form. Longer, formal reports usually require research, analysis, and documentation. Formal reports are usually divided into four or five sections.

Other kinds of written communications discussed in this chapter are records of meetings and news releases. Meeting records are prepared by a secretary or recorder, who follows a general set of guidelines. News releases, which usually concern an important company announcement or event, are submitted to various news media for release to the public. For this reason, most news releases are written by public relations personnel.

The advent of the electronic office has improved the organizational structure, environment, and quality of the traditional office. The trend is to merge information processing, word processing, and telecommunications into one integrated system.

Section 9.1　Writing Informal Reports

Objectives

After completing Section 9.1, the student should be able to:

1. Discuss the advantages of written reports versus oral reports.
2. Describe the basic style of informal reports and variations of that style.
3. Explain the importance of keeping file copies of informal reports.
4. Identify and appropriately use the three forms in which informal reports can be presented.
5. Explain what unsolicited reports are and how their subject lines differ from those of other reports.

Overview

Informal reports are written to transmit information within an organization. Such reports generally follow the memorandum style or some variation of it. They should be straightforward, factual presentations.

Teaching Suggestions

This section deserves extensive coverage because informal reports are so commonly used and so important in the business world.

Ask working students to bring in reports and compare them with those you provide as well as those in the text.

Exercise Keys

Practical Application (page 416)

A. The information requested would be best presented in table form, with such column headings as "Name of Computer," "Where Available," "Monochrome Display," "Color Display," "Other Features," "Price."

B. Answers will vary. The student should choose either the outline or the tabulation form for the report. This information would be presented in the form of a table that might look like this:

Closing Prices of AT&T, Dow Ch, and IBM for Dec. 26, 199– and Jan. 9, 199–

Stock	12/26/9–	1/9/9–
AT&T	19½	20⅛
Dow Ch	27½	27⅞
IBM	123¾	120⅜

C. The information would best be presented in table form, as follows:

Sources of Employees Hired in 19–

Source of Referred Employee	Number Referred	Number Hired*
State employment service	36	16 (44%)
College placement offices	27	19 (70%)
Private placement services	41	17 (41%)
Newspaper advertisements	53	10 (19%)
Unsolicited applicants	6	1 (17%)
Notices in service magazines	12	7 (58%)

*Number (and percent) of those referred who are hired

Section 9.2 Writing Formal Reports

Objectives

After completing Section 9.2, the student should be able to:

1. Identify the five main parts of most formal reports.
2. Define the purpose and scope of a formal report before writing the report.
3. Gather and document information for a formal report.
4. Organize information by means of an outline and headings.
5. Use an impersonal style in writing formal reports.
6. Observe the mechanics of English, spelling, and punctuation in report writing.
7. Describe and write letters of transmittal.
8. Determine when progress reports are necessary and write such reports.

Overview

Section 9.2 describes the purpose, structure, and style of formal reports. It also familiarizes students with the function and components of letters of transmittal and the frequent need for periodic progress reports.

Teaching Suggestions

Although students will encounter formal reports less frequently than informal reports, be sure that they understand the purpose, structure, and style of formal reports.

Emphasize that formal reports are generally prepared on a subject of great importance to a company. Also make sure that students understand the relationship between technical writers and researchers in report preparation.

As suggested in the text, stress the necessity of documenting all materials taken from another source when writing a report—and, of course, at all other times.

Exercise Keys

Practical Application (page 432)

B. Answers will vary but should encompass information similar to the following:

On March 31 you requested that I make a study of the dictation habits of executives of our company and prepare a report by May 1. As of today, I have interviewed all the executives and visited and interviewed three distributors of dictating equipment. I still must complete my library research, analyze the data, determine the conclusions and recommendations, and write the report. I expect to complete the report and have it on your desk not later than May 1.

C.   Questions that should be included are these:

1. How many hours each week, on the average, do you spend in the library?
2. At what time of the day are you likely to visit the library?
3. List the reasons you visit the library (to borrow books, to do research, to study).
4. Do you ask members of the library staff for assistance?
5. What reference sources do you use most frequently?

Students will probably suggest other questions that they consider pertinent.

D.   Sample report:

Employee Turnover
A Report for Michael Patel

Purpose of Meeting

On Wednesday, May 2, 19 — , a meeting was held in Conference Room A to discuss the growing problem of employee turnover. Attending were all supervisors, department heads, and corporate officers. Sophie Neal, Director of Personnel Relations, chaired the meeting.

Following are the main points discussed and the conclusions reached.

Annual Turnover Rate

The meeting was called to explore ways of reducing the annual turnover rate and to find ways of making the company a more desirable place in which to work.

Ms. Neal stated that the annual turnover rate for office employees is 15 percent; for manufacturing employees, 20 percent. This problem has become increasingly alarming, inasmuch as the rates are growing each year. Ms. Neal made the point that apparently morale is low and there is an atmosphere of general unrest.

Reasons for Leaving the Company

George Lincoln, of the Personnel Recruitment Section, outlined the principal reasons given by employees for leaving the company. Included in his list are the following reasons, stated in order of frequency.

Office:

1. Low salary.
2. Little opportunity for advancement.
3. Poor working conditions.
4. Friction with managers.
5. Difficult commuting.
6. Inadequate employee benefits.

Manufacturing:

1. Undesirable working conditions.
2. Low salary.
3. Friction with supervisors.
4. Little opportunity for advancement.

Considerable discussion followed Mr. Lincoln's presentation of reasons for leaving the company. A roundtable group of supervisors brainstormed on how each of these reasons could be eliminated.

Recommendations for Reducing Employee Turnover

The following points were suggested as possible courses of action in reducing labor turnover in the company:

1. Improve facilities by (a) redecorating offices and installing air conditioning and (b) replacing old furniture and equipment with modern and more efficient articles.
2. Encourage frequent departmental meetings to give employees an opportunity to express their opinions.
3. Institute training programs for supervisors.
4. Initiate a salary survey of similar businesses and comparable jobs.
5. Study promotion policies.
6. Obtain services of a management consultant to make recommendations concerning employee benefits.
7. Consider the possibility of hiring a personnel relations counselor to handle grievances.

Commuting Problem

Since commuting conditions are relatively poor, this fact may have caused a good deal of turnover in the past. It was brought out by Ms. Neal, however, that this problem may be considerably eased in the immediate future because a new bus route (direct from the Riverside area) will soon go into operation.

Responsibilities of the Manager

Managers should be alert to their responsibilities to all those people reporting to them. It was recommended that each manager talk informally about work conditions with each supervisor at least once every six months. Guidelines for inaugurating this semiannual employee check will be discussed at a meeting on June 5, when specific recommendations will be made for dealing with turnover at the departmental level.

Follow-up

At the August 18 meeting all managers should be prepared to offer concrete suggestions for easing the turnover problem. In the meantime, all managers should find out all they can about morale in their departments and issue a memorandum report of their findings by August 3.

Editing Practice (page 434)

1. Ms. Andrews, the new administrative assistant, is very proficient in computer operation.
2. Although her major is economics, she is also interested in public administration.
3. Spend an afternoon at the job fair to learn about job opportunities for recent college graduates.
4. In order to avert a strike, management conducted a discussion of fringe benefits with the employees.
5. The new manager decided we must pay cash because (a) he was not able to obtain any information about loans and (b) he did not know the procedure for making such loans.
6. When I returned the package of defective floppy disks, the store manager immediately refunded my money.
7. I liked the graphics in your report because they were readable and contained accurate and complete information.
8. Although he wanted to gather additional information for his report, Malcolm felt that he had already invested enough time and began the actual writing without it.
9. The credit manager had to call a special meeting to explain to the executives the very long and complicated report about the new billing system that was started recently for the Toledo branch.
10. The report on site possibilities here in Davenport was presented by the realty agents.

Section 9.3   **Keeping Meeting Records**

Objectives

After completing Section 9.3, the student should be able to:

1. Explain the function of the minutes of a meeting.
2. Identify and use seven general guidelines for recording the proceedings of a meeting.
3. Discuss how having the agenda of a meeting helps the secretary or recorder.
4. Describe and correctly use two acceptable formats for keeping minutes of meetings.
5. Describe the Interaction Method of conducting and recording the proceedings of meetings.

Overview

At one time or another nearly all business employees are called upon to keep the minutes of a meeting. In this section, students learn that such minutes serve as a permanent record of decisions reached and actions to be taken. The section also provides general guidelines and two of a number of acceptable formats for recording the proceedings of a meeting.

Teaching Suggestions

If any students have kept minutes for a meeting, ask what format they used and compare their answers to the two formats shown in the text. Ask students which of the two formats shown in the text they think is more effective. Have them give reasons for their answers.

Discuss with students the possible advantages and disadvantages of having a group recorder keep the collective record known as group memory. Have any students attended a meeting conducted according to the Interaction Method?

Exercise Key

Practical Application (page 438)

A.   Sample minutes:

Millstone Employees' Association Minutes

March 15, 19—

Absent: Holden, Yates, Witmer

The meeting was called to order in Room 5A of the Tyler Building by President Swensen at 5:30 p.m. on March 15, 19—. The following correction was approved in the February 15 minutes: The minutes should read that Ina Singer (not Rita Singer) was appointed chairperson of the Welfare Committee.

Karen Bjorn reviewed employee suggestions for January. Awards of $100 each were made for two suggestions submitted, and Ms. Bjorn is to make arrangements for presenting the awards at the spring banquet.

Jack Stuhlman presented revised written procedures for handling employee suggestions. These suggestions were accepted, with editorial revision to be made by a committee appointed by the president.

The meeting was adjourned at 6:15 p.m. The next meeting will be a dinner meeting at Jackson's Restaurant on April 21 at 6:30 p.m.

Section 9.4   Preparing News Releases

Objectives

After completing Section 9.4, the student should be able to:

1. Explain why public relations personnel usually prepare company news releases.
2. Give examples of the kinds of company information contained in typical news releases.
3. Identify two characteristics of a news release that increase the possibility of its being printed or broadcast.
4. Describe the form of a typical news release.
5. Explain why a news release should be written in paragraphs of decreasing order of importance.

Overview

News releases provide business organizations with publicity, advertising, public relations, and goodwill. Anything that will interest the public and enhance a company's image is suitable material for a news release. Section 9.4 shows students how to prepare news releases in an effective form and how to write them in such a way that news media will want to print or broadcast them.

Teaching Suggestions

Ask students how news releases can be considered sales devices. Remind them of the ways in which public relations letters serve a sales function. In what ways do news releases promote a company's product?

As suggested in the text, emphasize that public relations personnel usually prepare news releases because their intent is to present the public with a favorable image of the organization. Find out whether any students are planning a career in public relations.

As also noted in the text, stress the importance of using the journalistic style of putting the most impor-

tant information first and including who, what, why, how, and when in all news releases.

Exercise Key

Practical Application (page 443)

A. The suggested news release that follows is for a local paper.

NEWS from   The Association for Environmental
                 Protection
                 For immediate release
                 For further information call
                    (student's name) 555-3977

New Community Group to Push Conservation

AEP (Association for Environmental Protection), a new community organization, elected the following officers at its first meeting on Wednesday, October 8: Margot Hayden, president; (student's name), secretary-treasurer. Hayden has been active in environmental issues for many years. Professor Sidney Allen, chairperson of the Science Department of Mercer County College, will serve as technical adviser for the group.

AEP aims to publicize instances of local pollution, to investigate possible conservation measures in the area, and to make the community more conservation-oriented. The group plans to undertake appropriate projects and to make field trips. Membership is open to all. AEP will meet on the first Wednesday of each month.

B. NEWS from . . .   George Theopolus,
                         Vice President
                         Northwest Paper
                         Company
                         Portland, Oregon

Alvarez to Retire From Northwest Paper

The retirement of Philip Alvarez, president of Northwest Paper Company for the past 10 years, was announced today by George Theopolus, vice president. Alvarez, who has been with the company for 25 years, will retire at the end of the year.

Alvarez started his career with the company as a shop supervisor and became factory manager within 2 years. Shortly thereafter, Alvarez was named vice president and was elected president by the board of directors 10 years ago.

Following his retirement, Alvarez will serve as chairperson of the board of directors. He and his wife live in Seacrest. They have two married sons and one married daughter, all of whom live in Portland.

Alvarez is a graduate in accounting from Youngstown College, where he was class president during his senior year. He has served on the Portland Chamber of Commerce for 5 years, is a member of both Rotary and Kiwanis, and has headed the City Beautification Committee for the last 3 years.

Section 9.5 Communicating in the Electronic Office

Objectives

After completing Section 9.5, students should be able to:

1. Explain how the electronic office differs from the traditional one in terms of organizational structure, environment, and productivity.
2. Describe three major developments in business communication technology during the past 30 years.
3. Define the term *information processing.*
4. Explain the concept of word processing and two of its benefits.
5. Discuss the advantages of using desktop publishing programs.
6. Define the term *telecommunications* and identify the technology it embraces.
7. Discuss the benefits of teleconferencing, communication networks, and electronic mail.
8. Compose brief, clear messages for electronic transmission.

Overview

The advent of the electronic office has changed the methods but not the goals of business communications: Business communications must still be clear, complete, concise, consistent, and courteous. This section teaches students the functions and benefits of computerized information systems, including word processing and electronic communication systems.

Teaching Suggestions

The time line suggested in the text should help students of the computer age recognize that the electronic office is a very recent phenomenon. The development of the electronic office gives today's workers an immediate advantage over business workers of only a generation ago.

Have students share their research findings on projected innovations in equipment and service with the class. You could have them do this in oral reports or in written reports to be read in class.

If the business office of your school has a state-of-the-art communication system or even some of the technology mentioned in this section, arrange for a student tour of that office.

Exercise Key

Practical Application (page 451)

E.

1. Meet Phillip Goetz arriving Boston Friday morning Wemas Flight 15. Brief him Tracy-Phelps contract.
2. Order 7683 not arrived. If not shipped, ship 5 desks 5 chairs fastest method.
3. Computer printout March sales forecast lost. Airmail 2 copies immediately.

CHAPTER 10
DEVELOPING ORAL COMMUNICATION SKILLS

Oral communication, whether one-to-one conversation or the delivery of a formal speech, takes up a large portion of nearly every businessperson's workday. Those who can speak well not only convey information but also foster positive relationships with colleagues and good public relations. Another important component of the oral communication process, however, and one too often overlooked, is listening. The business setting requires active listening, that is, physical and mental preparation and concentration.

Section 10.1 Aspects of Oral Communication

Objectives

1. Discuss at least ten ways in which oral communication is used in business.

2. Identify at least six methods of communicating orally in business.
3. Explain how oral communication fosters an atmosphere for positive employee relationships.
4. Discuss how oral communication contributes to effective public relations.

Overview

Students often take oral communication for granted, not realizing its importance in the business world. Most business activity is conducted at least in part orally, and workers are often judged on the skill with which they communicate in one-to-one meetings and in groups.

Section 10.1 explains the various ways in which oral communication is used in business and the methods for ensuring effective oral communication. The section further points out the effects of good oral communication on interpersonal relationships among colleagues and on public relations.

Teaching Suggestions

Ask working students to estimate what portion of their job communication is oral versus written. How much of their oral communication is related to business matters and how much to social conversation?

Emphasize that interpersonal and public relations can be improved by oral communications that are positive and courteous. Poor oral communication skills hinder such relations with those inside and outside an organization.

Exercise Keys

Practical Application (page 458)

A. Answers will vary. Suggested activities for a student who selects the position of administrative assistant might include receiving telephone calls, reading notes from a meeting, placing telephone calls, receiving office visitors, requesting material or information from coworkers, and giving instructions to word processors.

B. Among the points that may be discussed, students should mention that effective communication skills:

1. Help college students get better grades on written assignments, contribute orally in class with greater effect, and get part-time employment.
2. Help business employees follow written and oral instructions accurately, communicate better with coworkers, and handle customers more effectively in face-to-face contacts and over the telephone.
3. Ineffective communication can lead to misunderstandings, mistakes of all types, ill feelings, incompleted work, delays, and so on.

C. Home: Engaging in social conversation, ordering services over the telephone, explaining problems to repair persons, taking messages for and relaying them to other family members, and so on.

School: Listening to lectures and instructions, serving on a committee, engaging in social conversation with classmates, participating in discussion at meetings, and so on.

Business: Selling merchandise in part-time job, talking to customers on telephone, giving information to supervisor, instructing coworkers, and so on.

Section 10.2 Sharpening Listening Skills

Objectives

After completing Section 10.2, the student should be able to:

1. Contrast hearing and listening.
2. Discuss active versus passive listening and explain when each is appropriate.
3. Prepare physically and mentally for listening.
4. Set listening priorities.
5. Listen with a positive attitude.
6. Concentrate on listening.

Overview

Although most employees spend more than a third of their business day listening, most of them remember only about a quarter of what they hear. Listening is an active skill that requires physical and mental preparation, a positive attitude, and concentration. Section 10.2 teaches students how to fulfill these requirements and to remember far more than the 25 percent average of what they hear.

Teaching Suggestions

Use the breathing analogy given in the text to impress upon students that many people make the incorrect assumption that listening is automatic. Then proceed in the rest of the section to show how listening is an acquired skill that students can improve dramatically.

As pointed out in the text, explain that the first step in improving listening skill is to determine the purpose of listening in each situation. Be sure students understand the difference between active and passive listening. Tell students to ask themselves whether they are listening to be informed or to be entertained. Emphasize that the former requires far more effort than the latter.

Instruct students to answer the questions in the listening checklist in the text. Have them write a brief report on the areas in which the most need to improve and how they plan to do so.

Exercise Keys

Practical Application (page 466)

B.

1. Yes. Periodic hearing tests are essential. If you have poor hearing, you will miss part of what is being said or misunderstand some of the speaker's words.
2. Yes. If you allow yourself to be distracted, you are certain to miss part of what a speaker says.
3. Yes. Unless you hear the complete thought, you are not really certain of what the speaker is trying to say.
4. Yes. No one can do two things at once and give adequate attention to both.
5. Yes. Observing the speaker helps you to understand what is being said. Besides, the speaker may feel insulted if the listener is looking away.
6. Yes. Unless you give full attention to the speaker's words, you cannot be sure of receiving the correct message.
7. Yes. Ideas and feelings reveal the speaker's attitudes.
8. Yes. Without this attitude your mind is closed to the chief source of new ideas—other people.

9. Yes. Whenever possible, clear up vague or ambiguous points right away. Otherwise, you may face problems later.
10. No. Disagreement or prejudice on the listener's part can prevent understanding of the speaker's message.
11. No. You should judge a speaker's message on the value of its ideas, the soundness of its arguments, and the conviction of the speaker.
12. No. Such action only serves to deprive the listener of the speaker's message.
13. No. If you listen carefully, you should be able to remember what the speaker has said.
14. No. Important points may be brought up after you have "tuned out" the speaker.
15. No. Impatience may close your ears to an important point in the message.

Section 10.3 Effective Oral Communication

Objectives

After completing Section 10.3, the student should be able to:

1. Discuss what constitutes good posture and appropriate hand and body movement when one is speaking.
2. Describe how grooming, cleanliness, and dress affect a speaker as well as his or her impact on listeners.
3. Identify and describe four qualities of speech.

Overview

Almost as important as what a person says is the way she or he delivers a message. Two factors—appearance and speech qualities—greatly influence the impression a speaker makes on listeners. Section 10.3 begins with a discussion of appearance, including effective body language, grooming, and dress. The section then goes on to describe four of the six qualities of speech: force, pitch, tone, and tempo. (The other two qualities, enunciation and pronunciation, are discussed separately in Section 10.4.)

Teaching Suggestions

Ask students how their first impressions of various speakers' appearance and voice qualities have affected their listening to the speakers' messages. Have students cite specific examples to explain their answers.

Have students practice reading aloud the sample sentences in the subsection on pitch to vary their voice level.

Exercise Keys

Practical Application (page 474)

B. Emphasize the italicized word in each of the following:

Marty mailed the letter yesterday morning.
Marty *mailed* the letter yesterday morning.
Marty mailed *the* letter yesterday morning.
Marty mailed the *letter* yesterday morning.
Marty mailed the letter *yesterday* morning.
Marty mailed the letter yesterday *morning*.

In each of the remaining sentences, proceed in the same manner, emphasizing first the first word, then the second, then the third, and so on.

Section 10.4   Enunciation and Pronunciation

Objectives

After completing Section 10.4, the student should be able to:

1. Explain by means of examples the difference between good and poor enunciation.
2. Identify several ways to learn how various words are pronounced.
3. Follow a four-step plan for improving enunciation and pronunciation.

Overview

Despite regional and cultural differences of speech throughout the United States, standard English should be familiar to students from listening to broadcast announcers. Section 10.4 explains the difference between enunciation and pronunciation and offers a plan for improving these speech qualities.

Teaching Suggestions

Have students practice enunciating and pronouncing the sample words and phrases in the text. Using a tape recorder will provide the students with helpful feedback.

Exercise Keys

Editing Practice (page 484)

1. portable, too
2. attendance, quite
3. mail, tomorrow; however,
4. their employees
5. Although we did consider the investment a year ago and decided against it at that time, perhaps the situation is different now, and you can tell us how the venture would now be profitable for us.
6. typing, taking
7. Seven, 6, overtime
8. believe, install, equipment
9. On May 12, 341 items disappeared before they could be loaded on the vans. We are at a loss to explain this disappearance.
10. Bill (or Jerome)

Critical Thinking (page 484)

Answers will vary, but students should suggest jobs — such as receptionist, manager, and administrative assistant — in which oral communication skills are an important part of the work.

Section 10.5   Communicating One to One

Objectives

After completing Section 10.5, the student should be able to:

1. Identify some of the ways that business workers orally communicate on a one-to-one basis.
2. Describe and follow eight guidelines for communicating one to one.
3. Explain how to communicate effectively with company visitors.
4. Discuss the major difference between communicating face to face and via telephone.
5. Plan the conversation before making a telephone call, place the call, and give your name and the purpose of your call first.
6. Answer telephone calls promptly and respond graciously.
7. Handle telephone complaints by listening carefully, expressing interest, and informing the caller of action that will be taken.

Overview

Although most students will readily understand the importance of one-to-one oral communication in a job interview (presented in Section 11.2), few will realize how much one-to-one communication will occupy them on the job. Face-to-face and telephone conversations are conducted with clients, customers, coworkers, and supervisors. Human relations skills are as important as oral communication skills in these situations. Section 10.5 covers these matters in depth.

Teaching Suggestions

As suggested in the text, stress the importance of routine business conversations. Alert students to some of the pressures and problems they will sometimes need to overcome to engage effectively in such conversations.

Have pairs of students demonstrate how to greet visitors to a company. Ask other students to comment on the techniques the greeter in each pair used. Did the greeter make a good first impression?

Again, emphasize the importance of courtesy in all human relations. Dealing effectively with the public on the telephone and face-to-face accounts for the success of many businesses.

Exercise Keys

Practical Application (page 492)

A. Mr. Jaeger's assistant might reply to each of the callers as follows :

1. "I'm sorry, Mr. Parrish. Mr. Jaeger is in conference and asked that he not be disturbed. May I take a message or have Mr. Jaeger call you back just as soon as he is out of the meeting?"
2. "Mrs. Jaeger, Mr. Jaeger is in a meeting and cannot be disturbed. Could I have him call you back, or would you like me to deliver a message for you when the conference is over?"
3. "I'm sorry, Ms. Cunningham. Mr. Jaeger is in conference and does not expect to be through until about 10:30. Would you prefer to wait, or could you come back at that time?" If Ms. Cunningham decides to wait, then the administrative assistant should make her comfortable and supply her with reading matter and perhaps a cup of coffee.
4. "Mr. Potts, Mr. Jaeger is in conference, but I'm sure he would want me to let him know that you

wish to speak to him. Just a moment, please, and I'll notify him." (Usually, the chairperson of the board is permitted to interrupt an executive at any time. The assistant has given the chairperson an opportunity to decline interrupting Mr. Jaeger. Furthermore, Mr. Jaeger can tell the assistant whether or not he is able to speak to the chairperson or whether the assistant should take a message.)

B. No key is required. Refer students to pages 489–491 for the information needed to write the memorandum. Encourage them to expand the discussion.

C. The receptionist might respond as follows:

1. "Good morning. May I be of assistance?"
2. "May I tell Mr. Nakama the purpose of your visit?" or "May I tell Mr. Nakama your name and the purpose of your visit?"
3. "Please tell me your problem. I'm certain there is someone who can help you straighten it out."
4. "Mr. Harris, you will have to see the building superintendent, Mr. Edwards. His office is in Room 566. Would you like me to telephone Mr. Edwards to see if he can see you now?"
5. "Yes, _____ (Check the appointment register for the correct name. If no name is listed, ask if you may have the person's name). Won't you have a seat until Mr. Rappaport can see you?"

D. The good listener should be sincerely interested in the message of the speaker, should be attentive, should be sympathetic to the needs of the speaker, and, where the occasion demands, should encourage the speaker to talk.

E. Three possible greetings are (1) "May I tell _____ the purpose of your visit?" (2) "May I tell _____ the name of the firm you represent?" (3) "Does _____ know the purpose of your visit?"

Critical Thinking (page 492)

One possible answer:

"Ms. _____ will be busy all day with conferences and cannot be interrupted. I will give her your message." Don't suggest that the caller call back or say that Ms. _____ will telephone the caller.

Section 10.6 Communicating in Groups

Objectives

After completing Section 10.6, the student should be able to:

1. Explain the difference between standing and ad hoc committees.
2. Describe and follow six basic rules for participating effectively in meetings.
3. Explain how teleconferencing works and identify the major advantage of teleconferencing over attending meetings in person.
4. Discuss the various kinds of advance work that can turn an ordinary meeting into a very profitable experience for all participants.
5. Prepare and lead successful meetings.
6. Discuss the key roles of the facilitator, recorder, group member, and chairperson in the Interaction Method of conducting meetings.

Overview

Group discussions, whether impromptu or informal meetings, are used in business to ensure that people understand their goals and agree on plans to reach them. This section explains how to communicate effectively in groups and how to prepare for and conduct successful business meetings.

Teaching Suggestions

Students' difficulties with communicating in groups will vary. Shyness, inattentiveness, aggression — all affect how the individual interacts with the group. You can use the class discussions to help individual students overcome their particular problems.

As suggested in the text, explain the necessity for tact when disagreeing with another member of the group or meeting participant. Note that tact is in essence a way of showing courtesy — the quality repeatedly emphasized throughout this chapter.

Relate this section to Section 9.3 on keeping minutes of meetings.

Exercise Keys

Practical Application (page 502)

A. Some steps are these:

1. Make certain that there are sufficient chairs.
2. Arrange the seats so that all members can see one another.
3. Provide pencils and paper for notetaking.
4. Make sure that the room is properly ventilated — not too warm or too cold.
5. Make certain that any audiovisual equipment required is available, is in working order, and is properly placed.
6. If an operator is necessary for visual aids, make certain that such person is available when needed.
7. Make sure that there is sufficient lighting (no blinking bulbs or burned-out bulbs).
8. Make sure that there is a copy of the agenda at each seat.

B. Here is an example of how the body of the memorandum might read:

There will be a meeting of all supervisors on Tuesday, June 15, at 9:30 a.m. in the conference room to discuss the orientation program for all new employees. In preparation for this meeting, I would like you to evaluate our present orientation program, to talk with new employees under your supervision who were hired since January 1 of this year, and to find out as much as you can about orientation programs in operation in other companies in our area. Please let me know which companies' programs you would like to examine so that we can avoid any duplication of effort.

As a result of our research and discussion, we will draw up a revised orientation program to be put into effect September 1 of this year.

D. The chairperson should set the example by making certain that the meeting room is in good condition before the meeting begins and by starting the meeting on time. The chairperson should organize the meeting so that it proceeds efficiently and should prepare an agenda and duplicate enough copies for each person who is to attend the meeting. In addition, the chairperson should conduct the meeting in an orderly fashion and give each person in attendance an opportunity to make a contribution.

F. Sample memorandum:

Memorandum
TO: Marietta Hart
FROM: (Student's name)
SUBJECT: Retirement Banquet
DATE: (Current date)

I am writing to remind you that at the meeting of the Employee Retirement Committee, you agreed to gather information regarding facilities for the retirement banquet and dance to be held on Saturday, October 15, at 7 p.m.

We anticipate that we will have approximately 32 retirees but that about 250 people will attend the banquet and dance. In addition, we expect to have 10 special guests. We will need space for an orchestra of 8 musicians, and we would like to have a stage available for the orchestra, special entertainment, and the retirement presentations. If there is any further information you will need to help you determine the proper facilities for this affair, please let me know immediately.

When you have acquired information regarding the available facilities, please circulate this information among the committee members.

Editing Practice (page 503)

1. There seems to be a discrepancy of $25 in our last statement.
2. We will be happy to replace the lamp base that does not match.
3. Although we should like to accept your application for credit, we think it is in your best interest that you continue to purchase on a cash basis. We should be glad to reconsider your application for credit at a later date.
4. We understand that you mailed your check to us last week, but we have not received it yet.
5. The merchandise is scheduled to arrive on the date you requested.

Critical Thinking (page 503)

1. A good discussion leader does not discourage participation and should not, therefore, evaluate the suggestions made. The leader might have asked, "How do you think this idea will work?"
2. This statement is a good one because it encourages elaboration of the plan.
3. This statement also is a good one because it encourages participation in the discussion.

Section 10.7 Preparing and Delivering a Speech

Objectives

After completing Section 10.7, students should be able to:

1. Determine the purpose of a speech, to whom it will be addressed, and how much time will be allowed for it before gathering information for the speech.
2. Gather information for a speech by reading about the topic and, when possible, speaking with experts on the topic.
3. Organize and prepare a speech so that the introduction states the purpose and arouses interest, the body contains a number of main points, and the conclusion summarizes the main ideas and, where appropriate, calls for action.
4. Practice delivering a speech, paying particular attention to body language and voice qualities.
5. Project confidence, a good appearance, and stage presence when delivering a speech.
6. Use an appropriate, brief introduction when introducing a speaker.

Overview

Because almost everyone is called upon at one time or another to "say a few words" to an audience, every business employee needs to know how to prepare and deliver an effective speech that will reflect favorably on his or her organization. Section 10.7 provides students with guidelines for previewing a speaking assignment, gathering and organizing information, and practicing and delivering the speech. In addition, this section explains how to introduce a speaker effectively.

Teaching Suggestions

Almost everyone is nervous about giving a speech; you can help your students overcome this by having them practice making speeches before the class or before smaller groups. A videotape machine is an excellent tool to provide the speaker with a playback of his or her speech. Use videotaping judiciously, however. As suggested in the marginal note, if students are uncomfortable about peers seeing their tapes, you might want to assure them that only you and the student will review the tapes.

Stress the reasons speeches should not be memorized or read. Inform students that reading and reciting usually bore audiences because of a resulting lack of feeling or voice inflection. People who read or recite their speeches can lose their place or train of thought and become thoroughly confused; this in turn causes the audience to become uncomfortable. Reading lessens eye contact with the audience, and so on.

Exercise Keys

Practical Application (page 515)

D. The student can be referred to the text, especially to the section dealing with practicing the speech. As pointed out in Section 10.7, it is important to have confidence, because the more confident the speaker feels about the subject matter, the more likely he or she is to be relaxed. If the speaker is relaxed, nervousness can be controlled. Excessive verbalizing, too, sometimes comes from nervousness and lack of confidence, as well as from inexperience.

E. Students should approach this assignment by looking for a clever but appropriate introduction. They may be referred to standard textbooks or handbooks on speaking. *Bartlett's Familiar Quotations* will also serve as a valuable reference for this type of assignment. With public figures, newspaper items may also serve to provide some interesting information about the speaker. When it is appropriate, the speaker's secretary may also be consulted for interesting information about the speaker.

F. Refer to the suggestions regarding closing remarks on page 515.

CHAPTER 11
COMMUNICATING FOR JOB RESULTS

Chapter 11 is probably the most important chapter in this text. All the learning that has taken place up to this point comes to fruition here, because the student's goal has been to prepare for a job and to succeed in that job. In this chapter, students learn to apply their communication skills to achieve job results.

Section 11.1   Communicating in the Job Search

Objectives

After completing Section 11.1, the student should be able to:

1. Apply the communication skills of reading, writing, speaking, and listening, as well as human relations skills, to the job search.
2. Assess personal characteristics, career goals, education, experience, and qualifications.
3. Seek a business position through various sources.
4. Prepare an effective résumé.
5. Write an effective application letter.
6. Properly complete an application form for a position in business.

Overview

In this section, students learn to apply their communication skills to the job search. Specifically, they learn how to analyze themselves and their qualifications, to assess the job market, and to "sell" themselves in a résumé, in an application letter, and on an application form.

Teaching Suggestions

Explain that while many earlier sections deal separately with the four basic communication skills, most business situations require the integration of these skills.

Be sure students understand that the application letter should not be a rehash of the résumé. The two documents serve very different purposes, as outlined in the text.

Exercise Keys

Practical Application (page 533)

A key for each of the Practical Applications in this section is not necessary. Check carefully to see that the student follows the sales letter pattern in the application letters. For the other employment letter situations, refer to the sample letters in the textbook as indicated for each Practical Application.

A. Sources regarding job openings, pages 520–521.

B. Letter of application, opening paragraph, page 527.

C. Letter of application, pages 525–530; résumé, pages 522–525; list of references, page 526.

By analyzing yourself and your qualifications, you can discover what is important to you and can narrow the choices of jobs that are most likely to suit you.

Section 11.2 The Effective Employment Interview

Objectives

After completing Section 11.2, the student should be able to:

1. Explain why it is essential to be well prepared for an employment interview.
2. Discuss three ways of gathering information about a company.
3. Prepare questions to ask the interviewer, including questions about opportunities for advancement, training, and travel.
4. Identify four items to take to an interview.
5. Anticipate and formulate answers to questions the interviewer is likely to ask.
6. Give a positive impression by being on time for the interview, appropriately dressed, and self-confident.
7. Answer questions and make statements in a positive, straightforward way during the interview.
8. Write a summary of opinions about the company and job and send a follow-up letter to the interviewer as soon as possible after the interview.

Overview

Because an effective employment interview is usually crucial to getting a job, it warrants as much or more preparation than any other business situation. In this section students learn how to prepare for a job interview, how to conduct themselves during an interview, and how to follow up the interview.

Teaching Suggestions

If time permits, have pairs of students role-play interviews; ask other students to critique the interviews. In addition, encourage students who have never been interviewed to go out on a few interviews to make themselves more comfortable with the process.

As suggested in the text, impress upon students that whereas the purpose of the résumé and application letter is to get an interview, the purpose of the interview is to get a job.

Exercise Keys

Practical Application (page 540)

A. The students can refer to the text for some of the answers to these questions and statements. The instructor will want to check for each of the following points in the answers:

1. Applicants want to work for a particular company because they (a) believe they will have a bright future with it, (b) are interested in the company's product or service, and (c) feel they can contribute to the company's success.
2. Students should be specific in saying what kinds of work they enjoy most — administrative duties, accounting, writing, selling, meeting people, and so on.
3. Although one doesn't dwell on what one likes to do least, an interviewer might ask such a question, and the applicant should be prepared for it. An answer might be "I do not enjoy working with numbers all day."
4. Students should look at the next five years with a realistic, but long-range, view.
5. The main points to emphasize here are interest, aptitude, and special training undertaken in order to secure such a position.
6. In answer to such requests as "Tell me about yourself," applicants should be specific about their (a) work experience, (b) education, and (c) reasons for applying for the job.
7. Although this question may not apply in all cases, it is important to face this issue in many instances. Generally acceptable answers are "I left to accept a job with a better future" or "I left to accept a job offering a better salary and better working conditions."
8. Reading, stamp collecting, participation in religious groups, team sports, school social activities — all may enhance the applicant's chances of getting the job. However, students should emphasize those activities that might have a relationship to the job.

B. Ten dos and don'ts in *preparing* for the interview:

DO	DON'T
1. Choose the type of work you like and prepare for a specific position.	1. Underestimate your abilities.
	2. Arrive late for the interview.

2. Prepare a résumé.
3. Analyze your strengths and weaknesses.
4. Anticipate questions that your interviewer may ask.
5. Be able to discuss your favorite courses in college.
6. Find out all you can about the company.
7. Be careful about your personal appearance.
8. Plan what you will say to the interviewer.

3. Take the first job that you find out about.
4. Go to the interview without the supplies you will need, such as pen and notebook.
5. Underestimate the importance of the interview and of preparing for it.
6. Go to the interview without knowing the name of the interviewer and the name and title of your potential employer.
7. Fold the résumé and put it in your pocket or purse.
8. Engage in idle conversation with the receptionist.

Ten dos and don'ts to be observed *during* the interview:

DO	DON'T
1. Refrain from smoking.	1. Be late for an interview.
2. Keep your voice well modulated.	2. Take anyone with you.
3. Look directly at the interviewer when speaking or being spoken to.	3. Place personal objects on the interviewer's desk unless you are invited to do so.
4. Control your nervous actions.	4. Toy with articles of clothing.
5. Maintain good posture.	5. Slump in your chair.
6. Refrain from talking too much or too little.	6. Chew gum.
7. Be pleasant to everyone you meet.	7. Interrupt the interviewer when he or she is talking.
8. Leave at once when the interview is over.	8. Show signs of nervousness.

9. Make a note of pertinent facts to be used later as follow-up.
10. Thank the interviewer for his or her time.

9. Criticize former employers or co-workers.
10. Make salary the main theme of your conversation.

C. Some questions are suggested on page 535 of the textbook, and the students may suggest additional questions.

D. Refer to page 539 of the textbook for a possible answer to this question. It is best to be noncommittal about such a controversial matter. For example, "Mr. Gustafson was a hard worker, and he insisted on very high standards. I got along quite well with him."

E. A sample follow-up letter:

Dear Ms. Peebles:

It was very pleasant meeting and talking with you yesterday about the position of public relations assistant that is open in the Williams Investment Company. I was especially interested to learn that you are a friend of Dr. Homer Casper, a teacher for whom I have great respect.

I am now more convinced than ever that I would like to work for Williams Investment. The position as assistant in your public relations department especially appeals to me, for it would involve some writing and working with the research unit. Writing was always one of my strong points in college. As a matter of fact, the two papers I prepared in my course in Market Research were my best.

If you wish to get in touch with me, I will be at home for the remainder of the week (telephone 555-9032).

Sincerely yours,

Critical Thinking (page 541)

1. *Analyze.*
The main purpose of the first interview is to determine whether or not the applicant has the qualifications and personality to justify the interview. If the applicant does not, the employer's time is not wasted. The interviews will be very similar in that both interviewers are trying to find out whether the applicant has something of value to offer the company. The second interview, however, goes into more depth about the specific job, opportunities for advancement, and so on.

Moreover, at the second interview, if the applicant is successful, the interviewer may discuss company policies, benefits, and the like.

2. *Evaluate.*

Any career decision must be carefully made. The company a person chooses to work for greatly shapes his or her future. Its stability, reputation, and economic status are all important factors to be considered. The employee does not want to be a "job hopper" and should be prepared to stick with this first job for a reasonable time.

Section 11.3 Communicating and Your Career

Objectives

After completing Section 11.3, the student should be able to:

1. Determine whether to telephone or to write a letter accepting a job offer.
2. Write a letter courteously declining a job offer.
3. Explain why resigning from a job requires tact and diplomacy.
4. Write a courteous resignation letter.
5. Summarize the value of good communication skills and interpersonal relations techniques to job success.

Overview

Section 11.3 explains how to use communication skills and human relations techniques in accepting, declining, and resigning from a job. In conclusion, it briefly summarizes the content of the text and reiterates the crucial role communication skills play in getting and keeping a job and in getting a better job.

Teaching Suggestions

After covering letters of job acceptance, decline, and resignation, use the remainder of this section to summarize and again emphasize the absolute necessity of having good communication skills if students are to succeed in the business world.

Exercise Keys

Practical Application (page 545)

A. Student answers will vary. See the sample letter of acceptance and the sample thank-you letter to the person used as a reference in Section 11.3.

B. Student answers will vary. See the sample letter in Section 11.3 about a change of mind in accepting a position.

Editing Practice (page 545)

1. You should make certain that nothing is done to change the procedure.
2. The ruling concerning tardiness takes effect today.
3. Mel was late because he had to pick up a report from another branch.
4. I have difficulty in distinguishing one from the other.
5. His name and title are to be printed under the last line in the return address on the envelope.

Critical Thinking (page 545)

Student answers will vary but should be based on material presented in this chapter.

SIXTH EDITION

COLLEGE ENGLISH AND COMMUNICATION

SIXTH EDITION

COLLEGE ENGLISH AND COMMUNICATION

KENNETH ZIMMER, Ed.D.
Professor Emeritus of
Business Education and
Office Administration
School of Business and Economics
California State University
Los Angeles, California

SUE C. CAMP, Ed.D.
Associate Professor of
Business Administration
Broyhill School of Management
Gardner-Webb College
Boiling Springs, North Carolina

GLENCOE

Macmillan/McGraw-Hill

New York, New York   Columbus, Ohio   Mission Hills, California   Peoria, Illinois

This book was prepared with the assistance of Visual Education Corporation, Princeton, New Jersey.

Illustration Credits

pages 209, 211: By permission. From *Webster's Ninth New Collegiate Dictionary* © 1990 by Merriam-Webster Inc., publisher of the Merriam-Webster® dictionaries; page 214: By permission. From *Webster's Collegiate Thesaurus* © 1988 by Merriam-Webster Inc., publisher of the Merriam-Webster® dictionaries; page 321: By permission from American Airlines, Marriott, Pencil Point Studio, Federal Express (Courtesy of Federal Express Corporation. All rights reserved.), American Heart Association (Copyright American Heart Association), and Hertz (Hertz is a registered trademark of Hertz System, Inc.)

Library of Congress Cataloging-in-Publication Data

Zimmer, Kenneth, 1921–
  College English and communication / Kenneth Zimmer, Sue C. Camp,
    p. cm.
  Rev. ed. of: College English and communication / Marie M. Stewart.
  Includes bibliographical references and index.
  ISBN 0–02–803015–X
  1. English language—Business English. 2. English language–
–Grammar—1950– 3. English language—Rhetoric. 4. Business
communication. I. Camp, Sue C., 1944– . II. Stewart, Marie M.,
1899– College English and communication. III. Title.
PE1479.B87Z55   1992
808′.06665—dc20   92–751
                                                                CIP

COLLEGE ENGLISH AND COMMUNICATION, SIXTH EDITION

Send all inquiries to:
GLENCOE DIVISION
Macmillan/McGraw-Hill
936 Eastwind Drive
Westerville, OH 43081

ISBN 0–02–803015–X (Student Edition)
ISBN 0–02–803016–8 (Instructor's Annotated Edition)

Printed in the United States of America.

2 3 4 5 6 7 8 9   RRD-C   99 98 97 96 95 94 93 92

CONTENTS

2 sections/wk

PREFACE

The business world of the 1990s is highly competitive and performance-oriented. To improve productivity and profitability, companies across the country spend millions of dollars hiring the best employees and upgrading the skills of their present employees. No matter what job you want and what specific skills you have, to succeed in business you need effective communication skills.

Why do employers demand communication skills from every employee? Experienced managers know that most business workers spend the greater part of each workday communicating — writing letters, listening to instructions, speaking to coworkers and to customers, and reading correspondence. Workers whose writing, speaking, listening, and reading skills are weak will perform ineffectively in most business environments because faulty communication leads to misunderstandings and errors. Workers who communicate effectively, on the other hand, generally do well in most job situations.

COLLEGE ENGLISH AND COMMUNICATION, SIXTH EDITION

College English and Communication, Sixth Edition, provides a comprehensive program to help you develop the proficiency in writing, listening, speaking, and reading that you will need for career success. The program — the text and the accompanying components — is designed to help you master the fundamental principles of communication, and it achieves this goal through its carefully planned, step-by-step presentation.

Understanding Communication. Because understanding the communication process is fundamental to effective writing, speaking, listening, and reading, Chapter 1 offers an introduction to the communication process — applied both to your personal life and to your business life. This chapter is designed to help you recognize the importance of communications skills and to master the fundamental principles of communication.

Grammar, Punctuation, and Style. Chapters 2 and 3 provide a thorough discussion of the principles of grammar, punctuation, and style — principles that you must master if you wish to write and speak effectively. Many examples illustrate proper usage. "Memory Hooks" aid the understanding and use of difficult-to-remember concepts, and "Checkups" within the text material provide immediate practice and reinforcement of the principles covered in these chapters.

Words.   The effective communicator must, of course, be able to use words skillfully both in writing and in speaking. *College English and Communication, Sixth Edition,* provides a continuing program to expand and refine your vocabulary. Chapter 4 introduces you to the reference tools that will make your writing less difficult and, at the same time, more effective. In this chapter you will learn techniques for using words precisely and for achieving variety in usage. In addition, Chapter 4 offers some basic methods for improving spelling.

The Craft of Writing.   Understanding the rules of grammar and having a wide vocabulary do not, of course, guarantee effective writing. Letters, memos, and reports must be planned if they are to achieve their goals. Chapter 5, "Sharpening Writing Skill," uses a building-block approach in presenting the techniques for planning and organizing messages. The steps begin with planning and then proceed to the units of writing — phrases and clauses, sentences, and paragraphs. The chapter concludes with some guidelines for revising.

Proofreading and Editing.   The important skills of proofreading and editing are vital to writers and document preparers alike. Chapter 6, "Developing Proofreading and Editing Skills," will give you an understanding of the proofreading and editing processes and their importance in producing error-free communications. Included is information on electronic "helps" such as grammar- and spell-check features of some word processing software programs and an introduction to proofreaders' marks.

Memos.   The most common form of business writing is the interoffice memorandum. Chapter 7 is devoted to this topic and includes information on the purposes, types, styles, and writing techniques of memos.

Letters.   Chapter 8 offers you the opportunity to apply all the writing techniques you've learned. After opening with a section on business letter style, the chapter covers letter formats and specific letter types — requests, claim and adjustment letters, persuasive letters, public relations letters, and social-business letters. In addition, a section on the use of form paragraphs and letters concludes the chapter.

Reports and Special Communications.   Reports are an important means of communicating information in business. Chapter 9 offers detailed coverage of these longer business communications. Besides memorandum reports and long reports, the chapter discusses minutes of meetings, news releases, and communication in the electronic office.

Oral Communication.   Speaking to coworkers, customers, and others is an important part of the business day for most people. Chapter 10 presents guidelines that will help you speak effectively in one-to-one and group situations.

Communication and Your Career.   During employment interviews and on the job, all the communication skills that you have developed will be tested.

In Chapter 11 you will discover how you can apply your communication skills to prepare for the job search, to make your interviews more effective, and to advance in your career.

EXERCISING YOUR SKILLS

College English and Communication, Sixth Edition, offers you several ways to exercise your communication skills both within selected chapters and in all section reviews.

- "Checkup" sections within Chapters 2, 3, and 4 provide immediate practice of skills just covered.
- End-of-section materials review the current section ("Practical Application") and add a variety of exercises in detecting and correcting errors in English usage ("Editing Practice").

ADDED FEATURES

Several new elements have been added to the sixth edition of *College English and Communication*.

- At the beginning of each chapter, you will find a brief outline of the chapter. At the start of each section, a list of student objectives provides a guide for your work in that section.
- Throughout the text a series of mini-features has been added. These features offer glimpses of a variety of language- and communication-related issues and situations not included in the body of the text. Displayed in the margin area of your text, these mini-features are grouped into five categories:
  - Living Language — an excerpt illustrating the richness and variety of the English language
  - Language Tip — an observation about the role of or the development of language today
  - Language Lapse — a quick check of your proofreading eye
  - Study Tip — a hint for making the best use of your study time
  - World View — a note about an issue in or a facet of international business

SUPPLEMENTARY MATERIALS

Besides the text, *College English and Communication, Sixth Edition*, includes a workbook of communication activities for students, instructor's editions of both text and workbook, print and microcomputer versions of the test bank, a booklet of case studies, a set of transparency masters, and an English-skills practice set for the microcomputer.

Activities for College English and Communication. A comprehensive book of skill-building activities, the student workbook provides additional exercises to improve communication skills. The exercises provide excellent reinforcement of the text principles section by section, as well as offering periodic reviews of preceding sections.

ACKNOWLEDGMENTS

We would like to thank the following educators for their invaluable comments and feedback on this revision: Cristina Brady, formerly of Bradford School, Pittsburgh, Pennsylvania; Joy L. Hanel, Mankato Technical College, Mankato, Minnesota; Sonja H. Litton, King's College, Charlotte, North Carolina; Sharon Occhipinti, Tampa College, Tampa, Florida; Jeannine F. Perkins, The Stuart School of Business Administration, Wall, New Jersey; James J. Quicker, Lakeshore Technical College, Cleveland, Wisconsin; Penny Stockman Sansbury, Florence-Darlington Technical College, Florence, South Carolina; Shirley Sloan, Jefferson Community College, Watertown, New York.

1

UNDERSTANDING COMMUNICATION

1.1 *EFFECTIVE COMMUNICATION IN EVERYDAY LIVING*

OBJECTIVES: After completing Section 1.1, you should be able to:

1. Name the purposes of communication and identify the two types of communication.
2. List the components of communication.
3. Describe the factors that influence communication.
4. Discuss how interpersonal skills can affect communication.

Communication, very simply defined, is the exchange of thoughts, messages, or information. Usually people think of speech as the primary means of communicating; however, long before children learn to speak, they are able to communicate. Almost from birth, it seems, a baby knows that crying makes people respond quickly with attention. Of course, communication skills increase in complexity after infancy, and over time listening and speaking, reading and writing become part of the communication process.

EFFECTIVE COMMUNICATION SKILLS

Learning to be a successful, effective communicator is somewhat like learning to be a good basketball player or a good chess player. Once you have learned the basic skills, you become better and better as you practice the skills and gain confidence.

Purposes of Communication

KEY POINT
The four main purposes of communication are to inquire, to inform, to persuade, and to develop goodwill.

Recall for a moment what you said to various family members, friends, and school or business associates today. Every statement you made and every question you asked — from "How do you feel today?" to "I just found a ten-dollar bill!" — fall into at least one of the following four main purposes of communication.

To inquire. "When did you learn to use this computer?"
To inform. "This computer is two years old."
To persuade. "You really will save time if you use a computer."
To develop goodwill. "Thank you for helping me buy a computer."

Types of Communication

Communication can be divided into two main categories: verbal and nonverbal. Verbal communication uses words to exchange both spoken and written messages. Logically, then, nonverbal communication is communication without words. Think about it. Without saying a single word, you can express your feelings with gestures, facial expressions, and body movements or positions.

The important combination of verbal and nonverbal communication, or, even more so, the lack of it, is easy to spot. For example, at some time or another, everyone has listened to a speaker who was an authority on a subject but who lacked any kind of nonverbal expression. Even if the subject interested you, you probably found it hard to keep your mind on the speech. Nonverbal communication can add emphasis and color to spoken words. It can even tell you whether or not to believe a speaker. Nonverbal communication plays an important role in clear, effective exchange of messages.

COMPONENTS OF COMMUNICATION

What can a speaker — even a great speaker — communicate if there is no one to listen? Keep in mind that communication can take place only if both a sender and a receiver are present. Each time you have a conversation with someone else, or exchange messages, you use these five basic components or steps of communication:

1. *Message sender.* The sender prepares or composes the intended message.
2. *The actual message.* The actual message is transmitted. It may or may not be the message the sender intended.
3. *Message transmission.* The message can be transmitted in a variety of ways including conversations, letters, memos, gestures, or a combination of these.
4. *Message receiver.* The receiver takes in or receives the message.
5. *Message interpretation.* The receiver interprets the message. The interpretation, of course, may be different from the intended message or the actual message.

Ideally, the intended message, the actual message, and the interpreted message will be the same. Miscommunication, however, occurs when two or three of the elements are different. For example, think about the following situation.

Even though Mark Reynolds, a college freshman, was upset with his semester grades, he knew he had to write home. He sent this *actual message* by letter to his parents: "I got only one D this semester." When his parents received his message, they developed the following *interpreted message:* "Mark

☐ SUGGESTION

Ask students to iden-
tify the message
sender, the actual mes-
sage, the message
transmission, the mes-
sage receiver, and the
message interpretation.
Discuss this question:
Were the actual mes-
sage and the intended
message the same?

got only one D this semester. That is much better than the three Ds he got last semester!"

Miscommunication occurred because Mark's *actual message* did not accurately convey the facts. Mark received only one D this semester, but he also received two Fs. Because his parents want him to do well, they interpreted his message in a positive way.

Keep in mind, therefore, that communication is effective only

1. If it enables the receiver to interpret the message exactly as the sender intended.
2. If it evokes the desired response from the receiver.
3. If it develops favorable relations between the sender and the receiver.

Avoiding Communication Breakdowns

Miscommunication and communication breakdowns can often be avoided by using the "feedback" technique. In the process of transmitting a face-to-face message, the sender can use clues to determine if the receiver is interpreting the message correctly. For example, one such device is the receiver's facial expressions that signal whether the message is clear or confusing. The sender can also ask questions to determine whether the message is being received accurately and to allow the receiver to question any content that is unclear.

Obviously, this technique is easier in face-to-face communication than in situations where the sender and receiver are separated. The wrong response, questions from the receiver, or no response may indicate a temporary breakdown in communication. Feedback cannot be achieved so easily with written communication, because receiver response is usually not immediate.

| W O R L D |
| V I E W |

Only 7 percent of
the world's people
speak English as a
primary language,
but nine out of ten
Americans cannot
speak, read, or
understand any
language but Eng-
lish.

—Gallup polls and
UNESCO studies

Means of Communication

As a message sender, you can transmit your message by verbal or nonverbal communication—that is, by spoken or written words or by body language. The receiver, in turn, must observe, listen, or read (or use some combination of the three) to receive and interpret the message. These, then, are the basic elements of communication. Their use involves the four communication skills—reading, writing, speaking, and listening.

FACTORS THAT INFLUENCE COMMUNICATION

Although the sender of a message knows the goals he or she wants to achieve, the sender must keep in mind several major factors that will influence the communication either favorably or unfavorably. A sender who is aware of these factors will better control them for a favorable effect on the communication process.

These factors are as follows:

1. The background of the receiver.
2. The appearance of the communicator or the communication.
3. The communication skills of the sender and receiver.
4. Distractions.

Background of the Receiver

The following four background elements can play an important role in determining the receiver's reaction to the message.

1. The *knowledge* the receiver already has about the facts, ideas, and language used in the message.
2. The *personality* of the receiver — particularly the emotions, attitude, and prejudices that are likely to influence the way the message is interpreted.
3. The receiver's *experiences* that are relevant to the message content.
4. The receiver's *interest and motivation* regarding the subject.

To understand how these factors can influence a receiver, imagine that you have just received a letter from a brokerage firm explaining an investment opportunity. If you have not made this kind of investment previously, your *knowledge* of securities is probably limited. Naturally, your reaction would be different from that of a person who is knowledgeable about many kinds of investments. If your *personality* is quite conservative, you have likely made sure that all your previous investments have been insured. However, if your *experience* with this brokerage firm has been good, your *interest and motivation* probably grew the minute you saw the tax advantages and potential profits available with this type of investment. The communicator who weighs all of these factors before preparing the message stands a greater chance that his or her message will be accepted by the receiver than the person who ignores these factors.

Appearance of the Communicator or Communication

What do these three situations have in common: (1) an unkempt speaker or salesperson, (2) a receptionist or telephone solicitor who does not speak distinctly, (3) a sloppy letter filled with errors? They all transmit their messages in an unfavorable way. Every communication you transmit can be your goodwill ambassador and can help achieve a positive reaction if you remember that appearances do make a difference.

Communication Skills of Sender and Receiver

The tools of language include careful selection of words and correct spelling or pronunciation of the words to express the intended meaning. How well the sender of the message uses these tools and how well the receiver interprets their use are major factors in the effectiveness of the message. Selection

√ REINFORCEMENT

Ask students to give examples of communication situations that would be affected by the four elements mentioned. A doctor, for example, would have to consider the background (knowledge) of the receiver when communicating with a patient.

√ REINFORCEMENT

Discuss the role that personal appearance and the appearance of written communications play in making a good first impression.

of the correct words is particularly important in cases in which there might be a language barrier—for example, if the receiver's first language is not English. Both the sender and the receiver have responsibility for effective communication. Something as simple as using the wrong word, making a grammatical error, or misusing a punctuation mark may change the intended meaning of the message.

Even if the receiver understands the message, his or her opinion of the sender may be influenced by the error. For example, a receiver may not do business with a company because of a poorly written sales letter. The receiver may feel that a company that is careless about its letters may also be careless about filling its orders promptly and accurately.

Each of these tools of language is discussed more fully in later sections of this book. Keep in mind, however, that these tools apply not only to writing but also to reading, listening, and speaking. If the communication process is to be successful, the message sender must be an effective writer and speaker, and the receiver must be an effective reader and listener.

Distractions

❏SUGGESTION

Discuss distractions that might be experienced by a student in class and by an employee in industry.

Under what circumstances is the message received? For example, is the room noisy? too warm or too cold? poorly lighted? Is the receiver more concerned with some personal problem? All such distractions draw the receiver's attention away from the message and interfere with communication. Sometimes the resulting lack of concentration can lead to incomplete communication and erroneous conclusions.

Distractions are usually easier to prevent in a speaking/listening situation because the surroundings can often be controlled or changed. In a writing/reading communication, however, the writer has little influence over the reader's surroundings. However, every writer can and should prevent the distraction of a sloppy-looking message.

DEVELOPING INTERPERSONAL SKILLS

The average person speaks about 18,000 words each day. (That many words could fill approximately 100 pages of a book.) Most of those words are spent communicating on a one-to-one basis or in situations involving only a few people. It makes sense, therefore, that everyone should develop effective interpersonal skills.

Understanding Human Needs

One significant factor in successful interpersonal skills is consideration for the needs and feelings of the receivers. Abraham Maslow, a famous psychologist, has divided human needs into five levels.

1. *Physical needs.* These needs include food, clothing, and shelter. Until these basic needs are satisfied, receivers can think of little else.

2. *Security needs.* Security needs include the desire to be safe from physical harm and mental abuse.
3. *Social needs.* These needs, which are evident in everyone's desire to be part of a group, can be met through family, social contacts, work relationships, or other group situations.
4. *Esteem needs.* Esteem needs are satisfied through a feeling of self-importance, self-respect, prestige, power, or recognition.
5. *Self-actualization needs.* These needs are met through a sense of achievement, competence, and creativity, and by helping others meet their own needs.

In order to communicate effectively, the sender must carefully examine each situation and assess the needs of the receiver, because needs motivate people to act or react in certain ways. In many cases, the first three needs (physical, security, and social) are satisfied. However, the last two needs (esteem and self-actualization) always have room for more satisfiers. By helping the receiver satisfy these two needs, the sender can improve communication.

As you consider the needs of the receiver, keep in mind that human relations is also important in successful communication. The human relations techniques described below can actually help you improve your communication skills.

Evaluate the Receiver and Each Communication Situation. The first thing you need to do is determine the needs and special circumstances of the person (or group) who is receiving your communication. Second, you must decide what would best motivate the receiver of your message to respond favorably. Third, you should empathize. In other words, you should imagine yourself in the receiver's situation. If you are writing a letter, for instance, try to visualize the receiver and his or her situation.

Demonstrate a Positive Attitude. A good communicator demonstrates a positive attitude. Two ways that you can show a positive attitude are by being considerate and by listening.

Be considerate of others. A good communicator is courteous, honest, and patient in dealing with other people and respects the opinions of others. This means using tact and diplomacy in some instances. It also means using words and terms that your receiver understands.

Be a good listener. A good communicator is also a good listener. It is important to listen carefully and let the person who is speaking know you are interested. Ask questions when you are unsure of the content of the message and take notes when appropriate.

Being considerate of other people and listening to them are certainly important aspects of effective communication. Both point up once again that communication, the exchange of thoughts, messages, and information, is a two-way process.

Practical Application

A. Define *communication* and list its four main purposes.
B. Explain the difference between verbal and nonverbal communication and tell why both are essential to effective communication.
C. Name the factors that influence communication and describe each one briefly. *background Bk, appearance, comm skills & S&R, Distraction*
D. List several basic human relations techniques that, if applied, could improve communication. *See page 7*

KEY
See page I-6.

asign

Editing Practice

Spelling Alert! Write each of the following sentences, correcting the spelling errors. A sentence may have more than one misspelled word.

1. Ms. Scalia wrote a recommendation letter to the <u>personel</u> manager.
2. Please give me your answer as soon as <u>posible</u>.
3. What time are <u>your planing</u> to leave for San Diego?
4. He finished the <u>report</u> <u>yesteday</u>.
5. Although Pete <u>shiped</u> the package last Tuesday, we did not <u>recieve</u> it until today.

KEY
Errors are underlined.
1. personnel
2. possible
3. you, planning
4. yesterday
5. shipped, receive

class

P.4 WORLD VIEW

Critical Thinking Skills

A. *Analyze:* Today, immediately after a conversation with a fellow student or employee, analyze what was said by jotting down answers to the following questions.

1. What was the intended message?
2. What was the actual message?
3. What was the interpretation of the message?
4. Were all three messages the same? If not, what, do you think, happened to cause a breakdown in communication?

KEY
Answers will vary.

B. *Analyze:* Tell which human need each of the following represents.

1. A burglar alarm system for your home
2. A sweatshirt with your school's name on it
3. The latest haircut
4. Fruits and vegetables
5. Election as president of a club or organization
6. A successful recording artist giving an unknown singer a chance
7. A smoke detector
8. A request for you to design and paint a mural in the public library
9. Owning an expensive car
10. Basic clothing

KEY
1. security
2. social
3. social
4. physical
5. esteem
6. self-actualization
7. security
8. self-actualization
9. esteem
10. physical

assign

WORKBOOK 1.1 A, C, D, F

1.2 *THE COMMUNICATION SKILLS: LISTENING, SPEAKING, READING, AND WRITING*

OBJECTIVES: After completing Section 1.2, you should be able to:

1. Discuss the relationship between and among the four communication skills.
2. Give examples to illustrate the importance of listening, speaking, reading, and writing skills in your life.
3. Explain how the four communication skills reinforce one another.

☐ **SUGGESTION**

Discuss the style and special characteristics of various news, weather, and sports announcers. List their strong and weak points.

KEY POINT

Communication is a two-way process that requires a sender and a receiver.

Look around you. There are many good communicators. Some of the people you identify as good communicators may be friends, members of your family, teachers, or supervisors. Others may be national figures, such as radio and television personalities and political figures. What makes these people effective communicators? What can you do to become a more effective communicator?

As we pointed out before, communication is a two-way process that requires a sender and a receiver. You cannot communicate in a vacuum. You cannot communicate by speaking if there is no one to listen. You cannot communicate by writing if no one will read your words. Each side — sender and receiver — must do its part.

As you have probably noticed, the communicators are paired: speaker-listener and writer-reader. Oral communication requires a speaker and a listener; written communication, a writer and a reader. Oral communication is most effective when the sender has good speaking skills and the receiver has good listening skills. Similarly, written communication is most effective when the sender has good writing skills and the receiver has good reading skills. If only half of the pair operates effectively, something is lost in the communication process. Suppose, for example, that someone writes a clear, step-by-step description of a certain business procedure. No matter how clear that message, some of it will be lost if the receiver does not give it full attention or does not know some of the words or references. The reader will not understand what the writer was trying to say. Communication, then, is a partnership in which each side has a responsibility.

COMMUNICATION IN YOUR LIFE

The communication skills — speaking, listening, writing, and reading — play important roles in many aspects of your life. Good communication skills will improve your chances of succeeding in your social, educational, and professional life.

Your Social Life

The communication skills you are likely to call upon most often in your social life are speaking and listening. You use your speaking skills to tell people about your thoughts, wants, accomplishments, and feelings. You ask questions to gain information and show interest. Speaking also comes into play as part of being a good listener. You provide feedback by letting the speaker know you understand, by offering advice, and by asking for more details. Of course, you need to use your listening skills in order to provide feedback.

Good listeners — those who understand what the speaker is saying and why — are much in demand. We often choose a good listener as a good friend: someone to turn to when we want to talk about our problems or fears or to share our triumphs or joys. Good listeners often reap the benefit of the experience of others and enjoy the satisfaction of close personal relationships.

Reading and writing skills play a role in social life, too. Through your reading of newspapers, magazines, and books, you can broaden your knowledge and understanding of the world and become a more interesting person. Reading gives you more information and ideas to share with others.

Perhaps writing is the communication skill that is least used in our personal lives today. Many of us tend to pick up the telephone rather than write a personal letter to a friend who lives some distance away. However, receiving a letter from someone we care about can be a great pleasure — and the letter can be kept and reread many times. We also need writing skills to send a note of appreciation, for example, or to express condolence to a friend or family member. In addition, we all have to use our writing skills when we take care of personal business correspondence, such as letters of request, complaints, and notifications of address change. Putting your business in writing puts it on record. You have a dated copy of the request, complaint, or notification, and so does the recipient.

Your Educational Life

Good communication skills are a great asset in the learning process. Education does not usually end with high school, college, or professional training. You may, for example, attend workshops on word processing and database software, telemarketing techniques, or management. In any type of schooling, your communication skills are tools that will help you learn and remember the subject matter.

Good listening skills help you absorb an instructor's lectures, explanations, and directions for assignments. Note taking enhances listening. It provides a record of the information you received and enables you to review that information at a later time. Speaking — asking questions, summarizing information, expressing ideas — is also an important part of the learning process. Your spoken feedback tells the instructor what you understand and what needs clarification. Your speaking skills will help you master the material.

In any kind of school, reading is one of the principal means of gaining course-related information. Reading is an efficient way to learn because it allows you to control the flow of information. You can reread a passage you have not fully understood, and you can take notes, which will help you when reviewing the material. Excellent writing skills can help you earn higher grades on research papers and tests. Writing about a subject helps you learn because you must think about the material and organize the information you have before you can start writing.

Your Professional Life

The four communication skills apply to the world of work in much the same way as they apply to your social life and your education. Getting along with other people and mastering new skills are basic elements in the business world. Perhaps the added element here is the need to polish your communication skills so that you can use them to persuade. The special applications of communication skills in business are discussed in Section 1.3, "Language and Communication Skills in Business."

COMBINING YOUR SKILLS FOR MORE EFFECTIVE COMMUNICATION

Listening, speaking, reading, and writing are important and useful skills in and of themselves. When used together, they reinforce each other, producing a higher, more efficient level of communication. Each of the four skills can be strengthened by combining it with the others. Take listening, for example.

Listening Skills

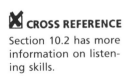
CROSS REFERENCE
Section 10.2 has more information on listening skills.

Listening is one of the primary means of receiving information. The problem with listening, though, is that if you miss something or forget part of what you heard, you cannot replay the message (unless, of course, you have recorded it). When you know something about the subject, however, when you have "read up on it" or "done your homework," you will find it easier to grasp the information presented orally. Reading, then, can reinforce listening; it helps you gain more from what you hear.

Speaking, too, can reinforce your listening skills. As mentioned before, good listeners ask questions to clarify points and elicit additional information. Speaking can also be used as a memory aid. Repeating a person's name right after you hear it, for example, will help you remember the name.

Writing reinforces listening skills on an ongoing basis. You jot down the name and address of a restaurant someone recommends, or you take a phone message for your sister. You take notes when your supervisor explains how a job should be done. You can then refer to your notes when you need them.

WORLD VIEW

Although English is becoming a global language, many know English as a second language and may have difficulty understanding it. People do not think in a second language the same way they do in their native language.

You can see how listening is assisted by the other communication skills when you consider how Lynn Shearer uses these skills in her job as an administrative assistant in a social service agency. Listening is an important part of Lynn's job. She attends staff meetings where she listens to case workers and senior staff discussing current problems and cases. To help her remember what was discussed and what she is supposed to do, Lynn takes notes. After a meeting she enters her notes on a word processor, creating a permanent record and handy reference. In the meetings Lynn often hears references to articles, books, or legislation. She finds that background reading helps her understand discussions at meetings. Lynn also uses her speaking skills in her job. She asks questions and supplies requested information at the staff meetings, and she spends some time each day on the telephone, answering questions and providing information about the agency. Lynn has discovered that reading, writing, and speaking have helped her become a more effective listener.

Speaking Skills

Speaking can be an excellent way to transmit information. Brian Healy, a data-processing instructor, spends much of his workday talking. He relies on notes to help him organize and present his lectures. He lists major points and supporting facts. His notes also include topics for class discussion and questions to help stimulate student interest. Brian knows that reading is an essential part of his job. He must stay up to date in the continually changing field of data processing. Reading and writing skills support his speaking skills. Listening is also important. An instructor must listen to students to find out what they understand and what needs clarification. Brian has found that students often bring up new ideas and interesting points that he can introduce to other classes.

CROSS REFERENCE

Chapter 10 has more information on speaking skills.

Reading Skills

It is clear that reading skills are important for students at every level. Ben Martinez works in a warehouse during the day and attends a community college at night. Ben found the reading assignments for some of his courses difficult at first. However, things improved when he started taking notes on his reading. Taking notes helped Ben organize and remember the information. These notes made studying for exams easier, since he could review the notes rather than the whole text. Ben discovered that he gets a lot more out of a class when he has read the assignment ahead of time. The lectures help him review basic material and clarify difficult points. Ben has also found that he likes participating in discussions when he is prepared for class. Talking about the material in class reinforces his reading and helps him master the material.

CROSS REFERENCE

Section 4.4 has more information on reading skills.

Writing Skills

Writing is a supporting skill in the cases discussed above, but in some jobs, writing is the primary skill. Sarah Haines works as a junior reporter on the

Somerville Sentinel. She has always liked to write and now has a chance to do it full time. Sarah, though, has found that listening, speaking, and reading skills are crucial in writing newspaper articles. For example, Sarah had to read the minutes of last year's town meetings to get the history of the new recycling program. She found that she needed details about recycling plans in other communities and more information about the technology involved. She spent the morning in the public library, reading and taking notes. Next, Sarah wanted to find out what various town officials and citizens thought about the new program. Was the proposed program worth the expense? Would it really help cut down the amount of garbage? Would the plastic bottles be processed and reused as promised? Sarah drew up a list of questions before conducting her first interview. When she asked questions, she listened carefully to the answers and took notes. Finally, Sarah had the material for her story, and she was able to plan what she was going to say and then to sit down at the computer and write.

As the examples above show, the four communication skills are interconnected. Though you may use one skill more often than the others in your job, the others play a vital supporting role. In addition, your listening, speaking, reading, and writing skills become stronger when reinforced by the other skills.

⊽ REINFORCEMENT

Ask students to list professional life situations that use all four skills: listening, speaking, reading, and writing. Discuss how the four skills are interconnected.

KEY
See page I-7.

KEY
See page I-7.

SECTION

REVIEW

Practical Application

A. Explain why communication skills are paired.
B. One of the communication skills is featured in each of the following examples. Explain how one or more of the other skills might be used in each situation to reinforce the main skill.

1. Listening to a neighbor's complaints about a barking dog.
2. Speaking to a group about the pros and cons of four popular word processing programs.
3. Writing a report about public opinion on local property tax rates.
4. Listening to an advisor in the school placement office explain what papers you will need to take when you go for a job interview.
5. Reading several consumer and photography magazines in the library that evaluate compact cameras. (You want to buy a compact camera.)

Editing Practice

Proofreading. Proper proofreading involves checking the spelling of each word and its meaning within the sentence. Proofread the follow-

REVIEW *cont.*

ing letter. On a sheet of paper, make a list of all the errors. Then rewrite the letter so that it is free of errors.

In accordance with our telephone <u>conservation</u>, we are <u>senting</u> you <u>corected</u> <u>specifacations</u>. Note that <u>instalation</u> of a two-way <u>comunication</u> systems is now required. Also, the <u>thermastat</u> is to be <u>re-located</u> to the <u>upstair</u> hall. Please send us your <u>revise</u> bid, <u>propperly</u> typed on your company <u>stationary</u>, no <u>latter</u> <u>then</u> Oct. 1.

Critical Thinking Skills

Analyze: Write a brief essay on letter writing. Give your opinion, supported by examples, on the following:

1. People don't write letters anymore.
2. Letter writing is a lost art.
3. Writing letters is a wonderful way to communicate with the people you care about.

KEY
Answers will vary.

1.3 *LANGUAGE AND COMMUNICATION SKILLS IN BUSINESS*

OBJECTIVES: After completing Section 1.3, you should be able to:

1. Explain the role of good communication in business.
2. Explain the difference between external communication and internal communication in business.
3. Discuss how writing, speaking, listening, and reading are all major communication skills in business.
4. Describe how sensitivity is the key to all communication.

√ REINFORCEMENT
Stress the importance of communication skills in career advancement.

Even if you have not settled on a specific career, you probably have a good idea of the field in which you want to work. Whatever job you eventually choose — accountant or computer programmer, secretary or sales representative, teacher or technician — you will need a thorough knowledge of your chosen field. Then, to get ahead in that field, you will have to become an effective communicator.

THE IMPORTANCE OF GOOD COMMUNICATION IN BUSINESS

No matter what your job is, your working day is basically an eight-hour flow of information. If you are a manager, you can choose to ignore this steady stream of information, or you can tap into the endless supply of ideas and solutions. If you choose to communicate not only by giving information but also by listening to the information provided by others, you will encourage team spirit, create a sense of unity, and increase employee morale and cooperation.

Imagine that you are an employee who has made suggestions for improvement in the department or company. How would you feel if your boss listened to your ideas and actually put some of them into effect? You would probably feel great. You might respond by working even harder than you were working before. You would have experienced effective communication.

Communication not only links members of a certain department but also serves as a vital link with people in other departments. In a company each department functions like a spoke in a wheel; all the spokes are needed for the wheel to function properly. If several spokes are missing, broken, or not aligned properly, the wheel becomes wobbly and eventually will break. Not only does good communication make a company operate efficiently, but it also creates a sense of unity — a team spirit — and a striving for common goals among its employees.

COMPONENTS OF BUSINESS COMMUNICATION

Communication that takes place in a company falls into two categories: external communication and internal communication. *External communication* is the transfer of information to and from people outside the company. Such communication most often persuades the recipients to respond favorably to company needs. A sales letter, for example, tries to get a potential customer to buy a product or a service. A job ad tries to attract qualified personnel to fill a certain position.

The goal of *internal communication* — the transmittal of information between persons within a business or organization — is slightly different from external communication. Within a company, communication is used to accomplish company objectives. People in management must, for example, let employees know when and how a specific job must be done. On the other hand, nonmanagement personnel use communication for understanding and clarifying when and how a specific job must be done. They also communicate to convince management that their knowledge and personal attributes qualify them for pay increases or promotions. Suggestions for improving products, services, and processes are other examples of internal communication.

The tone of internal and external communication is usually different. *Tone*, as it applies to communication, usually refers to the general quality or effect of a conversation, discussion, or speech. For example, in internal communication, a person's tone may be friendly and informal; however, in external communication the tone more often is polite and formal. As a student or employee, it is up to you to assess a situation and use the most appropriate tone. For instance, when telling a fellow student or colleague about an idea you have to make your school or company better, you would use different words, different phrasing, and a different tone than if you were making the same suggestion to the president of the college or the managers of your company.

External communication is more difficult, or more challenging, than internal communication because you are representing your company as well as yourself. Often, customers will transfer their opinions of you and your communication skills to the company itself. They will base opinions not only on what you say or write but also on your appearance and manner. In other words, the whole package counts.

❏ SUGGESTION

Discuss the importance of making a good first impression.

Although your physical appearance may not be so important as the content of what you say, it often creates a first impression. Keep in mind that the first impression you create will often influence how closely your customer or client will listen to what you have to say. As a result, your appearance can either work for you or against you.

DEVELOPING BUSINESS COMMUNICATION SKILLS

❏ SUGGESTION

Ask students to read articles on the changes in offices over the last 30 years. Discuss the articles.

During the past 30 years, traditional offices have been transformed by the addition of high-speed electronic equipment. In addition to the now-standard copying machines, today's offices have computers and word processors instead of typewriters, and fax machines hooked up to telephone lines. All of these new office machines help to make the transmitting of information faster and more efficient. However, machines like these can communicate only as effectively as the people who use them and the messages they carry.

Writing

A large percentage of the communication that takes place within a company is transmitted through the written word: memos, letters, announcements, and reports. Everything from a change in the health plan to a description of a departmental reorganization is usually put in writing in a memo or report and circulated throughout a company.

Writing is also an essential form of communication to people outside a company. Through letters, brochures, advertisements, and other printed material, a company sells its products or services, attracts new personnel, and builds its public image.

Who writes all these letters, advertisements, and reports? People just like you. Regardless of what job you are hired to do, you will have many occasions to pass on information that you have and that others need. What words you use and how you use them will not only reflect on you but undoubtedly will also influence someone's impression of the company you work for. After all, as a sender of communication you are representing the company to the receivers of your communication.

WORLD VIEW

If you're doing business with other countries, you should be aware of differences in etiquette and nonverbal communication. For example, most Europeans shake hands before and after social and business occasions. Japanese, on the other hand, usually bow instead of shaking hands.

✖ **CROSS REFERENCE**

Sections 1.3 and 10.2 give more information on listening.

⊕ **GLOBAL NOTE**

Tell students that companies must sometimes change product names or slogans before marketing products in other countries. For example, Chevrolet would have had a hard time selling its Nova model in Latin American countries. In Spanish, the phrase *no va* literally means "it does not go." Have students discuss the additional dimensions of communicating effectively on the international level.

Speaking

All the skills you need for communication through writing you also need for speaking. In addition, you need to be able to express your ideas verbally in a way that will capture the attention and interest of your listeners. Communicating through speech can take many forms. It can range from a formal presentation before a large group to an informal exchange with a colleague. Both situations are important, and both can affect how far you advance along your career path.

The president of a major corporation once pointed out: "People say that in big companies, it's so hard to get an idea through. . . . An idea that is going to demand the resources of the company needs a champion, and it needs a champion who has got the ability to convince others. Well, how is he going to do that? He's going to do it by the written and spoken word, and more of the spoken word."

Listening

Part of effective speaking involves the asking of questions to gain information and explanations. Too often, though, people who ask questions don't really listen to the answers. Executive Lee Iacocca has said that the ability to listen — or the ability to tune in to the needs and objectives of clients, customers, and colleagues — is the one skill that can make the difference between a mediocre company and a good company.

Being a good listener can also make the difference between being a mediocre employee and a good employee. Unfortunately, no one is born with good listening skills. Becoming a good listener takes conscious effort and continued practice to overcome the following listening blocks.

1. Not concentrating on what is being said.
2. Talking too much.
3. Thinking of responses while someone else is talking.
4. Not being interested in what is being said.
5. Having preconceived thoughts and opinions.

Think back to the most recent occasion in which someone told you how to do something new. Did you listen carefully and understand fully what you were supposed to do, or did you realize a few minutes later that you had actually missed or misunderstood certain steps in the directions? If you had to ask for the directions to be repeated, use the list of listening blocks to determine what prevented you from hearing all the directions the first time.

In business, those who listen carefully and follow directions accurately will usually be noticed and eventually rewarded. Being a good listener in business, however, can pay off in other areas as well. The old adage "What you don't know won't hurt you" certainly does not apply to business. In fact, the more you know, the better off you are.

Listening to the ideas of others can provide the basis for new ones of your own. From time to time, everyone has been in a brainstorming session in which one person's idea becomes the springboard for another idea, and that idea leads to yet another. This is an exciting and often rewarding process — and one that can develop only among good listeners.

Reading

CROSS REFERENCE

Section 4.4 gives more information on reading skills.

Information in business is passed along through either the spoken or the written word. Just as there are distractions to listening carefully, so are there distractions to reading and understanding the written word. Often just the clutter on a desk, the pressure of an immediate deadline, or even the uncomfortable temperature of a room can cause people to skim a memo or report and miss important points.

The advantage of reading over listening, of course, is that in most cases you have a second chance. You can go back and reread a memo or report to find the information you may have missed the first time. Often, however, if people did not read something carefully in the first place, they will not find the time to reread it later.

The ability to read carefully applies not only to the writing of others but also to your own writing. When you have finished an application letter, for example, do you proofread it carefully? Do you look for spelling errors or errors in punctuation? If you do not read your work carefully before sending it, you should not expect anyone else to read it seriously or thoughtfully.

LANGUAGE TIP

"Words are one of our chief means of adjusting to all situations of life. The better control we have over words, the more successful our adjustment is likely to be."

—Bergen Evans

Sensitivity: A Key Ingredient to Good Communications. To be a good writer, speaker, listener, and reader, you also need a sensitivity to others. Successful speakers and writers always consider their audiences. Before deciding what to say or write, effective communicators ask questions such as the following:

- Who will be hearing or reading what I have to say?
- What does my audience already know about my subject?
- What does my audience want to hear?
- How can I make my speech (or writing) interesting to my audience?

Likewise, careful listeners and readers are considerate of a speaker or writer. They put themselves in the other person's place, and they consciously try to eliminate all listening blocks or reading distractions. Careful listeners and readers try to give the speaker or writer their undivided attention and interest. This mutual sensitivity to the needs and concerns of others keeps communication flowing smoothly.

In business situations, you can demonstrate your sensitivity by consideration for the people you work with. This consideration might be expressed by keeping your emotions under control, doing your "fair share," giving credit for others' contribution, and being punctual.

In the upcoming chapters, you will read more about becoming a good communicator. Keep in mind that when poor communication creates a void, misunderstanding usually rushes in to fill that void. This is as true between two friends as between a manager and an employee.

It is clear that a communicator should be sensitive to the nature and needs of his or her audience. The good speaker and the good writer shape and adapt the communication to fit the audience. Since communication is a two-way process, sensitivity also comes into play for the recipient of the communication. The good listener and the good reader demonstrate their sensitivity to the communicator by keeping their minds open and focused on the subject in an effort to understand the message.

SECTION

REVIEW

Practical Application

KEY
See page I-8.

A. Define *internal communication* and *external communication* as they apply to businesses.
B. List the four skills needed to communicate effectively in a business and give an example of each skill.
C. Explain how sensitivity is the key to all effective communication.

Editing Practice

KEY
See page I-8.

Using Tact! Each of the following items lacks sensitivity to the reader. Rewrite each one to correct the problem.

1. We can't ship the shirt you ordered (catalog #456-861) until you tell us what color you want. Don't delay your order further. Send us the color today!
2. In our recent sales campaign, we sold 6,000 CD players. Your complaint is the only one we received. Even though 5,999 people were completely satisfied, we are shipping you a new CD player today.
3. The terms of our contract were clearly stated. We offered a discount if we received payment within 10 days. You took a total of 30 days to pay. Therefore, send us the $50 balance.

KEY
1. occasionally
2. supervisors, perfor-
   mance
3. dissatisfied
4. proofread, omitted
5. approximately
6. attorneys, defense
7. proceed

Spelling Alert! On a sheet of paper, rewrite each of the following sentences, correcting any spelling errors.

1. Mr. Huizinga <u>ocasionally</u> asks the members of his staff to work on Saturdays.
2. At the end of the year, all departmental <u>supervisers</u> must fill out employee <u>performence</u> appraisal forms.
3. The vice president was obviously <u>disatisfied</u> with the results of the survey.
4. When Peter <u>proofred</u> the report, he noticed that two charts had been <u>ommitted</u>.
5. Maryellen told us that <u>aproximately</u> 30 sales representatives were expected to attend the meeting.
6. The <u>attornies</u> for the <u>defence</u> and the prosecution agreed to settle out of court.
7. We will <u>procede</u> as soon as all the forms are signed.

REVIEW cont.

8. languages
9. OK
10. embarrassment

8. The applicant said he was fluent in three <u>langauges</u>.
9. The annual report was sent to the stockholders on Tuesday, February 11.
10. Proofreading letters carefully before sending them to clients will help avoid possible <u>embarassment</u>.

Critical Thinking Skills

KEY
Answers will vary.

A. *Evaluate:* Interview someone in business, asking questions such as the following. Then evaluate the importance you think communication has in that business.

1. Are written and spoken communications a big part of your job?
2. What kinds of communication problems do you often see?
3. Do you think that the ability to communicate effectively will play an important part in the advancement of your career? Explain why or why not.
4. What has your company done in the past to improve the communication skills of its employees?
5. What suggestions do you have to improve the communications within your company?

B. *Analyze:* Answer the following questions as honestly as possible. Based on your answers, analyze areas where you can improve your listening skills.

1. When a problem arises at work or at school, do you often react before getting all the facts?
2. After you receive the answer to a question, do you lose interest in the conversation?
3. Do you have a tendency to daydream at a meeting or during a lecture?
4. Do you ever finish other people's statements in order to save time?
5. Do you feel uncomfortable asking someone to repeat a set of directions or instructions?

class

WK BK 1.2
C, D, F

1.3
A, B, D

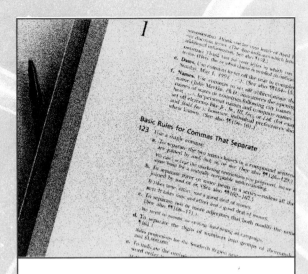

EXPANDING
LANGUAGE SKILLS

2.1 *LANGUAGE STRUCTURE*

OBJECTIVES: After completing Section 2.1, you should be able to:

1. Identify the eight parts of speech.
2. Distinguish between a subject and a predicate.
3. Compare and contrast phrases, clauses, and sentences.
4. Recognize and write grammatically correct sentences.

Imagine taking a newly arrived foreign-exchange student to her first baseball game. Although your friend understands basic English, would you expect her to comprehend terms such as *shortstop, double play, inning,* and *safe at home?* Of course not! Although none of these terms is difficult to understand, each will seem confusing — to a stranger.

Likewise, terms such as *adjective, infinitive,* and *predicate* will sound "foreign" and difficult to a beginner. However, each term is really simple to understand *with a little practice.* Just as understanding baseball terms helps the spectator discuss or explain the game, understanding some basic grammatical terms will help speakers and writers communicate more effectively. This section sketches a rough outline of English grammar and uses some of its basic terms. The terms are few — but pay close attention so that you will be sure to master the game!

THE PARTS OF SPEECH

√ **REINFORCEMENT**
Ask students to name the eight categories of language.

All the many thousands of words in our language can be grouped into eight categories: nouns, pronouns, verbs, adjectives, adverbs, prepositions, conjunctions, and interjections. These categories are called the "parts of speech." As you will see, each group describes a special *function* — that is, each category tells one way in which words can be used. Let's begin with nouns.

Nouns

The word *noun* is derived from a word meaning "name": A *noun* is the *name* of a person, place, or thing.

Persons: Professor Kayhart, Dr. Delfino, Ms. Webb, Corey, Jason, child, supervisor, clients, suppliers

Places: Omaha, Grand Canyon, West Coast, Japan, the Middle East, colleges, offices, factories, homes

Things: Corvette, Reeboks, subway, disk drives, x-rays, lessons, basketball, freedom, capitalism

Pronouns

Pronouns are words that *replace* nouns; for example, *I, you, he, she, it, we, they, me, him, her, us, them, my, your, his, her, our,* and *their.* Because they serve as substitutes, pronouns add variety to our speech and our writing and provide us with shortcuts.

He asked Maria to order a new coin dispenser. (Another way of saying "*Tim* asked Maria to order a new coin dispenser.")

She gave *them* the keys to *their* cars. (Another way of saying "*The parking attendant* gave *Fred and Mac* the keys to *Fred's and Mac's* cars.")

Checkup 1

Identify the nouns and pronouns in the following sentences. On a separate sheet of paper, label each noun (N) or pronoun (P). (Watch for nouns that have two or more words, such as *bulletin board.*)

1. They tested the product in Atlanta.
2. You and I should have gone to our assembly plant last March.
3. Indianapolis is the site of our newest division.
4. Perhaps we can rent a car in Des Moines and drive to the plant.
5. I am sure Joe Kettle will give us a map and some directions if we ask him.
6. Sol and Chris tell me the Midwest is their favorite part of the country.

Verbs

Verbs are commonly called "action words" because they give sentences life; they make sentences "move."

Our company *imports* Swiss chocolate and *uses* it in various desserts. (*Imports* and *uses* are verbs.)

Ms. Platt *bought* one Swiss chocolatier's inventory and *shipped* it to our Pennsylvania plant. (*Bought* and *shipped* are verbs.)

In fact, DeSuite Company *has been buying* chocolate from Switzerland since 1946. (*Has been buying* is a verb that consists of more than one word.)

Not all verbs indicate an obvious action; some merely show a "state of being," such as *am, is, are, was, were, be, been.*

Of course, I *am* happy about Julio's promotion, but his parents *are* thrilled. (*Am* and *are* are verbs that show "state of being.")

Julio *will be* a supervisor in March. By that time Greta *will have been* a manager for 12 years. (*Will be* and *will have been* are verbs. Note that each consists of more than one word.)

Checkup 2

KEY
Verbs are underscored for sentences 1 through 4. Sample verbs are provided for sentences 5 through 8.
5. completed, finished, met; started, began (action)
6. studies, reads, pre-pares (action)
7. was, is (being)
8. hope; passes (action)

Identify the verbs in the following sentences.

1. John is happy about his promotion.
2. Nancy was planning a new brochure for these products.
3. Janice hired two new assistants for her department after she promoted John.
4. Mr. Vernon has been in Cincinnati for about two weeks.

Now supply a verb for the blanks in the following sentences and indicate whether it is an action verb or a being verb. Use a separate sheet of paper.

5. Adriana _____ her degree requirements in June and _____ her new job the following month.
6. Now she _____ every night for her certification exam.
7. She _____ never one to wait until the last minute.
8. I _____ she _____ the exam.

Adjectives

KEY POINT
Adjectives describe nouns and pronouns.

Adjectives describe nouns and pronouns. In describing, adjectives limit or make more specific the noun or pronoun. Another word for limiting is *modifying*.

Adjectives may show "what kind of": *hectic* schedule, *interesting* article, *expensive* equipment. They may point out "which one": her *former* supervisor, *that* report, *those* folders. They may tell "how many": *one* employee, *several* clients, *few* tickets.

The words *a*, *an*, and *the* are special types of adjectives called *articles: a* printout, *an* employee, *the* magazine.

In the above examples, the adjectives describe nouns. When they describe pronouns, adjectives generally follow such verbs as *is, am, are, was, were, be,* and *been.*

She was *impatient* with the slow growth of her investment. (The adjective *impatient* describes the pronoun *she.*)

They were *nervous* before their presentation. (*Nervous* modifies or describes the pronoun *they.*)

Adverbs

KEY POINT
Adverbs describe adjectives, verbs, or other adverbs.

Adverbs are also modifiers; like adjectives, adverbs *describe* or limit. Adverbs describe or modify adjectives, verbs, or other adverbs.

Jean was *unusually* calm before she addressed the Lions Club. (The adverb *unusually* modifies the adjective *calm.*)

Herb *nearly* fell on his face as he tripped over the telephone cord. (The adverb *nearly* modifies the verb *fell*.)

He ran *extremely well* in the Boston Marathon. (The adverb *extremely* modifies the adverb *well*; the adverb *well* modifies the verb *ran*.)

Note that many adverbs end in *ly* and are therefore very easy to identify:

surely	immediately	badly
suddenly	successfully	happily

In fact, these adverbs are formed by adding *ly* to the adjectives *sure, sudden, bad, immediate, successful,* and *happy.*

Although most words that end in *ly* are adverbs, not all adverbs end in *ly.* Here are some adverbs that do not end in *ly:*

always	very	well	then
not	soon	here	never
much	quite	there	almost

Checkup 3

KEY
1. adjective, adverb
2. adverb, adjective
3. adjective, adverb
4. adjective, adverb, adjective
5. adjective, adverb, adjective

Identify the words in parentheses as either adjectives or adverbs.

1. A (large) shipment of plumbing supplies will arrive (here) on Monday or Tuesday.
2. Frank will forward the shipment (immediately) to the (new) construction site.
3. Several (experienced) plumbers are (eagerly) awaiting its arrival.
4. The (planned) development (surely) includes (several) parking areas.
5. The (original) architect was (more) interested in (large) apartments.

Prepositions

KEY POINT

Prepositions are used in phrases. They connect words and describe relationships among words.

Prepositions serve to connect words and describe relationships among words. Prepositions are always used in phrases, as shown below:

Preposition	Prepositional Phrase
in	in May, in the morning
for	for Helene, for us
by	by the parking lot, by tomorrow morning
of	of the company, of my supervisor
from	from Ms. Chu, from me

In addition to the prepositions listed above, there are many other commonly used prepositions, including these:

to	from	after	at
on	with	before	into
out	over	through	onto

Prepositional phrases are, obviously, very commonly used in sentences:

The technician left here *after the meeting* and went directly *to the airport.*

At the airport he boarded a plane *with his colleagues.*

The burglar leaped *out the window, over the hedge,* and *into the getaway car.*

Conjunctions

KEY POINT

Conjunctions are words that join words, phrases, or clauses.

Conjunctions are words that *join* words, phrases, or clauses. Note how the conjunctions *and, but, or,* and *nor* are used in these sentences.

Rebecca *and* Jayne attended the convention in Dallas. (*And* joins two words — the nouns *Rebecca* and *Jayne.*)

Their representatives did not go the bar *but* to the gym. (*But* joins two prepositional phrases.)

He will visit the housing project, *or* he will go to the mayor's office. (*Or* joins two clauses.)

Rena would not accept their gift, *nor* did she want them to join her coalition. (*Nor* joins two clauses.)

Checkup 4

KEY
1. P, P
2. C, P, P, P
3. P, C, P
4. P, C, P
5. P, P, C

Identify the words in parentheses as either prepositions (P) or conjunctions (C).

1. The letter (from) Mr. Delaney explained the reason (for) his cancelation.
2. Elise (and) Paula went (to) the toy fair (in) Seattle (with) Mr. Perretti.
3. Bob likes the bakery (on) the corner, (but) Marlene prefers the one (on) Connors Street.
4. Glen did not order more (of) these toys, (nor) has he ordered anything else (through) our purchasing department recently.
5. (With) Ms. Johnson's approval, the toy sale will begin (on) Wednesday (or) Thursday.

Interjections

KEY POINT

Interjections are words used alone that show very strong feeling.

Interjections are words used alone that show very strong feeling. Interjections are often followed by exclamation marks, as shown in the following examples.

Congratulations! All your hard work has finally paid off handsomely. (Note that the interjection *Congratulations* is treated as an independent sentence.)

No! I never dreamed we would get their account.

SUBJECTS AND PREDICATES

KEY POINT

A subject (usually a noun or pronoun) tells who is speaking, who is spoken to, or who or what is spoken about.

In addition to the parts of speech, you should know a few more important terms, including *subject* and *predicate*, the key elements needed to build a sentence. Let's look at subjects first. The subject in a sentence tells (1) who is speaking, (2) who is spoken to, or (3) who or what is spoken about. A subject is usually a noun or pronoun.

1. Who is speaking:
   I approved the proposal yesterday. (The word *I* identifies the subject of the sentence, the person speaking.)
   We approved the proposal yesterday. (The word *We* identifies the subject of the sentence, the persons speaking.)
2. Who is spoken to:
   You have been selected to attend the training session, Andrew. (The subject *You* identifies the person spoken to, *Andrew*.)
   You have been selected to attend the training session, Andrew and Pat. (The subject *You* identifies the persons spoken to, *Andrew and Pat*.)
3. Who or what is spoken about:
   Anthony is the manager of the Customer Relations Department. (Who is spoken about? Answer: *Anthony*, the subject of the sentence.)
   He is the manager of the Customer Relations Department. (Who is spoken about? Answer: *He*, the subject of the sentence.)

**W O R L D
V I E W**

Knowing a few words in another language will ease your way in international business. A foreign-language phrase book or dictionary will provide such basic expressions as "Good morning," "Nice to meet you," and "Thank you" in the customer's language.

In the above examples, the person spoken about is referred to by name, *Anthony*, and then by the pronoun *He*. Now note how sentences often can be rephrased without changing their meanings:

The manager of the Customer Relations Department is Anthony. (The subject of the sentence is *The manager of the Customer Relations Department*.)

Now that we have seen examples of *who* is spoken about, let's see examples of *what* is spoken about:

This insurance policy covers loss by fire and theft. (What is spoken about? Answer: *This insurance policy*.)

It covers loss by fire and theft. (What is spoken about? *It*, a pronoun that substitutes for *This insurance policy*. *It* is the subject of the sentence.)

Now note that subjects can be compound:

Anthony and Anne are the managers of the two departments.
(The subject is *Anthony and Anne*, the persons spoken about.)

KEY POINT

A predicate tells what the subject is, what the subject does, or what is done to the subject.

Now let's look at predicates. What is the predicate of the sentence? The *predicate* is simply the part of the sentence that tells what the subject is or does, or what is done to the subject.

Anthony and Anne *are the managers of these departments*. (The predicate tells what Anthony and Anne are.)

Checkup 5

Identify the subjects of the following sentences. For each subject, try to determine whether the subject is (1) the person(s) speaking, (2) the person(s) spoken to, or (3) the person(s) or thing(s) spoken about.

1. <u>The cables</u> will be laid by March 30.
2. <u>John Macallum</u> will be the account executive.
3. <u>I</u> agree that the original price was too high.
4. <u>The Ingram account</u> will be given to Joyce Van Heflin.
5. <u>Marta and Stan</u> will bring in several new accounts.

CLAUSES AND PHRASES

Words that are grouped together are classified as a *clause* if the group of words includes both a subject and a predicate. A group of related words that does *not* have both a subject and a predicate is called a *phrase*.

Clauses

KEY POINT

A clause is a group of related words that has both a subject and a predicate. A phrase is a group of related words that has neither a subject nor a predicate.

As you read above, a clause has both a subject and a predicate. If this group of words can stand alone — that is, the group of words makes a complete sentence — then it is an *independent* clause. If the group of words cannot stand alone, then the clause is called a *dependent* clause.

Review the following sentences. Note that each has a subject and a predicate and that each *can* stand alone. Each, therefore, is an *independent* clause.

James Northrop is a well-known expert in poultry breeding. (The subject is *James Northrop*, and the predicate is the rest of the sentence. Because this group of words *can* stand alone, this is an independent clause.)

A new software store is scheduled to open May 24 in the Waterville Mall. (Here, the subject is *A new software store*. The predicate is the rest of the sentence. Because this group of words *can* stand alone, this is an independent clause.)

Now read the clauses that follow. Each has a subject and predicate but cannot stand alone. Therefore, these are dependent clauses.

If Ms. Takazato accepts the nomination (This example is a clause; the subject is *Ms. Takazato*, and the predicate is the rest of the clause. But does this group of words make sense? No. This is a *dependent* clause. More information is required if this group of words is to make sense.)

When Mr. Cohen returns from vacation (Again, this example is a clause; the subject is *Mr. Cohen*, and the predicate is the rest of the clause. Once again, the words do not make sense by themselves. This group of words is a dependent clause. As you read this dependent clause, ask yourself this: "What will happen *when Mr. Cohen returns from vacation?*" Do you see that more information is required?)

Dependent clauses cannot stand alone as sentences; therefore, they must be joined to independent clauses to complete the meaning.

If Ms. Takazato accepts the nomination, she must resign her present position. (*She must resign her present position* is an independent clause. Thus the dependent clause *If Ms. Takazato accepts the nomination* is correctly joined to an independent clause.)

When Mr. Cohen returns from vacation, he will review all these blueprints. (Again, the dependent clause, *When Mr. Cohen returns from vacation*, is joined to an independent clause.)

Checkup 6

Determine which of the following groups of words are sentences and which are dependent clauses that are incorrectly treated as sentences. For each dependent clause, suggest an independent clause that would complete it.

1. Because Claire Hunt, the head nurse, will not return until next week, Thursday's meeting has been canceled.
2. Claire and Joel Martini will draw up the nurses' schedules.
3. Before the nurses meet to discuss their patients.
4. If Claire does not hire another nursing assistant by May 1.
5. When Florence meets with the nursing staff in her hospital.

Phrases

Phrases are groups of words that have neither subjects nor predicates. As you study the following three kinds of phrases, note that none has a subject or a predicate.

Prepositional Phrases. Prepositional phrases are phrases such as *for the interns, in the office, among them, at the seminar, with Michael Farmer, between you and me*, and *from Dr. Holzman*. The nouns and pronouns at the ends of prepositional phrases are not subjects; they are objects of the prepositions.

As you read the examples below, note how prepositional phrases can be used (1) as adjectives and (2) as adverbs.

1. As adjectives:
   The woman *with the clipboard* is Suzanne Chung. (Which woman? The prepositional phrase *with the clipboard* describes the noun *woman*. Therefore, because it describes a noun, this prepositional phrase serves as an adjective.)
2. As adverbs:
   Dirk sent the letter *to the chairperson*. (Sent it where? The prepositional phrase *to the chairperson* answers the question Where? This prepositional phrase serves as an adverb.)

Infinitive Phrases. An *infinitive* is the *to* form of a verb: *to drive, to study, to analyze, to review, to compute, to keyboard, to be, to have, to do,* and so on. An infinitive phrase includes the infinitive and any other words that are related to it. Infinitive phrases may be used (1) as nouns, (2) as adjectives, and, less frequently, (3) as adverbs.

1. As nouns:
    To develop sound training programs is the objective of this department. (The complete infinitive phrase is *To develop sound training programs;* the phrase is the subject of the verb *is.*)
2. As adjectives:
    Sheila McGuire is the manager *to ask about employment opportunities.* (Here the infinitive phrase *to ask about employment opportunities* modifies the noun *manager* and therefore serves as an adjective.)
3. As adverbs:
    Pat bent down *to remove the chewing gum from her shoe.* (Bent down for what reason? Here the infinitive phrase answers the question Why? The infinitive phrase *to remove the chewing gum from her shoe* therefore serves as an adverb.)

· M E M O R Y   H O O K ·

Because infinitives begin with the word *to,* they may sometimes be confused with prepositional phrases beginning with the word *to.*

	Infinitive	Prepositional Phrase	
I keyboard	to keyboard	to the committee	*I the committee No!*
I review	to review	to Professor Grant	
I accept	to accept	to me	

To avoid any possible confusion, remember that an infinitive is the *to* form of a *verb.* Simply test by using the infinitive as a verb: *I keyboard, you review, they accept.* Using this procedure with prepositional phrases will yield gibberish. Try it!

Verb Phrases. In a verb phrase, two or more verbs work together as one verb. In such cases, the main verb is always the last verb in the phrase; the other verbs are helping (or auxiliary) verbs.

The engineer *will complete* the calculations by noon tomorrow. (*Will complete* is a verb phrase. The main verb is *complete; will* is a helping verb.)

By noon tomorrow the calculations *will have been completed.* (The main verb is *completed,* the last word in the verb phrase. *Will have been* is a helping verb.)

Verb phrases are often interrupted by adverbs, as shown in these examples. Do not be misled by such interruptions.

The engineer will *soon* be showing his calculations to the traffic consultant. (The verb phrase *will be showing* is interrupted by the adverb *soon*.)

The traffic consultant has *already* been told about possible delays on metropolitan bus routes. (The verb phrase *has been told* is interrupted by the adverb *already*.)

Checkup 7

Are the words in parentheses prepositional phrases (PP), infinitive phrases (IP), or verb phrases (VP)? On a separate sheet of paper, write *PP*, *IP*, or *VP* for each group of words.

1. The chef's recipe (has been printed) and (will be submitted) (to the award committee) (by next Monday).
2. Mr. Heffner wants (to taste the recipe) when he goes (to the award dinner) (with Alma Brady).
3. (To become) a chef (at André's), you (must have had) at least five years' experience (at a three-star restaurant).
4. Several cooking classes (have been scheduled) (for André's best customers).
5. (To attend the cooking classes), customers (have been asked) (to pay) (in advance).

THE SENTENCE

We use sentences as our basic units of thought as we read, write, and speak. Our ability to use and to understand sentences effectively, therefore, determines our ability to communicate.

Review this section carefully to master this important topic.

What Is a Sentence?

 **KEY POINT**

A sentence is a group of words that expresses a complete thought.

Remember this definition: *A sentence is a group of words that expresses a complete thought.* Note especially the word *complete*. Writing incomplete sentences — called "fragments" — is a common but glaring error. You can distinguish between a complete sentence and a fragment by applying the "no sense/no sentence" rule. Look at the following examples:

Emily Clark wants to attend the conference because the theme of the meeting is electronic communications. (This is a complete thought. This group of words makes sense. This *is* a sentence.)

When we receive Mr. Wallack's approval, we will make a reservation for Ms. Clark. (This thought is complete. This group of words makes sense, so it is a sentence.)

If, however, you try to split off part of the sentence (see examples below), you would create a fragment.

Emily Clark wants to attend the conference. Because the theme of the meeting is electronic communications. (The first group of words is a sentence. The words *Because the theme of the meeting is electronic communications* do not make sense by themselves. The word *because* leads us to expect more. What happened *because the theme of the meeting is electronic communications?*)

When we receive Mr. Wallack's approval. We will make a reservation for Ms. Clark. (The words *When we receive Mr. Wallack's approval* do not make sense by themselves; the word *when* leads us to expect more. It is not a sentence. What will happen *when we receive Mr. Wallack's approval?* The second group of words is a sentence.)

In the examples above, the words *because* and *when* lead us to expect more. Each begins a clause that cannot stand alone. Note that the following words, like *because* and *when*, often introduce dependent clauses (clauses that cannot stand alone):

after	before	provided that	when
although	even if	since	whenever
as	for	so that	where
as if	how	than	wherever
as soon as	if	that	whether
as though	in case that	unless	while
because	in order that	until	why

Subjects and Predicates

REINFORCEMENT

A sentence must have a subject and a predicate.

Every sentence must have both a subject and a predicate. As we noted earlier, the subject of a sentence is that part that names (1) the person or persons speaking, (2) the person or persons spoken to, or (3) the person(s) or thing(s) spoken about. Here are a few more examples.

1. *I* requested additional copies. (*I* is the complete subject of the sentence, the person who is speaking.)
2. *You* should order a copy. (*You* is the complete subject of the sentence, the person or persons spoken to.)
    Order a copy. (Here the subject is still *you*, but this sentence is an imperative sentence — it is a request or an order. In such sentences, we are usually directly addressing the person spoken to; therefore, it is clearly understood that the subject is *you*.)
3. *That book* belongs to Daniel. *Those books* belong to Kristen. (*That book* and *Those books* are the subjects. *That book* is the thing spoken about; *Those books* are the things spoken about.)

4. *She* will attend the workshop. *They* will attend the workshop. (*She* and *They* are the subjects. *She* is the person spoken about; *They* are the persons spoken about.)

Every time you identify the subject correctly, you simplify your work in identifying the predicate. Reason: The predicate tells what the subject does, what is done to the subject, or the state of being of the subject.

Checkup 8

Are the following groups of words sentences, or are they fragments? Identify each as sentence or fragment; then rewrite each fragment to make it a complete sentence.

1. If Mr. Bartoli decides to change the policy.
2. Because both approvals are required for all checks over $5,000.
3. Our vice president initiated the policy in 1962.
4. Although her reasons were valid at that time.
5. Maureen or Elliot will be named chief accountant.

Simple and Compound Subjects

The *simple subject* is the main word in the complete subject — the core of the subject.

The *manager* of these hotels is Jack DeLorenzo. (The complete subject is *The manager of these hotels.* The main word or simple subject in this complete subject is *manager.*)

Two former *partners* in the Wolfe & Crowell accounting firm are scheduled to meet with us today. (The complete subject of this sentence is *Two former partners in the Wolfe & Crowell accounting firm.* Within this complete subject, the simple subject is *partners.*)

Because the subject of the first example is *manager*, not *hotels*, the correct verb must be *is.* Because the subject of the second example is *partners*, not *firm*, the correct verb must be *are.* As you can see, therefore, only by knowing how to find the simple subject will you be sure to make subjects and verbs agree.

Compound subjects are two or more equal subjects joined by a conjunction such as *and, but, or,* or *nor.*

The *drivers and loaders* in our company have announced that they will indeed strike if their demands are not met. (The complete subject is *The drivers and loaders in our company.* The main words in this complete subject are *drivers* and *loaders*, which are joined by the conjunction *and.* The compound subject is *drivers and loaders.*)

A *cruise* to the Bahamas or a one-week *vacation* in Cancun is going to be the first prize. (The complete subject is *A cruise to the Bahamas or a one-week vacation in Cancun*. Can you identify the main words in this complete subject? The main words are *cruise* and *vacation*, which are joined by the conjunction *or*. The compound subject is *cruise or vacation*.)

Normal Order: Subject, Then Predicate

The normal order of a sentence is subject first, then predicate.

Four members of the council were at last night's meeting of the zoning board. (The complete subject is *Four members of the council*. Because the complete subject precedes the complete predicate, this sentence is in *normal* order.)

At last night's meeting of the zoning board were *four members of the council*. (The words are the same, but the order is different. Now the predicate precedes the subject. This sentence, therefore, is *not* in normal order. It is in *inverted* order.)

Note that most questions are phrased in inverted order rather than normal order.

Has Alex checked on the estimated cost of this brochure? (Why is this question in inverted order? The subject is *Alex*, and part of the verb — the word *Has* — precedes the subject. Normal order: *Alex has checked on the estimated cost of this brochure*.)

Now let's see why it is important to be able to distinguish between normal order and inverted order. What, if anything, is wrong with this sentence?

Where's the blank disks that Peter left for us?

Many people almost automatically start sentences with *Where's*, *There's*, and *Here's*, even when these words are incorrect. Normal order quickly points out the error:

The blank disks that Peter left for us *is* where? (Simply put, "The disks . . . is where?" *Disks is* is incorrect, of course; we must say "Disks are.")

Not only in questions but also in statements is it important to spot inverted order. Note this sentence:

On the shelf in my office is the blank disks that Peter left for us. (In normal order, this sentence reads: "The blank disks that Peter left for us *is* on the shelf in my office." Of course, *disks is* does not agree. This error is masked by the inverted order.) It should, of course, read *disks are*.

Checkup 9

Practice identifying subjects and predicates. On a separate sheet of paper, write the simple subject or the compound subject for each sentence. Be sure to change inverted sentences to normal order first!

1. Has <u>Scot</u> written to the Internal Revenue Service for answers to these questions?
2. <u>Two printing companies and a travel agency</u> have shown interest in buying this property.
3. <u>The résumés that we received from all applicants</u> were exceptionally interesting.
4. <u>One woman in the first session that we conducted</u> asked about the availability of franchises in her city.
5. Sitting on my desk were <u>six large files on the history of the Firman account.</u>

SECTION

REVIEW

Practical Application

A. Name the part of speech for each word in parentheses in the following sentences. On a separate sheet of paper, write *noun, pronoun, verb, adjective, adverb, preposition, conjunction,* or *interjection.* For each phrase in parentheses, identify the phrase by writing *VP* (verb phrase), *IP* (infinitive phrase), or *PP* (prepositional phrase).

1. (Employees) should be encouraged (to make suggestions).
2. (Suggestions) are always welcome (in this organization).
3. A special bonus (will be given) (to employees) if their suggestions are implemented.
4. Stacy Moreno (and) Jack Kemper have (already) received bonuses for their (retooling) suggestion.
5. (Hooray!) (We) just (won) the computer sales contest (in) our district.
6. (Astrotech) finished second, (but) CompFast performed (very) poorly.
7. (In 1994), (Chicago) (or) St. Paul will be the site of (our) (national) convention.
8. (To choose between these cities) is a (difficult) task, but (we) will make the selection (in) October.
9. I (personally) (believe) that Tampa or San Diego would be a better (location) (for a winter meeting).
10. The (players) (should have known) the (rules) before (they) (entered) the game.

B. Identify the following clauses as dependent or independent. On a separate sheet of paper, write *D* or *I.*

1. When an increasing number of firms are striving for global competitiveness.
2. Before we see a significant upturn in the economy.

3. D
4. I
5. D
6. I
7. D
8. D
9. D
10. I

KEY
See page I-9.

KEY
See page I-10.

REVIEW cont.

3. One of the most important signs that we have seen in terms of consumer buying power.
4. Discount retailers are winning the battle.
5. While more aggressive managers are searching for multitalented employees.
6. The manufacturing sector has been hardest hit.
7. To the degree to which trainees will take direction.
8. If they really want Carlotta Morris to approve the merger.
9. As soon as the results of the taste test have been tabulated.
10. In about a week we should know which brand was the top choice.

C. Read each of the following sentences carefully. Then, on a separate sheet of paper, (1) change any inverted sentence to normal order, (2) write the complete subject, and (3) underline the simple or compound subject.

1. In late May or early June, Mr. and Mrs. Messineo will buy the Ashtons' beach property.
2. Their real estate agent found the property by accident.
3. Although the buildings and land were expensive, South Shore Bank approved the couple's mortgage application.
4. Located at the bottom of the hill are the only other houses on Hodge Road.
5. On the north side of the property are a guest cottage and a pool.
6. Jackie Messineo plans to use the guest cottage as a design studio.
7. As soon as the cottage is renovated, her two assistants will join her there.
8. Suppliers and past and potential customers will receive invitations to a studio open house on the Fourth of July.
9. Meanwhile, Dom Messineo has begun to look for a carpenter to make some minor improvements in the main house.
10. Shortly before the middle of July, the Messineo children and pets will arrive at their new summer home.

D. On a separate sheet of paper, (1) identify each complete sentence below or add the words needed to change a fragment to a complete sentence. Then (2) indicate the normal order of any inverted sentence and (3) identify the complete subject and the simple or compound subject for each sentence.

1. What is your decision?
2. As soon as we receive the auditor's report.
3. The two people in the accounting department who do that work.
4. The vendors and buyers agree with your suggestion.
5. Have you forgotten how to enter the data?
6. Where are the photographs for the Supershop advertisement?

REVIEW cont.

7. Although this system was in effect between 1962 and 1991.
8. At the November trade show in New Orleans, <u>they</u> will be able to examine our new software.
9. Stashed away in the green cabinet are <u>all the old files</u>.
10. Until Mr. Nicholson agrees to the reorganization plan that you submitted last April.

Editing Practice

The Word Processing Supervisor. Can you find any errors in the following excerpt from an informal note written by an employee?

Here's the samples you requested last Monday. If <u>there's</u> any more brochures left in the stockroom, I'll be glad to send them to <u>to</u>.

As a Matter of Fact . . . . Proofreading requires us to look not only for errors in grammar, spelling, punctuation, and so on, but also for inconsistencies and errors in facts. Read and correct the following excerpt from a business memo.

On September <u>31</u> we mailed Mr. Benson a check for $200, but we omitted the 8 percent sales tax on this total as well as the shipping charge of $10. Please send Mr. Benson a check for <u>$18</u> to cover the additional cost of the tax on $200 and the shipping expense.

Identify

KEY
Errors are underscored.
Here are
there are
too

KEY
September 30 (?)
$26

2.2 *VERBS*

OBJECTIVES: After completing Section 2.2, you should be able to:

1. List and provide examples of the four principal parts of a verb.
2. Explain what makes most English verbs regular rather than irregular verbs.
3. Define the term *verb tense* and identify the six most commonly used verb tenses.
4. Discuss the differences between transitive, intransitive, and "being" verbs.

Among the most serious and the most common errors we make as we speak and write are verb errors. Yet forming most verbs correctly is very easy, because most verbs follow one simple pattern, as you will see in the first half of this section. The verbs that do not follow this regular pattern are the ones that cause problems; these irregular verbs are discussed in depth in the second part of this section.

IDENTIFYING VERBS

As you read in Section 2.1, a *verb* is a word that describes an action, a condition, or a state of being. The following examples illustrate those three different kinds of verbs.

Action

Edith *signed* the agreement.
They *landed* on time at 4:15 p.m.
I *will speak* to the administrative assistants this morning.
Ms. Russo *is writing* the draft now.
Mr. Carlin *will be running* on the track during lunchtime.

The verbs *signed, landed, will speak, is writing*, and *will be running* all describe an action.

Condition

Edith *seems* pleased with the new clauses in the agreement.
They *felt* better on the ground.
The administrative assistants *became* restless during my talk.
Ms. Russo *appears* to be a good writer.
Mr. Carlin *grew* thirsty during his lunchtime run.

The verbs *seems, felt, became, appears*, and *grew* all describe a condition.

Being

Edith *is* happy with the agreement.
They *are* home at last.
I *am* happy to welcome the new administrative assistants.
Ms. Russo *will be* a likely candidate for promotion.
Mr. Carlin *was* very tired at the end of his run.

The verbs *is, are, am, will be*, and *was* do not describe actions or conditions in the sentences above, yet each is a verb. These verbs are "being" verbs.

Practice identifying verbs correctly—that's the first step in using verbs correctly.

Checkup 1

KEY
Verbs are underscored. When students suggest incorrect answers,

Identify the verbs in the following sentences.

1. Anne <u>asked</u> Carlo Mendoza to the dinner meeting.
2. The Acme Glass Company <u>wants</u> this property for its new plant.

dramatize how verbs
function by using the
incorrect answers *as if
they were verbs!* For
example, in sentence 1,
if a student says that
the verb is *meeting,*
say "I meeting, you
meeting, he meetings,"
and so on. The word
meeting cannot be
used as a verb, and
this simple test will be
useful to students.

3. Warren and Tim <u>are</u> at our branch office right now.
4. Helen <u>has accepted</u> the invitation.
5. The vice president <u>seemed</u> satisfied with the results of the campaign.
6. Lisa and Frank <u>were</u> in Little Rock when we <u>discussed</u> this proposal.

REGULAR VERBS

As we speak and write, the verbs we use indicate the time of the action, condition, or state of being. We form verbs to indicate present time ("I learn," "I am learning"), past time ("I learned," "I have learned"), and future time ("I will learn," "I will be learning"). Fortunately, most verbs in our language follow the same simple pattern to indicate time. These verbs are "regular" verbs.

Principal Parts of Regular Verbs

 **KEY POINT**

The principal parts of a verb are the present tense, the past tense, the past participle, and the present participle.

Knowing how to form the parts of verbs is necessary if you are to use verbs correctly in all instances. The principal parts of a verb are (1) the present tense form, (2) the past tense form, (3) the past participle, and (4) the present participle. From these four forms, all the variations of a verb are derived.

> ### ·MEMORY HOOK·
>
> How can you distinguish between the past tense form *called* and the past participle *called?* Answer: You cannot, except by seeing the word *in context.* Remember: A past tense form *never* has a helper; a past participle *always* has a helping verb.
>
> Bette *called* us at 9 a.m. (Here, *called* is a past tense form; it has no helping verb.)
> Matt came to tell us about the meeting, but Bette *had* already *called* us at 9 a.m. (Here, *called* is a past participle — the main verb in the verb phrase *had called.*)

Present Tense	*Past Tense*	*Past Participle*	*Present Participle*
move	moved	moved	moving
prepare	prepared	prepared	preparing
hire	hired	hired	hiring
call	called	called	calling
enter	entered	entered	entering
listen	listened	listened	listening

As you read this table, say to yourself "I move," "I prepare," and so on. Then notice that the past tense is formed simply by adding *d* to verbs that end in *e.* For verbs that do not end in *e,* add *ed: called, entered, listened.*

Further simplifying this pattern is the fact that the past participle is the same form as the past tense. And the present participle is formed by adding *ing* to the present form. (Of course, for verbs ending in *e*, you must drop the *e* before adding *ing: moving, preparing, hiring*.) Except for a limited list, all the verbs in our language follow this pattern.

Checkup 2

KEY
The missing verb forms appear in color.

On a separate sheet of paper, copy the following chart. Then fill in the missing parts correctly for each entry.

Present Tense	Past Tense	Past Participle	Present Participle
1. keyboard	keyboarded	keyboarded	keyboarding
2. elect	**elected**	elected	electing
3. order	ordered	**ordered**	ordering
4. indicate	indicated	indicated	**indicating**
5. remember	remembered	remembered	remembering
6. respond	**responded**	responded	responding
7. trust	trusted	trusted	trusting
8. use	**used**	used	using

Verb Phrases

REINFORCEMENT
The last verb in the verb phrase is always the main verb.

As you read in Section 2.1, a *verb phrase* consists of two or more verbs used together to function *as one verb*. The main verb in the phrase is *always* the last verb. The other verbs are helping or auxiliary verbs. Read these examples carefully.

    can *move*   did *prepare*   will *hire*

The main verbs in the above three examples are *move, prepare,* and *hire.* The verbs *can, did,* and *will* are helping verbs. Note that *move, prepare,* and *hire* are the present tense forms listed in the table on page 39.

    has been *moved*   have *prepared*   will be *hired*

The main verbs are *moved, prepared,* and *hired,* which are the past participles listed in the third column in the table. The verbs *has been, have,* and *will be* are helping verbs.

    are *moving*   is *preparing*   will be *hiring*

Again, the last word in each phrase is the main verb: *moving, preparing,* and *hiring,* which are the present participles listed on the chart. The words *are, is,* and *will be* are helping verbs.

Now note how verb phrases generally are used in sentences. Remember that the verb phrase can be interrupted by another word, most often an adverb.

Tomorrow Gene *will be moving* into his new office. (The verb phrase is *will be moving*, and the main verb is, of course, the last verb, *moving*.)

Jessica *has* also *been preparing* her résumé. (The verb phrase *has been preparing* is interrupted by the adverb *also*. The main verb is *preparing*.)

Zack's replacement *has* already *been hired*. (*Hired* is the main verb in the phrase *has been hired. Already* is an adverb.)

In questions, the verb phrase is often more difficult to identify, because, as you know, the sentence order is inverted. Finding the verb phrase in inverted sentences will be easier if you change the sentence to normal order first.

When *did* Mr. Herzog *return* all these cellular phones? (The verb phrase is *did return*.)

Have Lynn and Robin already *been working* on this system? (The verb phrase *have been working* is tricky to identify because of the inverted order and the interrupting adverb.)

Checkup 3

Identify the verb phrases in each of the following sentences. For each phrase, name the main verb.

1. Jonathan will be checking all these invoices tomorrow morning.
2. Anthony can complete this entire project by Friday.
3. The speaker will enter the auditorium by the rear door.
4. Have Alan and Ben already approved these diagrams?
5. Jason and Albert have been hoping for this news for many, many months.
6. Does Gregory really want another copy of this fax?

Verb Tenses

The *tense* of a verb is the form that tells the time of the action.

Present Tense. First, remember that *to call, to walk, to type, to listen, to enter,* and so on, are called *infinitives*. These forms without the word *to* are present tense forms:

I call	we call
you call	you call
he	
she } calls	they call
it	

√ **REINFORCEMENT**

Verb tenses for regular verbs are presented first in an effort to establish a foundation for students' understanding. Emphasize that the majority of verbs in our language do follow the rules of regular verbs.

As you see, there are only two present tense forms, *call* and *calls*. Use *call* to agree with *I, you, we,* and *they.* Add *s* for the present tense form to agree with *he, she,* and *it* and with singular nouns.

We *call* every morning. (*Call* with the pronoun *we.*)

He *calls* every morning. Brad *calls* every morning. (*Calls* with the pronoun *he* and the noun *Brad.*)

They *enjoy* assembly work. (*Enjoy* with the pronoun *they.*)

She *enjoys* assembly work. Alison *enjoys* assembly work. (*Enjoys* with the pronoun *she* and the noun *Alison.*)

The present tense is used to show action that is happening now. It is also used to indicate that something is always true (as in, "the sun *rises* in the east").

Past Tense. The past tense is formed by adding *ed* to the present tense form (or *d* if the present tense form already ends in *e*).

I called	we called
you called	you called
he ⎫	
she ⎬ called	they called
it ⎭	

□ **SUGGESTION**

The verb *to be,* which will be introduced later, is an exception to almost every rule. It has three present tense forms (*am, is,* and *are*) instead of the usual two, and it has two past tense forms (*was* and *were*) instead of the usual one. Delay this discussion until the students have mastered the general rules.

As you see, there is only one past tense form for a verb. (The only exception is the verb *to be,* which will be discussed later.) The past tense is used to indicate action that has already been completed.

Future Tense. To form the future tense of a verb, use *will* plus the infinitive form without the word *to.*

I will call	we will call
you will call	you will call
he ⎫	
she ⎬ will call	they will call
it ⎭	

This tense indicates action that is to take place in the future. In addition to these three tenses, each has a correlated "perfect" tense. As you read the discussion on these three perfect tenses, you will realize that they are very commonly used in our everyday conversation and our everyday writing.

Present Perfect Tense. The *present perfect tense* is used to show that an action began in the past and that it may still be occurring. This tense is formed by using the helping verb *has* or *have* with a past participle.

Amelia *has redecorated* the first floor of the house. (Present perfect tense for an action that was begun in the past.)

Quincy and George *have debated* the pros and cons of this issue for years. (Present perfect tense for an action that began in the past and may be still continuing in the present.)

Past Perfect Tense. The *past perfect tense* is used to show which of two past actions occurred first. To form the past perfect tense, use *had* plus the past participle of a verb.

Sam *had mailed* his check before he *received* the cancelation notice. (The verbs *had mailed* and *received* show *two* past actions. The past perfect tense *had mailed* tells us that this action is the *first* past one. After this action was completed, a second action occurred—Sam *received* something. *Received* is past tense, to show the second of the two actions in the order in which they occurred.)

Future Perfect Tense. The *future perfect tense* shows that an action will be completed by some specific time in the future. The action may have already begun, or it may begin in the future. The important point is that it will *end* by a specific future time. To form the future perfect tense, use the verb *will have* plus the past participle of a verb.

> The architect *will have completed* his sketches for the new wing long before the deadline. (*Will have completed* is a future perfect tense verb describing an action that will end by some specific time—*long before the deadline*—in the future.)

The Progressive Tenses. Closely related to the six tenses just discussed are the *progressive tenses*, which depict actions that are still in progress.

Present Progressive Tense. As its name indicates, the *present progressive tense* describes an action that is in progress in the present. To form this tense, use *am*, *is*, or *are* with a present participle.

> I *am using* this software program to prepare my income tax return. (*Am using* shows action in progress now.)

Past Progressive Tense. An action that was in progress at a certain time in the past is described by using *was* or *were* with a present participle.

> They *were reviewing* the field reports when Jenny Petroff arrived. (*Were reviewing* shows action that was in progress in the past.)

Future Progressive Tense. An action that *will be* in progress at a certain time in the future is described by using *will be* with a present participle.

> Maria *will be taking* the first part of her CPA examination next Thursday. (Is this action in progress now? No. In the past? Again, no. *Will be taking* shows an action that will be in progress in the future—specifically, "next Thursday.")

Conjugating Regular Verbs. The following table presents an overview of the rules we have been discussing. It is a *conjugation table* and indicates the three elements that determine verb forms: person (*I*, *you*, *he* or *she*, and so on), number (singular or plural), and tense. Every regular verb follows the same basic conjugation pattern shown here. When you are unsure about the correct form of a particular regular verb, check that verb against the table.

☐ SUGGESTION

The past perfect tense is often misused—not because it is such a difficult concept but because it is infrequently taught. Spend enough time on this topic to ensure that students do understand the simple way in which writers can order two past actions clearly for their readers.

☐ SUGGESTION

You may wish to include the "perfect" versions of these progressive tenses.

The present perfect progressive tense is formed by using *has been* or *have been* with a present participle: *has been working* or *have been working*.

The past perfect progressive tense is formed by using *had been* with a present participle: *had been working*.

The future perfect progressive tense is formed by using *will have been* with a present participle: *will have been working*.

CONJUGATION OF THE VERB *HOPE*	
Singular	*Plural*

Present Tense

Singular	Plural
I hope	we hope
you hope	you hope
he or she hopes	they hope

Past Tense

Singular	Plural
I hoped	we hoped
you hoped	you hoped
he or she hoped	they hoped

Future Tense

Singular	Plural
I will hope	we will hope
you will hope	you will hope
he or she will hope	they will hope

Present Perfect Tense

Singular	Plural
I have hoped	we have hoped
you have hoped	you have hoped
he or she has hoped	they have hoped

Past Perfect Tense

Singular	Plural
I had hoped	we had hoped
you had hoped	you had hoped
he or she had hoped	they had hoped

Future Perfect Tense

Singular	Plural
I will have hoped	we will have hoped
you will have hoped	you will have hoped
he or she will have hoped	they will have hoped

Present Progressive Tense

Singular	Plural
I am hoping	we are hoping
you are hoping	you are hoping
he or she is hoping	they are hoping

Past Progressive Tense

Singular	Plural
I was hoping	we were hoping
you were hoping	you were hoping
he or she was hoping	they were hoping

Future Progressive Tense

Singular	Plural
I will be hoping	we will be hoping
you will be hoping	you will be hoping
he or she will be hoping	they will be hoping

Remember — you substitute singular nouns in place of the pronouns *he* or *she* and plural nouns in place of the pronoun *them!*

Checkup 4

KEY
Use Checkup 4 to test students' ability to use the tenses correctly. As you review their suggested sentences, look for common errors such as using the past perfect tense in a sentence without a past tense verb and errors in subject-verb agreement.

On a separate sheet of paper, use each of the following verbs in a sentence.

1. had remembered
2. are listening
3. will have noticed
4. will be
5. have asked
6. wanted
7. has rejected
8. reviews

IRREGULAR VERBS

Most verbs follow the regular pattern shown above for forming the present tense, the past tense, the past participle, and the present participle. However, there are 50 or more commonly used irregular verbs that do *not* follow this pattern. The rest of this section discusses these irregular verbs.

Principal Parts of Irregular Verbs

Review the table on pages 45–46 in detail. During your review, try fitting some of the irregular verbs into the regular pattern. For example, say "speak, speaked" instead of "speak, spoke" or say "leave, leaved" instead of "leave, left." There is no alternative: We must memorize most of these forms, especially those that are used frequently.

PRINCIPAL PARTS OF IRREGULAR VERBS			
Present Tense	*Past Tense*	*Past Participle*	*Present Participle*
am	was	been	being
bear	bore	borne	bearing
begin	began	begun	beginning
bid (to command)	bade	bidden	bidding
bid (to offer to pay)	bid	bid	bidding
bite	bit	bitten	biting
blow	blew	blown	blowing
break	broke	broken	breaking
bring	brought	brought	bringing
burst	burst	burst	bursting
catch	caught	caught	catching
choose	chose	chosen	choosing
come	came	come	coming

PRINCIPAL PARTS OF IRREGULAR VERBS			
Present Tense	*Past Tense*	*Past Participle*	*Present Participle*
do	did	done	doing
draw	drew	drawn	drawing
drink	drank	drunk	drinking
drive	drove	driven	driving
eat	ate	eaten	eating
fall	fell	fallen	falling
fight	fought	fought	fighting
flee	fled	fled	fleeing
fly	flew	flown	flying
forget	forgot	forgotten	forgetting
freeze	froze	frozen	freezing
get	got	got	getting
give	gave	given	giving
go	went	gone	going
grow	grew	grown	growing
hang (to put to death)	hanged	hanged	hanging
hang (to suspend)	hung	hung	hanging
hide	hid	hidden	hiding
know	knew	known	knowing
lay	laid	laid	laying
leave	left	left	leaving
lend	lent	lent	lending
lie	lay	lain	lying
pay	paid	paid	paying
read	read	read	reading
ride	rode	ridden	riding
ring	rang	rung	ringing
rise	rose	risen	rising
run	ran	run	running
see	saw	seen	seeing
send	sent	sent	sending
set	set	set	setting
shake	shook	shaken	shaking
sing	sang	sung	singing
sit	sat	sat	sitting
speak	spoke	spoken	speaking
stand	stood	stood	standing
steal	stole	stolen	stealing
strike	struck	struck	striking
take	took	taken	taking
tear	tore	torn	tearing
tell	told	told	telling
throw	threw	thrown	throwing
wear	wore	worn	wearing
write	wrote	written	writing

Checkup 5

Correct any errors in the following sentences. Write *OK* for any sentence that has no error. Refer to the table on pages 45–46 if you must. (Hint: Remember that a past tense form *never* has a helper and that a past participle or a present participle *always* has a helper!)

1. Of course, Lynn <u>known</u> about the merger for several weeks.
2. Chris <u>had began</u> revising the merger papers before his supervisor asked him <u>to do so.</u>
3. In an effort to avoid a last-minute rush, Eric <u>come</u> in early yesterday and today.
4. Ask Kim who <u>has took</u> the company name off the building.
5. Has the bell rung yet?
6. Our profits <u>have grew</u> steadily over the past three years.

"Being" Verbs

KEY POINT

Only the verb *to be* has three present tense forms and two past tense forms; all other verbs (regular and irregular) have only two present tense forms and one past tense form.

The "being" verbs are the forms of the verb *to be*. They show no action. Study first the present tense and the past tense forms.

Present Tense

I am	we are
you are	you are
he ⎫	
she ⎬ is	they are
it ⎭	

As you see, there are three present tense forms: *am, is,* and *are*.

Past Tense

I was	we were
you were	you were
he ⎫	
she ⎬ was	they were
it ⎭	

There are two past tense forms, *was* and *were*.

Verb Phrases With Forms of *To Be*. As you saw earlier in this section, verb phrases are formed by using helping or auxiliary verbs with (1) the infinitive form *be*, (2) the past participle form *been*, and (3) the present participle form *being*.

1. *Be* with a helping verb: *will be, may be, can be, would be, might be,* and so on
2. *Been* with a helping verb: *has been, have been, had been, will have been, could have been, might have been,* and so on
3. *Being* with a helping verb: *am being, is being, are being, was being,* and *were being*

You will do well to memorize these eight "being" verbs: *am, is, are, was, were,* helper plus *be,* helper plus *been,* and helper plus *being.*

Because "being" verbs are so often used as helping verbs, be careful to distinguish between "being" verbs that are helpers and "being" verbs that are main verbs in the phrase.

Shelly *should have been* here by now. (The verb phrase is *should have been,* and the main verb is *been.* This verb phrase is a being verb.)

That contract *should have been signed.* (Now the verb phrase is *should have been signed. Should have been* is only a helping verb. The main verb is *signed.* Only the helping verb is a being verb.)

Ned Pierce *is* the vice president of telecommunications. He *was* formerly the director of technical services. (Both *is* and *was* are being verbs. There are no helping verbs.)

Checkup 6

On a separate sheet of paper, write the verbs and verb phrases in the following sentences. Identify each being verb that is a main verb by writing *B* next to the verb.

1. Of course, Judge Bancroft has been evaluating the union demands carefully.
2. Bill Vernon was the company's attorney at one time.
3. Both Caroline Hahn and Emily DeLucca have been members of the arbitration board for two years.
4. Carter McGinn, the management representative of our plant, is on vacation this week.
5. Our company is famous for its active involvement in the community.
6. Nevertheless, the local media have been siding with the union.

Were Instead of *Was.* Good writing requires that we sometimes use *were* instead of *was* after *if, as if, as though,* and *wish.* Whenever such statements describe (1) something contrary to fact, (2) something that is simply not true, or (3) something that is highly doubtful or impossible, use *were* instead of *was.* If, on the other hand, the statement *is true* or *could be true* (as often happens after *if*), then do *not* substitute *were* for *was.*

We wish it *were* possible for us to predict future stock prices, but SEC regulations prohibit us from making such claims. (It is not possible. Therefore, "We wish it *were*" is correct.)

If I *were* you, I would purchase this stock while it is still selling at 22. (Of course, I am *not* you — thus *were* is correct.)

If Michelle *was* here before us, she probably left a message with her assistant. (Michelle could indeed have already been here; thus this statement could be true. Do *not* substitute *were* for *was.*)

Checkup 7

On a separate sheet of paper, correct any errors in the following sentences. If a sentence has no error, write *OK.*

1. If I were Mr. Romanoff, I would reject the offer from Arctic Airlines.
2. At times Charles behaves as if he <u>was</u> the only travel agent in the country!
3. She has said that if she <u>was</u> younger, she would open her own travel agency.
4. Owen sometimes acts as if he <u>was</u> at a party instead of at the office.
5. If Lou was at the airport, I certainly did not see him.

Lie, Lay; Sit, Set; Rise, Raise

Like the being verbs, *lie* and *lay*, *sit* and *set*, and *rise* and *raise* deserve very special attention. To be able to use these verbs correctly, you must first understand the distinction between transitive and intransitive verbs.

Transitive Verbs. A *transitive verb* is a verb that has an object or a receiver of the verb's action. To find that object, say the verb and ask "What?" or "Whom?" The answer to that question is the direct object. Follow these examples:

1. Jessica accepted Harry's apology.
   a. Say the verb: *accepted.*
   b. Ask "What?" or "Whom?" Accepted *what?* Answer: Accepted *apology.* The object of the verb *accepted* is *apology.*
   c. Use the answer to determine whether the verb is transitive. Yes, *accepted* is transitive because it has an object, *apology.*
2. Ms. Milano invited Nancy to the executive dining room.
   a. Say the verb: *invited.*
   b. Ask "What?" or "Whom?" Invited *whom?* Answer: Invited *Nancy.* The object of the verb *invited* is *Nancy.*
   c. Transitive? Yes, *invited* is a transitive verb because it has an object, *Nancy.*

Sometimes the subject rather than the object of the sentence serves as the receiver of the verb's action. You can identify transitive verbs that are used this way because they include a being verb helper and a past participle.

The corner office *should have been given* to Adrienne Schwinn. (Do you have a being verb helper? Do you have a past participle? "Yes" to both questions. Therefore, this verb is transitive. What receives the action? Answer: *office.*)

The safari *was canceled*, according to William. (Again, we have a "being" verb helper, *was*, and a past participle, *canceled.* Thus we know that the subject, *safari*, receives the action of the verb. *What* was canceled? Answer: *safari. Was canceled* is a transitive verb.)

Marion has been nominated to the Executive Committee. (What is the verb in this sentence? Is it transitive? If so, explain why.)

Intransitive Verbs. Verbs that do not have objects are *intransitive verbs*.

Max Rosenthal *travels* very frequently. (Travels *what?* Travels *whom?* No answer. *Travels* is an intransitive verb.)

Cindy Wolfe *will sail* at noon, according to this itinerary. (The verb *will sail* has no object; it is an intransitive verb.)

Checkup 8

KEY
The complete verb phrase is underlined.
1. T
2. B
3. T
4. T
5. I
6. B

Identify the verbs and verb phrases in the following sentences. Then label each verb or verb phrase using *B* for "being," *T* for "transitive," or *I* for "intransitive."

1. A new program manager had been appointed as of last week.
2. Sandra will be in the studio shortly.
3. Our next broadcast will be televised on Thursday, August 18.
4. Has Don told Lee Edwards about the proposed script changes?
5. Apparently, both of them have left already.
6. As always, Bea has been very helpful on our crash project.

· M E M O R Y   H O O K ·

Now that you have learned to distinguish between transitive and intransitive verbs, you will have an easier task of using *lie* and *lay*, *sit* and *set*, and *rise* and *raise*. The letter *i* is the key. Use the *i* in *intransitive* to remember that the *i* verbs — *lie*, *sit*, and *rise* — are intransitive and, therefore, do not have objects.

*i*ntransitive   l*i*e   s*i*t   r*i*se

The other three verbs, *lay*, *set*, and *raise*, are all transitive.

Now review carefully the principal parts of the following irregular verbs.

Present Tense	Past Tense	Past Participle	Present Participle	Infinitive
lie	lay	lain	lying	to lie
lay	laid	laid	laying	to lay
sit	sat	sat	sitting	to sit
set	set	set	setting	to set
rise	rose	risen	rising	to rise
raise	raised	raised	raising	to raise

You will probably notice that one common trap is confusing *lay* in its present tense form with *lay* the past tense form of *lie*. How can you tell which is which? You can tell by remembering what you have learned about transitive verbs.

On Monday, Michael (lay, laid) the mail on the receptionist's desk.

After jogging, I usually (lie, lay) down for a short while.

Yesterday I (lie, lay) down for only five minutes or so.

Let's analyze these sentences. Does the first verb have an object? Yes, *mail*. Therefore, a transitive verb is needed. As you just learned, *laid* is the past tense form of *to lay*, so *laid* is correct, because *to lay* is the transitive verb.

In the second sentence, is there an object? No. (*Down* is not an object; it is an adverb.) Here you need a form of the verb *to lie*, so the answer is *lie* — I *lie* down.

In the third sentence, the word *yesterday* shows that past tense is needed. Whichever verb is correct, does it have a direct object? Answer: No. Thus the correct answer is *lay*, the past tense form of *lie*, an intransitive verb.

As you see, some thinking and analysis are needed when choosing among the forms of *lie* and *lay*, so do not choose hastily.

Now let's apply the same principles to the transitive verbs *set* and *raise* and to the intransitive verbs *sit* and *rise*.

Neil and Lena (sit, set) the materials on the windowsill before they left for lunch. (Is an object needed here? Yes. Which is the transitive verb? Answer: *set*. Set what? Set the *materials*.)

As soon as the temperature (rises, raises), the air conditioner will automatically go on. (What is needed, a transitive verb or an intransitive verb? Answer: intransitive, because the verb has no object in this sentence. Which, then, is the intransitive verb? The *i* verb, *rises*.)

Checkup 9

Practice your ability to use the verbs *lie*, *lay*, *sit*, *set*, *rise*, and *raise*. Write the correct word on a separate sheet of paper.

1. Les will (rise, raise) the roof when he hears about this problem.
2. When she works on special writing projects, Danielle generally (sits, sets) in this office.
3. According to the terms of the new contract, our salaries have been (risen, raised) by about 5 percent.
4. When you input the corrections on this report, please (sit, set) your margins for 15 and 70.
5. Tell the messengers to (sit, set) the display racks in the lobby.
6. Because Alan felt ill, he (lay, laid) down for about an hour this morning.

7. The certificates that you were looking for had been (lain, <u>laid</u>) carelessly on a lunchroom table.

8. All members, please (<u>rise</u>, raise).

SECTION

REVIEW

Practical Application

A. Identify the verb phrases in the following sentences. For the main verb in each phrase, tell where it belongs on the chart of principal parts—under (1) present, (2) past participle, or (3) present participle.

1. Anita <u>has visited</u> Charleston many times.
2. Next September 15, John <u>will have been working</u> for our firm for 25 years.
3. Larry <u>can finish</u> this assignment on Tuesday or Wednesday.
4. Karen <u>is being transferred</u> to Columbus in October.
5. <u>Have</u> they already <u>hired</u> a replacement for Stephanie?
6. You <u>should ask</u> Mr. Harrison for more help on this project.
7. Andy and Hank <u>will prepare</u> a rough draft for your approval.
8. The travel agent <u>is</u> now <u>preparing</u> a revised itinerary for you.
9. All new equipment <u>will have been ordered</u> by December 31.
10. The amended contract <u>should be retyped</u> before the end of the day.

B. Show your ability to form the principal parts of regular verbs by completing the following table. Use a separate sheet of paper.

Present Tense	Past Tense	Past Participle	Present Participle
1. instruct	instructed	instructed	instructing
2. disapprove	disapproved	disapproved	disapproving
3. appraise	appraised	**appraised**	appraising
4. assist	**assisted**	assisted	assisting
5. pack	packed	packed	packing
6. ensure	ensured	ensured	**ensuring**
7. bill	billed	billed	**billing**
8. cite	cited	**cited**	citing
9. argue	argued	argued	arguing
10. inquire	**inquired**	inquired	inquiring

KEY

Verb phrases are underscored; main verbs are given below.
1. visited (past participle)
2. working (present participle)
3. finish (present)
4. transferred (past participle)
5. hired (past participle)
6. ask (present)
7. prepare (present)
8. preparing (present participle)
9. ordered (past participle)
10. retyped (past participle)

KEY

The missing verb forms appear in color.

SECTION

REVIEW cont.

C. Identify the verb or the verb phrase in each of the following sentences. Label each choice transitive (*T*), intransitive (*I*), or being (*B*).

1. How safe <u>are</u> our airports?
2. Our firm <u>is studying</u> this question.
3. We <u>have been</u> very busy as a result.
4. Passengers at most airports <u>are arriving</u> more than an hour before flight time.
5. They <u>need</u> more time because of increased security checks.
6. Moreover, nearly all airports <u>have been banning</u> curbside check-in since the last terrorist attack.
7. As a result, of course, tempers <u>are rising</u>.
8. However, attempted highjackings <u>have been declining</u>.
9. We <u>should be finishing</u> our study in about a month.
10. Our findings <u>will be published</u> in *Travel & Leisure* magazine.

D. Correct any errors in the following sentences. Write *OK* for any sentence that has no error.

1. Richard has already <u>wrote</u> to the Securities and Exchange Commission concerning these violations.
2. The memo that I was looking for was <u>laying</u> on my desk.
3. When Mrs. Merriwether arrived, we <u>raised</u> to greet her.
4. At this morning's meeting, Carl laid out a comprehensive plan for our project.
5. Has Karen ever <u>flew</u> to Europe before?
6. Mark has <u>risen</u> that same objection at every meeting on procedures.
7. If I <u>was</u> David, I'd give it up.
8. The builder promised us that the foundation will have been <u>lain</u> no later than July 8.
9. Please lay all those packages on the conference room table.
10. Sharon has lent us $75 to buy the materials that we need.

Editing Practice

The Word Processing Supervisor. Check the following sentences for spelling errors. Write the misspelled words as they should be spelled. Write *OK* for any sentence that has no error.

1. At this morning's meeting with the manager of the <u>personel</u> department, we will discuss some specific problems concerning overtime pay.
2. Several of the <u>comittee</u> members offered suggestions that were <u>acceptionally</u> innovative.
3. We have also asked various <u>enployees</u> for ideas to solve these problems.

4. opportunity
5. received
6. appropriate invest-
   ments

KEY
Answers are under-
scored.

SECTION

REVIEW cont.

4. Opening this new store presents us with an excellent <u>oportunity</u> to expand our lines of merchandise.
5. This morning we <u>recieved</u> our first order from Glencoe Enterprises.
6. High-risk stocks are not <u>apropriate invextments</u> for Mr. Miller.

Editing Practice

The Right Word.   Select the correct word for each of the following sentences.

1. Rosemary suggested that we conduct a nationwide (pole, <u>poll</u>) of soft drink consumers.
2. According to Mr. DeFoe, the one-year freshness guarantee of Fruitfizz products is one of the (principle, <u>principal</u>) reasons for the company's success.
3. Fruitfizz has (<u>its</u>, it's) main plant in Waco, Texas.
4. Al and Rosemary are now planning (they're, <u>their</u>, there) trip to Fruitfizz.
5. We have estimated the total cost of the Fruitfizz campaign to be about $9,000; in any case, the actual cost cannot (<u>exceed</u>, accede) $10,000.
6. Has Mrs. Reeves already (collaborated, <u>corroborated</u>) this cost?

SECTION

2.3 *NOUNS: PLURAL FORMS*

OBJECTIVES: After completing Section 2.3, you should be able to:

1. State the basic rules for forming the plurals of most nouns.
2. Discuss solutions for forming difficult plurals.
3. Explain when to use a dictionary to determine how to form the plurals of nouns.
4. Analyze plurals that often cause grammatical errors.

When we say "several of our *clients*," or "one *client's* suggestion," or "all *clients'* orders," we do not ordinarily think of the difference in the spelling of *clients*, *client's*, and *clients'*. Because the pronunciation of all three forms is the same, in speaking we do not make errors when faced with a choice among these three words.

In writing, however, these three choices are not interchangeable. Each has its own distinct meaning and use. You must know, therefore, whether *clients* or *client's* or *clients'* is correct in a particular sentence. In Sections 2.3 and 2.4 you will master the use of plurals and possessives. With this knowledge you can solve some common spelling problems. This section emphasizes forming plural nouns correctly.

THE BASIC RULES

Although you probably know the basic rules for forming plurals, review them to make sure that you *always* apply the rules correctly.

Plurals of Common Nouns

Most common nouns form their plurals by adding *s* to the singular form:

service	services	commuter	commuters
employee	employees	diskette	diskettes
avenue	avenues	attorney	attorneys

However, nouns that end in *s*, *sh*, *ch*, *x*, and *z* form their plurals by adding *es* to the singular form:

class	classes
dash	dashes
wrench	wrenches
tax	taxes
buzz	buzzes

Plurals of Proper Nouns

Most proper nouns or *names* form their plurals by adding *s* to the singular form.

Urbanski	the Urbanskis
Keenan	the Keenans
Bromberg	the Brombergs

Proper nouns that end in *s*, *sh*, *ch*, *x*, and *z* form their plurals by adding *es*—just as common nouns ending in these letters form their plurals.

Ross	the Rosses
Walsh	the Walshes
Fitch	the Fitches
Dix	the Dixes
Herz	the Herzes

Plurals of Compound Nouns

A *compound noun* is a noun that consists of two or more words. Compound nouns may be written with a hyphen, with a space between the words, or as solid words. In any case, always make the main word or most important word in the compound plural.

bulletin board	bulletin boards
mother-in-law	mothers-in-law
attorney general	attorneys general
general manager	general managers
major general	major generals
editor in chief	editors in chief
chief of staff	chiefs of staff
notary public	notaries public
timetable	timetables

Plurals of Nouns Ending in Y

Singular nouns ending in *y* may form their plurals in one of two ways:

1. If the *y* is preceded by a vowel, add *s* to form the plural.

alloy	alloys
key	keys
money	moneys

2. If the *y* is preceded by a consonant, change the *y* to *i* and add *es*.

territory	territories
company	companies
faculty	faculties

Note that this rule does *not* apply to proper names ending in *y*. For proper names ending in *y*, add *s* to form the plural.

McCarthy	the McCarthys
Sally	two Sallys
Langley	the Langleys

ℹ INFORMATION

This exception demonstrates the effort to preserve the basic spelling of a proper name.

Checkup 1

Correct any errors in the following sentences. Write *OK* if a sentence has no error.

1. According to the article, one of the newly appointed editor in chiefs is Roxanne P. Chandler.
2. The terms of Mrs. Best's will were that her three son-in-laws must continue to operate her business.
3. Two Larries — Murphy and Resnik — work in the maintenance department.
4. The extra display materials and miscellaneous supplys are being stored in this closet.
5. Several lenss, including telephoto and wide-angle lenss, will be on sale at discounts up to 25 percent.

6. communities, counties
7. district attorneys
8. OK
9. Averys
10. OK

6. Most of the <u>communitys</u> in these two <u>countys</u> are popular because taxes are low.
7. The assistant <u>district attornies</u> who were assigned to this case are Ellen Hartwell and Connie Stern.
8. Both organizations have subsidiaries in Atlanta and in Portland.
9. Thomas Avery and his brother Jonathan are interested in buying this property, but the <u>Averies</u> have set a ceiling of $500,000 for both the building and the land.
10. The last three <u>attorneys general</u> were Republicans.

SPECIAL PLURALS

Certain plurals cause problems for writers because these forms follow no "regular" rules. For example, how would you form the plural of the abbreviations *Mr.* and *Mrs.?* When you have reviewed these special forms, you will have no difficulty forming these plurals.

Plurals of Titles With Names

When forming the plural of a title *and* the name used with it, make *either* the title *or* the name plural — *not both.*

Before we continue with this discussion, make sure that you know the plural forms of the commonly used courtesy titles *Mr., Mrs., Ms., Miss,* and *Dr.*

Singular	Plural
Mr.	Messrs.
Mrs.	Mmes.
Ms.	Mses.
Miss	Misses
Dr.	Drs.

Note the following:

1. *Messrs.* is derived from *Messieurs,* the French word for "Misters."
2. Likewise, *Mmes.* is derived from *Mesdames,* the French word for "My ladies," and is used as the plural of *Mrs.*
3. *Ms.* is considered nonsexist because it does not identify a woman's marital status, just as *Mr.* does not point out a man's marital status. The plural form of *Ms.* is *Mses.*

Now let's look at some examples of forming plurals of names with titles. Both plural forms are correct and mean the same thing.

Singular	Plural Title	Plural Name
Ms. Toto	the Mses. Toto	the Ms. Totos
Mr. Werner	the Messrs. Werner	the Mr. Werners
Mrs. Ford	the Mmes. Ford	the Mrs. Fords

Plurals With Apostrophes

In certain situations the apostrophe is used to form plurals. Specifically, to form plurals of lowercase letters and of abbreviations, use an apostrophe plus *s*:

For some reason, the *t*'s and *f*'s on this printer are illegible.

Our receptionist handles all *c.o.d.*'s for the office.

For plurals of capital letters, an apostrophe is needed only if adding *s* alone could be confusing; for example, *As* instead of *A's*, *Is* instead of *I's*, and *Us* instead of *U's* could be confusing. Use an apostrophe with the *s* to form these plurals.

In addition, an apostrophe is *not* required to form plurals in phrases such as *ups and downs, temperature in the 90s, dos and don'ts* and *in the 1930s.*

Plurals With Special Changes

☐ **SUGGESTION**

Remind students that some oddly formed plurals must be memorized.

Anyone who speaks English has certainly noticed (and perhaps had difficulty with) such oddly formed plurals as the following:

Singular	*Plural*
woman	women
child	children
mouse	mice
goose	geese
shelf	shelves
ox	oxen

Checkup 2

KEY
1. Miss Smiths (or Misses Smith)
2. 30s
3. I's
4. OK
5. Everetts
6. OK
7. men
8. Messrs.

Correct any errors in the following sentences.

1. Hugo asked us to send these flowers to the <u>Misses Smiths</u>.
2. This stock is now selling at 15, but it may soon reach the high <u>30's</u>.
3. Because of her illness, she received two <u>Is</u> for her incomplete courses.
4. Yes, the Messrs. Martin are indeed acquiring a controlling interest in that company.
5. The <u>Everett's</u> are staying with the vice president during the convention.
6. Carol and Mike Delos have managed our Orlando office since the 1960s.
7. Several of the <u>mans</u> on the committee objected to the suggestion.
8. The two junior partners are going in place of <u>Mr.</u> Prinz and Fenner.

DICTIONARY "MUSTS"

Despite the many thousands of words that form their plurals according to basic, simple rules, some words follow no basic pattern or rule. To form

plurals of such words, we must consult a dictionary. For example, plurals of words ending in *o*, *f*, and *fe* vary greatly. Study the following plurals carefully.

Plurals of Nouns Ending in *O*

Singular nouns ending in *o* preceded by a vowel form the plural by adding *s*. Some nouns ending in *o* preceded by a consonant form the plural by adding *s*; others, by adding *es*. Note the following examples.

Final *o* preceded by a vowel, adding *s* for the plural:

studio	studios	video	videos
folio	folios	ratio	ratios

Final *o* preceded by a consonant, adding *s* for the plural:

photo	photos	tuxedo	tuxedos
zero	zeros	memento	mementos

Final *o* preceded by a consonant, adding *es* for the plural:

motto	mottoes	hero	heroes
potato	potatoes	veto	vetoes
echo	echoes	cargo	cargoes

Note that nouns that relate to music and art and end in *o* form their plurals by adding *s*: *piano, pianos; alto, altos; oratorio, oratorios; solo, solos;* and so on.

Plurals of Nouns Ending in *F* or *Fe*

Plurals of nouns ending in *f* or *fe* are formed in one of two ways: (1) by changing the *f* or *fe* to *v* and then adding *es*; or (2) by simply adding *s*.

Change *f* or *fe* to *v*, then add *es*:

shelf	shelves	half	halves
life	lives	self	selves
wife	wives	knife	knives

Simply add *s*:

plaintiff	plaintiffs	proof	proofs
roof	roofs	safe	safes
belief	beliefs	chief	chiefs

Checkup 3

On a sheet of paper, write the correct plural forms of the following nouns.

1. tomato, mosquito
2. logo, ditto
3. leaf, thief
4. loaf, staff
5. strife, gulf
6. bailiff, handkerchief
7. volcano, concerto
8. radio, trio

i INFORMATION

Plurals of nouns of foreign origin that end in *um* are formed by dropping the *um* and adding an *a*.

i INFORMATION

Nouns that end in *is* in the singular are changed to *es* to form the plural.

i INFORMATION

Nouns that end in *us* in the singular are changed to *i* in the plural. Only *alumnae* shows the change from the singular *a* to the plural ending *ae*, which is common for feminine words in Latin.

i INFORMATION

It is commonly accepted to use *data* as a singular noun, as in "The data supports our theory." This usage is correct; some writers, however, prefer to retain the distinction between the singular *datum* and the plural *data*.

Plurals of Foreign Nouns

The plurals of foreign nouns are another category of dictionary "musts." As you will see in the following list, these plurals of words with foreign origin are not formed according to basic English rules.

Singular	Plural	Singular	Plural
addendum	addenda	crisis	crises
alumna	alumnae	criterion	criteria
alumnus	alumni	datum	data
analysis	analyses	hypothesis	hypotheses
axis	axes	synthesis	syntheses
bacterium	bacteria	syllabus	syllabi
basis	bases		

In addition to the above, some words of foreign origin have *two* plural forms—its "original" plural form (similar to the ones shown above) and an English plural form (a plural formed by treating the singular as if it were an English word).

Singular	Foreign Plural	English Plural
appendix	appendices	appendixes*
curriculum	curricula*	curriculums
formula	formulae	formulas*
index	indices	indexes*
medium	media	mediums*
memorandum	memoranda	memorandums*
nucleus	nuclei*	nucleuses
stadium	stadia*	stadiums
vertebra	vertebrae*	vertebras

NOTE: * indicates the plural form that is preferred in English usage.

Troublesome Forms

The following nouns are *always singular*. Use a singular verb to agree with them.

statistics (science)	molasses	genetics	physics
mathematics	civics	aerobics	
economics (science)	news	aeronautics	

The following nouns are *always plural*. Use a plural verb to agree with them.

statistics (facts)	jeans	winnings
auspices	tweezers	scissors
proceeds	riches	thanks
tidings	series	pants
belongings	antics	tongs
slacks		

The following nouns have only one form, which may be used either as a singular or a plural, depending on the intended meaning.

Chinese	French	moose	wheat
deer	sheep	odds	aircraft
politics	salmon	shrimp	corps

When modified by another number, the following nouns usually have the same form to denote either a singular or a plural number.

three *thousand* forms   four *score* years
five *hundred* applicants   two *dozen* seniors

Checkup 4

On a sheet of paper, write the correction for any error in the following sentences.

1. All three economists suggested the same <u>stimuluses</u> to help the American steel industry.
2. Sam's slacks <u>was</u> so long he tripped going up the stairs.
3. The proceeds from our raffle were given to a very worthwhile charity.
4. Many of the alumni are planning to attend the special celebration honoring Professor Inez Mendoza.
5. Scott always says that thermodynamics <u>were</u> his hardest subject.
6. By Monday we had received nearly two <u>hundreds</u> requests for brochures.
7. Enclose all cross references in <u>parenthesis</u>.
8. The Japanese was the first to cross the finish line.

SECTION REVIEW

Practical Application

A. Rewrite correctly any sentences with errors. Write *OK* if a sentence has no error.

1. <u>Are</u> there any recent news about the negotiations?
2. His article has two main <u>hypothesis</u>.
3. We have, of course, <u>already</u> notified the Mrs. Wallaces of the change in plans.
4. Because the goods that the shipper delivered <u>was</u> damaged, we returned the entire shipment to the manufacturer.
5. The cost of the new <u>facilitys</u> is expected to exceed $1 million.
6. Mrs. Lewis has announced that her two <u>son-in-laws</u> will be partners in her catering service.
7. The large <u>knifes</u> must, of course, be sharpened periodically to keep these machines performing properly.

8. hundred
9. Welshes
10. ourselves
11. Kellys
12. churches
13. yeas or nays
14. OK
15. journeys
16. CPAs
17. stereos
18. OK
19. territories
20. benches

8. Among the several <u>hundreds</u> competitors in this industry, none has had greater success than Peterson Plastics Inc.
9. Jordan and Joanne Welsh obviously enjoy operating their business; nonetheless, the <u>Welshs</u> have indicated a willingness to sell.
10. If we want the job done correctly, we'll have to do it <u>ourselfs</u>.
11. We tried to call Mr. Kelly several times, but none of the <u>Kellies</u> answered the telephone.
12. Alice Bonnell gives generously to various <u>church's</u> in this area.
13. Who won — the <u>yea's</u> or the <u>nay's</u>?
14. Since 1982 the <u>Marxes</u> have owned a controlling interest in Data Electronics.
15. All of Marco's sales trips seem to turn into memorable <u>journies</u>.
16. Perhaps 25 <u>CPA's</u> have already applied for the position that we advertised this morning.
17. Ludwig traded two <u>stereoes</u> for a CD player.
18. The premises are carefully guarded by security officers.
19. Each district manager is responsible for his or her sales representatives and their <u>territorys</u>.
20. Mr. Garmond said that the old <u>benchs</u> in the cafeteria will be replaced with comfortable chairs.

KEY
1. are
2. spoken
3. have been
4. OK
5. were
6. are
7. were
8. laid
9. women
10. set
11. OK
12. lying
13. 60s
14. glasses

B. Rewrite correctly any sentences with errors. Write *OK* for any sentence that has no error. (Note: In Sections 2.3 through 3.7, Practical Application B reviews some of the principles presented in earlier sections.)

1. On Jesse's desk <u>is</u> the January and February sales records that you wanted.
2. We have already <u>spoke</u> with Mr. Johanson about the shipping delays from Warner Chemicals.
3. I <u>been</u> meaning to speak to him about his sloppy appearance.
4. The market price of our corporate bonds has risen almost 15 percent in only three weeks.
5. Of course, I wish that I <u>was</u> able to buy you that sports car, but business is a little slow at the moment.
6. Winnings of any kind <u>is</u> taxable, according to IRS regulations.
7. In the conference room <u>was</u> just the two of us.
8. A prototype was <u>lain</u> on the table for all of us to inspect.
9. Several <u>woman</u> applied for the transfer.
10. Mrs. North suggested that we <u>sit</u> the projector on the shelf at the back of the room.
11. Miss Moffat thinks cryogenics is the right choice.
12. That carton has been <u>laying</u> there for two weeks.
13. The thermostat is generally set in the low <u>60's</u>.
14. Amber's new <u>glass's</u> make her look very studious.

SECTION

KEY

1. *toy*
2. *$84* (not *$94*)
3. *Mrs. Reisling* (not *Mr. Riesling*)
4. *Anne* or *Anna?*
5. Both model numbers are the same.

REVIEW cont.

Editing Practice

As a Matter of Fact . . . . In addition to checking for spelling and grammatical errors, writers and typists must check for inconsistencies and contradictions of facts within copy. Read the following statements to find any inconsistencies. Correct any errors in the following sentences. Write *OK* if a statement has no error.

1. Mrs. O'Day wrote to say the toy top she ordered does not work, so I asked her to return the <u>boy</u> and promised to replace it.
2. Your total cost will be $100 less a 20 percent discount plus a sales tax of 5 percent. Thus we will send you an invoice for <u>$94</u>.
3. When <u>Mrs. Reisling</u> pointed out that we had overcharged her, we apologized for the error and told <u>Mr. Riesling</u> we would correct her next statement.
4. <u>Anne</u> Loomis is the supervisor of customer relations. We suggest that you call <u>Anna</u> to discuss this problem with her.
5. Although we are out of stock of model <u>A199-2035</u>, we have plenty of model <u>A199-2035</u> in stock.

SECTION

2.4 *NOUNS AND PRONOUNS: POSSESSIVE FORMS*

OBJECTIVES: After completing Section 2.4, you should be able to:

1. Summarize the basic rules of forming the possessives of nouns.
2. Cite examples of correct possessive forms of compound nouns, of nouns showing joint ownership and those showing individual ownership, and of nouns used before gerunds.
3. Explain what to do when a noun that would ordinarily be in the possessive case is followed by an appositive.
4. Discuss the major pitfall in using possessive forms of personal pronouns.

Errors in the use of the possessive forms of nouns and pronouns are common — and very noticeable — in writing, if not always in speaking. There are, however, some easy ways to master the correct usage of possessive nouns and pronouns. Study this section to ensure that you do so.

□ **SUGGESTION**

Point out to students that the singular and the plural nouns here are treated the same because they do not end in *s*.

POSSESSIVE FORMS OF NOUNS

To begin, remember this rule: An apostrophe is *always* used with a noun to show possession. Now let's see some of the specifics of using the apostrophe with nouns.

✓ 1. For a noun that does not end in *s*, add an apostrophe plus *s*. This rule applies to *all* nouns, whether they are singular or plural.

The *man's* portfolio and the *woman's* report were in the board room.

The *men's* lounge is on this floor; the *women's* lounge is on the top floor.

✓ 2. For a plural noun that does end in *s*, add only the apostrophe.

The *executives'* meeting has been rescheduled.

Approximately two *months'* time has been allotted for the whole project.

The *Browns'* newest store is in New Brunswick.

✓ 3. a. For a singular noun ending in *s*, add an apostrophe plus *s* if the possessive form is pronounced with an added syllable.

One *witness's* comment was especially effective.

□ **SUGGESTION**

Ask students to pronounce the words *witness's* and *witness* as well as *boss's* and *boss* so that they can hear the added syllable.

My *boss's* recommendation was obviously helpful.

b. For a singular noun ending in *s*, add only the apostrophe if the possessive form is not pronounced with an additional syllable. Note that this rule applies mostly to proper names that would sound awkward with the extra syllable.

Bruce *Struthers'* selection will be announced on July 15. (The pronunciation of *Struthers's* would sound awkward.)

· M E M O R Y   H O O K ·

Remember that the possessive word always comes before the object of possession.

the *man's* portfolio (the portfolio of the man, the portfolio belonging to the man)
the *woman's* report (the report of the woman, the report belonging to the woman)
the *Browns'* newest store (the newest store of the Browns)
the *executives'* meeting (the meeting of the executives)
one *witness's* comment (the comment of one witness)

By separating the ownership words from the objects of ownership, you will be able more easily to apply the above rules.

Checkup 1

Correct any errors in the use of possessives in the following sentences. Write your corrections on a sheet of paper.

1. John Rileys' investments have risen dramatically in the last six months.
2. The actress's own account of Hollywood's glamorous past will appear in Sunday's newspaper.
3. Sam Canfield's goal is to rebuild his fathers business.
4. Elinor's latest article discusses womens nutritional needs, and she plans to write a book on the subject.
5. The applicants résumés are in the folder on your desk, Ms. Paoli.
6. No, we do not purchase our company cars; all our representatives vehicles are leased.
7. One mans report criticized the company's change in policy.
8. Our Travel Department makes all our supervisor's reservations for them.

POSSESSIVE FORMS IN SPECIAL CASES

Besides the basic rules of forming the possessives of nouns, there are a few special cases that need your attention. Study the following four discussions.

Compound Nouns

To form the possessive of a compound noun, make the *last word* in the compound possessive. If the last word ends in *s*, add an apostrophe; if the last word in the compound does *not* end in *s*, add an apostrophe plus *s*.

My *brother-in-law's* bid was accepted by the City Planning Department. (Bid belonging to my brother-in-law. *Law* does not end in *s*.)

Leroy did not win first prize; *someone else's* entry won highest honors. (The entry belonging to someone else. *Else* does not end in *s*.)

Several *vice presidents'* assistants participated in and contributed to the committee session. (Assistants of several vice presidents. The last word, *presidents*, does end in *s*.)

Joint Ownership? Separate Ownership?

To show joint ownership, add the apostrophe (or the apostrophe plus *s*) to the last part of the compound.

Susan and Randy's father is the one who started this restaurant in 1937. (The father of Susan and Randy. Note the singular noun *father* and the singular verb *is*.)

Isaac and Virginia's design studio is located in Hoboken. (Studio belonging to Isaac and Virginia.)

To indicate *separate ownership*, add the apostrophe (or the apostrophe plus *s*) to *each* part of the compound.

Bradley's and Marcia's mothers are the ones who started this service in 1980. (Here, we are talking about two different people—in other words, Bradley's mother and Marcia's mother.)

Irwin's and Vicki's agencies are located in Hartford. (Irwin's agency and Vicki's agency—two agencies, each separately owned.)

Before a Gerund

A *gerund* is a verb form that ends in *ing* and is used as a noun. A noun or pronoun used before a gerund must be in the possessive case.

Harry's proofreading was very helpful to us in meeting our schedule. *His* proofreading was very helpful to us. (Possessive *Harry's* or *His*, not *Harry* or *Him*, before the gerund *proofreading*.)

We were unaware of *Nancy's* leaving early. We were unaware of *her* leaving early. (The possessives *Nancy's* and *her* are needed before the gerund *leaving*.)

I appreciate your doing the potatoes for our fund raiser.

In Appositives

An *appositive* is a word or a group of words that explains or gives additional information about the word or phrase that comes before the appositive. When a noun that would ordinarily be in the possessive case is followed by an appositive, note that the appositive must then be in the possessive case.

Ms. Chang, our *bookkeeper's*, office is on the fifth floor. (Note that *bookkeeper*, not *Chang*, is made possessive.)

This kind of awkward construction can be avoided in most cases by rewriting the sentence.

The office of Ms. Chang, our bookkeeper, is on the fifth floor.

Checkup 2

KEY
1. OK
2. someone else's
3. vice presidents'
4. our
5. Neil and Anne's

On a sheet of paper, correct any errors in the use of possessives in the following sentences. Write *OK* if a sentence has no error.

1. Don and Sylvia's oldest daughter begins high school next September.
2. Revising the memorandum was <u>someone else</u> idea, not Adrian's.
3. As you know, the two <u>vice president's</u> reports are strictly confidential.
4. Juan was glad to hear about <u>us</u> working overtime to complete the project on schedule.
5. Neil and Anne were engaged last month; <u>Neil's and Anne's</u> wedding is now planned for November 11.

6. his
7. Mr. Clark's
8. Ella's and Bert's

6. Cindy and I said that <u>him</u> helping us was instrumental in meeting the deadline.
7. We surely appreciated <u>Mr. Clark</u> sending us the check early.
8. Yes, <u>Ella and Bert's</u> jobs are very similar.

POSSESSIVE FORMS OF PERSONAL PRONOUNS

You have seen that possessive forms of nouns *always* have apostrophes. In the following chart, notice that possessive forms of personal pronouns *never* have apostrophes.

Nominative Forms	Possessive Forms	
I	my	mine
you	your	yours
he	his	his
she	her	hers
it	its	its
we	our	ours
you	your	yours
they	their	theirs

Now study the following examples to see the correct uses of these pronoun forms.

Valerie asked *her* assistant to redo the report.

The first car is *ours;* the second one is *theirs.*

Please lend me *your* calculator; *mine* is at home.

Note that none of the above possessive pronouns has an apostrophe.

POSSESSIVE PRONOUNS IN SPECIAL CASES

The possessive forms discussed above are, unfortunately, easily confused with other similar words, which are compared below.

Its, It's

REINFORCEMENT

Teach students the standard trick of substituting the full phrase *it is* to test whether use of the contraction *it's* is correct. Do the same for other contractions.

The possessive pronoun *its* means "belonging to it" or "of it." *Its* is easily confused with the contraction *it's,* which means "it is" (note the apostrophe in *it's*). Use the contraction *it's* only when you mean "it is."

This laser printer is expensive and slower, but *its* legibility is superb. (Possessive pronoun *its.*)

Naturally, *it's* exciting to know that my brother is so successful. (*It is* exciting . . . .)

Their, There, They're

Their, there, and *they're* are indeed pronounced alike. But *their* is the possessive pronoun meaning "belonging to them," and *there* (notice the word *here*) identifies a place. *They're,* obviously, is a contraction; it means "they are."

Sally and Mac said that *they're* eager to begin *their* vacation. (*They are* eager . . . vacation "belonging to them.")

If we leave at 9 a.m., we should arrive *there* by 11. (*There* is an adverb that identifies a place; it answers the question *Where? There.*)

Theirs, There's

The pronoun *theirs* and the contraction *there's* are pronounced the same, but it is easy to recognize quickly that *there's* means "there is" or "there has." *Theirs* means "belonging to them."

The first seat is reserved for Dr. Pfeiffer; these three seats are *theirs.* (Seats "belonging to them.")

There's the manual we've been looking for! (*There is* the manual . . . .)

Your, You're

The possessive pronoun *your* means "belonging to you," and the contraction *you're* means "you are."

Leave *your* notebook on the desk if *you're* coming back later. (Notebook "belonging to you." If *you are* coming back.)

Our, Are

Actually, *our* and *are* should *not* sound alike when they are pronounced correctly. However, some people do pronounce *our* as if it were *are.* Thus errors in using *our* and *are* are more common in speaking than in writing.

Our district manager and *our* marketing director *are* planning a special tour for the visiting celebrities.

Whose, Who's

The possessive pronoun *whose* should not be confused with the contraction *who's,* which means "who is" or "who has."

Do you know *whose* shrimp cocktail this is? (Shrimp cocktail "belonging to whom?")

Do you know *who's* in charge of ordering the appetizers? (*Who is* in charge. . . ?)

Checkup 3

KEY
1. Who's (*or* Who is)
2. there's
3. it's
4. theirs
5. who's (*or* who is)
6. there
7. it's
8. OK

Correct any errors in the following sentences. Write *OK* if a sentence has no error.

1. <u>Whose</u> at the shop this morning, Jerry or Daniel?
2. As Mr. Cellini clearly explained, <u>theirs</u> only one problem involved: money.
3. Most of us prefer the red package because <u>its</u> so much brighter than the other choices.
4. The booth near the door is ours; the booth near the window is <u>there's</u>.
5. We will distribute the program when we know <u>whose</u> planning to speak at the conference.
6. John Duffy and his assistant Colette Leclaire will be <u>they're</u> when the conference begins.
7. Although it takes extra effort, <u>its</u> certainly worthwhile to request three estimates for such large conference expenditures.
8. Whenever you're ready to discuss these budgets, please call me.

SECTION REVIEW

Practical Application

KEY
1. marketing manager's
2. OK
3. who's (*or* who is)
4. woman's
5. Basses
6. Carole Franco and Diane Wilson's
7. you're
8. his
9. there's
10. children's

A. Correct any errors in the following sentences. Write *OK* for any sentence that has no error.

1. Each <u>marketing managers'</u> suggestion was discussed in great detail.
2. Are you aware that they're both CEOs?
3. Irena Alvarez, <u>whose</u> an excellent copywriter, has developed award-winning slogans for our products.
4. After hearing both sides, we agreed that the <u>womans'</u> latest complaint was completely justified.
5. Although the <u>Bass's</u> have owned this property only since 1985, Bob and Donna Bass have decided to sell.
6. <u>Carole Franco's and Diane Wilson's</u> boutique is one of the most successful in the city.
7. Let me know, please, whether <u>your</u> more interested in receiving monthly income or long-term capital gains.
8. Does Ms. Gregoris know about <u>him</u> offering to complete this assignment on a free-lance basis?
9. After we compared the two models carefully, we realized that <u>theirs</u> very little difference between them.
10. One of the most profitable departments in our Chicago store is the <u>childrens'</u> department.

11. bosses
12. it's
13. OK
14. his
15. it's

11. Denise's and Carl's <u>boss's</u> are both veterans of the Vietnam War.
12. Frankly, we're not sure that <u>its</u> possible to sell these yo-yos so cheaply and still make a profit.
13. When George and I heard about the two weeks' delay in the yo-yo shipment, we were not at all surprised.
14. Most of the members were in complete agreement with <u>him</u> rejecting the defective yo-yos.
15. Despite the fact that our competitor's yo-yos are very expensive, you must realize that <u>its</u> their unique design that offsets their high initial cost.

B. Correct any errors in the following sentences. Write *OK* if a sentence has no error.

KEY
1. yours
2. are
3. dozen
4. frozen
5. Wests
6. OK
7. OK
8. has been
9. Nick's
10. His
11. Gershwins
12. women's
13. weeks'
14. *i*'s, your
15. lying
16. else's
17. tomorrow's
18. rung
19. gone
20. analyses

1. Between you and me, the suggestion that I thought best was <u>your's</u>.
2. Everyone who saw Jill Kaplan's résumé agreed that her credentials <u>is</u> certainly impressive.
3. Beth requested about two <u>dozens</u> more booklets for our alumni.
4. To help us compete more effectively, the president ordered that all our list prices be <u>froze</u> immediately.
5. Harriet West and Gayle West are not related to each other; the <u>West's</u> are always among the top sales representatives in our company.
6. To celebrate their always-superior sales, we are giving the Mses. West a special award this year.
7. The leading actress's role is demanding—very demanding.
8. She <u>been</u> on stage during the entire first act.
9. <u>Nick</u> retyping the dialogue helped us save a great deal of time.
10. <u>Him</u> retyping the dialogue helped us save a great deal of time.
11. As you might imagine, there are few Ira <u>Gershwin's</u> writing for the theater today.
12. A well-known writer of <u>womens'</u> roles, Tom Ames is now doing TV sitcoms.
13. All of us are certain that the new musical will close in about four <u>weeks</u> time.
14. Dennis, remember to dot your <u>is</u> and mind <u>you're</u> p's and q's.
15. I was surprised to find so many messages <u>laying</u> on my desk when I returned from rehearsal.
16. Please check in someone <u>elses</u> office for a blank diskette.
17. We must revise the budget at <u>tomorrows</u> committee meeting.
18. After the alarm had <u>rang</u>, we went to the fire exit.
19. Emilio had already <u>went</u> to the meeting when we called him.
20. We studied all the <u>analysis</u> that our department managers submitted, and most of them were quite helpful.

REVIEW *cont.*

Editing Practice

Spelling Alert! Check the following excerpt for spelling errors. How many can you find? Write the misspelled words correctly on a sheet of paper.

As we explained, we are <u>intrested</u> in learning more about <u>goverment</u> <u>securitys</u>. According to the <u>materiel</u> we <u>recieved</u> from our broker, a <u>minimum</u> investment of $5,000 is <u>requrred</u>. The yield on primary issues is <u>currantly</u> <u>aproximately</u> 13.5 percent.

Call an Editor! Read the following excerpt. Then make any corrections necessary on a sheet of paper.

Mike and I had <u>spoke</u> with Dr. Merriam about training for our word processing operators before Dr. Merriam joined our company. Dr. Merriam and her husband are noted experts in information processing and have <u>wrote</u> many articles on this topic. <u>Copys</u> of some of <u>there</u> articles are enclosed. We are <u>planing</u> to begin the new word processing training program in early <u>Febuary</u>.

KEY
interested
government
securities
material
received
required
currently
approximately

KEY
spoken
written
Copies
their
planning
February

2.5 *PRONOUNS: NOMINATIVE AND OBJECTIVE FORMS*

OBJECTIVES: After completing Section 2.5, you should be able to:

1. Describe the two uses of nominative pronouns.
2. List three ways in which objective pronouns are used.
3. Discuss special problems in selecting the correct case form of pronouns and tell how to solve these problems.
4. Explain the intensive use and the reflexive use of pronouns ending in *self.*

When asked to identify the most important skills they seek in job applicants, most business executives put communication skills at the very top of the list. Indeed, when speaking or writing, workers are communicating their abilities to do their jobs well. To convince your colleagues of *your* ability to communicate well, you must be able to use the correct forms of nominative and objective pronouns and of pronouns ending in *self* in a number of different contexts.

CASE FORMS

In Section 2.4, you studied the possessive forms of pronouns. In this section, you will learn about the other two case forms of pronouns — the nominative and the objective forms — and about pronouns ending with *self*.

Nominative Form	Objective Form	Nominative Form	Objective Form
I	me	we	us
you	you	you	you
he	him	they	them
she	her	who	whom
it	it	whoever	whomever

Nominative Pronouns

Learn these two rules for using nominative pronouns correctly.

Subject of a Verb. *Rule 1:* When a pronoun is the subject of a verb, the pronoun must be in the nominative case.

> *I* have reviewed the menu carefully. ("*I* have reviewed," not "*me* have reviewed.")

> *She* and Mr. Costa will speak at the luncheon. (*She*, not *her*.)

> *Who* is the director of sales and marketing? (*Who*, a nominative pronoun, is the subject of the verb *is*.)

Complement of a "Being" Verb. *Rule 2:* As you know, the "being" verbs are *am, is, are, was,* and *were* and *be, being,* and *been* with helping verbs. A pronoun that completes the meaning of a being verb must be in the nominative case.

> Perhaps it was (they? them?) who sent us these samples. (*Was* is a being verb, and the pronoun that follows it complements the being verb. Therefore, the pronoun must be the nominative *they*.)

> It must have been (he? him?) in the convertible. (The nominative *he* is correct after the being verb *must have been*.)

Exception: One being verb has an exception. With the infinitive *to be*, do not use the nominative-case pronoun as the complement when *to be* is preceded immediately by a noun or a pronoun.

> When she first answered the telephone, Eva thought Robert to be (I? me?). (Is there a noun or a pronoun immediately before the infinitive *to be*? Yes, *Robert*. Therefore, do not use the nominative case — the answer is *me*. The "exception" rule applies.)

> The patients appeared to be (they? them?). (Is there a noun or a pronoun immediately before the infinitive *to be*? No, there isn't. Therefore, choose the nominative form *they*. The exception rule does not apply.)

To remember the exception rule about the infinitive *to be*, make this connection:

No subject — *Nominative* case

Let the *no* in the word *nominative* remind you to choose the nominative pronoun when there is *no* subject before the infinitive *to be*.

Checkup 1

On a sheet of paper, correct any errors in the use of pronouns in the following sentences. Write *OK* if a sentence has no error.

1. When Ms. Reynolds saw Clark's silhouette, she thought him to be I.
2. When a caller asks for you by name, you should reply "This is she."
3. Sam, if you were me, would you have hung up on the telephone salesperson?
4. All of us agree that the winner should be she.
5. Some drivers had suggested that the union delegate should be him.

Objective Pronouns

Use the objective-case pronoun forms *me, us, him, her, them,* and *whom* when they are objects of verbs, prepositions, or infinitives.

Mr. Nelson promoted *me* in July. (*Me* is the object of the verb *promoted.*)

Pam had already given a copy to *us,* so we bought an extra copy for *him.* (*Us* and *him* are objects of the prepositions *to* and *for,* respectively.)

To *whom* did Elmer send an Express Mail package on Monday? (*Whom* is the object of the preposition *to.*)

Ms. Weingarten plans to visit *them* next month. (*Them* is the object of the infinitive *to visit.*)

Use the objective-case pronoun forms for subjects of infinitives:

Ken wants *us* to travel to Minnesota in June or July. (*Us* is the subject of the infinitive *to travel.*)

Also, as you learned in the exception on page 72, use the objective-case pronoun following the infinitive *to be* whenever *to be* has a noun or a pronoun immediately before it.

When she first answered the telephone, Eva thought Robert to be *me.* (The noun *Robert* precedes the infinitive *to be;* the objective *me* is correct.)

SUGGESTION

If needed, spend extra time on these special problems. Incorrect use of nominative and objective case is frequent in speech and in writing.

Special Problems

In certain situations, selecting the correct case form may be confusing. The following discussion will help you in such situations.

Who and *Whom; Whoever* and *Whomever.*   You have already learned that the pronouns *who* and *whoever* are nominative forms, and the pronouns *whom* and *whomever* are objective forms. You also know that we use the nominative forms (*who* and *whoever*) as subjects of verbs and as complements of "being" verbs. Use the objective forms (*whom* and *whomever*) as you would use other objective forms — that is, as objects of verbs and objects of prepositions. Still, many people have trouble with these pronouns — usually because of complications in context.

· M E M O R Y   H O O K ·

You know that *him* is an objective form. Let the *m* in *him* remind you of the *m* in *whom* and in *whomever*, which are also objective forms. You may even substitute *him* to test whether an objective form is correct.

The consultant (who? whom?) Jay Haggerty recommended is Peter Chung. (Make this substitution: "Jay Haggerty recommended *(him)*." Because the objective form *him* is correct, the choice must be *whom*.)

Celeste doesn't know (who? whom?) the director has selected. (Make the substitution: "the director has selected *(him)*." The correct choice, therefore, is *whom*.)

We do not know (who? whom?) Russell Trent is. (Make the substitution: "Russell Trent is *(he)*." Because the nominative *he* can be substituted, the correct answer is *who*.)

In Interrogative Sentences.   Questions are generally worded in inverted order, meaning that the subject comes after the verb. Therefore, in applying the memory hook test to questions, change the sentence to normal order before substituting *he* or *him*.

(Who? Whom?) is the consultant Jay Haggerty recommended? (Normal order: "The consultant Jay Haggerty recommended is *(he)*." *Who* is correct because it complements the being verb *is*.)

(Who? Whom?) has the director selected? (Normal order: "The director has selected *(him)*." *Whom* is correct because *him* can be substituted.)

Of course, if the question is in normal order, simply substitute *he* or *him*.

In Clauses.   When *who* or *whom* (or *whoever* or *whomever*) is used in a clause within a sentence, you must (1) separate that clause from the rest of the sentence, (2) determine if the clause is in normal word order, and (3) proceed to substitute *he* or *him*.

1. Separate the clause, which *always* begins with the word *who, whom, whoever,* or *whomever.*

   We do not know (who? whom?) the caller could have been. (Separate the clause: "(who? whom?) the caller could have been.")

   Share this piece of information with (whoever? whomever?) you worked with on the Lenz account. (Separate the clause: "(whoever? whomever?) you worked with on the Lenz account.")

2. Change the inverted clause to normal order.

   (who? whom?) the caller could have been (Normal order: "the caller could have been (who? whom?).")

   (whoever? whomever?) you worked with on the Lenz account (Normal order: "you worked with (whoever? whomever?) on the Lenz account.")

3. Substitute *he/she* or *him/her* in each clause.

   the caller could have been *(he)* (Remember that a nominative form must be used to complete a being verb; thus *he* and *who* are correct.)

   you worked with *(him)* on the Lenz account (*Him* is correct; it is the object of the preposition *with.* Therefore, *whomever* is correct.)

   Note: Interrupters such as *I think, she says, you know,* and *we believe* should be omitted when selecting *who* or *whom* in clauses.

   The architect (who? whom?) I believe we should hire is Debra Levitt. (Separate the clause: "(who? whom?) I believe we should hire." Omit the interrupting words *I believe* and put the clause in normal order: "we should hire *(her)*." *Whom* is correct because *her* can be substituted.)

Checkup 2

Select the correct pronoun in parentheses in each of the following sentences.

1. Perhaps the person (who? whom?) you saw during the press conference was Jean McDonald.
2. Eleanor is the artist (who? whom?) should be assigned to this campaign.
3. The attendance committee can fine (whoever? whomever?) does not observe the regulations.
4. Mitch Chaffee, (who? whom?) we consider the best accountant in our company, will head the committee.
5. (Whoever? Whomever?) wrote this manual did an excellent job.
6. We asked Peter, (who? whom?) has much experience in tax matters, for his advice.

On a sheet of paper, correct any errors in the following sentences.

7. Do you know whom we should ask for a demonstration of this new copier?

8. OK
9. whoever
10. OK

8. No, I do not know whom Brian asked for permission to borrow a company car.
9. Please send a swatch to <u>whomever</u> asks for a sample.
10. Please send a swatch to whomever you want.

Pronouns in Compound Subjects or Compound Objects. Compound subjects or compound objects are nouns and pronouns joined by *and* or *or*. When the pronoun is part of a subject, use the nominative case. When the pronoun is part of an object, use the objective case.

Nominative in Subjects	Objective in Objects
Kevin and *I* want . . .	. . . for Kevin and *me*
Ms. Royce and *he* asked . . .	. . . asked Ms. Royce and *him*
She and *I* will write . . .	. . . written by *her* and *me*
They and *we* agree . . .	. . . agree with *them* and *us*

· M E M O R Y   H O O K ·

To simplify choosing the right pronoun in compounds, omit everything in the compound except the pronoun. Then say the sentence aloud, and the correct answer will be obvious.

Judy Sinclair and (I? me?) leave for Mexico City on Monday. (When you omit the words *Judy Sinclair and*, the answer becomes clear: "*I* leave . . . ," not "*me* leave.")

Sylvia sent copies to Mr. Chernof and (I? me?). (Omit the words *Mr. Chernof and*, and the answer becomes obvious: "sent copies to . . . *me*.")

Pronoun Phrases. When faced with pronoun choice in phrases such as *we supervisors* and *us supervisors*, simply omit the noun following the pronoun and test the sentence with the pronoun choices.

(We? Us?) supervisors met with the union delegates to discuss the issues in detail. (Omit the word *supervisors*, then say "*We* met with . . . " and "*Us* met with . . . " Which pronoun would you choose? The nominative *we*, of course!)

Pronouns with *Than* or *As*. Another pronoun problem arises in sentences such as "Roxanne has more vacation time than (I? me?)," and "This problem affects Aaron as much as (I? me?)." When the word *than* or *as* is used in such comparisons, it generally represents an incomplete clause. By completing the clause, you will make your choice easy.

Roxanne has more vacation time than I (have vacation time). (By completing the clause, you make it obvious that the clause is "*I* have vacation time," not "*me* have . . . ")

This problem affects Aaron as much as (this problem affects) me. (The missing words are *this problem affects*, which are deliberately omitted because they are repetitive and because the sentence makes perfect sense without them. But only by completing the clause will you easily be able to make the correct pronoun choice.)

Pronouns in Appositives. As you learned in Section 2.4, an *appositive* is a word or a group of words used to explain or give more information about a preceding word or phrase. Note the appositives in *italics* in the following sentences.

Lauren Schaeffer, the *principal owner of the conglomerate*, issued a statement to the press this morning. Her attorney, a *well-known financial analyst*, commented on Ms. Schaeffer's statement afterward. (The appositives, the words in italics, help give additional information about "Lauren Schaeffer" and "Her attorney," the words that precede the appositives.

A minor problem arises when choosing pronoun case in appositives such as these:

Two supporters of the amendment, Max Zellner and (she? her?), explained their reasons clearly.

We registered the bonds and delivered them to the co-owners, Paul Markham and (she? her?).

In such instances, follow the instructions of the Memory Hook below.

· M E M O R Y   H O O K ·

To choose pronouns in the preceding examples, (1) omit the words that the appositive renames, then (2) omit the other words in the compound — that is, *use only the pronoun.*

1. Omit the words that the appositive renames:

   . . . Max Zellner and (she? her?) explained their reasons clearly.

   We registered the bonds and delivered them to . . . Paul Markham and (she? her?).

2. Omit the other words in the compound — that is, use only the pronoun:

   . . . (she? her?) explained their reasons clearly. (You would not, of course, say "*her* explained." *She* is the correct pronoun.)

   We registered the bonds and delivered them to . . . (she? her?). (You would not say "delivered them to *she*." The correct pronoun is *her*.)

Checkup 3

On a sheet of paper, correct any errors in the use of pronouns. Write *OK* for any sentence that is correct.

1. The reprimands were sent only to <u>we</u> three smart alecks.
2. The procedure is to ask Dr. Humphreys or <u>I</u> to approve an advance.
3. The majority of the committee members voted for Tanya and <u>he</u>.
4. Do you agree that most of the speakers were not so well prepared as <u>her</u>?
5. Peter is surely a more effective speaker than <u>me</u>.
6. When she asked <u>we</u> students our opinions of the new program, we listed the specific changes that we wanted.
7. As you can see, Paul keyboards much more quickly and accurately than she.
8. Only Melissa Whiting or <u>him</u> has the authority to approve cash advances over $500.
9. Among the assistants who contributed to the campaign were our two new trainees, Nelson and she.
10. He quickly learned that none of <u>we</u> accountants wants to adopt the confusing new procedures.
11. Two of our account executives, Bob and <u>her</u>, leave for the West Coast tomorrow.
12. Between you and me, I know that Elizabeth Garcia will be selected regional manager when Mr. Seeley retires.

PRONOUNS ENDING IN *SELF*

The pronouns ending in *self (myself, yourself, himself, herself, itself, ourselves, yourselves,* and *themselves)* serve two functions: (1) to emphasize or intensify the use of a noun or another pronoun or (2) to refer to a noun or pronoun that has already been named in a sentence (called "reflexive use").

Intensive Use

Note how pronouns ending in *self* provide emphasis in these statements:

Suzanne *herself* announced the hostile takeover. (Much more emphatic than "Suzanne announced the hostile takeover.")

We requested Howard *himself* to write the ad copy. (Much more emphatic than "We requested Howard to write the ad copy.")

Reflexive Use

Pronouns that end in *self* refer to a noun or a pronoun that has already been named elsewhere in the sentence.

The sanitation workers paid *themselves* a compliment. (*Themselves* clearly refers to *sanitation workers.*)

Angela distributed all the copies but forgot to keep one for *herself*. (*Herself* clearly refers to *Angela*.)

Common Errors

A pronoun that ends in *self* must have a *clear* antecedent within the sentence. Furthermore, the pronoun must be positioned correctly in the sentence. Note these examples of common errors:

Gordon Weeks and *myself* developed the strategy. (To whom does *myself* refer? It has no antecedent in this sentence. Instead, the sentence should be "Gordon Weeks and *I* developed . . . .")

When we asked the painter for his advice, he said that he prefers spray painting *himself*. (Obviously, the man does not want to spray paint *himself!* Instead, the sentence should be ". . . he said that he *himself* prefers spray painting." The position of the pronoun ending in *self* must be correct.)

Checkup 4

On a sheet of paper, correct any errors in the following sentences. Write *OK* if a sentence has no error.

1. The felon himself pleaded for mercy.
2. When Elaine and myself suggested the idea, we did not realize how time-consuming the project would be.
3. Ms. Romero specifically said that she wants to join herself.
4. When they reviewed the estimates, they decided to cancel themselves.
5. The president herself will talk to the staff about the child care center.
6. As Bobbi and himself said, "It's too late now."

SECTION

REVIEW

A. On a sheet of paper, correct any errors in the following sentences.

1. Both of us thought the woman on the stage to be she.
2. We were delighted when Jess said, "I invited Danielle and him to the parade."
3. Last summer Jean and me went to our first training session.
4. Whom in your opinion is the most deserving contender?
5. The Messineos are the only ones whom I believe do not rent their beach house.
6. Invite whoever you think would enjoy the office Christmas party.
7. Us police officers were all suffering because of the mistakes of a few.

REVIEW cont.

8. she
9. he
10. him and her
11. OK
12. I
13. OK
14. he himself liked shooting
15. she
16. she
17. Jimmy's
18. OK
19. OK
20. whoever

8. Do you really think that Sebastian is smarter than <u>her</u>?
9. Two of my best friends, Joan and <u>him</u>, asked to be excused from the negotiations because of a conflict of interest.
10. We gave the toughest job to the best employees, <u>he and she</u>.
11. He signed the letters and mailed them to the Joneses and her.
12. If the price is right, Davy and <u>myself</u> will certainly sell our concession stand on the boardwalk.
13. Douglas himself will be in charge of filing the complaints.
14. When we asked the sheriff which of the two methods he preferred, <u>he said he liked shooting himself</u>.
15. The chief thinks that Ralph is more productive than <u>her</u>.
16. Are Delbert and <u>her</u> going out together regularly?
17. Jimmy and Miguel's wives make more money than Jimmy and Miguel.
18. Sam, if I were you, I would surely join the company's pension plan and begin making voluntary contributions like Jim and her.
19. Russ cannot handle the pressure as well as she.
20. Mr. Palmer's new assistants, <u>whomever</u> they may be, are in for a rude awakening.

KEY

1. me
2. who's
3. who
4. I
5. Alices
6. was
7. photos
8. were she
9. forgotten
10. is
11. employees'
12. OK
13. it's
14. sitting
15. lain
16. Doesn't
17. OK
18. There's

B. On a sheet of paper, correct any errors in the following sentences. Write *OK* if a sentence has no error.

1. Yesterday Ms. Rathbone invited Shelby and <u>I</u> to watch the parade from her front porch.
2. Ask Bill if he knows <u>whose</u> in charge of the cafeteria.
3. Melanie Harris, <u>whom</u> I know is a registered nurse, can help you.
4. She and <u>me</u> were in training together at Mt. Sinai Hospital.
5. The two <u>Alice's</u> were our supervisors there.
6. One of Melanie's first patients <u>were</u> the famous rock star Vanillie.
7. In fact, I think he gave her a couple of autographed <u>photoes</u>.
8. If I <u>was her</u>, I'd have the pictures framed.
9. Melanie, though, had <u>forgot</u> all about them until I reminded her.
10. Everyone in the admissions office at Mt. Sinai <u>are</u> always talking about how many people do not have health insurance.
11. With fewer and fewer companies paying for their <u>employee's</u> health insurance, a serious crisis in health care is imminent.
12. Dr. Karlan says the children from the ghettos are the people who suffer most.
13. I myself think <u>its</u> time we found a way to help these children.
14. The report is <u>setting</u> on the copy machine.
15. Emily must have <u>laid</u> in the sun too long to get such a bad sunburn.
16. <u>Don't</u> she know any better?
17. <u>Will</u> you and he please talk some sense into Marianne?
18. <u>Theirs</u> nothing more to worry about.

REVIEW cont.

Editing Practice

Plurals and Possessives.   On a sheet of paper, correct any errors in the use of plurals and possessives in the following sentences. Write *OK* for any sentence that has no error.

1. When your ready to begin reviewing the videotapes, just call us.
2. When we designed these playrooms, the childrens' safety and comfort were our main objectives.
3. Both companys are eager to compete for the Hillier account.
4. I believe that there ready now to meet with us to discuss the final details of the incentive package.
5. All of us appreciated him advising us on these financial matters.
6. On July 15 Harry will be eligible for one weeks' vacation.
7. Its obvious, in our opinion, that we have won the budget battle.
8. One of the editor in chiefs, Barbara McCloskey, convinced the publisher to release the article.

Using Your Word Processor.   You keyboarded the following on your word processor yesterday but did not proofread it. Please do so now.

Pleas review the enclosed cost estamate for the equipmant we are planning to purchase in Febraury. As you will see, the contract for maintenence is $500 a year, and instalation alone will cost nearly $2,000. Let's review this financail data carefully before we proceed.

2.6 *PREDICATE AGREEMENT*

OBJECTIVES: After completing Section 2.6, you should be able to:

1. State the basic rule of predicate agreement.
2. Explain how to determine whether a collective noun is singular or plural.
3. Describe other subjects that may be either singular or plural.
4. Identify relative-pronoun clauses and their antecedents.

PREDICATE AGREEMENT WITH SIMPLE SUBJECTS

Popular songs, television shows, and movies do little to avoid errors such as "he don't" and "I been." As a result, listeners and viewers hear such errors

CROSS REFERENCE

You may want to review predicates (Section 2.1) with students.

over and over so often that they may start to believe that "he don't" and "I been" are grammatically correct.

Well, they are *not!* Pay special attention to the agreement rules to make sure that you *do* avoid such errors in your speaking and writing.

In the first section of this chapter, you learned about predicates and simple subjects. Now let's review the way that these elements are related.

Basic Agreement Rule

A predicate must agree with its simple subject in number and in person. This statement is the basic rule of agreement for all sentences. A predicate always includes a verb, of course, and that verb must agree with its subject. In addition, if the predicate includes any pronouns that refer to the simple subject, those pronouns must also agree with the simple subject.

CROSS REFERENCE

Point out that *our vice president* is an appositive. See Section 2.5.

Agreement of Subject and Verb. Note how verbs agree with their subjects in the following sentences.

Ray Singleton *wants* to shorten the manufacturing schedule. (The verb *wants* agrees with the subject, *Ray Singleton* — both are singular.)

Ray Singleton, our vice president, *wants* to shorten the manufacturing schedule. (Neither the subject nor the verb has changed. *Wants* agrees with *Ray Singleton.*)

Two vice presidents *want* to shorten the manufacturing schedule. (Now the subject is the plural *vice presidents.* Therefore, the plural form *want* — not *wants* — is correct.)

REINFORCEMENT

For each noun, ask students to substitute pronouns; for example, *it* for *team, they* for *teams,* and so on. This practice will simplify their understanding of the next topic.

· M E M O R Y   H O O K ·

Although plural *nouns* usually end in *s* or *es,* an *s* ending on a *verb* indicates that it is a singular verb.

Singular Noun and Verb	Plural Noun and Verb
the *team wants*	the *teams want*
one *salesclerk has*	all *salesclerks have*
Mrs. Salerno is	*Mr. and Mrs. Salerno are*

Agreement of Pronoun With Subject. If the predicate includes a pronoun that refers to the subject, that pronoun must also agree with the subject.

The team wants to change *its* assignment in the company. The teams want to change *their* assignments in the company. (The pronoun *its* agrees with *team.* The pronoun *their* agrees with *teams.*)

Mrs. Salerno is eager to receive *her* dividends. Mr. and Mrs. Salerno are eager to receive *their* dividends. (*Her* agrees with *Mrs. Salerno.* In the second sentence, *their* agrees with *Mr. and Mrs. Salerno.*)

Checkup 1

Choose the correct verbs and pronouns in the following sentences.

1. Generally, the DeWitt Corporation (<u>does</u>? do?) not disclose (his? her? <u>its</u>? their?) acquisition plans.
2. All four managers (is? <u>are</u>?) going to bring (his? her? its? <u>their</u>?) analyses with (him, her? it? <u>them</u>?).
3. <u>Yolanda</u> (<u>wants</u>? want?) to open (his? <u>her</u>? its? their?) third store in the Shady Hills Mall.
4. The <u>union</u> (<u>has</u>? have?) changed (his? her? <u>its</u>? their?) demands since our last meeting with (his? her? <u>its</u>? their?) representatives.
5. That design <u>studio</u> (<u>is</u>? are?) very well respected as a leader in (his? her? <u>its</u>? their?) field.
6. Mary <u>Burroughs</u>, one of the senior partners, (<u>is</u>? are?) planning to sell (his? <u>her</u>? its? their?) share of the stock before (he? <u>she</u>? it? they?) retires next month.

Simple-Subject Agreement Problems

The most common problems concerning agreement of subjects and verbs are discussed below. Study them carefully.

Inverted Sentences. Agreement problems most often arise when the subject is difficult to identify, as in sentences with inverted word order — where the verb comes before the subject. These situations include questions and sentences or clauses beginning with *there*.

> On your desk (is? are?) the contracts that were done yesterday. (At first glance, the subject and verb may appear to be "desk *is*," but a closer look shows that the subject of this inverted sentence is *contracts*. The correct verb, therefore, is *are*.)

Sentences or clauses beginning with *there (there is, there are, there has been, there have been)* also are in inverted order.

> There (is? are?) still several openings. (Until you identify the subject *openings*, you cannot choose the correct verb, *are*.)

> Do you know whether there (is? are?) other copiers in the building? (The simple subject is *copiers*. Therefore, *are* is the correct verb.)

Intervening Phrases and Clauses. Another situation that may confuse the writer or speaker is words that separate the subject from its verb. Again, the trick is to identify the simple subject.

> The reason for the delays (is? are?) that half the department is out sick. (The subject is the singular noun *reason*. Therefore, the correct verb is *is*. Although the plural word *delays* immediately precedes the verb, *delays* is not the subject of the verb. *Delays* is part of the prepositional phrase *for the delays*.)

The treasurer, who must approve all expense vouchers signed by our sales managers, (has? have?) cut the travel budgets for all sales personnel. (The subject is *treasurer*, not *sales managers*. Therefore, the correct verb is *has*.)

Checkup 2

On a sheet of paper, correct any agreement errors in the following sentences. Write *OK* if a sentence has no error. (Be sure to identify the subject for each sentence.)

1. When we checked the directory, we found that there is only two stationery stores nearby.
2. Are you sure that there's no more than two stationery stores in the area?
3. The entire building, with all its offices, are to be painted during the summer.
4. The whole city, which consists of more than 800,000 people, are affected.
5. There is, as you already know, several reasons for the water shortage.
6. Did you know that there's a few individuals who water their lawns three times a week?

Pronoun Agreement With Common-Gender Nouns. When the gender of a noun is clearly masculine (*man, father, brother, son*) or feminine (*woman, mother, sister, daughter*), choosing between the pronouns *he* or *she, him* or *her,* and so on, is no problem. Common-gender nouns are those that can be either masculine or feminine, such as *employee, student, teacher, officer, owner, secretary,* and so on. The traditional rule is to use masculine pronouns to represent common-gender nouns. However, many writers now use pronoun combinations such as *he or she, him or her,* and *his or her* to avoid suggesting either masculine or feminine gender.

Every employee knows *his or her* role in the upcoming fire drill. (*His or her* agrees with the common-gender noun *employee.*)

An executive must be sure that *he or she* is familiar with the fire regulations. (*He or she* agrees with *executive.*)

When such combinations are used too often, they make the message difficult to read. In such instances, consider using plurals to avoid the need for pronoun combinations.

Executives must be sure that *they* are familiar with the fire regulations. (*They* agrees with *executives.*)

Indefinite-Word Subject. The words *each, either, neither, everyone, everybody, someone, somebody, anyone, anybody, no one,* and *nobody* are always singular.

When they are used as subjects, and when they modify other subjects, their predicates must be singular.

□SUGGESTION

In the first two examples, explain to students the difference between the pronoun *each*, which serves as a subject, and the modifier *each*, which describes the subject.

> *Each* of the printers *has* a 10-foot cable that connects *it* to the computer. (The singulars *has* and *it* agree with the subject *each*.)

> *Each* printer *has* a 10-foot cable that connects *it* to the computer. (Here *each* modifies the subject, *printer*. In all cases, *each* is singular.)

> *Anyone* in your precinct who *wants* to volunteer *his or her* time should be sure *he or she registers*. (*Wants*, *his or her*, *he or she*, and *registers* all agree with the singular *anyone*.)

Checkup 3

KEY

The simple subject is given in parentheses.
1. has, his or her (Nobody)
2. wants, his or her (Each)
3. OK (Anyone)
4. OK or he or she, his or her (executive)
5. has, its (Neither)
6. OK or his or her (officer)

On a sheet of paper, correct the following sentences. If a sentence has no error, write *OK*. For each sentence, identify the simple subject.

1. Nobody in these two departments <u>have</u> submitted <u>their</u> monthly expense report yet.
2. Each of the administrative assistants <u>want</u> to get <u>their</u> own computer.
3. Anyone who wants to participate in next week's training session must complete and return his or her form to the Personnel Department.
4. Every executive in this building is permitted to use these facilities if <u>he</u> shows <u>his</u> pass to the guard.
5. Neither of the service centers we visited <u>have</u> a parking lot for <u>their</u> customers.
6. Every corporate officer in the country is sure to want <u>his</u> senior staff members to take this course.

PREDICATE AGREEMENT WITH SPECIAL SUBJECTS

Remember the basic agreement rule: *The predicate must agree in number and in person with the simple subject.* As you review some especially troublesome agreement problems, keep this rule in mind.

Collective-Noun Simple Subject

A *collective noun* is one that refers to a group or a collection of persons or things; for example, *class, jury, audience, department, company, committee,* and *association.* Because a collective noun may be either singular or plural, its correct number may not be easily recognized. Use the following Memory Hook to help you.

When the class, jury, and so on, acts *as one group*, treat the collective noun as *singular*. When the constituents of the collective noun act *as individuals*, treat the noun as *plural*.

In other words, remember:

One group is singular.
Individuals are plural.

In a major case, the jury (does? do?) not give (its? their?) verdict quickly. (Is the jury acting *as one group*, or is the jury acting *as individuals*? Answer: As one group. Therefore, treat *jury* as a singular noun: " . . . the jury *does* not give *its* verdict quickly.")

The jury (is? are?) arguing about the charges. (Is the jury acting *as one group*, or is the jury acting as *individuals*? To argue, they obviously would be acting *as individuals*. Treat *jury* as a plural noun: "The jury *are* arguing about the charges."

Foreign-Noun Subject

Nouns of foreign origin do not form their plurals in the usual way. Review the list of foreign-origin nouns on page 60. Always be careful to determine first whether the noun is singular or plural before deciding on the correct verb to agree with such nouns.

The basis for her statements (was? were?) unsound. (*Basis* is singular; therefore, the predicate must be singular. *Was* is correct.)

The bases for her statements (was? were?) unsound. (*Bases* is plural; therefore, *were* is correct.)

Checkup 4

KEY
Errors are underscored.
1. were, their
2. are
3. are
4. have
5. are
6. are

On a sheet of paper, correct any errors in the following sentences. Write *OK* if a sentence has no error.

1. The faculty <u>was</u> assigned to <u>its</u> new offices in the recently constructed building.
2. In this book, parentheses <u>is</u> used for bibliographic references.
3. The economic stimuli that <u>is</u> being used by the Federal Reserve have been criticized by some experts.
4. Recent crises in the Middle East <u>has</u> caused great concern in the world.
5. The media we prefer for advertising our service <u>is</u> television and radio.
6. If you need more information, the criteria that we use to select meat for our restaurant chain <u>is</u> explained in detail in this report.

7. meets
8. OK

7. The honors class <u>meet</u> once a week.
8. The group has reached its decision and will announce it shortly.

Part, Portion, or Amount Subject

Other subjects that may be either singular or plural are those that refer to a part, a portion, or an amount of something. Thus *all, some, half, two-thirds* (or any fraction), and *none* may be either singular or plural. To decide, find the answer to "Part of *what*?" "Portion of *what*?" "Amount of *what*?" In other words, use the complete subject (not the simple subject) for your answer.

Some of the house (has? have?) been painted. (House *has*.)

Some of the houses (has? have?) been painted. (Houses *have*.)

A Number, The Number

A number is always plural. *The number* is always singular. (Note that an adjective before *number* has no effect on the choice.)

A number of tenants *have* questioned the new rent increase.
(*Have*, because *a number* is always plural.)

The number of tenants *is* declining. (*The number* is always singular, so *is* is correct.)

> **· M E M O R Y   H O O K ·**
>
> To remember the above principle quickly and accurately, picture the following:
>
> **Plural:** a
> **Singular:** the
>
> As you see, *plural* is shorter than *singular*, and *a* is shorter than *the*. So use this to remember that *a number* is plural and that *the number* is singular.

Checkup 5

On a sheet of paper, correct any errors in the following sentences. Write *OK* for any sentence that has no error.

1. The number of new ships <u>have</u> risen to six.
2. Luckily, none of the ships <u>were</u> damaged by the storm.
3. Nearly two-thirds of the city was affected by the transit strike.
4. We know that a number of workers <u>is</u> unhappy about the changes in our medical coverage.

5. Some of the machines, Hank told me, <u>was</u> not adequately inspected before shipment.
6. Some of the machine, as you can see, has already begun to rust.

PREDICATE AGREEMENT WITH COMPOUND SUBJECTS

To complete your study of predicate agreement, you will now work on predicate agreement with compound subjects joined by *and*, *or*, or *nor* and on one other predicate agreement problem: agreement with the relative pronouns *who*, *that*, and *which*.

Subjects Joined by *And*

A compound subject joined by *and* is plural and must take a plural verb.

Greg *and* Howard *have* applied for a business loan. (The compound subject *Greg and Howard* is plural; the plural verb *have applied* is correct.)

A construction company *and* a plastics distributor have filed for bankruptcy. (The plural form *have filed* is correct because the compound subject is joined by *and*.)

Two exceptions to this rule are possible:

1. If the two nouns joined by *and* refer to *one* person, then that subject is really singular and takes a singular verb.

My business partner *and* investment adviser *is* my sister, Joanne Delilo. (Although the compound subject is joined by *and*, obviously only one person is serving as *business partner* and *investment adviser*. The singular verb *is* is therefore correct.)

Strawberries *and* ice cream *is* going to be served for dessert. (*One* dessert, *strawberries and ice cream*, is the intended meaning.)

Note that if two different people or two different desserts were intended, the verbs would then be plural.

My business partner *and* my investment adviser *are* not in agreement on this issue. (Two different people are intended.)

Strawberries *and* ice cream are among the desserts included in the fixed-price lunch. (Here, two different items on the menu are referred to.)

2. If two or more subjects joined by *and* are modified by *each*, *every*, or *many a*, then the predicate is singular.

Each secretary and assistant *has* been asked to return the completed questionnaire to the personnel department by May 15. *Every* supervisor and manager *is* supposed to check the questionnaires. *Many a* factory, office, and store throughout the country *is* now following this procedure. (In each sentence, the predicate is singular because the subjects are modified by *each*, *every*, and *many a*. Members of the plural groups are being considered singly.)

Checkup 6

On a sheet of paper, correct any agreement error in the following sentences. Write *OK* for any sentence that has no error.

1. Broccoli and spinach is not at the top of most children's favorite-foods list.
2. As usual, every regular client and customer are eligible for the same special discount.
3. The letter and the envelope have two different addresses.
4. Many an auditor and business owner have complained to the IRS about their feelings on this new policy.
5. Ham and eggs are usually what I order for breakfast.
6. Each partner and associate in the accounting firms we contacted are writing to their representatives to show support for the legislation.

Subjects Joined by *Or* or *Nor*

For subjects joined by *or* or *nor*, simply match the predicate to the subject that follows *or* or *nor*.

The owner *or* her assistants (is? are?) going to discuss (her? their?) new winter clothing line at the sales meeting tomorrow. (Matching the predicate to the subject that follows *or*, the correct choices are *are* and *their*.)

The assistants *or* the owner (is? are?) going to discuss (her? their?) new winter clothing line at the sales meeting tomorrow. (Now the subject that follows *or* is the singular *owner*. Therefore, the choices are *is* and *her*.)

Neither the owner *nor* her assistants (knows? know?) where the French designer went. (Which subject follows *nor*? Answer: the plural *assistants*. The choice, therefore, is *know*.)

Either the three Japanese couturiers *or* SmartShirt (is? are?) going to present (its? their?) collection this afternoon. (The subject that follows *or* is *SmartShirt*, singular; thus the choices are *is* and *its*.)

Checkup 7

Select the correct words in the following sentences.

1. Either the salesclerks or Mr. Lehman (like? likes?) to present (their? his?) customers' clothes in special garment bags.
2. Neither Mr. Lehman nor the district managers (has? have?) endorsed the suggestion.
3. Alicia Martinez or her store managers (has? have?) always completed (her? their?) buying early in the season.

4. My brother-in-law or his associates (is? <u>are?</u>) often interested in purchasing unusual sportswear for (his? <u>their?</u>) stores.

5. Either her buyers or Alicia herself (<u>is?</u> are?) going to coordinate the fashion show.

PREDICATE AGREEMENT IN RELATIVE-PRONOUN CLAUSES

<u>SUGGESTION</u>

Show students that *who, which,* and *that* are not always relative pronouns. For instance, "Who is the clerk?" This example illustrates that *who* sometimes has no antecedent and is not a relative pronoun. Also, "Susan didn't know *that* the car had been sold." The word *that* has no antecedent. "Do you know *which* course has been canceled?" The word *which* has no antecedent.

The pronouns *who, that,* and *which* are called *relative pronouns* ~but not always~ because they *relate* to other words (called *antecedents*). The antecedent of the relative pronoun is a noun or a pronoun that is usually immediately before the relative pronoun.

Lucinda Schiff is one of those nitpickers *who* strive for perfection all the time. (The relative pronoun is *who,* and its antecedent is the noun immediately before it, *nitpickers.*)

The Super-Flo pump *that* is on the counter works efficiently and quietly. (If *that* is a relative pronoun, what is its antecedent? Answer: *pump.*)

This special offer is good until Friday, *which* is the last day of our sale. (The relative pronoun *which* refers to *Friday,* its antecedent.)

Note that in each sentence the verb in the relative-pronoun clause agrees with the antecedent.

☑ **REINFORCEMENT**

Help students see that omitting the relative pronouns *who, that,* and *which* focuses immediately on the correct agreement and makes finding the correct answer very easy.

· M E M O R Y   H O O K ·

To choose quickly the correct verb in relative-pronoun clauses, omit the relative pronoun and use the antecedent as the subject of the clause. For example, from the foregoing sentences the omissions would give:

nitpickers . . . strive
pump . . . is
Friday . . . is

Let's look at some other examples:

Elliott prefers one of those monitors that (has? have?) amber readouts on (its? their?) screens. (By omitting the relative pronoun *that,* you have *monitors . . . have . . . their.*)

Caroline Malley is one of those writers who (does? do?) (her? their?) best work under pressure. (Omit *who* and you have *writers . . . do . . . their.*)

Note: An exception is a clause preceded by *the only one.* Such clauses must take singular predicates.

Lynn is *the only one* of the partners who *has cast her* vote against the proposal. (*Has* and *her* are correct.)

Lynn is one of the partners who have cast their votes against the proposal

Checkup 8

On a sheet of paper, correct any errors in the following sentences. Write *OK* if a sentence has no error.

1. Barry is one of those stockbrokers who <u>calls his</u> clients once a month.
2. A.L. Landry and Co. is one of those dealers which <u>has</u> shown an interest in leasing <u>its</u> cars.
3. The company will soon close one of the several branch offices that <u>is</u> now operating at a loss.
4. Matthew is one of those proofreaders who always double-check their copy carefully.
5. Isabel prefers one of those offices that <u>has</u> modern furniture in <u>it</u>.
6. Audrey is the only one of the council members who wants to reapportion the voting districts in Los Angeles.

SECTION

REVIEW

Practical Application

A. On a sheet of paper, correct any errors in the following sentences. If a sentence has no error, write *OK*.

1. In the Emporium catalog <u>is</u> many different kinds of interesting gifts.
2. <u>Don't</u> Charles know how to move this equipment?
3. <u>Don't</u> you know how to move this equipment?
4. Every medical doctor in the country <u>have</u> been surveyed to see which option <u>they prefer</u>.
5. To exchange merchandise, each customer must show his or her receipt to the cashier.
6. <u>There's</u> the CDs that will be on sale next week.
7. Some of the shipments to Europe <u>has</u> been delayed by the winter storms lashing the continent.
8. The number of managers in the Detroit office <u>were</u> higher than the number of line workers in Flint.
9. Approximately three-fourths of her time, she says, <u>are</u> spent talking with customers about delays and errors.
10. During the convention, the engineering association <u>is</u> staying at two hotels downtown.
11. Because a number of people <u>has</u> complained about our billing policy, we are now reviewing it with our accounting department.
12. Half of the area in this warehouse has been converted to office space.
13. There's many a Tom, Dick, or Mary who wants just what you want.

14. is
15. hopes
16. was
17. were
18. was
19. are, their
20. OK

KEY
1. were
2. OK
3. is
4. OK
5. Huangs'
6. Where are
7. Messrs. Carson (*or* Mr. Carsons)
8. territories
9. understands
10. Doesn't
11. she
12. who, I
13. have, their
14. sisters-in-law
15. spoken
16. it's
17. he

14. Every invoice and package that we send customers <u>are</u> carefully checked first.
15. Neither Arnold nor Joanna <u>hope</u> to attend the New Delhi conference.
16. Every glass and bottle on the truck <u>were</u> broken in the accident.
17. The supervisor or the division managers <u>was</u> notified of the change in regulations.
18. Each editor, proofreader, and designer <u>were</u> invited to a full-day conference on the magazine's future plans.
19. As you probably already know, Mr. Mehta is one of those engineers who <u>is</u> always late in handling <u>his</u> paperwork.
20. Neither the floppy disks nor the manual is with the computer.

B. On a sheet of paper, correct any errors in the following sentences. Write *OK* for any sentence that has no error.

1. The family <u>was</u> arguing for several hours about the pros and cons of the move.
2. Unfortunately, nearly three-fourths of the goods were damaged during the hurricane.
3. Two forms of identification or a store credit card <u>are</u> required for cashing checks.
4. A store credit card or two forms of identification are required for cashing checks.
5. Have we received the <u>Huangs</u> response yet?
6. <u>Where's</u> the cable and the dust cover for this computer?
7. According to the rumor, the <u>Messrs. Carsons</u> are planning to sell the entire inventory.
8. The best sales <u>territorys</u> are in the northern part of Iowa.
9. Steve is the only one of the accountants who <u>understand</u> this procedure.
10. <u>Don't</u> Vivian prepare in advance for these inspections?
11. Either Ellen or Carla should have updated this data disk before <u>they</u> filed it.
12. Jason, my supervisor, <u>whom</u> did as much to win the new account as <u>me</u>, gave me all the credit.
13. A number of the products we developed <u>has</u> already passed <u>its</u> break-even points.
14. Both <u>sister-in-laws</u> have invested heavily in Janice's new business.
15. After Amelia and Phil had <u>spoke</u> with Ms. Trask, we understood why Ms. Trask reassigned the project.
16. Nancy and Carole objected to our candidates, but <u>its</u> not clear why they objected.
17. If <u>him</u> and I are selected, we will enjoy working on the Rodriguezes' beach house.

18. analyses
19. are
20. lie

18. All the analysis that we received from our detectives made the same point: we must tighten security.
19. In the old storeroom is the files that you'll need to write the background part of this report.
20. Excuse me, but I have to lay down before I fall down.

Editing Practice

Plurals and Possessives. On a sheet of paper, correct any errors in the following sentences. Write *OK* for any sentence that has no error.

KEY

1. women's
2. OK
3. knives
4. Davises
5. communities
6. lenses
7. ours
8. Ingrid's
9. theirs
10. Baileys

1. Ken's superb article on womens' rights appeared in last month's issue.
2. Her credentials for the position of development director for the college are excellent.
3. Among the cooking utensils that we import and sell are carving knifes, pots and pans, and baking items.
4. Although all were subpoenaed, only two of the Davis's appeared at the trial.
5. Our company underwrites the concert programs of several communitys in this part of the state.
6. Although several of the lens's were damaged, the insurance policy covers their cost.
7. This copier quickly duplicates and collates, but our's works just as well and costs less per copy.
8. No, I was not aware of Ingrid having completed her internship.
9. All these diskettes are ours; that box of diskettes is their's.
10. The Bailies indeed may be coming, but Mr. Bailey hasn't responded to his invitation yet.

KEY

accommodate

Using Your Word Processor. You keyboarded the following copy quickly but didn't have time to proofread it. Do so now.

We appreciate your request for information about the High-Top Inn. To answer your questions about convention facilities, we have enclosed our latest brochure.

As you will see in the brochure, the HighTop Inn can accomodate groups of from 20 to 300 people with equal ease — and with the same high-quality service that has made us famous for more than 40 years.

After you have read the brochure, please be sure to call Lynn Bandolo, our convention manager, at (800) 555-1234. Ms. Bandolo will be happy to answer any questions that you may have.

2.7 *ADJECTIVES*

OBJECTIVES: After completing Section 2.7, you should be able to:

1. Define and state the importance of adjectives in effective speaking and writing.
2. Identify and describe the various types of adjectives.
3. Explain how to form the comparative and superlative forms of descriptive adjectives.
4. Describe situations in which compound adjectives are and are not hyphenated.

Without adjectives, our speech and writing would be dull and lifeless. Used wisely, adjectives make nouns and pronouns interesting, vivid, and specific. This section will introduce you to the many kinds of adjectives and the ways that we commonly misuse adjectives. A mastery of the use of adjectives will help make *your* speech and writing better tools for communication.

IDENTIFYING ADJECTIVES

Any word that modifies or describes a noun or a pronoun is an *adjective*. An adjective usually precedes the noun it modifies. Some of the most commonly used kinds of adjectives are described below.

Articles

The words *a*, *an*, and *the* are called *articles*. Note how these special adjectives are commonly used:

The new administration gained *a* victory by allowing *an* enthusiastic work force to participate in high-level decision making.

Possessive Adjectives

The possessive adjectives *my, your, his, her, its, our,* and *their* and possessive nouns (*John's, Edna's, Gary's,* and so on) modify nouns.

Your partner reviewed *our* prospectus and submitted it to *Taylor's* manager.

Limiting Adjectives

Adjectives that tell "how many," "how much," or "in what order" are called *limiting adjectives*.

The *top ten* realtors in the state will share more than *fifty* prizes. (*Top* tells "in what order." *Ten* tells "how many realtors." *Fifty* tells "how many prizes.")

Each winner had sold *many* pieces of property. (*Each* modifies *winner; many* modifies *pieces.*)

Proper Adjectives

Proper nouns are very often used as proper adjectives:

Noun	Adjective
in *New York*	a *New York* hotel
near *Minneapolis*	two *Minneapolis* firms
to *Dallas*	*Dallas* residents

ISU is a SE Idaho "university"

Proper adjectives include words derived from proper nouns, such as *Mexican*, *British*, and *Israeli*.

Compound Adjectives

Two or more words joined to modify one noun or pronoun form a *compound adjective*.

Murray wanted a *long-term* contract but signed a *two-year* lease instead. (*Long-term* modifies *contract*, and *two-year* modifies *lease.*)

Descriptive Adjectives

The most commonly used adjectives are *descriptive adjectives* — the adjectives that describe or tell "what kind of."

In a *strong, clear* voice, Andrea rejected the *irresponsible* policies that some *real estate* companies use to lure *unsuspecting* consumers into buying *overpriced* and sometimes *worthless* property. (*Strong, clear, irresponsible, real estate, unsuspecting, overpriced,* and *worthless* are descriptive adjectives.)

Demonstrative Adjectives

The pronouns *this, that, these,* and *those* are also used as adjectives:

As Pronouns	As Adjectives	As Pronouns	As Adjectives
this is	*this* property	*these* are	*these* keys
that has been	*that* building	*those* might be	*those* tenants

Note that *these* is the plural of *this;* both *these* and *this* indicate nearness to the speaker. *Those* is the plural of *that*, and *those* and *that* indicate distance from the speaker. Never use the pronoun *them* as a substitute for *these* or *those!*

Please return *those* mortgages to Mr. d'Amato. (Not *them* mortgages.)

These kinds of problems arise often during our busy season. (*These* kinds, not *them* kinds or "these *kind*.")

REINFORCEMENT

Emphasize that when *this, that, these,* and *those* modify a noun, as they do in the second column examples, they function as adjectives.

this
these near

those
that far

Checkup 1

KEY

Use sentences 6 and 7 to illustrate adjectives that can be both compound adjectives *and* proper adjectives.

1. L, D, D, P
2. D, D, DM, D
3. L, C, DM, D, P & PR
4. L, P, D, DM, PR
5. P, C, D, P & PR
6. C & PR, DM, P, D, P & PR
7. P & PR, D, D, C & PR
8. DM, C, P, D

On a separate sheet of paper, identify the adjectives in the following sentences and label each *possessive* (P), *limiting* (L), *proper* (PR), *compound* (C), *descriptive* (D), or *demonstrative* (DM). Disregard articles.

1. The first realty office we opened has been a major success for our company.
2. A special class is being established for new agents to learn these important procedures.
3. Two well-known firms bid on this large building, which was formerly owned by Brian's mother.
4. In two weeks her older brother will join this company and will work out of the Atlanta office.
5. Our two-year forecast is an accurate one, in Harry's opinion.
6. The Los Angeles attorney who represents that company asked our office for additional information on Henderson's property.
7. One of Kelly's critical accounts is a new client who represents an East Coast broker.
8. These bonds are tax-free investments, according to their new prospectus.

COMPARISON ADJECTIVES

Descriptive adjectives can be compared. For example, *strong* and *clear* can be compared to show degrees of strength and clarity: *strong, stronger,* and *strongest; clear, clearer,* and *clearest.* These three forms of comparison are called the *positive,* the *comparative,* and the *superlative* degrees.

1. The positive degree expresses the quality of *one* person or thing.

   > a *strong* record
   > a *clear* message

2. The comparative degree allows us to compare that quality in *two* persons or things.

   > a *stronger* record
   > a *clearer* message

3. The superlative degree enables us to compare that quality in *three or more* persons or things.

   > the *strongest* record
   > the *clearest* message

 **INFORMATION**

Point out that *the* is required with the superlative degree, to label it as "the only one."

Now that we know how the three degrees are used, we need to know how they are formed.

LANGUAGE LAPSE

Catch the Lapse:
"Child teaching
expert to speak."

—*Birmingham Post
Herald*

[· · ·
[Child-teaching expert

Forming the Comparative and Superlative Degrees

The comparative degree is formed by adding *er* to the positive or by inserting the word *more* or *less* before the positive form. The superlative is formed by adding *est* to the positive or by inserting the word *most* or *least* before the positive form.

Positive	Comparative	Superlative
quick	quicker	quickest
funny	funnier	funniest
poor	poorer	poorest
decisive	more decisive	most decisive
	less decisive	least decisive

In addition, some very commonly used adjectives form their comparative and superlative degrees by changing the form to another word completely. Memorize these for quick reference.

Positive	Comparative	Superlative
good	better	best
bad	worse	worst
little	less	least
much	more	most
many	more	most

Selecting the Correct Forms

Adjectives of only *one* syllable are compared by adding *er* or *est* to the positive degree. Adjectives of *three* or more syllables add *more* or *less* or *most* or *least*. Adjectives of *two* syllables vary: some add *er* or *est*; others add *more* or *less* or *most* or *least*. However, these two-syllable adjectives are easy to compare because an error would be obvious: *more useful*, not *usefuler; most useful*, not *usefulest.* Conversely, *happier*, not *more happy; happiest*, not *most happy.*

Avoiding Comparison Errors

Making Double Comparisons. Do not "mix" the different ways in which adjectives can be compared—use only one at a time.

> *greatest*, not *most greatest*
> *better*, not *more better*

Comparing Absolute Adjectives. Adjectives whose qualities cannot be compared are called *absolute adjectives.* For example, a glass of water cannot be *fuller* or *fullest. Full* is already tops!

Here are some other adjectives that cannot be compared are:

accurate	empty	round	unanimous
complete	immaculate	square	unique
correct	perfect	supreme	
dead	perpendicular	ultimate	

Although they cannot be compared, the qualities of these adjectives can be approached, as indicated by the following:

more nearly accurate   *most nearly* correct
less nearly complete   *least nearly* perfect

You may hear (especially in advertisements) of products that are *most unique*, but *unique* really says it all. Remember that absolute adjectives cannot logically be compared.

Checkup 2

On a sheet of paper, correct any errors in the use of adjectives in the following sentences. If a sentence has no error, write *OK*.

1. Allen said that we had enough of the solvent, but the container was very empty.
2. Which refrigerator uses the most electricity, Model K123 or Model K987?
3. As you can see, Sasha is more happier now that he is working with the homeless.
4. Which is the largest shelter, Hill House or Mercy Center?
5. All of us agree that Dirk's suggestion is very unique.
6. The yellow container is obviously fuller than the blue container.
7. These offices are preferable to the offices on Maple Street because they are more quiet and more big.
8. Mr. Raymond is definitely a better instructor than Ms. Greene. In fact, he is probably the best instructor in the school.

KEY
Errors are underscored.
1. omit *very*
2. more
3. omit *more*
4. larger
5. omit *very*
6. more nearly full
7. quieter, bigger
8. OK

More Than Any Other, More Than Anyone Else

In "more than" comparisons, be sure to include the word *other* or *else* if the person or thing is being compared with *other* members of the same group.

Susan is *more* ambitious *than anyone else* in the Research Department. (With the word *else*, the sentence clearly says that Susan *is* a member of the Research Department. Without the word *else*, the sentence would indicate that Susan is *not* part of the Research Department but is being compared with people who are in this department.)

Brett is *more* productive *than any other* manager in my company. (Brett *is* a manager "in my company." Without the word *other*, this sentence would indicate that Brett is *not* a manager "in my company.")

Repeated Modifier

In the following examples, repeating the modifier *a* (or *an*), *the*, or *my* indicates that *two* different people are intended.

The accountant and *the* attorney (was? were?) formerly with the municipal government. (Repeating *the* shows that *two* people, an accountant and an attorney, are referred to. *Were* is the correct verb.)

The accountant and attorney (was? were?) formerly with the municipal government. (One person who is an accountant and attorney is referred to. *Was* is correct.)

For Added Polish

The following short discussions will help you make correct choices when referring to two or more than two persons or things.

Each Other, One Another. Use *each other* when referring to two in number; use *one another* when referring to three or more.

Emily and Fred work very creatively with *each other.* (Two people.)

Several postal employees commented to *one another* about the recent changes. (Three or more postal employees.)

Either, Neither; Any, Any One, No One, Not Any, None. Use *either* or *neither* when referring to one of *two* persons or things. When referring to *three or more*, use *any, any one, no one, not any,* or *none.*

Either of the mail carriers should be able to answer your questions. (There are only two mail carriers. Therefore, *either* is correct.)

Any one of the ticket agents in Penn Station will give you a train schedule. (There are more than two agents; *any one* is correct.)

COMPOUND ADJECTIVES

Hyphenate most compound adjectives that appear before a noun:

first-quality merchandise	*air-conditioned* rooms
no-fault insurance	*up-to-date* figures
tax-free bonds	*fund-raising* committees
two-mile trail	a *three-year* contract

When they appear after the noun, compound adjectives such as *air-conditioned* and *tax-free* retain the hyphen. Most other compounds do not. Use a dictionary to help you decide.

Before the Noun	After the Noun
a *well-known* writer	a writer who is *well known*
tax-free bonds	bonds that are *tax-free*
air-conditioned rooms	rooms that are *air-conditioned*

Longtime use has made the following compounds so familiar that they are no longer written with hyphens:

a *life insurance* policy	*real estate* services
high school teachers	*social security* benefits

□ **SUGGESTION**

Although not strictly related to adjective use, these two rules will help students enhance their writing skills.

□ **SUGGESTION**

Whether to hyphenate compound adjectives is one of the most vexing problems for writers—even for experienced writers. Advise students to use a dictionary or a writers' handbook to help them make their choices.

Checkup 3

KEY
1. three-time
2. any other
3. court-appointed
4. any other
5. anyone else
6. 15-minute question-and-answer
7. word-of-mouth
8. OK
9. either
10. each other

Apply the rules just presented by correcting the following sentences. Write *OK* for any sentence that has no error.

1. Benjamin Lee is a three time winner of the press writers' annual award.
2. Dana's suggestion is better than any suggestion that we have received so far.
3. Mr. Jefferson's court appointed attorney will probably be named this afternoon.
4. The Kaiser automatic coffeemaker is guaranteed to last longer than any electric coffeemaker on the market.
5. My supervisor, Sandra Weinstein, handles more contracts than anyone in our department.
6. Tom scheduled a 15 minute question and answer session after each presentation.
7. Marketing research has shown that word of mouth advertising is our best form of sales promotion.
8. My tax consultant and investment adviser is well known in financial circles.
9. Ask Sally or Ansel—any one of them should have a sample.
10. When Pat and Diana have more experience, they will work with one another very, very well.

SECTION REVIEW

Practical Application

KEY
1. duty-free
2. ten-minute
3. door-to-door
4. omit *more*
5. these (*or* those)
6. heavy-duty
7. OK
8. any other

A. On a sheet of paper, correct any errors in the following sentences. Write *OK* for any sentence that has no error.

1. Passengers may purchase gifts at the duty free shops here in the airport.
2. Every board member will give a ten minute summary of his or her views on the issue.
3. For security reasons, door to door soliciting is prohibited throughout the building.
4. Although the price is substantially higher, this television set is no more better than that one.
5. Most of them cables are inappropriate for computer equipment.
6. This particular model has a heavy duty motor that was especially designed for professional use.
7. Unless otherwise specified, each machine is equipped with a 120-volt, 10-ampere motor.
8. Of our branch offices across the country, the Cleveland branch receives more orders than any office.

REVIEW cont.

9. less
10. each other
11. any other
12. longer
13. types
14. OK
15. well ventilated

9. We evaluated both copiers carefully, and we decided to order the one that was <u>least</u> expensive.
10. Because they cooperated with <u>one another</u> so well, Rachel and Tony were able to complete their report two days ahead of schedule.
11. In only two years the new president of our company has expanded our overseas activities more than <u>any</u> president of this company.
12. Ollie and Myra have been with Warner Pharmaceuticals for several years, but I believe that Myra has been here <u>longest</u>.
13. No, these <u>type</u> of damages are not covered <u>by</u> your insurance.
14. Our three project managers always work closely with one another to meet their deadlines.
15. The room has no windows, but it is <u>well-ventilated</u>.

B. On a sheet of paper, correct any errors in the following sentences. Write *OK* for any sentence that has no error.

KEY

1. have
2. anyone else
3. its
4. OK
5. us
6. dozen
7. flown
8. he
9. manager's
10. analyses
11. whose
12. I
13. her
14. Willises
15. laying
16. she
17. I

1. There <u>has</u> been several promising applicants for the job.
2. Because of his seniority, Jesse receives a higher commission on net sales than <u>anyone</u> in our division.
3. The Sherman Stationery Company reported revenues of $2 million last year — <u>their</u> best year ever.
4. Whom has Harry selected to help him work on the landscaping, Bernie or her?
5. Ms. VanCleef wants <u>we</u> assistants to handle the details.
6. As of yesterday afternoon, we had received several <u>dozens</u> responses to the classified ad.
7. Has Felicia or Peggy <u>flew</u> to Denver before?
8. Although I am not sure, the person who called this morning could indeed have been <u>him</u>.
9. One <u>managers'</u> recommendation was to replace the company cars every three years.
10. Several of the <u>analysis</u> that were submitted were rather startling, in our opinion.
11. Please find out <u>who's</u> analysis this is.
12. Scot and <u>me</u> both enjoy working with the advertising agency on special promotions.
13. After you have met with Mr. Takeda and <u>she</u>, prepare a summary report of your discussion.
14. Deborah said that the <u>Willis's</u> were invited to the grand opening.
15. Next month we will begin <u>lying</u> our plans for the fall collection.
16. Two designers, Luis Morales and <u>her</u>, have been asked to prepare preliminary sketches.
17. Of course, Marcella and <u>myself</u> are convinced that we will scoop the other reporters.

REVIEW cont.

18. whom
19. has been
20. Messrs. Kennedy
    (*or* Mr. Kennedys)

18. At the moment, the candidate <u>who</u> Denise likes best of all is Larry Newman.
19. Joan <u>been</u> working in the human resources department ever since she was graduated from college.
20. If the <u>Messrs. Kennedys</u> are available, please confirm both the date and the time of our luncheon.

Editing Practice

Plurals and Possessives. Correct any errors in the use of plurals and possessives. Write *OK* for any sentence that has no error.

KEY
1. OK
2. Roger and Jane's
3. Nortons
4. it's
5. Terry's
6. their
7. accountant's
8. strikers
9. Sharon's
10. Smiths

1. My editor in chief's comment was, "Send a copy to the legal department for approval."
2. <u>Roger's and Jane's</u> newest yogurt stand will open on July 4 at the Westfield Mall.
3. Because Rose and Leslie Norton are well-known consultants in the nutrition field, the <u>Norton's</u> are certainly worth the high fee they charge.
4. Mr. Bellantoni does not think <u>its</u> worthwhile to spend so much money on a machine of limited use.
5. Elizabeth and I enjoyed <u>Terry</u> working with us on the color scheme.
6. As soon as you receive <u>there</u> tickets, please send them to the district managers.
7. Our <u>accountants'</u> brother is a well-respected builder in this community.
8. The <u>striker's</u> finally voted to accept the contract offer the city had originally presented.
9. <u>Sharon</u> managing the office has helped us to save time and to work much more efficiently.
10. If the <u>Smith's</u> accept the offer, our firm will then become the largest distributor of computer software in the state.

Using Your Word Processor. Proofread the following excerpt from a printout.

KEY
three-day
teamsters
coast-to-coast
Furthermore
well organized

A three day delay will cause us <u>teamster's</u> to take <u>coast to coast</u> action. <u>Furthmore,</u> let me assure you that we will be <u>well-organized.</u>

Homonyms, Anyone? Correct any errors in the use of homonyms—words that look or sound alike but have different meanings—in the following excerpt.

KEY
break
guerrilla *or* guerilla
seen, patience
right

Let's take a <u>brake</u> before these negotiations turn into <u>gorilla</u> warfare.

I've never <u>scene</u> Jim lose his <u>patients</u> before, but Fay simply will not admit that he is <u>rite.</u>

SECTION

2.8 *ADVERBS*

OBJECTIVES: **After completing Section 2.8, you should be able to:**

1. Discuss the ways in which adverbs are like adjectives and how these two parts of speech differ.
2. Explain how to identify the comparative and superlative forms of one-syllable adverbs and of adverbs ending in *ly*.
3. Name at least six conjunctive adverbs and six subordinating conjunctions and tell how each type is used.
4. Discuss several of the pitfalls of adverb use and ways to avoid them.
5. Define linking verbs and explain how recognizing linking verbs can help eliminate adjective and adverb confusion.

Like adjectives, adverbs modify or describe. You will see several similarities between adverbs and adjectives as you read this section, including some common confusions in their use.

IDENTIFYING ADVERBS

An *adverb* is a word that modifies an adjective, a verb, or another adverb. Adverbs answer questions such as "Why?" "When?" "Where?" "How?" "How much?" "To what extent?" Many adverbs are formed simply by adding *ly* to an adjective.

Adjective	Adverb
clear	clearly
happy	happily
perfect	perfectly
adequate	adequately
immediate	immediately

As you learned in Section 2.1, most words that end in *ly* are adverbs, but not all adverbs end in *ly*, as the following adverbs show:

also	never	soon
always	now	then
hard	often	there
here	quite	too
much	right	very

Note how adverbs are used in the following sentences.

Jack Alonzo arrived *late*. (Arrived when? Answer: *late*. The adverb *late* modifies the verb *arrived*.)

That is a *very* good data-processing program. (*How* good? *Very* good. The adverb *very* modifies the adjective *good*.)

She worked *quite* well under the pressure of the tight deadlines. (*How* well? *Quite* well. The adverb *quite* modifies another adverb, *well*.)

Some words can be used either as adjectives or as adverbs, depending on their position in the sentence.

He swallowed *hard* and then started to speak. (Here *hard* is an adverb that modifies the verb *swallow*.)

Henry complained that painting the garage was *hard* work. (Here *hard* is an adjective that modifies the noun *work*.)

COMPARISON ADVERBS

Adverbs can be compared in much the same way as adjectives. To indicate the comparative and superlative forms of a one-syllable adverb, add *er* or *est* to the positive form:

> fast, faster, fastest
> late, later, latest
> soon, sooner, soonest

For adverbs ending in *ly*, use *more* or *most* (or *less* or *least*):

quickly, more quickly, most quickly
quickly, less quickly, least quickly
confidently, more confidently, most confidently
skillfully, less skillfully, least skillfully

Certain adverbs form their comparative and superlative degrees by completely changing their forms:

> well, better, best
> badly, worse, worst
> much, more, most

CONJUNCTIVE ADVERBS

Conjunctive adverbs, as their name clearly tells, are adverbs that serve as conjunctions — words that *join*. These adverbs are also known as "transitional words."

accordingly	likewise	still	whereas
consequently	moreover	then	yet
furthermore	nevertheless	therefore	
however	otherwise	thus	

□SUGGESTION

Guide students through each example so that they see how each conjunctive adverb joins two independent clauses. Note that each independent clause can stand alone. Also point out the punctuation in each sentence.

These adverbs join two *independent* clauses, as shown in the following sentences:

Such fixed investments as bonds pay a higher interest rate; *moreover*, the investor receives regular payments of principal plus interest.

Our sales through June 30 are about 20 percent under budget; *however*, we expect to have a strong second half.

Note, again, that each sentence consists of two *independent* clauses joined by a conjunctive adverb.

ADVERBIAL CLAUSES

Subordinating conjunctions introduce *dependent* clauses that serve as adverbs modifying an adjective, verb, or adverb in the main clause. Here are some commonly used subordinating conjunctions:

after	before	unless
although	for	until
as	if	when
because	since	while

☑ REINFORCEMENT

Stress that these adverbial clauses cannot stand alone; they are dependent clauses. Read the clauses aloud to the class to dramatize that they are dependent.

Note the following examples of adverbial clauses introduced by subordinating conjunctions:

Cora Doyle will become the chief operating officer when Sidney retires. (The adverbial clause *when Sidney retires* modifies the verb *will become* in the main clause.)

Our new laptop computer will be successful *if we market it properly*. (The adverbial clause *if we market it properly* modifies the adjective *successful*.)

KEY

Review both correct and incorrect answers to make sure students understand the functions of simple adverbs, conjunctive adverbs, and subordinating conjunctions. Remind students that subordinating conjunctions always introduce adverbial clauses.

1. CA
2. SC
3. SA, SA, CA
4. SA, SC
5. SC, SA
6. SC
7. SC, SA

Checkup 1

Identify the italicized words in the following sentences by labeling each *simple adverb* (SA), *conjunctive adverb* (CA), or *subordinating conjunction* (SC).

1. The deadline for completion of the aircraft carrier is next Friday; our field supervisor, *therefore*, has approved our working overtime.
2. *If* you would like more information on this exciting new VCR programmer, call this toll-free number.
3. The new equipment works *quietly* and *efficiently*; it does not, *moreover*, require much maintenance.
4. Priscilla has been *very* busy *since* she opened her own accounting office.
5. *Since* Priscilla opened her own accounting office, she has been *very* busy.
6. We will review our progress on this prototype *when* Mr. Nielsen returns from New England.
7. *After* Raymond arrived *here*, everything changed.

8. Jack *always* works *diligently* on the end-of-year inventory, and he *usually* completes the inventory report *early*.

9. *Because* Toshi was busy, she stayed *here late* on Monday and Tuesday.

10. The client *specifically* indicated that she wanted spacious rooms; *accordingly*, our architects designed *very* large facilities.

PITFALLS

In speaking and writing, many people violate five principles of adverb use. These principles are neither tricky nor difficult, so you should be sure to avoid these pitfalls.

1. Position of the Adverb

Place an adverb as close as possible to the word that it modifies. Sometimes the meaning of a sentence can be changed by the position of the adverb.

Only Miss Berenson has a computer terminal in her office. (No one else has one.)

Miss Berenson has only a computer terminal in her office. (She has nothing else in her office, only a computer terminal.)

Miss Berenson has a computer terminal only in her office. (She has one nowhere else but in her office.)

2. Double Negative

Adverbs that have negative meanings (*scarcely, hardly, only, never,* and *but*) should not be used with other negatives.

Gregory *has scarcely* any money left in his R&D budget. (**Not:** Gregory *hasn't scarcely* . . . .)

On the noisy street, Pamela *could hardly* hear Frank. (**Not:** Pamela *couldn't hardly* . . . .)

Olivia *couldn't help suggesting* an alternative plan. (**Not:** Alicia *couldn't help but suggest* . . . .)

3. *Never or Not*?

Never and *not* are both adverbs, and both have negative meanings. *Not* expresses simple negation, but *never* means "not *ever*" (note the word *ever*). Use *never* only when an appropriately long time is intended.

Charlotte has *not* called me yet this week. (*Never* would be incorrect because the meaning "*not ever* . . . this week" would be wrong.)

I have *never* been to Greece. (*Never,* meaning "not ever," is correct in this sentence.)

4. *Where* for *That*

The subordinating conjunction *that* (not the conjunctive adverb *where*) should be used in expressions such as the following:

I read in a magazine *that* the Mellow Record Company is insolvent. (**Not:** I read in a magazine *where* . . . .)

We saw in the newspaper *that* the mayor has endorsed Claudia Olafson for governor. (**Not:** We saw in the newspaper *where*. . . . **But:** We saw the house *where* the famous writer once lived.)

5. *Badly* or *Worst Way* for *Very Much*

Too often, we hear people say *badly* or *in the worst way* when they really mean *very much*. Study these illustrations:

Janice said that she wanted a vacation *very much*. (**Not:** "wanted a vacation *badly*" or "wanted a vacation *in the worst way*.")

ADJECTIVE AND ADVERB CONFUSIONS

□SUGGESTION
Help students identify each action verb and each no-action verb. Their ability to do so quickly will determine their success in avoiding all the common adjective-adverb confusions.

Several adjective-adverb pairs cause special problems for writers and speakers. In the following pairs, the adjective is listed first.

Bad, Badly

Bad is an adjective; *badly* is an adverb.

Sara performs *badly* under pressure. (Performs how? *Badly*. The adverb *badly* modifies the action verb *performs*.)

The problem in selecting between *bad* and *badly* arises following no-action verbs:

Margaret felt (bad? badly?) when she heard about the layoffs. (Here, *felt* is a linking verb, not an action verb. The answer here will not modify the verb *felt* but the noun *Margaret*. Thus an adjective is required because an adverb cannot modify a noun. Margaret felt *bad*.)

The "being" verbs *am, is, are, was, were, be, been,* and *being* are all no-action, or "linking," verbs. In addition to these being verbs, verbs of sense such as *feel, appear, seem, look, sound, taste,* and *smell* can be used as no-action verbs. Remember that adjectives, not adverbs, must follow linking verbs.

Mr. Gunning was (angry? angrily?) when he heard about the delay. (The being verb *was* links the subject *Mr. Gunning* to the adjective *angry*. The verb *was* shows no action.)

Mr. Gunning appeared (angry? angrily?) when he heard about the delay. (Like *was*, the linking verb *appeared* shows no action; thus the adjective *angry* is correct.)

The refugees were (patient? patiently?). (Because the verb *were* indicates no action, the adjective *patient* is correct.)

The refugees seemed (patient? patiently?). (Like the no-action verb *were*, *seemed* links the noun *refugees* to the adjective *patient*; thus *patient* modifies *refugees*.)

Beware: Some of these verbs can also be used as action verbs. Analyze each sentence carefully.

Dr. Giordano felt carefully for a possible fracture. (Here, *felt* is an action verb; thus the adverb *carefully* modifies the verb *felt*.)

Real, Really; Sure, Surely

Real and *sure* are adjectives. Use the *ly* endings to remind you that *really* and *surely* are adverbs. In the following examples, note that you can substitute the adverb *very* or *certainly* whenever *really* or *surely* is correct.

Suzanne and Manny were (real? really?) dedicated to helping children with AIDS. ("*Very* dedicated" makes sense. The adverb *really* is correct.)

Paula (sure? surely?) was smart to exercise that stock option when the price was half its present price. ("*Certainly* was" makes sense. The adverb *surely* is correct.)

Good, Well

Good is an adjective, and *well* is an adverb. The adjective *good* can modify nouns and pronouns; the adverb *well* can modify adjectives and verbs.

Van generally prepares *good* presentations. (The adjective *good* modifies the noun *reports*.)

Van generally prepares presentations *well*. (The adverb *well* modifies the verb *prepares*. Prepares presentations how? Prepares *well*.)

Exception: Well can also be an adjective, *but only when referring to personal health*.

Because Amanda did not feel *well*, she left the office early. (Here, *well* is an adjective referring to a person's health.)

Remember the term *well-being* and you'll be sure to recall that *well* is an adjective only when it refers to health.

Some, Somewhat

Some is an adjective; *somewhat* is an adverb. To use *somewhat* correctly, test to be sure that you can substitute the phrase *a little bit*.

As we predicted, Ms. Feingold was (some? somewhat?) critical of the new training program. (Does "a little bit critical" make sense? Yes—thus *somewhat* is correct.)

As we predicted, Ms. Feingold had (some? somewhat?) criticisms of the new training program. (Does "a little bit criticisms" make sense? No—thus the adjective *some* is correct.)

Most, Almost

Most is an adjective, the superlative of *much* or *many*, as in *much, more, most*. *Almost* is an adverb meaning "not quite" or "very nearly."

(Most? Almost?) administrative assistants hope to become administrators. (Because "very nearly administrative assistants" makes no sense, *almost* cannot be correct. "*Most* administrative assistants" is correct.)

Jaclyn brought (most? almost?) enough hard hats for everyone at the work site. ("Very nearly enough hard hats" *does* make sense. *Almost* is correct.)

Checkup 2

On a sheet of paper, correct any errors in the following sentences. Write *OK* if a sentence has no errors.

1. Cynthia was <u>some</u> surprised by the news of her promotion.
2. Most of us in the real estate sales community found the reports <u>real</u> distressing.
3. After almost two years, the development plan has worked out very well.
4. Of course, she was <u>sure</u> justified in her request for equal salary.
5. Because you don't feel <u>good</u>, James, we suggest that you stay at home tomorrow.
6. Maria appeared <u>angrily</u> at the idea of closing the clinic.
7. Because of the recent problems, we were somewhat hesitant to discuss this sensitive issue.
8. Because this laptop computer is on sale, it is a <u>real</u> good bargain.
9. Needless to say, she and I felt <u>badly</u> when we heard that Mrs. Jordan was retiring.
10. Because she was rushed, Shula sketched the building badly.

SECTION REVIEW

Practical Application

A. On a sheet of paper, correct any adverb errors in the following sentences. Write *OK* if a sentence has no error.

1. All of us were glad when we read in the newspaper <u>where</u> the proposed amendment had been defeated.
2. Although this dinner special does smell <u>deliciously</u>, I really am not very hungry right now.

3. Only Harris and I
4. surely
5. frequently
6. did not tell
7. very much
8. OK
9. somewhat
10. bitter
11. clearly
12. bad
13. well
14. has scarcely
15. really
16. very much
17. well
18. did not receive
19. really
20. well

3. Harris and I <u>only</u> know about the planned expansion; no one else knows about it yet.

4. In our opinion, retaining our present retail prices should <u>sure</u> work very well during the forthcoming holiday sales.

5. Because Tim has been late so <u>frequent</u>, Ms. Gordon has spoken with him about the importance of arriving on time.

6. No, Sally, Mr. Lopez <u>never told</u> me that the Nesses left early this morning.

7. We immediately noticed that Louis had fallen and that he needed help <u>in the worst way</u>.

8. Elisabeth appeared very confident as she accepted the Thomas Hart Quality Award.

9. As you know, our sales decreased <u>some</u> during the summer months.

10. Did you notice that this water tastes very <u>bitterly</u>?

11. Because our offices are so close to the harbor we can <u>clear</u> hear the tug boats.

12. Needless to say, we felt very <u>badly</u> when we heard of your misfortune.

13. Follow these guidelines, Dolores, to make sure that you prepare your speech <u>good</u>.

14. The proposal that David and Francine submitted <u>hasn't scarcely</u> one new idea for our convention exhibit.

15. "We have," John said, "a <u>real</u> good chance of winning the contract."

16. According to Jackie, Mr. Campbell wants to buy her award-winning photograph <u>in the worst way</u>.

17. Yes, I do believe that <u>his suggestion</u> will work out very <u>good</u>.

18. Vic <u>never received</u> the samples from our San Francisco office, although the package was mailed more than a week ago.

19. As we expected, all the brokers are <u>real</u> concerned about the possible change in the commission schedule.

20. The credit for preparing the annual report so <u>good</u> must go to Marion.

KEY

1. did not complete
2. almost
3. has but
4. are

B. Correct any errors in the following sentences. Write *OK* if a sentence has no error.

1. Gabriella's estimates were due last Monday, but because she was so busy, she <u>never completed</u> them.

2. According to Peter's supervisor, Peter works <u>most</u> as quickly as Eleanor.

3. Last year, Elaine had three assistants in her department; since the budget cutbacks, however, she <u>hasn't but</u> one assistant.

4. Here <u>is</u> all the nuts and bolts that you asked for, Ms. Hammond.

5. I
6. Bradleys
7. well
8. have
9. has been
10. those (*or* these)
11. Where are
12. well
13. carefully
14. surely
15. kinds
16. he
17. I
18. There are
19. babies
20. Walshes

5. Of course, Barry and <u>myself</u> will be happy to help if you get extremely busy.
6. As you can well imagine, the <u>Bradleys'</u> were really pleased to learn that the interest on their <u>investments</u> is tax-free.
7. Mr. Flax sent Jeffrey to the infirmary because he wasn't feeling very <u>good</u>.
8. Neither the two managers nor the four assistants, in our opinion, <u>has</u> the time to devote to this extra work.
9. Because Joanne <u>been</u> dedicating all her time to the upcoming annual sales meeting, she has hired part-time help.
10. Seth and Donna will help you process all <u>them</u> invoices if you fall behind, Martin.
11. <u>Where's</u> the keys to the storeroom and the supply closet?
12. Sabrina has been doing very <u>good</u> since she was transferred to the accounting department.
13. Be sure to focus <u>careful</u> so that you get a crisp, sharp picture.
14. Carla <u>sure</u> does a superb job of handling customer complaints.
15. Are these <u>kind</u> of floppy disks available through our purchasing department?
16. Perhaps the two best adjusters in our office are Janet and <u>him</u>.
17. Of course, if Dana and <u>me</u> are selected to attend the convention, we will be really delighted.
18. <u>There's</u> about three or four ways to set up this trust fund.
19. The <u>babys</u> in the new formula advertisement must look healthy and happy.
20. Only the <u>Walsh's</u> have requested specific changes in the standard contract.

Editing Practice

Proofreading for Accuracy. Proofreading accurately requires more than spelling and grammar expertise — it requires accuracy in *every* detail. Check the following excerpt carefully. Does it have any errors?

The following discount schedule on purchases will become effective on <u>April 31</u>:

Over	Discount
$ 500	0.5%
1,000	0.75%
1,500	1.0%
2,000	1.25%
5,000	1.5%
10,000	1.75%
20,000	20.%

KEY
April 30
2.0%

REVIEW cont.

Using Your Word Processor. You are proofreading the following draft of a memorandum that you wrote. Before you print a copy, are there any errors that must be corrected?

The Office Trianing Center has recieved an overwhelming response to our recent proposal to add a basic programming course to our list of after-work course offerings. Begining on January 15, therefore, we will offer a variety of new programming courses; please see the enclosed catalog for a complete listing and time schedule.

If you are intrested in these new programing courses (or any other courses, for that matter), please complete the registration form and send it to the Training Center as soon as possible. Registration for each course will be limited to the first 20 aplicants. However, extra sections of the most poplar courses may be added to the shedule.

2.9 *PREPOSITIONS*

OBJECTIVES: After completing Section 2.9, you should be able to:

1. State the function of prepositions.
2. Explain why certain prepositions are used with certain words even though no rule is involved. Suggest the best ways to learn these combinations.
3. Identify several pitfalls in the use of prepositions, and cite the rules for avoiding those pitfalls.

Such prepositions as *for*, *in*, *of*, *on*, and *to* are used so often that we generally pay no attention to them. In order to avoid some common preposition errors, however, we must pay attention to those rules presented in this section.

☑ REINFORCEMENT

Ask students to find the object of the preposition in each phrase given in the examples. Point out the modifiers such as *the*, *our*, *new*.

IDENTIFYING PREPOSITIONS

A *preposition* is a connecting word. It is always connected to a noun or a pronoun, and the preposition combined with that noun or pronoun makes up a *prepositional phrase*. Note the following commonly used prepositions and some sample prepositional phrases.

Prepositions			Prepositional Phrases
about	but*	off	*off* the shelf
above	by	on	*above* the sink
after	except	over	*after* our mediation
among	for	to	*to* the new restaurant
at	from	under	*from* Gary and Mona
before	in	up	*before* your first lesson
below	into	upon	*into* the fray
beside	like	until	*like* that newspaper
between	of	with	*with* my partner

But is a preposition only when it means "except." In other cases, *but* is a conjunction.

The noun or pronoun that follows the preposition in a phrase is the *object* of the preposition. The phrase may include modifiers, for example, *new* in *to the new restaurant* modifies *restaurant*, which is the object of the preposition *to*. Also, the phrase may have compound objects, as in *from Gary and Mona*.

Because prepositional phrases often interrupt the subject and the verb in a sentence, your ability to make subjects and verbs agree will sometimes depend on your ability to identify prepositional phrases. Note the following:

The word processing operators *in this department* are reviewing the new rules carefully. (The prepositional phrase *in this department* separates the subject *operators* from the verb *are*. A careless speaker, therefore, may incorrectly say "department *is*," which is wrong, of course.)

One executive *on both boards* has agreed to serve as the liaison. (The prepositional phrase *on both boards* separates the subject *executive* from the verb *has agreed*.)

ℹ INFORMATION
Note that *in this department* serves as an adjectival phrase; it describes the noun *operators*. Likewise, *on both boards* describes the noun *executive* and also serves as an adjectival phrase.

Checkup 1

KEY
Prepositional phrases are underscored. In sentence 6, point out the compound object *you and me*, stressing the objective case *me* in this construction. Many people would incorrectly say "between you and *I*."

Identify the prepositions and the prepositional phrases in the following sentences.

1. The main reason for the delay is that Jill is still on the telephone.
2. Most of the invoices that Laura laid on my desk have been approved and sent to the Accounting Department.
3. Only one of the women indicated that she was dissatisfied with the new schedule.
4. Because Mr. Sanders was in a rush, Larry drove him to the airport.
5. On my desk are the instructions that you will need.
6. Between you and me, I do not believe that investing in that stock was a smart idea.
7. Nathalie went into the conference room, I think, with her assistant.
8. The final decision on the site of the midtown helicopter landing pad will be made by the planning board.

WORDS REQUIRING SPECIFIC PREPOSITIONS

Through years of use, certain expressions are now considered "correct," even though there may be no rule or logical reason to make them correct. Such usage, called "idiomatic usage," governs many expressions in our language. The use of certain prepositions with certain words is idiomatic. Long-accepted use has made it correct to use these prepositions, as in the following examples:

abhorrence *of*
abhorrent *to*
abide *by* a decision
abide with a person
abound *in* or *with*
accompanied *by* (attended by a person)
accompanied *with* (attended by something)
acquit *of*
adapted *for* (made over for)
adapted *from* a work
adapted *to* (adjusted to)
affinity *between*
agree *to* a proposal
agree *with* someone
agreeable *to* (*with* is permissible)
angry *at* or *about* a thing or condition
angry *with* a person
attend *to* (listen)
attend *upon* (wait on)
beneficial *to*
bestow *upon*
buy *from*
compare *to* the mirror image (assert a likeness)
compare *with* the reverse side (analyze for similarities or differences)
compliance *with*
comply *with*
confer *on* or *upon* (give to)
confer *with* (talk to)
confide *in* (place confidence in)
confide *to* (entrust to)
conform *to* (be in conformity *to* or *with*)
consist *in* (exist in)
consist *of* (be made up of)
convenient *for* (suitable for, easy for)
convenient *to* (near)

conversant *with*
correspond *to* or *with* (match; agree with)
correspond *with* (exchange letters)
credit *for*
deal *in* goods or services
deal *with* someone
depend or dependent *on* (but independent *of*)
different *from* (not *than* or *to*)
disappointed *in* or *with*
discrepancy *between* two things
discrepancy *in* one thing
dispense *with*
employ *for* a purpose
employed *at* a stipulated salary
employed *in*, *on*, or *upon* a work or business
enter *at* a given point
enter *in* a record
enter *into* (become a party to)
enter *into* or *upon* (start)
exception *to* a statement
familiarize *with*
foreign *to* (preferred *to* *from*)
identical *with*
independent *of* (not *from*)
inferior or superior *to*
need *of* or *for*
part *from* (take leave of)
part *with* (relinquish)
plan or planning *to* (not *on*)
profit *by*
in regard *to*
with regard *to*
as regards
retroactive *to* (not *from*)
speak *to* (tell something to a person)
speak *with* (discuss with)
wait *for* a person, a train, an event
wait *on* a customer, a guest

The idiomatic expressions that are used (and misused) most often are given special attention below. Be sure to learn to use these expressions correctly.

Agree With, Agree To

GLOBAL NOTE

Explain that doing business in a foreign language may be more difficult than students realize. Using an interpreter slows down the communication process because each speaker must pause to wait for the translation.

Use *agree with* when the object of the preposition is a person or idea; use *agree to* when the object is not a person or idea.

Does Henry *agree with* Mr. Vickers on the need to increase our discount to wholesalers? (Because the object of the preposition is a person, the preposition *with* is correct.)

Yes, Henry *agrees to* the proposal to increase our discount to wholesalers. (Here, the object of the preposition is *proposal;* because the object is not a person or idea, *agree to* is correct.)

Angry With, Angry At

Use *angry with* when the object of the preposition is a person; use *angry at* or *about* when the object is not a person.

Glenn appeared to be *angry with* Jacob because of the delay in shipment. (*With* is correct because its object is a person, *Jacob.*)

Glenn appeared to be *angry at* the delay in shipment. (Now the object of the preposition is not a person; thus *angry at* or *about* is correct.)

Part From, Part With

Part from means "to take leave of"; *part with* means "to relinquish," "to give up."
Part from is generally used when the object of the preposition is a person. *Part with* is generally used when the object is not a person.

As soon as we *part from* Tony Adams at the exhibition hall, we will return to the hotel. (*Part from* a person.)

Although we certainly appreciate the timesaving features of the new equipment, we hate to *part with* our familiar old machines. (*Part with*, meaning "to relinquish," "to give up.")

Discrepancy In, Discrepancy Between

Use *discrepancy in* when the object of the preposition is singular; use *discrepancy between* when the object specifically denotes *two* in number.

I checked this chart carefully, and I found no *discrepancy in* it, Ms. Williams. (Note that *one* chart is mentioned.)

Compare these two graphs carefully; then let me know if you find any *discrepancy between* the two. (Note that *two* graphs are mentioned.)

In Regard To, With Regard To, As Regards

The three terms *in regard to*, *with regard to*, and *as regards* are equally correct, but be sure to note that only the word *regard* (not *regards*) can be used in the phrases *in regard to* and *with regard to*.

Mark has already consulted Mr. Johanson (in? with? as?) regard to the changes in the agenda. (Either *in* or *with* is correct.)

(In? With? As?) regards the changes in the agenda, please be sure to consult Mr. Johanson. (Only *as* is correct—*as regards*.)

Note: In many cases, you can simplify and improve your sentence by substituting the word *about* for *in regard to*, *with regard to*, or *as regards*.

Mark has already consulted Mr. Johanson *about* the changes in the agenda.

Different From, Identical With, Plan To, Retroactive To

Memorize the correct prepositions that go with these phrases so that you will use them properly.

> different *from* (not different *than*)
> identical *with* (not identical *to*)
> plan *to* (not plan *on*)
> retroactive *to* (not retroactive *from*)

Checkup 2

On a sheet of paper, correct any errors in the following sentences. Write *OK* for any sentence that has no error.

1. When she discovered that the negatives had been carelessly handled, Ms. Cutter was angry at the messenger.
2. Rosemary plans on opening her own shoe store when she raises enough money to do so.
3. Of course, I was surprised to find several discrepancies in the budget he submitted.
4. We have already spoken with our assistants in regards to the need to tabulate the answers on each response form carefully.
5. Sharon said that the most difficult aspect of leaving our organization was parting from all her good friends.
6. Dennis methodically explained how the new fax machine is different than the old one.
7. Sue and I proofread both statistical tables; fortunately, we found no discrepancy in the two of them.

8. OK
9. to
10. with

8. No, I frankly do not agree with Louis concerning the need to upgrade our desktop publishing software.
9. According to the union leader, the contract will surely be retroactive <u>from</u> January 15.
10. Although this year's model looks different, it is really identical <u>to</u> last year's copier.

PITFALLS

When to use *between* and when to use *among* are among the preposition choices that trap many writers and speakers. Other pitfalls concern (1) adding unnecessary prepositions and (2) omitting prepositions that *are* necessary. Study the following to avoid the most common preposition pitfalls.

Between, Among

Use *between* when referring to *two* persons, places, or things, and use *among* when referring to three or more.

> The taste-test responses were divided *between* Marjorie and Horton. (Between two people.)

> The responses to our packaging were divided *among* our three free-lance tabulators. (Among three tabulators.)

Between may also be used to express a relationship of one thing to each of several other things on a one-to-one-basis.

> A separate agreement was signed *between* the parent company and each of the franchises.

Beside, Besides

Beside means "by the side of"; *besides* means "in addition to."

> Yes, the man seated *beside* Ms. McMann is Reginald Boonton, our guest speaker. ("By the side of" Ms. McMann.)

> Do you know who is scheduled to speak *besides* Mr. Boone? ("In addition to" Mr. Boone.)

Inside, Outside

Do not use the preposition *of* after *inside* or *outside*. When referring to time, use *within*, not *inside of*.

> The conference room door is the first door *inside* the main entrance. (Not *inside of*.)

> We expect to have our budgets completed *within* the week. (Not *inside of*.)

LIVING LANGUAGE

"I, for one, find the options for oral English as against written English quite useful—indeed, invaluable. Let oral English be the proving ground on which some succeed and others are slaughtered. . . ."

—Leo Rosten

All, Both

Use *of* after *all* or *both* only when *all* or *both* refers to a pronoun. Omit *of* if either word refers to a noun.

All the protesters blocked the clinic entrance. (*Of* is not needed.)

All *of* them were eventually arrested. (*Of* is required here.)

At, To; In, Into

At and *in* denote position; *to* and *into* signify motion.

Vivian arrived *at* the stockholders' meeting and immediately went *to* the podium. (*At* for position; *to* for motion.)

They went *into* the hotel and set up the display *in* the main ballroom. (*Into* for motion; *in* for position.)

Note: When either *at* or *in* refers to a place, use *in* for larger places and *at* for smaller places.

Edgar lives *in* Mercer County and teaches *at* the local community college. (*In Mercer County*, the larger place; *at the local community college*, the smaller place.)

Behind, Not In Back Of

Use *behind*, not *in back of*. *In front of*, however, is correct.

Until the audience arrives, place the microphones *behind*, not *in front of*, the curtain.

From, Off

From is generally used with persons; *off* is used with things. (*Off* is used with persons only when something on the person is physically being lifted away.) Never use *of* or *from* after *off*.

Get some extra staplers *from* Barbara. (Not *off Barbara*.)

After five minutes, take the cold compresses *off* your leg. (Something is physically being lifted away.)

Let's take these coffee cups *off* the conference room table. (Not *off of* the conference room table.)

Where, Not Where . . . At or Where . . . To

Adding *at* or *to* to *where* is an illiteracy.

No, I do not know *where* Dr. Torres is. (Not *is at*.)

Where did John go? (Not *go to*.)

Help, Not Help From

Do not use the word *from* after the verb *help*.

Although we wanted to leave early, we could not *help* asking Mr. Bart some questions. (Not *help from asking.*)

Opposite, Not Opposite To

Do not use the word *to* after *opposite*.

The Fifth Avenue bus stop is directly *opposite* that high-rise apartment building. (Not *opposite to.*)

Like, Not Like For

Omit the word *for* after *like*.

We told Ms. Adams that we would *like* her to visit the low-income housing project. (Not *like for.*)

Checkup 3

KEY
1. omit *at*
2. omit *from*
3. omit *to*
4. OK
5. into
6. omit *of*
7. among
8. into
9. beside
10. omit *of*
11. omit *of*
12. omit *for*

Correct any preposition errors in the following sentences. Write *OK* for any sentence that has no error.

1. I'm sure that the Director of Sales and Marketing knows where the two of them are <u>at</u>.
2. We know that Melanie cannot help <u>from</u> singing her theme song for the troops.
3. Please call his office to find out where Marvin has gone <u>to</u>.
4. I believe that the new computer store is opposite the railroad station.
5. Perhaps you should go <u>in</u> the new hotel to inspect its conference facilities.
6. We may attend these seminars at no charge if we attend outside <u>of</u> working hours.
7. The entire award of $10,000 was divided <u>between</u> Fred, Rosemary, and Vincent.
8. When we arrived at the resort, we immediately pulled <u>in</u> the garage.
9. Is the man seated <u>besides</u> Andrew the new sales representative you spoke of?
10. Let's leave all <u>of</u> these cassette recorders in the van.
11. Both <u>of</u> the police officers received awards for their part in organizing the community's Young Athletes program.
12. Peter's mother would like <u>for</u> him to be more ambitious.

REVIEW

Practical Application

A. On a sheet of paper, correct any errors in the following sentences. Write *OK* for any sentence that has no error.

1. Do you know yet what Mr. Dexter plans to do in regards to the insurance claims relating to the Johnstown flood?
2. We now know that the directions for assembling the workstation were inside of the package.
3. Beside all the department heads, the regional managers should receive a courtesy copy.
4. Have you asked Nancy where Roberta went to?
5. Tell all the visitors to park their cars in back of the building.
6. Leo and Agnes will take all of this equipment off of the conference room table.
7. Linda's recommendations were virtually identical to the recommendations we received from our branch office managers.
8. Of course, we would very much like for Mrs. Russo to be our guest at the banquet.
9. Ellen Maas plans on working next Saturday to prepare her presentation to the zoning board.
10. Unfortunately, Mr. Smyth, your name was taken off of our mailing list in error.
11. As a matter of fact, T. J. was angry at the vice president until he realized the reason for the transfer.
12. Marcia carefully proofread the statistical report to ensure that there was no discrepancy in it.
13. The restaurant that you mentioned is opposite to the library on West 79th Street.
14. Helen dislikes parting from the special pieces in her collection.
15. Who besides Raul will be transferred to the Chicago office?
16. Most of us could not help from wondering why the advertising manager was so enthusiastic about the Fruitfizz campaign.
17. If we ship the cars Tuesday, you should receive them inside of two weeks.
18. As all the invoices are received, they are divided among the three clerks in the accounting department for processing.
19. With regards to the possibility of staff cutbacks, I have been asked to make no comments to the press.
20. In terms of strength, this new plastic is no different than this metal.

B. On a sheet of paper, correct any errors in the following sentences. Write *OK* for any sentence that has no error.

1. A number of complaints about this new model has been received by our product manager.
2. Yes, Jodie generally works longer hours than me.

REVIEW cont.

3. who's *or* who is
4. whom
5. has its
6. Doesn't *or* Does not
7. me
8. is
9. these *or* those
10. to
11. is
12. whom
13. Ferraros
14. OK
15. really
16. well
17. she
18. his or her
19. I
20. with

3. Do you know <u>whose</u> in charge of the Maintenance Department?
4. Al Cardenas, <u>who</u> you met at the luncheon last Thursday, has been named head of the new division.
5. Each of our many branch offices <u>have their</u> own conference room.
6. <u>Don't</u> Phyllis want to attend the first session on Monday morning?
7. Don't Bernice and Alan want you and <u>I</u> to help them with their new feature film?
8. Among the stores that we manage <u>are</u> The Computer Wizard in the Edmonton Mall.
9. I think that you should order more of <u>them</u> sizes, because they're very popular.
10. Do these specifications conform <u>with</u> international standards?
11. The inventor of these two devices <u>are</u> revolutionizing traditional mousetraps.
12. If you were the head of this department, <u>who</u> would you select to be your assistant?
13. Have you already asked the <u>Ferraro's</u> whether they plan to vacation in Hawaii again this year?
14. In your opinion, who is the best sales representative in our company, Denise or he?
15. Teresa always does a <u>real</u> good job on the inventory reports.
16. Perhaps the reason Albert doesn't feel <u>good</u> is that he has poor eating habits.
17. Janet thinks that Lance writes better copy than <u>her</u>.
18. Every executive in the country will surely improve <u>their</u> management skills by reading Paul Drinker's informative new book.
19. Professor Stoddard said that you and <u>me</u> will receive a good raise because of our excellent work all year long.
20. No, I certainly was not angry <u>at</u> Mark for his blunt remarks about the quality of the exhibit.

Editing Practice

Using Business Vocabulary. From the list below, select the word that best completes each of the sentences. On a piece of paper, write the corresponding letter of the correct word for each sentence.

a. comptroller	d. hesitant	g. miscellaneous	j. unscrupulous
b. cumulative	e. inexhaustible	h. monopolize	
c. enumerate	f. irreparable	i. negligible	

1. At this morning's meeting we discussed _____ topics.
2. The insurance adjuster agreed that the damage is _____, and therefore she will authorize payment of our claim.
3. Michelle appeared somewhat _____ to discuss her plans to reorganize the warehouse space.

KEY
1. g. miscellaneous
2. f. irreparable
3. d. hesitant

REVIEW cont.

4. i. negligible
5. h. monopolize
6. c. enumerate
7. b. cumulative
8. a. comptroller
9. j. unscrupulous
10. e. inexhaustible

KEY
Students' answers will vary.

4. Fortunately, the amount of damage to the books was _____.
5. The instructor should not allow any one student to _____ the discussion.
6. To make this agenda clearer, _____ the topics in list form.
7. The first monthly column lists January sales; each succeeding column lists _____ sales for the preceding month.
8. Mr. Mobley, the _____ of our company, completed the requirements for an MBA degree in June.
9. She wrote a best-selling exposé of excessive profiteering by _____ companies during the oil shortage.
10. Our supply of this metal is virtually _____, but mining it is very expensive.

Writing Sentences. Each of the following words is a "must" for your vocabulary and your spelling lists. Do you know the meaning of each word? Can you spell each one correctly?

Write a sentence using each word correctly.

1. accommodate
2. campaign
3. dissatisfied
4. equivalent
5. exorbitant
6. guarantee
7. necessary
8. omission
9. potential
10. questionnaire

2.10 *CONJUNCTIONS*

OBJECTIVES: After completing Section 2.10, you should be able to:

1. Describe the three types of conjunctions and give examples of the use of each type.
2. Identify the pitfalls in the use of conjunctions and explain how to avoid those pitfalls.
3. Discuss ways of ensuring parallel structure with coordinating and correlative conjunctions.

As you will recall from Section 2.1, a *conjunction* is a word that is used to *connect* words, phrases, or clauses within a sentence.

The printer *and* the software are included in this low, low price. (In this sentence, the conjunction *and* joins the words *printer* and *software.*)

You may get a copy from my office *or* from the library. (The conjunction *or* joins two phrases, *from my office* and *from the library*.)

Wanda wants to buy this laser printer, *but* she is waiting for a sale. (The conjunction *but* joins the two main clauses.)

Writing varied sentences and punctuating them correctly become much simpler once you have mastered the uses of conjunctions. This section presents three different kinds of conjunctions, discusses the most common pitfalls in using conjunctions, and then considers parallel structure, an important topic that is closely related to conjunction use.

CLASSIFICATION OF CONJUNCTIONS

Three conjunction types are discussed below: *coordinating*, *correlative*, and *subordinating conjunctions*. As you will see, coordinating and correlative conjunctions connect two or more items of equal rank. Subordinating conjunctions, however, connect a subordinate clause to a main clause.

Coordinating Conjunctions

❏ **SUGGESTION**
At first, students may need help identifying the items that the conjunctions join. Help them find the words, phrases, and clauses in the example.

The four coordinating conjunctions — *and, but, or,* and *nor* — are very commonly used. Note that they connect only *like* elements of grammar: two or more words, two or more phrases, or two or more clauses.

Breakfast *and* dinner are included in the total price. (The conjunction *and* connects two words, *breakfast* and *dinner*.)

Breakfast, lunch, *and* dinner are included in the total price. (Here the conjunction *and* joins *three* words.)

Karen has been on the telephone *or* in meetings most of the day. (The conjunction *or* joins two prepositional phrases, *on the telephone* and *in meetings*.)

Mr. Marshall planned to spend the week at the convention, *but* he couldn't get a hotel room. (The conjunction *but* connects two independent, or main, clauses.)

Correlative Conjunctions

❏ **SUGGESTION**
Discuss with students the slightly different emphasis that the correlatives provide. For example, the meaning of the last example is "Henry intends to finish the report, *and* he plans to publish it. However, the use of *not only . . . but also* gives the sentence more emphasis than *and* provides. The word order "but he also plans" is correct.

Correlative conjunctions are *pairs* of conjunctions that are regularly used together to connect like elements. (Note, again, that both coordinating and correlative conjunctions connect *like* elements only.) The most commonly used correlative conjunctions are these:

> both . . . and
> either . . . or
> neither . . . nor
> not only . . . but also
> whether . . . or

Like coordinating conjunctions, correlatives connect words, phrases, or clauses—like elements of grammar.

Not only Bob *but also* Martha will take part in the ribbon-cutting ceremony next Wednesday. (Here the correlatives *not only . . . but also* connect two words, *Bob* and *Martha.*)

Henry has been working on his MBA thesis *not only* during the day *but also* long into the night. (Two phrases, *during the day* and *into the night,* are joined.)

Not only does Henry intend to finish his report, *but* he *also* plans to publish it. (Here two clauses are connected.)

Subordinating Conjunctions

Subordinating conjunctions join clauses of unequal rank. A subordinating conjunction introduces a subordinate (or dependent) clause and connects it to a main (or independent) clause.

Although we lowered the list price, sales failed to show a significant increase for the quarter. (*Although* is a subordinating conjunction, and it introduces the subordinate clause *although we lowered the list price.* Further, *although* connects this subordinate clause to the main clause.)

Ask Ms. DePalma for a registration form *if* you plan to apply for this course. (The subordinating conjunction *if* introduces the subordinate clause *if you plan to apply for this course* and connects this clause to the main clause.)

Study the following list of commonly used subordinating conjunctions so that you will be able to identify subordinate clauses.

after	before	provided that	when
although	even if	since	whenever
as	for	so that	where
as if	how	than	wherever
as soon as	if	that	whether
as though	in case that	unless	while
because	in order that	until	why

Checkup 1

On a sheet of paper, write the conjunctions used in the following sentences. Label each conjunction "coordinating," "correlative," or "subordinating."

1. Barry will discuss his findings as soon as he returns from his mission.
2. While Ms. Bernardo was on medical leave, her transfer was approved by the president of the company.
3. Have you already sent in both the completed registration form and your check?

4. coordinating
5. subordinating
6. subordinating
7. correlative
8. subordinating
9. correlative
10. coordinating

4. Our attorney <u>and</u> the president of Pennsylvania Steel carefully reviewed the price-fixing allegations.
5. Order today <u>if</u> you would like to receive this handsome ornament in time for the holidays.
6. You will save an additional 5 percent by enclosing your payment now, <u>unless</u> you prefer to be billed at a later date.
7. Frances, do you know <u>whether</u> Sergio <u>or</u> Larry has called this client yet?
8. Yes, I'm sure <u>that</u> Larry called him already.
9. Please ask <u>either</u> Marvin <u>or</u> Louise to investigate the cause of the accident.
10. You may pay 12 monthly installments, <u>or</u> you may save $100 by paying the entire amount before January 31.

PITFALLS

The following discussion focuses on the major conjunction pitfalls—mainly (1) choosing a conjunction that does not accurately convey the meaning intended and (2) choosing a preposition when a conjunction is needed.

But or *And*?

The conjunction *but* provides a contrast while *and* simply joins two elements. Use *but* when a contrast is intended.

The difference in price between the two models is minimal, *but* only one model is energy-efficient. (*But* for contrast.)

Who, *Which*, or *That*?

Use *who* to refer to persons and *which* to refer to objects. Never say or write *and who* or *and which*.

Send an invitation to Harry Pierson, *who* is the new research director. (*Who* refers to a person.)

We were instructed to send all recommendations to the Finance Committee, *which* is responsible for all capital-expenditure decisions. (*Which* refers to an object.)

That may be used to refer to persons, objects, or animals.

The speaker *that* you heard is Edwin Tobin, a well-known business lecturer. (*That* refers to a person. Note that *whom* could also have been used, of course.)

One process *that* you will find interesting is four-color separation. (Here, *that* refers to an object.)

The racehorse *that* Hilary sold has been insured for more than $1,000,000. (*That* refers to an animal.)

Since or *Because,* **Not** *Being That*

There is no such conjunction as *being that*. Use *since* or *because* instead.

Because I could not leave the house all day, Richie stopped by with a copy of the long-awaited report. (*Because,* not *Being that.*)

"The Reason Is That"; "Pretend That"

Do not say or write "the reason is *because*" and "pretend *like*." Instead, say "the reason is *that*" and "pretend *that*."

The reason for the sudden strike, according to informed sources, is *that* the company has threatened to lay off 1,000 workers. (Not *reason . . . is because.*) Of course, we cannot pretend *that* sales are healthy. (Not *pretend like.*)

Unless, **Not** *Without* or *Except*

Without and *except* are prepositions, and a preposition always introduces a prepositional phrase. Yet many writers and speakers incorrectly use these prepositions as substitutes for the subordinating conjunction *unless*. (*Remember:* A prepositional phrase consists of a preposition plus its noun or pronoun object and any modifiers.)

You cannot return this application *without* Ms. Ford's approval. (This sentence is correct. *Without Ms. Ford's approval* is a prepositional phrase: *approval* is the object of the preposition *without*, and *Ms. Ford's* is a modifier.)

You cannot return this application *unless* Ms. Ford approves it. (Again, this sentence is correct. The subordinating conjunction *unless* introduces a clause. An error occurs, however, when people incorrectly say or write *without Ms. Ford approves it.* The preposition *without* cannot introduce a clause.)

As, As If, As Though, **Not** *Like*

Remember that *like* is a preposition ("a car *like* mine") or a verb ("I *like* this model"). It is *not* a conjunction. Therefore, do not use *like* when *as, as if,* or *as though* is intended.

Celine acted *as if* she wanted to go home. (*As if,* not *like.*)

Checkup 2

Correct any errors in the following sentences. Write *OK* for any sentence that has no error.

1. She told Bill not to sit around <u>like</u> he has no work to do.
2. Please make sure that Ms. Ardell doesn't leave <u>without</u> she signs these letters.

3. but
4. that
5. who *or* that
6. as if *or* as though
7. unless
8. OK
9. as if *or* as though
10. unless

3. Ella's new job is not very glamorous, <u>and</u> she is really enjoying the challenge it presents.
4. According to the newspaper reports, the main reason for the sudden increase in oil prices is <u>because</u> OPEC has curtailed production.
5. Anne recommended several talented artists <u>which</u> have studios in the area.
6. Charles said, "It seems <u>like</u> artists have surrounded us."
7. No, Jonas, do not send this sample to Mr. Martin <u>without</u> you get official authorization from your supervisor.
8. Arlene was told not to send the sample unless she receives official authorization.
9. You certainly shouldn't act <u>like</u> you did not contribute to this success, Bernie.
10. Todd, please do not use any of these mailing labels <u>except</u> I specifically ask you to do so.

W O R L D   V I E W

Use a current almanac or an encyclopedia to learn about areas of the world in which your company does business. Check on location, climate, recent history, and political leaders. Such knowledge will help you understand the atmosphere in which business takes place.

PARALLEL STRUCTURE

Observing the rules of parallel structure will provide balance to your writing. Note the following examples:

This laser printer works quietly and quickly. (The conjunction *and* joins two parallel elements — two adverbs, *quietly* and *quickly*.)

This laser printer works quietly and with speed. (The same ideas are expressed here but not in parallel form. Now we have an adverb, *quietly*, joined to a prepositional phrase, *with speed.* These two grammatical elements are not alike; they are not parallel.)

Study the following subsections to ensure that you master parallel structure with coordinating and correlative conjunctions.

With Coordinating Conjunctions

Coordinating conjunctions connect *like* elements: an adjective with an adjective, a prepositional phrase with a prepositional phrase, and so on. Therefore, make sure that the elements before and after a coordinating conjunction match.

These delicate mechanisms are checked carefully and (regularly? with regularity?). (An adverb, *carefully*, appears before the coordinating conjunction *and*; therefore, the adverb *regularly* should follow *and*. Together, *carefully* and *regularly* achieve parallel structure.)

Writing the first draft is relatively easy, but (editing? to edit?) it is more difficult. (Which choice matches *writing*? Answer: *editing*. Both *writing* and *editing* are gerunds.)

Checkup 3

KEY
1. apply
2. exercising
3. courteous
4. in person
5. even immersed in water
6. helpful to everyone

Balance the following sentences to make them parallel.

1. Completing this course will help you understand the basics of finance and <u>applying</u> these basics to your job.
2. The <u>fitness</u> expert said, "Eating the proper foods is important, but <u>to exercise</u> is also important."
3. In my opinion, both applicants seem to be personable and <u>have courtesy</u>.
4. You may submit your application by telephone, by mail, or <u>you can come in person</u>.
5. This special new material can be bent, rolled, or <u>is even immersible in water</u>.
6. The receptionist we are seeking should be gracious in manner, <u>a person who helps everyone</u>, and loyal to the company.

With Correlative Conjunctions

As you already know, correlative conjunctions are used in pairs. To achieve parallelism with correlative conjunctions, simply make sure that the element that follows the first conjunction is the same as the element that follows the second conjunction.

Becky wants *either* Tom *or* me to choose the light fixtures for her new craft center. (The elements that follow *either . . . or* are a noun *(Tom)* and a pronoun *(me)*. Nouns and pronouns are considered like elements because pronouns are substitutes for nouns. Thus the phrase *either Tom or me* is parallel.)

The color blue is predominant *not only* in the center's furnishings *but also* on its walls. (Notice the parallelism of two prepositional phrases, one after each of the correlatives.)

Not only did Becky do all the painting, *but* she *also* built the cabinets and worktables. (*Not only* is followed by an independent clause, and *but also* is followed by an independent clause. The sentence is parallel. Do not be misled by the inverted order of the first clause.)

Checkup 4

KEY
1. either to
2. by either

Balance the elements joined by correlative conjunctions so that they are parallel.

1. In an effort to save fuel, we are trying <u>to either</u> form car pools or to use public transportation.
2. For 20 years the shop has been opened <u>either by</u> Mr. Forcini or his assistant.

3. skiing
4. went neither to
5. given either
6. colorfully illustrated

3. Among the activities I like best are both canoeing and to ski.
4. Maude neither went to the mountains nor to the seashore.
5. Higher discounts are generally either given to our best customers or to our employees.
6. This book is both well written and has colorful illustrations.

REVIEW

Practical Application

A. On a sheet of paper, correct any errors in the following sentences. Write *OK* for any sentence that has no error.

1. Store policy states that checks are not accepted without a manager's approval.
2. Store policy states that checks are not accepted unless a manager approves them.
3. Our manager neither feels that overtime work nor part-time help will solve the problem.
4. Vanessa seems to give away free samples of merchandise like they cost the company nothing.
5. Of course, Vanessa is neither stingy with the company's money nor with her own money.
6. The reason she is buying all those clothes is because she just won the lottery.
7. After a long discussion, they not only agreed to reprimand Vanessa but also to forbid her to give away any more free samples.
8. The small model sells very well, and the larger model is probably the better value.
9. The man which you saw in my office is the manager of our Dallas plant.
10. Because you looked like you were tired, we decided not to bother you.
11. Please do not mail this check without Clara signs it first.
12. Please do not mail this check except Clara signs it first.
13. The members of the arbitration board seem objective and to be impartial.
14. Your duties will include screening applicants and to interview candidates.
15. Being that you like American food, we thought we'd treat you to a hamburger for your birthday.
16. The deadline is only a few hours away, and we will be able to file the forms on schedule.
17. As I suspected, the reason total sales increased in the fourth quarter was because each regional office sponsored a sales contest.

KEY
1. OK
2. OK
3. feels that neither
4. as if *or* as though
5. stingy neither
6. that
7. agreed not only
8. but
9. whom *or* that
10. as if *or* as though
11. unless
12. unless
13. omit *to be*
14. interviewing
15. Because *or* Since
16. but
17. that

18. handling numbers.
19. that
20. unless

KEY
1. were
2. Stocktons
3. sell
4. me
5. nor
6. no
7. there have
8. plan to order
9. in regard to
10. that
11. because *or* since
12. that
13. doesn't *or* does not
14. has not called *or* did not call
15. I
16. OK
17. omit *the most*
18. are
19. you're *or* you are
20. OK

REVIEW cont.

18. You must test applicants for their skills in typing, filing, and to handle numbers.
19. When you are at the podium, pretend like you are talking to a few close friends.
20. Please do not throw out these tapes except I ask you to do so.

B. On a sheet of paper, correct any errors in the following sentences. Write *OK* for any sentence that has no error.

1. A large number of customers, according to Rory, was interested in our new cellular phones.
2. Mr. Rinaldo claims that the Stockton's are very eager to buy a cellular phone.
3. We are looking for one of those printers that sells for under $1,000.
4. Last week Mr. Carruthers invited Cora and I to visit his company's annual crafts exhibit.
5. The Messineo beach property is neither for sale or for rent.
6. No, Leonard, we have no computers and not any fax machines.
7. Yes, there's been a few problems with the new payment system, but we are confident that the new system will work out well.
8. Carolyn does not plan on ordering any new printers until she tests them for compatibility with our computers.
9. Have you received any more information in regards to the changes in our medical and dental coverage?
10. "When talking with your clients," our sales manager suggested, "pretend like our humidifiers are the only ones on the market."
11. We decided to purchase all our equipment from Super Computers Inc. being that SCI has such a great reputation for service.
12. Did you read in our company newsletter where we may form a company softball team?
13. Sam, don't Norma know about the four o'clock deadline for placing classified ads?
14. Nicole left a message with Dr. Ashford's service this morning, but Dr. Ashford never called back.
15. If you and me complete this layout today, we can take tomorrow off.
16. Jeanne neither completed the forms correctly nor mailed them to us on time.
17. We received many, many excellent suggestions; Kenneth's recommendation, however, was the most unique.
18. On the bulletin board in the main hallway is the announcements in regard to the upcoming staff meeting and the company picnic.
19. If your looking for value, quality, and durability, we honestly believe that the SCI computer should be your choice.
20. It's too cold to model those swimsuits at the lake; moreover, there's snow on the ground.

Editing Practice

Using Your Word Processor. Proofread "on-screen" the following excerpt from a memorandum that you wrote. Should any errors be corrected before you print a copy of this memo?

Begining March 15, account executives must sign each new-account form before sending the form to the sales department. Each account executive should proofread the form carefully to make sure that the client's name and address (as well as the details of the transaction, of course) are correct in every detail.

Remember that an error in the new-account form can delay shipments of merchandise to your client and cause errors in billing, both of which will contribute to poor customer relations. Lets strive to get it right the first time!

Plurals and Possessives. On a sheet of paper, correct any errors in the following sentences. Write *OK* for any sentence that has no error.

1. Among the people that were not able to attend were the Ross's, who have been in California since April.
2. One of the foremost childrens' clothing stores is Kids' Stuff, a nationwide chain whose headquarters is in New York City.
3. According to the newspaper, his three brothers are all majors general in the Air Force.
4. Most of the designs that we reviewed showed creativity and flair; however, we all agreed that her's was the best.
5. Retype this column of numbers, making sure that the zeroes and the decimals align properly.
6. I believe that some of the ratioes given in this table are incorrect; please check them carefully.
7. Julie and Mike's new apartment is only about ten minutes away.
8. Tonights' guest speakers, the Messrs. Klein, will surely entertain the audience.
9. Thank goodness my calculations do agree with your's.
10. No, I was not aware of Dean leaving early, but apparently the boss gave him permission to do so.

3

APPLYING THE MECHANICS OF STYLE

OBJECTIVES: **After completing Section 3.1, you should be able to:**

1. Use periods correctly to end sentences.
2. Identify when to, and when not to, use periods.
3. Correct errors in the use of periods.
4. Use question marks correctly after direct questions and in series of questions.
5. Use exclamation points correctly.

Punctuation marks do for writing what pauses, changes in pitch, and gesturing do for speaking: They provide the necessary road signs to help readers and listeners understand our messages correctly. The three punctuation marks discussed in this section — periods, question marks, and exclamation points — are used to end sentences. In addition, these marks have some other uses, which are also discussed in this section.

PERIODS

It's important to learn when to use periods and when *not* to use periods, as well as how to avoid some common pitfalls in using them.

When to Use Periods

Use periods (1) to end declarative or imperative sentences, (2) to end requests that are phrased as questions simply for the sake of courtesy, and (3) to end indirect questions.

After Declarative and Imperative Sentences. Declarative sentences make statements, and imperative sentences order someone to act.

All these contracts must be proofread carefully. (Declarative sentence.)

Proofread all these contracts carefully. (Imperative sentence.)

After Requests Phrased as Questions. In an effort to soften commands and orders, speakers and writers often phrase such orders as questions. Because such statements are not really questions, use periods to end these sentences.

Will you please send us your completed forms immediately. (Not a question — no answer is required.)

May we have the entire order shipped by the fastest method. (A polite way of saying, "Send the order as fast as possible." Not really a question.)

Will you be able to resurface the entire parking lot by Friday? (This question requires a yes-or-no answer and, therefore, requires a question mark rather than a period.)

After Indirect Questions. An *indirect question* is a question restated as a declarative sentence.

She asked me whether I had already sent a confirmation copy to Mr. Ortiz. (Stated as a declarative sentence, this sentence requires a period.)

Mark, have you already sent a confirmation copy to Mr. Ortiz? (Stated as a question, the sentence requires a question mark.)

Checkup 1

KEY
Punctuation is underscored and shown in color.

Which of the following sentences should end with periods and which should end with question marks?

1. May we schedule the meeting for Tuesday?
2. Karen asked Ms. Frost whether she plans to cancel the appointment.
3. May I have your completed questionnaire by Monday, May 5.
4. Jonathan, would you stop by my office this afternoon.
5. Dave asked permission to attend the grand opening.
6. Will you please send the remainder of the merchandise before the end of the month.
7. Submit your suggestions to your supervisor before December 31.
8. Did Mr. Russo say that the deadline is December 31?

When Not to Use Periods

Do *not* use periods in the following instances.

After Sentences Ending in Abbreviations. Do *not* use two periods for sentences that end with abbreviations. If a sentence-ending abbreviation requires a period, let that period serve both functions.

As you know, the reception will begin at 8 p.m. (Not *8 p.m..*)

After Headings or Titles or After Roman Numerals. Headings that are set on separate lines (for examples, see the headings in this textbook) should not be followed by periods. Also, roman numerals used with names or titles should not be followed by periods.

Peter Richardson III has been appointed assistant corporate counsel. (Not *Peter Richardson III. has been . . . .*)

After Numbers or Letters in Parentheses. Do not use periods after numbers or letters that are enclosed in parentheses.

Their portfolio consists mainly of (1) government bonds, (2) municipal bonds, and (3) utilities stocks.

LANGUAGE TIP
"One who uses many periods is a philosopher; many interrogations, a student; many exclamations, a fanatic."

—J. L. Basford

When numbers or letters are not in parentheses and are displayed on separate lines, use a period after each.

Their portfolio consists mainly of:
1. Government bonds.
2. Municipal bonds.
3. Utilities stocks.

Note: In the above example, each item in the list grammatically completes the introductory statement and, therefore, ends with a period. If each item did not grammatically complete the introductory statement, no period would be needed.

Their portfolio includes all of the following:
1. Government bonds
2. Municipal bonds
3. Utilities stocks

Of course, if each item in a list is a complete sentence or a long phrase, use a period.

After Even Amounts of Dollars. Except in tables (when it is important to align numbers), do not use periods or unnecessary zeros in even dollar amounts.

Thank you for sending us your $75 deposit so quickly. (Not *$75.* and not *$75.00*)

Checkup 2

On a sheet of paper, correct any errors in the following sentences. Write *OK* for any sentence that has no error.

1. For a limited time only, you can renew your membership for two years for only $125. a year.
2. The best presentation was given by the sales manager of Argosy Computers, Inc..
3. Have you heard that former Mayor William J. Clark III. has been elected to our board?
4. The enclosed materials include (1) a booklet describing the medical benefits program, (2) an application form, and (3) a postage-paid envelope.
5. By renewing your subscription now, you can save $39.00 over the newsstand price.
6. The survey polled the following employees:
   a. Commission sales representatives
   b. Executives
   c. Support personnel

Condensed expressions, found more frequently in spoken than in written English, are not considered incomplete sentences. Answers to questions are usually stated economically and are followed by a period. "Which branch office has the highest sales?" Response: The Raleigh office. Likewise, simple yes-or-no answers correctly end with periods.

☐ SUGGESTION

The period fault and the comma-for-period fault are common writing problems. Allow adequate time for students to master this point.

Pitfalls

Using a period at the end of an *in*complete thought is called the "period fault." Using a comma when a period is needed is called the "comma-for-period fault." Both are discussed below.

The Period Fault. An *in*complete thought is not a sentence and therefore cannot stand alone. Generally, joining the incomplete thought to a main clause will solve the problem.

> The company is planning to expand its sales force. Because it expects customer demand to rise dramatically next year. (The second group of words cannot stand alone. This dependent clause should be joined to the preceding independent clause as shown in the following example.)

> The company is planning to expand its sales force, because it expects customer demand to rise dramatically next year. (Now the dependent clause does not stand alone but is joined correctly to an independent clause.)

The Comma-for-Period Fault. A comma should *not* be used to join two independent sentences. A period is needed.

> Celia will answer these questions at our meeting next Monday, she will also discuss some changes in data processing. (A period should follow *Monday*, separating these two independent sentences.)

> Our fall catalog is enclosed, an up-to-date price list will be sent to you within the next two weeks. (Again, these two independent sentences should be separated by a period.)

Checkup 3

KEY

Note: If students suggest commas for the periods in sentences 6, 7, and 8, accept their answers as correct for now.
1. strategies, we
2. exhausted, he
3. opportunities. He
4. Tuesday. She
5. month. Our
6. afternoon when

Are there any period faults or comma-for-period faults in the following sentences? Make any necessary corrections. Write *OK* for any sentence that has no error.

1. As we decided at our recent meeting on marketing strategies. We must direct our advertising to the top manufacturing companies in the Northwest.
2. Although the budget had been completely exhausted. He recommended that additional funds be allocated to complete the project.
3. Frank is now exploring certain investment opportunities, he is especially interested in tax-exempt bonds.
4. Dr. Lo invited the entire staff to the luncheon next Tuesday, she will announce some promotions then.
5. Orders for CD-ROM drives and modems will be filled at the end of the month, our warehouse is currently out of stock.
6. The negotiations ended abruptly Friday afternoon. When the union representative walked out of the meeting.

7. safe because
8. workstations since

7. Seth placed the checks in Dan MacGrail's <u>safe. Because</u> they were cashier's checks.
8. We have gained nearly 25 percent more of the market for computer <u>workstations. Since</u> we launched our sales promotion campaign two years ago.

QUESTION MARKS

Use question marks after direct questions and in series of questions.

After Direct Questions

Direct questions always end with question marks.

Have you prepared your graphic presentation?

Mr. Abdul, have you received your airline tickets yet?

Should we stamp these cartons "Fragile"?

Gwen asked, "Where is the original copy of this memorandum?"

Sentences that begin as statements but end as questions are considered questions. Use question marks at the end of such sentences.

Betty Ann shipped all the software updates to the Atlanta office, didn't she? (The question at the end of the statement — *didn't she?* — requires a question mark at the end of the sentence.)

Lenny is planning to take the accounting course after work, isn't he? (Again, the question following the statement makes this an interrogative sentence. Use a question mark at the end of the sentence.)

In Series of Questions

When a sentence contains a series of questions, the series may be joined by commas and a conjunction (like other series) and end with one question mark. On the other hand, each question may be separated from the main sentence and may have its own question mark. Note the following examples.

Have you already sent this confidential report to the president, the executive vice president, and the treasurer? (The items in the series are joined by commas and the conjunction *and*. The sentence ends with a question mark.)

Have you already sent this confidential report to the president? the executive vice president? the treasurer? (Each item in the series is separated from the main sentence, and each ends with its own question mark. Note that a lowercase letter begins each item to show that it is connected to the main sentence.)

Will research centers be established in Chicago, in New York, and in Dallas?

Will research centers be established in Chicago? in New York? in Dallas?

Pitfall

So many questions include the word *why*, *ask*, or *how* that some writers automatically use a question mark at the end of any sentence with one of these words. However, many sentences with *why*, *ask*, or *how* are simply *indirect* questions — that is, declarative sentences.

> Ramon did not ask why the meeting had been postponed. (A statement. Period for an indirect question.)

> Ms. Mazur asked how we intended to cut two weeks from the schedule. (A statement, not a question.)

Checkup 4

Are periods and question marks used correctly in the following sentences? Make any necessary corrections. Write *OK* for any sentence that has no error.

1. Ask Jordan why the proposal is not <u>ready</u>?
2. When will Mrs. Strauss announce who <u>will</u> be in charge of the Accounting Department?
3. Henry knows how to use this spreadsheet program, doesn't <u>he.</u>
4. Pat asked Maria how she completed the assignment so <u>quickly?</u>
5. The cassettes that she is looking for are in that cabinet, aren't <u>they.</u>
6. Doesn't Robin know that the seminar has been canceled because <u>of</u> the budget cuts?
7. The manager asked how charts could be used to enhance the <u>report?</u>
8. Has Ms. Fulbright already met with the branch managers? the regional directors? the vice president of personnel?

EXCLAMATION POINTS

KEY POINT

Use exclamation points to show strong emotion or feeling.

During the typical day, we see many, many exclamation points as we read signs and advertisements: "Special Sale!" "Limited-Time Offer!" "Hurry! Place Your Order Today!" The exclamation point, of course, is used to show strong emotion or feeling. In business writing, the use of exclamation points is limited to special uses.

> Congratulations! We applaud you for winning the company's highest award.

> We won the park landscaping contract. What great news!

> Sandy, you exceeded your sales goals by 45 percent!

REINFORCEMENT

Encourage students to limit the use of exclamation points. Overusing exclamation points decreases their effectiveness.

Sometimes the exclamation point may replace a question mark when a question is really just a strong statement.)

> What happened to the fax machine! (This is worded like a question but really is an exclamation.)

> Do *not* overuse the exclamation point!

SECTION

REVIEW

Practical Application

A. On a sheet of paper, correct any errors in the use of periods, question marks, or exclamation points. Write *OK* for any sentence that has no error.

1. The lease must be signed by March 31, we should send it to our lawyer no later than tomorrow.
2. Jane is now comparing color copiers from various manufacturers. So that she will be able to make a wise choice.
3. This video recorder is not very expensive. Although it is obviously not the top-of-the-line model.
4. When you write to Midway Construction, be sure to ask for (1.) an itemized estimate, (2.) a breakdown of costs for parts and labor, and (3.) a schedule for completing the entire project.
5. Do you agree that the best suppliers are Ames Chemicals, Berg Industries, and Paulison Supply Company.
6. Did you ask Carla whether she has drafted the space ad that is due to the printer next week.
7. Brian asked Carla whether she has drafted the copy for the space ad.
8. Do you know whether we can obtain a grant for this project under Title II.?
9. Hyung is scheduled to return from Seattle on the 4:30 p.m. flight, isn't he.
10. The original purchase price was $13,500.00, but strong competition has resulted in a lower price of only $11,750.00.
11. Should we submit bids for the Blue Hills Shopping Center? the West Street Mall? the Fanwood Mall?
12. Raleigh can sign vouchers for up to $500, Megan can sign vouchers for up to $750.
13. Our financial adviser suggested the following alternatives. For investing in IRAs (Individual Retirement Accounts):
    a. Zero-coupon bonds
    b. Certificates of deposit
    c. Government securities
14. Colleen is going to Middletown next week, isn't she.
15. Steven wants to know whether the database has been updated?

B. On a sheet of paper, correct any errors in the following sentences. Write *OK* for any sentence that has no error.

1. Are you certain that she said to send all these cabinets c.o.d.
2. Mert appreciated us helping her with her annual report.
3. Mr. Karis, our assistant manager, asked whether these fax machines are also on sale?

KEY
Students' answers may vary. Some may use semicolons between independent clauses.
1. 31. We
2. manufacturers so
3. expensive, although
4. (1) . . . (2) . . . (3)
5. Company?
6. week?
7. OK
8. II?
9. he?
10. $13,500 . . . $11,750.
11. OK
12. $500. Megan
13. alternatives for
14. she?
15. updated.

KEY
Students' answers may vary.
1. c.o.d.?
2. our
3. sale.

SECTION 3.1 SENTENCE ENDERS **139**

4. There are
5. $950.
6. me.
7. harder
8. among
9. as if *or* as though
10. unless
11. sale when
12. now. Only
13. any other
14. doesn't *or* does not
15. goals. Her
16. customer's
17. copies
18. OK
19. is
20. was

4. There's only two or three word processors left in the building.
5. With the 10 percent discount, this copier will sell for only $950.00.
6. Please ask the Purchasing Department to send new forms to Gail and I.
7. Tabulating all these responses was more hard than we expected.
8. To make sure that we would be finished by the deadline, we divided all the invoices between Marie, Jason, and me.
9. Sometimes Fred acts like he were the president of this company instead of an assistant regional manager.
10. Pat, do not release these vouchers without your supervisor approves them.
11. We discontinued the sale. When we depleted our inventory.
12. You should sign up for this seminar now, only eight people will be accepted.
13. We predict that this advertisement will be more effective than any advertisement we ever placed.
14. Usually, Celeste don't like to take an early lunch hour.
15. Jessica is confident that she and her staff will exceed their sales goals, her group is only about $100,000 short of its target.
16. As you can see, each customers' account is carefully checked before a monthly statement is mailed.
17. Advance copys of the annual report will be delivered today.
18. Must all these specification sheets be approved by the president? the comptroller? the chief engineer?
19. Everett or Margaret are going to open the ceremonies next Saturday.
20. Only one of the supervisors were against the idea of reducing our total production for the next month.

KEY

1. his or her (or OK)
2. are
3. OK
4. have
5. is

Editing Practice

Are We in Agreement? On a sheet of paper, correct any agreement errors in the following sentences.

1. As you know, every consumer has the right to request a copy of his credit history.
2. On the shelf in Ms. Simon's office is the latest studies on industrial pollution.
3. One of the studies contains an analysis of the environmental impact of the proposed factory.
4. All tax records prepared before 1985 has been discarded, according to Mr. Yamoto.
5. The number of customers who asked for more information on the new credit accounts are surprisingly high.

6. has
7. are
8. his or her (or his)
9. has
10. are

6. The newspaper article said that some of the land <u>have</u> already been purchased by a major real estate developer.
7. Will, here <u>is</u> the VCR and the remote-control device that you requested.
8. Every executive in the country will be able to increase <u>their</u> productivity after reading this helpful study.
9. Pauline said that either Marisa or Raymond <u>have</u> been assigned to the mailroom.
10. Dependability and initiative <u>is</u> important for advancement to executive positions.

Spelling Alert! Correct any misspelled words in the following excerpt.

KEY
special
pieces
February

As a valued longtime customer of Fromm's Office Furniture Shop, you are invited to a <u>specail</u> one-day sale of quality merchandise. Among the items that will be reduced as much as 35 percent are desks, credenzas, chairs, and many other <u>peices</u> of office furniture, all from name-brand manufacturers.

Remember the date and the time: Saturday, <u>Febuary</u> 10, from 9 a.m. until 9 p.m.

SECTION

3.2 *SEMICOLONS, COLONS, AND DASHES*

OBJECTIVES: After completing Section 3.2, you should be able to:

1. Use semicolons correctly to join independent clauses.
2. Use semicolons and colons correctly before enumerations and explanations.
3. Use colons correctly to introduce an independent clause and for emphasis.
4. Use dashes correctly in sentences.
5. Correct errors in the use of semicolons, colons, and dashes.

In the preceding section you learned how periods, question marks, and exclamation points are used to *end* sentences. This section discusses three marks of punctuation that are used *within* sentences — semicolons, colons, and dashes. Each has its own specific function, as you will see in this section.

KEY POINT

Semicolons are used before the second clause in a compound sentence when the conjunction is omitted, before an introductory word that begins the second clause in a sentence, and before explanatory or enumerating words.

SEMICOLONS

Semicolons are intended to make the reader pause; by providing "timing cues," they guide the reader in understanding the message clearly. Semicolons are used (1) as indication of the omission of a conjunction, (2) before an introductory word that begins the second clause in a sentence, and (3) before explanatory or enumerating words.

As Indication of Omission of a Conjunction

A compound sentence has two or more independent clauses, which are usually connected by a comma or commas and a conjunction.

> The Office Training Center offers a variety of courses for personal enjoyment and professional development, and we encourage our employees to take advantage of these offerings. (This sentence is a compound sentence; it has two independent clauses connected by a comma and the conjunction *and*.)

The conjunction and comma in a compound sentence such as the one above may be omitted, and a semicolon may be used to replace them.

> The Office Training Center offers a variety of courses for personal enjoyment and professional development; we encourage our employees to take advantage of these offerings. (Here, a semicolon joins the two independent clauses, replacing the comma and the conjunction.)

Before a Second Clause Starting With an Introductory Word

In some compound sentences, the second clause starts with an introductory word such as the following:

accordingly	consequently	moreover
again	furthermore	nevertheless
also	however	otherwise
besides	indeed	therefore

REINFORCEMENT

Students must be able to identify independent clauses easily before they can master the use of semicolons. Be sure to discuss how each of the introductory words has its own unique meaning in the second clause. Use the text examples and the text and workbook exercises to illustrate the different meanings.

In such sentences, the semicolon provides the necessary pause between the independent clauses, and the introductory word tells the specific relationship between the two clauses, making the meaning clearer.

> Airline travel is increasingly costly; nevertheless, we are pleased to offer our best customers a special corporate rate. (The semicolon separates the two independent clauses, and the introductory word *nevertheless* signals the reader to contrast the two clauses.)

> This corporate bond offers a 7 percent after-tax return; consequently, we are increasing our total investment. (Again, the semicolon separates the two independent clauses and tells the reader to pause. The introductory word *consequently* establishes a specific relationship between the two clauses; it shows that the second statement is a result of the first statement.)

Note that the introductory word is not always the *first* word in the second clause.

> Airline travel is increasingly costly; we are pleased, *nevertheless,* to offer our best customers a special corporate rate.

> This corporate bond offers a 7 percent after-tax return; we are, *consequently,* increasing our total investment.

Before Explanatory or Enumerating Words

Use a semicolon before such terms as *for example, for instance,* and *that is* when they introduce an independent clause, an enumeration, or an explanation that is incidental to the meaning of the rest of the sentence.

> Elena is seeking to advance her career; for example, she has registered for two graduate-level economics courses at the university. (*For example* introduces an independent clause.)

> Raymond is now looking at several possible ways to cut expenses; for instance, leasing rather than buying delivery vans, using less expensive cartons and packing materials, and buying in larger quantities. (*For instance* introduces an enumeration.)

Checkup 1

Make any necessary corrections in the following sentences. Write *OK* for any sentence that has no error.

1. I will be attending a conference next week, however, my assistant will be available to answer your questions.
2. In the summer, we manufacture our winter line, in the winter, we manufacture our summer apparel.
3. The new policy states that we must request at least three estimates for such projects, accordingly, we have asked four architects to bid on this job.
4. The company reimburses employees for job-related courses; all employees are eligible.
5. Dr. Morley's presentation was interesting and informative, indeed, the local newspapers called it "fascinating"!
6. The board of directors has decided to open another factory, the new one may be located outside Milwaukee.
7. Vanessa will be promoted to office manager next month, we expect, therefore, to see many changes in procedures in the future.
8. We canceled the order because we have not been happy with the service from Premier Printers, besides, we already have an oversupply of brochures and order forms.

COLONS

Colons make readers pause and take note of what follows.

Colons Before Listed Items

When such expressions as *the following, as follows, this, these,* and *thus* are used to introduce a list of items, they are often followed by colons. The list may follow on the same line as the colon, or it may be typed on a new line.

At our department meeting next Wednesday, we will discuss these topics: (1) telemarketing strategies for next year, (2) the advertising and promotion budget, and (3) expansion of our storage facilities.

At our department meeting next Wednesday, we will discuss these topics:
1. Telemarketing strategies for next year
2. The advertising and promotion budget
3. Expansion of our storage facilities

Sometimes the words *the following, as follows,* and so on, do not directly lead into the list; for example, an "interrupting" sentence appears between the lead-in sentence and the list. In such cases, a period, not a colon, should be used.

Note that the schedules have been revised as follows. A new completion date is listed next to each model. (A period, not a colon, is used after *as follows* because the actual list does not follow directly. A sentence separates the lead-in *as follows* and the actual list.)

Colons Instead of Semicolons

You already have learned that semicolons are used before such expressions as *for example* and *that is* when these expressions introduce independent clauses, enumerations, and explanations that are incidental to the rest of the sentence. However, when the explanation or enumeration is anticipated, a colon is used instead of a semicolon.

Shawn cited two good reasons for postponing our decision: namely, the cost of computer hardware is dropping, and software for new applications will be on the market next year.

Colons to Emphasize

Writers use colons most often to emphasize important thoughts or words.

Mercedes quickly pointed out the most important factor: increased productivity. (The colon provides special emphasis to "increased productivity.")

Remember: Beginning Monday, no employee will be permitted to enter the laboratory without his or her identification badge. (More emphatic than "Please try to remember that beginning Monday. . . .")

Capitalizing After Colons

Capitalize the first word following a colon if (1) it begins a complete sentence requiring special emphasis or (2) it begins a sentence stating a formal rule.

The salary adjustment applies to only two groups of employees: hourly employees and commission employees. (Not a sentence; the first word is not capitalized.)

Peter cited one good reason for accepting the proposal: It will increase profits. (Complete sentence; the first word is capitalized because the sentence requires special emphasis.)

The first step is the most important: Create an outline for your report. (Complete sentence; the first word is capitalized because the sentence states a formal rule.)

Checkup 2

Correct any errors in colon use in the following sentences. Write *OK* for any sentence that has no error.

1. The changes in benefits affect these <u>areas,</u> medical insurance, dental coverage, and maternity leave.
2. The procedure for requisitioning office supplies has been changed as <u>follows:</u> Please notify your staff of these changes.
3. We finally discovered why the messenger had not arrived: He went to the wrong address.
4. Claudia gave these reasons for endorsing the ad campaign. Each reason is explained in her memo.
5. Only two people in our division were invited to the board meeting: <u>My</u> supervisor and Harry Sherman.
6. Check your document for spelling errors: <u>use</u> the spell-check feature of your word processing program.

DASHES

KEY POINT

The dash provides a pause, indicates that something important will follow, and draws special attention to what follows. The dash is stronger than the semicolon and the colon.

Dashes share some of the features of semicolons and of colons: All three make the reader pause — but dashes do so more forcefully. Compare, for example, the different impact of the punctuation in each of the following examples. Notice how the dash provides greater impact than either the semicolon or the colon.

Your advertising dollar will bring you the greatest return if you buy time on OKTV; this television network is the one that most viewers in this area watch night and day. (A good sentence, but not a forceful one.)

For the best return on your advertising dollar, do this: Buy time on OKTV, the television network that most viewers in this area watch night and day. (This is a better sentence, a more forceful one.)

Your advertising dollar will bring you the greatest return if you buy time on OKTV — the television network that most viewers in this area watch night and day. (The dash snaps off the main thought and thereby adds power to the rest of the message. This is the most forceful of the three sentences.)

The semicolon provides the needed pause between clauses. The colon provides more than a pause: It promises that something important will follow. The dash goes even further by drawing special attention to what follows the dash. Therefore, the dash makes the third example the strongest of the three. The punctuation marks discussed in this section allow the writer to guide the reader through the message. At the same time, they allow the writer to provide variety and interest to the message.

Forceful Summarizing, Forceful Repetition

In your writing it is sometimes necessary to summarize the main points of your message to make sure that your readers remember these key points. Repeating a key point is another technique that you can use to make a stronger impression on your readers. The same is true when you are speaking, of course. When you are summarizing or repeating main points, use a dash to separate the summary or the repetition from the rest of the sentence.

Challenging games, helpful business programs, educational software — all are available at the CompuCenter nearest you. (The dash provides forceful summarizing.)

Remember to get all your computer needs from CompuCenter — CompuCenter, the store with you and your computer needs in mind. (Forceful repetition. Here, the writer deliberately repeats the most important part of the message — the store name.)

Dashes With Afterthoughts

To add variety to their writing, to arouse the reader's curiosity, to soften a statement that might otherwise offend, to provide special emphasis — for all these reasons, good writers *plan* their afterthoughts.

Our Labor Day sale will surely save you money — and offer you some exciting *un*advertised specials! (To provide variety in writing style and to arouse the reader's curiosity.)

Of course, we wish that we could send you a review copy of our latest program as you request — but company policy limits the number of copies that we may send. (To soften a refusal.)

This catalog is sent only to our preferred customers — no one else receives one! (To reemphasize a statement.)

Checkup 3

KEY
1. galleries—
2. offer—
3. sample—
4. shape—
5. booklet—

Add dashes where needed. Write *OK* for any sentence that has no error.

1. Fine restaurants, department stores, art <u>galleries</u> these are among the many places where you will enjoy using your new SuperCard.

2. Our company is unable to take advantage of your discount <u>offer</u> at least for now.

3. Complete and mail the enclosed card for your free <u>sample</u> but don't delay.

4. Our reorganization plans seem to be taking <u>shape</u> but more about this later.

5. The complete set of cassettes, the cassette player, the instruction <u>booklet</u> all are yours if you order before May 31.

Punctuating Words Set Off by Dashes

At the End of a Sentence. When you want to set off words at the end of a sentence, only one dash is needed. The dash is placed before the words to be set off; a period, question mark, or exclamation point then ends the sentence. No spaces are used between a dash and the word or words it is setting off.

> This computer package has several features not usually found at this price — 20 megabytes of memory, dual disk drive, color monitor. (The dash precedes the words to be set off; then a period ends this declarative sentence.)

Note that no punctuation is used with the dash unless an abbreviation or quotation precedes the dash. No punctuation ever follows the dash.

> The contract was awarded to Motion Inc. — Ms. Forman approved the bid. (The period before the dash belongs with the abbreviation.)

Within a Sentence. To set off words within a sentence, two dashes are needed. Again, no punctuation is used with the first dash unless an abbreviation or quotation precedes the dash. The second dash may have a question mark or an exclamation point *before* it, but only if the words set off require a question mark or an exclamation point.

> Our new Director of Personnel — have you met her? — will head the committee. (The dashes set off a question; thus a question mark precedes only the second dash. Note that the sentence ends with a period.)

> Suzanne Glynn won — for the second consecutive year! — the company's Outstanding Achievement Award. (The words set off by dashes require an exclamation point. Note that the sentence ends with a period.)

> Many sales representatives in our district — Dan Conklin, Murray Stark, and Beatrice Webber are among them — have suggested changes in the incentive compensation plan. (No period before the second dash.)

Note in the above example that commas are used within dashes in the "usual" way.

REINFORCEMENT

Make sure students understand why complete sentences within dashes (or within parentheses, for that matter) do not end with periods but may end with question marks or exclamation points.

Checkup 4

Correct any punctuation errors in the following sentences. Write *OK* for any sentence that has no error.

1. Please send these display cases by Pacific Express to Ms. Rosario — she's still in San Francisco, isn't <u>she</u> — before she leaves for Houston.
2. The doors will open on Monday at precisely 9 a.m. — but I suggest that you arrive no later than 8:45.
3. It will probably be Hardy & Crew — do you <u>agree</u> — who will build the new facility.
4. Service, dependability, fair <u>prices</u>, — these are the reasons for dealing with O'Connell Business Systems.
5. After she won last year's award — there was a $5,000 cash <u>prize</u>. — she traveled in Europe for four weeks.
6. Friendly people, reasonable prices, expert skiing facilities — these are some of the reasons the Mountainview Inn is the most popular meeting place in the Rockies.

SECTION REVIEW

Practical Application

A. On a sheet of paper, correct any errors in the following sentences. Write *OK* for any sentence that has no error.

1. In long-term international trade transactions, these are the three major problem areas for <u>exporters</u> (1) losses, (2) delayed payments, and (3) political risks.
2. Here is the new policy: <u>accept</u> no credit cards for purchases under $25.
3. The manager of our Memphis office is Sharon <u>Vernon</u>, the manager of our New York office is Paul Jacobs.
4. A number of the employees polled were in favor of the four-day <u>workweek</u>, however, the majority favored keeping our present system.
5. Clothing from Milan, leather goods from Florence, foods from <u>Naples</u>, — these were among the items imported this week.
6. The rule is clear: <u>smoking</u> is prohibited in all public areas of the building.
7. The following changes in the insurance plan will become effective January <u>1</u>: Note that employees will not pay extra for the additional coverage.
8. The aluminum screens were due from the manufacturer on June <u>12</u>, however, the recent strike delayed the delivery.

9. inventory—
10. OK
11. speaker—
12. on interest
13. it?—
14. 11;
15. 11;
16. No
17. percent?—
18. OK
19. performance;
20. reaction: No *or* reaction—no

9. Our newest model is temporarily out of stock — all other models are in <u>inventory.</u> — but we will have more after Friday.

10. Three specialty stores — a cheese shop, an art supply store, and a bookstore — have signed leases in the new mall.

11. Susan Kelly is a dynamic <u>speaker,</u> — dynamic and very informative too.

12. Subscribe today to make sure that you hear the latest news <u>on:</u> interest rates, the bond market, stock prices, and much more.

13. The Fitness Center — have you ever visited <u>it</u> — has the most up-to-date equipment.

14. The original bylaws were approved on November <u>11</u>, however, they were later amended.

15. The original bylaws were approved on November <u>11</u>, they were, however, later amended.

16. Remember: <u>no</u> employee may enter the restricted area without security clearance.

17. At first the bank offered us a high interest rate — wasn't it over 12 <u>percent</u> — before we negotiated better terms.

18. The Tuckahoe Company has a virtual monopoly on these lower-priced modems; the Somoto Company has a virtual monopoly on the higher-priced modems.

19. Unfortunately, tickets are no longer available for the May 3 <u>performance</u>, more tickets may become available, however, if there are cancellations.

20. When we heard the rumor, both Maxine and I had the same <u>reaction, no</u> comment!

KEY

1. week's
2. whom
3. me
4. are
5. you're *or* you are
6. his or her
7. insist

B. Correct any errors in the following sentences. Write *OK* for any sentence that has no error.

1. The final copy of the long-term lease will be ready, according to Ms. Sanford, within one <u>weeks'</u> time.

2. Do you know whether the person <u>who</u> you spoke with is Mr. Casey, the head of the department?

3. Within the next six months or so, there should be opportunities for May and <u>I</u> to transfer to the Atlanta office.

4. Mr. D'Ambois, here <u>is</u> the revised statistics that you requested this morning.

5. Kathy said that we'll call a taxi whenever <u>your</u> ready to leave for the airport.

6. Any employee who wants to apply for a job listed on the bulletin board should leave <u>their</u> name with Ms. Chen in the Personnel Department.

7. As you probably know, Romulo Fernandez is one of those accountants who <u>insists</u> on meticulous record keeping.

8. operators
9. these *or* those
10. Besides
11. could
12. to begin
13. has already seen
14. doesn't
15. manufacturer;
16. There are
17. $50 because (*or* $50, because)
18. reasonable;
19. vehicle—
20. surely

8. Most of the word processing <u>operators'</u> in this department prefer this new computer system.

9. Kenneth reminded us not to mail <u>them</u> checks until Ms. Hadley has approved each one.

10. <u>Beside</u> her small condominium in New York, Dorothy owns a home in Princeton.

11. It was obvious that Pamela <u>couldn't</u> hardly wait to return home after her three-week tour of our overseas offices.

12. Did Dominick say that he plans <u>on beginning</u> his draft of the proposal this weekend?

13. Yes, Winston <u>already seen</u> Mrs. Keto about the revisions in the advertising copy.

14. Why <u>don't</u> James or Hilda head the committee meeting in Sylvia's absence?

15. We returned all the damaged merchandise to the <u>manufacturer,</u> the rest of the order was sent to our warehouse.

16. <u>There's</u> still extra catalogs in the supply room if you should need them, Carlotta.

17. We do not accept credit cards for purchases under <u>$50. Because</u> it is not profitable for us to do so.

18. The estimate, in our opinion, was certainly <u>reasonable,</u> in fact, it was only 5 percent over the price we paid two years ago.

19. We will lease cars from O'Connell Industry — the monthly cost is only $175 a <u>vehicle.</u> — as soon as we get official approval from our corporate headquarters.

20. Vito will <u>sure</u> be happier in his new position.

Editing Practice

Using Business Vocabulary. On a sheet of paper, fill in each missing word with the correct word from the list below.

a. allocated	e. fragile	i. persuasive
b. efficiency	f. grievance	j. resources
c. eliminate	g. itemize	
d. foreign	h. permissible	

1. Together, the union and management representatives established a (?) committee to hear employees' complaints.
2. All packages with breakable merchandise must be marked (?).
3. According to IRS regulations, it is not (?) to deduct commutation expenses.
4. Because we do not have the (?) to complete this complex assignment in such a short time, we hired an outside firm to do so.
5. Be sure to (?) the costs on each estimate before sending it to the Purchasing Department.

6. d. foreign
7. i. persuasive
8. a. allocated
9. c. eliminate
10. b. efficiency

KEY

Student answers will vary.
1. conscious
2. honest
3. avoid, shun, evade, disregard
4. liberal
5. periodic, recurrent
6. relieve, alleviate

SECTION

REVIEW cont.

6. Our vice president is now exploring opportunities to expand our (?) trade.
7. Everyone who works with Bob Kline knows how (?) he can be!
8. The total expense dollars were carefully (?) by the committee.
9. To process orders faster, we are now studying ways to (?) unnecessary, time-consuming steps in the handling of telephone and mail orders.
10. Clearly, the analysis shows that the new workstations will increase our overall (?).

Using Your Word Processor. A business writer should easily be able to supply a synonym for each of the italicized words below. Write your synonyms on a separate sheet of paper.

1. The board is *aware*, of course, of our consolidation strategies.
2. Bernice was *truthful* in describing the problems we are now facing.
3. A business worker cannot *shirk* his or her responsibilities.
4. Wilfred was indeed *generous* in sharing the credit with his staff.
5. Ted Sylvester has had *intermittent* problems in getting along with the research staff.
6. Several of these concessions will *mitigate* the present strain between management and labor.

SECTION

3.3 *COMMAS*

OBJECTIVES: After completing Section 3.3, you should be able to:

1. Use commas correctly in compound sentences and in series.
2. Use commas correctly after introductory words, phrases, and clauses and before certain kinds of subordinate clauses.
3. Use commas correctly to set off interrupting elements, appositives, and related constructions.
4. Use commas correctly with modifying adjectives and repeated expressions, for omissions, in direct address, and in numbers.
5. Correct errors in comma usage.

Effective speakers use pauses that enable their listeners to grasp and connect thoughts and to separate expressions that are not essential to the clarity of the message. Similarly, effective writers use commas to connect thoughts and to separate elements within sentences. You will find that using commas correctly will be an important asset to you in your business and personal writing.

A thorough discussion of the many uses of the comma follows. Study these applications so that you will be able to use commas correctly in all forms of business writing.

IN COMPOUND SENTENCES

☑ REINFORCEMENT

Help students see the difference between compound sentences and sentences with compound predicates. Only by understanding this difference will students be able to use commas correctly in compound sentences.

Note in the following sentences how commas are used with the conjunctions *and*, *but*, *or*, and *nor* to join two independent clauses.

Roberta moved to Chicago two weeks ago, and she started her new job with ABC Products today. (The comma and the conjunction *and* join two independent clauses.)

The Windham & Wilson Company originally planned to build a warehouse on the property, but it subsequently decided to sell the land instead. (The comma and the conjunction *but* join two independent clauses.)

Greg will send you a copy of the revised contract by overnight express, or he will fax it to you tomorrow morning. (The comma and *or* connect two independent clauses.)

Liza does not want to be transferred to the Boston office, nor does she want to stay in the Accounting Department. (The comma and *nor* connect two independent clauses.)

Reread the compound sentences above, noting that each clause can stand alone as a sentence. It is important to distinguish a compound sentence from a simple sentence with a compound predicate. As you know, a compound sentence has two or more independent clauses (each with a subject and a predicate). A simple sentence with a compound predicate has only one subject and a compound verb. A comma is *not* used to separate a compound predicate.

Roberta moved to Chicago two weeks ago and started her new job with ABC Products today. (*Roberta* is the only subject for the compound verb *moved* and *started*. No comma is needed.)

The Windham & Wilson Company originally planned to build a warehouse on the property but subsequently decided to sell the land instead. (The word *company* is the subject for the compound verb *planned* and *decided*. No comma is needed.)

Greg will send you a copy of the revised contract by overnight express or will fax it to you tomorrow morning. (*Greg* is the subject for the compound verb *will send* and *will fax*. No comma is needed.)

The exceptions to the use of commas in compound sentences are discussed on the following page.

No Comma Between Very Short Clauses

When the independent clauses are very short, the comma is usually omitted. Read the following examples aloud; as you do so, note that each sentence sounds "natural" without a pause before the conjunction.

> Shirley wrote the memo and Leo retyped it. (The two independent clauses are short; the comma can be omitted.)

> Jeff Belden attended the conference and Larry joined him there. (Again, two short independent clauses do not require a comma.)

Semicolons to Avoid Possible Misreadings

If either clause of a compound sentence already contains one or more commas, a misreading may result. To avoid misreadings, use a semicolon, not a comma, to separate the clauses.

> The issues to be discussed at tomorrow's meeting are paternity leave, increased health coverage, and flexible starting hours; and a company-sponsored child-care center will be the topic of next week's meeting. (The semicolon provides a stronger break and prevents this possible misreading: *and flexible starting hours, and a company-sponsored child-care center. . . .*)

When the two independent clauses in a compound sentence are very long, the brief pause of a comma may not be strong enough. A semicolon may be required. (Better yet, write very long clauses as independent sentences.)

> The findings of our research chemists clearly point to the possible effectiveness of polyvinyl chloride (PVC) as a replacement for the more expensive materials we are now using; and we fully support the need to fund further research to explore the uses of PVC for our entire line of products.

Checkup 1

Correct these sentences. Write *OK* for any sentence that has no error.

1. Mike declined the job offer, but Gail accepted it.
2. Curtis recommended Yvette, Ivan, and Samantha, and Sean recommended two of his staff members.
3. Bonnie does not plan to join the company softball team nor does she plan to rejoin the bowling league this year.
4. Our department manager will be promoted to district manager next month but her successor has not yet been chosen.
5. Wendy will chair the new committee, but will not be able to attend the first meeting.
6. I received the customer's letter this morning, and promptly began drafting a response.
7. We should revise these estimates, or we should request up-to-date bids.
8. The examinations began promptly this morning but ended late.

KEY
Errors are underscored.
1. offer
2. Samantha;
3. team,
4. month,
5. committee but
6. morning and
7. OK
8. OK

REINFORCEMENT

Help students see how commas are used in series. Stress that commas are used to separate items that precede the conjunction.

IN SERIES

A *series* consists of three or more items in a sequence. As you will see in the following examples, the items may be words, phrases, or clauses.

Marybeth took additional courses in accounting, statistics, economics, and public administration. (A series of words. Note that a comma is used *before* the conjunction.)

Many of our employees do volunteer work in hospitals, at shelters for the homeless, and for various charitable organizations. (A series of three phrases: *in hospitals, at shelters for the homeless, for various charitable organizations.*)

Gregory will be moving to our Honolulu office, Anne will take his place at headquarters, and Rhonda will become Anne's assistant. (A series of three independent clauses.)

When *Etc.* Ends a Series

Etc. means "and so forth." Never write *and etc.* because that would mean "*and and* so forth"!

When *etc.* ends a series, use a comma before and after it unless *etc.* ends the sentence.

According to the agenda, we will meet the dignitaries, take them to lunch, show them the plant, *etc.* (A comma before *etc.* No comma after *etc.* because *etc.* ends the sentence.)

We will meet the dignitaries, take them to lunch, show them the plant, *etc.*, according to the agenda. (A comma before and after *etc.*)

Semicolons Instead of Commas in Series

When the items in a series are long clauses or if the items already contain commas, use a semicolon to provide a stronger break between each item.

We should like you to do the following: arrange our goods into shipping units; transport them to the place where they are to be consumed; store them there if storage is necessary; and obtain a signed receipt showing the time of delivery and the condition of the goods. (You can see that a long pause is needed between the items.)

During the first six months of this year, Jack Shapiro attended sales meetings in Bangor, Maine; Hartford, Connecticut; Syracuse, New York; Wilmington, Delaware; and Baltimore, Maryland. (A semicolon to separate the parts of the series allows the reader to grasp the meaning immediately.)

When Not to Use Commas

Do not use commas in the following situations.

At the End of a Series. Do not use a comma after the last item in a series (that is, the item following the conjunction) unless the sentence structure requires a comma. Only the items preceding the conjunction are separated by commas.

Pedro, Lisa, and Carl will coordinate the training sessions for new employees. (No comma after *Carl*, the last item in the series.)

Pedro, Lisa, and Carl, who are supervisors in our headquarters office, will coordinate the training sessions. (The comma after *Carl* is required because of the interrupting clause beginning with *who*.)

With Repeated Conjunctions. When the conjunction is repeated between each item in the series, no commas are needed.

We will accept a personal check as payment if you have a valid driver's license or a major credit card or a current passport. (Because the conjunction *or* is repeated between each item in the series, no commas are needed.)

In Certain Company Names. Company names should be written exactly like their official names. Some companies write their names *without* a comma before *and*; others, *with* a comma. Follow the company preference. In all cases, no comma is used before an ampersand (&).

Balbach, McIntyre and Bridgeman bid on the contract. (Follows the official company name precisely.)

D'Amato, Weisel & Wilkens is an excellent consulting firm. (Never use a comma before an ampersand: &.)

Checkup 2

KEY
1. omit *and*
2. Starr &
3. etc.,
4. agendas,
5. messenger;
6. Andrea,
7. advertising;
8. train,

Correct any errors in the following sentences. Write *OK* for any sentence that has no error.

1. Every morning Ralph arrives early to make coffee, turn the copier on, water the plants, <u>and etc.</u>
2. Bartlett, <u>Starr, &</u> Haney received the BranFoods national advertising account.
3. Appliances, furniture, hardware, <u>etc.</u> will be on sale next week at all our outlet stores.
4. Alinda will order all the supplies, Carmen will print and mail the <u>agendas</u> and Barbara will handle registration.
5. You can send us the report by fax, modem, or <u>messenger</u> or if you prefer, you can send it by overnight express.
6. Please tell Seth, <u>Andrea</u> and Bettejean to submit their reports by Friday, and ask them to send copies to Ms. DeLeonetti.
7. Excellence Press prints all our brochures, pamphlets, and direct-mail <u>advertising</u>, catalogs, however, are printed by the Boston Printing Company.
8. You can use this laptop computer to create documents in the office, on a commuter <u>train</u> and at home.

Commas follow introductory words, phrases, and clauses to provide a needed pause and thereby prevent possible misreading or confusion.

Introductory Words

Commas follow introductory words at the beginning of sentences or clauses. Some of the most commonly used introductory words are listed below:

consequently	moreover	obviously
finally	namely	originally
first	naturally	therefore
however	no	yes
meanwhile	now	

Naturally, we were disappointed with the results of the survey. (The introductory word *naturally* is at the beginning of the sentence. A comma follows the word.)

The survey showed that our product was the least favored in consumers' opinions; naturally, we were disappointed with the results. (Here, the word *naturally* introduces the second clause in the sentence. Again, it is followed by a comma.)

We received the survey results this morning; we were, naturally, extremely disappointed. (In this example, the introductory word interrupts the second clause. Note that a comma is used before and after *naturally*.)

Introductory Phrases

Commas are often needed after infinitive phrases, participial phrases, and prepositional phrases.

After Infinitive Phrases. An infinitive phrase that begins a sentence or a clause is followed by a comma unless the phrase is the subject of the sentence or clause.

To finish her review, Jeannette will have to work overtime. (The infinitive phrase *to finish her review* introduces the sentence. It modifies the subject *Jeannette*.)

To finish her review is Jeannette's priority for today. (Here, the infinitive phrase is the subject of the sentence.)

After Participial Phrases. A participial phrase is always followed by a comma.

Waiting for the meeting to start, Hal reviewed his schedule for the week. (Use a comma after the participial phrase.)

Delayed by the heavy fog, Fiona's flight was two hours late. (Comma after a participial phrase.)

Do not confuse participial phrases with gerund phrases. A gerund phrase at the beginning of a sentence is always a subject. A participial phrase is always an adjective.

> Controlling costs carefully is every manager's responsibility. (*Controlling* is a gerund. The gerund phrase *Controlling costs carefully* is the subject of the sentence.)

> Controlling costs carefully, Claire was able to make the shop profitable in a very short time. (Here, *Controlling* is a participle — an adjective that modifies the subject, *Claire*.)

After Prepositional Phrases. Use commas after long prepositional phrases and prepositional phrases that contain verbs.

> For further information on product-support services, please refer to the appendix in the owner's manual. (Long prepositional phrase.)

> After securing the lucrative account, Laurene received a promotion as well as praise from the company chairman. (Note the gerund *securing* in the prepositional phrase.)

Do not use a comma if the prepositional phrase is short or if it flows directly into the main thought of the sentence.

> By next week the new telephone system will be installed and operational. (The prepositional phrase *By next week* is short and flows directly into the sentence.)

Introductory Clauses

A comma is needed after a subordinate clause that precedes a main clause. Note how the comma provides a necessary pause in the following example.

> When Tod Roosevelt returned, we met with the attorneys and discussed the terms of the contract. (Comma after a subordinate clause that precedes the main clause.)

To apply this comma rule, you must be able to identify the words and phrases that commonly begin introductory clauses. You will remember the following list better if you try using each word or phrase to introduce a clause.

after	how	though
although	if	till
as	inasmuch as	unless
as if	in case	when
as soon as	in order that	whenever
as though	otherwise	where
because	provided	whereas
before	since	wherever
even if	so that	whether
for	then	while

Checkup 3

KEY
1. tomorrow,
2. received,
3. printouts took
4. OK
5. therefore,
6. plan,
7. cafeteria,
8. days,
9. business requires
10. approved, moreover,

Correct any comma errors. Write *OK* for any sentence that has no error.

1. Between the close of business today and the start of business <u>tomorrow</u> we will have finished taking inventory.
2. As soon as orders are <u>received</u> they are entered into the computer and processed immediately.
3. Proofreading the computer <u>printouts, took</u> Tom and Connie all morning.
4. Proofreading the computer printouts, Tom and Connie worked carefully all morning long.
5. We should be able to leave Dallas Friday afternoon; <u>therefore</u> we should arrive home by 9 p.m.
6. Unless Sherri disapproves of our <u>plan</u> we will be able to begin next Monday.
7. To have lunch in the company <u>cafeteria</u> visitors must present a pass.
8. Unless you file a claim within 30 <u>days</u> you have no recourse.
9. To succeed in this <u>business, requires</u> persistence, determination, and drive.
10. Mr. Andersen finally gave his consent to the incentive-compensation plan; he <u>approved moreover</u> an additional bonus for the top sales representatives.

 WITH SUBORDINATE CLAUSE FOLLOWING MAIN CLAUSE

We have already seen that a subordinate clause preceding a main clause is always followed by a comma.

As we agreed at our last directors' meeting, we will review the commission rates for full-time and part-time sales representatives. (Comma after subordinate clause preceding a main clause.)

After Ms. Scott has made her final decision regarding staffing, she will meet with each department manager. (Comma after subordinate clause preceding a main clause.)

But when the subordinate clause *follows* the main clause, use a comma only if the subordinate clause offers *non*essential information — information not needed to complete the meaning. As you read the following examples, note how the subordinate clauses differ.

We will review the commission rates for full-time and part-time sales representatives, as we agreed at our last directors' meeting. (The words *as we agreed at our last directors' meeting* are certainly not critical to understanding the meaning of the sentence. They merely provide extra information. A comma separates nonessential words.)

☑ **REINFORCEMENT**

For students, the difference between essential and nonessential information may be rather subtle. Help students by reading the sentences aloud and explaining precisely why the information in one sentence is "extra" but is essential in another sentence. Have students create their own sentences for practice.

Ms. Scott will meet with each department manager after she has made her final decision regarding staffing. (No comma here because the clause *after she has made her final decision regarding staffing* is important to the meaning of the sentence. It provides *essential* information, *not* additional information. It tells precisely *when* "Ms. Scott will meet with each department manager.")

When writing such sentences, you will of course know the meaning you intend and will have an easier job of deciding whether a comma is needed or not.

WITH INTERRUPTING, PARENTHETIC, AND EXPLANATORY ELEMENTS

Interrupting Elements

Interrupting elements do not provide essential information. Use commas to set off interrupters.

The company's sales performance, naturally, has disappointed the stockholders. (Commas set off the interrupting word *naturally*.)

Each department's proposed budget, consequently, must be scaled down because of the loss in income during the last fiscal year. (Again, commas set off the interrupter *consequently*.)

Parenthetic Elements

As we speak and write, we add words, phrases, and clauses within sentences to emphasize a contrast, express an opinion, soften a harsh statement, qualify or amend the meaning, and so on.

Any change in these regulations, as I see it, must be approved by the legal committee. (The parenthetic expression *as I see it* is not essential to the meaning of the sentence and is set off by commas.)

The text of the annual report, but not the charts and the graphics, has been approved by the board of directors. (The parenthetic statement separated by commas emphasizes the contrast.)

Explanatory Elements

Additional information that is not essential to the meaning of the sentence is set off by commas. To determine this, read the sentence without the additional information to be sure it makes sense.

The systems analyst, suspecting a "virus" in the computer network, issued an advisory memo to all network users. (Read this sentence aloud. As you do so, note how you would pause at the beginning and at the end of the participial phrase *suspecting a "virus" in the computer network*. Use commas to set off such explanatory elements.)

Dr. Hoverman, who developed this vaccine, is a senior vice president. (The clause *who developed this vaccine* is set off by commas. Again, read this sentence aloud to note how you would pause before and after the explanatory element.)

Note, however, that clauses that *are* essential are not set off by commas.

Our firm has four senior vice presidents. The senior vice president who developed this vaccine is Dr. Hoverman. (In this sentence, the clause *who developed this vaccine* does not provide *extra* information; it specifies *one* of the "four senior vice presidents." Note that in reading this sentence aloud, you would *not* pause before and after the clause.)

Checkup 4

KEY
1. recruiter who . . . position is
2. Anna, . . . office,
3. alternative, . . . yesterday,
4. OK
5. attorney whom . . . consult is
6. received, . . . returned,
7. staff who . . . CPA is
8. supplies if
9. alternative, . . . think,
10. OK

Are commas used correctly in the following sentences? Make any necessary corrections. Write *OK* for any sentence that has no error.

1. The recruiter, who is interviewing applicants for this position, is Jason Bloom.
2. Anna waiting for the call from our Toledo office did not go out for lunch.
3. One possible alternative as we discussed yesterday is to delay this shipment until Trent & Fitch has paid its bills.
4. Cynthia Crain, who designs our brochures, met with the marketing director today.
5. The litigation attorney, whom you should consult, is Pat Reilly.
6. The interest received but not the principal returned is subject to taxation.
7. The only person on our staff, who is a CPA, is Arnold Rudolf.
8. Please order additional supplies, if the special discount is still in effect.
9. An effective alternative Larry and I think will be to postpone the production of these items until after the summer rush.
10. The department managers, but not the staff supervisors, must attend the hearing.

WITH APPOSITIVES AND RELATED CONSTRUCTIONS

The use of commas with appositives, degrees and titles, calendar dates, and state names is discussed below.

Appositives

An appositive is a word or a group of words that gives more information about a preceding word or phrase. When an appositive is not essential to the meaning, it is set off by commas.

The director of corporate communications, Andrea Patterson, is giving a seminar on desktop publishing. (The appositive, *Andrea Patterson*, offers additional information and is set off by commas.)

The president of our company, a well-known adjunct professor, is an expert in corporate finance.

When the appositive is very closely connected with the noun that precedes it, no commas are used to separate the appositive. One-word appositives frequently do not take commas.

His wife Tamara Wilkins will fly to the Cleveland office to be with him. (The appositive *Tamara Wilkins* is closely connected to the noun preceding it; therefore, no commas are needed.)

The year 1998 will mark the 100th anniversary of our firm. (Here, *1998* is essential to the meaning of the sentence. It is not set off by commas.)

Degrees, Titles, and Other Explanatory Terms

10 B

Several commonly used abbreviations offer additional information about the names that precede them. For example, *M.D.* following a person's name tells that he or she is a doctor of medicine, and *Inc.* following a company name tells that the firm has been incorporated.

Abbreviations such as *M.D.*, *Ph.D.*, and *D.D.S.* are always set off by commas.

Allen Chang, D.D.S., is a consultant to the Acme Dental Company.

Alice O. Bruno, Ph.D., is the director of research and development for the Allied Health Division of Sterling Products.

The abbreviations *Inc.* and *Ltd.* may or may not be set off with commas, depending on the preference of each company. Always follow the style shown on a company's letterhead.

The data-processing division of Sanford Enterprises, Inc., has moved to Columbus, Georgia. (*Sanford Enterprises, Inc.*, is the official company name.)

Ms. MacGrath works for Time Inc. in New York. (*Time Inc.* is the official company name.)

Like *Inc.* and *Ltd.*, the abbreviations *Jr.* and *Sr.* may or may not be set off with commas. Follow the preference of each individual when writing *Jr.* and *Sr.* or roman numerals after a person's name.

William D. Achison Jr. has been named to the Board of Directors. (Mr. Achison prefers no commas setting off *Jr.*)

Brooks Matthews, III, is the chief executive officer of Pinnacle Investors. (Mr. Matthews prefers commas setting off *III* following his name.)

Note that when commas are used to set off such abbreviations as *M.D.*, *Inc.*, and *Jr.*, they are used in pairs. Do not use a single comma to set off such abbreviations unless the abbreviation appears at the end of a sentence. If the person's preference is not known, do not use commas to set off *Jr.*, *Sr.*, or roman numerals after the name.

Calendar Dates

In month-day-year dates, the year is set off with two commas. In month-year dates, the commas are omitted.

On February 9, 1990, we purchased the land for this office building.

In February 1990 we purchased this land.

State Names

A comma is used to separate the city from the state and the state from the rest of the sentence.

The national sales conference will be held in Portland, Oregon, next April.

Checkup 5

Are there any comma errors in the following sentences? Make any necessary corrections. Write *OK* for any sentence that has no error.

1. A recruiter in the Personnel Department, Martha Salinger will represent the company at the job fair tomorrow.
2. Nehemiah Edwards, one of our engineers, lived in Boise Idaho for many years.
3. Next week James W. Preston, Jr. will be officially named to the board of directors.
4. Coakley & Givens, Inc. completed the architectural design for the new office complex in downtown Boston.
5. Two new staff writers, Betty Sanchez and Rick Barnes were recently hired by the *Fernwood Gazette*.
6. On December 31, 1998 our lease will expire.
7. One of our divisions Simco Chemicals has been very active in the field of pollution control.
8. Winnie Ackerman flew to Houston, Texas to meet with the inventor.
9. Send the damaged molds to Ames & Blackstone, Inc. as soon as possible.
10. His wife Patricia is a senior partner in a prominent law firm.

WHICH AND *THAT* CLAUSES

i **INFORMATION**

That and *which* are used interchangeably by many people, and students will encounter sentences like "The car which I bought cost $15,000." *Which* is used incorrectly in this example, but the absence of commas is correct. Whether the clause is essential or nonessential is the critical factor in punctuating the sentence correctly.

Clauses that are not necessary to the meaning of a sentence should be introduced by *which* and, of course, set off by commas. Clauses that are necessary to the meaning of a sentence are introduced by *that*. They are not set off by commas.

Only the inventory that is damaged will be sold at a 50 percent discount. (No commas separating a "that" clause.)

The damaged inventory, which includes VCRs and stereos, will be sold at a 50 percent discount. (The "which" clause gives additional information and is correctly set off by commas.)

❏SUGGESTION

Novice writers often fall prey to the pitfalls listed here. Be sure to discuss these common errors with students.

PITFALLS

Here are two more comma pitfalls that trap many writers: (1) using a comma to separate a subject from its predicate and (2) using a comma to separate a verb or an infinitive from its object or complement.

Comma Separating Subject From Predicate

Never separate a subject from its predicate by a comma.

All invoices from outside vendors, must be initialed by both the supervisor and the department head. (Wrong. No comma should separate the subject from its verb.)

All invoices from outside vendors, according to the accounting manager, must be initialed by the supervisor and the department head. (Correct. Now *two* commas separate a phrase that gives additional information.)

Comma Separating Verb From Object

Never separate a verb from its object with a comma. Likewise, never separate an infinitive from its complement with a comma.

Since 1985 Carol has been, one of the company's most prolific researchers. (Wrong. A comma should never separate a verb from its object.)

Most of the members were surprised to learn, that Frank resigned yesterday. (Wrong. A comma should never separate an infinitive from its complement.)

Checkup 6

KEY
1. outlet, . . . South,
2. products that
3. supplies that . . . catalog may
4. catalog, . . . form,
5. office are
6. OK

Find and correct any errors in the following sentences. Write *OK* for any sentence that has no error.

1. Our Newport News <u>outlet</u> which is one of the largest in the <u>South</u> is our company's most profitable revenue division.
2. Environmentalists have urged customers to boycott <u>products</u>, that have excess packaging.
3. All computer <u>supplies</u>, that are listed in our <u>catalog</u>, may also be purchased in our retail store.
4. The enclosed <u>catalog</u> which also includes an order <u>form</u> is yours at no extra charge for opening an account with us.
5. Several employees in our Oklahoma City <u>office</u>, are being considered for the new opening in our headquarters.
6. The board chairman is preparing his speech for the annual stockholders' meeting, which is to be held in the Grand Ballroom of the Astor Hotel.

WITH MODIFYING ADJECTIVES

When two or more adjectives separately modify a noun, use a comma to separate the adjectives. To test whether the two adjectives *separately* modify the noun, use the word *and* between the adjectives, as shown below.

Carlotta voiced her opinion in a forceful, logical way. (Comma between the adjectives *forceful* and *logical*. Note that the word *and* can be used between the modifiers: in a way that is forceful *and* logical.)

Jill and Gary are the most creative, most experienced, most versatile players on our squad. (Commas between the adjectives that *separately* modify the noun *players:* most creative *and* most experienced *and* most versatile.)

Note that no comma follows the last adjective—that is, no comma separates the last adjective from the noun.

We discussed conservative financial investments with our adviser. (You would *not* say "investments that are conservative *and* financial." Here, the adjective *financial* modifies *investments*, of course. But the adjective *conservative* modifies the unit *financial investments*. In other words, "financial investments that are conservative.")

Tim Warner's unique leadership style is his greatest attribute. (Using the word *and* between the modifiers *unique* and *leadership* makes no sense. These adjectives do not separately modify the noun *style*.)

Checkup 7

Insert commas as needed between adjectives in the following sentences. Test by using the word *and* between adjectives. Write *OK* for any sentence not requiring a comma or commas.

1. Chet is considered a brilliant reliable ambitious Wall Street analyst.
2. Luke and Rachel received an industry award for their fascinating documentary film on toxic wastes.
3. The latest marketing research reports are available in Mr. Luciano's office.
4. Their portfolio contains solid high-yielding investments.
5. Jonas & Westerly manufactures lightweight thermal blankets.
6. Ms. Kane has hired a creative dedicated staff of highly trained professionals.

FOR OMISSIONS, WITH REPEATED EXPRESSIONS, AND IN DIRECT ADDRESS

The comma is also used to save time and words, to emphasize an important thought, and to set off names and terms in direct address. These uses are discussed in this section.

Omissions

Sometimes writers can use the comma to avoid repeating words that have already been stated in the sentence. The comma makes the reader pause long enough to mentally supply the omitted words.

> Effective June 15, Mr. Hart will be in charge of the Bennett account; Ms. Dirkins, the Hastings & Ames account; Ms. Ellison, the Barker Fertilizer account; and Mr. Donnelly, the Henderson Trucking account. (Rather than repeat the words *will be in charge of* three times, the writer uses a comma after each name to indicate the omission and cause the reader to pause long enough to supply these words.)

Repeated Expressions

Repetition is one of the most effective ways to emphasize an important point. Repetitions, of course, must be planned if they are to be effective, and the repeated words must be separated by a comma.

> The manual says, "Never, never accept credit charges for amounts under $25." (Note the comma that separates the repetition *Never, never.*)

Direct Address

In writing, when we address people directly, we set off their names (or similar terms) with commas.

> As you may know, Mrs. Boudreau, this software program offers you direct on-line support.

> Without your continuing encouragement and support, dear sister, I would not have succeeded.

Checkup 8

Do the following sentences correctly illustrate use of commas for omissions, for planned repetition, and for direct address? Make any needed corrections. Write *OK* for any sentence that has no error.

1. Ms. Doyle we overwhelmingly endorse your proposal.
2. To complete the project on time, the staff will have to work long long hours.
3. The Detroit office is scheduled to be audited on August 3; the Milwaukee office August 10; and the Indianapolis office August 17.
4. Investing in that stock is a risky risky venture!
5. The reports confirmed that Brett & Umberto had contributed $10,000 to Senator Clay's campaign; Able Industries, $15,000; and Northern Commerce, $20,000.
6. Francis's comments were correct absolutely correct.

IN NUMBERS AND BETWEEN UNRELATED NUMBERS

Use a comma to separate thousands, ten thousands, hundred thousands, millions, and so on, in numbers of four or more digits. This function of the comma prevents misreading of numbers.

Our company payroll exceeded $1,500,000 last year and is estimated to be $1,800,000 this year.

During the past six months, CompuMart sold 5,368 Swift 386 computer systems.

When unrelated numbers are written together, a comma should separate them.

On May 10, 847 students will graduate from our M.B.A. program. (The comma slows down the reader and makes each number distinct.)

PITFALLS

Now that you know all the important uses of the comma, be sure to master the principles for *not* using a comma.

In Numbers

Never use commas in the following numbers, regardless of the number of digits: years, page numbers, house and telephone numbers, ZIP Code numbers, serial numbers, and decimals.

in 1991	2718 Magnolia Street	Kansas City, MO 64110
page 1318	201-555-2184	RD 14315789
12.75325		

In Weights, Capacities, Measurements

Never use a comma to separate the parts of *one* weight, *one* capacity, or *one* measurement.

The videotaped presentation runs for exactly 1 hour 18 minutes 20 seconds. (No commas to separate the parts of *one* time measurement.)

Checkup 9

KEY
1. 1995,
2. 2 hours 45 minutes

Did the writers of the following sentences fall into any of the comma pitfalls described above? Correct any errors. Write *OK* for any sentence that has no error.

1. By 1995 700 employees will have completed our new training program.
2. Surprisingly, the question-and-answer period lasted 2 hours, 45 minutes.

3. 1232 . . . 1336
4. 4840
5. OK
6. 80876
7. 9 feet 7 inches
8. OK

3. Refer to pages 1,232 through 1,336 for a detailed discussion of how to apply for federal grants.
4. In 1990 the medical supply company moved to 4,840 Crescent Avenue.
5. As you will see on Invoice 17-19853, 14 items were shipped, not 15.
6. My copy of Policy 80,876 is in my safe-deposit box.
7. The display cabinet is precisely 9 feet, 7 inches high.
8. Marielle invested her bonus of $7,200 in government bonds.

SECTION

REVIEW

Practical Application

A. Correct the following sentences. Write *OK* for any sentence that has no error.

1. To be well groomed and dressed appropriately, helps an applicant make a good first impression.
2. The contract was originally to be signed on March 15; last-minute revisions however have delayed the date until March 31.
3. When Mr. Marshall arrives we will begin the festivities.
4. To produce a professional-looking mock-up you may wish to include computer-generated charts and other graphics.
5. See the enclosed catalog for our line of modern-looking, ergonomic office furniture.
6. The budget was originally set at $9,000; actual expenses, however, totaled $12000.
7. Without your assistance Zack we would never have completed this project on schedule.
8. Katherine Quinn, Ph.D. is the director of the pharmaceutical division.
9. The new computer system, which Mr. Jerome ordered last week, was installed today.
10. We were amused to see the typographical error, that appeared in our competitor's latest brochure.
11. This fund prospectus will describe the advantages of such conservative investments as government bonds, municipal bonds and utilities stocks.
12. One of the most interesting analyses of the topic, appears in this economics journal.
13. Charlie will send you our annual report, as soon as we receive copies from the printer.
14. Her husband Martin is an investment banker in Los Angeles.
15. I suggest that you ask Schmidt, Davidson, & Associates to prepare an estimate.
16. The entire order will be shipped by truck, or by airfreight.

17. monitor,
18. from,
19. announcement that . . . merging shocked
20. stock, . . . broker,

17. For an incredibly low package price, you can purchase a computer with a 386 microprocessor, a keyboard, a color <u>monitor</u> and a dot-matrix printer.
18. The company's goal is to add to, not detract <u>from</u> the advantages it enjoys in the marketplace.
19. The <u>announcement,</u> that the rival companies were <u>merging,</u> <u>shocked</u> the industry.
20. Buying BioTek <u>stock</u> according to my <u>broker</u> is not a sound investment.

B. Correct any errors in the following sentences. Write *OK* for any sentence that has no error.

KEY
1. Virginia,
2. omit *and*
3. inexpensive
4. sit
5. OK
6. proposal's
7. whom
8. fallen,
9. Maxes
10. bids.
11. is
12. laid
13. lying
14. she
15. among
16. were
17. there
18. cost-effective?
19. OK
20. were

1. Our new showroom in Richmond, <u>Virginia</u> is scheduled to open in September.
2. Heat, electricity, water, <u>and etc.,</u> are included in these utility estimates.
3. The SuperSpeed copier is neither <u>inexpensive,</u> nor easy to service.
4. Whenever an error message appears on your screen, <u>set</u> down and consult your software manual.
5. By subscribing now, you can save $30 for two full years or $45 for three full years.
6. This <u>proposals'</u> opening paragraph is very confusing.
7. Is Allison James one of the consultants <u>who</u> we met in Washington?
8. Since the prices of laser printers have <u>fell,</u> we decided to purchase several for our publications department.
9. A job freeze, obviously, would hamper us from hiring the two <u>Max's.</u>
10. Deborah asked us to set up a meeting for next Wednesday to discuss the different <u>bids?</u>
11. Either Lisa or Ronald <u>are</u> planning to visit the branch office in Phoenix.
12. On March 20, 1992, the cornerstone was <u>lain</u> for the new convention center.
13. Harrison P. Smith, Jr., is <u>laying</u> in the middle of the corridor.
14. You and <u>her</u> will have to decide how to share the workload.
15. A disagreement arose <u>between</u> Alec, Tracy, Don, and Jerry.
16. Several bids, as he knows, <u>was</u> considered, but only one matched our budget.
17. Sue claims that <u>their</u> are hidden costs that no one has considered.
18. Isn't it apparent that their plan is not <u>cost-effective.</u>
19. In my opinion, you will have to reboot the computer using the systems diskette.
20. If I <u>was</u> in Austin, Texas, or in Santa Fe, New Mexico, I wouldn't be shoveling snow now.

REVIEW cont.

Editing Practice

Test Your Skills. You are applying for a position in a major corporation. You have been asked to take an editing test. Read the following excerpt from a letter addressed to shareholders. Make any necessary corrections.

Many of you have already seen the article in the November issue of *Consumer World* naming our hi-fi stereo videocassette recorder number one in each of ten categories tested. Needless to say, I am exceptionally proud of this accomplishment, and I congratulate all our sales representatives, service technicians, and engineers for achieving this singular honor.

How did we accomplish this goal? Through expert communication. Our sales representatives and service technicians accurately communicate to our engineers the needs and wants of our customers. Our engineers, in turn, design our products to satisfy not only our customers but also our service technicians. The result: a better product, an easier-to-service product.

3.4 *QUOTATION MARKS, PARENTHESES, AND APOSTROPHES*

OBJECTIVES: After completing Section 3.4, you should be able to:

1. Use quotation marks correctly for direct quotations, definitions, special expressions, unfamiliar terms, titles of articles, and so on.
2. Use parentheses correctly to enclose words that give additional information and references.
3. Use apostrophes correctly to form possessive nouns and contractions.
4. Combine other punctuation marks correctly with quotation marks and with parentheses in sentences.
5. Correct errors in the use of quotation marks, parentheses, and apostrophes.

Quotation marks serve primarily to tell the reader the exact words written or spoken by someone, but they also have other important uses. Parentheses share some (but not all) of the uses of commas and dashes. Apostrophes have one common use besides indicating ownership.

Knowing how to correctly use these three marks of punctuation will add to your written communication skill.

QUOTATION MARKS

The common uses of quotation marks are described and illustrated below.

For Direct Quotations

To indicate the *exact* words that someone has written or spoken, use quotation marks. In the following examples, note how commas, colons, and periods are used together with quotation marks.

Ms. Ornette said, "We invested in high-grade corporate bonds." (A comma precedes the direct quotation.)

"We invested in high-grade corporate bonds," Ms. Ornette said. (A comma ends the quotation, separating it from the explanatory words that follow the quotation.)

"We invested," Ms. Ornette said, "in high-grade corporate bonds." (Note how *two* commas are used to separate the interruption. The quotation marks still enclose the speaker's *exact* words.)

Ms. Ornette said: "We invested in high-grade corporate bonds. One reason is that a certain portion of the interest is exempt from taxation. Another reason is that the bonds are yielding more than other comparable investments." (Use a colon before a long quotation, including a quotation of more than one sentence.)

"We invested in high-grade corporate bonds," Ms. Ornette said. "One reason is. . . ." (Again, note that the interrupting expression is separated from the exact words of the speaker by a comma and a period.)

Remember that *indirect* quotations are not enclosed in quotation marks. Indirect quotations are often introduced by the word *that*.

She said that we invested in corporate bonds. (This example is an *in*direct quotation.)

For Quotations Within Quotations

Use single quotation marks for words quoted within other quoted material.

Mr. Laudenberger asked, "Did she say '16 days' or '60 days'?" (Note the position of the question mark *inside* the double quotation mark [because the question mark belongs to the entire sentence] but *outside* the single quotation mark.)

"In my opinion, this spreadsheet program is certainly not 'user-friendly,'" said Martina. (A final comma is placed inside both the single and the double quotation marks.)

Martina said, "In my opinion, this spreadsheet is certainly not 'user-friendly.'" (A period that ends a quotation is also placed inside both the single and the double quotation marks.)

For Definitions, Special Expressions, Unfamiliar Terms, Translations, and Slang

Use quotation marks to enclose definitions and special expressions following such phrases as *known as*, *marked*, and *signed*.

In computer terminology, *GUI* means "graphical user interface." (Quotation marks for definitions.)

Computer equipment known as "peripherals" includes printers, scanners, mice, and modems. (Quotation marks for expressions following *called*, *known as*, and so on.)

Note that words introduced by *so-called* do not require quotation marks since *so-called* itself provides them with sufficient emphasis.

Likewise, use quotation marks for unfamiliar terms and for translations.

The illustration below shows a "light pen," which is used to read bar codes. (Quotation marks for unfamiliar terms.)

Par avion is simply the French term for "by airplane." (Quotation marks for translations.)

Slang may be deliberately used to add punch to a message, to attract attention, or to make a point. (Of course, such uses should be limited.) Use quotation marks to enclose a slang expression, a funny comment, or a grammatical error.

There are only two selling days left in the month, but Tony Rella says the sales contest "ain't over yet!" (Quotation marks for intentional use of a grammatical error.)

The city editor said to "kill" that investigative report on contract fixing. (Quotation marks for a slang expression.)

Checkup 1

KEY
Errors are underscored.
1. 11,"

Are quotation marks used correctly in the following sentences? Add quotation marks as needed and correct any errors. Write *OK* for any sentence that has no error.

1. "The new catalog will be distributed to customers by April <u>11</u>" said Victor.

2. catalog," said Victor, "will
3. session," announced Mr. Caruso, "because
4. announced, . . . afternoon."
5. window of opportunity
6. "Fragile,"
7. 'Fragile.'"
8. "Barbara Myers,"

2. "The new catalog said Victor will be distributed to customers by April 11."
3. "Magda will attend only the morning session announced Mr. Caruso because she must meet an important client in the afternoon."
4. Mr. Caruso announced "Magda will attend only the morning session because she must meet an important client in the afternoon.
5. We concluded that the so-called "window of opportunity" is not open after all.
6. We marked all the cartons Fragile, of course.
7. Graham said, "Mark all the cartons Fragile."
8. The check was signed Barbara Myers, but the teller double-checked it with the signature on file.

For Certain Titles

Use quotation marks for the titles of articles, poems, lectures, chapters of books, essays, and sermons; and for mottoes and slogans.

She wrote "The Electronic Message," which appeared in October's issue of Modern Workplace. (Quotation marks for article title.)

In the preceding example, note that, while the article title is in quotation marks, the title of the magazine is underscored. In addition, book titles are underscored, as are the titles of newspapers, booklets, long poems, plays, operas, and movies.

His new book, Coping With Financial Success, was favorably reviewed in The New York Times. (Underscores for book title and for newspaper name.)

This book, Securing a Sound Financial Future, contains a chapter entitled "Bonds: Safe Investments for Unstable Times," which I highly recommend. (Quotation marks for chapter title; underscores for book title.)

Note that underscoring in typewritten or handwritten copy is equivalent to *italics* in printed copy. Note, too, that while chapter titles are enclosed in quotation marks, other book parts are not. Words such as *preface, index, introduction,* and *appendix* are not enclosed in quotation marks. They are capitalized only when they refer to other parts within a book.

Our economics professor wrote the preface to this volume as well as Chapter 7, "Analyzing Trends."

Punctuation at the End of Quotations

For a summary of how to use periods, commas, colons, semicolons, question marks, and exclamation points with quotation marks, study the following.

1. Periods and commas are *always* placed within the closing quotation mark.

"Performance appraisals," according to the company manual, "should be conducted one month before annual salary reviews."

2. Colons and semicolons are always placed *outside* the closing quotation mark.

> She disagrees that these stocks are "blue chips": American Metals, Inc.; Paige Industries; Clemson Rubber Company; and Verona Plastics.

> Mr. Somer thinks that all the estimates are "outside the ballpark"; for this reason, he is reconsidering the project.

3. Question marks and exclamation points may be placed either inside or outside the closing quotation mark depending on whether or not the question mark or exclamation point is part of the quotation. Follow these rules to decide.

   a. If the quoted words are a question, then the question mark belongs with those quoted words. Place the question mark *inside* the closing quotation mark.

> Edwin asked, "Do you think the computer has enough memory to run this graphics program?" (Only the quoted words make up the question; thus the question mark belongs with the quoted words—*inside* the closing quotation mark.)

> Treat exclamations the same way.

> Karen said, "I can't believe that we have run out of copier paper again!" (Only the words in quotations make up the exclamation; thus the exclamation point belongs with those words—*inside* the closing quotation mark.)

   b. If the quoted words do *not* make up a question (that is, if the quotation is part of a longer question), then the question mark belongs to the entire sentence. Place the question mark *outside* the closing quotation mark.

> Do you agree with Mr. DuPont that their responses to the directive were "flagrantly excessive"? (The entire sentence is a question; the quotation is only part of the question. The question mark belongs *outside* the closing quotation mark.)

> Treat exclamations the same way.

> Imagine calling these stocks "blue chips"! (The entire sentence is an exclamation; the quoted words are only part of the exclamation. The exclamation point belongs *outside* the closing quotation mark.)

Checkup 2

Correct any errors in the use of quotation marks. Write *OK* for any sentence that has no error.

1. Jerry said that the costs were "ridiculously overstated;" moreover, he said that he would prove his charges.

2. models"?
3. Taken."
4. "Waste not, want
   not"
5. OK
6. performers":
7. messenger!"
8. OK

2. Did Ms. Clancy specifically say "50 percent discount on all discontinued models?"
3. During her speech, she quoted a few lines from Robert Frost's well-known poem "The Road Not Taken".
4. Waste not, want not is an apt slogan for our cost-cutting campaign.
5. This book, Designing a Career, has a bibliography that I found very helpful.
6. She included these people in her list of "top performers:" Bernard Quinn, Dorothy Fishlock, and Duane Barrett.
7. Impatiently waiting for the documents to arrive, Robert exclaimed, "Where is that messenger"!
8. Did you hear that one of the major shareholders said he was "selling off his stock"?

PARENTHESES

Although commas, dashes, and parentheses share certain common uses, they should not be used interchangeably. Just as words that have similar meanings still have subtle distinctions, so, too, do commas, dashes, and parentheses have distinctions. The careful business writer is aware of these distinctions. Study the use of parentheses discussed below.

For Words That Give Additional Information

KEY POINT

Parentheses are correctly used to enclose words that give additional information and references.

Commas, dashes, and parentheses may be used to set off words that give additional information. The words set off by commas may be omitted, but they generally add something to the main thought. The words set off by dashes are often given additional emphasis by the dashes. The words set off by parentheses, however, are clearly de-emphasized; they may be omitted.

Sandy Evanson, our corporate librarian, has finally retired. (The words set off by commas may be omitted, but they do add something to the main thought.)

Ms. Fredericks personally selected four new employees—including Jim Kendall in our department—for the executive training program. (The words set off by dashes may be omitted; however, the writer deliberately uses dashes to draw attention to these words.)

In the past year, we lost only one account (Benson Plastics, which had small billings for the past three years). (The words in parentheses are extraneous; they contribute little to the main thought.)

For References

Parentheses are very useful for enclosing references and directions.

Refer to Appendix B (on page 742) for instructions on how to customize your keyboard.

Send your invoice and remittance (check or money order, no cash) in the preaddressed, postage-paid envelope.

Punctuation With Words in Parentheses

Parentheses may be used to enclose some of the words within a sentence, or they may be used to enclose an entire sentence.

Parentheses Within a Sentence. No punctuation mark goes *before* the opening parenthesis within a sentence. Whatever punctuation would normally be used at this point is placed *after* the closing parenthesis.

When we meet next Monday (at the weekly planning session), we will discuss the advantages of simultaneous engineering. (The comma that is needed after the clause *When we meet next Monday* is placed *after* the *closing* parenthesis, not *before* the *opening* parenthesis.)

Mr. Bellini suggested that we limit the number of overtime hours each week (to 5 hours for every employee), and a long discussion followed. (The comma needed to separate the two independent clauses is placed *after* the *closing* parenthesis, not *before* the *opening* parenthesis.)

Kilgore Electronics estimated a unit cost of $1.26 (see the itemized statement enclosed); however, this cost applies only to manufacturing 100,000 units or more. (The semicolon is placed *after* the *closing* parenthesis.)

Note that these rules do not affect any punctuation needed *within* the parentheses. Study the following examples:

As soon as we decide where we will hold our next product information meeting (probably Chicago, Illinois, or Washington, D.C.), we must immediately reserve 100 rooms for our sales representatives.

I would like to revise the last paragraph of the report I wrote (is it on this floppy diskette?) and ask Sal to comment on it.

If an independent clause in parentheses within a sentence is a question or exclamation, the question mark or exclamation mark is included within the parentheses. If the independent clause is a declaration, however, no period is used within the parentheses. Note, too, that when parentheses are included within a sentence, the first word in parentheses is not capitalized (unless, of course, the first word is a proper noun) even if the words in parentheses are an independent clause.

(no cap) indep clause

Paula Steig (she's the manager of contracts) is the person whom you should consult.

Parentheses for Complete Sentences. When the words enclosed in parentheses are entirely independent (that is, they are not part of another sentence), the first word in parentheses is capitalized and normal end punctuation is used before the closing parenthesis.

As you requested, we have amortized these costs over a 15-year period. (Please see Appendix A, page 105.)

Complete sentence: not w/in another sentence

Please be advised that payments received after the due date will not be credited to your account. (A late fee of $10 will be added to your next bill.)

Checkup 3

KEY
1. memorandum),
2. Industries (. . . Services") is
3. 15.)
4. move)?
5. OK
6. (we . . . so),
7. photocopies),
8. OK

Are parentheses used correctly in the following sentences? Correct any errors.

1. According to these new safety guidelines (see the attached memorandum,) we will have to revise our product specifications.
2. Abercrombie Industries, (formerly known as "Abercrombie Travel Services"), is expanding at a very rapid pace.
3. Take advantage of this exciting offer to upgrade your favorite word processing program for only $79.95. (This special offer ends July 15). Visit your software dealer today!
4. Do you think Kent will accept the transfer to the San Diego office (after all, it is a lateral move?)
5. Ms. Phelps insists that all these invoices (every one of them!) be processed by the end of the day.
6. If S&D merges with Renco Electronics (We think they will do so.), the newly formed company will be the largest manufacturer in the state.
7. Several errors in prices were printed in our new catalog (see the attached photocopies) and these must be corrected without delay.
8. The plan is to introduce the earphones at a special low price (say, $19.95); then, in three or four months, we can test the feasibility of raising the price.

APOSTROPHES 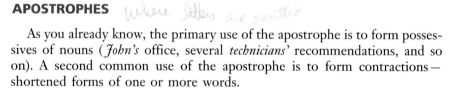 *where letters are omitted*

As you already know, the primary use of the apostrophe is to form possessives of nouns (*John's* office, several *technicians'* recommendations, and so on). A second common use of the apostrophe is to form contractions— shortened forms of one or more words.

KEY POINT

Apostrophes are used to form possessives of nouns, to form contractions, and to show omissions in dates ('92 for 1992).

SUGGESTION

We use contractions almost without thinking, so common are they in everyday speech. This is all the more reason to review contractions thoroughly to make sure that students do not misuse them, especially in creating errors in predicate agreement.

Contraction	Full Form
I'm	I am
you're, we're, they're	you are, we are, they are
she's, he's, it's	she is, she has; he is, he has; it is, it has
I've, you've, we've, they've	I have, you have, we have, they have
I'd, you'd, he'd, she'd, we'd, they'd	I had, I would; you had, you would; he had, he would; she had, she would; we had, we would; they had, they would
I'll, you'll, he'll, she'll, we'll, they'll	I will, you will, he will, she will, we will, they will

Contraction	Full Form
there's, where's	there is, there has; where is, where has
won't, don't, doesn't, didn't, can't, couldn't, wouldn't	will not, do not, does not, did not, cannot, could not, would not

Another use of the apostrophe is to show that the first two figures have been omitted from a year date, such as '93 as a shortened form of *1993*.

SECTION

REVIEW

Practical Application

A. On a sheet of paper, correct any errors in the use of quotation marks, parentheses, or apostrophes in the following sentences. Write *OK* for any sentence that has no error.

1. Dont Joel and Celeste realize that the fax machine is not for personal use?
2. As our attorney explained, *nolo contendere* is a legal term that means "no contest".
3. While adding a column of figures, Arthur exclaimed, "These numbers are wrong"!
4. The new billing system (its already operational) will save us time and will help us serve our customers better.
5. Maureen asked, "Which representative handles the Clifford Textiles account"?
6. "Perhaps" said Mrs. Vreeland, we should include a clause that gives us the right to renew this lease."
7. Check with Amanda (shes the supervisor of word processing) to find out whether the market research survey is ready yet.
8. Nearly 90 percent of our employees have signed up for the additional coverage. (Our survey had shown that the majority of them were very much interested in expanding their life insurance).
9. "We decided to ask the Finance Committee to review these budget changes," said Ms. McCrory, "naturally, we felt that the members would be interested in the reallocation of funds."
10. Since 1979 Seidel Alarm Systems has advertised its well-known motto: Safety With Confidence.
11. Mr. Wentland said "that candy canes will be distributed on December 15."
12. We will place signs in all the windows (each sign will read "Special Sale"!) and will advertise in the local papers.
13. After viewing my slides, Lee said, "Well done—just splendid!"
14. Jackie Howell, the consumer advocate on WFIT 83.8 on the FM dial enthusiastically endorsed our new car seat for children.

15. diagrams!''
16. floor?)
17. OK
18. couldn't
19. Confidential.''
20. degree . . . '84),

KEY
1. 15).
2. introduction,
3. Francis's
4. that the
5. rule:
6. $1,200,
7. has been
8. ''Planning . . .
   Moves,''
9. (1) . . . (2) . . . (3)
10. Croft;
11. 1265).
12. are
13. omit *and*
14. follow.'''
15. ''a

15. Stephen said, "Their so-called experts could not even read the schematic diagrams"!

16. Please take all these specification sheets to Ms. Mueller (is she still on the second floor) before you leave for lunch, Clyde.

17. One client asked whether all the bonds in the portfolio were rated "AAA."

18. Randall couldnt communicate the message to Mrs. Pryce because she was in transit between Sacramento and San Antonio.

19. Please make sure that the envelope is stamped "Private and Confidential".

20. When she completed her master's degree, (she was graduated in '84) Evelyn began working in our Legal Department.

B. On a sheet of paper, correct any errors in the following sentences. Write *OK* for any sentence that has no error.

1. A brief explanation of the new system is included (see pages 10 through 15.).

2. After skimming the "introduction," I decided to buy the book.

3. Francis' idea for modifying the design is brilliant, I think.

4. Beth suggested that, the type fonts be changed to give the report a more professional look.

5. Remember this rule, "No employee is permitted to enter the power plant without his or her identification badge."

6. Although the list price of this laser printer is $1,200.00, it sells for $999 in many discount computer stores.

7. Mr. Hawks said, "Because Kenneth been with our firm for more than 15 years, we will certainly miss him when he moves to Biloxi."

8. Ellen's article on job-hunting tips, Planning Your Career Moves, will soon be reprinted in several magazines.

9. The seminar will cover (1.) time-management techniques, (2.) interpersonal relations, and (3.) decision making.

10. "Without question, we have assembled the best possible team," said Ben Croft, "consequently, our product will be the best on the world market."

11. The Appendix lists several excellent sources for more information (see page 1,265).

12. In our storeroom is a carton of purchase order forms and an unopened package of floppy disks.

13. Miguel requisitioned printer ribbons, form-feed paper, file folders, and etc., for the department staff.

14. He asked, "What is a non sequitur?" She replied, "A non sequitur is a 'statement that does not follow."

15. "According to bank policy," said Ms. Marner, "A teller must verify the signature for any check over $500."

REVIEW cont.

16. company).
17. Skills."
18. 4750).

16. Joseph Pomerantz is the new director of marketing (he has been recruited from a rival <u>company.)</u>
17. If you read the book *Success Without Stress*, pay special attention to Chapter 5, "The Importance of Communication <u>Skills".</u>
18. If you need more information on the policy for merit increases, call Donna Gregus (extension <u>4750.).</u>

Editing Practice

The Editing Desk. Correct any verb errors in the following sentences. Write *OK* for any sentence that has no error.

KEY
1. has been
2. OK
3. Doesn't
4. OK
5. OK
6. gone

1. Janice said that she <u>been</u> to Puerto Rico twice within the past year.
2. Although a number of applicants were interviewed today, we have not yet hired anyone for the position of sales manager.
3. <u>Don't</u> Mr. Sonnenborn want to keep a duplicate copy of all these testimonials?
4. More than a million dollars was raised for the new youth center.
5. "The increasing number of new customers is encouraging," said Mr. Benedict.
6. Has Beatrice already <u>went</u> to the seminar at the Advertising Club?

3.5 CAPITALIZATION

OBJECTIVES: After completing Section 3.5, you should be able to:

1. Use capitals correctly for the first words of sentences, direct quotations, and items in outlines.
2. Use capitals correctly in headings and in titles of publications.
3. Correctly capitalize proper nouns and adjectives, titles, and names of commercial products.
4. Correct errors in capitalization.

The rules of capitalization help writers make words distinctive, emphasize words, and show that certain words are especially important. Some of the rules for capitalization are easy to remember because they are well known and long established. These rules are reviewed briefly in this section. Other capitalization rules may cause writers problems, however, and these pitfalls are also fully discussed here.

FIRST WORDS

Always capitalize the first word of:

1. A sentence or a group of words used as a sentence.

    That report must be finished by tomorrow morning. (Complete sentence.)

    Yes, *tomorrow* morning. (Group of words used as a sentence.)

2. Each line of poetry.

    Let the downpour roil and toil!
    The worst it can do to me
    Is carry some garden soil
    A little nearer the sea.
    — Robert Frost[1]

3. Each item in an outline.

    The results of the survey showed the following:
    1. Consumers dislike loud TV commercials.
    2. Viewers favor fewer commercial interruptions.
    3. Audiences respond to humorous commercials.

4. A sentence in a direct quotation.

    The attorney specifically said, "Be sure to get permission from the copyright holder to reprint this excerpt."

5. A complete sentence after a colon when that sentence is a formal rule or needs special emphasis.

    The retail chain's rule is: The customer is *never* wrong. (Rule.)

    Word processing experts stress this point: Always *save* your document. (For emphasis.)

    Also capitalize the first word after a colon when the material that follows consists of two or more sentences:

    She discussed fully the two main reasons for increasing prices: First, skyrocketing fuel prices have substantially increased shipping costs. Second, the cost of importing the raw materials has doubled in the past ten months.

6. A salutation.

    Dear Dr. Jackson:

7. A complimentary closing.

    Sincerely yours,

---

[1]From "In Time of Cloudburst," *Complete Poems of Robert Frost* (New York: Holt, Rinehart & Winston, 1958), p. 369.

MAIN WORDS

Always capitalize the main words of headings and titles of publications. The words that are *not* capitalized are articles, conjunctions, and short prepositions (that is, prepositions of three or fewer letters), unless they are the first word or the last word in the heading or title.

In this morning's edition of *USA Today*, under the headline "The Need for Financial Constraint and Strict Monetary Policy," Myra Sikorsky commended the House for its budget cuts. (*The* is capitalized in the title of the article because it is the first word. The preposition *for* and the conjunction *and* are not capitalized in the article title.)

You should read "What Small Investors Strive For," a well-written, perceptive article by Jonathan Millard that appears in the current issue of *Today's Investors* magazine. (Here, *for* is capitalized because it is the last word in the title.)

Hyphenated titles follow the same rules:

In "Out-of-Work Blues," Anne Replano tells job seekers how to retain their self-esteem and their sense of humor.

Checkup 1

KEY

Errors are underscored.
1. "Respectfully
2. Substantially
3. Always
4. -Management . . . and How to
5. OK
6. Hard . . . Laser . . . Modems
7. Yes,
8. for Men and Women in . . . *and*
9. All's
10. a

Make any needed corrections in the following sentences. Write *OK* for any sentence that has no error.

1. Whenever I send a letter to an elected official, I use the closing "respectfully yours."
2. Is this bid much lower than the other bids we received? substantially lower.
3. Remember: always keep receipts of all expenses.
4. An interesting and helpful article, in my opinion, is "Labor-management Problems And How To Avoid Them."
5. We must face the hard facts: Sales are down and layoffs are imminent.
6. We are now reviewing our needs for the following hardware:
   1. hard-disk drives
   2. laser printers
   3. modems
7. Is the fax machine on? yes, it's on.
8. He is now writing "Tips For Men And Women In Business" for *Business And Industry* magazine.
9. As Harriet closed the door, she said casually, "all's fair in love and war."
10. Tonight's meeting will include the following: A report by the treasurer, the minutes of the last meeting, and speeches by the candidates for city council.

LANGUAGE
LAPSE

Catch the Lapse:
"Marge and I are
insufferable
friends."

—Jane Ace

[inseparable]

NAMES OF PERSONS

Names of people are capitalized, of course. The problems surrounding the capitalization of names concern the use of prefixes such as the following:

O'. *O'Brien, O'Toole, O'Malley.* The prefix *O'* is followed by a capital letter and no spacing.

Mc, Mac. *McMillan, Macmillan, MacMillan.* The prefix *Mc* is followed by a capital letter and no spacing. The prefix *Mac* may or may not be followed by a capital.

D', Da, De, Di. *D'Amato, d'Amato; Da Puzzo, daPuzzo, DeLorenzo, De Lorenzo, deLorenzo; DiFabio, Di Fabio, diFabio.* Spell each name precisely as the person spells it.

Van, Von. *Van Fossen, van Fossen; van Hoffman; Von Huffman; von der Lieth, Von der Lieth, Von Der Lieth.* Follow the capitalization, spelling, and spacing used by each person.

In all cases, be sure to write each person's name precisely the way he or she writes it—this rule refers not only to capitalization but also to the spelling of and the spacing in names. Note, however, that even prefixes that begin with lowercase letters are capitalized when the surname is used without the first name.

Donald received a letter from Marie la Salle today. (She writes her name *la*.)

He thinks La Salle's comments about the proposal are valid. (When her first name is not used, capitalize *la* to avoid misreading.)

NAMES OF PLACES

Capitalize names of geographical localities, streets, parks, rivers, buildings, and so on, such as *South America, Main Street, Bryant Park, Delaware River, Medical Arts Building.*

Capitalize the word *city* only when it is a part of the corporate name of a city: *Dodge City,* but the *city of Boston.*

Capitalize the word *state* only when it follows the name of a state: *Kansas State,* but the *state of Kansas.*

Capitalize the word *the* in names of places only when *the* is part of the official name: *The Hague,* but *the Maritime Provinces.*

Capitalize *north, south, east,* and *west* whenever they refer to specific sections of the country and, of course, when they are part of proper names. They are not capitalized when they refer merely to direction.

We need a warehouse in the West in order to solve our present shipping problems and lower our shipping costs. (Specific part of the country.)

Her sales territory includes North Carolina. (*North* is part of a proper name.)

An industrial park is under construction 20 miles east of the city. (Here, *east* simply indicates direction.)

NAMES OF THINGS

Capital letters identify official names of companies, departments, divisions, associations, committees, bureaus, buildings, schools, course titles, clubs, government bodies, historical events and documents, and so on.

Jill and Bruce are taking Statistics for Business at Metropolitan College. (*Statistics for Business* is the official course title; *Metropolitan College* is the official name of the school.)

Jill and Bruce are taking a statistics course at a nearby college. (No capitals.)

Ms. Dimitrios is a consultant for the Hamilton Investment Company, which has offices here in the Fairchild Building. (Capitalize the official name of the company and the building.)

She is a consultant for a public relations company in this building. (No capitals.)

The Direct Mail Department has leased two entire floors in the Keystone Building. (Official department name; official building name.)

Capitalize the names of the days of the week, the months of the year, religious days and holidays, and the names of eras and periods: *Tuesday, Wednesday; March, June; Easter, Passover; the Roaring Twenties, the Middle Ages.* Do not capitalize the seasons of the year: *summer, fall, winter, spring.*

PROPER ADJECTIVES

Capitalize proper adjectives, which are adjectives formed from proper nouns; for example, *American, Canadian, Puerto Rican,* and so on. (Note that certain adjectives [*venetian* blind, *india* ink, *turkish* towel, and *panama* hat, for example] are no longer capitalized, because through many years of use they have lost their identification as proper adjectives. Consult a dictionary when in doubt.)

Checkup 2

KEY
1. Mexican
2. City
3. Von Spielmann . . . Inn . . . Lake
4. in . . . A Guide for
5. National Education Association . . . Building

Are capitals used correctly in the following sentences? Correct any errors. Write *OK* for any sentence that has no error.

1. Joanne DeAngello is the director of our <u>mexican</u> trade office.
2. The Decorative Textile Company has a showroom in Kansas <u>city</u>.
3. My associate <u>von Spielmann</u> owns and manages the Serenity <u>inn</u> on <u>lake</u> George.
4. Miriam's speech, "Women <u>In</u> Business: <u>a</u> Guide <u>For</u> Today's Executives," is both amusing and informative.
5. The <u>national education association</u> is exploring the possibility of moving its headquarters into the Chrysler <u>building</u>.

6. Our last <u>fourth</u> of <u>july</u> picnic was a smashing success, Hans von <u>hoffman</u> tells me.

7. Read "Doing Business In Japan — an Up-to-date Approach."

8. On the first <u>monday</u> in <u>october</u> we will meet to discuss our <u>Autumn</u> catalog.

PITFALLS

The following discussion presents some useful solutions to some of the typical problems writers face in using capitals correctly.

Short Forms

Writers often substitute one word for the complete name of a person, place, or thing. Such substitutions are usually lowercased when they are intended to indicate a specific person, place, or thing. Some short forms are capitalized if they are personal titles of high rank, organizational names, or governmental bodies.

The most recent biography of the Admiral is entitled *Nimitz in the Pacific.* (Here, *Admiral* is a personal title of a specific person.)

She has written a biography about an admiral who was famous in World War II. (Because *admiral* does not refer to a particular person, it is not capitalized.)

After the civil engineers completed their inspection of the Lakeview Bridge, they issued a report stating that the bridge needed routine repairs. (Lowercase the second use of *bridge*, because it is a common noun.)

The words *company, department, association, school, college,* and so on, are not usually capitalized when they stand alone, even though they may substitute for the official name of a specific organization.

Her company is considering a merger with Roebuck & Sellers.

Chad visited the museum during a recent trip to Philadelphia.

Ms. Roth is promoting two staff assistants in our department.

The terms *government* and *federal government* are not capitalized. *Federal* is capitalized, of course, when it is part of an official name, such as *Federal Communications Commission.*

Personal and Official Titles

Always capitalize a title written before a name.

Among the directors are Colonel Sanders, former Senator Elias, and Professor La Roche.

A title written after a name or without a name is capitalized when (1) it is a very high national or international title or (2) it is part of an address.

Javier Pérez de Cúellar, Secretary General of the United Nations, worked to obtain the release of the hostages. (Always capitalize this internationally known title.)

In yesterday's column, she discussed the President's economic policies. (*President* — referring to the President of the United States — is always capitalized.)

Anselm Fattimore, president of Vanguard Enterprises, Inc., plans to retire at the end of the year. (Do not capitalize *president* in such situations.)

Ms. Erica Godfrey, President
Godfrey Electronics, Inc.
1500 College Avenue
Racine, Wisconsin 53403
(Capitalize a title that is part of an address.)

When joined to titles, *ex-* and *-elect* are not capitalized. Also, *former* and *late* are not capitalized.

Among the dignitaries invited to the dinner was former Mayor Holland.

The late Senator John Heinz will be remembered for his strong stands on environmental issues.

Governor-elect Olins said that she would balance the state budget without raising taxes.

Next semester, ex-Senator Seeley will teach a course in political science.

Commercial Products

❏ **SUGGESTION**
Ask students to write sentences that have capitalization errors in them. Combine the sentences for a class exercise.

Distinguish carefully between a proper noun that is part of the official name of a product and a common noun that names the *general* class of the product. For example, you would write *Arch Saver shoes*, not *Arch Saver Shoes*, because the official brand name is *Arch Saver*. Note the following:

Kleenex tissues	Xerox machine
Coke (Coca-Cola)	Ping-Pong balls

Checkup 3

KEY
1. Data-Processing Department
2. west
3. president

Correct any errors in the use of capitalization in the following sentences. Write *OK* for any sentence that has no error.

1. The employees in the data-processing department collected contributions for the Children's Aid Society.
2. Laser Recordings is building a new plant and warehouse 15 miles West of Memphis, Tennessee.
3. Estevez Electronics will announce the appointment of a new President by this afternoon.

4. cars
5. Federal
6. supervisor . . . au-
   ditorium
7. OK
8. president
9. crackers
10. agency . . . coffee

4. Throughout the country we lease as many as 10,000 General Motors Cars.
5. The federal Deposit Insurance Corporation is not considering new banking regulations.
6. When your Supervisor returns, Homer, please ask her to meet with us in the Auditorium.
7. Send the original copy to the Manufacturing Division at our headquarters office, of course.
8. Esther Goodwin, President of Laser Recordings, has announced that her company will now manufacture videodiscs.
9. These Nabisco Crackers are low in sodium and high in fiber.
10. Which Agency currently has the Folgers Coffee account?

REVIEW

Practical Application

KEY
1. company
2. OK
3. vice president
4. "Cordially" . . .
   "Cordially
5. and Bonds: An
6. flight . . . Airport
7. Gallery . . . Library
8. manager . . . dis-
   trict
9. Restaurant . . . Day
10. Always
11. Midwest, . . . state
12. northern

A. On a sheet of paper, correct any capitalization errors in the following sentences. Write *OK* for any sentence that has no error.

1. Our Company now has exclusive distribution rights to these products anywhere on the East Coast.
2. According to reliable sources, the Governor will not seek reelection.
3. Marla Mendez, Vice President of Kline & Mendez Inc., purchased the property last week.
4. She suggests that we use "cordially" or "cordially yours" for less formal closings.
5. "Stocks And Bonds: an Investor's Guide" is the title of her recent article.
6. Severe winds delayed our Flight from O'Hare International airport yesterday.
7. When we were staying in Washington, D.C., we visited the National gallery and the library of Congress.
8. Before she was named Manager of the Chicago regional office, Melita was a supervisor in one of our District offices.
9. The Majestic restaurant will be closed on Thanksgiving day.
10. For years the policy has been the same: always plan your work and work your plan.
11. The company's distribution center is in the midwest, but its main office is located in the State of Georgia.
12. Trusty Truck Rentals is relocating to the Northern part of the city of Fort Wayne.

REVIEW cont.

13. states
14. West Coast
15. spring

KEY
1. as if he were
2. within
3. tickets,
4. well
5. federal govern-
   ment agency
6. OK
7. behind
8. Doesn't
9. help telling
10. Where are
11. beside
12. omit *at*
13. omit *to*
14. OK
15. Stuart?"
16. whom
17. OK
18. merger
19. head's
20. weeks, *or* staff,

13. For two weeks we will call on clients in the States of Iowa, Kansas, Nebraska, and Illinois.
14. Rowena hopes to find a position with a newspaper on the west coast.
15. Because of the success of our Spring fashions, we have exceeded our revenue goals for the year.

B. On a sheet of paper, correct any errors in the following sentences. Write *OK* for any sentence that has no error.

1. Martin, the assistant supervisor, sometimes acts like he was the president of the company!
2. The new communications system, according to the operations manager, will be completely installed inside of one week.
3. The travel agent sent our itinerary, airline tickets and hotel confirmations to the wrong address.
4. I installed a new hard drive in your personal computer, and it should work as good as any new PC you could purchase.
5. Do you know whether there is a Federal Government Agency that helps small businesses?
6. Yes, the official name of the agency is the U.S. Small Business Administration.
7. The maps that you're looking for are in back of those cabinets.
8. Don't Maureen know the way to the cafeteria yet?
9. When she saw the logo, Caryl could not help but tell the designers why it was inappropriate.
10. Where's the paper and crayons I requested this morning?
11. Is that young man standing besides Althea Watson the new summer intern?
12. Betty, do you know where Diana and Donna are at?
13. No, I do not know where they went to, Harold.
14. Do you have a purchase order form like this one in your file folder?
15. Merilee asked, "Why did you delete these files from the current directory, Stuart"?
16. One of the new installers who you met at this morning's orientation is Wilma's brother.
17. Elvera Fasano, former president of the Retail Jewelers Association, has been named to the Governor's committee.
18. The only one of the regional managers who was aware of the merger, was Andrew Abbate.
19. Each department heads status report must be submitted no later than August 31.
20. Because Cynthia has been working with our Denver staff for the last two weeks her assistant publisher has been handling these negotiations.

REVIEW cont.

Editing Practice

KEY
1. Since *or* Because
2. unless *or* without making sure
3. in regard to
4. among
5. to
6. OK
7. that
8. really

Using Your Word Processor. Edit the following sentences to correct any errors they may contain. Write *OK* for any sentence that has no error.

1. Being that we did not pay the bill within ten days, we cannot deduct the 2 percent discount.
2. Please do not schedule the meeting for next Friday <u>without</u> you make sure that Brian Sweeney is free to attend it.
3. One of the reporters asked her several questions <u>in regards to</u> the proposed government legislation.
4. This stack of new insurance claims will be divided <u>between</u> the three most experienced adjusters.
5. According to the announcement, the increases are retroactive <u>from</u> last January.
6. No one noticed that the inventory control number written on this form was different from the number on this computer printout.
7. We read in the company newspaper <u>where</u> Elliot has been on sabbatical.
8. As you can well imagine, Joy Madison was <u>real</u> happy when she heard that the contract had been canceled.

Using Business Vocabulary. On a separate sheet of paper, fill in the missing words with the correct words from the list below.

KEY
1. j. valuable
2. i. negotiate
3. g. irrelevant
4. b. bankruptcy
5. c. chronological
6. a. approximate
7. f. freight
8. e. extension
9. d. exhaustive
10. h. mandatory

a. approximate	e. extension	i. negotiate
b. bankruptcy	f. freight	j. valuable
c. chronological	g. irrelevant	
d. exhaustive	h. mandatory	

1. Stocks, bonds, and all other (?) securities must be locked in a fireproof vault overnight.
2. At tomorrow's meeting we will try to (?) a 15-year loan at 10 percent interest per year.
3. The other committee members thought that Evan's remarks were (?) and insensitive.
4. Because Norton Industries has been unprofitable for three years, (?) proceedings will begin early next month.
5. Please take these memos from Chairman Reo and arrange them in (?) order, beginning with January memos.
6. The (?) cost for the entire system is $10,000.
7. According to the contract, the shipper pays the (?) charges.
8. Because they could not meet the payment deadline, we have agreed to a 30-day (?) for the total balance.
9. The utility company announced that the (?) round of talks with the Metropolitan Power Commission has ended and that a rate increase of 10 percent has been approved.
10. Our company no longer has any (?) retirement age.

3.6 *ABBREVIATIONS*

OBJECTIVES: After completing Section 3.6, you should be able to:

1. Use appropriate abbreviations correctly before and after personal names.
2. Use abbreviations correctly in company and organizational names.
3. Use abbreviations correctly in addresses, units of measure, and expressions of time.

❑ **SUGGESTION**

Remind students to consult a dictionary or writer's handbook when they have questions about abbreviations.

Abbreviations provide writers with shortcuts, and shortcuts are certainly appropriate *at times*. As a business writer, you must know when abbreviations are acceptable — and when they are *not*. In addition, you must know the correct forms of those abbreviations.

PERSONAL NAMES

Study the following rules for using abbreviations before and after personal names.

Before Personal Names

Most of the titles used before personal names are abbreviations.

Singular	Plural
Mr.	Messrs. (from the French, *messieurs*)
Mrs.	Mmes. or Mesdames
Ms.	Mses. or Mss.
Miss	Misses
Dr.	Drs.

Other titles used before personal names are spelled out whether the full name or only the last name is given: *Governor* Billington, *Superintendent* Kuris, *Representative* Perez, the *Honorable* Jane W. Cleary, the *Reverend* Arthur Franks Jr., *General* Streeter, and so on.

After Personal Names

Academic Degrees and Similar Abbreviations. Abbreviations of academic degrees, religious orders, and similar abbreviations generally have internal periods: *M.D., D.D.S., Ph.D., D.V.M., Ed.D., S.J., D.D.* Check your dictionary whenever you are not sure of the abbreviation.

When such abbreviations follow a person's name, do *not* use *Mr.*, *Ms.*, *Mrs.*, *Miss*, or *Dr.* before the person's name. Use a comma before these abbreviations that follow names.

> Jane T. Prentiss, M.D. *or* Dr. Jane T. Prentiss (Not: *Dr.* Jane T. Prentiss, *M.D.*)

> Price S. Raymond, Ph.D. *or* Dr. Price S. Raymond (Not: *Dr.* Price S. Raymond, *Ph.D.*)

Other titles before the person's name may sometimes be appropriate:

> Reverend Peter Amendola, S.J.

> Professor Alicia P. Stevens, Litt.D.

Note that in a sentence, any such abbreviation following a name must be set off with *two* commas, unless the abbreviation ends the sentence.

> Jane T. Prentiss, M.D., is the subject of today's "Woman in the News" column.

Jr. and Sr. Omit the comma before *Jr.* and *Sr.* when either follows a person's name unless the person specifically uses a comma, as some people still do.

> Mr. Sloan P. Renwick Jr.

> Dr. A. Phillip Carlton, Sr. (Dr. Carlton *does* use a comma before *Sr.*)

> Do not use *Jr.* and *Sr.* with a person's last name only.

Initials

Initials are abbreviations of names; in some cases, the initials *are* names because they do not really "stand for" anything. Write an initial with a period and a space after it (always following, however, a person's individual preference).

> Will T. J. handle the arbitration case?

> Get approval from T. J. Forsythe before we leave today.

Note: Reference initials written at the end of memos and letters are usually written with no periods and no spaces. See Sections 7.2 and 8.2 for examples.

Checkup 1

Are abbreviations used correctly in the following sentences? Correct any errors. Write *OK* for any sentence that has no error.

1. Ms. Oliva wrote a letter to Paul C. W. Bradley Jr., but Mr. Bradley Jr. has not responded yet.

REINFORCEMENT
Review the need to have *two* commas set off any of these abbreviations. Likewise, when *Jr.* or *Sr.* is preceded by a comma (a style that is becoming outdated), it must also be followed by a comma (unless, of course, it ends the sentence).

KEY
Errors are underscored.
1. omit *Jr.*

2. Senator
3. OK
4. omit *Dr.* or *M.D.* (and, of course, the commas before and after *M.D.*)
5. Mr.
6. omit *Ms.* or substitute *Dr.* and omit *Ph.D.*, along with the commas.

2. Her constituents were pleased when <u>Sen.</u> Laughton announced she would run for reelection.
3. The property has been owned by the Messrs. Fleming since the 1970s.
4. Dr. Lucretia T. Harter, M.D., will be named director of the institute within the next few weeks.
5. His associate will oversee the project while <u>Mister</u> Kinsky is on vacation.
6. I read in the news that <u>Ms.</u> Jessica W. Taft, Ph.D., has resigned her university position.

COMPANIES AND ORGANIZATIONS

Always write the name of a company or an organization precisely as its *official* name is written:

Perkins & Burke Inc.
Olsten and Jonas, Inc.
Bits 'n' Bytes Unlimited
Magnolia Construction Company

Quick Contracting Co.
Landry Bros.
L. T. Marquette & Sons
The Loomis/Nettleton/Roth Group

Inc. and *Ltd.*

As with *Jr.* and *Sr.*, omit the comma before *Inc.* and *Ltd.* in company names. Again, however, always follow the *official* name.

Pam works for McCarter & Teisch in New York City.

Write to HiTech Wares, Inc., for more information. (Note *two* commas to set off *Inc.* within a sentence.)

All-Capital Abbreviations

Many names of organizations, associations, government agencies, and so on, are abbreviated in all-capital letters with no periods or spaces between the letters:

AAA	American Automobile Association
AFL-CIO	American Federation of Labor and Congress of Industrial Organizations
AT&T	American Telephone and Telegraph
FBI	Federal Bureau of Investigation
IRS	Internal Revenue Service
NASA	National Aeronautics and Space Administration
NYSE	New York Stock Exchange
OPEC	Organization of Petroleum Exporting Countries
UPS	United Parcel Service
USDA	United States Department of Agriculture

In addition, the call letters of broadcasting stations are always written in all-capital letters without periods.

WPAT-FM   WNBC-TV   KCBT   NPR

When *United States* is abbreviated (before the name of a government agency, for example), periods are used.

the U.S. Department of Commerce

BUSINESS ABBREVIATIONS

In addition to their use with personal names and in the names of companies and organizations, abbreviations are used in many other instances in business correspondence.

Address Abbreviations

Street Names. On envelopes, space restrictions sometimes make the use of *St.* and *Ave.* necessary. In letters, however (and on envelopes whenever possible), avoid abbreviating the words *Street, Avenue,* and so on. When abbreviations such as *NW, SW,* and *NE* appear after street names, use a comma to separate the street name from the abbreviation. (Note that the abbreviations *NW, SW,* and so on, should be spelled out in other cases.)

405 West Ninth Street
28 Kingston Boulevard
317 Cortelyou Avenue, NW

Post Office Box Numbers. The words *Post Office* may or may not be abbreviated with box numbers. In fact, the words *Post Office* may be omitted.

Post Office Box 605 *or* P.O. Box 605 *or* Box 605

City Names. Except for the abbreviation *St.* in such city names as *St. Louis* and *St. Paul*, do not abbreviate city names.

State Names. With inside addresses, use either (1) the two-letter abbreviations of state names or (2) the spelled-out name. The U.S. Postal Service prefers the two-letter state abbreviations on envelopes. In both cases, always use a ZIP Code.

Dr. Francine P. Snowden
1301 Westerly Avenue
St. Louis, MO 63121
or St. Louis, Missouri 63121

When state names are used elsewhere (that is, not on envelopes or with inside addresses), spell them out or, if abbreviations are appropriate, use the "traditional" state abbreviations, such as "Conn." or "Calif."

□ **SUGGESTION**
The U.S. Postal Service occasionally changes its guidelines for addressing mail. To remain current on this important issue, check with the post office about once a year.

Do not be surprised to see mail with computer-printed labels in all-capital letters with *no* punctuation and nearly everything abbreviated.

DR F P SNOWDEN
ST LOUIS HOSP
2500 CLARK ST
ST LOUIS MO 63121-1234

Units of Measure

General Use. In routine correspondence, units of measure are spelled out: *yards*, *pounds*, *kilograms*, *degrees*, *meters*, *gallons*, and so on. Use figures with units of measure.

Each swatch is about 3 inches by 4 inches.

We will need at least eight 1-liter containers.

The sample that we tested contained about 3 grams of zinc.

Technical Use. In technical work and on invoices, units of length, weight, capacity, area, volume, temperature, and time are usually abbreviated. Among the commonly used terms are these:

yd	yard, yards	g	gram, grams
in	inch, inches	kg	kilogram, kilograms
oz	ounce, ounces	m	meter, meters
pt	pint, pints	mm	millimeter, millimeters
gal	gallon, gallons	km	kilometer, kilometers
ft	foot, feet	L	liter, liters
lb	pound, pounds	cm	centimeter, centimeters

Expressions of Time

Write *a.m.* and *p.m.* in lowercase letters with periods but with no spacing. Always use figures with these abbreviations, and do not use *o'clock* with *a.m.* or *p.m.* Remember: *a.m.* means "before noon" and *p.m.* means "after noon."

The bus will leave at 8:30 a.m. on Thursday. (Not: 8:30 o'clock a.m.)

Days and Months

The days of the week and the months of the year should be abbreviated only when space forces the writer to do so (as in tables and lists). In such cases, use the following abbreviations. Note that *May*, *June*, and *July* are not usually abbreviated.

Days of the Week	**Months of the Year**
Sun., Mon., Tues. (or Tue.), Wed., Thurs. (or Thu.), Fri., Sat.	Jan., Feb., Mar., Apr., May, June (or Jun.), July (or Jul.), Aug., Sept., Oct., Nov., Dec.

No.

The abbreviation *No.* is used only before a figure: *License No. 465-75E, Patent No. 769,878,* and so on. Note that *number* is spelled out when it is the first word in a sentence and that it may be omitted after such words as *Room, Invoice,* and *Check.*

Have you found copies of the following purchase orders: Nos. 125-76, 125-89, and 126-13? When you do, bring them to Room 1272.

Number 5632 is the only outstanding check, Ms. Tobias.

The symbol # may be used on forms or in technical copy.

Miscellaneous Abbreviations

In addition to the abbreviations discussed so far, there are many more that are used in business, including these:

ASAP	as soon as possible
atty.	attorney
CAD	computer-assisted design
CEO	chief executive officer
ETA	estimated time of arrival
OTC	over the counter
PE	price-earnings (ratio)
reg.	registered
YTM	yield to maturity

Check a dictionary or other reference book for a complete list of terms and their acceptable abbreviations.

Checkup 2

Are abbreviations used correctly in these sentences? Correct any errors. Write *OK* for any sentence that has no error.

KEY
1. UAW
2. a.m.
3. Tuesday, March 7,
4. centimeters.
5. Minnesota,
6. pounds
7. New York, . . . New Jersey, . . . Rhode Island.
8. Fort Myers, Florida,

1. Mr. John Trevette, a U.A.W. official from Detroit, is the guest speaker at the rally tonight.
2. According to the revised agenda, the second session will begin promptly at 10:15 AM.
3. The Mayor has scheduled a news conference on Tues., Mar. 7, at 3:00 p.m.
4. The chip is about 2 inches long, which is equal to slightly more than 5 CM.
5. She now lives in St. Cloud, MN. where she works for KIBO radio.
6. Since the carton weighs more than 50 lb, we cannot ship it by Allied Parcel Service.
7. After she speaks in N.Y., Karen will travel to N.J. and to R.I.
8. Al Leonard moved to Ft. Myers, FL, after he retired from AT&T.

REVIEW

Practical Application

A. On a sheet of paper, correct any errors in abbreviation use in the following sentences. Write *OK* for any sentence that has no error.

1. Barbara Henry, a senior accountant at the <u>Saint</u> Louis office, will audit all the <u>MO</u> accounts.
2. One of our research chemists, <u>Dr.</u> Morris Anthony, Ph.D., holds Patent No. 987,789.
3. A reporter for <u>W.A.B.C.</u> interviewed two <u>VPs</u> of our firm.
4. Most of Lauren's territory is in the <u>NW</u> part of the state, isn't it?
5. Next semester <u>Prof.</u> Hoskins will teach Labor Relations at the Tucson campus of the <u>Univ.</u> of Arizona.
6. To save gas, just add 16 <u>oz</u> of Magic Oil to every 15 <u>gal</u> of gasoline.
7. <u>No.</u> 456-654 is the only file that is missing.
8. The committee members agreed to meet again on <u>Fri. a.m.</u>
9. Our guest speaker for the charity drive will be the <u>Rev.</u> Freeman J. Williams Jr.
10. Has <u>Mister</u> McCarthy had an opportunity to respond to this letter from the <u>US</u> Department of Labor?
11. This <u>U.S.D.A.</u> booklet offers helpful tips on nutrition.
12. Station WZXY-FM has almost 30 percent of the morning "drive time" audience.
13. Charlene once worked for the AAA in Ft. Wayne, IN.
14. Check the files for License <u>Number</u> 393-576, please, Alfred.
15. We renewed our lease on <u>Feb.</u> 1, 1991.
16. Packages weighing over 25 <u>lb</u> will be shipped at book rate.
17. Monica now works for <u>T.W.A.</u> in LA, doesn't she?
18. Steve reserved Room 2914 for the conference next Tuesday.
19. Louisa T. Clarkson, <u>M.D.</u> is the head of the Medical <u>Dept.</u>
20. Please call <u>Sen.</u> Kakutani's office to confirm our appointment.

B. On a sheet of paper, correct any errors in the following sentences. Write *OK* for any sentence that has no error.

1. Traffic circles in England are called <u>roundabouts.</u>
2. Yes, either Christina or José <u>are</u> going to supervise the completion of the project.
3. Mr. Hunter asked, "<u>why</u> did the attorney cross out this clause in the <u>contract</u>"?
4. Naturally, we're confident that our <u>Fall</u> list of trade books will sell extremely well.
5. On her desk <u>is</u> the sales report for the first quarter and the performance evaluation for each staff member.
6. As a result of our campaign, we raised more than $5,000 for <u>U.N.I.C.E.F.</u>

KEY

1. St. . . . Missouri
2. omit *Dr.* or *Ph.D.*,
3. WABC . . . vice presidents
4. northwestern
5. Professor . . . University
6. ounces . . . gallons
7. Number
8. Friday morning.
9. Reverend
10. Mr. . . . U.S.
11. USDA
12. OK
13. Fort, Indiana
14. No.
15. February
16. pounds
17. TWA . . . Los Angeles,
18. OK
19. M.D., . . . Department.
20. Senator

KEY

1. "roundabouts."
2. is
3. "Why . . . contract?"
4. fall
5. are
6. UNICEF

7. Doesn't
8. Blake's
9. omit *to*
10. lie
11. Who
12. New York
13. hard-working, de-
    pendable,
14. July;
15. September; *or* Sep-
    tember. The
16. Avenue
17. company
18. $2,000; *or* $2,000.
    Our
19. accountant's
20. contract, manage-
    ment

REVIEW cont.

7. Don't Priscilla need these graphs and charts for her presentation tomorrow morning?
8. When you finish, please call Ms. Blakes assistant to change our meeting to Friday afternoon.
9. Do you know where Sean has gone to, Louie?
10. Since we don't need to check these envelopes now, we can just let them lay there until tomorrow.
11. Whom has been named to head the Finance Committee?
12. All these terminals are connected to our mainframe computers in our N.Y. office.
13. Kim is indispensable because he is such a hard-working dependable experienced underwriter.
14. Our current inventory will last only until June or July, you should plan, therefore, to reorder in time for the summer rush.
15. AMC Plastics sent a deposit in September, the rest of the payment is due in November.
16. Send all purchase orders to the center on Third Ave. unless Mr. Conroy instructs you to do otherwise.
17. One co. on the West Coast has estimated the total cost to be under $10,000.
18. The total payment was $2,000, our current balance is approximately $450.
19. In my opinion, we should seek our accountants advice before the new fiscal year.
20. Although the union has not yet ratified the new contract. Management is conducting business as usual.

Editing Practice

Plurals and Possessives. Rewrite any sentences that contain errors. Write *OK* for any sentence that has no error.

KEY

1. who's *or* who has
2. Mike's
3. there
4. OK
5. Paulsons'
6. Rita's
7. OK
8. your
9. patients'

1. Do you know whose been assigned to handle the Brancusi account?
2. Mike keeping a chronological file is an excellent idea.
3. Obviously, their are still some problems to be resolved.
4. Miss Finderak's asking for a transfer surprised all of us.
5. The Paulsons home will be put up for sale as soon as the mortgage for their new home is approved.
6. Rita and Ellen's jobs are very different, even though they are both public health workers.
7. The first two suggestions are mine; the rest are theirs.
8. Mrs. Chu commented on you helping others to complete their projects.
9. The patient's lounge, which is now being redecorated, is on the second floor of the hospital.

10. weeks'

KEY
1. retroactive
2. attorneys
3. erroneous
4. equipping
5. corroborated
6. overrated
7. exaggerated
8. controlled
9. competent
10. pronunciation

SECTION

REVIEW cont.

10. In about three <u>weeks</u> time, we should know whether our budget has been approved.

Spelling Alert! Correct any spelling errors in the following sentences. Write *OK* if a sentence has no error.

1. Our decision to make the salary increases <u>retractive</u> to May has been approved by the Executive Committee.
2. The <u>attornies</u> both agreed that we should bring suit against the Hartland Corporation.
3. The newspaper reports were clearly <u>eroneous</u>; there is no truth to the allegations.
4. We are now <u>equiping</u> each store with its own computerized inventory-control system to help reduce out-of-stocks.
5. Mrs. Lerner <u>coroborated</u> Bob's statement concerning the sale of the LaSalle Street property.
6. In our opinion, the value of the building and the property is <u>overated</u> by as much as 30 percent.
7. To no one's surprise, the Widget Manufacturing Company has <u>exagerated</u> its share of the marketplace.
8. In carefully <u>controled</u> experiments, we proved that our product removes stains better than any other product on the market.
9. Abigail is not only a <u>compatant</u> systems analyst, but she is also a congenial and diligent coworker.
10. The <u>pronounciation</u> of *Messrs.* is "mes-ərz."

SECTION

3.7 *NUMBERS*

OBJECTIVES: After completing Section 3.7, you should be able to:

1. Determine when to express numbers in words and when to express them in figures in sentences.
2. Use ordinal numbers correctly in business communications.
3. Use correct punctuation and symbols with numbers.
4. Correct errors in the use of numbers.

❏**SUGGESTION**

Stress to students the importance of numbers in business correspondence. Letters, memos, and reports are usually filled with numbers.

Numbers, for obvious reasons, are commonly used in business to express sums of money, order quantities, discounts, time, measurements, percentages, addresses, dates, sales statistics, versions of computer programs, and so

SUGGESTION

Stress to students that errors in numbers can be expensive, time-consuming, and exceptionally disruptive.

on. Business writers know that the correct use of numbers is often critical to clear, accurate communication. Errors in number use can cause more than simple confusion; they can be expensive, time-consuming, and exceptionally disruptive. Be sure to master the following principles of number usage, and make it a habit to proofread numbers carefully whenever you write business messages.

USING WORDS TO EXPRESS NUMBERS

WORLD VIEW

Most countries outside the United States use the metric system of weights and measures. It is useful to know how to convert from one system to another. For example, a visitor from Japan who is planning to drive from Los Angeles to San Francisco may find it helpful to know the distance in kilometers as well as in miles.

Why is it important to know when to express numbers in figures and when to express them in words? One reason is that long-established use dictates certain rules. Another reason is that figures and words have different effects on different readers. The use of figures, for example, tends to emphasize a number, while the use of words tends to de-emphasize a number: *$100* is more emphatic than *a hundred dollars.* Thus we use figures when the number is a significant statistic or deserves special emphasis, while we use words for numbers in a formal message and for numbers that are not significant and need no special attention.

The business writer must know the general rules for expressing numbers in words and for expressing them in figures and must be able to manipulate the rules when it is necessary to achieve a greater degree of formality or to provide greater emphasis. First we will discuss when the writer should use words to express numbers. Then we will discuss when the writer should use figures to express numbers.

At the Beginning of a Sentence

At the beginning of a sentence use a spelled-out word, not a figure. If writing the word seems awkward, then reword the sentence so that the number does not occur first.

Ninety-two percent of the students we surveyed said that they prefer the new program. (Not: *92 percent.* . . .)

Of the students we surveyed, 92 percent said that they prefer the new program. (Better than *Ninety-two percent.* . . .)

Numbers From *One* Through *Ten*

In business correspondence, numbers from *one* through *ten* are generally spelled out.

Last month our representatives acquired nine new accounts.

Ms. Wrigley manages the Providence, Rhode Island, news bureau.

Their store was formerly on Fifth Avenue. (Note that numbered streets from *first* through *tenth* are also spelled out.)

Fractions

Fractions are expressed in words in general business correspondence.

About one-fourth of the people surveyed said that they were dissatisfied with their present long-distance carrier.

Only one-third of our sales representatives were at the Chicago meeting.

However, a mixed number (a whole number plus a fraction) is expressed in figures.

Our corporate headquarters is located on 8½ acres of land near the Blue Ridge Mountains.

Indefinite Numbers

Spell out indefinite numbers and amounts, as shown in these phrases:

a few million dollars
hundreds of requests
several thousand orders

Ages and Anniversaries

Ages are spelled out—unless, of course, they are significant statistics.

Len Barnwell, a staff writer, will be forty-two years old next week.

Winona Ames, who is in her late fifties, is our technology expert.

Angela Russo, 27, has been appointed director of marketing. (A significant statistic.)

When ordinal numbers (*1st, 2d, 3d, 4th*, and so on) are used for ages and anniversaries, they are generally spelled out.

his twenty-first birthday
our seventeenth anniversary

But when more than two words are needed to spell the number, or when special emphasis is desired, express the numbers in figures.

our town's 125th anniversary (Not *one hundred and twenty-fifth*.)
A 10th Anniversary Sale! (For emphasis.)

Centuries and Decades

Centuries are generally expressed in words.

the nineteen hundreds (But for emphasis, the *1900s*.)
the twentieth century
nineteenth-century factories

Decades, however, may be expressed in several ways.

the nineteen-nineties *or* the 1990s *or* the nineties *or* the '90s

Checkup 1

KEY

Errors are underscored.
1. eight
2. 1970s,
3. one-third
4. Forty-seven *or* According to this survey, 47 percent
5. OK
6. 3½ *or* 3.5
7. Sixteen *or* This morning, 16 applicants
8. thousand
9. OK
10. seventeenth-century

Correct any errors in number use in the following sentences. Rewrite the sentences if necessary. Write *OK* for any sentence that has no error.

1. The completed report, which should be about 8 pages long, will be duplicated and distributed tomorrow.
2. Bertell & Company bought this property in the late 1970's, when it cost less than $100,000.
3. Last year, less than 1/3 of our budget was spent on advertising.
4. 47 percent of the customers we interviewed valued quality over discounts, according to this survey.
5. Employees between the ages of 19 and 40 will pay only $18 a month for dental insurance; employees over 40 will pay slightly higher premiums.
6. Our Omaha district office is responsible for three and a half times more revenue than our next highest producer.
7. 16 applicants have already called about the apartment this morning.
8. Cyril, I think that we should reprint a few 1,000 more of these order forms.
9. We received hundreds of letters in response to our advertisement.
10. Mr. Carabelli thought the drawing might be the work of a 17th-century Dutch artist.

USING FIGURES TO EXPRESS NUMBERS

For Numbers Higher Than *Ten*

As you know, numbers from *one* through *ten* are spelled out. Numbers higher than *ten* are expressed in figures.

Last month 14 condominiums were sold at an auction.

This 16-page brochure describes our complete list of member services.

However, express related numbers in the same way. If any of the numbers are above ten, express all the numbers in figures.

In Conference Room B we will need 4 tables, 24 chairs, and 2 easel stands. (Because one of the related numbers is above ten, all are expressed in figures.)

Note: Figures are more emphatic than words because figures stand out clearly (especially when they are surrounded by words). Therefore, when greater emphasis is required for a number from *one* to *ten*, use a figure to express that number. For example:

for 10 minutes (More emphatic than *ten minutes.*)
a 3-year loan (More emphatic than a *three-year loan.*)

For Sums of Money

Sums of money are written in figures.

Clement's travel expenses totaled $536.75.

We have already exceeded the budget, which was $500. (Not *$500.00.* The extra zeros are unnecessary.)

We spent between $4,000 and $5,000. The unit cost is estimated to be 55 cents. (Not *$0.55.* Use the symbol ¢ in tables and in technical copy.)

Note that words *and* figures are often used to express amounts of a million or more.

$9 million or 9 million dollars
$12.5 million or 12.5 million dollars

To avoid misreading, be sure to repeat the word *million* in expressions such as this:

between $2 million and $3 million (Not *between $2 and $3 million.*)

Also be sure to treat related numbers in the same way.

between $500,000 and $1,000,000 (Not *between $500,000 and $1 million.*)

Remember that indefinite amounts are spelled out:

William's tax refund amounted to a few hundred dollars.

They bought about a thousand dollars' worth of antique china and crystal at the auction.

In Addresses

Use figures for house numbers except for *One.* For street numbers, spell out the numbers from *first* through *tenth.* Use figures for all other street numbers.

Our main office is located at One Broad Street. (Spell out *One* when it is a house number.)

The bookstore that was at 121 West 12 Street is now located at 94 West 14 Street.

When the house number and the street number are not separated by *East, West,* or a similar word, use the ordinals *st, d,* and *th* with the street number.

2131 96th Street (The ordinal *96th* helps to prevent possible confusion.)

ZIP Code numbers are, of course, always given in figures.

New York, New York 10020 (Note that no comma precedes the ZIP Code number.)
New York, NY 10020-1221 (Nine-digit ZIP Code number.)

Checkup 2

KEY
1. OK (significant statistics)
2. 270
3. 14
4. 12th
5. $4 million
6. $495,
7. OK
8. 8 . . . 9

Correct the following sentences. Write *OK* for any sentence that has no error.

1. Please note that the term of the loan is 2 years, not 4 years, as had originally been requested.
2. Commercial paper is an unsecured note that has a maximum maturity of two hundred <u>seventy</u> days.
3. To meet the project deadline, <u>fourteen</u> staff members volunteered to work on Saturday.
4. All these securities must be delivered by messenger to Ms. Catherine Reilly, 190 <u>12</u> Avenue, by 2 p.m. today.
5. The potential market for this product, according to our preliminary estimates, is between <u>$4</u> and $5 million.
6. The new software program has a list price of <u>$495.00,</u> but a local computer store is selling it at a 20 percent discount.
7. If you subscribe now, you will pay only 35 cents a day for your paper.
8. We now have <u>eight</u> terminals connected to our mainframes, our Denver office has <u>nine</u> terminals connected, and our New York office has 13 terminals connected.

With Units of Measure and Percentages

Use figures with units of measure and with percentages, as shown below:

Each office measures 10 feet by 12 feet.

This television screen measures 19 inches diagonally.

Each vial contains exactly 5 cubic centimeters of the serum.

We are offering a 20 percent discount on all refrigerators in the store.

Note: Use the symbol % only in tables and forms. In other cases, spell out *percent.*

With Decimals

Decimal numbers are always expressed in figures:

Mix this compound with water in a ratio of 4.5 parts compound to 1 part water. (A ratio may also be expressed as follows: 4.5:1 ratio of compound to water.)

When no number appears before the decimal, add a zero to help the reader understand the number quickly.

A very slight increase — 0.5 percent — was reported for the month of March. (Without the zero, the reader might read "5 percent" instead of "5 tenths of a percent.")

With *a.m.* and *p.m.*

As you already learned, always use figures with *a.m.* and *p.m.*

at 9 a.m.
between 11:45 a.m. and 12:30 p.m.

With *O'Clock*

With the word *o'clock*, either figures or words may be used. For greater emphasis and less formality, use figures. For more formality but less emphasis, use words.

You are cordially invited to join us at eight o'clock on Friday, the first of June, to celebrate the one hundredth anniversary of the founding of Marsh Enterprises. (*Eight o'clock* is more formal than *8 o'clock*.)

All regional booksellers are invited to a brunch and book-signing party to be held at the Warwick Inn on Saturday, September 14, at 11 o'clock.

In Dates

Use figures to express the day of the month and the year in dates:

March 19, 1993 (Not March *19th*, 1993.)

When the day is written before the month, use an ordinal figure or spell out the ordinal number.

the 4th of June *or* the fourth of June
the 21st of April *or* the twenty-first of April

Note: The ordinal figures are *1st, 2d, 3d, 4th*, and so on.

With Consecutive Numbers

REINFORCEMENT
Ask students to clip advertisements from the local newspaper showing the use and frequency of numbers in this form of business communication. Discuss the problems that could result if the numbers in the advertisements were incorrect.

Consecutive numbers should be separated by a comma when both numbers are in figures or when both are in words.

In 1992, 121 employees were promoted.

Of the original seven employees, two remain in the San Diego office.

But if one word is in figures and the other is in words, no comma is needed.

On May 12 two executives retired from Piedmont Industries Inc.

When one of the numbers is part of a compound modifier, write the first number in words and the second number in figures (unless the second number would be a significantly shorter word). Do *not* separate the numbers with a comma.

two 9-page booklets (But 200 nine-page booklets.)
fifty $10 bills (But 100 ten-dollar bills.)

Checkup 3

KEY
1. 1,
2. 3
3. 15,
4. 5½ or 5.5 . . . 2
5. OK
6. OK or 5th
7. OK
8. 10 . . . 12

Correct any errors in the following sentences. Write *OK* for any sentence that has no error.

1. The maturity date for this bond is July <u>1st</u>, 1998.
2. If the meeting is rescheduled for <u>three</u> o'clock tomorrow, all the committee members will be able to attend.
3. On March <u>15</u> 76 stockholders will meet with the president in the auditorium.
4. For best results, mix <u>five and a half</u> parts of Kleenall to <u>two</u> parts water.
5. The interest on this money market account is 6.5 percent.
6. The annual company picnic has been scheduled for the fifth of June.
7. The discussion will begin at 11:30 a.m. and will end by 12:45 p.m.
8. Although this room is small (it measures only <u>ten</u> feet by <u>twelve</u> feet), it will serve well as a storeroom.

KEY
1. 1.5 or 1½
2. First
3. 12.5 (or 12½) percent
4. seven
5. 6th or sixth
6. OK or $400 million
7. 19¢ . . . 16¢
8. OK
9. OK
10. 2,500
11. 67
12. 6.5 or 6½

SECTION

REVIEW

Practical Application

A. On a sheet of paper, correct any errors in number use in the following sentences. Write *OK* for any sentence that has no error.

1. According to the agreement, the monthly interest charge will be <u>one and a half</u> percent higher than the prime rate.
2. The sleek, new office building on <u>1st</u> Avenue is fully leased.
3. During the first quarter, our net operating profit was <u>12.5%</u> higher than for the same period last year.
4. Mr. Southerby approved overtime for the <u>7</u> people working on the Boorstin & Cutter account.
5. The first day of the sales conference is the <u>6</u> of June, isn't it?
6. The federal government has allocated a total of $400,000,000 to the mass-transit improvement program.
7. The unit cost for printing these brochures is <u>$0.19</u> in quantities of 10,000 but only <u>$0.16</u> for 25,000 or more.
8. Each lifelike reproduction stands 18 inches high and weighs about 10 pounds.
9. Whitney Glenning, age 32, is a full partner with the accounting firm of Peters, Ernest, and Charles.
10. According to our records, we have distributed about <u>two thousand five hundred</u> samples so far this month.
11. The <u>sixty-seven</u> cars that are now in our fleet will be replaced within the next six months or so.
12. We have three estimates for the cost of repaving <u>six and a half</u> acres of the parking lot.

13. 0.7
14. OK
15. two-thirds
16. four
17. thousand
18. $25
19. OK
20. OK

13. The difference between the estimated cost and the actual cost was minimal (only .7 percent).
14. Please pick up 250 twenty-nine-cent stamps at the post office today.
15. As many as 2/3 of our employees have indicated an interest in our evening training courses.
16. Ms. Steinbach said, "We expect to begin 1995 as a billion-dollar corporation thanks to the success of all 4 of our divisions."
17. A few 1,000 people are expected to attend the Trade Expo in the Lucas Convention Center.
18. If you order now, you may pay four monthly installments of $25.00 each.
19. Because we must follow the schedule closely, please start your session at 11:15 a.m. and end it no later than 12:30 p.m.
20. We have forecast an increase of 12.5 percent in gross sales and 14.5 percent in net income.

B. On a sheet of paper, correct any errors in the following sentences. Write OK for any sentence that has no error.

KEY
1. *Business Week*?
2. $15,000.
3. Governor
4. me,
5. sister, . . . Mendoza,
6. president
7. expensive, we
8. two-page
9. therefore,
10. is
11. 5; . . . issue,
12. two-week
13. doesn't

1. Do you subscribe to "Business Week"?
2. For the past several years, Ms. Rulinsky's commissions have averaged $15,000.00.
3. The governor has appointed one of our executive vice presidents to the new panel on corporate taxes.
4. Between you and I, Derrick, I doubt that this line of products will compete effectively.
5. Victor's older sister Dr. Rona Mendoza works for our Genetic Research Division in Honolulu.
6. Next Tuesday morning we will meet with Francis X. Smith, President of TykoToys Inc.
7. Because the cost of printing these full-color brochures is so expensive. We decided to spend the money on other forms of sales promotion.
8. We plan, for example, to run two page ads in major magazines.
9. The bonds that we discussed are rated "AAA"; therefore they are very safe investments.
10. The new procedure for obtaining approvals for cost overruns are detailed in this operations manual.
11. The deadline for the March issue is January 5, for the April issue February 4.
12. The recent rail strike caused a two week delay in shipping the lumber from our mills in the Northwest.
13. Brent, don't your supervisor want you to attend the training ses next month?

14. Company,
15. 15,
16. late, Carl,
17. you're *or* you are
18. likes
19. months,
20. 15.

14. Its major subsidiary, the AmCo Supply <u>company</u>, is responsible for nearly 60 percent of the parent <u>corporation's</u> profits.
15. When Kathe returns from Norway on June <u>15</u> we will discuss our new export agreement.
16. It may be too <u>late Carl</u> to run this ad in the July issue.
17. If <u>your</u> planning to sell this product for less than $10, you should <u>explore</u> less expensive packaging.
18. Larry Ruiz is the only one of the regional managers who <u>like</u> the idea of merging both smaller plants into one large plant.
19. Nancy and I reviewed the production schedules for the next two <u>months</u> but we were not able to find any easy way to expedite the product-completion date.
20. Send this draft to the district managers; ask each to respond by April <u>15th</u>.

Editing Practice

Using Your Word Processor. Proofread the following excerpt "on-screen." Correct any errors.

KEY
Principles
$50
February

Please send me 100 copies of your pamphlet, *Principals of Time Management*, which was advertised in the <u>November</u> issue of *Effective Management*. I have enclosed a check for <u>fifty dollars</u> to cover the cost of these pamphlets, including the mailing cost.

I would like to have the pamphlets by <u>Febuary</u> 21, when we will conduct a workshop for supervisors. Therefore, <u>I would</u> be happy to pay any extra charge for shipping the pamphlets to me by that date.

CHAPTER

4

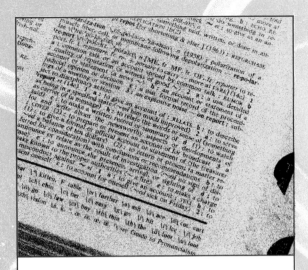

USING WORDS EFFECTIVELY

4.1 *USING THE DICTIONARY AND OTHER REFERENCE MATERIALS*

OBJECTIVES: After completing Section 4.1, you should be able to:

1. Use a dictionary to obtain information about the spelling, hyphenation, pronunciation, etymology, and meaning of words.
2. Use a thesaurus to find words that will make your expression more precise.
3. Use a dictionary of synonyms to add variety to your vocabulary.

❑**SUGGESTION**

Have available an unabridged dictionary, a thesaurus, a dictionary of synonyms, a spelling and hyphenation book, and a handbook of style. Let students use these references when working on writing assignments.

Words are the devices we use to communicate messages in speaking and in writing. When we speak or write, we create pictures with words — just as artists create pictures with paints. To be effective in your communications, you must learn to use words — the tools of language — effectively. Increasing the number of words in your vocabulary will broaden the range of tools at your command.

The English language is an incredible storehouse that contains an estimated one million words. For every occasion, there is a word, or several words, to communicate exactly what you want to say. Although you have thousands of words stored in your memory, finding or identifying the right one can sometimes be difficult. Fortunately, help is available in three valuable reference books: a dictionary, a thesaurus, and a dictionary of synonyms. Using these books will not only help you locate a word for a particular occasion but also enrich your vocabulary for future occasions. As you expand your vocabulary and sharpen other verbal tools, you will become a more effective speaker and writer.

THE DICTIONARY

❑**SUGGESTION**

Make transparencies of dictionary entries to use as bases for discussion of the kinds of word information that can be found in a good dictionary.

The dictionary is the most used and most useful reference work for those in search of the *right* word. Learning to use the dictionary is part of learning to use the language. Every successful writer, office professional, editor, proofreader, and student should keep a dictionary within reach and be adept at using it.

The choice of a dictionary is important. A standard abridged (concise) dictionary serves the needs of most students and office workers.[1] A pocket-

---

[1]The dictionary used as the source for this discussion and throughout this text (except where noted) is *Webster's Ninth New Collegiate Dictionary*, Merriam-Webster, Inc., Springfield, Mass., 1990.

**L I V I N G
LANGUAGE**

The name *Webster*
has become almost
synonymous with
the word *diction-
ary.* It seems that
adding *Webster* to
the title helps sell
dictionaries. *Web-
ster* refers to Noah
Webster, whose
first dictionary was
published in 1806.
After Webster died
in 1843, his name
was sold but not
registered. Now
anyone can use
Webster.

from *The New York
Times*

sized dictionary should not be your standard dictionary reference, because such dictionaries contain too few words and provide limited information about each word.

For our purposes we will divide dictionary information into two kinds: "Word Information" and "Other References."

Word Information

The primary use of the dictionary is to find information about specific words—their spellings, definitions, synonyms, and whatever other information is available to help the communicator. As an example of the extensive information provided by a good dictionary, read the entry for the word *business* as it appears in the dictionary (see below).

> **busi·ness** \ˈbiz-nəs, -nəz\ *n, often attrib* (14c) **1** *archaic* : purposeful activity : BUSYNESS **2 a :** ROLE. FUNCTION ⟨how the human mind went about its ~ of learning —H. A. Overstreet⟩ **b :** an immediate task or objective : MISSION ⟨what is your ~ here at this hour⟩ **c :** a particular field of endeavor ⟨the best in the ~⟩ **3 a :** a usu. commercial or mercantile activity engaged in as a means of livelihood : TRADE. LINE ⟨in the ~ of supplying emergency services to industry⟩ **b :** a commercial or sometimes an industrial enterprise ⟨sold his ~ and retired⟩; *also* : such enterprises **c :** usu. economic dealings : PATRONAGE ⟨ready to take his ~ elsewhere unless service improved⟩ **4 :** AFFAIR. MATTER ⟨a strange ~⟩ **5 :** movement or action (as lighting a cigarette) by an actor intended esp. to establish atmosphere, reveal character, or explain a situation — called also *stage business* **6 a :** personal concern ⟨none of your ~⟩ **b :** RIGHT ⟨you have no ~ hitting her⟩ **7 a :** serious activity requiring time and effort and usu. the avoidance of distractions ⟨immediately got down to ~⟩ **b :** maximum effort **8 a :** a damaging assault **b :** REBUKE, TONGUE-LASHING **c :** DOUBLE CROSS
> ***syn*** BUSINESS, COMMERCE. TRADE. INDUSTRY. TRAFFIC mean activity concerned with the supplying and distribution of commodities. BUSINESS may be an inclusive term but specifically designates the activities of those engaged in the purchase or sale of commodities or in related financial transactions; COMMERCE and TRADE imply the exchange and transportation of commodities; INDUSTRY applies to the producing of commodities, esp. by manufacturing or processing, usu. on a large scale; TRAFFIC applies to the operation and functioning of public carriers of goods and persons. ***syn*** see in addition WORK

This dictionary entry provides extensive information about the word *business.*

❑ SUGGESTION

Using a transparency
of the dictionary page
that shows the word
business will facilitate
your explanation.

Spelling. First the dictionary entry tells how the word *business* is spelled. Many people face a problem at this point because they do not know the possible spelling patterns for the sounds in a word. Section 4.3, "Mastering Spelling Techniques," provides the hearing and seeing skills needed for finding words in the dictionary. Here are some other guideposts for good spelling:

- Be sure that you see the letters in their correct order; for example, *neither*, not *niether.*
- Be sure that you have not inserted letters that are not there, as *athaletic* instead of *athletic.*
- Be sure that you have included all the letters that are in the word; for example, *mortgage*, not *morgage* or *business*, not *busness.*
- Be sure that the word is not some other word that is spelled somewhat like the one you are seeking. *Read the definition.* Suppose you want to

write this sentence: "Ms. Ribera sent me *(complementary/complimentary)* tickets to her concert." You need to verify the spelling of *compl?men-tary*. In the dictionary you will find *complementary*, followed by the definition "serving to fill out or complete." This definition is not the meaning you want. But look under *complimentary* and you will find "given free as courtesy or favor." Now you know that the word you seek is *complimentary*.

- Many words have more than one spelling. The dictionary shows spellings that are equally correct by joining them by *or*. For example, the dictionary entry for *adviser* reads "adviser *or* advisor." This indicates that both spellings are standard and both are commonly used. When one spelling is less commonly used, the dictionary joins them by *also*: "lovable *also* loveable" shows that both spellings are used, but the second less commonly so.
- Pay particular attention to compound words to determine whether they are written as one word *(checkpoint)*, two words *(check mark)*, or a hyphenated word *(drip-dry)*.
- Be sure to include any accent marks that are part of a word. For example, *exposé* is a noun that means "the revelation of something discreditable"; but *expose* is a verb that means "to deprive of protection; to cause to be visible."

Hyphenation. Sometimes a word must be divided at the end of a line of writing. Unless the word is divided at a certain place or places, the reader may be confused and will be delayed. Here is an example of this kind of problem:

Please sign and return the enclosed statement promptly if you want a refund.

Dictionary entries use centered periods to indicate the correct places for hyphenating words: *com · mu · ni · cate; con · trol; ap · pre · ci · ate*, but *ap · pre · cia · tive*.

Capitalization. The dictionary may show if a word is to be capitalized when it is not the first word of a sentence. For example, the word *south* is usually not capitalized, but when it refers to a specific region, it *is* capitalized.

Pronunciation and Division Into Syllables. Immediately after the regular spelling of a word, the dictionary shows the word's phonetic spelling. This feature indicates how the word should be broken into syllables, how each syllable should be pronounced, and which syllable or syllables should be accented. If phonetic symbols are new to you, refer to the section of the dictionary that explains them. Many dictionaries have a convenient phonetic guide on every page or on every other page.

Look again at the sample dictionary entry. The dictionary shows that the pronunciation of *business* is *biz-nes*. The hyphen indicates syllable breaks. *Webster's New Collegiate Dictionary* and some other dictionaries show major and minor stresses by placing an accent mark *before* the stressed syllable or syllables. In this text we place an apostrophe *after* a syllable to show that the syllable is stressed, and we show only major, not minor, stresses.

Word Origin. A word's origin, also called its "etymology" or "derivation," is interesting and informative and often fixes the word's meaning in memory. The origin of the word *radar*, for example, is shown as "*ra*dio *detecting and ranging.*" This information will help us remember the word's correct meaning and spelling. Words that are formed, like *radar*, from the initial letters of a compound term are called "acronyms." When you know their etymologies, acronyms are easy to remember.

Definition. A good dictionary lists all of a word's definitions, usually in the order in which they developed. Often the dictionary gives examples of the word's use in more than one sense. For example, see page 209, where the entry for *business* shows several examples of the word's use.

Inflectional Forms and Derivatives. The dictionary shows the irregular plural of nouns, the past tense and participial forms of irregular verbs, and the comparative and superlative forms of irregular adjectives and adverbs. After the definition of the noun *contract*, for example, are its derivative noun *contractibility* and its derivative adjective *contractible*. The entry for the irregular verb *fall* gives its past tense, *fell*, its past participle, *fallen*, and its present participle, *falling*.

Synonyms. For many entries the dictionary also lists synonyms — words that have almost the same meanings as the entry. The entry for *invent*, shown below, lists three synonyms. Note that although they have what the dictionary calls a "shared meaning element," each synonym has its own distinct shades of meaning. Edward Mellanby did not *invent* vitamin D, but he did *discover* it. The Wrights did not *discover* the airplane, but they did *invent* it. Synonyms for the entry word are often shown in small capital letters.

in·vent \in-'vent\ *vt* [ME *inventen*, fr. L *inventus*, pp. of *invenire* to come upon, find, fr. *in-* + *venire* to come — more at COME] (15c) **1** *archaic* : FIND, DISCOVER **2** : to devise by thinking : FABRICATE **3** : to produce (as something useful) for the first time through the use of the imagination or of ingenious thinking and experiment — **in·ven·tor** \-'vent-ər\ *n* — **in·ven·tress** \-'ven-trəs\ *n*
syn INVENT, CREATE, DISCOVER mean to bring something new into existence. INVENT implies fabricating something useful usu. as a result of ingenious thinking or experiment; CREATE implies an evoking of life out of nothing or producing a thing for the sake of its existence rather than its function or use; DISCOVER presupposes preexistence of something and implies a finding rather than a making.

The last six lines of this entry offer synonyms for *invent* and explain the differences.

Illustrations. A good dictionary sometimes uses illustrations to make a word's meaning clear. Illustrations are especially helpful in understanding definitions of terms that denote complex physical forms and objects. The meanings of some of these terms, in fact, are difficult to grasp from words alone but become clear at once after looking at an illustration. Can you visualize a *teasel* without the aid of an illustration? a *pantograph?* a *blockhouse?* After looking at the illustrations in a good dictionary, you will have no difficulty understanding these terms.

Other Information

A good dictionary provides much more than just word information. For instance, a good abridged dictionary contains a guide to the organization and use of the dictionary, explanatory notes about the kinds of information contained at each entry, a key to phonetic symbols, a guide to correct punctuation, a list of abbreviations used in the word entries, and more. Here are some of the special sections you may find helpful.

Signs and Symbols. This section consists of signs and symbols frequently used in such fields as astronomy, biology, business, chemistry, data processing, mathematics, medicine, physics, and weather.

Biographical Names. The names of famous people, each with the proper spelling and pronunciation, are listed under this heading. Biographical data such as dates of birth and death, nationality, and occupation are also given. This section may be useful for checking the pronunciation of names or for identifying unfamiliar names encountered in reading or conversation.

Geographical Names. This section provides information about places — name, pronunciation, location, population, and so on. This section, therefore, can be helpful when checking the spelling of places mentioned in correspondence.

Handbook of Style. This very useful section contains rules on punctuation, italicization, capitalization, and plurals; citation of sources; and forms of address.

W O R L D
V I E W

A knowledge of prefixes will help you understand the difference between the words *export* and *import.* The root *port* comes from the Latin *portare,* meaning "to carry." The prefix *im-* means "in" or "into"; the prefix *ex-* means "from" or "out of." Thus imports are carried in, while exports are carried out.

ELECTRONIC REFERENCE TOOLS

Although the dictionary remains the primary reference for spelling, hyphenation, word definitions, and synonyms, you should be aware that many word processing programs now provide electronic reference tools to use on the computer screen. These tools include automatic hyphenation, spell-checkers, dictionaries, and thesauruses. The computer user can quickly check for spelling and typographical errors. However, spell-checkers cannot replace careful proofreading, since they will not catch errors of context and usage. A spell-checker, for example, would find no errors in the following:

The boy *run own* the *bill* and saw *and* alligator.

It should read:

The boy ran down the hill and saw an alligator.

The words *run*, *own*, *bill*, and *and* are correct spellings but incorrect usage. Only careful proofreading of the text will identify and correct errors of this sort.

Several other software programs can help identify certain weaknesses and errors in writing. Overuse of passive voice, lack of variety in sentence structure, wordiness, and certain errors in grammar can be pointed out. Although such software programs can be very helpful, they should not replace detailed proofreading and editing.

THE THESAURUS

❏ **SUGGESTION**

Transparencies showing selected pages of a thesaurus will enhance your discussion of the thesaurus.

If you know a word, the dictionary will give you its meaning. The thesaurus works the other way around: if you have a general idea of the meaning you want to convey, the thesaurus will give you a choice of specific words to express it. The thesaurus offers a selection of different expressions related to the same idea. Look up the general idea, and then choose the word or expression that best fits your meaning.

Roget's International Thesaurus and *Webster's Collegiate Thesaurus*, two popular references, are arranged differently. *Roget's* has two parts: the main section, which lists synonyms and associated words, and the index to the main section. For example, to find a synonym for the adjective *careful*, look up *careful* in the alphabetic index. There you will find these seven entries, each followed by a key number:

careful
    adj. attentive 530.15
        cautious 895.8
        conscientious 974.15
        economical 851.6
        heedful 533.10
        judicious 467.19
    interj. caution 895.14

The key numbers refer to numbered paragraphs in the main section. Thus, if *cautious* is closest to the idea you wish to convey, turn to entry number 895 in the main section (organized numerically) and find paragraph 8 for a listing of synonyms.

Webster's Collegiate Thesaurus is organized like a dictionary, with one list of entries arranged in alphabetic order. To find synonyms for *careful*, just turn to the entry *careful*. Within this entry the capital letters for the word *CAUTIOUS* indicate that more information can be found at that entry, which is also in alphabetic order.

Whichever thesaurus you select, learn to use it properly. A thesaurus can be useful when you want to (1) find the most suitable word for a given idea, (2) avoid overusing a word by finding a suitable synonym, (3) find the most specific word, or (4) replace an abstract term.

careful *adj* **1** *syn* CAUTIOUS, calculating, chary, circumspect, considerate, discreet, gingerly, guarded, safe, wary
rel attentive, heedful, observant
2 closely attentive to details or showing such attention < *careful* workmanship >
syn conscientious, conscionable, exact, fussy, heedful, meticulous, painstaking, punctilious, punctual, scrupulous
rel accurate, nice, precise; deliberate, studied; foresighted, provident, prudent; critical, discriminating, finical, finicky; observant, particular, religious; duteous, dutiful, intent
con disorderly, lax, negligent, slack, slipshod, slovenly; heedless, neglectful, remiss
ant careless

cautious *adj* marked by careful prudence especially in reducing or avoiding risk or danger < a *cautious* approach to marriage >
syn calculating, careful, chary, circumspect, considerate, discreet, gingerly, guarded, safe, wary
rel alert, vigilant, watchful; cagey, canny, cozy, foresighted, precautious, shrewd; forethoughtful, prethoughtful, provident, prudent; calculating, scheming, shrewd; expedient, judicious, politic
idiom on one's guard, on the safe side, playing it safe
con daring, rash, reckless, venturesome; headlong, impetuous, precipitate
ant adventurous, temerarious

These two entries from *Webster's Collegiate Thesaurus* show that there are many alternatives for the words *careful* and *cautious*.

To Find the Most Suitable Word

Imagine that you are a writer of advertising copy, working on an advertisement about the new fall fashions. One aspect you wish to emphasize is the smartness of the clothes. Using your thesaurus, you can find that *smart* may be expressed as *chic, fashionable, dapper, well-groomed, dressed up,* and *dressy,* among a number of other words and expressions.

To Avoid Overusing a Word

 **INFORMATION**

The search feature of most word processing programs can find and count how many times a particular word or phrase has been used in a document.

Suppose you have written a paper in which you use the word *great* over and over. Consulting the index of your thesaurus, you find a list of other adjectives, such as *grand, chief, important, large,* and *famous.* When you check these references, you discover additional words and expressions that are synonyms of *great.* You now have at your disposal a wide choice of words that you can use in place of *great.*

To Find the Most Specific Word

Sometimes you have a general word for an object or idea in mind, but you want to use a more specific word. For example, you may be discussing the possibility of taking a *trial* vote, but that is not the specific word you are seeking. You look up the word *vote* in your thesaurus, and among the many choices shown is the expression *straw vote,* which is precisely the expression you are seeking.

To Replace an Abstract Term

Imagine that you are writing a memorandum and that you wish to replace the word *precipitous* in the phrase *"a precipitous decision."* Among the substitutes that you would find in your thesaurus are *hasty, abrupt, hurried,* and *sudden.*

A thesaurus such as *Roget's International Thesaurus* or *Webster's Collegiate Thesaurus* is a writer's tool that you will turn to more and more often as you become more adept in its use. A good thesaurus can help you create the flavor, color, and fresh images that will make you an effective writer.

THE DICTIONARY OF SYNONYMS

A single example will show the value of a dictionary of synonyms. *Roget's International Thesaurus* lists approximately a hundred types of hats. If you need only to be reminded of the exact name of a familiar type of hat (for example, *fedora*), then the thesaurus ends your search. But what if you don't know the difference between a fedora and a beret, a bowler and a busby, a derby and a homburg, or a shako and a toque? Then you have to return to the dictionary and look up each of these words until you find the definition that matches the description given you ("a felt hat with a lengthwise crease in the top"). Clearly, this kind of search will take time.

A dictionary of synonyms not only *lists* words of similar meaning (as does a thesaurus) and *defines* words of similar meaning (as does a dictionary), but also lists synonyms and gives brief definitions, pointing out what distinguishes one synonym from another — all in one place. A dictionary of synonyms can save many long searches through the dictionary.

SECTION

REVIEW

Practical Application

A. Using a thesaurus, list five words that can be used to replace the underlined word in each of the following phrases:

1. A pleasant weekend
2. An interesting film
3. A good dinner
4. A good neighbor
5. A good mechanic

B. For a speech she was preparing, Denise referred to the following people. Using a dictionary, indicate the pronunciation of each name and provide some identifying information about the person.

1. Cellini
2. Pepys
3. Lehman
4. Walesa
5. Goethe

C. In the same speech, Denise referred to the following places. Using your dictionary, indicate the pronunciation of these places and where they are located.

1. Beijing
2. Gloucester
3. Rijeka
4. Leman Lake
5. Sault Sainte Marie

D. The following words should be part of your vocabulary. For each, write the correct pronunciation and the most common definition. Then correctly use each word in a sentence.

1. excise
2. lien
3. bankruptcy
4. ecology
5. depreciation
6. franchise
7. mortgage
8. accrual
9. incumbent
10. cartel

E. The writer of the following sentences confused two similar words. Replace the incorrect word with the correct one. Define both the correct and the incorrect one.

1. We located an excellent cite for the plant in Missouri.
2. The secretary gave the clerk some good advise.
3. John Dietz was formally employed by our company.
4. The supervisor informed all personal of the new vacation policy.
5. Althea Simone designed the new stationary for our office.

F. In each of the following pairs, which is the preferred spelling?

1. traveling, travelling
2. saleable, salable
3. centre, center
4. envelope, envelop (noun)
5. installment, instalment
6. judgement, judgment
7. sizeable, sizable
8. advisor, adviser

Editing Practice

Hidden Pairs. From each group of words below, two can be matched because they are similar in meaning. Find each pair. Write the letters that indicate the pairs.

    Example: (a) practice (b) proscribe (c) placate (d) preempt (e) appease
    Answer: c and e

1. (a) wield (b) procure (c) dispense (d) obfuscate (e) obtain
2. (a) circumstance (b) sanitation (c) cenotaph (d) situation (e) accident
3. (a) dispense (b) depreciate (c) spend (d) disburse (e) disperse

KEY
1. site
2. advice
3. formerly
4. personnel
5. stationery

KEY
1. traveling
2. salable
3. center
4. envelope
5. installment
6. judgment
7. sizable
8. adviser

KEY
1. b, e
2. a, d
3. c, d

4. b, d
5. b, d
6. b, c
7. c, d
8. a, b

REVIEW cont.

4. (a) dispatch (b) keep (c) locate (d) retain (e) indicate
5. (a) unlawful (b) illegible (c) ineligible (d) unreadable (e) uncouth
6. (a) deny (b) alleviate (c) ease (d) impound (e) obfuscate
7. (a) wretched (b) depicted (c) obsolete (d) antiquated (e) meticulous
8. (a) new (b) innovative (c) despicable (d) deplorable (e) neutral

4.2 *IMPROVING VOCABULARY POWER*

OBJECTIVES: After completing Section 4.2, you should be able to:

1. Make more careful and precise use of words in writing and speaking.
2. Avoid using words that are not correct, that are overused or out of date, or that are not appropriate for the audience.

▲
▽ **CRITICAL THINKING**

Ask students to name words they "like" and words they "dislike." How do these words affect them? Why do these words affect them? A previous experience? The pleasant or unpleasant sound of a word?

N REINFORCEMENT

Remind students that correct speaking and writing are the marks of an educated person. The inability to communicate effectively can limit advancement opportunities.

Words not only communicate ideas but also stir the emotions, either favorably or unfavorably. Words can lift spirits, inspire action, or soothe injured feelings. If chosen without care, words can hurt, confuse, and possibly even enrage the receiver. This fact is all too clear to anyone who has ever had to say, with downcast eyes, "I'm sorry — I did not mean it that way."

The words that you use in writing and speaking can earn you the respect and admiration of those with whom you communicate, or they can mark you as unimaginative — and even uneducated. The words you use can even brand you as insensitive. If you want to be an effective communicator, you must be precise in your use of words. To achieve this precision, you must know many words, and you must use the right word at the right time. Also you must be concerned with correctness in the words you use, you must avoid overusing words, and you must be able to predict how listeners or readers will interpret the words you use. Following the guides presented in this section can be a first step toward becoming an effective communicator.

THE CORRECT WORD

Careful speakers and writers know the difference between correct usage and illiterate usage. This difference is not merely a matter of what some authority somewhere declares to be correct. Illiterate usage is illiterate because it does not make sense. Consider the word *irregardless*. We can break it into three parts to reveal its confused meaning: *ir regard less*. When attached to the end of a word, *-less* means "without." *Hopeless* means "without hope"; *regardless* means "without regard." Attached to the beginning of a word, *ir-* means "not" or "without." *Irrelevant* means "without relevance." *Irregardless*, then, means "without without regard." It makes no more sense than *irhopeless* does. Although your listeners or readers may understand what you mean, the illiteracy will tell something about you.

Irregardless, like some other illiteracies, probably came about as the result of combining parts of two correct expressions, *regardless* and *irrespective of*. Another cause of illiteracies is mispronunciation. If *relevant* is mispronounced, for example, we may hear the mysterious word *revelant*. Does it mean "revealing"? Does it have anything to do with revels? While the listener ponders this concept, the speaker may say many intelligent things that the listener will not hear.

Other illiteracies arising from mispronunciation are *irrepair'able* for *irrep'arable*, *renumeration* for *remuneration* (although *enumeration* is correct), *hunderd* for *hundred*, *strinth* for *strength*, *compare'able* for *com'parable*, *nucular* for *nuclear*.

Mistrust and avoid any words that you cannot find in the dictionary.

HOMONYMS

Words that look or sound alike — but have different meanings — are known as *homonyms*. Choosing the incorrect word (although it may sound or even look correct) is one of the most frequently committed errors in word usage.

For example, the tenants of a large apartment building receive a letter urging "all the *residence* to protest the proposed rent increase." This important message might be ignored simply because the writer cannot distinguish people, *residents*, from a place, *residence*. Another letter writer might place an order for a ream of *stationary*, much to the amusement of the *stationer* supplying it.

The chart entitled "Easily Confused Word Pairs" lists some homonyms that every business writer should know and should use correctly.

Pseudohomonyms

Pseudohomonyms are words that sound somewhat alike but have different meanings. They are called "pseudo" because, when pronounced correctly, these words do *not* sound exactly alike. For example, the statement "Smathers, Delgado, and Hull placed orders for $800, $1,000, and $1,300, respectfully," is incorrect. The communicator has confused the word *respectfully* (meaning "courteously") with *respectively* (meaning "in the order given"). The pseudohomonyms that give the most trouble are listed in the chart "Easily Confused Word Pairs."

EASILY CONFUSED WORD PAIRS

Homonyms

ad add
aisle isle
allowed aloud
altar alter
ascent assent
assistance assistants
attendance attendants
aural oral
bail bale
base bass
berth birth
born borne
brake break
canvas canvass
capital capitol
cereal serial
cite sight site
coarse course
complement compliment
core corps
correspondence correspondents
council counsel
dependence dependents
desert dessert
discreet discrete
dew do due
dual duel
foreword forward
forth fourth
foul fowl
gorilla guerrilla
grate great
hear here
hole whole
idle idol
instance instants
intense intents

lean lien
leased least
lessen lesson
lesser lessor
loan lone
mail male
medal meddle
miner minor
overdo overdue
pain pane
passed past
patience patients
peace piece
pedal peddle
plain plane
presence presents
principal principle
raise raze
rap wrap
residence residents
right write
sole soul
some sum
stake steak
stationary stationery
straight strait
taught taut
their there they're
threw through
to too two
vain vane vein
waist waste
wait weight
waive wave
weak week
weather whether

Pseudohomonyms

accede exceed
accept except
adapt adopt
addition edition
adverse averse
advice advise

affect effect
allusion illusion
anecdote antidote
appraise apprise
carton cartoon
casual causal

EASILY CONFUSED WORD PAIRS

Pseudohomonyms

clothes	cloths	fiscal	physical
choose	chose	formally	formerly
conscience	conscious	ingenious	ingenuous
cooperation	corporation	later	latter
dairy	diary	liable	libel
deceased	diseased	loose	lose	loss
decent	descent	dissent	moral	morale
deference	difference	our	are
desert	dessert	persecute	prosecute
detract	distract	personal	personnel
device	devise	precede	proceed
disburse	disperse	quiet	quit	quite
disprove	disapprove	reality	realty
elicit	illicit	recent	resent
eligible	illegible	respectfully	respectively
emigrate	immigrate	statue	statute
eminent	imminent	suit	suite
expand	expend	than	then
facilitate	felicitate		

Spelling

If you were a business executive, would you hire an engineer whose résumé listed a degree in *compewter* science? You would look even less kindly on an applicant who wrote to request a position as a *fial* clerk. Poor spelling would make you doubt that these people could do the jobs that they sought. The poor speller has few excuses, because everyone has access to a dictionary.

Business executives complain more about the poor spelling of employees than about any other fault in the use of language. In the world of business, improving your spelling improves your career prospects. You can improve your spelling by giving careful attention to the similarities and differences between homonyms or pseudohomonyms and to the suggestions in Section 4.3 at the end of this chapter. The most important step to improved spelling, however, is developing the dictionary habit.

WORDS SUITED TO THE AUDIENCE

In a speech to a social club, a computer specialist would lose the attention of the audience if, in discussing how a computer could be useful to everyone, he or she used such technical terms as *backups*, *checkdisk*, and *batch file*. But if the speaker used nontechnical terms, such as *made copies of, asked the computer how much space has been used and how much remains*, and *a file composed of a number of directions*, the speaker could better hold the attention of the audience. Using a specialized vocabulary that is unfamiliar to an audience is as serious a mistake as speaking in a foreign language that is unknown to an audience. Real communication takes place only when a speaker chooses words geared to the interest and knowledge of that audience.

WORDS WITH DIFFERENT SHADES OF MEANING

English offers many ways to describe the same basic facts with altogether different implications. A solitary person, for example, might be called a *wall-flower*, a *recluse*, or a *rugged individualist*. The wrong choice of terms can distort the speaker's or writer's intentions and perhaps even offend someone.

Only an unskilled writer or speaker would use the word *cheap* to mean *inexpensive*. Certainly no salesperson would make that mistake. *Cheap* means "worthless or shoddy"; *inexpensive* refers only to cost, not to quality. Sometimes an *inexpensive* suit is a bargain; a *cheap* suit never is.

A gracious host would never introduce an honored guest as "notorious for his gifts to charity." *Notorious* means "*un*favorably known." *Famous* may be either favorable or unfavorable. *Infamous* does not mean "unknown" but "having a reputation of the worst kind."

Whenever in doubt about a word's meaning, check the dictionary before using the word. If there is no time to look up the unknown word, then phrase your idea in a way that avoids the unknown term.

WORDS TO AVOID

Building a successful business or a successful career requires building goodwill. Because words play a vital part in establishing goodwill, a skilled communicator chooses words and phrases that the listener and reader can both understand and appreciate. In general, this means choosing positive rather than negative terms, presenting information directly and without repetition, and using fresh and current expressions rather than old, stale ones. The information below will help you avoid words that will hamper your efforts to create goodwill.

Avoid Negative Words

Which of the following paragraphs is more likely to build or retain customer goodwill?

You neglected to specify the sizes and colors of the dress shirts you ordered. We cannot ship with such incomplete order information.

The four dozen dress shirts you ordered will be on their way to you just as soon as you tell us what sizes you want and in what colors — white, tan, or blue.

Although the second paragraph is the obvious selection, note that both paragraphs try to say the same thing. The second paragraph is positively worded and avoids such unpleasant expressions as "you neglected" and "cannot ship with such incomplete information." Negative words are almost sure to evoke a negative response. The customer reading these negative words may cancel the order or may choose a different supplier for future orders.

Words create negative responses when the reader feels blamed or accused. Most expert business writers consider *failed, careless, delay,* and *inexcusable* negative words, regardless of how the words are used, and recommend avoiding these words. Actually, such words are unpleasant primarily when they are accompanied by *you* ("you failed") or *your* ("your delay"). "Your oversight," "your error," "your claim" signal the reader to react negatively; but "our oversight," "our error" — though not necessarily wise choices of words — carry a different impression entirely.

The following words sound negative when used with *you* or *your* and thus cannot promote good business relationships.

blunder	damage	inability	regret
careless	defective	inadequate	trouble
claim	delay	inferior	unfavorable
complaint	error	mistake	unfortunate
criticism	failure	neglected	unsatisfactory

Avoid Unnecessary Words

Words that are repetitious are a waste of the reader's or the listener's time. Such words clutter the message and can distract, delay understanding, and reduce emotional impact. The italicized words in the following expressions are unnecessary and should be omitted.

adequate *enough*	meet *up* with	*free* gratis
as yet	modern methods *of today*	inside *of*
at above	over *with*	my *personal* opinion
up above	*customary* practice	rarely (seldom) *ever*
both alike	*connect up*	repeat *back* or *again*
new beginner	continue *on*	refer *back*
cooperate *together*	*and* etc.	*exact* same
same identical	*as to* whether	*true* facts
lose *out*	*past* experience	

Avoid Out-of-Date Words

Words that are out of date suggest that the speaker or the writer is behind the times. Imagine the reaction to a sign that said ESCHEW SMOKING! In certain uses, the words below have a similar effect.

advise or state (for *say, tell*)	kindly (for *please*)
beg	party (for *person,* except in legal work)
duly	same ("and we will send you same")
esteemed	trust (for *hope, know, believe*)
herewith (except in legal work)	via

Avoid Overused Words

Replacing overused words with more exact and colorful terms can change a dull communication into a bright and compelling one. The adjective *good* is overused and weak: a *good* maneuver, a *good* negotiator, a *good* speech, a *good* worker. Instead, for greater interest, say: an *adroit, clever,* or *skillful* maneuver; a *patient, forceful,* or *wily* negotiator; an *eloquent, informative,* or *engrossing* speech; an *able, efficient,* or *industrious* worker.

Adjectives such as *awful, bad, fine, great,* and *interesting* are also overused. Often these adjectives have no more meaning than a grunt or a moan. The following sentences show how meaningless these words can be.

1. The new guidelines on hiring workers will result in a *bad* situation.
2. The meeting last Thursday was *great,* and the resolution passed was *great* too.
3. Kari Michaels gave an *interesting* sales presentation.
4. We have an *awful* backlog of orders.
5. Mr. Heald was a *fine* employee who worked for this company for 40 years.

While these vague, dull terms deaden the sentences, the choices below impart life and zest.

Sentence 1: *difficult, painful,* or *troublesome* situation
Sentence 2: *important, productive,* or *memorable* meeting; *constructive, salient,* or *eloquent* resolution
Sentence 3: *informative, enlightening,* or *educational* sales presentation
Sentence 4: *enormous, gigantic,* or *overwhelming* backlog
Sentence 5: *loyal, diligent,* or *exemplary* employee

By substituting more precise adjectives for the imprecise and overworked *great, awful, bad, interesting,* and *fine,* you will create more vivid or informative descriptions. Words, like people, become less effective when overworked. Examine your own speech and writing to discover the words that you overwork.

Avoid Overused Expressions

To be *brutally frank, you know,* if a *goodly number* of clichés are *like part and parcel* of your *manner of speaking,* then it is *like crystal clear* that your English is a *far cry* from *passing with flying colors* the *acid test of top-notch, A-number-1 King's English according to Hoyle.* How is it possible that so many words can say so little! Most of those words are parts of overworked expressions that long ago lost their strength. In other words, if you rely on such clichés, your English is weak.

Clichés say much about you. The use of clichés exposes a lack of imagination—the tendency to repeat the familiar, even when the familiar is not worth repeating, rather than to think of new and forceful expressions. Clichés waste time, obscure ideas, and bore readers and listeners. Your imagination is sure to provide better expressions once you resolve to avoid clichés.

Some commonly overused words and expressions, together with suggested substitutions for them, are listed below.

For	Substitute
along the lines of	like
asset	advantage, gain, possession, resource
at all times	always
by the name of	named
deal	agreement, arrangement, transaction
each and every	each *or* every
face up to	face
factor	event, occurrence, part
field	branch, department, domain, point, question, range, realm, region, scene, scope, sphere, subject, theme
fix	adjust, arrange, attach, bind, mend, confirm, define, establish, limit, place, prepare, repair
inasmuch as	since, as
input	comment, information, recommendation
in the near future	soon (or state the exact time)
line	business, merchandise, goods, stock
matter	situation, question, subject, point (or mention what is specifically referred to)
our Mr. Smith	our representative, Mr. Smith
proposition	proposal, undertaking, offer, plan, affair, recommendation, idea
reaction	opinion, attitude, impression
recent communication	letter of (give exact date)
say	exclaim, declare, articulate, express, assert, relate, remark, mention

WHAT TO STRIVE FOR

Avoiding hackneyed words and expressions is like giving away worn-out clothes: now you must find something to replace them. There are reference books to help you in the search for variety in expression, but you cannot expect to find ready-made words and phrases to express every idea. To achieve variety in word usage requires creativity. To develop creativity, you need to understand, study, and apply the following suggestions.

Become Word-Conscious

Curiosity is your natural ally in building an effective vocabulary, so use it to your advantage. Remember a word you see or hear for the first time (or write it down) until you can get to a dictionary. Find the meaning of the new word and fit the meaning into context. Becoming word-conscious means satisfying your curiosity every time you encounter a new word.

Once you become word-conscious, you will be amazed to discover how many new and interesting words you come across each day. You will hear new words in class, on the job, on radio and television, and in the movies and the theater. You will see new words in newspapers, magazines, textbooks, novels, advertisements, and even on package labels.

Keeping a notebook of new words will speed your progress. Keep a record of words and their definitions and review them from time to time. If you hear a new word, be sure to note its pronunciation. If you read a new word, be sure to note its spelling. New slang expressions are worth noting too. You should always label them as slang, however, and realize that they are inappropriate in most business situations.

Learn to Use Word Tools

A good vocabulary is a vast and complex structure that must be built piece by piece. Your own inborn curiosity will give you the necessary energy to build your vocabulary, but you will also need the right tools: a dictionary, a thesaurus, and a dictionary of synonyms. Besides making vocabulary building easier, these tools will ensure that your vocabulary will be strong and lasting.

Select Suitable Synonyms

Choosing suitable synonyms is the most direct means of achieving variety in your vocabulary. A synonym, as you know, is a word that has the same or nearly the same meaning as another word; for example, *old*, *aged*, *venerable*, *exhausted*, and *seasoned* are synonyms. Although synonyms have the same basic meaning, each synonym has a different shade of meaning. To select the synonym that best expresses a specific idea, you must go beyond the basic idea and learn the distinctions.

Instead of using the overworked word *bad*, for example, you might look in the dictionary and find these synonyms: *evil*, *ill*, *rotten*, and *naughty*. These synonyms cannot be used interchangeably. The dictionary entry is instructive: Murderers are worse than *naughty*, and mischievous children at their worst do not deserve to be called *evil*. But both *naughty* and *evil* are more vivid than saying "The murderer is very bad," or "The children aren't too bad." By using each of the synonyms for *bad* in appropriate cases, you introduce variety and color.

Sometimes a dictionary will refer you to another entry for synonyms. For example, when looking for synonyms under the adjective *precise*, you will read "see *correct*." There, under the entry for *correct*, are listed the synonyms *correct*, *accurate*, *exact*, *precise*, *nice*, and *right*. If no synonyms are listed for the word you seek and there is no reference to another entry, you can create a phrase to achieve variety. Under the word *explore*, for example, the dictionary lists no synonyms, but look at its definition: "to investigate, study, or analyze;

to look into; to examine minutely; to make or conduct a systematic search." Thus, instead of using *explore*, you can make a phrase to fit: "*study* the options," "*examine* the records *minutely*," "*systematically search* the files."

An excellent source of synonyms, of course, is the thesaurus. With the help of the thesaurus you can avoid trite expressions and develop variety in word usage. For instance, suppose you are preparing a report in which you claim "Capable office workers are few and far between." You wish to avoid the expression *few and far between*, partly because it is trite and partly because it does not exactly express the thought you would like to convey.

The dictionary will provide limited assistance here. The word *few* is defined as "consisting of or amounting to a small number." The thesaurus, on the other hand, gives many additional similar words and phrases; for example, *sparseness, handful, meager, small number, hardly any, scarcely any, scant, rare,* and *minority.* So you might say, "Capable office workers are in scant supply."

Use Appropriate Antonyms

An *antonym* is a word that means *exactly* the opposite of another word. For example, *light* is an antonym of *dark*. Antonyms may also be "created" by using such prefixes as *il-, in-, ir-, non-,* and *un-* before a word. For instance, *legible* becomes *illegible; credible, incredible; abrasive, nonabrasive; acceptable, unacceptable;* and so on.

Facility in the use of antonyms opens broad possibilities to the communicator. While *additional* reading sounds like an added burden, *unrequired* reading sounds as if it might even be fun. It is sad when the dead are *forgotten*, but sadder still when they are *unmourned*.

Choose Picture-Making Words

Picture-making words make readers or listeners "see" what is being described — often with themselves in the picture. A scarf with an *intricate pattern* is difficult to visualize, but *a violet and jade patchwork pattern* calls an image to mind. Notice that more specific words are better at picture-making. Since the thesaurus is the best aid in the search for specific terms, it is a treasure house of picture-making words as well. Let's say that you start with a vague description like a *big, hairy dog*. The thesaurus can supply more specific terms for *big* and *hairy dog* like *hulking* and *St. Bernard*. You can complete the picture by visualizing it more fully and then describing what you see: a *hulking St. Bernard leaving a trail of coarse, white hairs on the carpet*.

Advertising copywriters must make each word count, since each word is costly to the client. The copywriter's language is sometimes extravagant, but it always makes pictures. A shirt has *windowpane* checks; an evening gown has *spaghetti* straps; children's overalls come in *crayon-bright* colors. Notice the colorful words in the following advertisements:

> On land or on sea, our indestructible deck shoes are packed with quality, stem to stern.

Get all four of these garden gems. Crown your garden with the sparkling beauty of these aristocratic irises.

Using picture-making words will improve your messages, whether spoken or written, but developing this skill requires much work and practice. You can develop it, however, if you force yourself to visualize a complete picture of what you want to describe, and then consult the thesaurus until you find the most specific descriptive terms that apply. First comes the idea, then the full picture, and finally the right words. If you see this process through, you will be able to hold the attention of your readers and listeners.

Practice Using New Words

A new word really becomes a part of your vocabulary only when you write it or speak it correctly. As soon as you are certain that you understand the meaning and shades of meaning of a new word, use it in business and social conversation or correspondence. Each new word makes possible greater variety and precision in word usage. Verbal variety and verbal precision increase your power to express and advance your views.

KEY
1. exceeded
2. canvass
3. averse
4. access
5. edition

KEY
1. dispersed
2. a disinterested
3. effect
4. physical
5. counsel
6. assistance

SECTION *REVIEW*

Practical Application

A. Which words in the following sentences are used incorrectly? Write the incorrectly used word and next to it the word you would use in its place.

1. Their prices <u>acceded</u> the usual market price.
2. Please <u>canvas</u> the committee members on the zoning issue.
3. Mr. Pierce is <u>adverse</u> to changing the work schedule.
4. The reservations clerk could not gain <u>excess</u> to the hotel vault.
5. Which <u>addition</u> of the book did you use?

B. In each of the following sentences, select the word in parentheses that correctly completes the thought intended.

1. The senator's reassuring speech (disbursed, dispersed) the crowd.
2. As one of the signers of the contract, he is not (a disinterested, an uninterested) party to the negotiations.
3. Being caught in a traffic jam for hours had no apparent (affect, effect) on her mood.
4. All the (fiscal, physical) assets of the restaurant are to be sold at auction.
5. He was appointed (council, counsel) in the company's legal section.
6. The report was prepared with the (assistance, assistants) of the research staff.

REVIEW cont.

7. biographical
8. awhile
9. past
10. slight

7. Bill Dubois was asked to prepare a (bibliographical, biographical) description for his employer to use in introducing the speaker to the audience.
8. He waited (awhile, a while) before calling his lawyer.
9. Your account is long (passed, past) due.
10. The designer made a (sleight, slight) change in the pattern.

KEY
See page I-23.

C. Recast each of the following negative sentences in positive terms.

1. Not until today did your letter reach us, too late for our special offer, which ended last week.
2. There is no excuse for misunderstanding my clear instructions, even if you were interrupted while I was talking.
3. Since you failed to state whether you want legal- or letter-size, we cannot send the filing cabinets that you ordered.
4. I will not be in the office on Tuesday, so I will be unable to help you then.
5. Do not use a box number address when sending a letter by an overnight delivery service because the letter cannot be delivered without a street address.

KEY
See page I-23.

D. Substitute more precise words for the overworked words in the following phrases.

1. fix a date
2. a good meeting
3. a fine program
4. fix the letter
5. a bad presentation
6. a fine supervisor
7. a good secretary
8. a great film
9. a fine building
10. fix this error

KEY
See page I-23.

E. Find original replacements for the clichés italicized below.

1. a worker who never *leaves you in the lurch*
2. must stop *passing the buck*
3. get it done *somehow or other*
4. *ironing out the bugs in* our procedure
5. thought about *calling it quits*
6. he *gets on his high horse*
7. she *racked her brains*
8. he *sets no store by*
9. she *made short work of it*
10. likes to *toot her own horn*

KEY
See page I-24.

F. Write an antonym for each of the following words.

1. reliable
2. implausible
3. exorbitant
4. lengthen
5. sensitive
6. fascinating
7. trivial
8. synthetic
9. openly
10. encourage

SECTION

REVIEW cont.

Editing Practice

Picture-Making Words. Rewrite these sentences, substituting exact, picture-making words for the italicized words.

1. The high waves *hit* the side of the ship.
2. They felt *good* sitting on the rug in front of the fireplace.
3. When he lit the cigar despite their objections, they all *looked* at him through the smoke.
4. When the bus finally arrived, they were all *very cold*.
5. His words *set off* the crowd, which *moved* in a body toward the barricades.

SECTION

4.3 *MASTERING SPELLING TECHNIQUES*

OBJECTIVES: After completing Section 4.3, you should be able to:

1. Describe the rule of doubling a final consonant, giving examples to illustrate the rule.
2. Discuss at least three other spelling principles that almost always hold true.
3. Name two ways to ensure the correct spelling of words for which there are no rules.

ℹ️ INFORMATION

The dictionary and a spelling and hyphenation book are standard references for correct spelling. However, spell-checkers, available with most word processing programs, are helpful in detecting spelling errors. CAUTION: If a word is a correct spelling but an incorrect usage, the error will not be detected by the spell-checker.

A poor speller may ask: "So long as the reader understands the meaning of my message, why does it matter whether a word is misspelled?" One might reply, "So long as you are clothed, why does it matter if your clothes are dirty or if you are wearing a purple tie with a bright orange shirt?" The answer should be obvious. The misspelled word, the dirty clothing, and the questionable choice of colors all convey an impression to the observer that says that this person does not care, is not knowledgeable, or is lazy. These negative feelings will result in negative reactions. Furthermore, the reader must waste time deciphering the mystery that pretends to be a word, since the writer did not take time to consult the dictionary. The reader must bear a burden that belongs to the writer, and naturally the reader feels annoyed.

Poor spelling makes both you and your organization look inept. Your employer may be reluctant to let you represent the organization in dealing with customers or clients. As a result, your opportunities for advancement will be limited. Therefore, you should make every possible effort to overcome any spelling difficulties you may have. A good start in this direction is to study and apply the principles presented in this section.

GUIDES TO CORRECT SPELLING

Although there are many variations in the spelling of English words, some spelling principles always hold true. Every writer must know and be able to apply these principles — the basic guides to correct spelling.

Final *Y*

Many common nouns end in *y: company, industry, entry, territory, warranty, supply, day, attorney, survey.* The spelling of the plurals of these common nouns depends on whether the *y* is preceded by a consonant or a vowel. If preceded by a consonant, the *y* is changed to *i* and *es* is added: *company, companies; industry, industries; entry, entries; territory, territories; warranty, warranties; supply, supplies.* If preceded by a vowel, the *y* is not changed. Only *s* is added: *day, days; attorney, attorneys; survey, surveys.*

Ei and *Ie* Words

Among the most frequently misspelled words are these: *believe, belief, deceive, deceit, perceive, conceive, conceit, receive, receipt, relieve,* and *relief.* The word *Alice* is a clue to their correct spelling. In *Alice* we see the combinations *li* and *ce.* These combinations can help you remember that the correct spelling after *l* is *ie (believe);* after *c, ei (receive).*

· M E M O R Y H O O K ·

To help you spell *ie* and *ei* words correctly, memorize the following:

Write *i* before *e*
Except after *c*
Or when sounded like *ay*
As in n*eigh*bor or w*eigh*.

Exceptions: Words with long *e* sound (*either,* caff*ei*ne, s*ei*ze) and for*eig*n, h*eig*ht, forf*ei*t.

Endings *Ful, Ous, Ally, Ily*

To spell the endings *ful, ous, ally,* and *ily* correctly, a writer needs to remember the following:

The suffix *ful* has only one *l: careful, skillful, masterful, beautiful, meaningful.*

An adjective ending with the sound "us" is spelled *ous*: *previous, various, miscellaneous, humorous, obvious.*

The ending *ally* has two *l*'s: *financially, originally, incidentally, basically, finally.*

The ending *ily* has one *l*: *necessarily, hastily, busily, gloomily.*

Doubling a Final Consonant

Knowing when to double and when not to double a final consonant is easy for the person who can determine the sound.

Words of One Syllable. If you can hear the difference between long and short vowel sounds, you can tell whether or not to double the final consonant of a one-syllable word. If the vowel sound is long, do *not* double; if the vowel sound is short, double the final consonant. Exception: Do not double the final consonant of words ending in *w* (saw) or *x* (fix).

hope	hoping *(long vowel)*	hop	hopping *(short vowel)*
mope	moping *(long)*	mop	mopping *(short)*
plane	planing *(long)*	plan	planning *(short)*
pine	pining *(long)*	pin	pinning *(short)*
scare	scaring *(long)*	scar	scarring *(short)*
stripe	striping *(long)*	strip	stripping *(short)*
tape	taping *(long)*	tap	tapping *(short)*
weed	weeding *(long)*	wed	wedding *(short)*
mix	mixing *(ends in x)*	let	letting *(short)*

Words of More Than One Syllable. The only rule needed is this one: Double the final consonant if the last syllable of the base word is accented, if the vowel sound in the last syllable is *short*, and if the suffix to be added begins with a vowel.

commit	committed, committing
equip	equipped, equipping
occur	occurred, occurrence, occurring
omit	omitted, omitting
prefer	preferred, preferring (*but* preference)
regret	regretted, regretting
transmit	transmitted, transmitting

In each of the following words, the accent is on the *first* syllable; therefore, in the preferred spelling, the final consonant is *not* doubled.

benefit	benefited, benefiting
cancel	canceled, canceling (*but* cancellation)
differ	differed, differing
edit	edited, editing
equal	equaled, equaling
offer	offered, offering
travel	traveled, traveler, traveling

Checkup 1

On a sheet of paper, correct any misspelled words in the following sentences. Write *OK* for any sentence that has no error.

1. First, she tried scrapping the ice off her windshield.
2. Are you refering to Gene Davis in accounting or Jean Davis in marketing?
3. I cannot conceive of a more fitting ending for your story.
4. The day we got the Carnegie account was truly momentus.
5. Jasper wandered around in the zoo looking for the monkies.
6. I believe the Burnside file is in the green filling cabinet.
7. Be sure to take your reciept when you return your laptop computer to CompuWorld.
8. All our competitors are envius of our state-of-the-art color monitor.

DICTIONARY ALERTS

Everyone needs to use a dictionary, even the best of spellers. However, no one has time to look up every word encountered. Therefore, one skill you should acquire is to learn how to recognize the types of words that are most likely to be misspelled—spelling pitfalls. These pitfalls alert careful spellers to the need to consult the dictionary.

The most common spelling pitfalls are presented here so that you, too, will be alert to certain combinations that send even excellent spellers to the dictionary. You may have your own personal spelling pitfalls. Identify them and use the tools you've learned to help avoid them. *Remember:* Use the dictionary whenever in doubt, but especially if the word in question contains one of these prefixes or suffixes.

Word Beginnings

Words beginning with the prefixes *per, pur* and *ser, sur* present a spelling difficulty because the prefixes sound alike. If you are not absolutely certain of the correct spelling of any given word, check the spelling in a dictionary. Study the following words:

perimeter	purloin	serpent	surmount
perplex	purpose	servant	surplus
persuade	pursuit	service	surtax

Word Endings

The following groups of word endings are tricky because they have similar sounds or because they may be pronounced carelessly. The spellings of these endings, however, differ. Do not try to guess at spellings of words with the following ending sounds.

"unt," "uns." If the endings *ant, ance, ent, ence* were always clearly enunciated, they would present no problem. However, because they are so often sounded "unt" and "uns" and because there are so many words with these endings, they are spelling danger spots. They must be spelled by eye, not by ear. Some common words with these endings are listed below:

accountant	compliance	dependent	existence
defendant	maintenance	incompetent	independence
descendant	perseverance	permanent	interference
tenant	remittance	silent	violence

"uhble," "uhbility." The sound "uhble," which might be spelled *able* or *ible*, is another trap. The alert writer consults a dictionary in order to avoid misspelling this ending. Some common "uhble" and "uhbility" words are the following:

changeable	availability	collectible	credibility
movable	capability	deductible	flexibility
payable	predictability	illegible	possibility
receivable	probability	reversible	visibility

Checkup 2

On a separate sheet of paper, correct any misspelled words in the following sentences. Write *OK* for any sentence that has no error.

1. Mitch, do you realize that your perpose in being here is to sell vacuum cleaners?
2. The judge asked the defendent to rise.
3. Ask Joe to take the returnible bottles to the market on his way to work.
4. I was pursuaded that he was perfectly sincere in apologizing for the interruption.
5. Your handwriting is completely illegible.
6. Will Mr. Harrington come back here, or is his transfer to Dallas permanant?

"shun," "shus." Words ending in "shun" might be spelled *tion, sion,* or even *cian, tian, sian, cion,* or *xion.* The ending "shus" might be *cious, tious,* or *xious.* Learn the spelling of the words listed here, but at the same time, remember never to trust a "shun" or a "shus" ending.

ambition	ignition	anxious	malicious
collision	profession	conscientious	pretentious
complexion	suspicion	conscious	suspicious
dietitian	technician	fictitious	superstitious

"shul," "shent." The ending that sounds like "shul" is sometimes spelled *cial* and sometimes *tial.* A "shent" ending might be *cient* or *tient.* Look at the following words and learn how they are spelled, but never take chances on the spelling of any word ending in "shul" or "shent."

artificial	omniscient
beneficial	deficient
judicial	efficient
essential	impatient
partial	proficient
substantial	quotient

Checkup 3

KEY
1. conscientious
2. OK
3. beneficial
4. complexion
5. ambitious
6. anxious

On a sheet of paper, correct any misspelled words in the following sentences. Write *OK* for any sentence that has no error.

1. Charlotte is a capable and <u>consciencious</u> dietitian.
2. Although I was conscious of his presence in the doorway, I did not turn around until he spoke.
3. Andy found the orientation meeting very <u>benefitial</u>.
4. Saralee's bright blue eyes and rosy cheeks were set off by her pale <u>complection</u>.
5. The new assistant seems very efficient and very <u>ambicious</u>.
6. Peter's attorney explained that the questions were just part of routine judicial procedure, but Peter was still <u>ankcious</u>.

"ize," "kul." The ending "ize" might be spelled *ize, ise,* or even *yze (analyze).* A "kul" ending could be *cal* or *cle.* A careful writer, therefore, consults a dictionary for words with these endings. Study the following "ize" and "kul" words:

apologize	advertise	identical	obstacle
criticize	enterprise	mechanical	particle
realize	improvise	statistical	spectacle
temporize	merchandise	technical	vehicle

ar, ary, er, ery, or, ory. *Stationary* and *stationery* end with the same sound, but they are spelled differently. Words that end in *ar, ary, er, ery, or,* or *ory* should be recognized as spelling hazards; you should always verify each spelling. Memorize the spellings of the following words:

calendar	advisory	debtor
customary	advertiser	inventory
grammar	adviser	laboratory
temporary	customer	realtor

"seed." Although only a few words have "seed" endings, they are often written incorrectly because the ending has three different spellings. When

W O R L D V I E W

Be aware that the British rules for spelling and punctuation differ somewhat from ours. For instance, in England the word *labor* is written with *ou* instead of *o (labour)* and the word recognize is written with an *s* instead of a *z (recognise).*

studying the following list of "seed" words, memorize these facts: (1) The *only* word ending in *sede* is *supersede*, and (2) the *only* words ending in *ceed* are *exceed*, *proceed*, and *succeed*. All other "seed" words, then, must be spelled *cede*.

sede	ceed	cede	
supersede	exceed	accede	precede
	proceed	cede	recede
	(*but* procedure)	concede	secede
	succeed	intercede	

Checkup 4

On a sheet of paper, correct any misspelled words in the following sentences. Write *OK* for any sentence that has no error.

1. Nancy proceeded to circle the date on her calander.
2. The realter is supposed to come by tomorrow afternoon to look at our house.
3. Please explain the grammar lesson preceeding Figure B.
4. Little particals of dirt prevented the typewriter keys from functioning properly.
5. I hope you realise what a spectacle you are creating.
6. The store will not be open to customers tomorrow because we need to take inventory of the merchandice.

YOUR SPELLING VOCABULARY

Business writers cannot take the time to verify the spelling of every word. They must, therefore, take the time to learn the correct spellings of the words used most often in their communications. Knowing how to spell troublesome words requires more than memorization. You must analyze each word and fix in your mind its peculiarities, as illustrated by the analyses of the following twenty words.

accommodate (two *c*'s, two *m*'s)   occasion (two *c*'s, one *s*)
aggressive (two *g*'s, two *s*'s)   occurred (two *c*'s, two *r*'s)
believe (*ie*)   precede (*cede*)
chief (*ie*)   privilege (*vile*)
convenient (*ven*, *ient*)   proceed (*ceed*)
definite (*ni*)   receive (*ei*)
develop (no final *e*)   recommend (one *c*, two *m*'s)
embarrass (two *r*'s, two *s*'s)   repetition (*pe*)
forty, fortieth (only *four* words without *u*)   separate (*par*)
ninth (only *nine* word without *e*)   until (only one *l*)

REVIEW

Practical Application

A. Without using a dictionary, write the correct forms of the words enclosed in parentheses on a sheet of paper. Then check your answers in a dictionary.

1. The wheat sale proved (advantage) to both the United States and the Soviet Union.
2. According to the warranty, the manufacturer is responsible for the (maintain) of the typewriter.
3. It was (presume) of the customer to go to the head of the line.
4. We are (scrap) the ineffective procedures.
5. Chris had (plan) to go by plane but ended up taking a bus.
6. Tina made it (abundant) clear that she preferred to remain in Tulsa.
7. What are the (eligible) requirements for entering the contest?
8. It would be (waste) to dispose of the contents too (hasty).
9. Herman is the one in the blue (stripe) suit.
10. Is Gabe Hart on the (advise) board?

B. Make any spelling corrections needed in these sentences. Write *OK* for any sentence that has no error.

1. Raoul has been <u>faxxing</u> the information to me as soon as he receives it.
2. If you can't print this report by noon tomorrow, the order must be <u>cancelled</u>.
3. Joan <u>siezed</u> the opportunity and is now president.
4. Mae knew Keith was in a good mood when she heard him <u>huming</u>.
5. Mrs. Smith retired from the business after <u>bakking</u> about a million cookies.
6. Archibald Crane could never be called a <u>lovible</u> boss.
7. From Glen's comment, Emily <u>infered</u> that the company was in financial trouble.
8. She drew up a list of the <u>uncollectable</u> accounts yesterday.
9. Apparently, sales have been declining <u>steadely</u>.
10. Employee morale is still <u>noticebly</u> high, however.
11. With firmness of purpose, the firm will <u>sermount</u> its present crisis.
12. After such a late lunch Judy won't be <u>dinning</u> early tonight.
13. The union <u>rebeled</u> when management called for employee salary reductions.
14. Now the two sides are <u>confering</u>, thank goodness.
15. The first day of the electronics show is <u>Wensday</u>.
16. Mr. Cunningham was very <u>embarassed</u> that he could not remember the name of the new vice president.

KEY

occasion
recommend
accommodations
privileges
separate
enclosed
brochure
notify
truly

KEY

1. however, still, nevertheless, yet
2. mechanics, workings, basics
3. strong leader, forceful personality, bulwark
4. hard work, industry, diligence, perseverance
5. in excellent condition, working perfectly
6. Today, In this age, Now

KEY

1. g. secede
2. a. delinquent
3. b. perplexed
4. j. visualize
5. i. retrieval

REVIEW cont.

C. On a sheet of paper, write the misspelled words in the following letter. Next to each misspelled word, write the correctly spelled word.

Dear Ms. Renchik:

We would like to take this occassion to reccommend our newest hotel, Casa Grande. Your reservation at Casa Grande guarantees first-class accomodations and all the priviledges that go with them. You may apply now for seperate personal and business rates far below those of other deluxe hotels. You will find inclosed a broshure describing the new Casa Grande. If you have any questions, please notefy us.

Very truely yours,

Editing Practice

Why Be Trite?   Rewrite these sentences, using lively and different words for the trite italicized expressions.

1. Pen-based computers may well be the ultimate portable; *be that as it may*, they initially will be very expensive.
2. Jonathan is more interested in the *nuts and bolts* of the notebook computer than in its sales or advertising.
3. Our new office manager is a *tower of strength.*
4. She advanced in the company by *the sweat of her brow.*
5. Despite heavy use, the old typewriter is *none the worse for wear.*
6. *In this day and age*, mastery of English is essential for a business career.

Using Business Vocabulary.   On a sheet of paper, write the letter and the correct word from the following list to complete each sentence.

a. delinquent   f. principle
b. perplexed   g. secede
c. personal   h. supersede
d. personnel   i. retrieval
e. principal   j. visualize

1. Several nations are threatening to (?) from the economic alliance and form their own group.
2. Matt Turner suggests that we turn over all (?) accounts to a collection agency.
3. Isabel was (?) by Doug's contradictory phone messages.
4. The slides helped us (?) the components that Theresa was describing.
5. We have a sophisticated (?) system for all our stored files.

6. h. supersede
7. c. personal
8. e. principal
9. d. personnel
10. f. principle

6. Granting them exclusive rights to market our products will (?) all earlier licensing agreements.
7. Mr. Kowalski wrote a (?) note to Ms. Bordon to congratulate her on her promotion.
8. The lecturer stressed that economic recovery was her (?) concern.
9. The (?) in our laboratory are well-trained, experienced researchers.
10. Although we stand to gain little from the lawsuit, Mr. Boskin feels it is a matter of (?).

SECTION

4.4 *IMPROVING READING SKILL*

OBJECTIVES: **After completing Section 4.4, you should be able to:**

1. Identify four types of reading and explain the differences among them.
2. Explain how to increase your reading speed.
3. Discuss three ways to improve your reading comprehension.

Reading and vocabulary are closely related. Reading will increase your vocabulary, and increasing your vocabulary will make you a better reader. Of course, there is more to effective reading than just knowing the words. Good readers read fast, but they also understand and remember what they read.

ASSESSING READING SKILL

☐ **SUGGESTION**

If you do not have time to devote to reading skill, you should at least emphasize its importance in business so that students will take steps to improve their skill on their own.

Skillful reading is essential for success in college or in business. Students are tested on what they have read, and employees are often held accountable for actions based on their reading. An employee who can read quickly and efficiently may be able to handle more work than a slow reader. Because reading speed sometimes affects how much work the employee can do, it may affect the employee's value to the company. Reading speed, then, is one important measure of reading skill.

Speed, however, counts little if the reader does not understand what is being read. Reading well requires much more than moving your eyes rapidly over the words on a page. The reader must comprehend ideas and absorb information. Therefore, reading comprehension is a second important measure of reading skill. Do you fully understand the material that you read? Does it take you much longer than other people to read material at school or at work? If your reading speed and comprehension need improvement, you can benefit from the following reading-improvement program.

IMPROVING YOUR READING SKILL

Many people have benefited from reading-improvement courses offered by schools, business organizations, and private institutes. You can also do several things on your own to improve your reading skill.

Adjust Rate to Material and Purpose

 **KEY POINT**
The purpose for reading should determine the speed.

You should adjust your reading speed to the kind of material you are reading and to your purpose for reading it.

Reading for Pleasure. When you are reading for entertainment — novels, magazines, newspapers, etc. — you do not need to absorb every detail or remember a long list of specific facts. You should be able to read this kind of material quite rapidly — at a rate of about 400 words per minute.

Reading for Specific Data. When you are looking for specific names, dates, or other items of information, you should be able to locate the items by skimming a page, without reading every word. Use the same skimming technique when you want to identify the most important ideas in reading matter. Then, stop only to read significant phrases.

SUGGESTION
Prepare a display or a transparency that illustrates the different types of material that one may have to read every day: a newspaper clipping (for pleasure), a section from a telephone directory (for specific data), a set of instructions (for retention or analysis), or a purchase order (for checking and copying).

Reading for Retention or Analysis. This kind of reading includes textbooks and other materials that present content you need to master. You may need to memorize information or analyze the concepts so that you can interpret, explain, or apply the material to other situations. This kind of reading, therefore, requires a slower reading rate.

Checking and Copying. This kind of reading includes such activities as proofreading typewritten or printed copy, checking invoices, and verifying the accuracy of information on a computer screen that was keyboarded from a printed or handwritten document. Checking one copy against another or one column of figures against another calls for great concentration because an error of one digit, one letter, or one syllable could change the entire meaning or accuracy of a document. As a result, such reading must be done carefully, with close attention paid to every detail.

Increase Reading Speed

 **CROSS REFERENCE**
Additional information on proofreading and editing is presented in Chapter 6.

You will always read light novels faster than you read complicated material. However, you can improve your speed of both types of reading by following these suggestions.

Add to Your Vocabulary. Enlarging your vocabulary will help you read faster and improve your comprehension. You will have fewer unfamiliar words to look up, and you will understand complex concepts more easily.

Read in Thought Units. Since all words are not of equal importance, read in thought units rather than word by word. You can develop your visual span of a thought unit by forcing your eyes to take in more words at each pause. With fewer pauses on each line of print, you will naturally read faster. For example, read the following lines.

1. unyqpr
2. table magazine television driver
3. Read in thought units

Although you had no difficulty reading each of these lines, you should have spent progressively less time on each line. In the first line, you had to read each letter individually; in the second, you read each word separately; but in the third, your eyes could take in and read the whole sentence with one glance.

You should be able to read a line in a newspaper column with only one or two eye pauses and to read a book-width line with only four or five eye pauses.

Keep Your Eyes Moving from Left to Right. Always force yourself to concentrate on what you are reading so that you do not have to go back to read a phrase a second time.

Avoid Vocalization. Avoid spelling or pronouncing the words—even silently—as you read them. Such vocalization limits you to reading only as fast as you can read aloud.

Read Only Word Beginnings. Many words can be identified by reading only their beginnings. For example, you should be able to recognize the complete words from these first syllables: *remem-, sepa-, funda-, catal-,* and *educa-.* Then you should be able to tell from the rest of the sentence whether the exact ending of each word should be *remembering* or *remembrance; separate, separately,* or *separation;* and so on. For instance: *Did he remem-(remember) to sepa-(separate) the old catal-(catalogs) from the new catal-(catalogs)?*

Practice Rapid Reading. By following the above suggestions, exercising your willpower, and continually practicing rapid reading, you are certain to increase your reading speed.

Improve Reading Comprehension

 **KEY POINT**

Comprehension (understanding) and retention (remembering) are more important than reading speed.

Even more important than reading speed are comprehension (understanding) and retention (remembering). Many of the suggestions made for increasing reading speed will also contribute to greater comprehension. However, here are some additional hints.

Scan or Preview Material. Before actually beginning to read, look over the material, noticing main headings and subheadings. Also look at illustrations and read captions and numbered passages. This preliminary survey will help you determine your purpose for reading and will also let you see at once the important points. Consequently, after completing your reading of the whole piece, you will have read the most important points twice. Thus, your memory of these parts will be reinforced.

Take Notes. To help you remember what you have read, take notes that include the main ideas. How do you find these main ideas? Usually writers deal with only one main idea per paragraph, and they often place that main idea in the first sentence in the paragraph. In addition to the main idea, you should also note the facts, examples, and key ideas that explain, support, or develop each main idea.

Reread and Review. How often you reread or review material will depend on its difficulty and on the use you plan to make of the information it contains. Often, quick skimming or rereading of your notes will be adequate for review if the first reading was done carefully.

If you follow the suggestions made in this section and apply yourself seriously to a reading-improvement program, you will see results. Not only will you be able to read more in the same amount of time, but also you will get more from what you read.

REVIEW

Practical Application

A. To test your reading speed, have someone time you with a stopwatch (or a watch with a second hand) as you read the following selection.

Microcomputers are low-cost, powerful systems that contain hardware components almost identical to display word processors. They differ from display word processors in not being "dedicated" solely to word processing. Often the size of the microcomputer is the only distinguishing characteristic of appearance. Display word processors usually are larger than microcomputers.

The development in the late 1970s of sophisticated word processing software for the microcomputer led to the widespread use of these microcomputers in the office. Word processing software programs make it possible for documents and other forms of written communication to be prepared on microcomputers. Many of the software programs available for microcomputers provide the ease of operation that often is associated only with dedicated word processing systems.

Microcomputers with word processing capability now provide large and small business organizations with a low-cost office productivity tool. Today, clerical, professional, and executive personnel use microcomputers with word processing capability to create documents quickly, easily, and accurately. Many professional workers create their documents at the keyboard and later turn them over to clerical support personnel for formatting and printing.

Minicomputer and mainframe computer systems are bigger and more powerful than word processors and microcomputers. Data processing activities, such as payroll preparation and maintenance of personnel and inventory records are examples of the information that is handled on these systems. As with microcomputers, word processing applications are handled through the use of specially designed word processing software programs.

Word processing represents a challenge for the worker who enters the business world. It provides an opportunity to learn new skills, use existing skills, and explore new careers. The word processing office has been called the office of the future. The future is now. (234 words)

How long did it take you to read the selection? Use the following chart to compute your reading speed. Because the selection is 234 words long, your speed is 234 words a minute if you took 1 minute, 117 words a minute if you took 2 minutes, and so on.

15 seconds	936 wpm
30 seconds	468 wpm
1 minute	234 wpm
1½ minutes	176 wpm
2 minutes	117 wpm
2½ minutes	98 wpm
3 minutes	78 wpm
3½ minutes	68 wpm
4 minutes	58 wpm

KEY
Line 1: attitude, difference, outward, expression. *Line 2:* personality, involves, attitudes, toward. *Line 3:* employer, toward, general, attitude(s), toward. *Line 4:* respond, suggestions. *Line 5:* righteous, indignant, indifferent. *Line 6:* attitude, negative, responses, positive. *Line 7:* response, suggestions, criticism(s), thoughtfully. *Line 8:* according, judgment, resulting. *Line 9:* self-improvement.

B. One excellent reading habit that will help you improve speed is to read only the beginnings of familiar words rather than the entire words. Test your ability to do this by reading as rapidly as possible the following paragraph, in which the endings of some familiar words have been omitted.

The right atti____ makes all the diff____ in the out____ expres____ of your pers____. This inv____ your atti____ toward your work, tow____ your emp____, tow____ life in gen____. You reveal your atti____ tow____ people in the way you resp____ to sugg____. You can reject them in a self-right____, almost indig____ manner. Or you can adopt an indiff____, "don't care" atti____. These are both neg____ resp____. The pos____ resp____ is to accept sugg____ and crit____ thought____ and graciously. Then you can act upon them acc____ to your best judg____, with resul____ self-impr____.

C. Copying amounts of money, form numbers, dates, and other figures often results in errors because of reading carelessness. Com-

REVIEW cont.

pare the original list (A) with the copied list (B) to determine if any items have been copied incorrectly.

List A	List B
1. 789836B	789863B
2. 4328765	4328765
3. $2786.54	27866.54
4. 9833V39	9833V39
5. LT817745	LT187745
6. u897V229	U897v229
7. Wjkti	wkjti
8. July 23, 1987	July 23, 1978
9. 23 gross @$32	32 gross @23
10. S768R3456J789	S768R3546J789

Editing Practice

Preparing a Digest of a Letter. Secretaries and administrative assistants often read incoming letters for their employers. When a manager is very busy or on a business trip, he or she may ask the secretary or administrative assistant to prepare a short digest (summary) of each letter. Using phrases instead of complete sentences, write a digest of the following letter.

Dear Mr. Stacy:

Thank you for arranging to visit our Woodland plant on October 16 to give us some suggestions for improving the work flow in both our accounting office and the manufacturing plant.

Unfortunately, it will be necessary for me to be out of town on October 16 on a business trip. I will be returning on October 20 and would like to suggest some alternative dates for your visit. Will you telephone me before the sixteenth to let me know if either October 24 or November 2 would be convenient for you? In the event that neither date is satisfactory, please suggest an alternative date.

I would appreciate your bringing with you the pamphlet on telephone systems that you told me about at lunch last week.

Very sincerely yours,
Margaret Stern

5

SHARPENING
WRITING
SKILL

5.1 *PLANNING FOR EFFECTIVE WRITING*

OBJECTIVES: After completing Section 5.1, you should be able to:

1. Explain why planning is an important and necessary part of effective writing.
2. Discuss the three elements that should be considered before writing any business communication.
3. List three ways of making replies to business correspondence faster and easier.

Businesses need to plan for every contingency. Whether interest rates rise or fall, whether inflation worsens or eases, whether times bring boom or recession, businesses must be ready for whatever happens. The success of any business operation depends in large measure on planning and organizational skill.

Written communications are a major business activity. The vast market for word processing products and electronic mail equipment shows the key role of written communications in business. Still, recognizing this importance may not prepare you for the following statistic: Every year business correspondents write the equivalent of 300 letters for every person in the United States. This figure does not include the millions of direct-mail advertising pieces and interoffice memorandums and reports produced every year.

Like other business operations, written communications require careful planning and organization. In order to contribute to the success of your company, you will need the planning and organizational skills required by all business operations. Dashing off a letter without using these skills can lead to serious mistakes in business. The purpose of this section is to equip you with the planning and organizational skills that good business writing requires.

THE MECHANICS OF PLANNING

Writing successful business communications is a serious and difficult job. In order to write a successful business communication, the writer must first think through the task at hand: *why* is the communication being written, *what* information is to be conveyed, and *how* can the message be made most effective? Only then can the writer hope to produce a clear, convincing message.

Determining Your Purpose

Every forceful business letter has a guiding purpose. Everything in the letter, from the salutation to the complimentary close, is done to achieve that purpose. Usually the purpose is simple: to persuade a supplier to extend further credit; to request prices for supplies; to order supplies; to sell a product; to promote goodwill. As you face each writing project, begin by writing down the purpose of the letter or memo. You might make notations like the following.

Request prices and delivery information on printing supplies.

Order 12 dozen computer disks.

Congratulate an employee's daughter who has just been graduated from college.

Persuade a potential customer to try our water filter system.

Assembling the Information

REINFORCEMENT

Remind students to get all needed information before beginning to write. They will save time and avoid the interruption of having to stop to check something.

After you define the purpose of your letter, your next step is to gather all the information necessary to achieve that purpose. Making sure you have all essential information before you begin to write prevents needless interruptions for finding or verifying details. Unless you do the proper research before writing a letter, you will probably have to write another letter answering questions about the information you left out of the first letter. Although follow-up letters are sometimes unavoidable, a carefully planned first letter should get the job done.

Suppose, for example, that you are asked to write a routine letter requesting a rush price quote on letterhead stationery from your regular printer. You quickly remit this letter:

Please quote us your best price for 2,000 pieces of our company's stationery.

Two days later you receive a letter from the stationery supplier asking these questions: Do you want second sheets for the stationery? If so, how many? Do you want matching envelopes? If so, how many? Do you want single sheets of stationery or do you want stationery that can be continuously fed? In the past, your company has ordered printed stationery and engraved stationery; which do you want on this order? Your previous letterhead showed the five-digit ZIP Code. Do you want to keep this ZIP Code or change it to the nine-digit ZIP Code that the U.S. Postal Service now recommends?

Obviously, you should have assembled all the pertinent information before writing the letter, as in the following notes. (The numbers in parentheses are discussed in the next section.)

Remind rush; request expedite (5)
Charge it to our account (4)
Need 2,000 sheets of letterhead (2)

Need 500 second sheets (2)
Request parcel delivery service (4)
Need 2,500 envelopes (2)
Request engraved (3)
Request quote, not placing an order (1)
Change to nine-digit ZIP Code; provide the ZIP Code (3)
Letterhead and second sheets should be single sheets that will not be used in a continuous-feed printer (3)

Orderly Presentation

REINFORCEMENT
Point out to students that reading information not presented in an orderly fashion can be compared to missing the beginning of a movie. We often miss the central idea as well as crucial supporting details.

Your notes now cover all the necessary information. You have jotted them down, however, without regard to the best order for presenting the information in your letter.

The final step in assembling the information is to number your notes in the most logical order. (The numbers in parentheses after the items listed in the preceding discussion illustrate how to present these topics.) Now you have assembled the facts for a successful letter.

The Social Framework—The Letter as a Visit

KEY POINT
A letter substitutes for a visit. Even though the letter pertains to business, it has a social aspect.

You now know *why* you are writing and *what* you must say, but something essential to a good letter is missing. It is the same thing that is missing from the following visit.

Steven Chin walks into Staley Office Supply and sees the owner, Emily Staley. He walks straight toward her and says, "Sixteen number 2 pencils, 1 electric pencil sharpener, 12 boxes paperclips, 14 yellow legal pads."
Ms. Staley replies, "One hundred fifty-four dollars and ninety-five cents."
Mr. Chin hands Ms. Staley a check. Ms. Staley hands Mr. Chin a package.
Exit Mr. Chin.

Why is this scene so strange and unreal? Neither Steven nor Emily acts as one human being does on meeting or visiting another. They both ignore the inescapable social framework of their business transaction. A kind of social framework exists even in written business communication, particularly the business letter. When writing a letter you must visualize the reader and think about his or her interests. This visualization will help you convey your message in a friendly yet businesslike way.

Business letters that include only the necessary facts are lacking in the same way as the strange visit described above. Just like a visit, a good letter must contain the following social elements:

1. Greeting: "Good morning, Ms. Staley."
2. Statement of purpose: "I came to your store because my office is almost out of supplies."
3. Business of the occasion: Steven specifies what he needs.
4. Leave-taking: "Good-bye, Ms. Staley, and thank you for helping me so promptly."

LANGUAGE TIP

"Whatever we conceive well we express clearly."

—Boileau

This procedure is the outline for a personal visit. It could also be the outline for a visit by mail.

Greeting. The salutation is the greeting of a letter. If the letter is written to an individual, the salutation should be *Dear Mr. Carson* or *Dear Mrs. Bonner,* not the cold *Dear Sir* or *Dear Madam.*

ℹ INFORMATION
The purpose is usually presented first to give it emphasis.

Purpose of the Visit. When making a personal visit, you follow the greeting with a statement of the purpose of the call. Similarly, after the salutation, the opening paragraph of a letter tells the reader what will be discussed in the letter. Here are three examples of opening paragraphs that state the purpose of the call:

Your September 1 letter expressed an interest in our group health and accident insurance policies. Enclosed is our latest brochure, which gives some of the general information you requested.

Thank you for requesting information on our May 18 sale, which will liquidate our stock of antique desks. The dates, times, and terms of the sale are listed on the attached sales sheet.

Your application letter and résumé have been received and reviewed by our Human Resource Department. We feel that your education and experience could qualify you for a management trainee position with our company.

Business of the Call. Here is the "meat" of your call. If, for instance, you were writing that letter ordering stationery, here is where you would make the orderly presentation of the facts that the supplier will need.

Leave-Taking. Sometimes a letter has another paragraph that becomes a part of the leave-taking. Consider the following examples:

Thank you for giving us the opportunity to serve you. We appreciate your business.

You can rely on our staff to give you creative suggestions to promote your products. Contact us for advertising that gets results.

Your quick response in replacing the goods damaged by the recent tornado made our grand opening a success. Thank you for the special effort you made in our behalf.

Advertising in your newspaper brought many new customers to our store.

👤 KEY POINT
Avoid these two writing pitfalls: (1) using participial closings and (2) offering thanks in advance.

If you add another paragraph, there are two pitfalls to avoid. First, never use a participial closing, an *ing* expression, such as *Wishing you the best of luck in your new venture, we are . . .* or *Looking forward to seeing you at the conference, I am . . . .* Instead, simply write, *We wish you the best of luck in your new venture.* Or, *I am looking forward to seeing you at the conference.* Second, never offer thanks in advance. To do so would be presumptuous. Express gratitude for a favor or a service when you can acknowledge it, not before.

In all letters, the complimentary closing completes the leave-taking and affords the writer a last chance to set the tone of the communication. The choice ranges from the cold *Very truly yours* to the warm *Cordially*. An incongruous closing can be confusing, as shown in the following examples:

This letter is to inform you that we are seeking an eviction order to remove you from the offices in our building.

Cordially yours,

We are delighted that you have accepted our invitation to appear at the benefit dinner to be held in your honor.

Very truly yours,

BEYOND THE MECHANICS

A mastery of the mechanics of planning, although necessary for effective business writing, takes us only so far. If we stopped there, our letters would have limited influence on our readers. Courtesies, facts, and reasoned arguments are not the only ways in which a letter can guide the reader's judgment. Planning must go beyond the mechanics if we are to influence our readers in ways more subtle than extending normal courtesies, stating the facts of our business, and presenting arguments. Every letter carries with it a certain atmosphere. The techniques that follow will show you how to create an atmosphere in which your message will appear at its best.

Atmosphere Effect

All of us have had the experience of meeting someone and immediately deciding "Oh, what a bore!" If asked the reasons for our judgment, we probably couldn't offer any. We know only that something about that person registered an impression and we cannot reason it away. For want of a better term, we might call this impression the "atmosphere effect."

It is important to use impressions, or atmosphere effect, to work for us in our business writing, so that our readers will think, "I'd like to do business (or I like doing business) with this company."

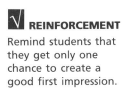 **REINFORCEMENT**

Remind students that they get only one chance to create a good first impression.

First Impression.   The reader's first impression on opening a letter might be "a quality firm," "a very ordinary company," or even "a shoddy operation." To create a desirable atmosphere effect, the stationery must be of good quality, the letterhead design attractive, the typing imprint uniform, the right-hand margin even, and the corrections not discernible.

Further Acquaintance.   After registering the first impression created by your letter, the reader looks for confirmation. Correct and polished grammar, spelling, punctuation, word usage — all these are needed to solidify the first impression of "quality firm." Avoid using clichés like *attached hereto*, *the writer*, and *under separate cover*; otherwise, the atmosphere effect of your letter would be that of a stale, unprogressive business operation.

Paragraph Length.   Paragraph length is a key factor in creating a good first impression. The length of paragraphs in a letter is so important to atmosphere effect that it merits special treatment (Section 5.4).

As you plan your letter, remember that reading can be *hard work*. You do not want your reader to open your letter, see a densely packed page, and think "What a job to wade through this material!"

Facilitating Action

We often tend to follow the course of least resistance. We complete immediately the tasks that are easy and put off those tasks that will take time and effort. Recognition of this human tendency suggests ways of increasing the chances of getting quick and favorable responses to your letters and memorandums.

Reply Copy. A reply copy is a duplicate that is sent with the original letter. This device is effective when the reader can reply by writing answers in the margin of the copy. The reason for its effectiveness is that the reader is relieved of the chore of planning and composing a reply.

For example, suppose you are president of a statewide photography association and are writing to give one of your colleagues a choice of dates for the annual meeting and to ask for recommendations for a speaker for that meeting. If you send a reply copy, your colleague can answer your letter by writing in the margin *January 21* and *Dr. Cardenas, Professor of Graphic Arts Technology at Midvale College*. What do you think are the odds that you will get a quick answer?

When you assemble information for a letter that will be accompanied by a reply copy, one of your notes should be *Call attention to reply copy*. When you are composing that letter, be sure that you convey to the reader the no-work-involved idea. For example, say something like:

> Just jot your comments in the margin of the enclosed copy and return it to me.

Enclosed Card or Return Slip. Another method of bringing about a prompt and favorable response is to enclose a card or return slip with the letter. Suppose your firm, The Chef's Supply Center, is planning a new campaign for customers. Your job is to write the promotional copy that will go to thousands of people on a newly obtained mailing list. Management has decided to offer each potential new customer a free copy of the company's latest discount catalog. A postage-paid, addressed return card will be enclosed.

The psychological motivation for your letter will be financial gain — making money by saving money — and the spur to action will be a final paragraph such as:

> You will start to save money just as soon as you fill out and return the enclosed card. No postage is necessary.

Attached Perforated Form. Still another means of facilitating action is to use a perforated return form that can be detached from the letter. This method can be just as effective as a separately enclosed slip and is much easier to prepare and mail.

The Chef's Supply Center

Cooking Equipment, Dishes, Glasses, Cutlery
Dover, Delaware

Yes! Please send me your latest money-saving catalog.

Name _____

Street _____

City _____ State _____ Zip _____

Positive words such as *yes* and *money-saving* help make this return card an effective way to stimulate action.

When you write this type of letter, be sure to include a paragraph that calls attention to the form. For instance:

> To renew your subscription — and to receive a bonus of four free issues! — fill in the form at the bottom of this page, tear it off, and mail it *today*.

Watch That *If!* Our readers almost always have a choice of what to say in response to our messages. When reminded of the choice, however, people are more likely to decide against a new proposal. The writer, therefore, should never remind readers that they have a choice. Always assume that the readers will act favorably. Your confidence will help make the case for your proposal.

If is the word that indicates a choice; and *if* is the word to watch. Perhaps we can illustrate this bit of psychology by rewording the last two examples.

> If you would like to receive the latest edition of our money-saving catalog, just fill out and return the enclosed card. No postage is necessary.

> If you wish to renew your subscription — and win the bonus of four free issues! — fill in the form at the bottom of this page, tear it off, and mail it *today*.

The *if* in either of these examples suggests to your readers that they might *not* like to receive or wish to renew — and the chances are that they will go along with the *not*. Be aware that the *if* in each of these paragraphs is the word that risks losing the order.

Rereading Your Letters

A business writer's extra polish is the final check of each communication. After you finish your letter-writing stint for the day, reread the letters as if

CROSS REFERENCE

Discuss the merits of having someone else read your letter—particularly if it is important. Refer the students to Chapter 6 on proofreading and editing.

they were addressed *to* you, not sent *by* you. From this fresh and different viewpoint, you should be able to spot any errors you have made, either in language or in psychology. Often the difference between employees who receive raises and promotions and those who do not is this kind of attention to detail. Don't be satisfied with "That's good enough." Although additional time and effort are involved, your intelligence tells you that only by spending that time can you produce a first-class product.

SECTION

REVIEW

Practical Application

A. Assume that you are inviting Tom Edelman, a management consultant, to speak to your business communications class. Ask him to speak for 30 minutes on the role communication plays in making a business successful. Tell him you would like a 10-minute question-and-answer session after his talk. Work with a classmate to plan the letter. First, list the items that should appear in the letter. Use your imagination to supply needed details such as time and place.

KEY

Students' answers will vary, but look for such things as time, date, place, topic, type of presentation, and name and address of school.

KEY

Students' letters will vary.

B. Using the information you developed in the previous exercise, write the first draft of the letter.

KEY

Students' answers will vary. A suggested order is given.
a. 4
b. 6
c. 9
d. 2
e. 7
f. 5
g. 8
h. 3
i. 1

C. As the owner of a retail computer company, you have decided to introduce your products to fourth-, fifth-, and sixth-grade children. You have made the notes below about your educational program. Now, number them in the order in which they should appear in a letter that could be written to respond to inquiries from parents.

4 a. Time will be 6:30 to 8:30 p.m.

6 b. Application blank is enclosed.

9 c. Call 555-2861 for additional information.

2 d. Class runs for two weeks.

  e. Cost is $25 per child.

5 f. Enclose a brochure giving details on program, equipment, and software.

  g. Class is limited to the first 15 applicants.

3 h. Dates are June 1–5 (Monday through Friday) and June 8–12 (Monday through Friday).

1 i. Thank you for asking about our computer education program for elementary students.

D. Using the notes you have just arranged, write the letter.

KEY

Students' answers for D through F will vary.

E. List three business writing situations that could effectively use a reply copy.

F. Choose one of the business situations from Application D and write a letter that could use a reply copy.

REVIEW cont.

Editing Practice *⁹/₂ in class ✓*

Trimming Extra Words. Redundancy is the unnecessary repetition of an idea. Reading the same thing twice can be time-consuming and confusing. Which word or words in the sentences below can be omitted to eliminate redundancies? Write *OK* for any sentence that is correct.

KEY

Students' answers will vary. Suggested omissions are given.

1. again
2. and without error
3. afternoon
4. and customary
5. and on time
6. past performance
7. downward
8. OK
9. of his money
10. exact

1. Thinking that her associates had not heard her the first time, Elisha repeated the comment ~~again.~~
2. The consultant announced that both answers to the question were correct ~~and without error.~~
3. Can you attend the meeting tomorrow ~~afternoon~~ at 4:30 p.m.?
4. Our usual ~~and customary~~ procedure is to mail the invoice the same day the merchandise is shipped.
5. Kevin tries to be punctual ~~and on time~~ for his appointments.
6. Our p~~ast performance~~ history of real estate sales indicates an increase each May.
7. Della reported a ~~downward~~ decrease in the quality of raw materials.
8. Computers can be used to control inventory and predict trends.
9. Steven will get a refund ~~of his money~~ because the product was defective.
10. After examining all pertinent information, Allison and Florence reached the ~~exact~~ same conclusion.

5.2 *STRUCTURING PHRASES AND CLAUSES*

OBJECTIVES: After completing Section 5.2, you should be able to:

1. Recognize and correct errors in thought units composed of words, phrases, and clauses.
2. Recognize and correct errors in pronoun references.
3. Correct *this* and *thus* faults.

In the writing of every message, a writer must group words with care; otherwise, the reader will be confused. Small differences in the grouping or placement of words can make huge differences in meaning.

Consider the following example:

Calling the meeting to order, the new autofocus camera drew the praise of the marketing director.

When the meeting was called to order, the new autofocus camera drew the praise of the marketing director.

While we can understand how a new autofocus camera might please the marketing director, even in this age of technological miracles we cannot expect an autofocus camera to call a meeting to order. In order to avoid the confusion and embarrassment that accompany such a ridiculous statement, the writer must learn to place together words whose meanings belong together.

A combination of words that properly belong together is called a *thought unit*. When the writer correctly places the words of a thought unit, the reader can understand the meaning quickly and easily. When the writer incorrectly places the words of a thought unit, however, the reader may get a completely mistaken idea of the writer's meaning. Sometimes the mistaken idea is laughable, but in business such mistakes are more likely to cause serious problems, as in the example below.

If our new Integrated Stereo components don't satisfy you, just fill out the enclosed warranty forms and send them back to us—we'll pay the postage.

The difference between the cost of mailing the warranty forms and the cost of mailing the stereo components would be considerable. Does the pronoun *them* stand for the forms or the components? Let's hope that the writer's employer won't mind paying the postage for both.

The first step in developing your writing skill is to learn to structure phrases and clauses in a way that makes your meaning unmistakable. This section will show you how.

WORDS IN THOUGHT UNITS

Sometimes a confusing, laughable, or simply false meaning is conveyed because a single word is not connected with its proper thought unit. The following advertisement is an example of a misplaced adjective.

Gigantic men's clothing sale begins today!

Placement of the words seems to indicate that *gigantic men's* is a thought unit. However, few men want to be described as *gigantic?* The correct thought unit, of course, is *gigantic sale.* Therefore, the copywriter should have written the ad as shown below.

Gigantic sale of men's clothing begins today!

Misplaced adverbs, too, can lead to confusion:

The idea for changing our sales emphasis came to me after I had opened the meeting suddenly.

The thought unit *opened suddenly* is incorrect. The *idea came suddenly*, and so the sentence should read as follows:

> The idea for changing our sales emphasis suddenly came to me after I had opened the meeting.

PHRASES IN THOUGHT UNITS

Incorrectly placed phrases, as well as incorrectly placed words, can change the meaning of a message completely. Expert writers edit their work carefully to see that they have placed phrases correctly. An expert writer would reject the following sentence:

> This hard drive can be installed by anyone who has studied the computer manual in ten minutes.

Obviously, no computer manual could be studied in ten minutes, but someone who had studied the computer manual for a reasonable length of time could probably install a hard drive in ten minutes. The sentence, therefore, should read:

> This hard drive can be installed in ten minutes by anyone who has studied the computer manual.

Now read the following classified advertisement and see the confusion that results from an incorrectly placed thought unit.

> **For rent:** Three-room apartment for working couple with balcony only.

This ad might bring to the real estate office only those couples who already have a balcony. How many couples can there be, however, who have a balcony but don't have an apartment? The ad should say:

> **For rent:** Three-room apartment with balcony for working couple only.

Two misplaced phrases can be even worse than one. Imagine receiving a direct-mail advertisement that contained the following sentence:

> Our interactive high-resolution games are guaranteed to give you hours of entertainment without qualification for your home computer.

The correct thought units are *games for your home computer* and *guaranteed without qualification*. The following revision would be more likely to encourage you to order a game or two:

> Our interactive high-resolution games for your home computer are guaranteed without qualification to give you hours of entertainment.

CLAUSES IN THOUGHT UNITS

Misplacing a car is a bigger mistake than misplacing a bicycle. We shouldn't be surprised, then, to learn that a misplaced clause can have even more devastating consequences than a misplaced word or phrase. How would the public react if the president of your company made this announcement?

> Our goal in marketing is to encourage the public to try our products until our pet foods become better known.

The sentence sounds as if once the products are better known, no one will want to buy them. Moving the *until* clause clears up the matter.

> Until our pet foods become better known, our goal in marketing is to encourage the public to try our products.

Because clauses pose a special hazard, since they often are used to explain people's motives. Consider the following statement:

> Ms. Dearborn hardly noticed the flowers that were sent by her husband because she was concentrating so intensely on the labor contract she was negotiating.

Imagine the loving note that Mr. Dearborn must have sent with the flowers: "Thank you so much for concentrating intensely on the labor contract. I will always remember this moment as one of the most touching in our life together."
Unless Mr. Dearborn is an official of the labor union, he could hardly be expected to send his wife either the note or the flowers as described above. More likely the following sentence better describes the situation:

> Because she was concentrating so intensely on the labor contract she was negotiating, Ms. Dearborn hardly noticed the flowers that were sent by her husband.

Now Ms. Dearborn's reason for taking little notice of the flowers is easy to understand.

AMBIGUOUS *WHICH* CLAUSES

The word *which* is a pronoun that refers to another word in the sentence. If the word referred to is unclear, confusion will result. A mark of the expert writer is the ability to place a *which* clause with the word modified, explained, or amplified.
Here is an example of one misuse of a *which* clause — simple misplacement.

> Our gallery has a book on important nineteenth-century American paintings, which you can purchase for a special price of $19.95 plus postage.

Placing *which* immediately after *paintings* alters the meaning of the sentence. Can the *paintings* be purchased for only $19.95? The writer of the sentence above actually intended to say that the book could be purchased for $19.95. Accordingly, the *which* clause should have been placed as follows:

> Our gallery has a book, which you can purchase for a special price of $19.95 plus postage, on important nineteenth-century American paintings.

While clear and a definite improvement, the rewritten sentence would gain force and polish if the *which* clause were removed as in the version below:

For a special price of $19.95 plus postage, you can purchase our gallery's book on important nineteenth-century American paintings.

Another misuse of a *which* clause will be familiar to all. Although it is perfectly acceptable for *which* to refer to a broad idea rather than to a single noun, the writer must take extra care to see that the reference is clear. Pronoun reference in the sentence below is ambiguous:

Further resistance to the board of directors will only jeopardize your job, which neither of us wants.

The problem here is that the *which* clause may refer either to the broad idea *will only jeopardize your job* or to the single noun *job*. Although most of us can guess the meaning intended, incorrect interpretations come more easily. *Which* seems at first to belong to the thought unit *your job*. If neither of the persons referred to wants the job, why should either one care whether the job is jeopardized? A clearer statement of the sentence's intended meaning would be as follows:

Further resistance to the board of directors will only jeopardize your job, and we do not want to jeopardize your job.

Here is an example of a *which* clause making clear reference to a broad idea:

Ms. Bergen predicted that an out-of-court settlement would be reached, which is precisely what happened.

Used with care, *which* clauses perform valuable service. In the sentence below, the *which* clause achieves a degree of clarity that would be difficult to equal in as few words.

Read clause 5, which contains the productivity standards under the new contract.

WHO DID WHAT?

In business communications, as in any other kind of communication, it is essential that the writer make it absolutely clear *who* has done or will do a specific thing. Sometimes, however, the writer confuses the thought by having the wrong person or thing connected with an action, and so the intended meaning is not conveyed to the reader. Such a violation of the thought-unit principle can cause doubt or uncertainty as to *who* did *what*.

If not satisfied, we will refund your money.

Consider the thought unit *If not satisfied, we*. The meaning here is that *we* are the ones who might not be satisfied. If a customer returned the goods and asked for a full refund, the manufacturer could refuse on the grounds that the manufacturer was well satisfied with the customer's money. The correct meaning is immediately apparent to the reader when the sentence is revised.

If you are not satisfied, we will refund your money.

Occasionally, if the who-did-what principle is violated, the sentence becomes ridiculous, for an object, not a person, seems to be performing an action.

Receiving the customer's urgent request, the order was immediately processed by Jerry.

The thought unit *Receiving the customer's urgent request, the order* suggests that the order was receiving the request. This kind of phrasing shows a serious lack of communication know-how. In this revision, Jerry performs the action:

Receiving the customer's urgent request, Jerry immediately processed the order.

Here is another illustration of this type of error:

After climbing to the top of the tower, the whole city lay spread before us.

What does the thought unit *After climbing to the top of the tower, the whole city* mean? How could a city climb to the top of the tower? Revised, the sentence would read:

After climbing to the top of the tower, we saw the whole city spread before us.

A who-did-what violation, sometimes called a *dangler*, does not necessarily occur at the beginning of a sentence. For example, note the error in the following sentence:

Ms. Waters saw the prospective customer leaving the stockroom.

As written, the thought unit is *customer leaving the stockroom*. Where was Ms. Waters when she saw the customer, and why was the customer in the stockroom? Most likely it was Ms. Waters who was leaving the stockroom. In order to eliminate the confusion, the writer must change the sentence:

Leaving the stockroom, Ms. Waters saw the prospective customer.

INDEFINITE, CONFUSING PRONOUN REFERENCES

Each pronoun borrows its meaning from a noun. When the writer fails to make clear which noun a pronoun refers to, the pronoun loses its meaning or assumes an incorrect and unintended meaning. One vague or mistaken pronoun reference can garble an entire message. The careful writer checks each pronoun used in order to make certain that its reference is clear.

Confusing *He* or *She*

When you use either the pronoun *he* or the pronoun *she*, you must make certain that the antecedent is clear. If more than one man or more than one woman is mentioned in the sentence, you should take special care to place the pronoun as near as possible to the person referred to. The following sentence leaves the reader wondering "Who returned from the meeting?"

> Mr. Consodine asked Richard to write a report immediately after he returned from the regional sales meeting.

Does the *he* in this sentence refer to Richard or to Mr. Consodine? If the reference is to Mr. Consodine, then the sentence should be revised as follows:

> Immediately after he returned from the regional sales meeting, Mr. Consodine asked Richard to write a report.

If, on the other hand, Richard is the one who attended the meeting, then the sentence should read:

> Immediately after Richard returned from the regional sales meeting, Mr. Consodine asked him to write a report.

Indefinite *It*

 **REINFORCEMENT**

Ask students to collect errors (similar to the ones shown in this section) in letters, memos, newspapers, and so on.

Using the pronoun *it* to refer to something that is not immediately clear is a common offense.

> I will place the football in punt position, and when I nod my head, kick it.

Kick what? This indefinite *it* could result in a painful injury, wouldn't you say? The indefinite *it* must be replaced by the noun to which it should refer. The revised sentence reads:

> I will place the football in punt position, and when I nod my head, kick the ball.

Inept writers tend to use the pronoun *it* as a catchall word, even if there is no antecedent to which the *it* can refer.

> It is Sarah's unique style of management that has contributed greatly to the success of her department.

In this example the *it* reference is vague and serves only to make the sentence wordy. Consider how much more effective the sentence would be if it were written:

> Sarah's unique style of management has contributed greatly to the success of her department.

Other Indefinite Pronoun References

Speakers who are uncertain of their sources frequently use the careless "they say" as a reference. Writers who use the same vague reference are considered amateurish; in written communication, references must be definite and exact. For example, read the following sentence:

> They say that the joint venture between Eastern Rail/Road Transport, Inc., and the Baltic republics will be launched early next year.

Who is meant by *they* in this sentence? A lack of definiteness earmarks a poorly trained writer. A precise writer would present the information this way:

> *International Market News* reports that the joint venture between Eastern Rail/Road Transport, Inc., and the Baltic republics will be launched early next year.

Another type of indefinite reference that is puzzling and annoying to a reader is illustrated in this sentence:

> Although I dictated all morning on Tuesday, the word processing operator input only two of them.

The slipshod *two of them* is vagueness carried to an extreme. Two of what? stories? letters? reports? news releases? A clear and explicit thought could be communicated by writing:

> Although I dictated all morning on Tuesday, the word processing operator input only two of the letters.

CORRECTING THE *THIS* AND *THUS* FAULTS

 **KEY POINT**

A common writing fault is the use of *this* or *thus* to refer to an entire preceding thought.

A common writing fault is the use of *this* or *thus* to refer to an entire preceding thought. This lack of precision sometimes forces a reader to read a sentence several times to understand the writer's meaning. This inexact use of *this* and *thus* can spoil an otherwise fine writing performance.

> Employees can't find parking spaces. This has existed since we hired 50 new employees.

To what does the *this* refer? *This* refers to the *shortage of parking spaces*. Stating the point specifically makes the meaning clear.

> Employees can't find parking spaces. This shortage of parking spaces has existed since we hired 50 new employees.

Now read the following sentence, which is another example of unclear word reference.

> Clement Browne was promoted to branch manager, thus confirming everyone's opinion that he is the most qualified person for the position.

Thus, as used here, is ambiguous. The thought could have been expressed more clearly and more directly as follows:

> The fact that Clement Browne was promoted to branch manager confirms everyone's opinion that he is the most qualified person for the position.

REVIEW

Practical Application

KEY
See page I-26.

A. Rewrite each sentence, making sure all thought units are clear.

1. Manuel took the computer out of the box, which everyone had been waiting to see.
2. After breaking for lunch, the meeting reconvened.
3. Because of design defects, the manufacturer recalled the Model Zoom lawnmowers.
4. Exotic-looking men's ties are fashionable this season.
5. Hold the two pieces in place with your fingers and glue them together.
6. Walking on crutches, stairs were difficult to climb for Rick.
7. Having forgotten to save the document before turning off the computer, the report had to be reinput by Susan.
8. Sitting close to the window, the skyscrapers were clearly visible.
9. People often buy things with credit cards that they don't need.
10. The new computers, with little or no training, can be operated by good keyboarders.
11. Cooking in the microwave oven, Ned finds that he spends less time in the kitchen.
12. Your rental agreement says that you may not have animals or children unless caged.
13. After doing much planning, the budget finally balanced.
14. The mixer truck was wrecked by a substitute driver only half full of cement.
15. We have a brochure of our diverse financial services, which we will give you upon request.
16. The acerbic theater critic's review hurt ticket sales.
17. When walking through the office, the printer noise was distracting to the visitors.
18. Covered with proofreader's marks, Ms. Kantor sent the draft back for corrections.
19. After working a 12-hour shift, his head ached and his feet hurt.
20. To remove paint without scraping, you should plan on a two-hour soak in solvent.

KEY
See page I-26.

B. These sentences have confusing pronoun references. Rewrite them, making the specified corrections.

1. Alice saw Katie when she was in Chicago last week. (Alice was in Chicago.)
2. Len and Judd researched the topic, but he did the actual writing of the report. (Judd wrote the report.)
3. Dan told Charlie that his explanation was not clear. (Dan's explanation was not clear.)

4. They think that more test trials are needed for the new arthritis treatment. (*They* refers to Dr. Anne McCurry and Dr. Ben Lawson.)
5. Although we interviewed 30 applicants, we hired only 3 of them. (*Them* refers to laboratory technicians.)
6. It is a positive attitude that can make the difference between success and failure. (Remove the *It*.)
7. The computer terminal is on my desk. Don't move it for any reason. (*It* refers to the computer terminal.)
8. It may be a good idea to rearrange the desks in this office. (Remove the *It*.)
9. Ms. Nichols was offered a five-year lease or a ten-year lease. She will probably sign it next week. (*It* refers to the longer lease.)
10. Martha asked Caroline to review the contract as soon as she received it. (Martha received the contract.)

C. Rewrite each sentence, correcting the *this* or *thus* references.

1. The meeting adjourned without our taking any action or making any decisions thus causing us to be dissatisfied.
2. When we transferred the files, several folders were misplaced. This was not Dexter's fault.
3. When the power was unexpectedly interrupted, several computer files were damaged. This will cause us to work late.
4. The company's top designer was not able to work with us because she was on vacation when we launched the project. This has affected the quality of our project.
5. Steven ignored his father's good advice thus proving that he was stubborn.

Editing Practice

Pronoun Practice. Correct the pronoun errors in the following sentences. Write *OK* for any sentence that has no error.

1. Its not clear which letter arrived first.
2. Warren, Elizabeth, and him volunteered to work overtime for two weeks.
3. They are planning to ride with us to the convention.
4. Who's request should be granted?
5. Will you give your recommendations to William or I?
6. What one of the account representatives will be transferred?
7. Whom is going to the meeting in Houston next week?
8. The article was written by she last summer.
9. The fee will be divided between you and I.
10. Durability and appearance are it's strong points.

KEY
See page I-26.

KEY
1. It's
2. he
3. OK
4. Whose
5. me
6. Which
7. Who
8. her
9. me
10. its

REVIEW cont.

Using Your Word Processor.   Correct the typographical errors in the following sentences.

1.   After the meeting, all the managers wemt to the cafeteria for lunch.
2.   The discussion during lunch helped us understand how the group reallly felt about the new procedures.
3.   Everyone thought we should accept the the new procedures.
4.   Most of the procedures were designed to improve efficiency adn safety.
5.   Efficiency and safety definitely important.

5.3 *WRITING EFFECTIVE SENTENCES*

OBJECTIVES: After completing Section 5.3, you should be able to:

1. Phrase messages positively by choosing the right combination of words that are balanced and effective.
2. Use planned repetition for emphasis, and identify and remove distracting words.
3. Use subordination properly, and correct *so* and *and so* faults.
4. Use the active and passive voices appropriately.

A good business communication flows smoothly. Unaware of sentences, clauses, and phrases, the reader absorbs the continuous flow of ideas. Nothing interrupts the reader's concentration — no awkward phrases, vague references, or imbalanced constructions.

Because a good letter moves so easily for the reader, the reader may feel that the letter flowed as easily from the mind of the writer. In actuality, however, the letter as it first occurred to the writer was probably much the same as a first draft of anyone's writing — full of awkward phrases, vague references, choppy sentences, and imbalanced constructions. The writer took the time, however, to look and listen for problems in the rough draft and then applied the writing techniques needed to eliminate the problems.

Becoming an effective business writer takes time and practice. It is a cumulative skill. In other words, you cannot forget what you learned in the previous sections. You must combine that knowledge with what you are learning now and what you will learn in later sections.

WORD USAGE

Words combine to make sentences, and sentences combine to make paragraphs. You cannot write a good paragraph without using the right words. Here are some suggestions for improving written communications.

1. Use positive words.
2. Use planned repetition of words to emphasize important points.
3. Identify and revise combinations of words that produce harsh or awkward sounds.

Positive Words

KEY POINT

Positive words can help the writer achieve the desired response. Negative words encourage a negative response.

Positive words are pleasant to hear and to read. They are words that create a receptive, pleasant impression in the mind of a reader. Consequently, the skilled writer deliberately uses words that produce this desirable psychological effect. The words in the first list cause a positive response, and the words in the second list cause a negative response.

Positive Words

success	eager	agreeable	courage
profit	easy	fun	welcome
happy	capable	enjoy	pleasure
integrity	cheerful	warmth	advancement

Negative Words

failure	cannot	complaint	no
loss	difficult	blame	problem
sad	incapable	apologize	sorry
dishonest	anxious	damage	wrong

Negative sentences should be reworded to make them more positive.

Negative: We were not late in our deliveries last month.
Positive: All our deliveries were made on schedule last month.

Planned Repetition of Words

REINFORCEMENT

Another example of unplanned repetition—Sam is very pleased to introduce the very qualified consultants.

Although careless repetition of words shows a lack of imagination, *planned* repetition can sometimes achieve striking emphasis of an important idea. Repeating the words *too* and *easy* in the following examples helps to emphasize each point.

She arrived too late too often to keep her job.

He did the easy things the easy way, and he was easy to replace.

A major goal of any advertisement is to make readers remember the name and purpose of the product. Sometimes this goal is accomplished by simple repetition of the name. Clever writers manage to vary the order of the repeated words to prevent monotony. Consider the clever and purposeful transposition of the words below.

> Flexicise Workouts will add muscles to your body, and Flexicise Workouts will add body to your muscles.

The Sound of Words

Excessive repetition of sounds can make tongue twisters that detract from the message. Even when reading silently, the reader cannot ignore sentences like:

> Sylvie sold seven slinky silk shifts on Saturday.

Sound repetition can cause problems other than tongue twisters. Although easy to say, the following sentence is hardly a pleasure to hear:

> Steer your weary, dreary body to O'Leary's Health Spa.

Avoid unpleasant sounds, and do not attempt to write business letters that sound musical or poetic. The letter, like everything else in business, has a particular function. For the greatest effect, concentrate on that function.

PROPER SUBORDINATION OF IDEAS

 **KEY POINT**

The most important thought is expressed as a main clause, and the lesser idea is written as a subordinate clause.

Proper subordination of ideas depends on the ability to determine the difference between an important idea and a lesser idea. The important thought is expressed as a main clause, and the lesser idea is properly written as a subordinate clause. The principle can be remembered as follows: "Main idea — main clause; subordinate idea — subordinate clause." Consider the following sentence:

> I was just about to ship your order when your request for additional supplies arrived.

Which idea is more important, the fact that *I was about to ship your order* or the fact that *your request for additional supplies arrived?* The arrival of the request for additional supplies is the more important idea; therefore, it should be expressed as the main clause. The sentence should read:

> Your request for additional supplies arrived just as I was about to ship your order.

 **KEY POINT**

When a sentence contains two ideas of equal importance, divide the sentence into two main clauses.

Coordination Versus Subordination

When a sentence contains two ideas of equal importance, divide the sentence into two main clauses. For example, consider the following:

> The work is difficult, but the rewards are great.

On the other hand, writing power is diminished when the writer fails to see that the thoughts belong not in two main clauses but in a main clause and a subordinate clause.

> Other committee members were equally qualified, but the research director chose Herbert as the chairperson.

This sentence places equal stress on what the writer considers to be two main ideas. The emphasis should properly be placed on the director's choosing Herbert even though others were qualified. For force, as well as for clarity, the sentence should be written:

> Although other committee members were equally qualified, the research director chose Herbert as the chairperson.

Interrupting Expressions

Some writers unwittingly destroy the forcefulness of proper subordination by writing the lesser idea as an interrupting expression. For instance, read this sentence:

> You are, considering the risks involved in such an investment, very fortunate.

The main thought, *you are very fortunate*, is interrupted by the lesser idea, *considering the risks involved*. This interference with the flow of the main thought is so distracting that the force of the statement is lost. Properly written, the sentence reads:

> Considering the risks involved in such an investment, you are very fortunate.

Correcting the *So* and *And So* Faults

Whenever you read a sentence that uses *so* or *and so* to introduce a clause, you can improve the sentence greatly by substituting a more meaningful conjunction. Notice how weak the connection is between the two clauses in the following sentence:

> Elena has been a dedicated literacy volunteer for ten years, so we gave her a special tribute at last night's fund-raising dinner.

The first clause gives the reason for the second clause. *Because* is a better choice for joining clauses that give causes and results. The following sentence is stronger, clearer, and more polished than the version above.

> We gave Elena a special tribute at last night's fund-raising dinner because she has been a dedicated literacy volunteer for ten years.

And so is not a two-word conjunction. They are two conjunctions used to form some vague connection between two clauses. Consider the following sentence:

> Mr. Velez is a talented artist, and so we recommend that you hire him.

The first clause is the reason for the second. The relationship is easier to detect in the following revision:

We recommend that you hire Mr. Velez because he is a talented artist.

ACTIVE VERSUS PASSIVE VOICE

Voice is that property of a transitive verb that shows whether the subject acts or is acted upon. Any verb phrase composed of a past participle with a "being" verb helper is in the passive voice: *will be shipped, has been sent, was done, is frozen.* In the active voice, the subject is the doer of an action; in the passive voice, the subject is acted upon.

The software company sent us a program upgrade. (Active voice.)

A program upgrade was sent to us by the software company. (Passive voice.)

The active voice expresses thoughts in a stronger, livelier way than does the passive voice. Compare these two sentences:

Your order will be shipped on Monday, July 8. (Passive voice.)

We will ship your order on Monday, July 8. (Active voice.)

Both sentences state the same information, but the active voice sentence is more direct. In the following pair of sentences, note that the sentence using the active voice makes a stronger selling point than does the weak, passive sentence.

Last year our telephone systems were sold to three out of every four new businesses in the city. (Passive voice.)

Last year, we sold our telephone systems to three out of every four new businesses in the city. (Active voice.)

The passive voice has its uses in business writing, usually to soften the impact of negative news. In the following sentences, note how the sentence using the passive voice is the more diplomatic of the two.

Because the college did not send us a copy of your transcript, we cannot consider your application to our program at this time. (Active voice.)

Your application to our program will be considered when a copy of your transcript is sent to us by the college. (Passive voice.)

BALANCING TECHNIQUES

Parallel structure is a must for similar parts of a sentence. A noun should be parallel with a noun (or a pronoun), an adjective with an adjective, and a phrase with a phrase. For example, look at this sentence.

The new staff assistant is eager, diligent, and has much knowledge.

Lack of parallel structure causes the sentence to lose momentum. The writer erroneously coordinated two adjectives and a clause. The revision below is strong to the end. The writer has coordinated the three adjectives, making the sentence grammatically parallel and effective.

The new staff assistant is eager, diligent, and knowledgeable.

In the paragraphs that follow, you will study techniques of balancing comparisons, modifiers, verbs, prepositions, conjunctions, and clauses. Studying these paragraphs will help you write with greater force and consistency.

Balancing Comparisons

Comparisons are balanced only if they are complete. They can be complete only if they include all the necessary words. The omission of one necessary word can throw a comparison out of balance.

Recent studies show that women spend more money on eating in restaurants than men.

As written, the sentence could mean that women spend more money on eating in restaurants than they spend on men. The comparison lacks balance, as well as sense, because an essential word is omitted. One word, properly placed, can make the meaning of the sentence clear.

Recent studies show that women spend more money on eating in restaurants than men spend.

Or the sentence could be rearranged.

Recent studies show that women spend more money than men do on eating in restaurants.

Here is another imbalanced comparison:

Ms. Ridgeway's role in the corporation is more than a financial analyst.

This sentence lacks sense because essential words have been omitted. The following revision improves the clarity.

Ms. Ridgeway's role in the corporation is more than that of a financial analyst.

An imbalanced comparison like the one that follows provides a chance for skillful revision.

Celia can program just as well, if not better, than George.

Disregarding the words set off by commas, the sentence reads as follows: "Celia can program just as well than George." Of course, no one would say "as well than." The first revision below is acceptable, but the second one is a much better sentence.

Celia can program just as well as, if not better than, George.
Celia can program just as well as George, if not better.

Balancing Modifiers

KEY POINT

Omitting one small word can change the sentence meaning.

Omission of single-word modifiers can destroy the balance of a sentence in several ways. Such an omission can produce, for example, this illogical message:

The company is hiring a receptionist and field engineer.

Failure to write "*a* field engineer" makes "a receptionist and field engineer" the same person. Dim, indeed, is the prospect of hiring a person who can serve in this dual capacity.

Modifiers should be repeated when necessary. What is wrong with this sentence?

The supervisor requested a secretary, mail clerk, and administrative assistant.

Because the modifier is not repeated with each member of the series, *a* is understood as the modifier for all three parts of the series. However, "a administrative assistant" would never be acceptable writing. For balance, the series should read, "a secretary, a mail clerk, and an administrative assistant."

Do you see why the next sentence is out of balance?

Mr. Brodsky speaks often of his parents, wife, and children.

The modifier *his* is the correct modifier for all three members of the series and is technically correct; however, a writer with a "feel" for language would repeat the modifier *his* to achieve a fullness and roundness of tone. The following revision sounds much better:

Mr. Brodsky speaks often of his parents, his wife, and his children.

Balancing Verbs

Structural balance demands that whenever the parts of verbs in compound constructions are not exactly alike in form, no verb part should be omitted. The following sentence breaks this rule:

Rhonda always has, and always will, do a good job.

Omitting the past participle *done* with the auxiliary *has* causes the meaning to be "Rhonda always has do and always will do a good job." The verbs in this compound construction are not exactly alike in form; therefore, no verb part should be omitted. The sentence should be revised.

Rhonda always has done and always will do a good job.

The following sentence shows the same kind of error:

Your revised report was received today and copies sent to the members of the advisory committee for their comments.

The omission of the auxiliary verb after *copies* structures the sentence like this: "Your revised report was received today, and copies was sent to the members of the advisory committee for their comments." The plural noun *copies* requires a plural verb; therefore, the sentence must read:

> Your revised report was received today, and copies were sent to the members of the advisory committee for their comments.

Balancing Prepositions

The omission of a preposition can also throw a sentence off balance. Some words must be followed by specific prepositions. When two prepositional constructions have the same object, you must use, in each construction, the preposition that is idiomatically correct. Failure to supply the correct preposition results in a mismatch.

> Senior documentation writers must demonstrate expertise and knowledge of software programming.

In this illustration *expertise* and *knowledge* form a compound, both parts of which are modified by the prepositional phrase *of software programming. Of* is the preposition used with both *expertise* and *knowledge*. However, it is incorrect to say "expertise of software programming." The correct preposition to use with *expertise* is *in*. To be balanced the sentence should read:

> Senior documentation writers must demonstrate expertise in and knowledge of software programming.

Balancing Conjunctions

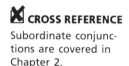

CROSS REFERENCE
Subordinate conjunctions are covered in Chapter 2.

In speech, subordinating conjunctions, particularly *that* and *when*, can often be omitted without causing any confusion. In writing, however, such omissions may destroy the balance of the thought units of a sentence and thus confuse the reader. Read the following example aloud:

> Marc often talks about the time he had neither money nor position.

If this were an oral communication, the speaker could make the meaning clear by pausing slightly after the word *time*. The reader, however, might see the thought unit as *Marc often talks about the time he had*, with the result that the words following *had* would not make sense. The reader would have to reread the sentence to get the meaning. In business communications, you want the reader to get the message the first time it is read. The sentence should be written as follows:

> Marc often talks about the time when he had neither money nor position.

The following sentence may also be misread:

> I searched and discovered the contract folder was missing.

The reader may see *I searched and discovered the contract folder* as one thought unit. The subordinating conjunction *that* adds clarity.

> I searched and discovered that the contract folder was missing.

In informal writing, subordinating conjunctions may be omitted if their omission will not confuse the reader.

We do have the stationery you requested.

Balancing Clauses

❏ **SUGGESTION**

Stress that effective business writing is a cumulative skill.

Another mark of writing distinction is to avoid incomplete (elliptical) clauses whenever failure to write the complete clause would confuse the reader. In the sentence "You are a faster typist than I," the meaning "than I am" is clear. But listen to this:

Did Mr. Norville pay the bill or his accountant?

This sentence could be interpreted as follows: "Did Mr. Norville pay the bill, or did he pay his accountant?" It could also be interpreted this way: "Did Mr. Norville pay his bill, or did his accountant pay the bill?" The following sentence clarifies the intended meaning:

Did Mr. Norville pay the bill, or did his accountant pay it?

SECTION

REVIEW

Practical Application

KEY
See page I-27.

A. The sentences below repeat like sounds too often. Rewrite the sentences to make them less distracting to the reader.

1. The lawyer summarized some of his comments.
2. The cashier's check, of course, cleared up the confusion.
3. Miss Pellettieri missed Miss Carr's call.
4. The board became bored by noon.
5. A pair of paralegals perused the law publications in the library.

KEY
See page I-27.

B. Rewrite each sentence by using positive words.

1. I failed to finish the report by noon, but I will finish it by 5 p.m.
2. Your qualifications and lack of experience do not match our hiring needs at this time.
3. Discuss any complaints about your cable TV service with our 24-hour customer representatives.
4. Installation instructions should not be difficult to understand.
5. Cashiers should not be dishonest.

KEY
See page I-27.

C. Rewrite these compound sentences, subordinating the less important ideas.

1. The copier was broken, and we could not distribute the report that was typed yesterday.
2. My train was late, and I missed my first appointment.

3. You did a superb job on the project, and you will get a bonus.
4. The sales figures were not accurate, and we underestimated our losses.
5. You are the most qualified applicant, and we are going to employ you.

KEY
See page I-27.

D. Rewrite each sentence, correcting the *so* and *and so* faults.

1. The contractor was concerned about the rising cost of raw materials, so he added 5 percent to his estimated price.
2. He injured his foot while operating the forklift, and so he has applied for Worker's Compensation benefits.
3. My flight to Atlanta was canceled, so I spent an extra night in Washington.
4. Dolores has been promoted, so we wonder who will be named to fill her position.
5. The shipment was damaged in transit, and so I refused to accept it.

KEY
See page I-28.

E. Rewrite each sentence in accordance with the directions.

1. Gary was praised by Mrs. Bonney when his design was accepted by the committee. (Change to the active voice.)
2. We cannot accept your credit application because of your short employment history. (Change to the passive voice.)
3. The new vacation policy was discussed by the department managers. (Change to the active voice.)
4. The new procedures were outlined by Susan Sokolovsky, and the details were filled in by Jim Conte. (Change to the active voice.)
5. The state legislature passed the proposed education budget. (Change to the passive voice.)

KEY
See page I-28.

F. Rewrite each sentence, correcting the balancing problems.

1. Her business acumen is equal, if not sharper than, theirs.
2. Did Jeanne call the client or her assistant? (Who called the client?)
3. I have, and will continue to try, to contact her.
4. The latest survey shows that women own more stock than men.
5. In his briefcase were a calculator, pen, file folder, and umbrella.
6. Sarah reminded me about the time she had neither money nor employment.
7. I have much respect and confidence in Ms. Nelson's decisions.
8. Armstrong Investment Specialists advertised for a mailroom assistant and account executive.
9. We need temporary personnel to keyboard documents, to proofread correspondence, and answering the phone.
10. Daria's communications skills are as good, if not better than, those of her coworkers.

REVIEW cont.

Editing Practice

Choosing the Right Word. On a separate sheet of paper, write the word that correctly completes each sentence.

1. The board of directors plans to (adapt, adopt) its first policy manual.
2. Most employees can (access, excess) the computer files by telephone.
3. Elisabeth gave me some helpful (advice, advise) when I was graduated from college.
4. Please order some letterhead (stationary, stationery).
5. Much planning (preceded, proceeded) the warehouse expansion.
6. Rafael (lead, led) the trainees in sales last quarter.
7. The report (cited, sighted) several studies that support our position.
8. Brendan Sullivan, (formally, formerly) a director, chairs the board.
9. The customers are completely satisfied with (their, there) purchases.
10. Demetria is more qualified (than, then) Gwen.

5.4 BUILDING EFFECTIVE PARAGRAPHS

OBJECTIVES: After completing Section 5.4, you should be able to:

1. Write paragraphs that have one main idea, sentences that have one main thought, and messages that have a definite purpose.
2. Write paragraphs that are no longer than six to eight lines.
3. Use transitional devices to make all communications flow more smoothly.
4. Use variety in sentence length and sentence structure to make communications more interesting.

Writing effective paragraphs requires writing good sentences and combining the sentences to get the message across to the reader. Even though sentences may be grammatically correct, they may not contribute positively to the paragraphs they compose.

In a paragraph, sentences should be positioned so that the series of thoughts expressed supports a single, more general, main idea. If sentence structure is faulty or if paragraph organization is poor, the whole communication will fail.

ONE MESSAGE, ONE IDEA, ONE THOUGHT

Each business communication should have one message. Each paragraph in the message should have one main idea. Each sentence in a paragraph should have one main thought, and that thought should support the main idea of the paragraph.

MESSAGE CONTROL

Business communications, such as letters and memorandums, should be limited to one main message. Two or more main messages within a communication can cause confusion or can cause one message to seem more or less important than another message.

If a message does not have a definite purpose, it should not be written. If a business writer sends numerous, insignificant communications, readers routinely receiving them will soon categorize all mail from that writer as unimportant. This categorization will cause an isolated important communication not to get the attention it deserves.

PARAGRAPH CONTROL

Achieving paragraph control requires the writer to focus on one main idea. All sentences in the paragraph should help support the main idea.

Before writing even the first sentence of a paragraph, the writer should have clearly in mind the main idea of the paragraph. The writer must know where the paragraph is going before attempting to guide the reader there. The writer who does not know what conclusion the paragraph is to have should stop writing and start thinking.

Paragraph Length

In general, a paragraph should have no more than six to eight lines. If the development of one thought requires more than six to eight lines, the writer should carry that thought over to another paragraph. Readers seem to need a visual break (paragraphs) but not a continuity break (interruption in message content).

Transitional Devices

The polished communication carries the reader along by interest in its message, by the rhythm and momentum of its words, and by the seamless transitions between paragraphs. Skillful use of transitional words and phrases can move the reader through the communication—from one idea to another—without a break in continuity that could detract from the message.

Writers can ensure this continuity by using appropriate transitional words or expressions. Here is a partial list of such transitional words and expressions.

accordingly	for this purpose	moreover
after all	further	nevertheless
again	furthermore	notwithstanding
also	hence	on the contrary
at the same time	however	on the other hand
besides	in addition	similarly
consequently	likewise	still
equally important	meanwhile	therefore

Let's look at the long paragraph below, which would benefit both from incorporating transitional expressions and from being broken into shorter segments.

We are sorry that you did not enjoy our Modern Magellan Nature Tour of the Amazon in Brazil last month. We feel that our literature gave you an accurate impression of what to expect. Our literature states, "Modern Magellan Nature Tours are not for the faint of heart. Our naturalist-guides take you to the most remote and primitive areas remaining on Earth. You'll see all the natural wonders that the area of your choice has to offer. You'll look down from the peaks, look up at the waterfalls, and see eye to eye with birds and beasts." This paragraph does not say explicitly that you are going to wake up and find a 30-foot anaconda in your tent. But everyone knows the anaconda is a snake native to the Amazon. You must admit that faint of heart is exactly what you were when you discovered the snake curled around your cot. Of the 42 members of your tour group, only one other complained. He felt the tour lacked excitement. We are now trying to arrange something more stimulating for him. I am afraid that we must refuse your request. We cannot arrange another tour for you or refund the money you paid for the first tour. We clearly stated this no-refund policy in our brochures.

There are various editing possibilities for this paragraph, but one revision might go like this:

We are sorry that you did not enjoy our Modern Magellan Nature Tour of the Amazon in Brazil last month. We do feel, however, that our literature gave you an accurate impression of what to expect. Our literature states, "Modern Magellan Nature Tours are not for the faint of heart. Our naturalist-guides take you to the most remote and primitive areas remaining on Earth. You'll see all the natural wonders that the area of your choice has to offer. You'll look down from the peaks, look up at the waterfalls, and see eye to eye with birds and beasts."

Although our literature does not say explicitly that you are going to wake up and find a 30-foot anaconda in your tent, the anaconda is an animal native to the Amazon. Of the 42 members of your tour group, one person said that he felt the tour lacked excitement. We are now trying to arrange something more stimulating for him.

I regret that we must refuse your request: We can neither arrange another tour for you nor refund the money you paid for the first tour. As we indicated in our brochures, the price of the tour cannot be refunded.

Paragraphing Decisions

Paragraphing decisions can create an attractive, uncluttered format that can make business communications easier to read and understand. Here are some simple paragraphing suggestions that can improve a communication's appearance and readability.

Obviously, content must determine paragraphing decisions. However, when it is practical, adjust paragraph length to fit the guidelines below. These are guidelines, *not* hard-and-fast rules.

1. Keep the first paragraph short, usually two to five lines.
2. Have middle paragraphs average four to eight lines, and make them longer than the first and last paragraphs.
3. Keep the last paragraph short, usually two to five lines.
4. Vary paragraph length.
5. Use several short paragraphs instead of one tremendously long paragraph to create an uncluttered appearance.
6. Combine several short paragraphs to avoid a choppy appearance.
7. Avoid a heavy appearance (all paragraphs too long).
8. Avoid a top-heavy appearance (beginning paragraphs too long); avoid a bottom-heavy appearance (ending paragraphs too long).
9. Use an odd number of paragraphs. Three paragraphs look better than two, and five paragraphs look better than four.
10. Even with guidelines for paragraph length, remember that each paragraph should have one main idea.

SENTENCE CONTROL

Long sentences tend to be harder to understand than short ones. Yet, short sentences can seem choppy and boring. What is the solution to the sentence-length problem? Variety.

Variety in Length

Most sentences should range in length from 10 to 20 words. This range is a guide. To provide variety, some sentences will have fewer than 10 words; others will have more than 20 words.

Extremely long sentences seem to bury the main thought. Beyond a certain length, sentences seem to grow weaker with each added word. This unnecessary length frustrates most readers. Overly long sentences may be

KEY POINT

Paragraphing decisions can be an important tool in improving appearance and readability.

SUGGESTION

Stress that these suggestions for making paragraphing decisions are *guidelines*, not rules.

KEY POINT

Most sentences should be from 10 to 20 words long.

REINFORCEMENT

Stress that extremely long sentences seem to bury the main thought.

grammatically correct, but often they are wordy. Look at the following example:

> Thank you for informing us in your letter of May 30 that you still have not received the illustrated *Complete Guide to Organic Gardening* that we shipped to you by parcel post on or about last May 1, but there's no need for you to worry, because we are going to start inquiries with the post office and perhaps file an insurance claim, meanwhile sending you another copy of this excellent handbook on the techniques of successful gardening without chemicals.

The reader has to swallow far too many words merely to learn that another copy of the desired book will be sent. The writer was correct, of course, to point out that the post office is to blame for the delay. The writer could have expressed that thought better, however, in a separate sentence. Study the following revision:

> Thank you for letting us know that your copy of the *Complete Guide to Organic Gardening* has not reached you. We are mailing you a new copy at once.

On the other hand, a succession of short sentences weakens writing, because the reader is jerked along from thought to thought.

> I received your proposal yesterday. The messenger delivered it about 10:30 a.m. Your approach to automating subway turnstiles is interesting. We have a manufacturing committee meeting next week. I will present your proposal at that time.

An expert would never write such a stop-and-go communication. Instead, the expert would smooth out the bumps like this:

> Your proposal arrived by messenger yesterday morning. In my opinion, your specifications for automating subway turnstiles are excellent. I intend to present your proposal to the other members of the manufacturing committee when we meet next week.

In some situations, the planned use of short sentences can be very effective. Short sentences are useful to bring out a series of important facts, to emphasize a point, and to break up a series of longer sentences.

> The Shutter Machine camera is made especially for quick-moving action photography. Its motorized film-advancer prepares you for your next shot a fraction of a second after you press the shutter. You just focus and shoot! Its easy-open back permits you to insert a new cartridge faster than you can in any other camera. You can reload in 15 seconds! Best of all, the Shutter Machine is equipped with a built-in computerized flash that works on a rechargeable battery. The camera provides flash when it's needed! See your dealer for complete details.

Variety in Structure

Communications that lack variety lack interest. One sure way to produce a dull communication is to use only simple sentences. Equally dull is a commu-

REINFORCEMENT
Stress to students that a succession of short sentences can jerk the reader from thought to thought.

REINFORCEMENT
Planned use of short sentences can be effective.

nication with all compound sentences or one with all complex sentences. Study the following paragraph:

> Your new Metro Motors truck costs more and offers more features. The diesel engine is durable, and you will enjoy its trouble-free operation. The engine uses less fuel while idling, and it uses less fuel on the road. Diesel trucks stand up to years of wear and have high resale value. You chose the right truck, and the years will prove it.

Too many compound sentences and too many *ands* make the above paragraph dull. See what an improvement structural variety makes in the following version.

> Your new Metro Motors truck costs more, but it offers more features too. Because the diesel engine is durable, you will enjoy years of trouble-free operation. You will use less fuel both when idling and when moving. Furthermore, because diesel trucks stand up to years of wear, they have high resale value. The years will prove that you chose the right truck.

SECTION REVIEW

Practical Application

KEY
See page I-28.

A. Edit the following paragraph, making sure that each sentence has one main thought and that each sentence supports the main idea of the paragraph. If the paragraph contains more than one main idea, break it into two or more paragraphs.

The operator's body should be erect; he or she should sit well back in the chair and lean forward slightly from the waist. Feet should be placed firmly on the floor. The body should be about a handspan from the front of the keyboard. Sitting too close to the machine can cause bottom-row errors, just as sitting too far away can cause top-row errors. Likewise, sitting too far to the left or right causes errors of the opposite hand. Keyboarding speed increases only through practice.

KEY
See page I-28.

B. The following paragraph uses short, monotonous, simple sentences. Rewrite the paragraph, varying the sentence structure. Some sentences will be combined.

There will be a reception on Wednesday, September 26. It will honor Graham C. Dobbs. He has been the corporation counsel for 30 years. He is retiring on September 30. The reception will begin at 5:30 p.m. in the corporate dining room. Everyone is invited to say goodbye.

KEY
See page I-29.

C. Paragraphs should have one main idea. Each paragraph below contains one sentence that does not relate to that main idea of the paragraph. The sentence, however, does relate to the main idea of another paragraph. Rewrite the letter, putting the sentences in the *right* paragraph.

Dear Mr. Morris:

Thank you for requesting information about Lakeview Family Campground. Baby-sitting services are available ($4 per hour) through the local teen club.

Free activities include morning aerobic workouts, afternoon water games, and nightly movies. Shuttle bus service to the village, panoramic boat tours, and water skiing — all reasonably priced — are offered daily.

You may select various optional services, which are available at very low rates. Cable television, water connections, and electrical hookups are the most popular selections. Each Saturday night, the camp recreation director arranges such free entertainment as puppet shows, folk singing, and short plays.

The enclosed brochure lists our rates. Our grounds, arranged to provide privacy, can comfortably accommodate tents, camping vehicles, and mobile homes. Please phone us soon to make sure that you get the reservations you want.

Sincerely yours,

D. Rewrite each incorrect sentence. Write *OK* for any sentence that has no error.

1. Where <u>was</u> the cases shipped?
2. Julia Daniels and <u>myself</u> will give the presentation on Monday afternoon.
3. Before being considered, each applicant must send <u>their</u> résumé.
4. The committee on civil rights <u>meet</u> tomorrow at 7 p.m.
5. The supervisor spoke sharply to Grace and <u>I</u>.
6. Bill Hovanic and <u>me</u> were invited to attend the ceremony at which the Technical Innovation award will be presented.

Editing Practice

One Word or Two? Some words can be written together or separately, depending on the context of the sentence. In the following paragraphs, words have been incorrectly written together or incorrectly written separately. Rewrite the paragraphs, correcting the errors.

Thankyou for telling us about your experience with our products. Eventhough we have strict quality control procedures, some defective products maybe getting by our inspectors.

Of course, comments like yours help us improve. We have all ready initiated actions that maybe helpful. Inasmuchas we respect your opinion, we plan to try your suggestions for awhile and monitor the results.

Your special order is already and will be shipped sometime later today. We sincerely appreciate your business.

KEY
1. were
2. I
3. his or her
4. meets
5. me
6. I

KEY
Errors are underscored.
Thank you
Even though
may be
already
may be
Inasmuch as
a while
all ready
some time

5.5 *REVISING FOR EFFECTIVE WRITING*

OBJECTIVES: **After completing Section 5.5, you should be able to:**

1. Explain the importance of revising your written communications.
2. Improve your writing by reviewing the organization of your work and checking its organization and tone against a checklist of key questions.
3. Improve your writing by reviewing the language and checking it against a checklist of key questions.

Imagine that you have just finished writing the last word of the last sentence of a report that you will turn in to a teacher or to a supervisor. Is your report really finished? Is it the best that it can be? The answer to both questions is the same: *no*. All good writers know that they need to revise, edit, and proofread their written work before submitting it. Some writers go through the three procedures—revising, editing, and proofreading—simultaneously, and some writers focus on one procedure at a time. This section deals primarily with *revising* your written work; editing and proofreading are discussed in Chapter 6.

WHAT IS REVISING?

KEY POINT

A time lapse between writing a document and reading it for revision purposes enhances the writer's ability to identify errors and passages in the text that can be improved or should be refined.

Revising involves "seeing again." In other words, when you revise, you have to stand back from your work and "see it again" with fresh eyes in order to improve the writing. To do that, you need to find a little extra time so that you can put your work aside for a few hours or even for a day. Then you should be able to read what you have written more objectively—as others may read it.

Reading your written work aloud is one technique you can use to help identify awkward sentences and other problems that might be overlooked in a silent reading. Another revision technique is to ask a friend, classmate, or coworker to read your work and tell you whether everything is clear and makes sense. Such comments are often valuable, but, as the author of the work, you still have the final say. Therefore, you must evaluate your reader's comments to decide whether or not the suggestions would improve your work.

CHECKING PURPOSE, AUDIENCE, AND TONE

Revising is not a hit-or-miss procedure. You need to ask specific questions when revising any piece of writing. To begin the revision process, you should always ask:

Is the Purpose of the Letter, Memo, or Report Clear?

If your purpose, for example, is to persuade your reader to take a certain action, does that message come across clearly and with no possibility of being misunderstood?

The second question you should ask concerns the suitability of the writing.

Is the Writing Tailored to the Audience?

Suppose you wrote a memo to new employees about company copying and mailing procedures. Did you consider that your audience — the new employees — know very little about the company, its policies, or other procedures? Did you use any terms, abbreviations, or references that might not be understood by the new employees?

Is the Tone Appropriate for the Audience?

As you consider your audience, you should also consider the tone of your work. *Tone* usually refers to the general effect a piece of writing creates. For example, your writing could be formal or informal, serious or humorous, or positive or negative. Although seldom stated directly, the tone is inferred by the reader through the choice of words and other elements of style. For example, if you were writing a memorandum to a supervisor, you would avoid a negative, critical tone — even if you were reporting on some aspects of company procedure that needed improvement. To keep the attention of your audience, you should establish a positive, upbeat tone that offers constructive suggestions for dealing with problem areas.

REVIEWING THE ORGANIZATIONAL STRUCTURE

After answering the basic questions about clarity of purpose, audience suitability, and appropriateness of tone, you should examine the organizational structure of your writing. Is it logical? To be logical, you should have a strong introduction that states the main idea or purpose. The middle paragraphs should sufficiently support or explain your stated purpose, and the conclusion should summarize your ideas or arguments. One way to make sure that your writing has a logical organization is to prepare an outline before you begin to write. Then make sure that you follow that outline carefully as you write.

Sticking to the Point

As you review the structure of your writing, pay particular attention to any sentences that seem to stray from the main idea of each paragraph. Such sentences usually contain unnecessary details or information that should be removed from your work because they detract from the message and create confusion. For example, if you were making the point in a report that good math skills are necessary for all entry-level jobs in your company, you would be wandering off the subject if you described your own math training.

Including Transitions

REINFORCEMENT

Transitions help the reader move smoothly from one idea, sentence, or paragraph to another.

If your paragraphs are complete and if you have presented them in a clear, logical order, you should then make sure that you have included effective bridges or transitions between ideas, sentences, and paragraphs. Below is a list of some common transitions you could use to show how things, ideas, or events are related in time (chronological order), in location (spatial order), in significance (order of importance), and in relationship to one another (developmental order). Some sentences illustrating the use of transition words follow.

TRANSITIONS			
Chronological	*Spatial*	*Importance*	*Developmental*
after	above	even more	also
as soon as	ahead	finally	besides
first	behind	first	despite
at last	below	more important	for example
second	higher	most important	however
later	inside	one reason	therefore
meanwhile	outside	to begin with	while

Chronological: *After* he receives the photographs, Peter will put the report together.

Spatial: *Behind* the cabinet, covered with dust, was the long-lost letter.

Importance: *More important*, I believe this meeting will be mutually beneficial.

Developmental: *Therefore*, in recognition of Maureen Nagy's outstanding contribution to the company, we are naming her "Employee of the Year."

Choosing a Title

Keep in mind that a title of a report or any document is your reader's first impression of your writing. It should be short, clear, and informative; it also needs to catch the reader's favorable attention. Remember that the tone of the title should match the tone of your report.

A good idea is to develop a revision checklist to use when revising anything that you write. You might start with a checklist such as the following.

Revision Checklist 1: Organization and Tone

1. Is the purpose clear?
2. Is the work suited to the audience?
3. Is the tone appropriate?
4. Does it follow the outline prepared in advance?
5. Is the organization of the work logical?
6. Does the material have a strong introduction, middle, and conclusion?
7. Do any sentences wander away from the main idea of each paragraph?
8. Are appropriate transitions used to connect one idea to another or one paragraph to another?
9. Is the title of the report clear and informative?

REVIEWING THE LANGUAGE

Once you are confident that the paragraphs and sentences in your writing are effective, take one more close look at the words that comprise those paragraphs and sentences. First, make sure that each word is used correctly. If you are unsure of the meaning of a word, either look it up to make sure the word is appropriate or find an alternative word that expresses your exact meaning.

Now determine whether the words you have chosen will have the effect you intend them to have. The purpose of all writing, of course, is to transfer your thoughts and ideas — as completely and as forcefully as possible — to someone else. Some words accomplish that purpose more easily than others.

Using Colorful, Vivid, Specific Words

To understand the power of words, imagine that your reader's mind is a television set. Then determine what your reader will see on that make-believe television screen after reading your message. Will the images be vivid and clear or will they be hazy and dull? For example, what do you think readers will picture in their minds when reading the following two statements.

Statement 1

Our new building is well located and the apartments are comfortable.

Statement 2

Our new high-rise building is located on a quiet, tree-lined street near the center of town; the apartments are spacious and equipped with all the latest modern conveniences.

If several people read the first statement, each reader probably would imagine a different scene. One might visualize small, cozy apartments in a small building. However, another reader could just as easily see an entirely different type of apartment building on a very different street because the words used in the first statement are general and vague.

When you revise, therefore, always examine your writing to make certain that the nouns, adjectives, and verbs are precise and sufficiently descriptive to convey your message. Use a thesaurus or a dictionary to find replacements for dull or overused words.

Avoiding Unnecessary Repetition

While reviewing your choice of words, check to see whether you have used the same words or expressions over and over. Readers sometimes become annoyed at such unnecessary repetition. For example, if you find that you have repeatedly used the word *told* throughout a report, consult a thesaurus for alternative words, such as *related, announced, declared, asserted, directed,* or *replied.* You will avoid repetition and at the same time describe more clearly the various ways people speak or make statements.

Creating Sentence Variety

Most people write exactly as they speak, and most people begin sentences with the subject. The monotony of this sentence structure is much more noticeable in a letter or report than it is in conversation. Therefore, if you tend to begin sentences the same way, add some variety. For example, occasionally begin a sentence with an adverb or prepositional phrase.

Subject

Employees often have to wait in line for 15 minutes in the cafeteria.

Adverb

Often employees have to wait in line for 15 minutes in the cafeteria.

Prepositional Phrase

In the cafeteria, employees often have to wait in line for 15 minutes.

Using the Active Voice

Another important step in the revision process calls for checking verbs to see if they are in the active voice wherever possible. In active voice the subject is the doer of the action; in passive voice, the subject is the receiver of the action. Your writing will be much livelier if you use the active voice. *(See Section 5.3 for more information about active and passive voice.)*

Active Voice

The president of the company read the long-awaited announcement.

Passive Voice

The long-awaited announcement was read by the president of the company.

Revision Checklist 2: Language

1. Do I know the meaning of the words I have used?
2. Can I replace any dull or overused nouns, adjectives, and verbs with more colorful, specific words?
3. Have I unnecessarily repeated any words or expressions?
4. Have I consulted a thesaurus or dictionary to make my writing clearer and more forceful?
5. Did I vary my sentence beginnings?
6. Have I used the active voice whenever possible?

Once you have revised your text by carefully reviewing its organization, tone, and language, you can move on to the other steps in writing effectively. These steps are proofreading your text for errors and editing the text to make sure it is clear, consistent, and correct. Proofreading and editing are discussed in Chapter 6.

SECTION REVIEW

Practical Application

KEY
See page I-29.

A. Define the word *revising*.
B. Why is revising a necessary step to take when you have finished writing a letter or a report?
C. What are transitions? How should they be used?
D. How will using the active voice make your writing better? Give an example.
E. How can a thesaurus be helpful when you are revising?

Editing Practice

KEY

Students' answers will vary. Suggested synonyms are given.

1. mishap; stumbled, tripped
2. sluggish; foreman, supervisor
3. noticed, observed; delicate, exquisite

Use a Thesaurus! Use a thesaurus to edit the following paragraphs. For each underlined word or combination of words in the following sentences, find a more colorful synonym in a thesaurus. Then rewrite the sentences on a separate sheet, replacing each underlined word with a synonym. Finally, read each sentence to yourself with the new words to see how much clearer each image is.

1. Jack's <u>accident</u> occurred when he <u>fell</u> on the step.
2. The <u>slow</u> elevator drives my <u>boss</u> crazy.
3. Everyone <u>saw</u> the <u>pretty</u> box on her desk, but no one knew what was inside it.

REVIEW cont.

4. devoured
5. narrated, recounted;
hilarious

KEY
Errors are underscored.
his or her
environment
specially
waste—
recycle

KEY
See page I-29.

4. I quickly ate the food on my plate.
5. She told us a funny incident that happened the day before.

Proofreading on Screen.   You have been asked to write a memorandum on recycling for the company's Environmental Committee. Proofread the copy on the computer screen and correct any errors before you make a printed copy.

We would like to urge every member of this company to do their part for the envirnment. In each department, you will find specialy designated containers in which to place cans and bottles. You will also find boxes in which to place paper for recycling. Please make an effort to avoid waste, — especially of paper — and to recyle.

Critical Thinking Skills

Evaluating.   Read the following paragraph and list ways in which it can be revised. Then revise the paragraph, making as many improvements as possible.

Employees are spending too much time in the coffee room. They are spending their time drinking coffee, rather than doing their work. The coffee room was first accomplished five years ago. It might be stopped by the senior officers if people don't stop misusing the privilege of using it. I would be very sorry to see that happen.

Applying.   Find a letter or report that you have written recently, and use the two revision checklists to revise it.

6

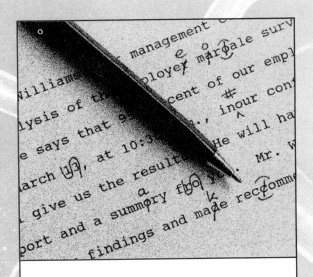

DEVELOPING PROOFREADING AND EDITING SKILLS

6.1 *THE PROOFREADING PROCESS*

OBJECTIVES: After completing Section 6.1, you should be able to:

1. Explain why teamwork is important in the proofreading process.
2. Explain why proofreading your own work is essential.
3. Follow the five steps in proofreading.
4. Use revision symbols when proofreading.

Proofreading is the process of examining a document to find errors and omissions that should be corrected. Sometimes, proofreading is a verification process, such as checking a letter typed from a handwritten rough draft. There may be no document for comparison, however, when proofreading your own work. In either case, you should look carefully for errors in capitalization, content, format, grammar, word usage, number usage, punctuation, spelling, typing, and word division.

To be a good proofreader—to be able to identify errors—you must be familiar with each type of error mentioned above. If you are unsure of a spelling, a usage, and so on, rely on reference sources. You may, for example, see the word *accomodation* and wonder whether it is spelled correctly. After checking a dictionary, you change the word to *accommodation*.

The proofreading process should begin in the early stages of document preparation and continue through each step, including the final copy. In other words, before keyboarding from shorthand notes, a handwritten draft, or a typewritten or printed draft, check the document for errors. When using a word processor, proofread the document on the screen. Also, proofread the final copy to make sure that it is typed or printed correctly.

RESPONSIBILITY FOR QUALITY

Business writers are responsible for the quality of their communications no matter who prepares the final document. Errorless communications are important because of the impressions they make on the receiver. Frequently a letter may be the first or only contact someone has with your organization. A carefully prepared letter with no errors projects a quality image and helps build goodwill, while a letter with errors projects a careless or disinterested image on the part of the writer. Likewise, a memo written to a colleague or supervisor can convey a message of competence or carelessness.

Office personnel sometimes overlook the proofreading process, because each person expects someone else to do it. The keyboarder may think that the document originator will proofread each communication. The document originator may think that the keyboarder will find and correct all errors before submitting the document for signing. Ideally, proofreading is a team effort. Both the keyboarder and the document originator should carefully proofread each document. The final responsibility, however, definitely rests with the person signing the document.

PROOFREADING FOR YOURSELF AND FOR OTHERS

Proofreading is an essential step in the writing process, whether you are proofreading your own work, a coworker's writing, or your employer's writing. As a student or as an office professional, you must get into the proofreading habit. Grades will suffer if errors are found on a research paper, and a potential salary increase or promotion may be lost if errors are found in a sales report you prepared. Habitual proofreading problems may even result in a loss of one's position.

In a business situation, you may have responsibilities for writing memos or reports. You would, therefore, need to proofread your own work. Often, a coworker, realizing the importance of an error-free document, will ask you to check his or her work for errors. If you keyboard business letters, reports, or other correspondence, you must fulfill this essential step in document preparation.

Proofreading your own writing is usually considered more difficult than proofreading the work of others for two reasons. First, you, as the writer, may tend to be overconfident, believing that you corrected all errors during the keyboarding process. Second, you may be overly familiar with the document, causing you to "read" what you intended to keyboard, not what you actually keyboarded. Have you ever had this experience? A friend reads something you wrote and almost immediately finds an error that escaped your detection. This friend provided the benefit of a fresh set of eyes and so was neither overconfident of keyboarding accuracy nor overly familiar with the document.

Technology offers some assistance in proofreading for spelling and keyboarding errors. Most word processing programs have spell-checkers that will locate words they do not recognize from their "built-in" dictionaries. However, these programs will not locate a misused word if it is correctly spelled. For example, the error in the following sentence would be undetected if you relied on a spell-checker alone: "The letter was *form* (should be *from*) Frank." Some spell-checkers will find repetition errors like this one: "He gave me *the the* calendar."

Software programs have also been developed that will check for usage errors. These programs locate a possible error, but you as the writer must make the final decision. You must ask yourself these questions: Is what I typed correct? Should I make a change? What is the correct usage?

Proofreading on the computer screen is similar in many ways to proofreading a printed page. However, you must condition your eyes and mind to this different medium. Three particular techniques have been useful in finding errors on screen:

1. Scroll through the document, proofreading line by line as each line comes up on the bottom of the screen.
2. Move the cursor through the document checking each word as the cursor encounters it.
3. Use a piece of paper to guide your eye as you proofread line by line down the screen.

Try each method and select the one that works best for you.

Some writers make the mistake of waiting until they print the document before proofreading it. You should do your first proofreading on the screen, make the necessary changes and corrections, then print a copy. You should also proofread the printed copy to make sure that your changes were entered correctly. Experience will help you build confidence and skill in proofreading on the computer screen.

Whether proofreading your own correspondence or that of other business writers — on the screen or on a printed copy — you must detect and correct errors. Accurate documents are a goal of a good business communicator.

IMPORTANCE OF PROOFREADING

REINFORCEMENT

Have students collect communications with errors. Highlight the errors with a yellow marker and post on a bulletin board.

REINFORCEMENT

Discuss the reasons for verifying that changes and corrections have been made. Answers include these: Changes or corrections indicated on a draft can be overlooked. New errors may be introduced in the proofreading process. Adding or deleting text may change paragraphing or paging, causing awkward placement.

Uncorrected errors create a bad impression. They also can cost your company money and cause various types of problems. Consider these two examples.

Suppose, in a handwritten draft, you quoted a price of $32,453 for a new desktop publishing system. When the final copy was keyboarded and mailed to the customer, the price was incorrectly listed as $23,453 by transposing two figures. If not detected, this simple transposition of numbers could cost your company $9,000. Correcting the error after the customer receives the incorrect quotation would cause ill will and, possibly, the loss of business.

Suppose, on a travel itinerary, the airplane departure time was erroneously listed as 10:50 instead of the correct time of 10:05. This simple transposition could cause the recipient to miss the plane.

In both examples, efficient proofreading would have resulted in the error being caught. For this reason, executives encourage the detection and correction of errors to prevent problems. Therefore, it is essential that you approach proofreading in a systematic way.

STEPS IN PROOFREADING

There are five major steps one must follow for efficient proofreading:

1. Quickly scan for such obvious problems as format errors. Is the date included in letters and memos? Do all headings in a report follow the same format?

CAPITALIZATION	Capitalize a letter	texas	Texas
	Lowercase a letter	This	this
	Capitalize all letters	Cobol	COBOL
	Lowercase a word	PROGRAM	program
	Use initial capital only	PROGRAM	Program

CHANGES AND TRANSPOSITIONS	Change a word	price is only $10.98 $12.99	price is only $12.99
	Change a letter	deductable	deductible
	Stet (do not make the change)	price is only $10.98 are	price is only $10.98
	Spell out	2 cars on Washburn Rd.	two cars on Washburn Road
	Move as shown	on May 1 write him	write him on May 1
	Transpose letters or words	hte time the of meeting	the time of the meeting

DELETIONS	Delete a letter and close up	strooke or strooke	stroke or stroke
	Delete a word	wrote two two checks	wrote two checks
	Delete punctuation	report was up to date	report was up to date
	Delete one space*	good # day	good day
	Delete space	see ing	seeing

INSERTIONS	Insert a word or letter	in the office buildhg	in the office building
	Insert a comma	may leave early. . . .	may leave early, . . .
	Insert a period	Dr Maria Rodriguez	Dr. Maria Rodriguez
	Insert an apostrophe	all the boys hats	all the boys' hats
	Insert quotation marks	Move on, she said.	"Move on," she said.
	Insert hyphens	up to date report	up-to-date report
	Insert a dash	They were surprised --even shocked!	They were surprised —even shocked!
	Insert parentheses	pay fifty dollars $50)	pay fifty dollars ($50)
	Insert one space	may leave	may leave
	Insert two spaces*	1. The new machine 2 #	1. The new machine

*Use marginal notes for clarification.

FORMAT SYMBOLS: BOLDFACE AND UNDERSCORE	Print boldface	Bulletin
	Remove boldface	Bulletin
	Underscore	Title
	Remove underscore	Title

FORMAT SYMBOLS: CENTERING	Center line horizontally	] TITLE [

FORMAT SYMBOLS: PAGE AND PARAGRAPH	Begin a new page	. . . order was delivered today by *pg* common carrier. We have all the . . .
	Begin a new paragraph	. . . order was delivered today by common carrier. We have all the . . .
	Do not begin new paragraph (run in)	. . . order was delivered today by common carrier. *No ¶* We have all the materials . . .
	Indent five spaces	*5* We have the raw materials in our warehouse. Production will . . .

FORMAT SYMBOLS: SPACING	Single-space	ss XXXXXXXXXX XXXXXXXXXX
	Double-space	ds XXXXXXXXXX XXXXXXXXXX
	Triple-space	ts XXXXXXXXXX XXXXXXXXXX

2. Read carefully for correct content, making sure no words were omitted or repeated.
3. Read for correct capitalization, grammar, word usage, number usage, punctuation, spelling, keyboarding, and word division.
4. As a separate step, check all numbers and technical terms for accuracy.
5. After the proofreading process has been completed and the marked changes or corrections have been made, verify that these changes or corrections were correctly made and that no new errors were introduced.

PROOFREADERS' MARKS

Proofreaders' marks are a quick, simple way to indicate changes or corrections on handwritten, typed, or printed documents. Study the proofreaders' marks on pages 291–292. You will need to know how to use these when proofreading business communications.

REVIEW

Practical Application

A. On a sheet of paper, write *Yes* if the names are the same in both columns. Write *No* if they are different.

1. John R. Kimble	John R. Kimble
2. Nicole Negbenebor	Nicole Negbenebor
3. Angela R. Smith	Angela P. Smith
4. Dr. Richard Lee	Mr. Richard Lee
5. Janet Bethea Ramsey	Janet Betha Ramsey
6. David Scott, Jr.	David Scott, Jr.
7. Rebecca C. Martinas	Rebecca C. Martines
8. C. Jon Christopher	C. John Christopher
9. Robin Renee Champion	Robin Renee Champion
10. Mrs. Roberta Delgado	Mrs. Robert Delgado

B. On a sheet of paper, write *Yes* if the items are the same in both columns. Write *No* if they are different.

1. $212,845,321.32	212,845,321.32
2. 905-682-1482	905-682-1482
3. June 27, 1995	June 27, 1995
4. 1991–1995	1981–1995
5. 125,673,281	125,683,281
6. 489 pages	498 pages
7. 28284-4916	28284-4916
8. 10:38 a.m.	10:38 p.m.
9. 214-887-6875	214-887-6785
10. 1,875 pounds	1,875 pounds

C. On a sheet of paper, write each sentence, making the indicated changes.

1. Dr. Sam Martinez autographed copies of his latest book, <u>Healthy Eating for Busy Executives</u>.
2. His letter was mis‿interpreted by the ~~the~~ newspaper editor.
3. Phils Sandwich Shop opens daily at 10:30 a.m.
4. The camera, were shipped February 10 and the film.

REVIEW cont.

5. Mrs. Anderson, I appreciate your willingness to participate (our/in) charitable interests.
6. The shipment will arrive in ③ days.
7. Many business expenses are tax deductible.
8. Tom and Mariel are looking forward to Their Summer Vacation.
9. Alexandra went to Mexico, and to south America.
10. We need a new Zip CODE Directory.

Editing Practice

Choosing the Right Word. On a sheet of paper, make a list of words used incorrectly in the following paragraph. Beside each incorrect word, write the correct word that should have been used.

In the passed ate weaks, my assistance have placed twenty adds in you're newspaper. As you may no, their was some confusion about the invoice. Your paper accidentally build us twice for the same advertisements.

Will you please make an appropriate adjustment to our account. Advertising with you has been affective in increasing our sales, and we plan to buy more advertising space soon.

KEY

Errors are underscored.
1. passed; past
2. ate; eight
3. weaks; weeks
4. assistance; assis-
   tants
5. adds; ads
6. you're; your
7. no; know
8. their; there
9. build; billed
10. affective; effective

6.2 THE EDITING PROCESS

OBJECTIVES: After completing Section 6.2, you should be able to:

1. Define editing and understand how it differs from proofreading.
2. Explain why experienced writers complete more than one draft of every business communication.
3. Apply the six Cs of editing.

☐**SUGGESTION**

Complete the related Practical Application as each topic is discussed.

Editing is the process of revising a document to improve it. Obviously, proofreading (see Section 6.1) is a part of editing. In fact, it is hard to tell exactly where proofreading stops and editing begins.

As you begin writing a document, assume that your initial writing is a draft. The term *draft* is used because very few people can write a truly effective communication on the first attempt. Often, there may be more than one draft, particularly in complex explanations or information. Experienced writers realize the value of revising their work as many times as necessary to make each document as nearly perfect as possible.

On the first draft, you should be concerned only with content and an orderly presentation of information. Then you should begin the editing process that leads to perfection. Editing not only helps improve the quality of your document but also helps improve your skill as a writer.

Editing skill is important for anyone involved with written communication. The purpose of editing is to make the document as effective as possible. Editing includes detecting and correcting errors (proofreading) and improving a document by seeking an affirmative response to these questions:

1. Is it clear?
2. Is it complete?
3. Is it concise?
4. Is it consistent?
5. Is it correct?
6. Is it courteous?

THE SIX Cs OF EDITING

Is It Clear?

□ **SUGGESTION**

Complete Practical Application A, which relates to clarity.

Business communications are written to get action—not to entertain or increase the vocabulary of the reader. Good business writers use simple words and proper English and make every effort to avoid trite language.

Trite language involves using words and phrases that have lost their effectiveness because of overuse. Using a participial closing in a letter is a good example: "Expecting to hear from you soon, I remain . . ." Another example involves using "business" language: "Enclosed herewith, please find my check." "My check is enclosed" is much easier to understand.

Is It Complete?

□ **SUGGESTION**

Complete Practical Application B, which relates to completeness.

A complete message includes all necessary information. Because the writer is so familiar with the message, omitted details are not always obvious to the writer. These missing details may, however, be obvious to the reader. Imagine receiving a party invitation that gives only the hour, place, and kind of party. The message is incomplete without the date. A lot of extra communication may then be required to clarify the situation.

Is It Concise?

□ **SUGGESTION**

Complete Practical Application C, which relates to conciseness.

Unnecessary words, phrases, clauses, sentences, and paragraphs are a barrier to effective communication. Needless repetition of words decreases the effectiveness of your message because the reader must read a lot of words to get a little information.

Is It Consistent?

□ **SUGGESTION**

Complete Practical Application D, which relates to consistency.

Business messages should be consistent in fact, treatment, and sequence. A message is consistent in fact if it does not contradict itself, an established fact, or a source document.

Treating similar items the same way results in consistency in treatment. For example, when listing both men's and women's names, use courtesy titles for all or none of the names. Failing to indent one paragraph in a letter when all others are indented is an error in treatment.

Consistency of sequence (alphabetical, chronological, or numerical) improves content flow. Using alphabetical sequence often avoids conveying unintentional bias when mentioning two or more people.

Some businesses have their own set of rules for treatment; others follow a published guide, such as *The Gregg Reference Manual.*

Is It Correct?

❏ **SUGGESTION**
Complete Practical Application E, which relates to correctness.

Accuracy in content, typing, and mechanics (capitalization, grammar, spelling, punctuation, and so on) makes the message more effective. Proofreading to eliminate these kinds of errors is definitely a part of the editing process.

Is It Courteous?

❏ **SUGGESTION**
Complete Practical Application F, which relates to courtesy.

Courtesy in a business communication means that it is eye-pleasing, reader-centered, and positive. Here are some suggestions for achieving courtesy:

- Create an eye-pleasing communication by using several short paragraphs instead of one long one. Using a table format or a list (when appropriate) instead of the traditional paragraph format often looks better and makes reading easier.
- Make a communication more reader-centered by using a "you" tone instead of an "I" tone. Another method involves personalizing by inserting the reader's name in the body of the message.
- Achieve a positive communication by avoiding such negative words as *can't, don't, error, mistake, no,* and *not.* Use tactful language that preserves reader integrity. Also, use active rather than passive voice when making positive statements.

WORD PROCESSING AND EDITING

❏ **SUGGESTION**
Encourage students to double-space drafts. Additional space for proofreaders' marks makes proofreading, editing, and correcting the document easier.

Advances in office technology have led to a renewed emphasis on editing. Even though word processors and computers with word processing software have made editing easier, this automated equipment is only as good as the person operating it.

Automated equipment has simplified editing through machine functions that allow text manipulation. Small or large amounts of text can be inserted, deleted, or moved from one point in the document to another.

As you are editing your own work on the computer screen, you can move words, paragraphs, or pages without having to rekeyboard the entire document. Suppose, for example, you are reading a letter to a client you have just drafted. You notice that the fourth paragraph should logically be placed before the third. Using simple word processing commands, you can quickly move the paragraphs. Being able to move pages or other large segments of text is especially useful in writing business reports.

The proofreaders' marks for editing shown below will be helpful if you are revising a hard copy that you have keyboarded or that has been keyboarded for you. Once the changes have been indicated on the hard copy, it is a simple process to make the changes on the computer screen. Be sure to proofread the document after it has been printed to make sure all the indicated changes have been made correctly.

The material to be manipulated can be identified on the printed copy by marking the beginning and the end of the segment with a vertical line and labeling the block with a letter of the alphabet. Use marginal notes as needed for clarification as shown in the chart of proofreaders' marks.

PROOFREADERS' MARKS FOR EDITING

Revision	Edited Draft
Identify block	/A/and the catalog/will be mailed.
Insert identified block	Your order [A]will be mailed.
Delete identified block	Your order /A/and the catalog/will mailed
Move identified block*	Your order /A/and the catalog/will be *move* [A] shipped. The invoice [A]will be mailed.
Query identified block*	Ed will retire at the age of/96/ B ?[B] (Are the numbers transposed? Verify age.)
Query identified block*	Make my reservation for/June 31/ C ?[C] (June has only 30 days. Verify date.)
Query conflicting blocks*	Call me Monday/morning at/8 [D] ?[E] /E/p.m./ (Morning or p.m.? Verify time.)

*Use marginal notes for clarification.

These symbols are used to indicate text manipulation functions and to query the accuracy of the copy.

Another use of block identification is to mark a hard-copy text segment that should be checked for accuracy before the final document is printed or typed. Identified blocks are marked with a query (question mark) in the margin.

Machine functions also make it necessary for identical changes (usually called *global changes*) to be entered only once. Suppose, for example, the name *Sandra DeJong* was used five times in a document. After keyboarding, you became aware of the correct spelling, *Sandra De Jonge*. Using the global function, you would have to make the correction only once; the other four changes would be made automatically. A marginal note can indicate a global change.

KEY
See page I-31.

REVIEW

SECTION

Practical Application

A. Are the following sentences clear? Rewrite them, changing difficult words to easier words, correcting English, and eliminating trite wording.

1. Your company can <u>utilize</u> a facsimile machine.
2. <u>Looking forward to hearing from you soon, I remain</u> . . .
3. <u>In compliance with</u> your request, enclosed <u>herewith</u>, <u>please find</u> a copy of your sales slip.
4. Matthew was <u>kind of</u> tired after his business trip.
5. We should be able to <u>ascertain</u> the information by Monday.

KEY
1. Time omitted
2. City omitted
3. Quantity omitted

B. Are the following sentences complete? What detail is missing from each one?

1. All assistant managers will meet Thursday, October 21, in the manager's office.
2. Mail the refund to Mr. Antonio Marta, 621 West Magnolia Avenue, Tennessee 37916-4483.
3. Please ship the white copier paper ($3.48 per ream) immediately to Mr. Fred Dingler, 1442 South State Street, Charlotte, NC 28244.

KEY
Underscored words should be deleted.

C. Is each sentence concise? Rewrite each sentence, omitting all unnecessary words.

1. Please respond by <u>the date of</u> December 1.
2. Enclosed <u>herewith</u> is a copy of your magazine advertisement.
3. You can make the cord long enough by joining <u>together</u> the two shorter cords.
4. Our new manager seems to be <u>of</u> about forty years of age.
5. Connect <u>up</u> the printer to the computer.

KEY
See page I-31.

D. Rewrite each sentence, correcting any inconsistencies.

1. Please order these two books for our company resource center: COMPUTERS MADE EASY and Common Computer Uses.

2. We will monitor our air conditioning costs closely during June, August, and July.
3. Three invoices have not been paid: 2216, 2214, and 2215.
4. Dixon, White, and Clary asked for the same vacation week.
5. Mr. Randy Matz, Dr. Wilma Johnson, and Steven Horowitz have applied for the transfer.

E. Rewrite each sentence, correcting any errors.

1. I offered the position to Julie Schlagenhauf last <u>monday</u>.
2. Can you have the <u>recomendation</u> ready by July 10?
3. Mr. Ruiz gave me the <u>the</u> Davis file yesterday afternoon.
4. Lisa will be in <u>Tampa Florida</u> for two weeks.
5. Donna Davenport, one of our directors, <u>are</u> going to represent us at the conference.

F. Rewrite these sentences, making them more positive and achieving the "you" tone.

1. Unfortunately, we can't ship your order because you carelessly omitted your shirt size. Write to give us your size.
2. Please do not hesitate to call our toll-free number if you can't read and understand the instructions on your microwave oven.

   Personalize the message by adding the name *Ben* within these sentences. Remember to use a comma before and after the name.

3. Thank you for the work you did on the Kansas project.
4. I can always depend on you to find a solution to any public relations problem our company may have.

   Change the sentence to active voice.

5. The award was presented to John Torres by our manager.

Editing Practice

Editing Corrections.   Rewrite the following paragraph, making the indicated changes. Assume that Monday is July 1.

   Nancy Threlkeld will assume the position of Director of Employee Activities on Monday, July 1. In this position, she will be in charge of and responsible for athletic teams, organizations, trips, and all other social events sponsored by our company. On Wednesday, July 3, she will attend a conference to learn about activities offered by other companies. She will have a meeting Tuesday, July 3, at 2:30 p.m., in the Recreation Hall, to get your suggestions for August and September activities.

KEY

Errors are underscored.
1. Monday
2. recommendation
3. omit second *the*
4. Tampa, Florida,
5. is

KEY

See page I-31.

KEY

See page I-31.

7

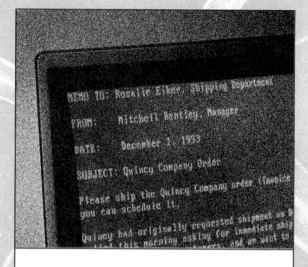

MEMO TO: Rosalie Eiker, Shipping Department

FROM: Mitchell Bentley, Manager

DATE: December 1, 1993

SUBJECT: Quincy Company Order

Please ship the Quincy Company order (Invoice
you can schedule it.

Quincy had originally requested shipment on
led this morning asking for immediate ship

WRITING

MEMORANDUMS

7.1 Memo Purposes and Writing Techniques

7.2 Memo Types and Memo Style

7.1 MEMO PURPOSES AND WRITING TECHNIQUES

OBJECTIVES: After completing Section 7.1, you should be able to:

1. Name four advantages of memos.
2. List six uses of memos.
3. Describe how the tone of a memo is tailored to the person to whom the memo is addressed.
4. Identify the organizational elements of a memo.
5. Describe the use of special formatting and mechanical techniques in memos.

Memorandums represent more than 50 percent of written communications in businesses today. Memos, as they are often called, are written to someone within your own organization. Letters, on the other hand, are written to people outside your organization. Memos can be used within a department, between departments, and between company branches at different geographic locations.

IMPORTANCE OF MEMOS

☐ **SUGGESTION**

Stress that memos are important, even though they do not go outside the organization.

Memos can be as important and as complex as the communications sent outside your organization. Two employees in different departments of the same company, for example, must agree on a position before either of them can write to one of the company's customers or suppliers. Unless they reach agreement themselves before communicating with an outsider, the employees may unknowingly make conflicting statements. Such poor internal communication is certain to confuse the outsider and to embarrass the employees.

When the matter is important or complicated, employees within an organization will want to put it in writing. This is why the memo is an essential part of business life.

ADVANTAGES OF MEMOS

 KEY POINT

Memos are quick, inexpensive, convenient, and provide a written record.

Memorandums have become popular because many people in business recognize the need for effective internal communication. Organizations are larger and more diversified. Branches or divisions of a company are often located in different states or even in different countries. Many people's efforts must be coordinated. Memos seem the logical way to exchange messages.

Memos Are Quick

Memos offer speed in reaching many people simultaneously. Phoning many people or visiting them individually takes considerable time and often adds the inconvenience of not reaching a person on the first, second, or even third attempt.

Memos Are Inexpensive

Saving time is saving money. Because memorandum formats are simple to produce, memos save time. Because they are usually done on lightweight, inexpensive paper, they decrease both stationery and postage expense. Electronically transmitted memos eliminate both of these expenses and provide very quick communication.

Memos Are Convenient

Memos offer easy access to people not seen on a regular basis. Memos also minimize any interruption that the receiver may experience. Reading a memo requires less time than a phone call or a personal visit, because, with a phone call or a visit, limiting conversations to the matter being discussed is difficult.

Memos Are a Written Record

Details of conversations are often confused or forgotten. Memos can serve as a written record for both the reader and the writer. They can clarify instructions or information given orally. In many situations a well-written memo can help prevent misunderstandings.

PURPOSES OF MEMOS

KEY POINT

Memos are used to
inquire, to inform,
to report, to remind,
to transmit, and to
promote goodwill.

Memorandums have a variety of purposes. The main purposes are to inquire, to inform, to report, to remind, to transmit, and to promote goodwill.

To Inquire

Use memos to request information, action, or reactions.

When is the software consultant coming?

Will you ship the Henderson order today?

Will you please review this bid and give me your opinion of it?

To Inform

Use memos to communicate procedures, company policies, and instructions.

Our safety procedures require a 15-minute rest period for every four hours of work.

⊕ GLOBAL NOTE

Discuss the fact that many countries place certain restrictions on the importation and exportation of goods. These goods may include plants, animals, foods, pharmaceuticals, currency, weapons, or technology. Have students choose a country and find out what restrictions apply. Students should present their findings in a memo to their supervisor.

Company policy permits escorted visitors (sixteen years old and older) to tour our plant.

Use your key card to enter the Third Avenue gate.

To Report

Use memos to convey organized data.

Below is our schedule for the completion of North Brick Road.

Here is a list of the supplies we will need.

To Remind

Use memos as reminders about overdue reports, important meetings, and so on.

Did you send me your travel itinerary?

Is our appointment with the Southern Telcom representatives on your calendar for Monday, April 3, at 2 p.m. in the conference room?

To Transmit

Use memos to tell readers about an accompanying message. The memo could describe, explain, or simply identify the enclosure.

Attached are the time sheets I asked you to distribute to all hourly employees.

Enclosed is a printout listing the names and home addresses of all regional managers.

REINFORCEMENT

Ask students to write one example for each of the memo uses. These can be similar to the ones in the text.

To Promote Goodwill

Use memos to establish, improve, and maintain goodwill. These memos could congratulate, welcome, or convey a "pat on the back."

Congratulations on your promotion.

Welcome to Huntley Industries.

Your advertising designs got us the Wright order. Thanks for a great job!

TONE OF THE MEMO

The tone of a memo depends largely on the position of, and the writer's relation to, the person to whom the memo is addressed. In some ways, the choice of tone is easier in business settings than in many social settings: Relationships are often clear between two people on different levels within an organization. In general, the writer of a business memo chooses a more formal tone when addressing top management than when writing to an equal or a subordinate, unless the writer knows that the addressee prefers an informal tone.

Even within clear corporate structures, of course, there will be times when the writer is not certain what tone to use in a memo. The best course in these cases is to choose a middle way—neither too formal nor too casual. Avoid using contractions like *you'll* and *here's*, but do not resort to elevated, artificial, or stilted language either. Stick to business. For example:

> Here is the report on last month's stereo sales, with the changes that you requested yesterday. The figures on Model A26 are now broken down to show the number of those stereos sold in each sales region. In addition, the appropriate tables now have an added line showing Model A26 sales by region for the same period last year.

Subject matter also helps to determine the choice of tone for a memo. A memo announcing the schedule of the company's bowling team would obviously have a lighter tone than a memo justifying costs that ran over budget. The more serious the topic, the more serious the tone.

ORGANIZATION OF THE MEMO

 **KEY POINT**

Memorandums should have these organizational elements: a statement of purpose, a message, and a statement of future action to be taken.

The form and the tone of a memo are means to help the writer convey his or her message. The memorandum's organization is another means to the same end. A memorandum tries to "sell" its readers a point of view. This situation holds true whether the writer wishes to convince a superior of the need for new office equipment or to convince someone under the writer's supervision of the need to maintain high work standards. The memo is more likely to achieve its goal if it is brief and to the point without seeming brusque or incomplete. A memo is usually even more sparing in its use of words than a good letter.

The organization in the body of a memorandum should be simple and clear. Only three elements are needed: (1) a statement of purpose, (2) a message, and (3) a statement of future action. An example of a simple memo is shown on page 305.

Statement of Purpose

The subject line of a memorandum tells the reader what the memo is about but does not usually state the writer's reason for writing. Often the writer can make the purpose clear simply by referring to an earlier memo (whether written or received) or to a previous meeting or telephone conversation. Here are some examples of how a writer can state the purpose of a memo.

> At the Advertising Department's last meeting, I was asked to investigate and report on the comparative costs of print and broadcast advertisements in the Northeast. Here is a summary of what I found.

> I received the attached memorandum from Dr. O'Hara this morning. I think you will agree that it shows the need for some changes in our hospital admission procedures.

INTEROFFICE MEMORANDUM

To: Susan C. Rostagno, Advertising and Display

From: James Roe, Garden Department

Date: July 1, 19--

Subject: August Newspaper Advertisements

Purpose   Our semiannual garden supply sale is planned for August 29 through September 19. We will need to run ads in the local newspapers to announce it.

Message   I would like to meet with you to discuss copy preparation and photography and to provide you with samples and suggestions.

Future
Action   Would you let me know when it is convenient for you to meet to plan these ads?

Jim

JR

mbc

This brief memo contains the three organizational elements—purpose, message, and future action.

Message

After the statement of purpose, the writer should go directly to the main points of the message. The object is to help the reader grasp the main points as easily as possible.

We could admit patients more quickly and efficiently if we gave them a checklist to complete. The checklist would take the place of the long-answer forms now being used.

A new form has been designed to simplify taking telephone orders. A copy of that form is attached.

Statement of Future Action

The body of the memorandum should usually end with a statement of future action to be taken or with a request for further instructions, as illustrated in the following example:

I will send further details about the proposed checklist if you wish, including an estimate of the amount of time such a checklist would save.

LANGUAGE TIP

Confusables:
biweekly—
(1) occurring every two weeks; (2) occurring twice a week [actually a wrong meaning; avoid it]
semiweekly—
occurring twice a week
fortnight—two weeks [it means 14 nights];
fortnightly—
occurring every two weeks.

SPECIAL TECHNIQUES FOR MEMOS

Memos, like letters, can be effective or ineffective, depending on how they are written. Here are some suggestions for increasing memo effectiveness.

Writing for Greatest Effectiveness

1. Cover only one major topic in each memo. When memos cover too many topics, a main thought may go unnoticed or may not receive the attention it deserves.
2. Consistently use a simple familiar heading that includes, but is not limited to, information such as *DATE, TO, FROM,* and *SUBJECT.* People getting messages from you regularly will know exactly where to look for specific information. Of course, if your company uses printed memo forms, the heading has already been standardized. (Detailed information on memo components and types appears in Section 7.2.)
3. Choose a brief but appropriate subject line. Subject lines should identify the topic – not give all the details.
4. Present the key idea first. The idea presented at the beginning will usually receive the most emphasis.
5. In most instances, use a personal, pleasant, and somewhat informal tone. You will know most of your receivers because they are in your organization. Special situations, however, such as writing to your superiors or reprimanding an employee, may require a more formal treatment.
6. Strive to make memos clear, complete, concise, consistent, correct, and courteous.

Even though written primarily to people that you know, memos still should accomplish the purpose you had when you wrote them. Taking too many shortcuts can decrease effectiveness.

☑ REINFORCEMENT

Divide students into seven groups. Ask each group to compose, keyboard, and print a memo that illustrates one of the special formatting and mechanical techniques. Assign each group a different technique. Make transparencies of the memos and show them to the class.

Special Formatting and Mechanical Techniques

Formatting and mechanical techniques can simplify the overall organization and thereby encourage further reading. Some suggestions follow.

1. Use enumerations to list important items.

    Please do the following things before tomorrow morning:
    1. Make 25 copies of the inventory report and the sales report.
    2. Collate and staple the reports and put a copy in each manager's folder.
    3. Call the managers to remind them of the meeting.

2. Use solid capitals and centering to emphasize an important detail.

    Tomorrow at 8:30 a.m. Sam Dubinski will be here to discuss our
    NEW PROFIT-SHARING PLAN
    Please arrange for as many staff members as possible to attend. . . .

3. Use columns with headings to make reading and understanding easier.

Below are the inventory figures you wanted:

Number	Product	Cases
Y-3346	Wallpaper	1,300
Z-4384	Cushions	2,856
M-8729	Curtains	1,438
L-4778	Comforters	1,143

4. Use underlining and side headings to show natural breaks in a memo.

Our new vacation policy rewards continued employment.
<u>Employees—Six Months or Less</u>
Employees who have been with the company six months or less will receive one-half day of paid vacation for each month of full-time employment.
<u>Employees—Seven to Eleven Months</u>
Employees who have been with the company seven to eleven months will receive three-fourths of a day of paid vacation for each month of employment.
<u>Employees—One to Two Years</u>
Employees who have been with the company one to two years will receive fourteen days of paid vacation.

5. Use bullets to emphasize several points.

Here are some things I want to discuss with you at our meeting:

- Orientation program for new employees
- Stock purchases by employees
- Employee training programs
- Education benefit program
- Severance plan

6. If you are using a word processing system that offers these features, use boldface printing and italics when appropriate.

Invest in our **U.S. GOVERNMENT SECURITIES FUND.**
This investment offers *safety* and *growth*.

7. Use color coding to attract attention. For example, use yellow paper for all messages from the accounting department. Or use a colored highlight pen to attract attention. The color used would have a special meaning: for example, blue could be used for general announcements (Our profits are up); red could signify needed information (All expense reports must be turned in by June 6).

A Word of Caution. If these techniques are overused, they will become commonplace and their benefit will be lost. Use them appropriately and sparingly.

REVIEW

Practical Application

A. Answer these questions.

1. In what writing situation would a memorandum be more appropriate than a letter?
2. In what writing situation would a letter be more appropriate than a memorandum?

B. List and discuss the advantages of memorandums.

C. Memorandums have the following uses:

a. To inquire	d. To remind
b. To inform	e. To transmit
c. To report	f. To promote goodwill

On a separate sheet of paper, write the letter of the use that best describes a memo that accomplishes each of the following:

1. Identifies an attached prospectus
2. Asks about the servicing of company vehicles
3. Announces a new security policy
4. Congratulates someone who has been transferred to Monte Carlo
5. Lists sales figures for the last three months by division
6. Asks about a holiday schedule that was due last week
7. Explains company bonus policy
8. Welcomes a new employee
9. Asks your opinion on a specific matter
10. Gives instructions for ordering new equipment

D. What are the three basic parts of the body of a memo? After you have answered this question, complete the assignment that follows.

After six months' full-time employment, employees are eligible for tuition reimbursement for evening and Saturday courses taken at local colleges. Employees must have the course approved before they enroll. George Earl, personnel manager, requires each applicant to write a memorandum requesting approval. The memo must list the course, the credit hours, the dates of the course, the college, the cost, and how successful completion of the course will benefit the company.

You want to take Data Processing 101 at Cranbury Community College. The course begins the first Monday of next month and meets each Monday for 12 weeks. The cost is $250 for three credit hours. Write the body of a memo persuading Mr. Earl to reimburse your tuition costs. Then identify the three basic parts of the body of your memo.

E. What are some formatting and mechanical techniques that can be used with memos? Why should you be cautious when using special

REVIEW cont.

techniques in memo writing? After you have answered these questions, complete the following assignment.

In her memo of July 15, your supervisor, Amanda Plowright, asked you to give her a list of sales by region for April, May, and June. They are, respectively, Region 1 — $23,494, $22,577, $19,482; Region 2 — $33,458, $32,332, $25,854; Region 3 — $21,589, $21,887, $20,492. Write the body of a memo giving this information in columnar form.

Editing Practice

Possessives, Plurals, and Contractions. Rewrite each incorrect item by adding, moving, or deleting apostrophes to make the sentences correct. Write *OK* for any sentence that has no error.

1. <u>Lets</u> walk over to <u>Lisas</u> office.
2. Two trainees are working in the <u>mens</u> sportswear department.
3. <u>Its</u> almost time for our annual safety inspection.
4. Most <u>manager's</u> agree with the Art <u>Departments</u> new procedures.
5. Until Bonnie's car is repaired, she is driving her <u>daughter-in-laws</u> car.
6. <u>Luke</u> and Dawn's faces were sunburned after the softball game.
7. One <u>witnesses'</u> statement agreed with <u>Jons</u>.
8. Two employees must check the lock on the bank <u>vaults'</u> door.

KEY

1. Let's . . . Lisa's
2. men's
3. It's
4. managers . . . Department's
5. daughter-in-law's
6. Luke's
7. witness's . . . Jon's
8. vault's

7.2 *MEMO TYPES AND MEMO STYLE*

OBJECTIVES: After completing Section 7.2, you should be able to:

1. Describe the various types of memos and the circumstances under which each should be used.
2. Identify the headings that should appear at the top of a memo form.
3. Explain how to write complete, correct, and effective memos.

KEY POINT

Memos are a vital link in achieving an organization's objectives.

Effective communication skill is essential for business success. Even though memos are internal, they are a vital link in achieving an organization's objectives. Successful internal communication can also be vital in achieving your career objectives. In this section, we shall concentrate on the various types of memos and on memo style. Selecting the appropriate type of memorandum for a particular purpose and following proper memo style will help you communicate successfully with other members of your organization.

TYPES OF MEMOS

Memorandums come in different formats, depending on their usage. Some of the most frequently used are described here.

The Typical Memo Format

The typical memo format is probably the most familiar and the most frequently used. The headings can be keyboarded as shown below, or they can be part of a printed form. Headings may be in all capitals or initial capitals as shown. The trend is to use initial capitals only, because this style is easier to keyboard on automated equipment.

☐ **SUGGESTION**

Ask students to bring examples of memo forms, carbonized sets, scratch pads, memo pads, message memos, and so on, or catalogs advertising these items. This collection would make an attractive bulletin board display.

A typical memo format.

```
                          Memorandum

     Date:      December 1, 19--

     To:        Rosalie Eiker, Shipping Department

     From:      Mitchell Bentley, Manager

     Subject:   Quincy Company Order


     Please ship the Quincy Company order (Invoice 2385) as soon as you
     can schedule it.

     Quincy had originally requested shipment on December 10 but called
     this morning asking for immediate shipment.  Quincy is one of our
     largest customers, and we want to cooperate if at all possible.

     Let me know if there are any delays.

                              MB

     lk
```

From the Desk of

Josephine Paxton

Omar:

When will the budget be ready?

Jo

Jo

10/25

4:45 p.m.

From the Desk of

Omar Rustin

Jo :

The budget will be ready tomorrow.

Omar

10/26

8:10 a.m.

Informal notes are very useful when communicating on the job. They are used to communicate brief—usually one-thought—messages and can be handwritten or typed.

The Informal Note

Informal notes (handwritten or typed, sometimes on printed forms) are very useful in the communication process. Jo wrote the memo (see above left) after the office closed, and Omar responded (above right) early the next morning.

Printed Forms

Using printed forms for specific purposes is a time-saver when communicating the same kinds of information frequently. Three examples are the standard memo (shown on page 312), the message memo (shown on page 313), and the routing slip (also shown on page 313).

Standard Memos.   Printed interoffice memo forms make it easier both to write and to read memos. Most companies use memo forms printed in two sizes: 8½ × 11 inches and 8½ × 5½ inches. Often, printed memo forms come in convenient snap-out sets. These provide an original for the ad-

INTEROFFICE MEMORANDUM

```
      To:  Winifred Johnson

    From:  Joyce Mercado

    Date:  July 9, 19--

 Subject:  Special Requests


          Several community colleges and high schools in the area have asked us
          about stocking videotapes in the following areas:  Shakespearean
          plays, American literature, aerobics, first aid, and reading
          tutorials for children.

          I think we can increase our business by working with schools and
          parents.  No other video company is carrying a rental inventory of
          educational materials.

          Will you please check the availability and the cost of tapes in these
          areas and provide me with a list by July 15.

                                        JM
```

This printed memo form includes the company's name and the words *Interoffice Memorandum,* as well as the guide words *TO, FROM, DATE,* and *SUBJECT.*

dressee, copies for two or three other intended readers, and a file copy for the writer. Many companies still choose to produce interoffice memos on the typewriter or word processor as the need arises. These companies give up the convenience of the snap-out forms but do gain the advantage of complete flexibility — preparing as many or as few copies as are needed for every occasion. Although memos written on computers do not use printed forms, many word processing programs can be set up to provide a memo format.

The heading of a printed memo form, such as the one shown above, usually includes (1) the name of the company, (2) the title *Interoffice Memorandum* (or *Interoffice Memo*), and (3) the guide words *TO, FROM, DATE,* and *SUBJECT.* In a large organization, the heading may also include *Department, Location,* and *Telephone Extension.*

Message Memos. Message memos are used to record phone messages and messages from visitors.

Routing Slips. Routing slips systematically channel messages to specified people. If the same routing is not used often, the names and office numbers can be left blank. If the same routing is used often, print the names and office numbers on the form as shown on page 313.

```
┌─────────────────────────────────┐   ┌─────────────────────────────────────────┐
│  MESSAGE  MEMO                   │   │              ROUTING  SLIP                │
│                                  │   │  Please read the attached information.    │
│  TO: ___Jim Silver___           │   │  Initial and date                         │
│                                  │   │  this form.  Send both to the next        │
│  FROM: __Susan Dexter__         │   │  person on the list.                      │
│                                  │   │                                           │
│  OF: _Dexter Company, Inc._     │   │  Name          Office   Initials   Date   │
│                                  │   │                                           │
│  __✓__ Phoned                   │   │  Anita Bledsoe    106   _____   _____      │
│                                  │   │                                           │
│  _____ Came to Visit            │   │  Ben Huang        104   _____   _____      │
│                                  │   │                                           │
│  __✓__ Please Call at           │   │  F. M. Latham     105   _____   _____      │
│        (803) 555 - 6124         │   │                                           │
│                                  │   │  Will Lutz        107   _____   _____      │
│  _____ Left This Message:       │   │                                           │
│                                  │   │  Tim Rucker       109   _____   _____      │
│  _____      │   │                                           │
│  _____      │   │  Lena Stevenson   108   _____   _____      │
│  _____      │   │                                           │
│  _____      │   │  Peter Wolensky   110   _____   _____      │
│                                  │   │                                           │
│  TAKEN BY: R. Carver            │   │  Return to:  Linda Branscomb, Office 210. │
│  DATE: 6/4  TIME: 10 a.m.       │   │                                           │
└─────────────────────────────────┘   └─────────────────────────────────────────┘
```

Printed forms, such as message memos and routing slips, are used to save time on the job. These forms allow the user to mark items on a preprinted list or to fill in labeled lines to complete a standard form.

MEMO STYLE

The *TO* Line

The writer fills in the *TO* line with the name of the person who is to receive the original of the memo. (If the writer chooses to add an appropriate courtesy title — Ms., Miss, Dr., Mrs., or Mr. — he or she should be consistent in using the title.)

> TO: Carl Martin
> TO: Stephanie Grimaldi
> TO: Rodolpho Gonzalez

The writer should include the addressee's job title when

1. The writer wishes to show deference:
   TO: Rodolpho Gonzalez, Chief Executive Officer
2. The addressee has more than one job title and the writer's message concerns the duties that belong with only one of the titles.
   TO: Stephanie Grimaldi, Chair, Employee Committee on Community Relations (Ms. Grimaldi is also the director of personnel.)

```
                          MEMORANDUM


          DATE:      October 4, 19--

          TO:        Branch Managers--Distribution Below

          FROM:      Gerry Nordstrom, General Manager

          SUBJECT:   Meeting for Branch Managers


          The Employee Relations Department has announced improvements in the
          employee benefits plan.

          A meeting to explain our new benefits package will be held on Monday,
          October 10, at 10 a.m. in the conference room adjoining my office.

          Please read the enclosed comprehensive booklet about the package and
          let me know if you have any questions about it.

                                      GN

          dk
          Enclosure


          Distribution:

          Michael Baxter
          Amy Dillingham
          Jon Henderson
          Andrew Poplin
          Madge Wray
```

This type of memo shows how a distribution list is typed. Note the *TO* heading. These guide words are typed in all-capital letters.

3. The addressee happens to have the same name as another employee, or a very similar name, so that the writer must make clear which of the two people is intended to receive the memo.
    TO: Carl Martin, Assistant Chief Engineer (Carol Martin is the production manager.)

In large companies, it may be helpful to include address information in the *TO* line of an interoffice memo. For example:

TO: Antonio Pappas, Room 3301, Benefits Office

TO: Michelle Gold, Laboratory 3, Research Department

If the memo is going to more than a few people, the writer should consider typing "Distribution Below" on the *TO* line and placing the list of recipients at the end of the memo under the heading *Distribution*. Placing the distribution list at the bottom gives the memo a more balanced appearance and spares the readers the chore of reading the long list of names until after they have read the heart of the memo — its message.

The *FROM* Line

It is usual for the writer of a memo not to use a courtesy title before his or her own name. If required, the writer may include a job title, department affiliation, room number, and telephone extension.

FROM: Edith L. Fitzpatrick, Researcher, Investment Department, Room 2403, Ext. 988

The *DATE* Line

In both letters and memos, the date should be written in full rather than abbreviated or given in figures only.

DATE: December 19, 19 — (*or* 19 December 19 —)

The day-month-year style is used in military correspondence.

The *SUBJECT* Line

The writer should state the subject of a memo clearly and briefly. Only in exceptional cases — such as technical matters — should the subject of the memo require more than a single line. The example below says all that is necessary; the rest should be left to the body of the memo.

SUBJECT: Request for Additional Personnel

The Body

The memo, unlike the business letter, includes no salutation. Instead, the writer leaves two blank lines beneath the subject line, then goes directly to the body of the memo. The body is single-spaced (if the message is unusually short, it may be double-spaced). The block paragraph style is usual, but paragraphs may be indented. Many organizations determine these matters according to a style of their own; thus new employees should ask if there is a "house" style for memos.

The Signature

The writer's initials are optional. If included, they should be typed a double space below the body of the memo, starting at the center. (Typing or signing the full name is unnecessary because the full name appears after *FROM*.) Most writers also *sign* their initials on each memo (either next to the name on the *FROM* line or near the initials at the bottom of the memo).

Below the signature initials, the typist includes his or her own initials and any notations (for example, enclosure notations and copy notations) that may be needed. Thus the end of the memo may look like this:

ELR

cb
c John W. Palmer

For more details, see a comprehensive reference manual.

KEY
See page I-33.

KEY
Students' designs will vary.

KEY
Students' designs will vary.

KEY
See page I-33.

SECTION

REVIEW

Practical Application

A. Answer these questions.

1. What kinds of information are transmitted in message memos?
2. What is the purpose of routing slips?
3. When are distribution lists used in memos?
4. List three reasons why a memo writer would include the addressee's job title on the *TO* line.
5. What two types of notations might be needed below the initials of the typist of a memo?

B. Design and produce (type or print) a form for handwritten, one-way (no space allowed for response) memos. The form should include the necessary headings, should be 8½ × 5½ inches, and should have lines on which to write.

C. On a sheet of paper, design a memorandum form that you will have printed. Your design should look as much like the finished product as possible. Follow these instructions:

1. Choose your business.
2. Use your creativity to choose a company name and logo (illustration) that will be printed on the memo.
3. Include the form title "Interoffice Memo" and appropriate headings.

D. You are an assistant to the director of a firm that imports fabrics for the fashion industry. The director has instructed you to report on the fabric choices of prominent designers for the fall season. After analyzing the collections of major designers, you have learned that the usual cold-weather fabrics—wools, cashmeres, mohairs, flannels, and corduroys—will be common. But you have also found prominent use of other fabrics—cotton and rayon. In addition, you have noted occasional use of silks, especially silk crepe de chine.

REVIEW cont.

Write a memorandum with typed or handprinted headings that presents this information so that the director can understand it at a glance.

E. Match the following words with their definitions:

1. Line listing the topic
2. Writer's initials
3. Written communication within a company
4. List of persons receiving a memorandum
5. Reason for writing

a. Distribution
b. Memo
c. Signature
d. Purpose
e. Subject

Editing Practice

Missing and Extra Words. Rewrite the following paragraph, omitting the repeated words and adding omitted words.

Aaron Singer of Caralia Draperies will be be here tomorrow morning at 10:30 to show us his line window treatments. His best-selling draperies are bow and ribbon swags and eyelet tiebacks. Our our competitors are doing quite with these two styles of, and we have lost some business because do not have them.

Punctuation Check. Correct any punctuation errors in the following sentences. Write *OK* if a sentence has no error.

1. All Bennington Bros. tools have a 5-year warranty; in our experience however most tools last for 10 or more years.
2. Ms. Pirelli wrote a check for $250.00 for the college's scholarship fund.
3. May we expect your shipment by July 1?
4. We have not yet received payment for last month's order nor have we been paid for goods sent the previous month.
5. If the dates change please let me know immediately.
6. You will be glad to hear, that our new office will be open for business on September 15.

CHAPTER 8

Nippon Company Inc
Sumire Building 2D
20-08 Ebishu 1-chome
ku, Tokyo 112

WRITING BUSINESS LETTERS

SECTION

8.1 *BUSINESS LETTER STYLE*

OBJECTIVES: **After completing Section 8.1, you should be able to:**

1. Identify both the standard parts and the optional parts of business letters.
2. List the order in which letter parts appear in business correspondence.
3. Explain the use and need for each letter part.
4. Describe the letter formats acceptable in business.
5. Discuss four or more techniques for achieving a positive, lasting impression with business letters.

KEY POINT

Both appearance and content are important.

Think about the people you have seen within the last twenty-four hours. Were any two people dressed exactly alike? Did any two people say precisely the same thing?

Chances are that except for such uniformed workers as police officers, fire fighters, and restaurant employees no two people that you have seen recently were dressed alike. The *appearance* of each person was different (either *slightly* or *very* different) from that of the others. Moreover, the *content* of the conversations you had with various people was probably different. In other words, the *style* of each person differed from that of the others.

These two style factors — *appearance* and *content* — can also be used to describe a business letter. How did the letter *look*, and what did the letter *say*? The appearance and the content of a business letter make up that letter's *style*, just as a person's manner of dress and the content of his or her conversation contribute to that person's *style*.

The style of a business letter contributes as much to that letter's success as a person's style contributes to his or her success. Obviously, then, if your business letters are to achieve their goals, you must first learn how to control the *appearance* and the *content* of a letter, both of which will be discussed in this section.

REINFORCEMENT

Emphasize that first impressions formed by a reader about the writer of a letter and the company he or she represents are based first on appearance and then on content.

THE FIRST IMPRESSION: *APPEARANCE*

Imagine receiving a letter from someone who is applying for a job with your firm. Further, imagine that the envelope is very messy — and that the letter looks even worse. The letter is folded awkwardly, is wrinkled, and appears to have smudges and smears everywhere. As a busy executive, how much time would *you* sacrifice from your workday to read the contents of this letter? Probably not very much.

Letters that do not make a good first impression simply do not get serious attention from busy professionals. The first step toward making a good impression is to use an acceptable letter format.

Business Letter Parts

□ SUGGESTION

Refer to the illustration on page 324 as you lecture on each letter part. Explain why optional parts are not always required.

Letter *format* refers to the placement of letter parts on the page. Before we discuss various formats, let's review letter parts. All the letter parts are illustrated on page 324. Note that in the following material *optional* parts are labeled; all other parts listed are *always* included in business letters.

1. Letterhead. The term *letterhead* can refer to either (1) the printed information at the top of business stationery or (2) the actual sheet of paper itself.

The printed information always includes the company's name, full address, and phone number. The letterhead may also include other information — for example, the company's slogan, a listing of its divisions, names of key personnel, or the company's logo (a symbol that identifies the company). See page 321 for illustrations of letterheads. Note that the company's address and telephone number may appear at the top or the bottom of business stationery.

When the letterhead is typed rather than printed, the information should be attractively arranged, starting 1 inch from the top of the page (line 7). Word processing equipment simplifies keyboarding a letterhead such as the following:

Electronic Designs Unlimited
575 Harborview Drive
Chelsea, Massachusetts 02150
800-555-0123

2. Date Line. The first item below the letterhead is the date of the letter.

3. Inside Address. The inside address repeats the information that is shown on the envelope; for example:

Ms. Camille R. Barry
General Manager
Habitat Wallcoverings, Inc.
85 East Perth Road
Conway, AR 72032

Thus the inside address includes the name of the person to whom the letter is addressed, the person's title, and his or her company's name and full address.

4. Attention Line (Optional). The attention line is an optional letter part. When it is used, the attention line may appear in one of two places. (1) It may follow the inside address; in this case the inside address does not include a *person's* name, only the *company's* name. (2) It may be placed on the first line of the inside address.

Well-designed letterheads help readers form positive first impressions of the sender.

LANGUAGE LAPSE

Catch the Lapse: "Abraham Lincoln wrote the Gettysburg Address while traveling from Washington to Gettysburg on the back of an envelope."

—Louis Untermeyer

[. . . wrote the Gettysburg Address on the back of an envelope while traveling . . .]

The attention line is used by writers who want to stress that the letter is technically intended for the *company*, not the *person*. A general salutation—such as *Ladies and Gentlemen:* —is used to show that the company is being addressed. See the letter on page 324 for an example of an attention line in the first position noted above.

5. Salutation. The salutation, which is the letter equivalent of saying "Hello," immediately precedes the body of the letter. Unless the letter is written to someone known very well and is rather informal, the salutation includes a courtesy title such as *Mr.* or *Ms.* If the letter is intended to be less formal and more friendly, then the salutation will contain the addressee's first name.

Dear Ms. Grant:	Dear Sir or Madam:
Dear Jim:	Ladies and Gentlemen:

Note the colon in each of the above examples. Traditionally, the salutation ends with a colon. However, *in the block letter format*, some writers drop both the colon after the salutation *and* the comma after the complimentary closing (see below). They reason that the vigorous, aggressive block format does not require the traditional punctuation marks after the salutation and the complimentary closing.

6. Subject Line (Optional). Another optional part is the subject line, which is used to identify quickly the topic of the letter. When a subject line is used, it immediately follows the salutation. See the letters on pages 324 and 325.

7. Body. The body, the main part of the letter, is typed single-spaced with an extra line of space between paragraphs.

8. Complimentary Closing. The "Good-bye" of the letter, the complimentary closing is an ending such as the following:

Cordially,	Cordially yours,
Sincerely,	Sincerely yours,

9. Company Signature (Optional). Some writers (and companies) prefer using a company signature; others do not. When it is used, the company signature appears below the complimentary closing. See the letter on page 324.

10. Writer's Identification. The writer's identification consists of the writer's name and title.

11. Reference Initials. Reference initials are the *typist's* initials—a way of identifying who typed or input the letter.

12. Enclosure Reminder (Optional). When something is sent along with the letter, the word *Enclosure* (or *Enclosures*) is typed beneath the reference initials.

13. Transmittal Notation (Optional). When the letter and enclosure(s) are to be sent by some means other than First-Class Mail—for instance by Certified Mail, Federal Express, and so on — the writer may indicate this fact by writing, for example, *By FAX* below the enclosure notation. See the letter on page 329.

14. Copy Notations (Optional). When a copy of the letter is to be sent to a third party, the writer may indicate this fact by writing, for example, *c: David Fischer* below the reference initials (or below the enclosure notation or enclosure and transmittal notations). The abbreviation *c* followed by a colon *(c:)* means "copy."

15. Postscript (Optional). The postscript *belongs* to the body of the letter but is positioned at the *end* of the letter — deliberately or as an afterthought. Because it is part of the body of the letter, it is typed in the same way that the paragraphs in the body of the letter are typed. Postscripts may be indicated by writing *PS:* or *PS.* before the message.

PS: Be sure to bring a copy of your report with you.

Business Letter Formats

KEY POINT

Acceptable business formats are: block, modified block, modified block with indented paragraphs, and simplified format.

Now that we have reviewed the parts of business letters, let's look at the various acceptable formats for letters. As you proceed, note that the *sequence* of the letter parts (including the optional parts) does not vary from one letter format to another. The differences in formats primarily are concerned with whether or not a particular part is indented.

Block Format. In the *block* letter format, all letter parts begin at the left margin. Because there are no indentions, the block style is easy to set up and, therefore, very popular. See page 324 for an example of a letter in block format.

Modified Block Format. Long popular, the *modified block* format (as its name hints) differs somewhat from the basic block style — namely, the date line, the complimentary closing, and the signer's identification line are indented so that they start at the center of the page. See page 325 for an example.

Modified Block Format—With Indented Paragraphs. One variation of the standard modified block format involves indenting the paragraphs five spaces rather than starting them at the left margin. See page 326 for an example.

Simplified Format. In an effort to simplify letter writing, the Administrative Management Society (AMS) developed what it calls the *simplified letter style.* Illustrated on page 327, the simplified letter:

1. Begins each part at the left margin (except unnumbered lists, which are indented five spaces).
2. Omits the salutation and the complimentary closing. As a substitute for the salutation, the first paragraph always includes the addressee's name.
3. Has an all-capital subject line.
4. Has an all-capital writer's identification line, which includes both the writer's name and the writer's title all on one line.

CONSOLIDATED
CONSTRUCTION COMPANY

75 Oakwood Terrace • Elgin, Illinois 60120 • 312-555-1550

December 8, 19--

Little Creek Inn
200 Irving Lane
Little Creek, CA 92358

ATTENTION: MS. CYNTHIA GRECOS

Ladies and Gentlemen:

Subject: Accommodations for Annual Conference

We would like to explore the possibility of holding next year's
National Sales Conference at the Little Creek Inn. Our meeting is
scheduled to begin on Sunday, June 16, and end on Saturday, June 22.
We will require single rooms for a minimum of 325 employees and guests
for the entire week.

Our needs for meeting rooms are described in the enclosed tentative
agenda for our week-long conference. The times of the meetings,
breaks, and meals are specified in this agenda, as well as the
approximate number of attendees for each session.

Will you please provide us with brochures and pamphlets describing
your room accommodations, dining facilities, and sports and
recreational facilities? Also, please suggest menus for the scheduled
lunches and dinners that are listed on the enclosed agendas and
estimate the approximate cost per person for both the rooms and the
meals.

After we have had an opportunity to review your brochures and
estimates, I would like to visit the Little Creek Inn so that I may
have the pleasure of <u>seeing</u> your highly praised resort.

Sincerely yours,

CONSOLIDATED CONSTRUCTION COMPANY, INC.

(Ms.) Doris P. Weingart

Doris P. Weingart
National Sales Manager

acd

Enclosure
c: Tyrone Pernell

The **block format** is considered very streamlined. In the block format every part begins at the left margin, so it is easy to type.

CONSOLIDATED
CONSTRUCTION COMPANY

75 Oakwood Terrace • Elgin, Illinois 60120 • 312-555-1550

December 8, 19-- ↓6

Ms. Cynthia Grecos
Convention Manager
Little Creek Inn
200 Irving Lane
Little Creek, CA 92358 ↓2

Dear Ms. Grecos: ↓2

SUBJECT: ACCOMMODATIONS FOR ANNUAL CONFERENCE ↓2

We would like to explore the possibility of holding next year's
National Sales Conference at the Little Creek Inn. Our meeting is
scheduled to begin on Sunday, June 16, and end on Saturday, June 22.
We will require single rooms for a minimum of 325 employees and guests
for the entire week. ↓2

Our needs for meeting rooms are described in the enclosed tentative
agenda for our week-long conference. The times of the meetings,
breaks, and meals are specified in this agenda, as well as the
approximate number of attendees for each session. ↓2

Will you please provide us with brochures and pamphlets describing
your room accommodations, dining facilities, and sports and
recreational facilities? Also, please suggest menus for the scheduled
lunches and dinners that are listed on the enclosed agendas and
estimate the approximate cost per person for both the rooms and the
meals. ↓2

After we have had an opportunity to review your brochures and
estimates, I would like to visit the Little Creek Inn so that I may
have the pleasure of seeing your highly praised resort. ↓2

Sincerely yours, ↓4

Doris P. Weingart

Doris P. Weingart
National Sales Manager ↓2

acd
Enclosure
c: Tyrone Pernell

The **modified block format.** The optional subject line may be typed in all-capital letters centered below the salutation, as shown here, or in capital and lowercase letters typed at the left margin, as illustrated in the block letter on page 324.

FWP

Finance Weekly Publications, Inc.

One Wall Street
New York, New York 10005

A Global Industries Company
212-555-2000

November 28, 19-- ↓6

Mr. Jerome P. Kirsch
840 Woodland Avenue
Lawrenceville, NJ 08648-2540 ↓2

Dear Mr. Kirsch: ↓2

    Thank you for calling to tell us that you have not
been receiving your issues of FINANCE WEEKLY since you
moved to your new home. We have corrected our oversight
so that normal service can now resume. ↓2

    As you suspected, your address-change notice had not
been processed. Of course, your new address has now been
included in our weekly subscriber mailing list. In fact,
you will probably receive the first December issue around
the same time you receive this letter. ↓2

    Mr. Kirsch, I am sending, under separate cover, the
two issues of FINANCE WEEKLY that you missed. If you miss
any future issues, please call me toll-free at 1-800-555-
1212. ↓2

                    Sincerely, ↓4

(Ms.) Marcia Alcott

Marcia Alcott
Circulation Manager ↓2

jpc ↓2

    PS: To apologize for our being late with two issues
of FINANCE WEEKLY, I am sending you the new FINANCE WEEKLY
ALMANAC as soon as it is available. I hope that you will
enjoy using this popular reference book, which sells for
$9.95 at newsstands nationwide.

The **modified block format with indented paragraphs** has an "executive look." Note that the postscript is formatted like the paragraphs—that is, indented five spaces.

Finance Weekly Publications, Inc.

One Wall Street
New York, New York 10005

A Global Industries Company
212-555-2000

November 28, 19-- ↓6

Mr. Jerome P. Kirsch
840 Woodland Avenue
Lawrenceville, NJ 08648-2540 ↓2

SUBSCRIPTION DELAY ↓2

Thank you, Mr. Kirsch, for calling to tell us that you
have not been receiving your issues of FINANCE WEEKLY
since you moved to your new home. We have corrected our
oversight so that normal service can now resume. ↓2

As you suspected, your address-change notice had not been
processed. Of course, your new address has now been
included in our weekly subscriber mailing list. In fact,
you will probably receive the first December issue around
the same time you receive this letter. ↓2

Mr. Kirsch, I am sending, under separate cover, the two
issues of FINANCE WEEKLY that you missed. If you miss any
future issues, please call me toll-free at 1-800-555-1212. ↓5

(Ms.) Marcia Alcott

MARCIA ALCOTT - CIRCULATION MANAGER ↓2

jpc ↓2

PS. To apologize for our being late with two issues of
FINANCE WEEKLY, I am sending you the new FINANCE WEEKLY
ALMANAC as soon as it is available. I hope that you will
enjoy using this popular reference book, which sells for
$9.95 at newsstands nationwide.

The **simplified format** has every letter part beginning at the left margin. It does *not* have a salutation or a complimentary closing; instead, it always has an all-capital subject line and an all-capital writer's identification line. Note, too, the use of the addressee's name in the beginning of the first paragraph.

Other Letter Formats

In addition to the formats just discussed, you will find the personal-business and the social-business letter formats useful.

Personal-Business Letter Format. Personal-business letters generally are not typed on letterhead stationery. Instead of a letterhead, a *return address* was traditionally typed at the top of the page, with the date immediately following it. Now, however, the return address is usually placed directly beneath the writer's name, at the bottom of the letter, as follows:

John K. Fitzpatrick
John K. Fitzpatrick
307 Franklin Avenue
Detroit, MI 48207

See page 329 for an example of the personal-business letter format.

Social-Business Letter Format. A special format is sometimes preferred for letters written to business associates when the subject matter is more social than business. For samples of this format, see Section 8.6, "Writing Social-Business Messages."

Formatting Guidelines

Letters. Whichever letter style a writer selects, the letter must be keyboarded and formatted properly. The margins must be adequate, the spacing between parts should adhere to certain standards, and so on.

The letters illustrated on pages 325 through 327 have notations that show the number of lines of space generally left between letter parts. Use these notations to guide you in the vertical spacing of letter parts.

Generally, try to achieve a line length of 5 inches. When a letter is short (under 75 words) or long (over 225 words), you may want to vary the line length and make other changes that will help you prepare an attractive, balanced letter. In such cases, you may find the following guidelines helpful:

Words in Body	*Line Length* 10-P	12-P*	*Date Typed On*	*From Date to Inside Address*	*Space for Signature*
Under 75	40 (4")** Side margins 2¼"	60 (5") 1¾"	Line 13 (Ln 2")	6 lines (Ln 3")	3–6 lines
75–225	50 Side margins 1¾"	60 1¾"	Line 13	6 lines	3 lines
Over 225	60 Side margins 1¼"	70 1⅓"	Line 13	6 lines	2–3 lines

*10-P = 10-pitch type, also called pica; 12-P = 12-pitch type, also called elite.
**In some word processing programs, lines are indicated in inches.

August 2, 19--↓3

Akita Industries of America
120 Highland Parkway
Riverside, CA 92504 ↓2

Attention: Service Department ↓2

Ladies and Gentlemen: ↓2

In April I purchased your Akita "1600" letter-quality
printer and, at the suggestion of the Akita dealer, a
tractor-feed attachment. According to the Akita dealer,
the tractor-feed attachment would "pay for itself" because
it would allow me to use continuous-form paper and print
page after page automatically, without monitoring the
printer. I had to admit that it certainly sounded well
worth the $125 price tag.↓2

Imagine my disappointment when my Akita printer <u>regularly</u>
miscued in vertical spacing from one line to another! Two
or three times on every page, the printer "returns" less
than a full line of space, causing copy to be overprinted
and, of course, messy and illegible. Please see the
enclosed sample.↓2

An authorized Akita service center has installed a new
motor that is supposed to solve the problem, but the
linespacing problem persists. Despite its higher price, I
bought the Akita printer because Akita has a reputation
for dependability. Will you please prove to me that this
reputation <u>is</u> well deserved by telling me how I may get my
printer serviced and working properly?↓2

Please call me at 201-555-2184 or write to me at the above
address. ↓2

                              Sincerely,↓4

                              Harold P. Cornwall

                              Harold P. Cornwall
                              119 Sumter Avenue
                              Fanwood, NJ 07023

Enclosure
By Certified Mail

This **personal-business letter** uses a modified block format. The writer's name at the end of the letter is immediately followed by the writer's full address.

Envelopes. To prepare standard business envelopes (called No. 10 envelopes), follow these guidelines:

1. Begin typing the mailing address on line 14, about 4 inches from the left edge.
2. Use a block style and single spacing.
3. Always be sure to include the ZIP Code. Also, leave only one space between the state and the ZIP Code.

See page 331 for illustrations of two properly typed envelopes.

If you are not using standard-size stationery or envelopes, or if you need specific formatting instructions, refer to a typing manual or business writing handbook.

THE LASTING IMPRESSION: *CONTENT*

INFORMATION

Making a positive, lasting impression in a letter helps establish and maintain good business relationships.

As important as it is to make a good first impression, it is even more important to make a positive *lasting* impression. With your business letters, the lasting impression will be made by the content of your messages, by the combined effect of the *words* you use.

Your words will determine whether your reader considers you out of date, verbose, and pompous instead of modern, businesslike, and down to earth. Your words will convince your reader that you are the best person to do business with — or the worst.

Pay attention to the following techniques for ensuring that your words will support the most positive image of you and your company.

Use Current Expressions

Expressions, like fashions, change. Few people today would choose the cumbersome, confining clothes worn a few generations ago. In letter writing, fashions change too. Some expressions are just as old-fashioned as celluloid collars and high-buttoned shoes, but many people continue to use them in business letters. Make sure that you know the expressions that are out of date so that you can avoid them; but also make sure that you know and use current — not slang — expressions in your letters.

Use	Do Not Use
say, tell, let us know	advise, inform
now, at present	at this time, at the present time, at the present writing
as, because, since	due to the fact that, because of the fact that
regarding, concerning, about	in re
if, in case	in the event that
please	kindly
for	in the amount of
according to	in accordance with

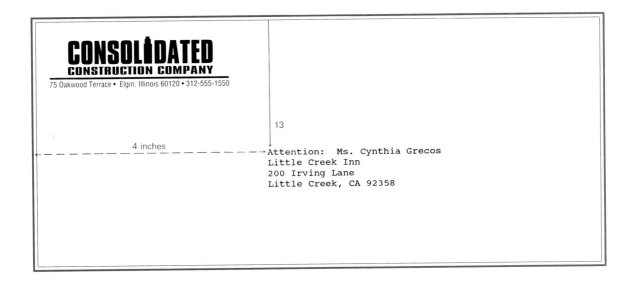

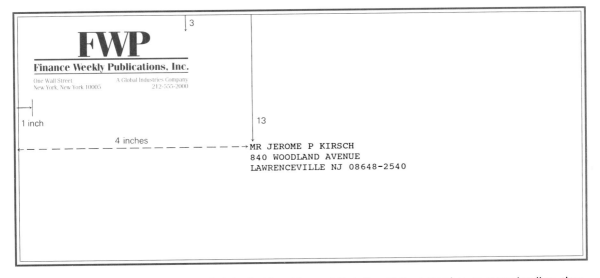

The envelope information should parallel the inside address of its letter. If the letter has an attention line, then the envelope should have an attention line. Note that the attention line (in this case on the first envelope) should appear on the first line of the mailing address. When the address appears in all capital letters, no punctuation is used. Note the use of the ZIP Code and the ZIP + 4 Code on these envelopes, which were prepared for the letters on pages 325 and 326.

Eliminate Redundancy

Redundancy in writing or in speech results from using words that are unnecessarily repetitious; for instance, using *free gratis* for *gratis*. Since *gratis* means "free," *free gratis* means "free free." The following list includes some common redundancies that you should avoid.

Use	Do Not Use	Use	Do Not Use
about	*at* about	enter	enter *into*
above	*up* above	etc.	*and* etc.
alike	*both* alike	experience	*past* experience
beginner	*new* beginner	identical	*same* identical
check	check *into*	otherwise	*as* otherwise
connect	connect *up*	practice	*customary* practice
continue	continue *on*	repeat	repeat *again*
converted	*converted over*	same	*exact* same
cooperate	cooperate *together*	together	*both* together

Use Plain, Simple Words

Even some people who would never *say* "I have amended and rectified the errors" sometimes *write* such fancy prose. Of course, a simple "I have corrected the errors" says it all!

The goal of a business letter is to convey a message efficiently and politely, not to show off the writer's vocabulary. Don't use a fancy word, a long word, or an impressive-sounding word when an *everyday* word will communicate your meaning just as well.

For example, saying "We are appreciative of your felicitations" certainly sounds fancy, but is it better or clearer than simply saying "We appreciate your best wishes"? Also, imagine writing "The store and all its appurtenances were sold" instead of "The store and its furnishings were sold."

Similar to using overly fancy words is using jargon inappropriately. *Jargon* is technical language that is common in a certain profession or trade—but foreign outside that trade. For example, if someone in the pharmaceutical industry were talking with a colleague about a *time signature* (a set of directions telling a patient how to use a prescribed medicine), that person would certainly be communicating appropriately. But using the term *time signature* with someone who is not in the pharmaceutical industry would probably cause confusion.

Moral: Keep it *simple*.

Be Concise

Imagine that you're having an extremely busy day when you receive a letter that begins with this paragraph:

In reviewing your proposal—in response to which we have arrived at a decision—we considered everything fully and completely. We looked at the financial aspects of the proposal, and at the practical aspects of the proposal, and at the managerial aspects of the proposal. We don't just jump into things.

It's not our way. To the best of our knowledge, ability, and belief, we overlooked nothing before reaching our decision, which is final, irrevocable, and nonnegotiable. I'm afraid that we have decided that the proposal is unworkable under present economic conditions, circumstances, regulations, and restrictions.

Would you be eager to continue reading? Definitely not. If the writer had considered your time and your needs, perhaps the letter would have come to the point sooner, as in this revision:

Thank you for sharing your proposal with us. We explored every aspect of the proposal—financial, practical, and managerial. Despite its positive features, we concluded that your proposal would not succeed in the current economic climate.

Get to the point and do it quickly (without being abrupt, curt, or rude, of course). Cut irrelevant words, sentences, or paragraphs. You will save your time and your reader's, and you will improve your letter.

Be Specific

Clear writing is a reflection of clear thinking and is therefore *specific*. Note how the following statements are unclear, how they mislead the reader.

Mr. Nevins assigned the project to Arthur, but *he* is attending a conference in Phoenix. (To whom does *he* refer—to Mr. Nevins? to Arthur?)

Mrs. Carney wants the information sent by fax and the report transmitted by modem, but *it* is not complete yet. (What does *it* refer to?)

The effective business writer knows the value of being specific.

Mr. Nevins assigned the project to Arthur, but Arthur is attending a conference in Phoenix.

Mrs. Carney wants the information sent by fax and the report transmitted by modem, but the information is not complete yet.

Don't keep the reader guessing: Be specific.

Be Coherent

Help the reader see specifically *how* your thoughts are interrelated by using such "connecting words" as the following to tie your ideas together:

because	thus	on the other hand
since	for example	nevertheless
naturally	of course	therefore
however	as a result	as a matter of fact

For example, read the sentence below without the italicized words to see how *nevertheless* and *because* contribute to the coherence of the sentence.

The attorney advised them not to sign the contract unless certain clauses were amended. *Nevertheless*, they signed it *because* only then could they start work.

Be Complete

In an effort to be concise, some writers become "word shy" and become *too* concise — abrupt, really. As a result, they omit essential information. For example:

Dear Mr. Petersen:

We would like to order 20 more beach chairs — the same kind we ordered last time.

Thank you.

Although the writer may know all the specifics — the purchase order number, the date of the original order, the catalog number, the price, and so on — the reader may *not* have this information right at hand and may have to spend time checking files to find information that the writer should have included.

Be sure that your messages are complete:

Dear Mr. Petersen:

Please send us 20 of the same beach chairs you shipped to us on April 12 (Invoice 755-123) — that is, 20 wood and canvas folding beach chairs (Castaways Catalog No. A970-5588).

In April we paid $32.11 for each chair. The enclosed purchase order, therefore, is for $642.20 plus shipping charges. Please let me know if there is any change in this price.

As usual, Mr. Petersen, please ship this order to us by Allied Delivery Service.

Sincerely,

SECTION REVIEW

Practical Application

KEY
See page I-34.

A. Using the simplified letter style, write a letter to your instructor stating whether you think the simplified style is appropriate for all business letters. Include your reasons why or why not.

KEY
Students' answers will vary.

B. Using the letter style you prefer, write a letter to your instructor explaining how the style selected is superior to the other styles discussed in this section.

KEY
See page I-34.

C. Modernize the following expressions.

1. In re your letter of 27th last, . . .
2. At the present writing we have still not received . . .
3. Please be advised that your dividend will be $6,000, not $600.
4. In the event that August 14 is an inconvenient date, kindly let us know when you would like the speakers delivered.

5. Due to the fact that property sales are down because of . . .

D. Find and eliminate any redundancies in the following sentences.

1. <u>Prior</u> foresight would have saved us these cost overruns.
2. The same <u>identical</u> error message appeared the last time I used this word processing command.
3. Unless the whole staff cooperates <u>together</u>, we won't finish the manuscript in time for spring publication.
4. Their management styles are <u>both</u> alike.
5. The heating system has been converted <u>over</u> from gas to solar power.

E. Make the following sentences clearer and more forceful by using simple words.

1. From the expression on Michael's face, we knew that he was engaged in deep <u>ratiocination</u>.
2. The managing partner <u>discommended</u> the proposal.
3. Phyllis was the <u>cynosure</u> of the labor negotiations.
4. His dark blue suit was in every way <u>comme il faut</u>.
5. Her remarks <u>precipitated</u> a <u>veritable brouhaha</u>.

Editing Practice

Updating Vocabulary. Rewrite these excerpts from business letters, eliminating all outmoded words and expressions.

1. I would like to make an appointment at your earliest convenience.
2. Hoping to hear from you soon, I remain, Sincerely yours,
3. Kindly advise us of your decision in the very near future.
4. At the present writing, we are revising the production schedule.
5. Due to the fact that manufacturing costs are rising, we must increase prices accordingly.
6. Thank you in advance for your assistance in this matter.
7. We have received your order for a scanner and are shipping it at the present time.
8. Enclosed please find our remittance.
9. In the event that you have a better suggestion, please advise me of it as soon as possible.
10. Research was not part of the director's purview.

Using Your Word Processor. Are there any spelling errors in this paragraph?

Because we specialize in the needs of <u>attornies</u>, our building is uniquely equipped to serve lawyers. Each suite already has a large room furnished with <u>shelfs</u> and tables—ideal for a legal <u>liberry</u>. In addition, there are rooms <u>suitible</u> for large and small meetings and, of course, several private offices.

KEY
Omit the underscored words.

KEY
For underscored words substitute:
1. thought
2. disapproved
3. guiding star *or* leader
4. proper
5. caused, real, uproar

KEY
See page I-34.

KEY
attorneys
shelves
library
suitable

8.2 *WRITING AND ANSWERING REQUESTS*

OBJECTIVES: **After completing Section 8.2, you should be able to:**

1. Write request letters and answers to requests that are complete, precise, reasonable, and courteous.
2. Answer requests promptly and use a positive approach.
3. Be helpful in answering requests.
4. Apply general sales techniques in responding to requests.

Some of the most routine business tasks involve requests of some kind — for example, asking for appointments, reserving conference rooms, obtaining price lists and catalogs, asking for copies of reports and studies, seeking technical information about goods and services, and asking favors. If writing requests is a common business task, then answering requests is obviously equally common. In this section you will learn how to get favorable responses to your requests and how to answer requests most effectively.

WRITING REQUESTS

KEY POINT

Follow these guidelines in writing requests: Be complete, be precise, be reasonable, and be courteous.

REINFORCEMENT

Stress the fact that the person making the request knows what he or she wants, when it is needed, why he or she wants it, and so on. The reader does not. In such a situation, many of us will assume that it is obvious why we need the information or when we need it. But it may not be obvious to the reader.

Although requests are truly routine, they are not to be treated routinely. What is more, extraordinary requests require extraordinary planning and writing skills! Whether you are simply asking an office supply company for a copy of its catalog or asking a busy, important executive to go out of her way to speak at your conference, follow these guidelines in writing requests:

Be complete.
Be precise.
Be reasonable.
Be courteous.

Be Complete

When writing a request, always ask yourself, "What can I provide the reader to make sure that he or she has *all* the information needed to grant the request?" Also, "Will any more information be helpful for some reason?" Consider the following situations:

You are requesting information about CD-ROM systems for a report that you are preparing. Tell the reader the purpose of your request. He or she might have additional materials to share with you or might grant the request solely to get publicity for his or her company.

INTEROFFICE MEMORANDUM

To: George Huizinga, Office Manager

From: Dorothy Monroe, Mailroom Supervisor

Subject: Need for Another Postage Meter

Date: January 23, 19--

Our use of postage has more than doubled in the last six months. The volume of outgoing first-class letters has risen from an average of 390 a day to almost 1,000. The increase in second-class mailings has been almost as great. In the same period, postal rates have gone up 18 percent. It is no wonder that our postage meter seems to run out of postage every day.

Simply putting more postage in the meter would help but would not solve the problem. It is company policy never to leave the mailing of a completed first-class letter until the next day. Since most outgoing first-class letters reach the mailroom between 3 and 5 p.m., there are only two hours available for processing approximately 800 letters. Using a single meter, we simply do not have enough time to place postage on every item.

The result, I am afraid, has been late delivery of some company mail. During the past week, we have received three complaints about this from outside the company and two complaints from within.

I am sure that you will agree that another meter is needed. I have obtained a purchase order and filled it out for your signature, and I would be grateful if you would authorize the purchase as soon as possible. I will send a member of my staff to get the second meter as soon as I receive authorization.

DM

Whether a request is routine or is complicated, it should be complete. It should also be precise, reasonable, and courteous.

You are assuming the reader will remember facts from your last letter or your last conversation. Don't assume! Repeat the model or type, the catalog number, the price, the preferred shipping method, and so on.

You are ordering extra stock to qualify for a quantity discount. Be sure to mention the discount you expect.

You are having something shipped to an address other than the one in your letterhead. Tell the reader where the materials are to be shipped. Don't assume the reader knows because he or she has handled your requests before; the order may be processed by someone else this time.

Put yourself in the reader's place so that you can better understand how the reader might feel and what information he or she might need to know. Note, for example, how the requests on pages 337 and 339 successfully answer "Who?" "What?" "Why?" "When?" and "Where?"

In your effort to be complete, however, do not be tempted to give the reader an excessively detailed description or needless information. Decide whether it will help the reader to know that you are planning to write a report. If it will help, include this fact in your request; if it is likely to be useless information, omit it. Likewise, decide whether you must include the model or type, the catalog number, and so on. If all this information is already included in the enclosed purchase order, then there may be no need to repeat it in the letter too.

Be Precise

From time to time, newspapers have reported stories of the wrong convicts being released because the approved release form listed the wrong convict number. Although an error in your written requests may not have such strong repercussions, the error, nevertheless, may be very embarrassing, troublesome, costly, and time-consuming.

Learn to be a good proofreader. Don't delegate the entire responsibility to others. Share the proofreading of your request letters and memos with your secretary, your assistant, or a colleague. Look for ways to ensure accuracy such as reading to each other statistics in the letter against statistics in the original invoice. List statistics in a table (rather than in sentences) if the table format makes the information easier to comprehend. See page 340 for an example of a letter that illustrates how to be precise.

Be Reasonable

Even people who are usually reasonable will sometimes make unreasonable requests when faced with job pressures or when they do not fully understand that what they are requesting is exceptionally difficult or time-consuming or complicated.

Make a conscious effort to avoid presenting unreasonable requests. Consider your request *from the reader's perspective.* Are you asking too much of someone's time? Are you taking advantage of a colleague's influence? Are you

CROSS REFERENCE
Section 6.1 provides more information on proofreading.

REINFORCEMENT
Emphasize that being reasonable and courteous are part of standard business etiquette. This standard applies in communicating face to face, on the telephone, or in writing. Inexperienced office workers may not realize that a written request may be unreasonable or impolite.

The Seduto Agency

13 East Taylor Road   White Plains, New York 10604   914-555-9300

September 13, 19--

Ms. Frances P. O'Flaherty
Training Director
National Insurance Institute
500 Independence Way
Cleveland, OH 44015

Dear Ms. O'Flaherty:

I read with interest in <u>Insurance Today</u> about your new training booklet, "The 100 Most-Asked Questions About Casualty Insurance." This booklet sounds as if it will be especially suited for training our new personnel.

Ms. O'Flaherty, will you please send us 30 copies of this booklet? I have enclosed a check for $42 to cover the cost of the booklets and shipping.

Because we are planning to use these booklets on September 30 for a training session, we will be glad to pay any additional costs for first-class or Priority Mail shipping to ensure that we receive the materials in time. In this case, please bill me for any additional costs.

Sincerely yours,

Anthony Seduto

Anthony Seduto
President

jt
Enclosure

A request letter should answer the questions "Who?" "What?" "Why?" "When?" and "Where?"

WESTWOOD ART STUDIO
One Sun Valley Road
Baltimore, Maryland 21211
301-555-7575

August 14, 19--

H & W Graphic Arts Supply Inc.
9100 State Street
St. Paul, MN 55101

Attention: Order Department

Ladies and Gentlemen:

Please ship the following materials to us airfreight and bill
our account.

Quantity	Item (Catalog No.)	Unit Price	Total ↓2
12	Nonskid rulers, 18" (138255)	$ 5.00	$ 60.00
1	Leroy Lettering Set (211501)	313.00	313.00
1 doz.	Ebony drawing pencils (07824)	3.00	3.00
5 gal	Best-Test Rubber Cement (119590)	19.90	99.50
			$475.50

We would appreciate receiving the entire order within two weeks.
Please charge the total to our account (No. 47/344).

Sincerely,

Beatrice Keller

Beatrice Keller
Office Manager

dbc

Listing information in a table format often helps the writer to communicate precisely.

asking for a character reference from someone who hardly knows you? Can you reasonably expect this person to expend such effort on your request? Consider these factors before making a request.

Be Courteous

Courtesy is a must in business communications. Whether you are requesting something that is legally or morally due to you, something that you have paid (or will pay) for, something that is yours and should be returned, or something that the reader should be delighted to send to you — in every case, you should be courteous in writing your request. Just as you deserve common courtesy, you must show common courtesy.

Although few people intentionally write discourteous requests, in their rush to complete a job, to place an order, to mail a letter, and so on, people *do* sometimes write impolite requests. For example, read this request for a free videotape describing vacation time-shares:

> I saw your ad in *Leisure Days* magazine about a free videotape describing vacation time-shares at Morning Glory Resorts. Send one to me at the address in the letterhead.

The reader *did* advertise free videotapes, obviously in the hope of selling vacation time-shares. Does this mean, however, that the reader of the request letter does not deserve common courtesy? Of course not! The writer would have shown more thoughtfulness, more respect for the reader, by writing the request along these lines:

> I was very much interested to read in *Leisure Days* magazine that you have a free videotape describing vacation time-shares at Morning Glory Resorts. My husband and I are avid golfers and tennis players, and your resort sounds as if it is the ideal place to spend our two-week summer vacation each year.

> We are also interested in buying a two-week time-share at a ski resort during the month of January. If you would please send us information about time-shares at winter resorts as well as the free videotape about Morning Glory Resorts, we would be most appreciative. We look forward to watching the videotape, which you can send to our business address on the letterhead.

The writer might have reaped additional benefits from this revised, more courteous request. The reader will gladly send not only the free videotape advertised in the magazine but also any information about vacation time-shares at winter resorts, because the writer took the time to state specific needs and did so *courteously*.

When communicating a request, write the request that *you* would like to receive if you were the reader.

ANSWERING REQUESTS

Each request letter and memorandum illustrated above deserves a response from the reader. Common courtesy dictates that a reply be sent.

Common courtesy also dictates that the response be written *promptly*. Whether the response is an easy-to-write positive reply or a more difficult rejection, the reader should not be kept in suspense. Also, the writer should try to *help* the reader as much as possible, even if the request must be refused.

Writing a response — whether the reply is positive or negative — presents an opportunity to promote goodwill and to make a sale. Thus the response should be *sales-minded*. In addition, the response (like the request) should be *specific* and *complete*.

As you can see, then, answering requests requires the writer to:

Be prompt.	Be specific.
Be helpful.	Be complete.
Be sales-minded.	Be positive.

Let's take a closer look at each of these six rules for answering requests.

Be Prompt

Many companies have policies requiring their employees to respond to letters within 48 hours — some, within 24 hours. Why? Because the companies realize that being prompt in replying is simply good business.

Even when an inquiry cannot be answered in detail, common business courtesy demands that a reply (at least an acknowledgment of the request) be sent *promptly*. For example:

Dear Mr. Miller:

Your recent request for a price quotation for four 5,000-watt alternators (Bitco No. 4700) is being handled by Beverly Jenrette. Bitco, the manufacturer, now has these alternators on back order. Ms. Jenrette is checking with Bitco to determine how soon these alternators will be available and what the price change (if any) will be.

Ms. Jenrette expects to have this information for you by October 15. In any case, she will write to you before then to give you an update on your request.

Sincerely yours,

This prompt response (1) acknowledges the request, (2) tells the potential customer specifically who is taking care of his request, and (3) tells him when he can expect an answer. The writer in this situation would send a copy to Ms. Jenrette and place another copy in a tickler file — a reminder file — for October 15.

Because promptness is both a courtesy and a sign of good business, your reader will always be impressed by your promptness. Therefore, take advantage of situations in which your promptness will be a plus. Note how one writer capitalized on a quick response:

When I received your request in this morning's mail, I checked immediately to make sure that we could process the color slides you requested for your March 19 meeting. I am pleased to tell you that we can process and deliver the slides by. . . .

Modern business writers use word processors to help them save time in answering requests promptly—especially when replies must be written in large volumes. As you will see in Section 8.7, word processing equipment permits writers to develop individually personalized letters in a fraction of the time it would take to do so without such equipment.

Another shortcut that allows writers to achieve promptness when faced with large volumes of responses is to *print* a card or letter. The card or letter may have blanks that the writer can quickly fill in, or it may simply give a printed message with no blanks. Despite their lack of personalization, printed responses allow a company to respond to hundreds or thousands of requests *promptly*. Imagine, for example, the number of responses a nationally famous magazine would need to send as a result of advertising a half-price subscription offer! Without printed "Dear Subscriber:" responses, such as the one on page 344, prompt replies would be impossible. Printed responses certainly do serve a purpose.

Be Helpful

 **KEY POINT**

In responding to a request, provide additional help or information whenever possible.

A customer or a potential customer who asks for information expects to receive assistance, whether the customer is asking in person, on the telephone, or in writing. Not only does the customer expect assistance, but management also *wants* its employees to offer their assistance to customers, suppliers, and coworkers.

When responding to a request, try to understand why the person is asking for help and remember why your company wants you to help. Remember, too, that you are the expert. Whether or not you can grant the request, consider whether there is something additional you can do to help the person. Do you know of a store where the person can find the product he or she needs? Do you know of a company that makes the product he or she is looking for? Do you know of a book that covers the very topic the person wants to research? Do you know of a service organization that can help the person?

Note how the writer of the following letter did more than fill the request—the writer anticipated Ms. Harrison's interest in a closely related product. Good sales expertise? Good business? *Both!*

Dear Ms. Harrison:

It's good to know that you are considering ImageMaker, our telephone facsimile transmitting system. One of our most popular items, the ImageMaker will enable you to send any graphic design 24 by 24 inches or smaller to any office in the world equipped with an ImageMaker and a telephone. The ImageMaker should be particularly valuable to you and your partner-architects in other cities. Now you won't have to wait days to react to one another's latest sketches.

A wonderful complement to ImageMaker is our reducing, high-resolution photocopier, the ImageReducer. With no discernible loss in precision, the ImageReducer will reduce graphic designs as large as 48 by 48 inches to 24 by

FWP

Finance Weekly Publications, Inc.

One Wall Street
New York, New York 10005

A Global Industries Company
212-555-2000

Dear Subscriber:

THANK YOU...

for renewing your subscription to FINANCE WEEKLY. We received your
payment, and we have credited your account.

In the coming year, we know that you will continue to enjoy all the
feature stories and the up-to-the-minute reporting on important
financial news--the kind of information for which you rely on FINANCE
WEEKLY.

We encourage you to take a moment to complete the "From the Reader"
card that is included in every issue. By quickly checking the
features you most like, you can help ensure that future issues of
FINANCE WEEKLY will continue to serve <u>your</u> interests and meet <u>your</u>
needs.

Sincerely,

(Ms.) Marcia Alcott

Marcia Alcott
Circulation Manager

lmg

This printed form letter helps a publisher acknowledge all its subscription renewals *promptly.*

24 inches—small enough to transmit by the ImageMaker. The combination of ImageMaker and ImageReducer will save not only the transit time of mailing or of shipping by airfreight but also the cost.

We very much appreciate your interest in our products and would be happy to demonstrate them for you soon.

Sincerely,

Although it is rather easy to be helpful when you are granting a request, you can also be helpful in many situations when you cannot grant the request, as the writer of the following letter proves:

Dear Mrs. Gonzales:

I wish that we were able to fill your recent order for the 15-millimeter, f/2.8 Caxton underwater lens. Although we generally carry this superb lens, we are currently out of stock, and Caxton will not be shipping more until September or October.

Because you mentioned that you wanted the lens for your upcoming scuba diving trip, I called another supplier to find this lens. Good news: The F Stop, a photography specialty store, has the lens that you want. You may call the F Stop toll-free at 800-555-1800.

Good luck! And please be sure to try us again *next time*.

Sincerely,

This letter has certainly won a friend for the writer's company—just by being helpful.

Be Sales-Minded

❏ **SUGGESTION**
Discuss how responding to a request offers the possibility to make a sale.

Whenever you respond to a request letter, you should look for possible ways to make a sale. After all, whether you work in the Sales Department or not, your company depends on sales to make a profit and to pay your salary.

Of course, the "hard sell" approach is rarely effective; you will not make much progress by bluntly saying "Buy this product!" Yet you can help sell your company's products or services. Two ways that you can be of help have already been discussed—by responding promptly to requests and by being helpful. Both will make your readers appreciate the quality customer service that your company provides and will convince them to deal with your firm.

In addition to these indirect sales techniques, there are several direct ways to help sell your company's goods and services when responding to requests. For example, if you are sending a potential customer a catalog, include *both* an order blank *and* an addressed envelope to make it easy to place an order. If a customer complains about having had to wait a long time to receive a previous order, take a few minutes to write an apology and an explanation—better yet, tell the customer to write directly to you next time so that you may personally help track down the order. Such "extras" are really techniques for selling.

Can you uncover the indirect selling methods the writer of this letter used?

Dear Mr. Neumann:

Thank you for asking about the service contract for Gorden's Model-X radial-arm saw. We are pleased to share some information with you.

Mr. Neumann, the enclosed booklet includes a list of all the specific items that are covered by our service contract. In fact, it also lists (in equally large print) the few items that are *not* covered in the contract, so that there will be no "surprises" if something should happen to the product; you will know exactly what is covered. The Gorden management insists that we stand behind all our products and that we inform our customers precisely *how* we stand behind our products. By doing so, we avoid the unfortunate experience that you described in your letter.

May I make a suggestion? Because service is such an important factor in your buying decision, I recommend that you ask your local Gorden dealers how they rate the service of two or three of the brand names that they sell. (A list of dealers in your area is enclosed.) Further, I invite you to visit Peter Cleary of Cleary & Sons in Woodmere, which I believe is just a few miles from you. Mr. Cleary has operated an authorized Gorden service center for more than twenty years. Not only will visiting Peter be informative, but this also will give you a chance to meet the person who would service any Gorden product that you own.

Of course, please review the enclosed booklet. Then let me know of any way that we can be helpful. You may call me toll-free at 800-555-9250 whenever you have any questions for us. We would be delighted to be of service.

Sincerely,

Throughout the letter the writer stresses what is most important to the reader — *service.* The writer:

1. Provides a booklet that gives all the details of Gorden's service contract.
2. Subtly *challenges* the reader to visit the Gorden service center nearest his home (a "see for yourself" test).
3. Adds a personal touch by providing him with the name of the local service center manager.
4. Gives the reader a toll-free number, and asks him to call if he has any questions.

As you respond to requests, look for ways in which you can help sell your company's goods or services.

Be Specific

The need to *be specific* is a general rule; it applies, of course, to any letter or memorandum, whether the message is a request, a response to someone's request, or any other type of communication.

When acknowledging receipt of money, for example, cite the exact amount:

We appreciate receiving your check for $1,250 in payment of invoice 17290.

When discussing dates, times, airline flight numbers, or other specific statistics, cite them clearly.

I am delighted to accept your invitation to discuss my career in textile design with your students. It has been a long time since I visited the Design Institute, and I look forward to our discussion on April 28 at 3 p.m. As you suggested, I will bring samples of my newest designs to share with your students.

As I mentioned in our conversation earlier today, I will arrive at LaGuardia at 2:30 p.m. on Monday, July 8, on Northeast Airline flight 741. . . .

When you receive something of value, acknowledge its receipt, including any specific information that is appropriate. Remember that your letter will become part of the reader's files — proof that you received the important package.

Your portfolio of industrial photographs arrived this morning. When Carrie Foster, our art director, returns from vacation next week, she will call you to discuss the prints she has selected for the September issue of *Modern Manufacturing*.

When acknowledging receipt of an order, include the date of the order and the purchase number. Although the reader already knows this information, it is repeated because the letter will be filed for future reference. In addition, mention how the materials will be shipped, when the reader can expect to receive the merchandise, and so on.

We are delighted that you are taking advantage of our annual stock-reduction sale. Your order 575, dated June 20, will be shipped by Reliable Parcel Service this afternoon. As you requested, the merchandise will be delivered to your Central Avenue store.

Be Complete

❏ SUGGESTION
Discuss ways to make sure your responses to requests are complete.

Again, the need to *be complete* is a general rule. Although many writers try to be complete, important information is often omitted because of carelessness.

One way to make sure that your responses are complete is to underline the specific points in the request letter. Another way is to note in the margin each answer to a specific point in the request letter. The underlined points or the marginal notes serve as excellent outlines in writing the reply. For example, when Marion Schaeffer received the letter of inquiry illustrated on page 348, she made marginal notes to make sure that her response, illustrated on page 349, would be *complete*.

One technique that fosters completeness is listing major points item by item. In this follow-up letter, which confirms the various points agreed upon

April 2, 19--

Ms. Marion Schaeffer
Sales Manager
Electrostatic Cleaner Company
896 Kingston Avenue
Chicago, Illinois 60613

Dear Ms. Schaeffer:

I am very much interested in the Electrostatic electronic
air cleaner that was advertised in the March issue of Home
Products. There are some questions I would like answered
about your air cleaner to help me decide whether yours is
the one that best suits my needs.

   1. Under what principle does your air cleaner work? *agglomerate*

   2. Where does the unit have to be mounted? *Vertical, horizontal,*

   3. How often does the collecting cell have to be /8 mos. *underneath*
       washed?

I should appreciate your answering these questions in time
for me to make a decision by May 10.

                    Very truly yours,

                    James A. Daughtrey

                    James A. Daughtrey
                    1783 Lincoln Boulevard
                    Westwood, Virginia 23205

Jotting comments in the margin of a request letter helps the recipient to be thorough in responding.

Electrostatic Cleaner Company 896 Kingston Avenue • Chicago. Illinois 60613

April 24, 19--

Mr. James A. Daughtrey
1783 Lincoln Boulevard
Westwood, Virginia 23205

Dear Mr. Daughtrey:

Thank you for your interest in the Electrostatic electronic air cleaner. I am
delighted to answer the questions you have asked about the model advertised in
Home Products.

    1. This model, FL-190-A, operates on the agglomerator principle. The
dirt particles are charged and collected on the cell plates in the
conventional way, but as they build up on the cell, they "agglomerate" or
break off in chunks, which are easily retained by the special pad on the
clean-air side of the cell. This method of air cleaning, used successfully
for many years in commercial installations, eliminates the need for frequent
washing of the cell.

    2. The unit may be mounted either horizontally or vertically in any
forced-air system, or it may be placed underneath a furnace.

    3. The cell may have to be removed and washed in a good nonsudsing
detergent once every 18 months or so. This procedure will be necessary only
if the cell is especially sticky or greasy.

I am enclosing a folder that describes the unit in more detail, gives price
information, and lists the dealers in your area who carry this model. You
will find that there is no finer air filter on the market, that its
installation is flexible, and that its price is competitive.

Please let us know if you have any further questions.

                              Very sincerely yours,

                              Marion Schaeffer
                              Marion Schaeffer,
                              Sales Manager

rej
Enclosure

By answering the reader's questions in the same order as they appear in the original request, the writer makes
this response more effective.

during a telephone conversation, the writer enumerates five specific items that were covered in the conversation:

Dear Eve:

I am writing to confirm our telephone conversation of this afternoon regarding the first Reyes Stores Celebrity Amateur Golf Tournament. We reached agreement on the following points:

1. Jessica Moran will handle liaison with the charities that will benefit from the tournament's proceeds.
2. You will be responsible for recruiting celebrities to play in the tournament alongside local amateurs.
3. I will coordinate plans with both the Amateur Golfers' Group and the Tappen Hill Golf Club.
4. The tentative date for the tournament is June 23, 19—.
5. A Coordinators' Committee formed of members of Reyes Stores' management will have full charge of financial arrangements for the tournament.

Please let me know if you see the need for any further arrangements. Thanks for your help in organizing this important public-service event.

Cordially,

Be Positive

 **KEY POINT**

Written responses that deny a request require tact and diplomacy.

The need to *be positive* is especially important when handling problem requests. Saying no to people who have applied for credit, who do not qualify for discounts, whose warranties have expired, who have asked for confidential information, who have requested contributions that must be turned down — these situations require extra tact and diplomacy from the writer. Remember: Whatever the cause of the problem, the writer's goal is to keep the reader's goodwill.

To begin, consider the contrast between the statements listed below. Note how the "positive" statements say no without greatly hurting the reader's ego.

Negative	Positive
Your product does not meet our specifications.	Our engineers believe that the brand we selected is closest to our specifications.
You do not meet our standards for this particular job.	Although your qualifications are excellent, we feel that we must continue to search for someone who meets all the unique qualifications for this job.
In view of your poor payment record, we are unable to grant you credit.	We shall be glad to evaluate your credit record after you have settled some of your obligations.

Negative	Positive
We must say "No."	Unfortunately, we cannot say "Yes" at this time.
Your prices are too high.	Perhaps, when you have adjusted your prices to make them more competitive, we shall be able to do business with you.

Note how the above "negative" comments stress *you* while the "positive" comments stress *we*. Always avoid saying "Because of your mistake . . ." or "You failed to . . ." Placing blame on the reader will accomplish nothing. Remember, preserving goodwill toward your company should be your goal in all business writing.

Although it is important to phrase your comments in a positive manner and avoid placing blame, you should not hide behind false statements in refusing a request. If at all possible, try to share with the reader some of the genuine reasons that his or her request is being rejected.

> Layoffs this year have reduced our staff, and as a result our remaining employees' work load has increased.

> As much as we would like to help you with your research project, gathering all the information you requested is beyond our present resources. As you can imagine, Ms. Granger, we simply cannot afford to take so much time away from our usual duties.

Perhaps the most positive aspect of such refusals is to hold out hope for the future.

> Perhaps next year we will be able to . . .

> Of course, we will keep your application on file so that . . .

Once again, remember to put yourself in your reader's place. When you consider your reply *from your reader's perspective*, you will seek creative ways to be positive.

SECTION REVIEW

Practical Application

KEY
See page I-36.

A. Write a letter to Alvarez Office Furniture, 1199 Memorial Boulevard, Des Plaines, Illinois 46043, to order a desk. Before writing the letter, jot down answers to each of the following questions:

Why are you writing?
What kind of desk are you ordering?
How do you want to pay for and receive the desk?

REVIEW cont.

When do you want the desk?
Where do you want the desk delivered?

KEY
See page I-36.

B. Find in magazines or newspapers two advertisements that invite you to write for additional information about goods and services. Write a letter to each company to ask for a catalog, sample, brochure, or other descriptive information.

KEY
See page I-36.

C. Write a letter to the Superintendent of Documents, U.S. Government Printing Office, Washington, D.C. 20402, asking for a list of publications about an occupation that interests you.

KEY
See page I-36.

D. An advertisement for Rainbow Images Copiers has interested you in a new color copier. Write the company asking for the names and addresses of authorized dealers in your area.

KEY
See page I-36.

E. At a meeting of the Consumer Awareness Club, someone proposes subscribing to the periodical *Consumer Reports*, published by Consumers Union, Mount Vernon, New York 10962. One club member has heard that a group of people can subscribe to the magazine and the *Annual Buying Guide* at reduced cost. You volunteer to request information from Consumers Union about group subscriptions. Write the request letter on behalf of the club.

KEY
See page I-36.

F. A valuable century-old lithograph was given to you as a gift. Write the Old Prints Museum requesting its booklet *Care and Preservation of Lithographs*.

KEY
See page I-36.

G. How many ways can you express "please" and "thank you" without using the actual words? Consider yourself *good* if you find five ways; *excellent* if you find eight.

KEY
See page I-37.

H. Steven Crowell, 23 Saltway Drive, Saltway, Florida 33596, requested from your company, Allword Publishing Inc., a copy of your new magazine, *Video Visions*. Demand has exceeded expectations, and the first issue has sold out. Write an appropriate response to Mr. Crowell.

KEY
See page I-37.

I. Gladys Simon, sales manager for Bermuda Beauty Lawn Products, 1132 South Market Avenue, Claremore, Minnesota 54335, has received an order from the Howard House and Garden Shop, 853 Wallace Street, Dearfield, Illinois 62705. The order, dated March 1, is large and is the first received from Howard House and Garden Shop. John Rosetti, the manager of Howard, wants to know the terms of payment and how and when the merchandise is to be shipped. Write Ms. Simon's reply to Mr. Rosetti.

KEY
See page I-37.

J. Alice O'Toole, director of public relations for Advantage Office Systems and Networks, 332 Phillips Avenue, Manchester, New

Hampshire 03110, has telephoned Craig Curtis, chief advertising consultant for New England Best Business Consulting, 212 Crofts Street, Peterborough, New Hampshire 03484, and asked him to make a presentation on "Advertising in the Electronic Age" at the convention of the New England Advertising League. The presentation is to take place on June 24 at the Merrick Hotel in Cambridge, Massachusetts 02138, starting at 4:30 p.m. Mr. Curtis is to make a 40-minute presentation and then participate in a 20-minute discussion period. The meeting will be held in the Peerless Ballroom and will be followed by dinner at 5:30. Mr. Curtis is invited to the dinner as a guest of the Advertising League. Write the letter that Ms. O'Toole should send to Mr. Curtis to confirm all the details of his participation in the convention.

KEY
See page I-37.

K. Mrs. John Fletcher, 2224 Humbolt Street, Akron, Ohio 44313, owner of an Infinite Video Computer Game System, made by Infinite Video, 833 West San Pedro, Mountain View, California 94041, has sent a defective unit to the factory for repair. Unfortunately, there is a shortage of a usually abundant silicon integrated circuit, or "chip," needed to repair the game system. Integrated circuits have been ordered from the manufacturer but are not expected for two weeks. Write a letter explaining the delay and telling Mrs. Fletcher when to expect the return of her repaired unit.

KEY
See page I-38.

L. The Association of Office Managers has asked you to speak at its monthly meeting on January 15. The topic is to be "Streamlining Office Systems." Since you didn't receive the invitation until January 8, you do not think that enough time remains for you to prepare a good speech. Write a note of refusal to the chairperson, Marilyn Novack, 8788 North Filmore, Blacksburg, Virginia 24060.

KEY
See page I-38.

M. You are a new employee in the sales office of a manufacturer of motion picture projectors, screens, and accompanying audio equipment. Your predecessor has been fired, leaving behind a stack of half-finished correspondence. How would you revise the following draft of a letter left in the out-basket?

Ms. Rita D'Amico
1100 Rosemont Drive
Indianapolis, Indiana 46226

Dear Madam:

Your order for a Zapamatic movie outfit has reached us. As manufacturers, we do not deal directly with the buying public. Therefore, we cannot fill your order as requested. Contact Hagen Camera Retailers, 668 Northpoint Street, Indianapolis, Indiana 46221. Let us know how you make out.

Yours truly,

REVIEW cont.

Editing Practice

Using Your Word Processor.   Edit and rewrite the following paragraph, correcting all errors.

KEY
complete
calendar
refrain

Please send me the compleat two-volume set of *Marketing and Distribution.* I understand that for the price of $53.99 I will also receive a one-year subscription to *American Business Today,* along with a callendar for business executives. Please refrane, however, from placing my name on any mailing lists.

KEY
See page I-38.

Updating Correspondence.   Rewrite these excerpts from letters, replacing any dated expressions.

1. The information in your application has been duly noted.
2. We wish to extend our thanks to you for taking the time to complete the questionnaire.
3. I have before me your letter of October 10.
4. Up to the present writing, we have not received your payment for last month.
5. We will be sending the fax card to you under separate cover.
6. I am enclosing an invoice in the amount of $210.98.
7. In the event you will be unable to accept the offer, please advise.
8. I am sending herewith the prospectus for Oakgrove Condominiums, Ltd.

8.3 *WRITING CLAIM AND ADJUSTMENT LETTERS*

OBJECTIVES: After completing Section 8.3, you should be able to:

1. Gather the appropriate facts needed to write a claim letter that is complete and accurate.
2. Evaluate claim letters received and make adjustments based on appropriate considerations.
3. Write effective adjustment letters.

Whether a business is a multinational conglomerate or a small family store, it will have customers who claim that they received fewer items than they ordered; damaged goods; the incorrect size, color, or model; unsatisfactory merchandise; and so on. Each customer's letter must be answered, of course, and each situation must be studied. The business must determine first whether the claim has any merit and then how the merchandise was damaged or why the wrong item was shipped so that the same mistake will not happen again. In many cases an *adjustment* will be made — the customer will receive a full or a partial credit, will be allowed to exchange the merchandise, or will be granted a refund.

Not only will a business *receive* claim letters, but it will also *write* claim letters to its suppliers. The ability to write convincing claim letters and negotiate satisfactory adjustments is a strong business asset. It is essential, therefore, that an effective business communicator be able to write claim and adjustment letters.

WRITING CLAIM LETTERS

The person who writes a claim letter believes, of course, that he or she has been wronged. Indeed, the claim is justified if the writer:

1. Ordered Model R-75 but received Model R-57.
2. Requested 150 booklets but received only 100.
3. Requested size 10 but received size 14.
4. Enclosed full payment but was billed anyway.
5. Specified brand Q but received brand T.

Sometimes, however, the writer *intended* to order brand Q but forgot to specify this particular brand. Or neglected to proofread the order letter or purchase order and did not correct the "100" booklets to "150." Or wrote the check for full payment but did not enclose it. The first step in making a claim, therefore, is to get the facts — *before* you write your claim.

Get the Facts

Before you make a claim, try to find out what happened and why. If part of the order is missing, is there a packing slip that clearly says the rest of the order will be shipped separately? Check your original order to be sure that the "missing" merchandise *was* ordered.

If merchandise was damaged, should you write your claim to the supplier or should you write it to the shipping company? You will be embarrassed if you write a strong letter to the supplier and later discover that the shipping company was at fault — or worse, the shipping department in your own company.

If the wrong merchandise was delivered, check the original order first. Then try to find out if, perhaps, anyone telephoned a change in the order before you write your claim letter.

When you write a claim letter, you should be relying on facts as the basis of your claim. Until you have sufficient facts, do not write the letter. When you do have all the facts, use them to describe the claim completely and accurately.

Describe the Claim Completely and Accurately

It is especially important to be complete and accurate when you are writing a claim letter because in effect you are making an accusation. Both to make a convincing argument and to be fair to the reader, you should present all the facts and you should do so accurately.

Read, for example, the following letter. As you do so, note how the writer cites all the necessary details — size, quantities, times, descriptions, and so on.

Dear Mr. Congdon:

We have received your invoice for twenty-five 100-pound bags of polypropylene resins of injection-molding grade. When we placed this order 17 days ago, we stressed the need for speedy delivery of the resins and were promised delivery within 10 days. Your invoice for 25 bags arrived on the tenth day, but we received none of the resins until the fifteenth day, when we received only 5 bags.

We would appreciate your checking your records to make sure that all the resins have been shipped. If so, please check with the shipping company at once. Our customer desperately needs the items to be made from these resins and is understandably upset that we have not delivered them as promised. We are counting on you to help us make up for lost time.

Please let us know the minute you find out what has happened to this vital shipment of resins. We will hold your invoice until we receive all 25 bags of resins. Then, of course, we will be happy to send payment.

Sincerely yours,

The writer not only tells the reader *everything* that happened concerning the materials that were ordered but does so in chronological order. By giving complete information and delivering it accurately, the writer makes an honest, believable claim.

Let's look at another example of a claim letter that is both complete and accurate.

Dear Ms. Draper:

I was distressed to receive your notice of March 1 indicating that you have canceled my home owner's insurance policy No. AZ1843687 for failure to pay the premium of $350 due on January 15.

On January 4, I mailed check 186 for $350. On January 17, the check, endorsed by your company and stamped "Paid," was returned to me. I reported this information to you on the back of a notice of cancellation mailed to me January 30. Since I received no further word from you, I assumed that the matter had been straightened out satisfactorily.

I am enclosing a photocopy of the front and back of my canceled check. Would you please send me a notice of the reinstatement of my insurance?

Very truly yours,

STUDY   TIP

It is little service to the reader to print windy, dozen-page letters of no quality when a few quoted phrases and a sentence of summary would have conveyed the nature of most of them.

—John Skow

The letter gives *all* the details — completely and accurately — so that the insurance company can quickly correct its error. Note, however, that even though the above letter is filled with facts, it does not accuse, threaten, or demand.

Avoid Accusations, Threats, and Demands

The goal of the claim letter is to get the missing merchandise, to correct the billing error, to return the damaged goods — in other words, to get results, not to blame someone, to threaten, or to demand. For example, assume that the above letter to the insurance company was not answered in a reasonable time. What would you do? Write a threatening letter? Demand that the company send you a formal apology? These are reactions, not solutions. Writing a letter saying "You know very well that I paid my premium" or "You failed to reply" or "I will sue you" would be a waste of time.

Instead, writing a reasonable letter, this time addressed to the president of the agency that handles your insurance, would probably get results:

Dear Mr. Kovacs:

I am enclosing a photocopy of a letter I wrote to your main office on March 5. My letter has not yet been acknowledged, and I am concerned about whether my home owner's insurance is in force.

I should very much appreciate your looking into this matter for me and providing written notification regarding the status of my insurance policy.

Very sincerely yours,

Without threatening, demanding, or accusing, the letter will get results. After all, if you were the president of the agency, would you overlook this letter? The president would obviously understand that the next step is legal action.

Suggest Reasonable Solutions

The opposite of accusing, demanding, or threatening is suggesting reasonable solutions. Remember: Except in rare circumstances, you are dealing with honest business people who have made a mistake *and realize it*. By suggesting reasonable solutions, you strengthen your chance of getting a just settlement quickly. For example, if you placed an order and received only part of it, one solution might be to indicate that you will accept the missing portion if it arrives by a specific date, as shown by the following statement:

We will gladly accept the 25 camping tents if they reach us by May 15, the first day of our Great Outdoors Savings Spectacular.

Or suppose that you were overbilled $100 on an order. In this case, you might say:

Our records indicate that we were billed $650 for the merchandise on our purchase order 3290, dated July 7. The figure should have been $550. Therefore, please credit our account for $100 and send us a credit memorandum for this amount.

It is usually best to suggest the kind of solution that you consider acceptable. If you received defective merchandise, for example, you might request replacement of the merchandise, cancellation of the order, a credit of the amount to your account, or substitution of a similar item that meets your needs. By suggesting a solution, you will let the company know what kind of action you want taken. When your suggestion is reasonable, there is a good chance that the company will follow it.

As you see, then, to make the best claim for your case, you should:

Be sure of the facts.
Describe the claim completely and accurately.
Avoid accusations, threats, and demands.
Suggest reasonable solutions.

EVALUATING CLAIMS AND MAKING ADJUSTMENTS

❏ SUGGESTION
Skill in evaluating claims fairly goes beyond the scope of this text. Use this discussion to provide students with an overview of the kinds of factors that should be considered before writing the adjustment letter.

Several qualities are required to evaluate a claim, determine a fair adjustment, and approve the adjustment: business experience; company authority; familiarity with company policy, industry standards, and consumer laws; and common sense. You are essentially playing the role of judge; but since you have a vested interest in the case, being impartial is even more difficult. Yet an equitable adjustment requires you to be reasonable, fair, honest, and impartial in making your decision.

Making the right decision, therefore, is a difficult task. The sources of evidence that you must weigh are the company, the claimant (the person making the claim), the transaction, and, in some cases, the law. Let's look at each source to see how it influences or affects the final decision.

The Company

Your company, like most other companies, is ethical in its dealings. (You would not want to be associated with a company that is not.) Ask yourself the following questions to determine the extent of your company's responsibility in causing the claim. Do you know, without a doubt, that the company is not at fault? Could anyone in the company have made a misleading statement? Could the advertising be misinterpreted? Could your records be at fault? Is it possible that someone in the company made a mistake? If such questioning reveals an element of blame on the part of the company, you, the adjuster, will probably decide to honor the claim, at least in part.

The Claimant

To help you evaluate the claimant's share in causing the claim, ask questions like these: Could the claimant be mistaken? Is the claim, if true, the kind that a reasonable person would make? Has the claimant provided all the information you need to check the claim and place responsibility for it? Does the claimant have a record of fair dealings with your company? Even if you find that the claimant *is* wrong beyond any doubt, does good business sense tell you that perhaps the claim should be honored anyway?

The Transaction

The answers to the following questions will help you arrive at an equitable decision about the transaction. Did your company carry out all its obligations — both explicit and implied — to the customer? Has your company made any claims with reference to this product such as, "Double your money back if you are not absolutely satisfied"? Were any misleading statements made to the customer by your sales personnel? Is there evidence of faulty materials or workmanship in the product? Were the instructions for use of the product clear and complete? If you find a defect either in the product or in the handling of the transaction, you should decide in favor of the claimant. This correction is just one more application of the almost universal business rule of trying to please the customer.

Sometimes you will have to seek further information before you can answer the above questions. You may need to question some of your coworkers or to write the claimant before you have all the facts at your disposal. The following letter is an example of an inquiry addressed to the claimant.

Dear Mrs. Parker:

Thank you for your October 17 letter reporting a malfunction of your Healthguard water purifier. We are sorry that you are having problems with the purifier, a product that is usually quite reliable.

We have looked in vain for a copy of your warranty agreement, which should be on file here. The period of the warranty is normally one year. If you could send us the number from the top right corner of your receipt, we could date the purchase. If you do not have the receipt, then please give us the name of the dealer from whom you made the purchase and the approximate date of purchase.

As soon as we receive the information, we will be happy to make an adjustment.

Sincerely yours,

When you receive the necessary information, you will be able to make an equitable decision on the claim.

 **REINFORCEMENT**
Stress the need to get the required approvals. Once on the job, students will need to be very careful about what they say in all letters and will need to develop a sense for what may be legally dangerous to the company.

The Law

In some cases, there may be laws that will affect your decision. Laws intended to protect consumers, for example, allow a consumer to cancel certain contracts within three days "without penalty or obligation." State or local laws may apply in special situations in your industry.

In any case, you should realize that there are potential legal problems in some situations. Although you now know that you should not threaten when making a claim, many writers will threaten you with legal action in their first claim letters just because they believe that making such threats will get results. Does your company have a policy that requires all employees to notify the Legal Department any time there is a possibility of a lawsuit? Whether it has such a policy or not, you *should* notify someone in authority (perhaps your supervisor *and* the Legal Department) whenever a lawsuit is even remotely possible.

WRITING ADJUSTMENT LETTERS

After probing all the sources of evidence and reviewing all the facts in a claim, you may determine that (1) the claim is indeed allowable, (2) the claim is only partially allowable, or (3) the claim is not allowable. Now comes the task of using your writing skill to respond to a claim letter with an adjustment letter.

An Allowable Claim

Mistakes occur in every business. What separates a well-run business from a poorly run business is not simply a matter of *whether* the company makes mistakes but *how it handles* its mistakes.

Question: What do you do when the error is yours? Answer: Admit that it was your fault, without quibbling or trying to avoid responsibility. Note the following letter:

Dear Dr. Hargrove:

Thank you for your December 9 letter reporting a problem with your new barometer.

From your description of the problem, we believe that your aneroid barometer was mistakenly calibrated for use as an altimeter. We manufacture altimeters and aneroid barometers using the same mechanism—only the calibrations are different. Somehow our normally efficient production staff and inspectors must have placed the wrong model number and name plate on the mechanism that you received. We are reviewing our procedures in an effort to prevent this kind of mistake from happening again.

We are very sorry for our mistake, and we have shipped you a new barometer by airfreight. We hope our error did not spoil any of your weather forecasts.

If we can be of further assistance to you, Dr. Hargrove, please don't hesitate to write or call.

Sincerely yours,

The writer obviously admits the error without quibbling and certainly strives to keep the customer's goodwill. In an effort to maintain goodwill, in fact, some companies will even grant doubtful claims if the costs are not exorbitant. In this way they develop excellent reputations among their customers and gain new business.

A Partially Allowable Claim

Allowing a claim is rather easy. Slightly more difficult is reaching a compromise with a claimant. For instance, if the transaction involves a heavy piece of equipment worth $10,000, the manufacturer will probably be reluctant to exchange the equipment and pay for double shipping charges besides. Yet that may be what the claimant asks for.

Suppose, for example, that a recent purchaser of a commercial automatic film processor wants to exchange the processor. The customer states that the processor is unsatisfactory because the developed film comes out wet instead of dry. You feel certain that the problem is caused by failure of the small fan under the drying hood. Replacement of the fan will take one of your technicians ten minutes and cost you only $25. Exchanging the entire processor, which weighs 200 pounds and is valued at $9,000, will be expensive because of shipping costs. Moreover, the customer will have to wait at least three weeks for a new processor. You decide to seek a compromise adjustment.

How much of an adjustment a company makes in a case like this depends on company policy. You believe that the customer will be satisfied with the processor after the fan is replaced. You are also willing to offer the customer a $100 discount toward the purchase price as compensation for the inconvenience caused by the failure of the fan. Your letter describing this proposed adjustment might read as follows:

Dear Ms. Solfano:

We very much regret that your new SuperSpool Rapid Film Processor is not working properly. The problem sounds to us as if the fan under the drying hood is at fault. Although we thoroughly test each processor before it leaves our plant, the machines are sometimes damaged by rough handling in transit.

Exchanging your processor for a new one would require subjecting another unit to the hazards of shipping. In addition, you would be without a processor for at least three weeks. We seriously question the wisdom of exchanging the entire unit when only one small component is the cause of all the trouble.

We realize that the fan's failure has inconvenienced you, Ms. Solfano, and we want you to be satisfied with our products and our service. We believe that the following adjustment is a fair one. We can send a service technician to your plant with a new drying fan. Replacement of the defective fan should take only ten minutes, and you can test the processor immediately to make sure that everything is working properly. In addition, we have enclosed a $100 discount certificate.

If this adjustment is satisfactory, please call our service center at 555-2243 to make an appointment at your convenience. We will make sure that someone answers your call promptly.

We are also confident that your SuperSpool Rapid Film Processor will provide good service for years to come.

Sincerely yours,

The writer is trying to reach a fair settlement with the customer. Nonetheless, Ms. Solfano may reply by asking to be compensated for all the film wasted as a result of the fan's failure.

A Nonallowable Claim

❑SUGGESTION

Point out that in an effective letter, the writer is never defensive.

Although a business may strive to satisfy its customers and may have the easiest claim policy in its industry, it will encounter situations in which claims simply cannot be allowed. One customer, for example, may try to return a perfectly good lamp that he ordered simply because he no longer wants that style. Another customer may wrongly insist that she ordered merchandise before a price increase. If the business granted such claims once, of course, it would set a dangerous precedent. Besides, it would be poor business to do so. Whatever the reason, the company is faced with the uncomfortable but necessary task of saying no to a customer.

Assume, for example, that you are employed by Essex Distribution Company, a computer products wholesaler. Last month you featured a special offer on the complete Epic Model KL computer system. In your mailer to dealers, you specifically stated that you are discounting your current inventory of the KL model by 30 percent "to make room for new inventory." Many dealers took advantage of the superb discount offer. You specifically stated in the mailer that this sale was a "clearance sale" and that no returns would be permitted.

Patrice Clemente, manager of the Metropolitan Computer Center, purchased 50 of the Epic KL systems, sold 20, and then asked permission to return the remaining 30 systems. Because Metropolitan is a good customer, in the past you have "bent the rules" to allow Ms. Clemente special return privileges for unsold merchandise. However, you simply cannot accept the 30 Model KL systems. You must write to Ms. Clemente to tell her this, but you must also try to retain her goodwill—and her future business. To do so, perhaps you would send the following letter:

Dear Ms. Clemente:

Thank you for complimenting us on our special offers on the top brand names in computers. We at Essex pride ourselves on being the number-one computer distributor in the state, and we sincerely appreciate having the opportunity to do business with the number-one computer store in the state, Metropolitan Computer Center.

As you know, Ms. Clemente, no other distributor has offered such a drastic discount on Epic computers as our recent 30 percent discount. We did so, frankly, because we were forced to make room for new inventory, and to do so, we simply had to clear our stock at the time of the special sale. That's why we specifically stated that the sale was on a no-return basis. I'm sure that you, too, have been faced with similar situations.

As much as we would like to help you, we really cannot accept a return of 30 Epic KL systems. For one reason, we now have on order more than 500 of the new Epic XP system. As you can imagine, these 500 systems will take up much warehouse space as well as inventory dollars. We are also increasing our inventory of other major brands so that we can continue to deliver to dealers like Metropolitan all computer merchandise in the minimum amount of time. By serving you better, of course, we help you to serve *your* customers better.

May I make a suggestion? A few days ago Bill Kline of Computer World (in the Warren Mall) was eager to get more Epic Model KL systems. Perhaps you can arrange to sell your stock to Mr. Kline. Of course, if I should hear of any other dealers who are looking for Epic KLs, I will be sure to call you.

By the way, let me give you some "advance notice" of a special sale we are planning for next month. We will be offering the popular Speedex disk drive for only $125 and the Lark 2400 modem for only $195!

Sincerely yours,

Although the reply is obviously "no," the letter:

1. Has a positive tone throughout.
2. Acknowledges Ms. Clemente's claim courteously.
3. Explains specifically why the claim cannot be granted and cites reasons.
4. Suggests a possible solution for clearing her excess stock.
5. Maintains the customer's goodwill by giving her advance notice of an upcoming sale and by showing appreciation for her business.

SECTION REVIEW

Practical Application

KEY
See page I-39.

A. The City-Wide Newspaper Delivery Service, 322 Oxford Street, Detroit, Michigan 48226, has billed you for a month's delivery of both daily and Sunday newspapers. You ordered only the daily newspaper, however, and that is all you received. The delivery service has charged you $7.20 for 24 issues of the daily newspaper and $3.40 for 4 issues of the Sunday newspaper. For an adjustment to your bill, write to Benjamin Davis, the customer service representative for the City-Wide Newspaper Delivery Service.

KEY
See page I-39.

B. Benjamin Davis receives your letter seeking an adjustment to your monthly bill (see A above). His records confirm your claim that you ordered and received only daily newspapers. Compose the adjustment letter that Mr. Davis should send in response to your claim.

KEY
See page I-39.

C. Review the letter of adjustment addressed to Ms. Solfano (page 361) concerning the problem film processor. Assume that Ms. Solfano is not satisfied with your offer to replace the fan and to give her a $100 discount. Instead, Ms. Solfano agrees to accept replacement of the fan, but she also wants full compensation for all film wasted as a result of the defective fan. You decide to write Ms. Solfano offering to send a claims adjuster to her photography business to examine the wasted film and determine its value. But you also decide not to commit yourself at this point to pay for all film wasted. Write the letter.

KEY
See page I-40.

D. After visiting Ms. Solfano's photography business (see C above), your adjuster tells you that five 100-foot rolls of 12-inch-wide film were ruined because the fan failed. Since the film is valued at $.50 per foot, the cost of the film wasted is $250. Your adjuster says that the fan is definitely the immediate cause of the wastage. The adjuster adds, however, that Ms. Solfano should have stopped running the processor and called for service after the first roll or two of film were ruined. Decide how much compensation Ms. Solfano is entitled to, and write a letter to her either accepting or denying her claim to compensation for all 500 feet of wasted film.

KEY
See page I-40.

E. Write a letter for William Roland, the manager of Le Crépuscule, a French restaurant located at 665 Darien Street, Omaha, Nebraska 68108. Today Mr. Roland has received a new, heavy-duty commercial food processor, but his chef shows him that it does not slice foods as precisely as advertised. Write the manufacturer, Whirling Wonder Kitchen Co., One Bluegrass Way, Lexington, Kentucky 40506, requesting replacement of the food processor.

KEY
See page I-40.

F. You work in the Claims and Adjustments Department of Whirling Wonder Kitchen Co. You receive a letter from the manager of Le Crépuscule (see E above) requesting replacement of a food processor that is not slicing evenly. You know from experience that uneven slices usually result from a damaged slicing disk. Write Mr. Roland, the manager of Le Crépuscule. First, ask whether the food processor performs correctly with other attachments, such as the two-bladed knife and the shredding disk. Explain that if the machine does correctly dice, chop, grate, grind, and shred, the problem is definitely the damaged slicing disk. Offer to replace the slicing disk at no cost if this is the problem.

Editing Practice

KEY
See page I-40.

Applied Psychology. Rewrite the following sentences so that each promotes goodwill.

1. There is no chance that we can deliver your order on time because many smarter consumers placed their orders before you.
2. Because you were careless and forgot to write your taxpayer's identification number on the form, we are returning it to you.
3. You must be too lazy to open your mail, because we have already written you once about this matter.

REVIEW cont.

4. Your October 3 letter fails to explain satisfactorily your delay in paying.
5. Your inability to operate computer equipment means that we will have to send a technician to your office.
6. We will repair the cabinet that you claim was damaged in transit.
7. You are the only person who ever found our sunscreen product unsatisfactory.
8. You neglected to send us the sales receipt for your stolen watch when you filed your claim.
9. You complained that order 977 did not arrive on time.
10. You made a mistake of $27 on our March 15 invoice.

8.4 *WRITING PERSUASIVE LETTERS*

OBJECTIVES: After completing Section 8.4, you should be able to:

1. Explain why sales letters can be more effective than radio or television commercials.
2. Explain the value of knowing the target audience when writing sales letters.
3. List the five objectives of sales letters.
4. Describe the various approaches needed when writing collection letters.

We may live in the age of electronics, but traditional sales letters remain an important tool of modern business. Next to the face-to-face visit of a sales representative, sales and other persuasive letters represent the most effective direct contact a business can have with the customer. You should know the guidelines for writing sales letters, because most business letters are really sales letters written to promote the sales of goods or services.

WRITING SALES LETTERS

Businesses spend millions of dollars on sales letters every year because letters have two major advantages over radio or television advertisements.

KEY POINT

Sales letters have two major advantages over radio and television advertisements: (1) Letters can be read and reread, and (2) Letters can be more direct and personal than mass media commercials.

First, letters give recipients something they can put their hands on and see or read more than once. Second, letters, which are sent to a carefully selected audience, can be more direct and personal than commercials, which are produced for a mass audience.

Targeting Audiences

Think about the sales letters you receive. They range from offers to sell magazines or insurance to invitations to collect a free prize when you visit a time-share condo in your area. Do you think that everyone on your street or in your town gets the same sales letters that you do? You might be surprised to learn that marketing specialists make a living by choosing very select target audiences for different products and services. A target audience is a group of potential customers chosen on the basis of certain characteristics such as age, geographic location, income, or lifestyle.

If the new product, for example, is construction equipment, the target audience will be contractors who might be able to use such equipment. If the product is a new line of children's clothing, the target audience will be families with young children. Of course, finding the target audience is not always as easy as in the two preceding examples. Companies that want to sell a new product for businesses, such as a color laser printer, may have to do extensive research to determine the best target audience.

When the target audience for a product is the general public, the challenge facing the market researchers and writers of sales letters is to determine which of the following buying motives most likely will appeal to the readers.

Understanding Buying Motives

Identifying Wants and Needs. In general, people buy products and services to satisfy specific needs and wants. People's needs are, of course, vital but relatively few: food, shelter, clothing, and perhaps transportation. People's wants, by contrast, are endless. People want not just any food, but delicious food; not just any shelter, but a comfortable apartment or house; not just any clothes, but the latest fashions. Most people also want security, status, the approval of others, health, personal attractiveness, conveniences (such as microwave ovens and garage door openers), and various forms of recreation and entertainment.

While people are usually aware of their wants in a general way, they may not know how a new product or service would fulfill any of those wants. The job of a sales letter writer, therefore, is to convince people that a specific product or service will satisfy one or more of their wants.

Satisfying Wants and Needs. To make readers interested in a product or service, a sales letter writer must show how purchasing the item will provide the readers with prestige, good health, fun, beauty, savings, romance, freedom from drudgery, and so on. For example, the following list indicates the kinds of personal wants and needs that can be satisfied by the products and services shown.

❑SUGGESTION

Ask students to read articles on how companies target audiences.

❑SUGGESTION

Help students distinguish between needs and wants.

Product or Service	Want or Need
Central air conditioning	Comfort
Stocks and bonds	Profit
Insulation	Savings, comfort
Microwave oven	Convenience
Toothpaste	Health and attractiveness
Home swimming pool	Recreation
Outdoor lighting	Security
Hair color	Personal attractiveness
Ice cream	Eating pleasure
Charitable contributions	Self-esteem
Pizza delivery	Convenience
Fast sports car	Prestige

OBJECTIVES OF SALES LETTERS

After identifying the target audience's motives for buying a particular product or service, the writer proceeds to write the sales letter. Keep in mind, however, that there is no standard formula for all sales letters. They can vary in length, organization, and content. However, an effective sales letter generally accomplishes the following five objectives.

1. Attract the reader's attention.
2. Establish a close relationship with the reader.
3. Appeal to one or more specific buying motives.
4. Persuade the reader to act.
5. Give the reader an opportunity to act.

Attracting Attention

A sales letter must immediately attract favorable attention. The appearance of a sales letter often makes the difference between whether it is read or tossed into the wastebasket. Because appearance starts with the envelope, sales letters often come in envelopes that promise big prizes, valuable certificates, and great savings inside. Recently, creative advertisement writers have taken advantage of computers to add personalized attention-getting questions to envelopes—such as the example shown below: "What would you do, Melba Jones, with a million dollars?" Many readers would react by opening the envelope to see what they have to do to get a million dollars.

Once a reader opens the envelope, other factors come into play. For example, heavy-stock stationery and an engraved letterhead give an appearance of importance or the facsimile of a telegram gives the appearance of urgency. An enclosed free sample is another good way to get a reader's attention.

Establishing Familiarity

To keep the sales prospect reading, the writer needs to establish a familiar tone with the reader. One way to achieve this goal is to refer to the reader as

Magazines, Inc.
2389 Lexington Avenue
New York, NY 10001

What would you do,
Melba Jones, with a
million dollars?

```
Ms. Melba Jones
347 Beacon Street
Winchester, MA 01890
```

Word-processing equipment makes it easy to add a personalized question on the envelope to attract the attention of the reader.

you as often as possible. Another good device for establishing a mood of familiarity is to start the letter with a rhetorical question. If you combine these two techniques, you might come up with an opening sentence such as the following.

Isn't it time you took a really good photograph?

or

Would you like to lose 5 pounds in a week?

Other techniques that can be used in the first paragraph to establish a familiar tone with the reader include (1) using imperative sentences; (2) using informal punctuation such as dashes, exclamation points, underscores, ellipses, and parentheses; (3) using contractions; (4) using short, informal sentences; (5) repeating the reader's name in the letter; and (6) complimenting the reader. The sentences that follow are additional opening lines that illustrate these techniques.

Opening	Product or Service
Protect your family with Burglar Beware.	Security system
Now! Do it . . . don't wait a minute longer. Health — happiness — fitness: they're all yours at Exercise World!	Fitness Club
Mr. and Mrs. Engles, don't you want your child to get better than average grades?	Encyclopedias

Music Clubs of America

6877 56th Street ★ Newington, CT 06111

Mr. Roy Hamilton
87 Timber Creek Road
Hendersonville, NC 28739

Dear Mr. Hamilton:

Did you know that . . .

> . . . psychologists claim that people who listen to
> music "get more out of life"?

> . . . lovers of music control stressful situations
> better than people who do not listen to music?

> . . . listening to good music is considered one of
> the least expensive yet most highly rewarding
> pleasures?

Yes, you probably knew these facts, Mr. Hamilton,
because you have purchased several CDs of popular music in
the past year. For you and all the other people who
appreciate popular music, we have assembled more than a
thousand of the top tunes from the '50s and '60s and
packaged them in two long-playing CDs--all of the highest
quality and all played by the original artists. The price
of each CD? A remarkable $25.25.

That's right. For only $25.25 you can own both CDs
described on the enclosed brochure. If this offer sounds
as if it is an exceptional opportunity to add to your
collection or to purchase superb gifts for friends--well,
you're right . . .

Does the enclosed brochure include the favorite
songs you love but seldom hear? Probably. But don't look
too long because we expect our limited supply to be
depleted very, very quickly.

We won't say any more because we know that the
brochure--and the $25.25 price--will sell these fantastic
CDs for us. To reserve one or more sets, just check the
appropriate box on the enclosed return card and mail it to
us. That's all you have to do. We will bill you later.

Sincerely,

Edward Hoey

Edward Hoey
President,
Music Clubs of America

The sales letter makes the reader's response to the offer very easy. All he needs to do is check his selections; his name and address are already printed on the postage-paid return card.

Appealing to Buying Motives

Now comes the time for the writers of sales letters to take advantage of market research and other knowledge about the target audience of the sales letter. They need to make a connection between the features of the product or service and the presumed buying motives of the reader. The goal, of course, is to induce the reader to buy. Incentives to buy are called *sales appeals*, and they are the main act of the sales letter. Keep in mind, therefore, that the envelope, the stationery, and the opening line only set the stage. Notice how the following excerpts use sales appeals to stimulate the reader's buying motives.

Sales Appeal	Buying Motive
Your family will ask for more each time you serve Grandma's Best macaroni and cheese.	Family approval
You can get twice the work done in half the time if your employees use Famous Maker computers.	Convenience and economy
You can relive all your happy moments time and time again if you catch them with a Video-Play camcorder.	Enjoyment
Don't drive just any car. Drive a car that people will notice. Drive an elegant Tempest Turbo-Supreme!	Personal status

The sales appeal brings the reader to the point of wanting to buy a product. The writer must then nudge the reader just a little further by persuading that person to act on his or her desire to buy.

Persuading Someone to Act

To increase the pressure on the reader to say "Yes, I want to buy this!" the writer often uses the techniques that help develop a close relationship between writer and reader. The most effective of these techniques is the rhetorical question. Although a sales letter may contain several rhetorical questions at various points, a question can be used most effectively after the sales appeal. For example, after the virtues of the product have been described and the sales appeal has been made, imagine how effective questions such as the following could be.

Do pressures, deadlines, and difficult people leave you feeling frazzled?

Are your fuel bills too high?

Would you like to be free from back pain?

After answering "Yes" to rhetorical questions like these, readers are as ready to act as they will ever be. The writer's job, however, is still not over.

Providing the Opportunity to Act

What happens if the reader feels the urge to buy but all the stores are closed? If the reader has to wait too long, probably the urge to buy will lessen. Therefore, writers of sales letters include at least one of the following opportunities for the reader to act immediately.

1. Enclose a postage-paid reply card.
2. Include order forms.
3. Provide coupons.
4. List a toll-free, 24-hour telephone number.

The sample letter on page 369 tells the reader simply to "check the appropriate box on the enclosed return card and mail it to us. That's all you must do. We will bill you later."

The Sales Letter Campaign

A series of sales letters is sometimes written to prospective customers — particularly to sell high-priced items. In fact, as many as eight letters may be sent, depending on the nature of the product, its cost, and the nature of the market. Professional writers might use a different appeal in each follow-up letter, in the hope that one of the appeals might ultimately persuade the reader to take action to buy the product or service. Usually the letters are spaced about ten days apart and are kept relatively short.

WRITING CREDIT AND COLLECTION LETTERS

KEY POINT
The goal of credit and collection letters is to get customers to pay their bills without damaging the goodwill relationship between the customer and the company.

KEY POINT
Guidelines for maintaining goodwill in credit and collection procedures are as follows: Make sure customers understand credit terms; assume customers will pay; send additional reminders and follow-up letters.

Another type of persuasive letter is the collection letter, a letter in which a company reminds certain customers that they have not paid their bills. Collecting an overdue account, of course, is not an easy task because no one likes to ask for money. Yet businesses must ask — or lose money. The goal, therefore, is to get customers to pay without losing their goodwill. You can achieve this goal by adhering to the following guidelines.

Making Sure Customers Understand Credit Terms

The terms of credit should always be explained to the customer at the time credit is granted. In fact, the law requires such explanation. In commercial credit (between wholesaler and retailer), it is also advisable to review credit terms pleasantly, but firmly, when acknowledging a customer's first order. If the terms are 30 days net, then expect your money in 30 days and do not hedge with weak statements like "We hope you will send your check in 30 days." Instead, say, "Our terms are 2 percent discount if you pay within 10 days; the net amount is due in 30 days."

FB

FOX BROTHERS CLOTHIERS

894 SW 90TH STREET
PLANTATION, FLORIDA 33317

Just a reminder . . .

Have you overlooked sending us your monthly payment for
your charge account at Fox Brothers Clothiers?

Your payment for the amount due below will be greatly
appreciated. If you have already mailed it, please ignore
this reminder.

        Credit Account: 345-872
        Amount due: $250.56
        Minimum due: $25.98

This impersonal printed form is a gentle reminder that an account is overdue.

KEY
See page I-41.

Assuming Customers Will Pay

When a customer first fails to pay a bill on time, it is wise to assume that this failure is an oversight. Therefore, if the usual monthly statement does not produce results, companies often send the customer a second statement a week or ten days later. Sometimes this second statement is stamped "First Reminder" or "Please Remit." Some credit departments even use humorous reminders — such as the imprint of a rubber stamp of a drawing of a finger with a string tied around it. Others use impersonal printed forms such as the one shown on page 372.

Most customers will respond to gentle hints that their accounts are overdue. Remember, therefore, that the first reminder should never be an attack. Rather, it should be a highly impersonal nudge.

Sending Additional Reminders and Follow-up Letters

If there is no payment after a second statement and a reminder, most companies will send a series of three to five follow-up letters before turning the account over to a lawyer or a collection agency.

In a five-letter follow-up series, the first follow-up letter, though clear and firm, should still give the customer the benefit of the doubt. The second letter, which should be mailed no later than 15 days after the first letter, should remain friendly and courteous but should be firmer and more insistent than the first. The third letter should be even more insistent and forceful, and the fourth letter should demand payment. The fifth letter, then, should state what legal action will be taken if the delinquent customer fails to take advantage of this last opportunity to pay. The goal of this last letter, of course, is to scare the reader into paying the bill in order to avoid legal action.

SECTION

REVIEW

Practical Application

A. (1) What two advantages do sales letters have over radio or television commercials?
    (2) Define the term *target audience.*

B. (1) List the five objectives of sales letters.
    (2) Name some ways that prospective buyers can act immediately after they finish reading a sales letter.

C. Identify three rules for writing collection letters.

D. After looking through magazines, newspapers, catalogs, and sales letters that you have received, list at least ten different types of sales appeals you find. Prepare your list under these three headings: (1) Type of Product, (2) Trade Name, and (3) Sales Appeal.

E. Write a sales letter — including an attention-getting envelope — that asks young married couples to buy a mobile home. Be sure to

REVIEW cont.

attract the readers' attention, set up a close relationship, appeal to a specific buying motive, persuade the readers to act, and give them an opportunity to act.

Editing Practice

KEY
See page I-42.

Promoting Good Public Relations. Rewrite the following excerpts so that they will be more diplomatic.

1. You claim that your VCR was not tested after it was repaired.
2. Why would we deliver the furniture free if you have never bought anything from us before and may never buy anything from us again?
3. Because you didn't include your warranty number, we won't repair your CD player.
4. Don't expect a discount if you don't remember to include your coupons.
5. If you don't pay your bill immediately, you'll be sorry.

8.5 *WRITING PUBLIC RELATIONS LETTERS*

OBJECTIVES: After completing Section 8.5, you should be able to:

1. Write a letter effectively promoting a new business.
2. Write a letter encouraging charge account use.
3. Apply general public relations techniques to the writing of routine business letters.

Public relations is concerned with the business of influencing the public's feeling or attitude toward a company or an organization. Business and industry spend many millions of dollars a year on magazine and newspaper advertisements, radio and TV commercials, billboard signs, cards, posters, and letters intended not only to sell a specific product but also to promote good public relations. Favorable public relations with a business means that the public has a positive opinion of the company or organization; unfavorable public relations, a negative opinion.

Major corporations have public relations departments that specialize in creating favorable images of their firms and minimizing the negative impact when their firms get "bad press." You may not work in the Public Relations Department; however, as an employee, you will certainly affect your company's public image.

Question: When will you have an opportunity to influence public opinion about your company? Answer: Whenever you communicate with the public as a representative of your company — when you talk with or write to anyone outside the company, you have an opportunity to affect the public's attitude toward your firm. Your communication skills, therefore, can contribute to your firm's favorable public image, as you will see in this section.

SPECIAL PUBLIC RELATIONS OPPORTUNITIES

❑ SUGGESTION

Help students see that public relations letters and advertisements are intended to help sales without specifying particular products. Thus there is an ulterior motive to public relations advertisements and letters because they attempt to sell indirectly. Ask students to cite popular public relations advertisements they have seen.

You have seen signs that say, for example, "Working Hard to Keep You and Your Family Safe . . . COLUMBO SMOKE DETECTORS." This sign is not designed specifically to sell Columbo's Model 121-E smoke detector or to sell Columbo's line of products but to promote the Columbo Company in general. The ad is designed to convince you that the Columbo Company has your safety in mind. Why? So that when you *do* shop for smoke detectors, you will (subconsciously or otherwise) select Columbo — a name you can trust.

The PR specialist looks for opportunities to show the company in the best possible light. When an employee receives a commendation from his or her community for civic work, the company might send a press release to various newspapers to share this good news with the public. The good civic work of one of its employees helps to enhance the firm's image. On the other hand, the PR specialist tries to minimize anything the public could interpret in a negative way. For instance, if a store is expanding, the noise and dust of the construction work may irritate passersby. The PR specialist may place sidewalk signs, such as the one illustrated on page 376, in key locations for passersby to see. Reason: To explain and apologize for the temporary mess and show that the store shares its neighbors' concerns about the noise and dust.

Unfavorable public opinion can ruin a firm. If a newspaper report states or implies that the All-Natural Breads Company uses chemical preservatives and artificial coloring despite claims that their breads contain only natural ingredients, public opinion of that company will certainly drop — even if the report is later proved false. Consumers who remember the negative report may start buying another brand if they doubt the integrity of the company.

Knowing the benefits of good public relations, all businesses strive to create — and to keep — a favorable image of their organizations in the eyes of the public. An oil company may televise a short film showing the public that the company strives to protect the environment wherever it drills for oil. A well-known, reputable person may narrate the film to lend it additional credibility. At no time does the narrator say "Buy your oil and gas from _____." Instead, the narrator points out all the beneficial things the company is doing for the public.

To help build a favorable image of Kale's among its neighbors and its customers, the store places signs at key locations for passersby to see.

Here are some specific situations in which public relations specialists seek to influence public opinion.

1. A commuter bus company is operating at a deficit. Although fares have increased 200 percent in the past five years, the company is still losing money and must ask for another increase. Of course, the bus company is sensitive to the opinions of its customers; it needs their understanding and their support. The PR department of the company may place advertisements in newspapers, may purchase radio time, may issue circulars to riders, and may write letters to leading citizens in order to explain why fares must be raised.

2. A private water main on the grounds of a manufacturing plant bursts, submerging a low stretch of a nearby public road in two feet of water. The company provides a detour road on its own grounds, posts large signs with directions to drivers, apologizes to the community, and employs someone to direct traffic until repairs are complete. In addition, the company publishes apologetic letters in the local newspapers, explaining how the accident happened and what steps are being taken to prevent a recurrence.

3. The president of the utility company that provides electricity to customers in a large metropolitan area publishes a full-page letter in several newspapers apologizing for the recent disruptions in service. The letter also states that plans for modernizing a major power plant are under way and that the pass-along fuel tax currently charged on customers' bills has been eliminated.

4. A large public school system plans to use modular scheduling in all its schools starting next fall. A news release is issued to newspapers, and a letter is written to parents and to various civic organizations to inform the public of this new development.

5. A university hospital has received a large endowment. In recognition and appreciation, the administration renames one of the hospital's pavilions

after its benefactor. The hospital's PR director writes to alumni and members of the medical profession to announce the gift and the new name of the pavilion. In addition, a press release is issued to the newspapers.

6. A consumer protection agency spokeswoman announces that several accidents have been caused by defective XYZ-77 tires. The XYZ Corporation prepares a news release helping customers to identify the tires in question and outlining how they may then be checked or replaced. In addition, XYZ writes to its retailers and to all customers who have bought its "77" model tire.

The public relations specialist tries to win friends and customers when faced with the opportunity to:

Promote a new business.
Invite someone to open a charge account.
Announce a special privilege or service to preferred customers.
Offer special incentives to encourage charge customers to use their credit cards.
Welcome new residents (new *potential customers*) to the community.
Congratulate someone for a special achievement.
Invite someone to a lecture, art show, demonstration, or film.
Wish customers a healthy, prosperous New Year.
Thank someone for his or her business.

Let's take a closer look at some of these special PR opportunities.

Promoting a New Business

To promote a new business, the first step toward establishing good public opinion is to announce the grand opening — for example, in a letter such as this one:

May we introduce you to —

Constance Devane

chef and managing partner of Maple Grove's newest and most exciting restaurant:

A SPLENDID AFFAIR

Chef Devane, a graduate of the American Culinary Arts Institute and author of two best-selling cookbooks, has practiced her culinary magic in several fine restaurants in New York City and Boston. *Good Food Magazine* has hailed Constance Devane as "one of America's most creative young chefs."

Dining at A Splendid Affair is the ultimate dining experience. Surrounded by understated elegance, you and your guests will be attended by a well-trained staff who will describe in mouth-watering detail the tempting appetizers, entrees, and desserts that Chef Devane and her staff will prepare for you.

Reservations are necessary, and all major credit cards are accepted. A smaller dining room is reserved for our guests who smoke so that our nonsmoking guests can dine in a smoke-free atmosphere.

Join us at A Splendid Affair for a relaxed evening of fine dining and unmatched service.

Cordially,

This letter alone, however, is only one step in a PR campaign. To effectively promote this grand opening requires newspaper ads, spot announcements on local radio stations, circulars, and press releases, all focused on the general theme and tone of this letter. Together, these messages make up a PR campaign that will surely reach the potential diners who live or work in the Maple Grove area.

Then, to continue the campaign, the general manager of A Splendid Affair would send a thank-you letter to each diner who signed the guest book. Note how this follow-up letter continues to build on the image of A Splendid Affair as offering a unique dining experience.

Dear _____:

It was our pleasure to have you dine with us this week. Chef Devane and the staff at A Splendid Affair hope that you will be our guest again soon.

Although reservations are required, the management makes exceptions for our patrons who wish to entertain unexpected visitors or business clients from out of town. We believe that A Splendid Affair is the perfect setting to seal an important personal or business relationship or to celebrate a special occasion.

We promise to provide you and your guests with the finest food and service every time you dine with us at A Splendid Affair.

Cordially,

To continue the momentum, soon after its grand opening the general manager of A Splendid Affair might send each patron a printed card announcing a change in serving hours and a special fixed-price menu. The card might be phrased as follows:

We are pleased to announce that A Splendid Affair is now open from 12 noon until 2 P.M. on weekdays to serve lunch to you and your guests. Chef Devane will oversee the preparation of luncheon dishes to delight your discerning palate.

During the evening hours, we now offer a fixed-price complete dinner menu in addition to our à la carte menu of different specialties each evening.

Be our guest for lunch at A Splendid Affair, and in the evening dine sumptuously on five- or seven-course meals Chef Devane has created for our new fixed-price menu.

Through these PR communications, A Splendid Affair seizes every opportunity to put its name before potential customers in a favorable light.

Encouraging Charge Account Use

Because so many sales today are charge account sales, public relations is often employed to increase credit card use. The end result of increased credit card use is, of course, sales.

One obvious step toward increasing credit card use is to invite cash customers to open a charge account. The invitation letter will include, of course, an application form. From time to time, the store may have employees distribute applications to customers.

Another way to increase credit card use through public relations letters is to create a special occasion "for charge card customers only." Because charge customers usually buy more than cash customers and return to the store again and again, it is to the store's advantage to develop a sale exclusively for charge customers. Note the following letter:

Dear Mrs. Daly:

You are invited to a special courtesy shopping day at Bender's next Friday, August 5. As a valued charge customer, you will enjoy double privileges. In the splendor of the Tropical Promenade on the fourth floor, you will sip complimentary refreshments while you see a preview of the latest fall fashions. You will also be entitled to make purchases in every department at special bonus savings not advertised to the public.

The fashions to be modeled will not be placed on our selling floors until August 19. We want you, a valued charge customer of Bender's, to have first choice. Your Bender Charge Card is your ticket to this spectacular shopping event. Tell your friends about this exclusive event if you must—but please come alone. This special show and sale is just for YOU from your friends at Bender's.

Cordially yours,

A well-run business knows not only its most frequent charge customers but also its least frequent charge customers. Yet another way to encourage charge account purchasing, therefore, is to aim a special letter at credit card holders who seldom use their cards. One clever writer developed this unique, intriguing letter for inactive charge card holders:

Dear Customer:
You've
Earned
50¢   Is it worth 50 cents a line to you to read this
$ 1.00   letter?
   1.50   We'll gladly pay you that amount—but only if you
   2.00   read the entire letter.
   2.50   Now, we reason this way: You really are a valued
   3.00   customer. But lately you haven't been in even to say
   3.50   "Hello." We would like you to come back; we would
   4.00   like to see you often; we would like you to reopen
   4.50   your account. We think that it is better for us to
   5.00   have a longtime customer like you on our books

5.50	than a new customer whom we don't know. And
6.00	since it would cost us at least $12 to open a *new* ac-
6.50	count, we would rather pass this amount on to you.
7.00	So we say, "Here is a $12 credit on the house."
7.50	Come in and select anything you wish from our ex-
8.00	tensive stock of nationally advertised clothing and
8.50	shoes for the entire family. Invest in that household
9.00	appliance — food processor, microwave oven — you
9.50	have been dreaming about. Or do your gift shopping
10.00	early for such items as diamonds, watches, stereos,
10.50	and glassware.
11.00	The enclosed credit of $12 is your down pay-
11.50	ment.
$12.00	Why not come in tomorrow?

Cordially yours,

Handling Other Special Opportunities

KEY POINT

Astute businesspeople look for opportunities to improve public relations.

The sharp businessperson has an eye for opportunities to improve public relations — and takes every advantage of those opportunities. For example, a clothing store manager with a list of names of newborns might take the opportunity to congratulate the proud parents with this letter:

Dear Mark:

You're a mighty discerning young man to have chosen the parents you did, and that's why I'm writing this letter to you instead of to them. Congratulations!

Here's your first pair of long pants. A little early, perhaps, but I want you to get used to coming to B&G's for all your clothing needs. Your dad has been a friend of ours for some time now. We like to think he is well satisfied with his purchases, and we hope you'll bring him in to see us often.

Tell you what: If you'll come in with your dad one year from now (I'll remind you), I'll have a present for you that you can really use.

Sincerely,

Note how the following letter stimulates holiday sales:

Dear Dad:

Mind if we slip a small string around that index finger of your left hand?

Not that we think you're absentminded. Far from it. But just in case the press of business has made you suffer a temporary lapse of memory, we thought it would be helpful to remind you that May 12 is Mother's Day. You hadn't forgotten? Good.

We know you'll also remember that Kale's is the store where Mother would purchase her own gift if she were doing the shopping. We have all those lovely things that women appreciate — jewelry, boudoir sets, manicure sets, leather-crafted desk sets, luxurious handbags, elegant luggage.

Drop in this week for a chat with our gift specialist, Mrs. Lopez. From years of experience, Mrs. Lopez knows the gifts that women cherish forever. She can help you choose the perfect gift for this occasion.

Cordially yours,

For examples of how to *create* special occasions, see the letters illustrated on pages 382 and 383.

EVERYDAY PUBLIC RELATIONS OPPORTUNITIES

i **INFORMATION**

Common, everyday business transactions provide opportunities for public relations.

Unless your job is in the Public Relations Department, you may not have all the special PR opportunities that have been discussed so far. But the techniques will be useful, because you *will* have everyday opportunities to improve public relations for your company.

Whenever you reply to routine requests, for example, you have opportunities to build your company's image. In Section 8.2, "Writing and Answering Requests," you read the following paragraph in a routine reply:

> Mr. Neumann, the enclosed booklet includes a list of all the specific items that are covered by our service contract. In fact, it also lists (in equally large print) the few items that are *not* covered in the contract, so that there will be no "surprises" if something should happen to the product; you will know exactly what is covered. The Gorden management insists that we stand behind all our products and that we inform our customers precisely *how* we stand behind our products. By doing so, we avoid the unfortunate experience that you described in your letter.

Note that the writer does not *sell a product* here; the writer *sells the company*. In other words, the writer employs good public relations techniques in replying to a routine request for information.

Assume that you are working for a California hotel that specializes in convention meetings. You might have the opportunity to write a letter such as this to a valued customer:

> Dear Mr. Gould:
>
> All of us here appreciate your thinking of the Little Creek Inn as *the* place to hold your annual sales conventions. Thank you for the compliment!
>
> For several years now, you have used our facilities to host your special dinners, to demonstrate products to customers, to train your new representatives, and to lodge your employees and guests whenever they are in our area. We do, indeed, make special efforts to make all your meetings successful, because your appreciation of our efforts always shows.
>
> Mr. Gould, we sincerely enjoy serving you, your employees, and your customers. Thank you for doing business with us.
>
> Cordially yours,

As you see, then, public relations is part of every letter you write for your company. When you write your letters, even *routine* letters, look for ways to incorporate the good public relations techniques discussed in this section.

the
sp⬤rts
shop

101 East Adams
Chicago, Illinois 60603
312-555-1234

January 2, 19--

Ms. Francine Byrd
21 Victor Street
Mankato, MN 56001

Dear Ms. Byrd:

Let's talk about golf. Yes, I know that there's snow on the ground
and not a leaf on the trees. The fairways aren't fair, and the
temperature is unmerciful.

But January is golden weather at The Sports Shop. The floor is abloom
with the most fantastic selection of golf balls, clubs, bags, shoes,
carts, jackets, caps--everything you can imagine. Come stand under
our palm tree and see our fresh white rows of golf balls, the
roll-a-way Bermuda Rug putting green, the warm, gleaming woods, and
the sunny golf fashions. Once the golfers in your family get their
hands on these, can spring be far behind?

To make The Sports Shop even warmer, we've slashed prices by 25
percent. Why not come down and get a little bit of spring right now,
at our fabulous Spring-in-January sale.

Sincerely yours,

Conway Isaacson

Conway Isaacson
Manager

The Sports Shop *creates* a special occasion—a "Spring-in-January" sale!

DePaul Finance Company
201-555-9580 • Route 22 • Mountainside, New Jersey 07092

June 12, 19--

Mrs. J. P. Crane
120 Raritan Road
Scotch Plains, NJ 07076

Dear Mrs. Crane:

Congratulations--your Chevrolet sedan is all yours as of today. The
enclosed canceled note is evidence that you've completed all the
payments.

You don't owe us any more payments, but we feel we owe you this one
last statement--a statement of how pleased we are with you as a
customer. You made every payment right on time. We hope you'll call
on us again whenever you need financing.

The enclosed certificate entitles you to preferred credit privileges
at the lowest available rates. Just present this certificate to any
of our branch offices for fast service on loans of any kind. As long
as we have money to lend, we'll be pleased to help you.

Cordially yours,

Karen Anne LoPresti

Karen Anne LoPresti
Vice President

ge

The writer makes an opportunity to contact a former customer. While thanking her for her patronage the
writer also reminds her that she has credit privileges with DePaul Finance Company the next time she considers
making a purchase that will require financing.

REVIEW

Practical Application

KEY
See page I-42.

A. Suppose that you are a college graduate with five years of business experience as (1) an administrative assistant in an attorney's office, (2) a travel agent in a large agency, or (3) a tax accountant in a public accounting firm.

   You decide to set up your own (1) legal secretarial service, (2) travel agency, or (3) tax accounting business. You choose to begin promoting your new business by writing a letter and sending it to 100 businesses in the community. You wish to emphasize both your business experience and your excellent college education. Write a letter that includes all the details that will improve your chances of succeeding in your own new business.

KEY
See page I-42.

B. Develop a letter that encourages charge customers of a retail store to use their charge accounts. Use your ingenuity in making the letter different from others you have seen.

KEY
See page I-43.

C. You are the manager of Vanguard's Department Store. Vanguard's has always provided charge cards without charging any fee other than interest. Extremely high interest rates and tight credit force you to introduce a $15 annual fee for charge cards in order to cover Vanguard's own increased borrowing costs. Write a letter explaining this new store policy tactfully. *Remember:* Your customers are accustomed to paying no fee, and you are imposing the fee through no fault of the customers.

KEY
See page I-43.

D. You work for Newlook Decorators, an interior decorating firm that is introducing a new line of furniture and decorations this spring. A special preview showing of the new line is planned for charge customers, including family and friends, at the Newlook showroom, 657 Woodside Avenue, March 21, from six until nine in the evening. You are assigned to write a letter of invitation. Admission will be by ticket only, and you are enclosing a ticket with each invitation. The general public will not see the new line until March 28. Write a letter that makes the most of this occasion.

KEY
See page I-43.

E. You are manager of Lindemann's Hardware Store, an established business on the outskirts of a large city. Traditionally, your customers have come from the city. New towns and neighborhoods are springing up beyond city limits, however, and you are looking for a way to develop business with the residents of these new areas. You decide to write a letter, enclosing a discount coupon worth $5, that invites each resident of the new areas to visit your store. Write an appealing invitation addressed to new residents.

REVIEW cont.

Editing Practice

Editing to Improve Writing Techniques.   Edit the following sentences to improve any poor writing techniques.

1. Arriving to pick up the package, I asked the messenger to wait while the cover letter was signed by Ms. Drake.
2. Employees must now submit their health insurance claim to Robert Bergman in the personnel office.
3. Ellen borrowed the dictionary which was on my desk.
4. Judy said she couldn't find any stamps for the letters after looking in the desk drawers.
5. You can use either of these four spreadsheets as a model for your training course.
6. In order to prepare the inventory report, all the figures will be needed by you.
7. Within two days after I sent my request to Ms. Medina, a reply was received from her.
8. There is no future for the business communicator who is careless or indifferent to the techniques of writing.
9. The mail would remain in the out-basket for hours and sometimes days.
10. Our engineers have made many improvements in design, and so we shall be able to produce a better product.
11. The committee must complete the research, assembling of facts, and writing the report.
12. In his writing, Simon consistently used unnecessarily big words, thus making his communications ineffective.
13. Perry always has and always will be a team player.
14. Clifford is one of the brightest if not the brightest summer interns in the program.
15. He felt the furniture was too expensive.

Plurals and Possessives.   Indicate the correct plural or possessive forms of the words enclosed in parentheses.

1. The managing partner reviews new (attorney) briefs each week.
2. (Marie and Laura) telephone, which they share, is on Marie's desk.
3. All the (secretary) in this company speak Spanish fluently.
4. The two (general manager) reports were in agreement.
5. My (boss) hotel reservation needs to be changed.
6. Mr. Harvey gave Glenn a box of monogrammed (handkerchief).
7. All the (analysis) that have been submitted support this proposal.
8. Each choir member sang two (solo).
9. The (president-elect) adviser on environmental policy will speak at a conference of environmental scientists next week.

10. utilities
11. Children's
12. whose
13. its
14. chintzes
15. Lynches

10. For good investments, buy stock in public (utility).
11. (Children) clothing is on sale at great savings today.
12. Professor Pepper is a man (who) experience is highly regarded.
13. Although the system is costly, (it) motherboard can be upgraded.
14. Many (chintz) are used for making curtains.
15. The (Lynch) are remodeling their showroom.

8.6 WRITING SOCIAL-BUSINESS MESSAGES

OBJECTIVES: After completing Section 8.6, you should be able to:

1. Use the correct social-business letter format both on plain stationery and on printed stationery.
2. Write effective congratulatory letters, thank-you letters, and condolence letters.
3. Correctly write—and reply to—formal invitations.

❏ **SUGGESTION**

Discuss with students how traditions may differ from family to family, region to region, and so on.

❏ **SUGGESTION**

Ask students to identify different ways in which their friends or relatives might congratulate them on special occasions. Then make the point that, in business, the way to communicate congratulations, appreciation, or sympathy is through a well-written social-business letter.

When you buy a new car or a new home, start a new business, get a promotion, or get married, you expect your lifelong friends and your closest relatives to congratulate you—to show somehow that they share the joy of the occasion. On the other hand, if you suffer the loss of a loved one, you expect those same friends and all your other close relatives to show their sympathy for you. Common courtesy and tradition require people to communicate their congratulations or their sorrow in these instances.

In business, likewise, common courtesy and tradition demand that business workers congratulate one another on special occasions, send letters of condolence when a business associate suffers the loss of a loved one, reply properly to a formal invitation, write a thank-you note for a special favor or gift, and so on. Just as you would appreciate hearing from your coworkers and business associates in these situations, you should let them hear from you whenever appropriate.

Writing *social-business communications*, as they are called, is considered difficult only by those people who have had little experience writing such messages. By reading this chapter, studying the sample letters, and practicing the exercises, you will prepare yourself to tackle all your social-business correspondence and develop your messages expertly.

SOCIAL-BUSINESS LETTER FORMAT

As you learned in Section 8.1, the *format* of a letter refers to the arrangement of letter parts on the page.

On Company Letterhead

For a social-business letter typed on company letterhead, use the social-business letter format illustrated on page 388. As you see, this social-business letter format has its letter parts in the usual position *except the inside address*, which is placed last, positioned at the bottom of the page. In addition to this format change, the social-business letter has a change in the usual punctuation pattern for business letters: The salutation ends with a comma rather than with a colon. Reference initials, copy notations, and so on, are not included.

Some companies provide *monarch* letterhead or *baronial* letterhead for social-business and other letters. (Monarch stationery measures 7¼ by 10½ inches; baronial, 5½ by 8½ inches rather than the standard 8½ by 11 inches.) Many people consider these sizes especially fitting for executive correspondence.

Whether you are using monarch or baronial letterhead or standard-size stationery, follow the same format described. Note that for baronial stationery, a shorter line length — say, 4 inches — must be used. See page 389 for an illustration of a social-business letter typed on monarch stationery.

On Plain Stationery

When a social-business letter is typed on stationery with no printed letterhead, follow the same format as for personal-business letters, but use a comma after the salutation. See the letters illustrated on pages 391 and 392.

CONGRATULATIONS LETTERS

KEY POINT
Congratulatory letters can be an effective public relations tool.

Special honors and special events provide ideal PR opportunities. They present you with an appropriate occasion to say "Congratulations!" Your reader will appreciate your thoughtfulness, and you will certainly win favor both for yourself and for your company. *Remember:* Everyone wants to be respected and admired, and a congratulatory message shows your respect and admiration for someone's accomplishment or recognition.

For Promotions

Suppose you read in a trade magazine that Helene Adams, a woman who worked in your bank a few years ago, was promoted to vice president for Amesville Bank & Trust Company. During the three years that you worked together, you and she were friendly. Since she left, you have seen her at various banking industry meetings and conventions, the two of you have served together on a banking industry committee, and you have had lunch

Jansen Construction, Inc.

The Jerry Building • 1200 Amboy Highway
Lubbock, Texas • 806-555-1111

March 13, 19-- ↓6

Dear Ms. Herz, ↓2

Please allow me to express my congratulations on your promotion to Senior Vice President. All of us at Jansen Construction offer you our best wishes in your new position. ↓2

In the two years since you joined Hillside Building Supplies, you have been instrumental in making your firm the number one source for materials for all major construction projects in this area because of your personal involvement in every project. As a result, contractors have come to expect fair prices, high-quality materials, and reliable, on-time deliveries from Hillside. With your help, we can now estimate project costs accurately and develop schedules precisely. As you can imagine, we genuinely appreciate the pleasure of working with you. ↓2

Ms. Herz, we hope that your promotion will not reduce the opportunities we will have to work together. In any case, we wish you success in your new position. ↓2

Sincerely, ↓4

Hector P. Lopez

Hector P. Lopez
Manager
Purchasing Agent ↓5

Ms. Carolyn Herz
Senior Vice President
Hillside Building Supplies
50 Excelsior Avenue
Lubbock, Texas 79409

Prepare in modified block format, this message illustrates the two unique features of social-business letters: (1) the inside address is positioned at the bottom of the letter and (2) the salutation ends with a comma, not a colon. This letter was prepared on standard 8½- by 11-inch letterhead stationery.

Ruck, Moser & Naldi
Members, New York Stock Exchange
Stocks Bonds Mutual Funds Options
One Essex Plaza Atlanta, Georgia 30341
1-800-555-3000   404-555-3200

June 3, 19-- ↓6

Dear Jack, ↓2

Congratulations! I'm very happy to hear that you've been named to head our new branch office in Albany, and I wish you success as our newest branch manager. ↓2

After working with you for more than 15 years and living next door to you equally long, Jack, I simply don't know how I'm going to function here without my best friend. Conversation at the watercooler is sure to suffer! Moreover, I'll have to start driving to work <u>alone</u> for the first time in years. ↓2

Seriously, Jack, I've often told you that you should be a branch manager because you have all the talents and skills necessary for the job. I know, therefore, that you'll be very successful. I expect to hear soon that our Albany branch office is <u>the</u> number one office in the country. Let me know whenever I may be helpful, of course. ↓2

Sincerely, ↓4

Harold W. Porter

Harold W. Porter
Senior Counsel ↓5

Mr. John J. Haggerty
121 Raymond Street
Atlanta, GA 30341

Prepared in block format, this social-business letter was typed on monarch (7¼- by 10½-inch) letterhead station-ery. Note the inside address positioned at the bottom of the letter and the comma ending the salutation.

with her from time to time. Should you send her a note congratulating her on her promotion? Of course!

Your note might follow this example:

Dear Helene,

How delighted I was to read in *The Banking Journal* that you were recently promoted to Vice President of Amesville Bank & Trust. Congratulations!

Having had the pleasure of working with you, I know very well that you have worked hard and have fully earned that promotion. I also know that there isn't a nicer person in the entire banking industry. For both reasons, I'm truly happy for you.

Needless to say, Helene, I wish you success in your new position. I know that I'll be hearing more good news about you in the future.

Sincerely,

The message is clear: You really *are* pleased by Helene's good fortune. You are sure to make her happy — and to solidify a business friendship — by letting her know how pleased you are.

The degree of friendliness or informality of your congratulatory note will depend on the specific relationship you have with the reader. For two more examples of similar congratulatory notes (one more formal and the other more friendly), see the letters illustrated on pages 389 and 391.

Congratulatory letters often are also written to employees of the same company. In fact, it is virtually *mandatory* for executives to acknowledge promotions of employees in their company. The following letter is written to a valued employee:

Dear Preston,

Congratulations to you on your promotion to District Manager. You certainly are "the right person for the right job."

Catherine Paine has been talking about promoting you to this position since she became Marketing Manager six months ago. All of us in management are equally convinced that you will be able to continue to turn in the high sales volume that the Southern District is well known for.

In any case, Preston, I certainly am happy to welcome you to the sales management team for our Consumer Division, and I wish you success in your new position.

Sincerely,

For Anniversaries

A coworker's anniversary also calls for written congratulations. Note the friendliness and informality — and the sincerity — of this letter:

Dear Gene,

Congratulations on your tenth year with Vector Products Inc. I remember your first day with the company, when Len Denaro introduced you to me and

```
                              Current Date




Name
Address
City, State ZIP Code

Salutation

      Thank you for asking about our fall bus tours through the New
England states.  Our "Fall Color Tours," as we call them, are some of
our most popular excursions.

      Enclosed is our brochure that lists
tours.  The pictures will give you an i
views and the historical sites that you

      Please complete and return the encl
as possible.  Space is limited, and the

      You owe yourself a luxurious trip.
details.  All you have to do is have a g

                              Since

                              TERR


                              Betty
                              Manag

??
Enclosure
```

Terrific Tours, Inc.
P.O. Box 2310, Atlanta, GA 30301 404-555-8124

```
                              May 21, 19--


Ms. Meredith Larson
3628 Garwood Road
Atlanta, GA 30306

Dear Ms. Larson:

      Thank you for asking about our fall bus tours through the New
England states.  Our "Fall Color Tours," as we call them, are some of
our most popular excursions.

      Enclosed is our brochure that lists the dates and costs of the
tours.  The pictures will give you an idea of some of the breathtaking
views and the historical sites that you will enjoy.

      Please complete and return the enclosed reservation form as soon
as possible.  Space is limited, and the tours are filling fast.

      You owe yourself a luxurious trip.  We take care of all the
details.  All you have to do is have a good time!

            Sincerely,

            TERRIFIC TOURS, INC.

            (Ms.) Betty Weaver

            Betty Weaver
            Manager

dk
Enclosure
```

This is Form Letter A of Terrific Tours, Inc. The body of the letter remains the same; only the highlighted date line, address, salutation, and reference initials change.

```
                              Current Date



          Name
          Address
          City, State ZIP Code

          Salutation

          Your reservations for Number have been
          popular tours, "Name of Tour."  You wi
          your selection of your vacation packag

          Your deposit for Deposit has been rece
          of Balance within ten days of the date

          As soon as the detailed itinerary is f
          personal copy.  Please call us if you

                                    Sinc

                                    TER


                                    Bett
                                    Mana
          ??
```

Terrific Tours, Inc.
P.O. Box 2310, Atlanta, GA 30301 404-555-8124

```
                              July 10, 19--


          Mr. Sherman Arthur
          Post Office Box 1824
          Atlanta, GA 30301

          Dear Mr. Arthur:

          Your reservations for two have been confirmed for one of our most
          popular tours, "Country Music Exposition."  You will definitely be
          pleased with your selection of your vacation package.

          Your deposit for $500 has been received.  We will need the balance of
          $900 within ten days of the date of this letter.

          As soon as the detailed itinerary is finalized, you will receive your
          personal copy.  Please call us if you have any questions.

                                    Sincerely,

                                    TERRIFIC TOURS, INC.

                                    ( Ms. ) Betty Weaver

                                    Betty Weaver
                                    Manager

          dk
```

Form Letter B of Terrific Tours, Inc., has variables in the *body* of the letter. The highlighted items are those that change from letter to letter.

example, include the person's name within a sentence. "I look forward to seeing you, Ms. Tate, Friday, at 2 p.m."

2. If readers find out that they have received a form letter, they may feel somewhat disappointed. A manager, for example, wrote you a congratulatory message when your son finished college. You felt good about the letter until your coworker showed you one exactly like it when his daughter finished college. The purpose of the letter was goodwill, and the goodwill was lost.

3. Using form letters and boilerplate can be abused. Some business writers use them when they are inappropriate or when they do not quite fit the situation.

TYPES OF FORM LETTERS

Executives often find that they are repeatedly writing the same content in response to frequently occurring—almost identical—writing situations. When this happens, they should invest some time and effort in developing general responses that can be used and reused. These general responses fall into three main categories.

Form letters
Form letters with variables
Letters with form paragraphs

Form Letters

Form letters are used to respond to identical situations. The letter shown on page 401 would be used to respond to any general inquiries about fall bus tours. The entire body of the letter remains the same; the date, inside address, and salutation are the only changes. These letter parts are highlighted in the example.

Form Letters With Variables

Form letters with variables are used when similar, but not identical, responses are needed. In addition to the date, inside address, and salutation, other details are changed throughout the body of the letter. These changes are called *variables*. On page 402, the letter on the left shows the form letter with the variables highlighted. The letter on the right is in finished form, with specific information added for the variables.

To simplify requests for form letters and form letters with variables, printed request forms are used. The example shown on page 404 requests form letter B, which uses variables. List the variables in the order in which they should appear in the letter.

REQUEST FOR FORM LETTER

Form Letter Requested: _____ *B* _____

Requested by: _____ *Betty Weaver, Manager* _____
Date Requested: _____ *July 9, 19 — —* _____
Date Needed: _____ *July 10, 19 — —* _____

Name: _____ *Mr. Sherman Arthur* _____
Address: _____ *Post Office Box 1824* _____
City, State, ZIP: _____ *Atlanta, GA 30301* _____

Salutation: _____ *Dear Mr. Arthur* _____
Variables (if applicable):
Number: _____ *Two* _____
Name of Tour: _____ *Country Music Exposition* _____
Deposit: _____ *$500* _____
Balance: _____ *$900* _____

Special Instructions: _____ *None* _____
_____
_____

Completed by: _____ *D. K.* _____

This form makes composing a form letter easy. The writer specifies the particular form letter, indicates the addressee, and lists any variables in the body of the message.

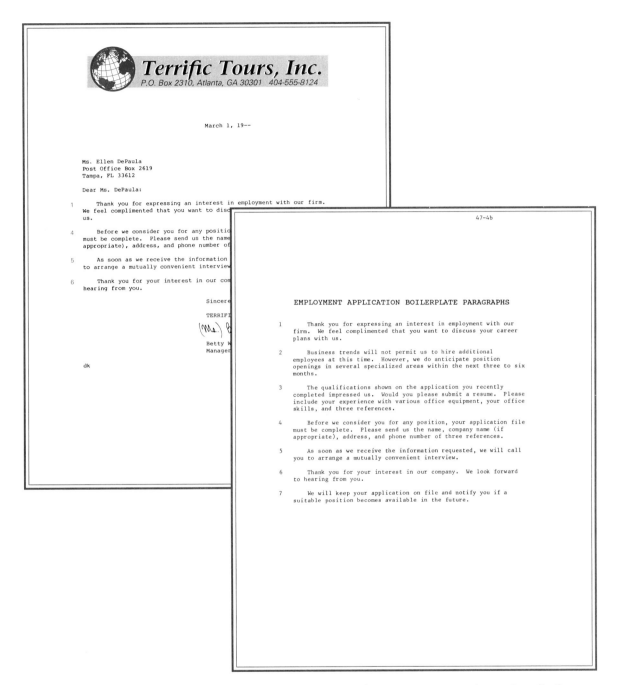

Note how the seven form paragraphs shown here cover a range of responses to an employment application. Paragraphs can be selected to make up an appropriate response.

Letters With Form Paragraphs

For similar writing situations that occur frequently but vary in content, experienced business communicators use form or boilerplate paragraphs. Paragraphs dealing with most common situations are written. Each paragraph has a number. Instead of dictating each letter, the executive gives the transcriber the date, inside address, salutation, and a list of paragraphs (by number). Sample boilerplate and a letter are shown on page 405.

Using the word processing program on a computer makes writing letters with form paragraphs even easier. Boilerplate paragraphs and complete letters can be stored on disk and retrieved and altered as necessary. Only the variables need to be input. As a result, routine letters can be prepared quickly and efficiently.

SECTION 2

REVIEW

Practical Application

A. List and describe the three main categories of form letters.

B. Denis Prior, Post Office Box 2849, Birmingham, AL 35238, recently visited your office and completed an application. You want to arrange an interview with him as soon as he sends his résumé. Because he applied for a job in the office, you are interested in his office skills and his experience with various office equipment. You also need three references.

   Select four of the seven form paragraphs (see page 405) that can be appropriately combined in a letter to Mr. Prior. On a separate sheet, list the paragraph numbers in the order that you would present them.

C. On a separate sheet, design a form to request a letter with form paragraphs. Be sure that your request form has space to provide all needed details. After designing the form, make two photocopies of it. Complete a request for the letter to Mr. Prior (Application B) and one to Ms. DePaula (see page 405).

D. You own a motel in a very popular coastal area. Write a form letter to respond to general inquiries. In the letter, mention that you are enclosing a brochure listing the various kinds of accommodations and the rates.

Editing Practice

Missing Words. A word has been left out of each of the following sentences. Select a word that will correctly complete each sentence.

1. A helpful highway gave us directions to your plant.

KEY
See page I-46.

KEY
Paragraphs: 1, 3, 5, and 6.

KEY
See page I-46.

KEY
Students' answers will vary.

KEY
Sample answers.
1. highway *patrol officer*

406 CHAPTER 8 WRITING BUSINESS LETTERS

2. *had* trouble
3. *to* participate
4. area *is*
5. *and* radio

2. We were late for the ceremony, because we trouble with our car.
3. Most of the employees have decided participate in the dental insurance program.
4. Our sales representative in your area Carla White.
5. Newspaper advertisements radio advertisements aroused our interest.

Missing Letters. A letter has been incorrectly omitted from some of the words in the following sentences. Correctly write each incorrect word.

KEY
1. three
2. envelope
3. installations
4. equipped
5. arrangements

1. On which floppy disk did you store the thre documents?
2. Inside the large manila envelop is a photocopy of the stock certificates.
3. Rhonda Jackson oversees the modular furniture instalations for our corporate clients.
4. The camping trailer is equiped with a gas stove.
5. Alex Magruder is the agent who makes all the travel arangements for our company's executives.

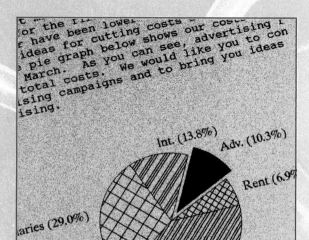

PREPARING REPORTS AND SPECIAL COMMUNICATIONS

9.1 *WRITING INFORMAL REPORTS*

OBJECTIVES: After completing Section 9.1, you should be able to:

1. Write an informal report in correct memorandum form.
2. Use a variety of forms of presentation for an informal report.
3. Prepare and present an unsolicited report.

ℹ️ INFORMATION

Discuss the fact that reports use many different styles and that those in this text are only examples. Each business may have its own report style, which must be learned by those who prepare reports. If possible, have available some real business reports to show the variety of report styles.

In the business world, a report is probably the primary method for providing information. This information is intended to help executives, supervisors, managers, department heads, and others to understand their roles and perform their duties more effectively. Many of these people also write reports to supply others with essential information. Therefore, anyone who wishes to succeed in today's business world must be able to gather information and prepare reports.

A report may be given orally, but usually it is written. Any important information should be in written form so that there is some record that may be referred to in the future. "Put it in writing" is the basic principle behind most reports.

The values of a written report, compared with an oral one, are obvious. An oral report may be misunderstood. Important information in an oral report may be quickly forgotten, especially statistical data. Even a forceful oral report will grow weaker with each passing day, whereas a written report can be referred to again and again. Each reading of the report reinforces the message conveyed in the report. Moreover, a precise and permanent record exists in the report itself.

One way to classify reports is according to the length of the report—*informal* (shorter reports) and *formal* (longer) reports. Because formal reports usually require extensive research, documentation, investigation, and analysis, the style of the presentation is usually different from the style used for a short report. You will learn how to prepare a formal report in Section 9.2. But first let's discuss informal reports, the type you will probably prepare most often, at least in the early years of your career.

👤 KEY POINT

The memorandum form is used for writing informal reports. Usually the standard memo heading (To, From, Date, and Subject) is used. However, this heading can be adjusted to fit individual or company preferences.

STYLE OF INFORMAL REPORTS

In Chapter 7, you learned how to use a memorandum as a means of corresponding with other employees within an organization. The same memorandum form is used for writing informal reports, hence the name *memorandum report*.

The memorandum report begins with the same information contained in the memorandum you learned to use for interoffice correspondence:

To:
From:
Date:
Subject:

Whether you use this form exactly as it is or adapt it will depend upon the circumstances of your work. *How* you use the above outline will depend on a number of variables.

To

The way you address the person to whom the report is going depends primarily upon the degree of formality or informality of your office atmosphere. For instance, if everybody addresses the boss by his or her first name and the boss approves, and if the report is of a personal nature, you might write:

To: Sam Whitman

But suppose you know that the report will be read by other persons besides the boss or that the report will be filed for future reference. Then it would be better to write:

To: Mr. Samuel Whitman

From

The *From* line should match the tone of the *To* line. For example, the first two lines of a very informal memorandum report written only for the personal information of the boss would appear as:

To: Sam Whitman
From: Kim Mason

For a report that is not for the exclusive information of the boss or that is to be filed for future reference, a more formal *From* line would be preferable. Keep in mind that all readers are likely to know the boss, but they may not know who you are. Therefore, you might need to include more information about yourself. You might write:

To: Mr. Samuel Whitman
From: Ms. Kimberly Mason, Administrative Assistant

Subject

The *Subject* line should be a comprehensive, yet clear and precise, statement that will prepare a reader for rapid assimilation of the information given in the report. Composing a good subject line, therefore, requires a high degree of skill.

Let's look at some illustrations. Here are two possible subject lines for a sales manager's report to the vice president in charge of sales.

Subject: Sales Projections

Subject: Third-Quarter Sales Projections, by Product

Of course, the first subject line would be meaningless to the vice president. He or she could not tell what the report is really about without reading the report itself. The second example, however, would orient the reader immediately.

Suppose that you are a personnel director and receive a report with a subject line like this one:

Subject: Employee Absenteeism

Possibly you have forgotten that you asked for a report on some phase of employee absenteeism. If that is the case, the above subject line will not refresh your memory or help you quickly grasp the facts presented in the report. Wouldn't the following subject line be more helpful?

Subject: Causes of Employee Absenteeism, January 19—

Date

Because conditions change so rapidly, facts presented on one date may not be valid at a later date. Therefore, every report should show the date on which it was written. In addition, think how frustrating it would be to search for an undated report in the files — a report that could prove very valuable if only you knew when it was written!

Wherever dates are given in the body of a report, those dates must be specific. Instead of writing, "Last Friday, we sent. . . ," you would write, "On Friday, May 10, 19—, we sent. . . ."

Adapting the Memo Form

Although the memo form we have been using is the one most frequently used, there are variations that may sometimes be more appropriate. For example:

Erin Burke
February 28, 19—
Causes of Employee Absenteeism, January 19—

This adaptation shows the writer — Erin Burke — and gives the date; but it states the subject as a heading or title. The assumption is that this report would go only to the person requesting the report and, therefore, requires no additional name. However, if an addressee's name is necessary, the body of the report could start like this:

Mrs. Alvarez: The causes of employee absenteeism in January 19— are as follows:

Before you sit
down to work on a
report, make sure
that you have all
the necessary tools
on hand—your
notes, all relevant
data and corre-
spondence, basic
reference works (at
least a dictionary,
thesaurus, and
style guide).

File Copies

Whenever you write an informal report, even if you think it is not important, be sure to make a copy for your own files. Anything important enough
to put in writing is important enough to be retained. You may never need to
refer to your file copy, but you cannot be certain that you or someone else in
the company will not need some of the information contained in the report
sometime in the future. One way to guard against lost or misaddressed reports is to file a copy of every report you write in a folder marked "Reports."

PLANNING AND WRITING INFORMAL REPORTS

Many people, including some correspondents, think that writing involves
merely sitting down and dashing off a few words. This widespread but false
notion is partly responsible for the fact that good business writers are scarce
and, therefore, very much in demand.

In fact, first-class writing of any kind involves hard work and results from
much thought, careful planning, and excellent training. Before you can write
informal reports of the highest quality, you need to study, think about, and
apply the following principles.

Be Clear, Complete, Correct, and Concise

REINFORCEMENT

Stress the importance
of writing quality in
preparing reports. Re-
ports should be clear,
complete, correct, and
concise.

As you know, *concise* writing should still be complete writing. To be concise, you must say everything that needs to be said, but you must say it in the
fewest possible words.

You are also well aware that your writing must be clear and complete. You
would not write a "fuzzy" sentence like this:

Tom Bennett told Mr. Delgado about the construction delays at the industrial
park, and he said he would have the report on his desk by Friday.

Instead, you would write a clear, complete message, such as this one:

Tom Bennett told Mr. Delgado that he would have the report on the
construction delays at the industrial park on Mr. Delgado's desk on
Wednesday, October 20, 19—.

All reports must be correct in every detail. Perhaps we should use the
stronger term *accurate*, because any information important enough to be reported must be more than substantially correct; it must be completely accurate. For example, if you are asked to report the number of free-sample
requests that come in on a given day, you'd better be sure that you give an
exact, not an approximate, count.

Wording

KEY POINT

A report is a straight-
forward, factual pre-
sentation.

The wording of reports differs from that of letters. A letter is designed to
do more than convey a message, for its accompanying purpose is to win new

customers or clients for the company and to retain old ones. Therefore, the tone of a letter is warm and friendly. A report, on the other hand, is a straightforward, factual presentation—and it should be worded as such.

As an illustration, read the following opening paragraph of a letter answering a request for information about your company's free tuition program for employees.

> In response to your April 10 request, we are pleased to tell you that we do provide free tuition for employees taking work-related courses in local schools under the following circumstances: (Then you would itemize and explain the circumstances under which your company pays the tuition for its employees.)

Now, note how the wording changes when the same information is given in a report:

> Employees taking work-related courses in local schools will be reimbursed for tuition when the following requirements have been met:
> 1. The course has been approved in advance by the employee's supervisor.
> 2. The employee earns a grade of "B" or better.
> 3. The employee has been with the company for one year or more.

FORMS OF PRESENTATION

 **KEY POINT**

There are three basic types of presentations used in reports: paragraph form, outline form, and table form. Computer-generated spreadsheets are often part of formal and informal reports.

How brief or how detailed should your informal report be? Should you give the requested information in a single paragraph? Should you present the information in outline form? Should you tabulate the information?

Because you are preparing the report, you are the one who must answer these questions. Only you are close enough to the situation to know why the report was requested, to project the probable uses of the information, and so on. In order to make a wise decision about the form your report should take, though, you must be familiar with the different types of presentations and their uses.

Paragraph Form

The paragraph form is used for the presentation of a simple fact. For example, if your boss has requested that you report how many hours of overtime were paid the previous month—and you are certain that the only statistic your boss wants is the total number of hours—you might write the following in a memo-style report:

> In the month of March 19—, the total number of hours of overtime in the Accounting Department was 15 hours.

Or, if you want to give a little extra information, you might add to the above statement:

> There are 35 employees in the department, and 7 employees (20 percent) accounted for the 15 hours of overtime.

Outline Form

If, however, you know that your boss has a personal interest in the staff, you might correctly believe that you should list the names of the persons who worked overtime. You could present all the information necessary in outline form, as follows:

Information regarding overtime in the Accounting Department during March 19— is as follows:

1. Total employees in department: 35
2. Total hours of overtime: 15
3. Employees working overtime: 7 (20 percent)
   Mark Petrone, 2 hours
   Cynthia Rogers, 2 hours
   Ruth Stein, 2 hours
   Kenneth Ulrich, 1 hour
   Alicia Velez, 3 hours
   Robert Williams, 4 hours
   Steven Wimmer, 1 hour

Note how the outline form is used to highlight the suggestions in the memo shown on page 415.

Table Form

In some cases, the most effective way to present information is in table form. The advantage of a tabulated presentation is that the reader can more easily see the total situation at a glance without wading through a great many words. Obviously, the decision to tabulate should be influenced by the amount and the kind of information to be included and also by the writer's projection regarding the uses to which the information is likely to be put. In table form, the example overtime report would look like this:

ACCOUNTING DEPARTMENT OVERTIME MONTH OF MARCH 19—		
Employee	*Hours*	*Reason*
Petrone, Mark	2	To complete January billing
Rogers, Cynthia	2	To prepare for business trip
Stein, Ruth	2	To prepare expense statement
Ulrich, Kenneth	1	To complete checking cost estimates
Velez, Alicia	3	To prepare cost analysis
Williams, Robert	4	To analyze travel expenses
Wimmer, Steven	1	To complete January billing

Total employees: 35
Overtime hours: 15
Total employees working overtime: 7
Percent of employees working overtime: 20

INTEROFFICE MEMORANDUM

To: Ms. Elizabeth Wang   From: Peter White

Subject: Increasing Credit Card Use   Date: May 5, 19--

Our firm has issued 2,320 credit cards to customers during the past 12 months. However, a survey made recently by our credit department indicates that only 40 percent of these credit card holders have made purchases exceeding $50 during this period. The average charge is $35.

A national study recently made by the American Credit Association revealed that the average single purchase by credit card holders is $75. This figure would seem to indicate that we are not getting the maximum benefits from the credit cards we issue and that we should be able to increase our volume of credit business by encouraging greater use of credit cards by our customers.

I am, therefore, recommending that we undertake a campaign to encourage customers who hold our credit cards to make greater use of them. The initial steps of this campaign should include the following:

1. Preparing folders encouraging new customers to apply for credit cards. An application form should be a part of this folder, which would be available not only in the credit office but also at numerous locations within our stores.

2. Placing full-page advertisements in all regional newspapers, explaining how customers can use their credit cards more extensively without getting into economic difficulties.

3. Buying television time for spot announcements with a theme similar to that of the newspaper advertisements.

I would suggest that representatives from both the credit and the marketing departments form a committee to plan the strategies of this program not later than the end of this month.

I will be happy to discuss any aspects of these suggestions with you at your convenience.

PW

as

Ideas for increasing efficiency, productivity, or profitability are often welcomed. Note how the subject line in this unsolicited report appeals to the reader's interest.

UNSOLICITED REPORTS

An unsolicited report is, quite simply, one that you make on your own initiative rather than one you are asked to prepare. In business, any idea for increasing efficiency, productivity, or profit making will usually be welcome. It's advisable to put your idea in writing so that you can present it in the most complete, logical, and generally effective manner. See the unsolicited report shown on page 415.

How do you go about preparing and submitting an unsolicited report? Before you begin to write, consider these details.

To

You will want to direct your suggestion or idea to the person who has the authority to put it into effect. Usually this person will be your boss; but even if it happens to be someone else, courtesy and protocol demand that the suggestion be routed *through* your boss *to* that other person. For example:

> To: Mr. Dan Spivack (your boss)
>   Ms. Antonia Dawson (the "authority" person)

Subject

In any report, the subject line should tell the reader what the report is about. In an unsolicited report, though, you should slant the wording of the subject so that it will appeal to the reader's particular interest. For example, if you know that your boss is particularly interested in increasing new subscriptions, your subject line might read:

> Subject: Suggestions for Increasing New Subscriptions

KEY
See page I-48.

SECTION

REVIEW

Practical Application

A. Your supervisor, Ms. Marion Hoskins, is considering the purchase of a personal computer so that she can perform some of her office responsibilities at home during the evenings and weekends. She asks you to check the prices of various personal computers available in your community in terms of number of disk drives and memory. Ms. Hoskins has specified what she needs, so you will investigate only models that meet her specifications. You obtain the following information: (1) *ACI*, monochrome display $1,200 and color display $1,495; *Tecniq*, monochrome display $1,400 and color display $1,680; *Saporo*, monochrome display $999 and color display $1,300; and *CompPute*, monochrome display $2,200 and color display $2,600. All carry 1-year warranties, and service contracts are available after the expiration of the warranty. Both the *ACI* and the *Tecniq* are available at Super Computer and each comes with a carrying case. The *Saporo* is available at Red Barn Computer Sales, and the company will extend its warranty for 6 additional months if the system has not required service during the first year. The *Comp-Pute* is available at CompPute, Inc., which will provide a free spreadsheet program with each purchase. Organize this information into a concise, easy-to-read memorandum and submit it to Ms. Hoskins.

B. Select two stocks or bonds that are listed in your local newspaper's stock market report. From the information that is provided in the newspaper, write an informal report about the status of these two securities during the past five days. Address the report to your instructor.

C. Prepare a tabulation report, similar to the one on page 414, for the following information:

Sources of Employees Hired During the Year 19—: The state employment service referred 36 candidates; 16 were hired. Local college placement offices referred 27 candidates; 19 were hired. Private placement services referred 41 candidates; 17 were hired. Newspaper advertising resulted in 53 candidates; 10 were hired. Unsolicited applicants included 6 candidates; 1 was hired. Notices in employee service magazines resulted in 12 candidates; 7 were hired.

D. From *one* of the following areas — accounting, word processing services, marketing, personnel, or communications — indicate three subject lines that would be likely for short reports. For example, a possible subject for a short report in the marketing area might be "Sources of New Clients."

Editing Practice

Using Your Word Processor. Can you find any spelling or homonym errors in the following excerpt from a magazine's circulation department report?

Newsstand sales plus subscription sales of the magazine acceded 1.5 million copies in the month of December. Clearly, the principle reason for this sharp increase in sales is that our radio and television advertising in November and December was well planned. In fact, we expect sales of our Febuary addition to reach 1.6 million copies; sales should than level off in the months of March and April and (as usual) decrease over the summer months.

KEY
See page I-48.

KEY
See page I-48.

KEY
Students' answers will vary.

KEY
exceeded
principal
February
edition
then

9.2 *WRITING FORMAL REPORTS*

OBJECTIVES: After completing Section 9.2, you should be able to:

1. List and describe the functions of the main sections of a formal report.
2. Explain how to plan and write a formal report.
3. Explain how to write progress reports while preparing a formal report.
4. Describe the mechanics of report writing.

KEY POINT

Formal reports, as compared to informal memorandum reports, are usually longer. Formal reports often cover more complex problems and questions that often require extensive study or investigation prior to the actual writing process.

SUGGESTION

Impress upon students that employees who can plan and write reports are highly valued in business organizations. In addition, such employees have a direct influence on what the organization does.

How do formal reports differ from the memorandum reports that you learned to write in the previous section? Formal business reports, in addition to being longer than the informal memorandum report, are usually concerned with more complex problems or questions necessitating investigation, analysis, research, and documentation. Some typical formal report subjects might be an analysis of the methods of marketing a company's products; a study to determine how to modernize a particular aspect of a business, such as a study to determine which type of computer accounting and billing system to install; or an experiment to determine how to improve the quality control of a product.

The writing of a formal business report may require weeks or even months of extensive research and reading related to the topic of the report. The completed report could contain anywhere from several pages to more than a hundred pages. Regardless of its length, however, a formal report must be accurately documented and well written, because often the report is the basis upon which a company decides whether or not to spend many thousands of dollars.

Who generally does the actual writing of a formal report? Not everyone is capable of writing an effective formal report. Even though an executive or an engineer or other technician may conduct the research that is the basis for the report, often a secretary or an administrative assistant will be closely involved in the preparation of the report itself. Your skill in writing formal reports will enhance your value to your employer.

Some companies conduct a considerable amount of research and write many reports concerning various research projects. Such companies often hire specialists (sometimes called "technical writers") to put the material assembled by the researcher into report form. If the researcher writes the report, the technical writer can assist the researcher in preparing the report. Technical writers earn high salaries because of their expertise, which is in short supply.

GLOBAL NOTE

Some products come with documents printed in two or more languages. Have students bring examples of such documents to class. Discuss reasons for the use of multilingual materials (saves cost and simplifies storage, shipping, and handling).

You have a head start in learning how to write longer formal reports because you have already learned how to write informal reports. This knowledge is an excellent background for learning how to write the more complex formal report.

PREPARING TO WRITE FORMAL REPORTS

Not all reports look alike. There are some variations in the style and form used in formal reports. These variations are usually determined by the nature of the subject being investigated. For example, a technical report that specifies the requirements for manufacturing computer components may be organized in outline form with very little text. Similarly, the reports of chemists, engineers, and other scientists are likely to include many tables, charts, and graphs, with a relatively small amount of narrative interpretation. On the other hand, many business reports are mainly narrative, possibly with some tabular material. Despite this variation in the style and form, most formal reports include these main sections:

Introduction
Summary
Body
Conclusions and recommendations
Supplementary material

Before commencing the actual writing of the formal report, the writer-investigator must first determine the purpose and the scope of the report. To make this determination, the investigator must gather reliable facts, assemble and analyze those facts, draw conclusions from the factual analysis, and, finally, make recommendations that are reasonable in view of company needs.

Defining Purpose and Scope

Why is the report being written? The answer to this question should appear in the introductory section of the report. For example, in a study to determine whether a company should disband its word processing center and let each department handle its own communication needs, the purpose of the report might be stated as follows:

1. To determine current methods of preparing communications.
2. To determine the efficiency of these methods.
3. To determine the feasibility of returning responsibility for correspondence and report writing activities to individual departments.

A report writer must avoid selecting a topic that is too large in scope to be handled effectively. The experienced report writer, therefore, clearly defines the scope of the problem and sets boundaries that keep the research within reason. For example, think how difficult it would be to do research involving

"Telephone Techniques of Office Workers." This topic is much too broad in scope to be treated in one report, if it could be treated at all. The topic needs to be limited to a more specific group. A revision that would be more practical might read "Telephone Techniques of Customer Representatives of the Arco Electronics Company."

Gathering Information

"No report is stronger than the facts behind it." A term used by computer specialists — *GIGO* (pronounced *guy-go*), standing for "garbage-in, garbage-out" — expresses this idea vividly. The value of any report depends on the quality of the material going into its production. If "garbage" goes in, "garbage" is bound to come out. With reliable facts behind it, a reliable report can be written; with questionable data, only a questionable report can result.

In gathering information and documenting it, writers should be familiar with the authoritative references in their fields. There are, of course, many general references that everyone needs. Such standard sources as the *Readers' Guide to Periodical Literature*, *The Business Periodicals Index*, *The New York Times Annual Index*, *Facts on File*, and *The World Almanac* are invaluable helps to every writer.

In each field of business, such as accounting, marketing, or office administration, there are basic references as well as current periodicals that should be reviewed frequently by report writers. Naturally, anyone doing research must first learn how to find and use books, periodicals, card catalogs, data bases, and various indexes.

When data is to be obtained in other ways, such as through the use of questionnaires or personal interviews, other research techniques will be needed.

Working Bibliography. In consulting the various reference works pertinent to the subject, the writer should make up a list of the books, periodicals, reports, and other sources to be used as references in the report. This preliminary list of sources is called the *working bibliography*. If the writer makes each entry of the working bibliography on a separate card (5 by 3 or 6 by 4 inches), the final bibliography of sources actually used will be easier to assemble. The writer will also find the bibliography cards useful when footnoting material in the report.

A book card for a working bibliography should contain all the following information:

> Author's full name (last name first)
> Complete title (and edition, if there is more than one)
> Name and location of publisher
> Date of publication (latest copyright date)

In addition, it is helpful to include for the writer's own use the library's call number for the reference. The following illustration shows a bibliography card that has been prepared for a book reference.

> Banks, Michael A., and Ansen Dibell
>
> _Word Processing Secrets for Writers,_
> Writers Digest Books, Cincinnati, 1989

This bibliography card for a book shows author, title, publisher, place of publication, and date.

When consulting a magazine, newspaper, or other periodical, the writer prepares a bibliography card like the one below. This card should show the full name of the author, the title of the article (in quotation marks), the name of the publication (and location, if a newspaper), the date, volume, and number of the publication, and the page numbers.

> Singe, Kioshi
> "Minicomputers and Word Processing"
>
> _The Journal of Office Competency,_
> April 1989, pp. 72-76
> Vol. 8, No. 4

Be sure that a bibliography card for an article includes the date, volume and issue numbers, and page numbers as well as author, article title, and periodical title.

Avoid plagiarism by following a simple rule: When taking notes from published sources, use quotation marks around any material that you copy word for word. When you reach the writing stage of your report, you can either quote and acknowledge the source or summarize the material in your own words.

Notetaking. The writer also uses cards for taking notes. Cards are much more practical for this purpose than sheets of paper because cards are sturdy and can be sorted and re-sorted easily.

The ease with which material can be organized and a report can be written depends to a large extent on how well notes have been made from reading. Most good writers take more notes than they need. This practice gives them a great deal of information, which they can "boil down" to the essentials before writing the report.

When you take notes from your reading, be sure to identify each source carefully. Always use a new card for each new source or topic. Normally, summary statements or phrases with page references are sufficient for note cards. Whenever you use a quotation, however, be sure to copy the statement exactly, enclose it in quotation marks, and list the number of the page from which the quotation was taken. Later, when you are organizing the material for writing, you might include a brief subject reference at the top of each card; for example, if you are tracing the development of a product, you might identify references by "year," "developer," or "site of development."

ORGANIZING THE REPORT

After all the material related to the topic has been collected and studied, the writer can begin to organize the report. At this time, the note cards should be revised, sorted by topic, and tentatively organized into a logical sequence for the report.

Outline

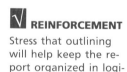

REINFORCEMENT

Stress that outlining will help keep the report organized in logical units.

Using organized note cards as a guide, the writer creates an outline to serve as the structure, or framework, of the report. The outline should be kept as simple as possible. While determining the outline, the writer should keep in mind the kinds of topic headings the report requires. If outline entries are carefully thought out, many of them can be used as topic headings in the final report. The writer should keep in mind the following points in making the outline:

The purpose of the report is to convey information accurately and efficiently.

A good report structure gives the reader a sense of movement; one thought naturally leads into another.

The outline is a time-saver when the writer starts writing.

The outline should be arranged to present material in logical units and in logical sequence.

Headings

Most books, articles, and business reports use headings to indicate the organization of the material. Headings of equivalent weight should be styled alike. For example, the main divisions of an article, a report, or a chapter in a book may be centered, and the subdivisions of each main heading may be typed as paragraph headings. When there are more than two divisions, however, the following arrangement of headings should be used:

CENTERED FIRST-ORDER HEADING

Side Second-Order Heading

    Run-In Third-Order Heading. Text follows on the same line. . . .

If the report writer is consistent in the use of headings, the reader will better understand the report's organization and content. Consistency should be observed in the form as well as in the style of the headings. In general, a topic form is preferred to a sentence form. For example, "How to Write Reports" is preferable to "This Is How to Write Reports."

WRITING THE REPORT

There are considerable differences between the informal writing style of business letters and memorandums and the writing style commonly found in formal reports. These differences are examined in the following discussion.

Writing Style

 **CROSS REFERENCE**
Remind students of the discussion in the previous section about the variety of report styles in informal reports. The discussion on variety also applies to formal reports.

Long business reports are important documents upon which management bases many of its high-level decisions. Consequently, such reports tend to be written in a serious, formal style, usually in the third person. The impersonal style helps the writer avoid interjecting a personal tone that might weaken a report by making it seem merely a statement of one person's opinions and beliefs, instead of a sound evaluation of the data gathered for the report. Of course, usually only one person, the writer, is evaluating the facts, but the more the writer can de-emphasize the *I* and cite facts to back the evaluation, the more objective and more persuasive the report will be.

A poor report writer presenting a report on letter-writing practices might make these statements:

It seems to *me* that the modified block style of letter takes too much time to type.

Personally, *I* would *prefer* to use the simplified letter for all company correspondence.

Even though most of the other departments prefer mixed punctuation, *I* have a strong *preference* for open punctuation, which *I* feel we should adopt.

Even though the facts may provide a sound basis for the evaluations given in the examples above, these sentences do not seem objective because the writer has used so many personal references. In addition, the writer has not shown *how* judgments are drawn from the data gathered.

On the other hand, the good report writer knows that merely stating a judgment will not persuade anyone to accept it, no matter how soundly based on fact and reason the judgment may be. Therefore, the expert writer uses an impersonal style and relates all evaluations to the facts found in the study. This writer carefully avoids any expressions that may imply that the evaluations are based on personal opinions instead of sound reasons and facts. Instead of the sentences given above, the expert writer would write the following:

The evidence revealed by this survey indicates that the modified block style of letter takes 15 percent more typing time than the simplified style.

Use of the simplified letter style would be appropriate for New Visions Entertainment, Inc., because the style has the modern look of simplicity and is also faster and easier to type.

Three of the five departments studied use mixed punctuation; however, adoption of open punctuation would have the following advantages: (Explanation of these advantages would follow.)

The same impersonal writing style illustrated above should characterize every section of the report. Remember that making it possible for the reader to reason from the facts presented is an important factor in the success of any business report.

Title Page

The title page usually includes the complete title of the report, the name and title of the author, the name and title of the person for whom the report is prepared, and the date the report is submitted. These items should be attractively arranged on the page. A typical title page is shown on page 425.

Table of Contents

This section is prepared after the report has been completed. One commonly accepted form is illustrated below.

CONTENTS

THE FEASIBILITY OF ESTABLISHING
A WORD PROCESSING CENTER
AT
Reliable Medical Underwriters Inc.

Prepared by

Sandra Link
Director of Administrative Services

Submitted to

Harold Kaminsky
President

June 10, 19--

This title page shows the complete title of the report, the name and title of the author, the name and title of the person for whom the report is prepared, and the date the report is submitted.

Introduction

The introduction section tells the reader why the report was written, how the data was gathered, and what the report does or does not do.

Suppose that Harold Kaminsky, president of Reliable Medical Underwriters Inc., has assigned Sandra Link, the director of administrative services, the job of investigating the feasibility of establishing a central word processing unit, in order to improve the company's correspondence function and also to cut costs. In such a report, Ms. Link would include in the introduction the *purpose* and *scope* of the report, as well as a description of the *procedures* followed to collect and analyze the data presented in the report.

Purpose and Scope. First, the writer should state why the report was written. Next, the writer should clearly list the basic objectives of the report:

This report was prepared at the request of Mr. Kaminsky, president of Reliable Medical Underwriters Inc. The purposes of the report are:

1. To determine what practices are used in preparing communications in each department of the company.
2. To determine what equipment is used to prepare communications in each department.
3. To determine the costs involved in preparing communications.
4. To determine whether the establishment of a word processing center would improve the quality of company communications and/or decrease the cost of producing company communications.

In addition, a brief statement of the scope of the investigation may be included in this section.

This investigation is limited to the communication practices in the home office of Reliable Medical Underwriters Inc. in Lexington, Massachusetts.

Procedures. The introductory section of the report should describe the methods that were used to collect and analyze the data. Here is an example:

Information for this report was collected through interviews with all supervisors responsible for correspondence in each department and all technical writers. The questionnaire shown in Appendix C of this report was sent in advance and was completed by each supervisor and each technical writer. The responses to the questionnaires were reviewed carefully and were analyzed during the final interview conducted by Monica Alvarez. Major manufacturers of word processing equipment were contacted, and each manufacturer presented a demonstration of its equipment. In addition, current periodicals were consulted to compare the results of this survey with recommended practices for handling communications in other companies.

Summary

As a convenience for the busy executive, the summary is placed early in the report (following the introduction). A summary section contains the most significant information in capsule form, which is helpful to the reader who cannot take time to read the entire report. When time permits, the reader can complete the reading of the report. The length of the summary may range from one paragraph to four or five pages, depending on the amount of material that has been gathered. The following example is the opening paragraph of the summary of the feasibility study to determine whether a word processing center should be established at Reliable Medical Underwriters Inc.:

SUMMARY

This study recommends that a word processing center be established at the home office of Reliable Medical Underwriters Inc. and shows that such a center would improve correspondence practices and decrease correspondence costs. The specific data gathered during this investigation resulted in the following conclusions that led to the above recommendation:

1. More time than is necessary is expended in both the dictation and the transcription processes.
2. There is a great variation in letter styles used throughout the company.
3. Correspondence often is not answered for as long as two to three days after it is received.
4. Many letters that are individually written could well be form letters.

Body

The body is the actual report. In this section the writer tells what research was done, how it was done, and what the writer found. Writing this section should present no great difficulties if the writer follows a carefully prepared outline and has good notes. The writer should stick to accurate, verifiable facts and present them in a clear, concise manner. The suggestions given in Chapter 5 for forceful, clear writing apply also to the writing of reports.

Conclusions and Recommendations

❑ SUGGESTION
Point out that the writer should become thoroughly informed before coming to a conclusion. A conclusion should be based on solid information that can be documented.

This section can easily be the most important one in any report, for it is here that the real results of the report appear. The writer's conclusions tell the busy executive, on the basis of the most reliable data available, "Here is what the report tells us."

Personal observations should be kept to a minimum—conclusions should be drawn only from the facts. In the light of the conclusions and from experience with the company, the writer can make recommendations. As a guide to making worthwhile recommendations, the writer should refer to the listed purposes of the report. As a rule, there should be at least one recommendation for each stated purpose.

By referring to the purposes stated in the introduction of the report on the feasibility of establishing a word processing center at Reliable Medical Underwriters Inc., the writer might include the following conclusions and recommendations:

CONCLUSIONS AND RECOMMENDATIONS

From an analysis of the data gathered in this study, the following conclusions are drawn:

1. Current dictation and transcription practices waste time.
2. Almost half the letters that are individually written could be form letters or could make use of form paragraphs.
3. Little use is made of available dictation equipment.
4. Most of those who dictate do not know how to dictate properly.
5. Secretaries are rarely permitted to compose letters.
6. Only half of the secretaries have word processing equipment.
7. A variety of letter styles is used, depending upon each writer's preference.

With these conclusions in mind, the following action is recommended:

1. Establish a word processing center, using a dedicated word processing system.
2. Make dictation equipment available to each dictator.
3. Provide each dictator with instruction in how to dictate properly and how to use dictation equipment properly.
4. Adopt the simplified letter as the standard letter style to be used throughout the company.
5. Keep comparative communication costs as a basis for determining whether word processing centers should be established in the branch offices of the company.

Supplementary Information

Supplementary information, which is given after the conclusions and recommendations, provides substantiating data for the report. One or all of the features discussed below may be included.

Illustrations. A formal report can often be enhanced by including graphics or illustrations. When should graphic displays be used to supplement the material in your report? Consider using graphics when any or all of the following situations occur:

1. The information — ideas, facts, or figures — being presented is complex, and illustrations will help simplify it.
2. Visuals can reinforce the logic of your conclusions and recommendations.
3. You are comparing or contrasting two sets of data or analyzing trends.
4. Statements need to be documented, and tables and other displays will provide the necessary information.

What kinds of graphic or visual displays should be included? The kind depends on the information you are presenting and your purpose in presenting this information. The possibilities include:

1. Tables — to provide a visible comparison of two or more sets of data and ready access to information.

2. Bar graphs — to depict relationships between fixed groups of data or to compare or contrast two sets of data.
3. Line graphs — to illustrate trends or how sets of data have changed over a period of time.
4. Circle graphs (pie charts) — to show the relationships between parts and a whole.
5. Diagrams, flowcharts, organizational charts — to simplify complex relationships or operations.
6. Photographs — to document information or statements.

How graphic displays are prepared varies from company to company. Unless you are a business writer with artistic ability, you may wish to have visuals prepared by your corporate art department or by an independent artist or agency. Another alternative is to use a graphics software program to prepare visuals. Several excellent programs that produce sophisticated, professional-looking graphic displays are available, and they are easy to learn.

Appendix. The appendix consists mainly of supporting information to back up the material in the body of the report. Long tables, charts, photographs, questionnaires, letters, and drawings are usually placed in this section. By including such material at the end of the report, the body of the report is freed from the kind of detail that makes reading difficult.

Bibliography. This section is an alphabetic listing of all the references used in the report. Bibliographic entries are listed in alphabetic order by author. Forms for book and periodical entries are shown below.

Books

Braun, Harold F., *Communication Procedures*, Westly Book Company, New York, 19—.

Schrag, A. F., *How to Dictate*, McGraw-Hill Book Company, New York, 19—.

Periodicals

Greene, Arnold, "Word Processing Centers," *The Office Worker*, Vol. XV, No. 6, 19—, pp. 89–100.

Zane, Anthony, "Cutting Communication Cost," *The Executive*, Vol. IV, No. 3, 19—, pp. 34–38.

Letter of Transmittal

A short letter of transmittal shown below, composed after the report has been completed, accompanies the report. It is written in the form of a memorandum and usually contains such information as:

A reference to the person who authorized the report.
A brief statement of the general purpose of the report.
Appropriate statements of appreciation or acknowledgment.

Reliable Medical Underwriters, Inc.

To: Mr. Harold Kaminsky, President

From: Sandra Link, Director of Administrative Services

Date: June 10, 19--

Subject: Attached Report on the Feasibility of
Establishing a Word Processing Center

On April 30, 19--, you authorized a feasibility study concerning the
establishment of a word processing center. This study is now
completed. The results of the study, together with my conclusions and
recommendations, are contained in the attached report.

The results are significant, and I hope that they will be of value to
you. Much credit should be given to Monica Alvarez, my assistant, who
conducted several of the surveys and helped a great deal with the
organization and writing of this report.

If you wish, I shall be glad to discuss the report with you at your
convenience.

                              SL

ma
Enclosure

When a formal report is intended for a person within the organization, the letter of transmittal is prepared in the form of a memo.

Progress Reports

As indicated earlier, it may take months to complete an investigation and prepare the finished product, the written report. When such is the case, it is a good idea to keep the person who requested the investigation informed as to the progress being made. How many progress reports will be called for depends upon how much time elapses following the original request.

A progress report generally is made in memorandum form. Suppose that you were requested on April 30 to make an investigation of the feasibility of establishing a word processing center at Reliable Medical Underwriters' home office. On May 15, you might prepare the following memorandum:

You asked me on April 30 to investigate the feasibility of establishing a word processing center. I have now completed all the preliminary investigation and am ready to analyze the data I have gathered. I am also in the process of investigating word processing equipment available from the leading manufacturers. I expect to complete all my investigation and analysis by May 30 and to have the report completed on or before June 10.

MECHANICS OF REPORT WRITING

√ **REINFORCEMENT**

Stress the importance of making a good first impression with the appearance of a report. Obviously, content is important; however, the content may not be read as thoroughly if the reader forms a negative first impression.

An immaculate physical appearance, expert placement, and careful attention to the mechanics of English, spelling, and punctuation emphasize the importance of the finished report. For this reason, mechanics, as well as organization and writing style, are important in preparing the report.

Of course, all the mechanics of English, spelling, and punctuation discussed in earlier chapters apply to report writing. Some suggestions for setting up a report are also necessary, and they are presented in the following paragraphs.

1. Use common sense and show variety in paragraphing; try to avoid too many long and too many short paragraphs. Keep in mind that the topic sentence, telling what the paragraph is about, frequently comes first. Also, the closing sentence is often used to summarize the meaning of the paragraph.

2. Be generous in using headings. Take care to leave plenty of white space around major headings, tables, and other display materials. Be sure that all headings of the same value within a section are parallel in wording. For example:

Nonparallel	*Parallel*
Writing the Introduction	Writing the Introduction
The Body	Writing the Body
How to Write the Closing	Writing the Closing

i **INFORMATION**

Point out that students should footnote ideas that are taken from someone else or another source, even though students are not quoting the material word for word. Taking credit for an idea presented by someone else is a form of plagiarism, in the same way that using the words of someone else without enclosing those words in quotation marks is plagiarism.

3. Use footnotes to give credit when the ideas of others are used, either verbatim or modified. A footnote may be placed at the bottom of the page carrying the footnoted item, or all the footnotes may be listed at the end of the report. Footnotes should always be numbered consecutively, whether they appear at the bottom of each footnoted page or are grouped at the end of the report. The information usually given in a footnote includes the footnote number, author, book or periodical title, publisher, place and date of publication, and page numbers. Since footnote styles may vary, it is advisable to consult the company's reference manual or a standard reference manual.

4. Select carefully any tables, charts, diagrams, photographs, drawings, and other illustrated materials used to supplement the writing. To promote better understanding of the contents, choose the items that contribute most to the report. Try to eliminate any items that are not pertinent.

5. Observe these rules of good manuscript form:
   a. Type all reports on standard $8\frac{1}{2}$- by 11-inch paper. Legal-size paper will not fit standard office files.

b. Use double spacing except for long quotations (usually three or more lines), for which single spacing is preferred. Of course, type on only one side of the sheet. Consult a standard style manual for other spacing details.

c. Leave ample margins. Commonly accepted margins are these:
Left margin: 1½ inches to allow for side binding.
Other margins: 1 inch.
First page only: When it contains the title, allow a 2-inch top margin.

d. Always prepare at least one file copy.

e. Traditionally, the first page is not numbered when it contains the title. All other pages, beginning with 2, should be numbered in the upper-right corner.

f. Follow this pattern for any material presented in outline form:
I.
   A.
      1.
         a.
            (1)
               (a)

6. Bind the report attractively. Many types of binding, from the single staple to an elaborate sewn binding, can be used. Reports that are subject to frequent, rigorous use should be placed inside a special hardback report folder for protection. Do not rely on a paper clip to bind the report; the chances of losing part of the report are very high.

SECTION

REVIEW

Practical Application

A. In memorandum report form, write a report for your instructor that describes the function of each of the following parts of a report:

1. Title page
2. Table of contents
3. Introduction
4. Summary
5. Body
6. Conclusions and recommendations
7. Supplementary material

B. Write a progress report for your employer, Charlotte Hopkins, using the following information:

1. Nature of the study: dictation habits of executives at ABC Company.

2. Assigned March 31; due May 1; progress report April 16.
3. Completed so far: interviews with 20 executives, the total number of executives in the company; visits and interviews with three distributors of dictating equipment.
4. Remaining research: library research, analysis of data gathered, determination of conclusions and recommendations. Add any additional items you think should be included.

KEY
See page I-49.

C. Prepare a questionnaire that might be suitable for gathering data for a report on "Library Usage by College Students." The class will discuss the validity and wording of the questions submitted by the class members.

KEY
See page I-49.

D. You have been asked by your department manager, Michael Patel, to attend a meeting on employee turnover and to write a report based on the information presented at the meeting. From the notes you took, prepare a report, supplying other data that you think might be appropriate. Here are your notes:

1. Annual turnover rate: manufacturing employees, 20 percent; office, 15 percent.
2. Reasons given for leaving the company (in order of frequency): Manufacturing — working conditions undesirable, higher salary in another company, friction with supervisors, little opportunity for advancement. Office — better salary, little opportunity for further advancement, poor working conditions, friction with managers, difficult commuting, inadequate employee benefits.
3. Recommended actions: Improve facilities by (1) redecorating offices and installing air conditioning and (2) replacing old furniture and equipment with modern and more efficient articles; encourage frequent departmental meetings that will give employees an opportunity to express their opinions; institute training program for supervisors; initiate a salary survey of similar businesses and similar jobs; study promotion policies; obtain services of a management consultant to make recommendations concerning employee benefits; consider the possibility of designating a personnel relations counselor to handle grievances.
4. Department managers are to consider the turnover problem with reference to their experiences with employees under their supervision, are to be prepared to discuss the problem further, and are to make recommendations at a special meeting to be held on August 18. Prior to this meeting, by August 3, managers should submit a memorandum on morale in their departments.
5. In the discussion, it was brought out that there seems to be an atmosphere of unrest and that morale is generally low. It was also pointed out that the commuting problem may be eased shortly,

REVIEW cont.

when the proposed new bus route (direct from the Riverside area) goes into operation.

Editing Practice

Editing for Writing Power. Edit and rewrite these sentences for the purpose of improving writing power.

KEY
See page I-50.

1. Ms. Andrews is the new administrative assistant, and she is very proficient in computer operation.
2. Her major is economics, but marketing also interests her.
3. Spend an afternoon at the job fair, and there you can learn about job opportunities for recent college graduates.
4. Desiring to avert a strike, a discussion of fringe benefits was held.
5. Not having been able to obtain any information about loans; and as he did not know the procedures for making such loans, the new manager decided we must deal on a cash basis.
6. The manager refunded my money, when I returned the floppy disks.
7. I liked the graphics in your report. They were readable. They contained accurate and complete information.
8. Although wanting information for his report, but he felt he had invested enough time, Ed began the writing without it.
9. The report to the executives about the new billing system that was started for the Toledo branch, was long and complicated so then the credit manager had to call a special meeting to explain it.
10. The report on sight possibilities was given by the reality agents.

9.3 *KEEPING MEETING RECORDS*

OBJECTIVES: After completing Section 9.3, you should be able to:

1. Record and prepare for distribution a set of minutes for a meeting.
2. Explain the role of group recorder at meetings conducted by the Interaction Method.

Every organization, business or social, has meetings and must keep a record of what happens at these meetings. These records of the proceedings of meetings, called *minutes*, are another type of report used in business. The minutes serve as a permanent record of the decisions reached and the actions that are to be taken. The minutes can also be used to inform those who were not at the meeting of what took place. At one time or another, most business employees will serve as recorder in a group or committee and be responsible for keeping an accurate set of minutes. For this reason, you should know how to prepare minutes.

RECORDING THE MINUTES

The accurate recording of the proceedings of all meetings is an important function, for the minutes usually serve as the only historical record of a meeting.

There is probably no one best way to record what happens at a meeting. If an agenda of the meeting has been prepared beforehand, the secretary or recorder should receive a copy. The agenda lists briefly the business to be transacted and acts as a guide to the person who presides at the meeting. The agenda also helps the secretary check to be sure that all scheduled items are accounted for in the minutes. Much of the success of good notetaking revolves around the personal efficiency of the secretary. However, any secretary preparing to record the proceedings of a meeting should find the following general guidelines helpful:

1. Record the time and place of the meeting.
2. List the persons attending and those absent. In a small group, actual names can be given; in a large group, however, it is usually sufficient either to state the number of people present, such as "Forty-five members were present," or to list the names of the absentees only.
3. In the opening section of the minutes, mention the fact that the minutes for the previous meeting were read and approved, amended, or not approved.
4. Record the important points in the discussion of each item on the agenda. Presenting supporting facts helps those who were present recall the discussion and informs those who were not present. Papers read during the meeting are often attached to the final typewritten minutes because it is usually not possible for the secretary to record verbatim all such information.
5. Record verbatim all resolutions and motions, as well as the names of the persons who introduced and seconded the motions. If this information is not recorded when the motion is made, the secretary should request that the motion be repeated or even put in writing so that the exact motion is recorded.
6. Type the minutes first in draft form so that they can be edited before being prepared in final form. Sometimes, the secretary may want to get another person's approval before issuing the minutes in final form. The secretary signs the minutes, thus certifying their accuracy according to his or her notes. Sometimes the presiding officer countersigns them.

 **KEY POINT**

Minutes are the written record of a meeting.

◻ **SUGGESTION**

Point out that minutes for a social group are similar to minutes that would be kept for a meeting conducted in a business setting. You might determine if there are any students in the class who have kept minutes for a social group. Also point out that the form used for minutes varies.

```
                    ASSOCIATION OF BEST COMPANY EMPLOYEES

                    MINUTES OF MEETING OF April 19, 19--


TIME, PLACE,        The monthly meeting of the Association of Best Company
ATTENDANCE          Employees was held in the Blue Room at 5:30 p.m.  The
                    president, Jan Dixon, presided.  All members and
                    officers were present.

MINUTES             The minutes of the last meeting, March 15, 19--, were
                    read and approved.

OFFICERS'           Treasurer:  The treasurer reported receipts of $650,
REPORTS             disbursements of $150, and a balance of $967 as of
                    April 1, 19--.  Tony Valenti moved the acceptance of
                    the report.  Anne Terry seconded the motion.  Motion
                    carried.

COMMITTEE           Chairperson William Ferris presented the report of the
REPORTS             nominating committee.  The nominees are:

                              President:        Meg Andrews
                              Vice President:   James Brown
                              Secretary:        Antonio Valdez
                              Treasurer:        Garth Kimberly

                    Rosa Sanchez moved that nominations be closed and that
                    a unanimous ballot be cast for the slate of officers
                    presented by the committee.  The motion was seconded by
                    Yamen Abdulah.  Motion carried.

UNFINISHED          Plans for the Annual Retirement Dinner to be held
BUSINESS            June 30 were discussed.  Tory's Inn and Edwin's were
                    suggested for this event.  The president will report to
                    the group at the next meeting about these restaurants.

NEW                 The president reported that the Board of Directors is
BUSINESS            considering a policy change regarding tuition
                    reimbursement for college courses taken.  The change
                    would involve getting approval for each course in
                    advance.  The feeling of the group was to recommend to
                    the board that the words "unless prior approval is not
                    feasible" be added to this change in policy.

ADJOURNMENT         The meeting adjourned at 6:15 p.m.

                                        Respectfully submitted,

                                        Ivy Lewis
                                        Ivy Lewis
```

This two-column format for minutes uses topical headings.

```
                    MINUTES OF THE MEETING

                            of the

                      Board of Directors

                     Best Company, Inc.
                       April 10, 19--

    Presiding:   Sandra Michel

    Present:     Dale Thompson
                 Marta Maez
                 Jo Ann Keith
                 Frank Ericson
                 Hideko Chang

    Absent:      Samuel Smyth


    The meeting was called to order at 11 a.m. by Ms. Michel.
    The principle topics for discussion concerned recommended
    changes in two company policies, one related to donations
    to charitable organizations and the other related to
    reimbursing employees for tuition for college courses.

    With reference to donations to charitable organizations,
    Ms. Keith proposed that all donations be limited to a
    maximum of $300.  After some discussion, the Board agreed
    and voted unanimously to add this limit to the present
    policies concerning charitable donations.

    Mr. Ericson proposed that tuition reimbursement should be
    made only if the employee has received prior approval of
    the course submitted for tuition reimbursement.  The
    present policy does not require that approval be given in
    advance.  Mr. Chang was opposed to the change and
    suggested that this proposal be tabled until the next
    meeting.  In the meantime, employee opinion regarding the
    change should be sought.  The board voted to table the
    proposal until the May meeting and asked Mr. Chang to
    consult with the Executive Board of the Associated
    Employees regarding pros and cons of this change.  The
    meeting adjourned at 12:30 p.m.

                        Respectfully submitted,

                        Kenneth Dorsey
                        Kenneth Dorsey, Secretary
```

The proceedings of the meeting are written in complete detail in this format for minutes.

7. Make one copy of the minutes and file it in the folder, notebook, or binder used for this purpose. Usually minutes are duplicated and sent to each person present at the meeting or to designated officers who would be interested in the business of the meeting.

FORMAT OF MINUTES

![i] INFORMATION

Companies or organizations may specify a particular format for minutes. New employees or new members of an organization who are asked to take minutes should ask to see copies of the most recent minutes.

Various formats are used for meeting minutes. The main issue, however, is to make sure that all the essential information appears in a neat, well-arranged form. Some organizations prefer to emphasize the main points on the agenda by using a standardized format.

The minutes on page 436 illustrate an acceptable format. Notice the standard pattern and the topical headings that are used for all meetings of this group and the way in which the motions and discussion are summarized.

Other groups use a more traditional format (as shown on page 437) in which the proceedings of the meeting are written in rather complete detail.

MINUTES PREPARED BY A GROUP RECORDER

![person] KEY POINT

In the Interaction Method, a group recorder writes the ideas—as they are presented—on a chalkboard or on large pieces of paper. The collective record is later printed and is called the group memory.

In some organizations, meetings are conducted according to the Interaction Method,[1] a system designed to encourage people to participate actively in meetings. (See Section 10.6.) The minutes of the meeting are taken by someone designated as the "group recorder." The role of the group recorder is to write down ideas as they are exchanged, using the actual words of the speaker. The recorder stands in front of the group and writes on large sheets of paper so that the members of the group can see what is being recorded. The collective record that is created is called the *group memory*.

KEY
See page I-50.

SECTION *REVIEW*

Practical Application

A. Assume that you are the secretary of the Millstone Employees' Association, charged with the responsibility for taking minutes at all meetings and distributing copies to each member. From the following information, prepare in a concise format the minutes of the latest meeting:

1. The meeting, held in Room 5A, Tyler Building, was called to order by President Karl Swensen at 5:30 p.m., March 15, 19 — .

2. Correction in minutes of preceding meeting (February 15) approved: Ina Singer, not Rita Singer, was appointed chairperson of the Welfare Committee.

---

[1]Michael Doyle and David Straus, *How to Make Meetings Work*, Wyden Books, 1976, pp. 83–87.

REVIEW cont.

3. Karen Bjorn reviewed employee suggestions for January. Awards of $100 each for two accepted suggestions were approved. Bjorn to make arrangements for presenting the awards at the spring banquet.
4. Revised written procedure for handling employee suggestions presented by Jack Stuhlman. Accepted with editorial revision to be made by appropriate committee.
5. Meeting adjourned at 6:15 p.m., with the understanding that the next meeting would be a dinner meeting at Jackson's Restaurant, April 21, to begin at 6:30 p.m.
6. The following members were absent: Holden, Yates, Witmer.

B. Do research about how meetings are conducted using the Interaction Method. Try to interview people who have attended such meetings. Then write a report that explains how the method works and that states whether you think meetings conducted this way are more productive.

Editing Practice

Spelling Check. Correct any spelling errors in the following paragraph.

Harrison, who dislikes meetings, thought the comittee meeting was a waist of time. Everyone else, of corse, disagreed. Alice Croft chairred the meeting and encouraged the members to participat fully. Clark recorded the minuets — a task that he enjoys and takes seriusly. We were all accomodating and listened to one another's ideas. Accept for Harrison, we all left the meeting convinced that a productive meeting had been adjorned.

KEY
B. Reports will vary.

KEY
committee
waste
course
chaired
participate
minutes
seriously
accommodating
Except
adjourned

9.4 *PREPARING NEWS RELEASES*

OBJECTIVES: After completing Section 9.4, you should be able to:

1. Explain the purpose of a news release.
2. Write a news release, using the correct form.

Publicity, advertising, public relations, goodwill — all these terms denote the effort of a business to get its name, its reputation, and its product before the public. In fact, large companies — even schools and colleges — today employ a public relations staff, whose job is to attract favorable public attention to their organizations.

Public relations specialists use a particular type of report called a *news release* to inform the media of newsworthy events. They hope that the media will prepare a story for publication or broadcast, based on the news release. Knowing how to prepare news releases is another way of making yourself valuable to your employer.

THE FUNCTION OF THE NEWS RELEASE

An important means of getting the planned publicity of business into the hands of the public is the news release. Whenever a business plans an announcement or an event that it considers newsworthy or capable of enhancing its public image, its public relations personnel prepare and submit a news release to various news outlets for publication or broadcasting. Such a news announcement may concern the appointment of a new company president after a meeting of the board of directors; it may tell of a large local expansion in a company's plant, which will increase the work force and have a great impact on the economy of the community. The news announcement may publicize the introduction of a new line or new product, or it may concern the awarding of some honor (perhaps for long, faithful service) to a member of the organization. Any item that will interest the public and create goodwill for the organization is an appropriate subject for a news release.

Any news story sent by a company must, of course, be approved for release. In large companies, the director of public relations would have this responsibility. In small companies, individual department heads might handle their own news and distribute it in keeping with company policy, or releases might be issued from the office of the president or of one particular executive.

To be printed or broadcast and thereby serve its purpose, the release must be newsworthy; that is, the contents of the release must be of sufficient interest to the public. Naturally, the writing style of the news release, as well as the form in which it appears, will have a strong effect on the news editor who decides whether or not the story is worth printing or broadcasting.

◩ REINFORCEMENT

Emphasize that businesses value highly a favorable image in the community. Often a company hires a public relations firm or establishes its own public relations staff to maintain this favorable image. This image is a great part of what a business considers one of its assets—goodwill.

ℹ INFORMATION

Again, there is no one prescribed form for a news release. However, there are some rules that should be followed in preparing a news release that will provide greater assurance that it will be published.

THE FORM OF THE NEWS RELEASE

With hundreds of releases coming to their desks each week, news editors will select for publication or broadcast the items that require the least amount of rewriting, everything else being equal. Therefore, the news release must give complete, accurate information in a "news style" of writing that presents the facts in a clear and interesting way.

Many organizations use a special form for issuing news releases. These forms are arranged so that editors can get to the heart of the story without wasting time. Like a letterhead, a news release form usually contains the name and address of the company or organization and the name, address, and telephone number of the person responsible for issuing the release to the public.

1. The news release is double-spaced with generous margins for possible changes by the news editor.
2. The writer includes a tentative headline in all-capital letters to identify the story. An editor, of course, will change this title to fit the space requirements and style of the publication or broadcast.
3. The news release indicates the time when a story may be published. In the example, note the prominence of the phrase *For Immediate Release*. A release may be sent to the media before an event occurs so that news will reach the public at almost the same time the event takes place. For example, if a company plans to announce a million-dollar gift to a local hospital at a banquet on Saturday, June 25, the release might read *For release after 6 p.m., Saturday, June 25*.
4. In a long release, subheads may be inserted between parts of the release to relieve the reading monotony and to guide the editor who wants to scan the story.
5. If there is more than one page to the release, the word *MORE* in parentheses is added at the end of the first and each intermediate page. At the end of the last page of the release, the symbol -×××-, ###, o0o, or -30- (adapted from the telegrapher's abbreviation *30*, which means "the end") is typed to indicate the end of the release.

WRITING THE NEWS RELEASE

 **KEY POINT**

The opening paragraphs should summarize the story and present the most newsworthy information first, including *who, what, why, how,* and *when.*

However good the form of a written communication, the subject and the words determine whether the release will be read and used. In writing a news release — just as in writing letters, memorandums, and reports — certain guides will help the writer develop an effective writing style and will improve the chances of getting the release printed. Especially important is the arrangement of paragraphs in the news release.

The opening paragraph of a news release should summarize the entire story and should present the most newsworthy information first. In this opening section, the writer should give the *who, what, why, how, when,* and *where* of the news story in such a form that this paragraph can stand by itself. If, for example, an announcement is to be made of the appointment of Pamela Browning as international marketing director of New Millennium Electronics, Inc., a poor lead paragraph might read:

> Hayden Bartholomew, president of New Millennium Electronics, Inc., announced today the appointment of Ms. Pamela Browning as international marketing director.

Hayden Bartholomew is not the person the article is about; therefore, the lead paragraph should read:

> Ms. Pamela Browning has been named international marketing director of New Millennium Electronics, Inc., by its president, Hayden Bartholomew.

1678 State Street
Boston, Massachusetts 02102
617-555-3405

News Release
Emanuel Gomez
Director of Public Relations

```
          Ralph Greene
          Manager
          Boston News Bureau
          617-555-7500


For Immediate Release                    May 30, 19--


        GLORIA ATWATER NAMED PERSONNEL DIRECTOR

             OF LORIMER NATIONAL BANK


     Boston, May 30, 19--.  Gloria Atwater has been named

personnel director of Lorimer National Bank in Boston by

its president, Mark Rider.

     Ms. Atwater succeeds George Abel, who retired from the

bank on April 15 after serving for 30 years.

     The new personnel director joined the Lorimer National

Bank in Covington a year ago as a training director.

Before that, she was a business education teacher and

guidance counselor at Lexington High School.  Ms. Atwater

is a graduate of the University of Massachusetts and a

member of the Boston Chamber of Commerce.

                         -xxx-
```

A news release must give complete, accurate information in a "news style" of writing. Note that this company has a special preprinted form for its news releases.

KEY POINT

The first one or two paragraphs should provide a complete story. The rest of the release provides additional details.

KEY
See page I-51.

KEY
See page I-51.

Each succeeding paragraph should supply background facts in the order of decreasing importance. In this way, editors who need to shorten the release because of space or time limitations can easily shorten the story from the bottom up. For example, notice that the first two paragraphs in the news release illustrated on page 442 make a complete news story by themselves. The remainder of the copy provides additional details. A common practice is to include quotations from an official or other important person commenting on the news in the release.

REVIEW

Practical Application

A. The AEP (Association for Environmental Protection) held its first organizational meeting in your community last evening. Margot Hayden was elected president, and you were elected secretary-treasurer. The technical adviser is Professor Sidney Allen, chairperson of the Science Department of Mercer County College. The group plans to meet monthly on the first Wednesday of each month. Its aims are to publicize instances of local pollution and toxic waste dumping, to investigate possible conservation measures in the community, and to recommend publicity to make the community more conservation-oriented. Write a news release about the organization — its officers, aims, plans — for your local newspaper. Supply any additional facts that you feel are needed.

B. Your boss, George Theopolus, vice president of Northwest Paper Company of Portland, Oregon, requests that you write a news release for the news outlets in the Portland area announcing the retirement of the company president, Philip Alvarez, at the end of this year. The newspaper may make the announcement immediately since the board of directors has already regretfully accepted Mr. Alvarez's notice of retirement. Alvarez has been with the company for 25 years, serving as president for the last 10 years. He started his career with the company as a shop supervisor and then became factory manager within 2 years. Alvarez became a vice president shortly thereafter and remained in that position until 10 years ago, when the board of directors elected him president. Following his retirement, Mr. Alvarez will serve as chairman of the board of directors. Alvarez lives in Seacrest with his wife. They have two married sons and one married daughter, all of whom live in Portland. Alvarez is a graduate in accounting from Youngstown College, where he was class president during his senior year.

REVIEW cont.

Alvarez has served on the Portland Chamber of Commerce for 5 years, is a member of both Rotary and Kiwanis, and has headed the City Beautification Committee for the last 3 years. Using an acceptable format, write a news release. Supply any information that should be included.

Editing Practice

Supply the Missing Words. Indicate a word or words that you think would make sense if inserted in the blank space within each sentence.

1. If this booklet does not give you the . . . you desire, please write us again.
2. Thank you for being so . . . in filling our order for eight laser printers.
3. We are happy to tell you that your . . . has been established at the Crawford Hotel.
4. We hope that we shall have the pleasure of serving you whenever you have . . . to use our repair service.
5. Once you know the . . . of a credit card, you will never shop without your card.
6. Please sign the original copy and return it to us in the enclosed envelope, retaining the . . . for your files.
7. We understand that your company will probably . . . to purchase as much as $3,000 worth of office supplies monthly on your new charge account.
8. We hope that your clerical staff will . . . some means of checking purchases made by persons of the same name but of different addresses.
9. Of course, we have taken steps to see that there is no . . . of this error.
10. We hope that our business dealings will be . . . pleasant and profitable.
11. The report . . . the data that had been gathered by the newly appointed committee.
12. The new telephone system was . . . just before the Christmas rush began.
13. An office worker's . . . is judged not only by the volume of work completed but also by the accuracy of the work.
14. All the payroll . . . were noted on the check stub.
15. Government . . . are available to many different groups and organizations.
16. We recently . . . a state-of-the-art computer system for the accounting department.

KEY

1. information, details
2. accurate, prompt, helpful
3. credit
4. the opportunity, the need
5. advantages, convenience
6. copy, second copy, duplicate
7. wish, desire, plan
8. find, discover, devise
9. repetition, recurrence
10. both, mutually
11. summarized, analyzed, presented, verified
12. installed, completed
13. efficiency, value
14. deductions
15. grants, funds
16. bought, purchased, installed

9.5 COMMUNICATING IN THE ELECTRONIC OFFICE

OBJECTIVES: After completing Section 9.5, you should be able to:

1. Describe the electronic office.
2. Define *information processing* and *word processing*.
3. Describe telecommunications.
4. Compose electronic messages.

❑**SUGGESTION**

Ask students to develop a time line tracing the developments in office automation.

Technology has definitely had an impact on business communication. For years, the only equipment used in an office was the typewriter, the telephone, and the calculator. Now, the electronic office is equipped with computerized information processing systems, including word processing and electronic communication systems.

Although technology has drastically changed the ways messages are created, transmitted, and received, the standards for business communications have not been lowered. Effective communication must still be clear, complete, concise, consistent, correct, and courteous; and human relations techniques still must be applied.

THE TRADITIONAL OFFICE

To understand why the electronic office was needed, we must first look at the traditional office.

Organizational Structure

Most offices were composed of secretaries, typists, and clerks who handled the paperwork for a business. Each executive had a full-time secretary who did a variety of tasks such as typing, filing, and duplicating. Work loads varied considerably. For example, one secretary might have been extremely busy while the secretary in the adjoining office had idle time. A secretary often had idle time when the executive was away from the office. When a secretary was temporarily away, however, work would pile up.

Environment

Although some authorities were predicting a paperless office, what came instead was a paper explosion. The availability of convenience copiers and the ease of getting computer printouts seemed to encourage businesses to create mounds of paperwork—some of it necessary and some not. Filing cabinets were filled to capacity. Computer printouts were stacked on every available surface.

Desks were cluttered with correspondence, folders, message pads, and a variety of error correction material (erasers, correction tape, and correction liquid).

Productivity

There were enough people in the traditional office, but they were not working efficiently enough. Office costs were rising, but the amount and quality of the work was not increasing. Information was not readily available for executives, and this situation hampered decision making.

THE ELECTRONIC OFFICE

□ SUGGESTION

Ask students to research projected innovations in equipment and services that may be available in the next five to ten years.

The need for improved environment, organization, and productivity caused management to look for ways to improve the office. Many innovations were introduced to speed the processing of information.

Organization

In many cases, management restructured the organization to provide for adequate supervision. Office personnel were given new titles and responsibilities that did not tie them to a specific executive. This new structure allowed them to progress through career paths that were visible and accessible.

Environment

LIVING LANGUAGE

Many ideas grow better when transplanted into another mind than in the one where they sprang up.

—Oliver Wendell Holmes, Jr.

Technology improved the environment. *Word processing* equipment provided an easier way to produce correction-free communications that eliminated the various correction materials and repeated retypings. *Electronic storage systems* (tapes, disks, and so on) reduced the number of filing cabinets, the stacks of computer printouts, and the proliferation of unnecessary copies. *Electronic distribution systems* were used to deliver messages within the office, to branch offices, and to other destinations. For example, *voice mail* helped to solve the telephone tag problem (repeated failure to make contact by phone even though both parties are trying). Voice mail stores the actual voice. *Facsimile (fax) machines* were developed to transmit exact copies of already completed handwritten and typewritten information as well as graphs, illustrations, and photos.

Productivity

Information systems helped managers reach decisions by making the necessary data readily available. One innovation that saves time and increases accessibility is the *executive workstation*. The executive workstation may be a microcomputer operating independently or a computer terminal linked to the company's main computer. Without leaving the office, an executive can examine information and make the calculations necessary to provide an informed, timely decision. Automated equipment simplified tasks and increased the amount of work completed by executives and other business personnel.

BUSINESS COMMUNICATION TECHNOLOGY

During the last 30 years, technology has provided major developments for the electronic office: information processing, word processing, and telecommunications. In some offices, these three developments are operated independently. However, the trend is to merge them into a total system—an information processing system.

Information Processing

❑ **SUGGESTION**

Ask a local executive to speak to your class on the communications technology used at his or her firm.

Information processing is the manipulation of data by electronic means to collect, organize, record, process, distribute, and store information for decision-making purposes. It can relieve office personnel of routine, time-consuming, repetitive work. For example, a *spreadsheet* program—a computerized version of an accountant's ledger—will perform numerical calculations and recalculate totals when one or more numbers are changed. Spreadsheets allow businesses to keep and update accounting, inventory, and sales records and to schedule operations and maintain cost controls. Many companies also rely on *data base* programs to store and organize facts and figures in electronic files, to compile and maintain lists of customers and their addresses, to generate mass mailings and lists of past-due accounts, and to keep track of inventory.

❑ **SUGGESTION**

White collar crime as it relates to communication security is an interesting topic for group research and discussion.

Much of the information processed and stored in a computer is either confidential or necessary for the continued success of company operations. For this reason, management should protect company records from accidental security breaks, from unintentional destruction, and from unauthorized access. Many states are passing laws covering electronic "snooping."

The possibilities and applications offered by information processing systems are seemingly unlimited. Word processing, of course, is one of the major functions of information processing.

Word Processing

Even though the term *word processing* is fairly recent, office personnel have been processing words for years. They have taken spoken, written, and typed words and presented them in final typewritten form. Today, however, technology has simplified the production of the final form. The concept of word processing involves taking ideas and using automated equipment to produce them in final form. Once the idea is entered into the equipment, it becomes a *document*.

Word processing equipment evolved from the automatic typewriters that appeared on the market in the 1960s. Since that time, there have been many improvements and developments by different vendors. One of the main benefits of word processing equipment is that it has text-manipulation capabilities. In other words, text can be added, deleted, moved, corrected, and revised before the final document is printed. In addition, after a document has been printed, it can be stored electronically. Once a document has been stored, it can be retrieved at a later time to make revisions or copied to create new versions. The use of word processing equipment has saved companies countless hours formerly spent keyboarding correspondence and other communications on a typewriter.

Word processors have keyboards that are similar to typewriter keyboards. As information is entered using this keyboard, the document appears simultaneously on a screen. The operator can read the document, make needed changes, and when sure that the document is correct, initiate a print command. The revised document is then printed at a speed that far exceeds the speed of superior typists. Because changes were made before printing, there are no messy corrections in the final copy.

The word processing function is accomplished by dedicated word processors, microcomputers with word processing software, and a company's main computer. *Dedicated word processors* are designed and used primarily for word processing applications, although some of them also have calculating functions. *Microcomputers* have word processing capabilities usually through a *software program* — a set of instructions — that was written specifically for that purpose. Some companies use computer terminals to access word processing capabilities stored in a program run by their main computer.

❑ **SUGGESTION**
Try to arrange a field trip to a company that uses desktop publishing. Students need to see all the steps from idea conception to finished product.

In recent years *desktop publishing* (DTP) programs have gained popularity. These specialized software programs enable the user to lay out pages that combine text generated by a word processing program and illustrations created on a graphics software program. Many companies have reduced costs by producing their own professional-looking brochures, booklets, and catalogs using desktop publishing programs and laser printers.

Word processing in the electronic office saves valuable time and resources and reduces operating costs. Although investing in word processing equipment may be costly, the initial outlay is quickly recovered by increased productivity and higher-quality communications.

Telecommunications

Telecommunications is the transmission of information by telephone lines, satellites, or networks. Because of rising postage costs and the need to speed up message delivery, many companies are using telecommunications of various types to transmit information. The telephone call is a simple but familiar form of telecommunications. However, voice is not the only way that data can be transmitted electronically. Today printed words and graphic images may also be sent electronically.

REINFORCEMENT

As part of a newscast, television anchors often interview distantly located celebrities and other newsworthy people using teleconferencing. Discuss the advantages of using teleconferencing in newscasting.

Teleconferencing. Teleconferencing allows a group of people in different locations and even different time zones to meet and confer electronically. Teleconferencing offers text, audio, and video capabilities. By means of teleconferences, executives can reduce the time and cost of traveling to meetings. Companies can deliver training and development seminars to employees in different locations.

Communications Networks. The ability of different pieces of electronic equipment to communicate has facilitated the transfer of information from one place to another. The automated office does not consist of isolated equipment operating independently. Communication lines link computers to other computers, word processors, printers, and data bases. These communication networks can be set up within an organization for internal communications, or they can be used to communicate with other organizations that have compatible equipment.

Electronic communications travel by various means in today's computerized world. Many business offices are linked by:

1. Modems — devices that enable computers to send and receive documents by converting electronic signals into signals that can travel by telephone line.
2. Fax machines — devices that "read" documents and translate them into signals transmitted via telephone line to other fax machines, which convert the signals and print "facsimile" documents on paper.

Electronic Mail. Millions of messages are sent every day by electronic mail. Messages are relayed from the sender's terminal through a central computer to the receiver's terminal, where they are stored until read. The advantages of electronic mail are that it eliminates the need for the sender and receiver to communicate at the same time, as the telephone requires, and it eliminates the time needed by the postal or other delivery service to deliver a message in paper form.

Composing Electronic Messages. Electronic messages are usually sent when speed is required. Because telecommunications convey a sense of importance and urgency, recipients pay more attention to them than they would to letters that arrive by mail.

Businesses still use some older types of telecommunications such as the telegram, the Telex (the direct exchange of messages by teleprinters), and the Mailgram, a combined service of Western Union and the U.S. Postal Service. In these telecommunications, brevity is important because the cost of sending a message is based on the number of words. Therefore, it is permissible to compose a telecommunication without using complete sentences and to dispense with some typical courtesies of the business letter.

Although many companies now prefer to communicate by fax machines, modems, and electronic mail, someday you may be asked to compose and send a telegram or a telex message. However quaint this skill may seem to you, knowing how to compose brief but clear messages is an important busi-

LIVING LANGUAGE

Style, in its finest sense, is the last acquirement of the educated mind.

—Alfred North Whitehead

ness skill. In the following illustration, notice how the telegram expresses in 11 words the essentials of what the letter says in 85 words.

Letter	Telegram
We would like to have you check our letter of May 1 and the accompanying purchase invoice, Number A751C. We requested that you deliver the furniture to our store to reach us by August 1. However, we have planned a summer sale that is to begin on June 15 and would like to advertise this furniture if we can be certain that it will be in stock when we announce the sale. Please let us know promptly if delivery can be made by May 30.	Confirm immediately if order A751C can be delivered by May 30.

Electronic communication plays a key role in the business world today. Learning about the technology and its applications is essential for success in business communications.

SECTION REVIEW

Practical Application

A. Contact three companies that sell word processing equipment. Ask them to send you advertising brochures describing their equipment. If you were an author working on a novel, which one would you choose? If you needed to produce letters and mailing lists, which would you select? Be sure to consider the functions you would need and the price.

B. Interview someone who has work experience in both the traditional office and the electronic office. Report the interview in dialogue form as follows:

Student: What kinds of equipment did you use in the traditional office?

Office Employee: I used a typewriter, a telephone, and an adding machine.

C. Review an article on business communication technology. Write a one-page summary.

D. List the people with whom each of these professionals might be communicating: doctors, lawyers, teachers, and secretaries.

REVIEW *cont.*

E. Revise the following telecommunications so that none exceeds 15 words. Aim for brevity, clarity, and completeness.

1. Phillip Goetz expects to arrive in Boston on Wemas Flight 15 on Friday morning. Please arrange to pick him up at the airport and brief him on Tracy-Phelps contract en route to board meeting.

2. Our Purchase Order 7683 for four mahogany desks and matching executive chairs has not arrived, and our inventory is depleted. If the order has not yet been shipped, arrange shipment for six of each by fastest method.

3. The computer printout of the March sales forecast was lost and never reached us. Please airmail two copies immediately.

Editing Practice

Spelling Alert! Rewrite the paragraph below, correcting the problems with numbers.

Too secretaries wanted two trade their to typewriters four won word processor that they would share. They felt this would work because each secretary types only for hours per ate-hour day. Each secretary works four five executives. The tin executives agreed two the trade.

10

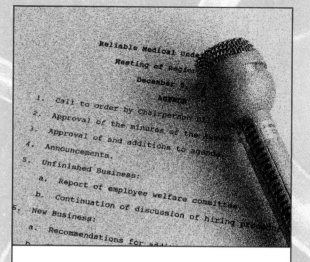

DEVELOPING ORAL COMMUNICATION SKILLS

10.1 *ASPECTS OF ORAL COMMUNICATION*

OBJECTIVES: After completing Section 10.1, you should be able to:

1. Explain the importance of oral communication in today's business world.
2. Describe the various forms of oral communication.

❏ SUGGESTION

Ask students to point out the positive aspects of the receptionist's behavior and to discuss why the receptionist's actions make a favorable impression.

As you enter the reception area of the Sterling Building, you are greeted by the warm smile and friendly voice of the receptionist asking, "May I help you?" You reply, "I have a ten o'clock appointment with Mr. Welden." The receptionist tells you, "Mr. Welden's office is on the twentieth floor, Suite 2059. May I please have your name so that I may telephone Mr. Welden to let him know that you are on your way up to see him?" The receptionist then directs you to an express elevator that stops on the twentieth floor. Likely you are already favorably impressed with the Sterling Company, based on this first encounter with one of its employees.

As you step from the elevator on the twentieth floor into the tastefully furnished office of the Sterling Company, you notice a number of employees busily engaged in a variety of activities. A young man approaches you. "Good morning, (your name); I'm Josh Brown, Mr. Welden's administrative assistant. Mr. Welden will be with you as soon as he completes an overseas telephone call. Please make yourself comfortable. Would you like a cup of coffee or tea?"

As you glance around the busy office, you notice several employees quietly engaged in telephone conversations. In a corner of a partitioned section, someone is explaining and demonstrating how to operate a new copying machine. In a glass-enclosed conference area, a small group is gathered around a table listening to an explanation of some figures on a flip chart. A young executive in another office is using a dictation machine. You notice on a nearby bulletin board an announcement of a sales training workshop; another posting announces a meeting of the Office Employees' Association next Monday morning.

√ REINFORCEMENT

Ask students who work to discuss the role of oral communication in their jobs.

Your communication instructor was right — oral communication *does* play an important role in the daily activities of every office employee! Then, as you are shown into Mr. Welden's office, you realize how fortunate you are to have had some training in oral communication. You are about to be interviewed for a position that you very much want, and you are going to make your training in oral communication work for you.

CRITICAL THINKING

Ask students to explain why the last statement in this paragraph is true.

THE IMPORTANCE OF ORAL COMMUNICATION IN BUSINESS

Even before you began to work, you were convinced of the importance of oral communication in the business world. This conviction will grow stronger each day. From the receptionist who greeted you in the lobby to the president on the top floor, information is continually being transmitted orally from one employee to another, from employees to customers and vendors on the outside, and from customers, vendors, and other outsiders to employees of the firm. The success of any business organization depends, to a very large degree, upon the success of its members in making themselves understood and in persuading others to accept their ideas.

Although written communication is important in transacting business, oral communication is used more often and by more people. Some business positions require the use of oral communication almost exclusively, and the people who fill these jobs are hired on the strength of their ability to speak well. The sales representative, the office receptionist, the switchboard operator, the person who handles customer service or complaints—all these people must be highly skilled in oral communication. The office or factory supervisor, the public accountant, the personnel manager, the bank teller, the business executive, and the secretary are only a few of the other workers who make extensive use of oral communication in carrying out the responsibilities of their positions.

If you aspire to a position of leadership in business, your ability to speak forcefully, persuasively, and convincingly will play a vital role in helping you achieve your goal. At meetings and conferences, speakers will include employees of various levels, company directors, clients, and outside consultants. On many occasions, you will do much of the talking. You will seek to solve grievances of employees; you will conduct meetings and small group discussions; you will give talks to employees, to the public, and to business and professional groups. In your daily contacts with supervisors and coworkers, you will use oral communication for reporting, instructing, reprimanding, giving information, and asking for information. This ability to communicate effectively is important to every business leader.

THE ROLE OF ORAL COMMUNICATION IN BUSINESS

Oral communication is used by business employees in a variety of ways and in a variety of settings. Business employees depend upon oral communication when engaged in such activities as the following:

REINFORCEMENT

Ask students to provide additional specific examples of the use of oral communication for each of these activities.

- *Selling goods and services.* All salespeople, whether they are selling goods or services, rely on their oral communication ability to help them make sales. Both the insurance agent who calls on you at home and the retail salesperson who asks, "Would you like a tie to go with that shirt?" are using their oral communication abilities to sell. The airline ticket agent who assists you in arranging a business trip is also using oral communication skills.

GLOBAL NOTE
Point out that most businesspeople who visit the United States speak some English. However, as a courtesy, the host company should find out if foreign visitors would like translation or interpreting services arranged.

- *Giving instruction to an individual or a group.* The teacher, whether performing in a school situation or in special business or industrial classes on the job, depends on oral communication. The sales manager who conducts special training classes for sales representatives must be an effective oral communicator. Even the computer programmer who must instruct a new assistant relies heavily on oral communication.

- *Explaining or reporting to supervisors, subordinates, and those on the same level.* The sales manager may report orally to the vice president in charge of sales. The supervisor in the office interprets a new company policy for employees. An employee explains a grievance to the supervisor. The general manager's secretary tells the file clerk to pull all correspondence with a particular company.

- *Giving information to customers and potential customers.* A customer calls a floor covering and carpet store for information about the sizes, colors, and prices of ceramic tile; another customer telephones for advice about the best method of cleaning recently purchased carpeting.

- *Giving formal speeches before groups.* The president of a company is asked to give a speech before the members of the Rotary Club. An accountant is invited to talk to a college class in advanced accounting. The administrative assistant to the vice president of marketing in a large cosmetics firm is asked to address a group of college students on "The Wide-Ranging Responsibilities of an Administrative Assistant."

- *Participating in social-business conversations.* The office manager telephones the secretary of Kiwanis to schedule a luncheon meeting. A sales representative congratulates two former associates who have gone into partnership.

- *Interviewing employees and prospective employees.* The personnel manager and the section supervisor interview applicants for an accounting position. The supervisor discusses an employee's merit rating at the end of the probationary period.

- *Acquiring information necessary to conduct the everyday affairs of business.* The credit manager of a department store calls the local credit bureau to determine the credit rating of a new customer. The mail clerk telephones the post office to find out which class of mail to use for a special mailing the company is planning. The accountant visits the Internal Revenue Service office to discuss methods of figuring depreciation on equipment. A secretary telephones a travel agency to get information about flights to Seattle.

- *Purchasing goods and services.* A homeowner asks an insurance company representative questions about expanding the coverage on her house. The purchasing agent telephones a stationer to order a filing cabinet. The manager of a truck fleet inquires about a truck-leasing plan.

- *Providing service for customers and potential customers.* The credit manager explains to a customer the procedure for opening a charge account. The section manager in the bedding department tells a customer why bedding can't be returned for exchange or refund.

- *Participating in meetings.* A sales manager conducts a meeting of the Sales Executives Club. A corporate librarian contributes ideas for the convention of the Northeastern Corporate Librarians Association to the members of the planning committee.
- *Participating in informal discussion with fellow employees.* The receptionist takes up a collection to buy a gift for a coworker who is in the hospital. The mail room supervisor organizes a committee to plan the office picnic. The new sales promotion manager invites the employees in her department to an informal get-together at her home.

These are just a few examples of oral communication activities that may be observed every day in business — activities that rely for their success almost wholly upon effective oral communication.

STUDY TIP

How much of communicating is listening? If you are conversing with one person, your share of the "talking time" is not more than 50 percent of the conversation. If the group is larger, each member's share of time is decreased. Use more than your share only if the group agrees.

FORMS OF ORAL COMMUNICATION IN BUSINESS

Oral communication in business occurs in many different forms. Some forms are used more frequently than others. Among the most commonly used methods of oral communication are the following:

- Face-to-face conversation — interviews, sales, social-business situations, informal discussions with coworkers.
- Telephone conversation — with an employee in another office, with customers, with suppliers.
- Conversation via interoffice communication devices — between an executive and a receptionist, between a sales representative on the selling floor and a clerk in the stockroom.
- Dictation and recording — dictating a letter to a secretary, using a dictating machine for dictating letters, recording meetings electronically.
- Radio and television appearances — giving interviews or reporting information.
- Formal speeches — debates; panels; addresses to employees, the public, customers, or professional groups.
- Group discussions or meetings — leading employee group discussions, participating in stockholders' meetings and in meetings of business and professional organizations.
- Instruction — teaching training classes for sales representatives, users of information processing systems, and retail store employees.

Each of these methods of communication requires a slightly different technique. The difference may be in the amount and kind of prior preparation, the manner in which the voice is projected, or the style in which the speaker makes the presentation. For example, speaking over the telephone requires a knowledge of how far the telephone mouthpiece should be held from the lips and how much the speaker's voice should be projected. A radio or telephone presentation may be read from copy and, therefore, requires a knowledge of how to read without giving the impression that you *are* reading. Leading a meeting requires a knowledge of parliamentary procedure. Teaching a class requires that the teacher know how to ask questions properly. Participating in a panel or in a group discussion requires the ability to think quickly and to put thoughts into understandable language without hesitation.

EFFECTIVE BUSINESS RELATIONSHIPS THROUGH ORAL COMMUNICATION

Regardless of what position you hold in business, the effectiveness of your oral communications with people both inside and outside the company will have an important influence on your personal success. Furthermore, your verbal contacts can influence the success of the company that employs you. When employees get along with one another — with those on the same job level as well as with those on levels above or below them — they are likely to be more productive. Moreover, satisfactory interpersonal relationships among employees also contribute to better relationships with those outside the company. The result of effective public relations is almost certain to be increased business.

How does oral communication help develop the most desirable atmosphere for effective employee relationships in business? By establishing an environment that provides for a free flow of information and ideas between management and employees. When employees can discuss their ideas and concerns freely and easily, morale is likely to be high — and when morale is high, work efficiency is greater. Personal conferences with employees, committee meetings, group conferences, and informational speeches that provide for question-and-answer sessions are some of the primary situations in which oral communication contributes to improved relations among employees and between management and employees.

How does oral communication contribute to effective public relations? By ensuring that every spoken communication with a customer is a positive experience. Although business spends considerable time and money planning and writing carefully worded letters and advertising copy to keep customers and to win new ones, often the oral contacts are overlooked. Successful businesses do not neglect the importance of oral communication and, therefore, train their employees in areas such as speaking in public, using correct telephone techniques, and leading group discussions.

The manner in which a customer is treated on the telephone or in person is just as important in developing goodwill as is the written communication — sometimes even more important. *All* employees — salespersons, secretaries, receptionists, accountants — create a public image of the company they represent by the manner in which they speak to customers and potential customers. A curt or rude employee can cause a business to lose sales — and even to lose customers of long standing. Every employee a customer comes in contact with *is* the company. Therefore, the telephone conversation or the face-

KEY POINT

Public relations can be improved by ensuring that spoken communications with customers are a positive experience for the customer.

to-face conversation must, through the words and tone used by the employee, make these customers feel that their interests are important and that the company wants them to be satisfied.

IMPROVING YOUR ORAL COMMUNICATION SKILLS

The beginning of this section illustrated how oral communication can influence a person's initial impression of a company. The receptionist's greeting certainly contributed to the positive impression of the company. Also, it was clear that a variety of oral activities played an important role in the performance of many employees' daily tasks.

The manner in which you use your oral communication skills on the job can either help or hinder you in performing your everyday activities and advancing to higher positions. The remaining sections of this chapter provide you with the opportunity to learn techniques for improving your oral communication skills when dealing with both coworkers and the public.

KEY
Answers will vary. See page I-53 for an example.

SECTION **REVIEW**

Practical Application

A. For each of the following business positions, indicate the oral communication activities that you think would be typical in that position:

1. Accountant
2. Retail salesclerk
3. Administrative assistant
4. Personnel interviewer
5. Receptionist

KEY
See page I-53.

B. Be prepared to discuss each of the following topics:

1. The Importance of Communication Skills for Success in College
2. The Importance of Communication Skills for Success in Business
3. How Ineffective Communication Leads to Problems

KEY
See page I-53.

C. Under three headings—Home, School, Business—list as many oral communication activities as you can.

KEY
Students who have practiced reading this material several times should be able to read the paragraph more smoothly than those

D. Practice reading aloud the following instructions for talking on the telephone so that you do not sound as though you are reading the material or have memorized it.

Clear enunciation is extremely important if you wish to be understood by the listener. Each word and each syllable must be pronounced distinctly. Your voice should be well modulated, and you should move your lips,

SECTION

who are reading it for the first time.

tongue, and jaw freely. Hold the mouthpiece about an inch from your mouth, speaking directly into the transmitter. Keep your mouth free of gum, candy, and other objects that could affect your pronunciation or cause you to slur your words. You can usually tell if your words are being heard clearly by the number of times the listener asks you to repeat what you have said.

KEY
Answers will vary.

E. Without using any gestures or diagrams, give oral directions for the following situations:

1. How to walk to the nearest shopping area from your school.
2. How to get to the administration office of your school from the classroom in which your communication class meets.
3. How to fold a letter for insertion in a No. 10 envelope.

KEY
Answers will vary.

F. Orally describe an object without telling the class what the object is. If you have described the object clearly, the class should be able to identify it from your description.

SECTION

10.2 *SHARPENING LISTENING SKILLS*

OBJECTIVES: After completing Section 10.2, you should be able to:

1. Explain the difference between active and passive listening.
2. Cite examples of listening for pleasure and listening for information.
3. Explain how physical and mental preparation can improve listening skills.
4. Name four ways to improve listening concentration.

KEY POINT

Businesspeople spend more of their day listening than they do talking, reading, or writing.

You may be surprised to learn that you spend more of your time listening than you spend talking, reading, or writing. Surveys have shown that the majority of businesspeople spend roughly 70 percent of their working day engaged in oral communication; about half of that time is spent listening. However, most people remember only about 25 percent of what they hear. They hear but do not really listen. *Hearing* is a passive activity that involves your ears; *listening* is an active skill that involves your mind as well as your ears. Almost everyone could improve his or her listening skills.

LISTENING—A NEGLECTED SKILL

Listening is a little like breathing. You began listening many years ago without ever studying how to listen or being aware of the way you were listening. Listening is different from the other communication skills in that you were not taught to listen. When you were learning to talk, someone corrected you if you made mistakes or mispronounced words. Learning to read and write involved even more formal instruction and practice. Most people assume that listening is automatic, but it is really an acquired skill.

The first step in becoming a better listener is to make listening less auto-matic. You need to be aware of the kind of listening that is required in each situation and to learn how to make your listening more productive.

ACTIVE AND PASSIVE LISTENING

Basically there are two kinds of listening: passive and active. Passive listen-ers absorb just enough of the speaker's words to keep a conversation flowing, but they actually understand little of what is being said. Often passive listen-ers let the speaker's inflection or tone of voice signal when they should react by nodding, smiling, or saying "I see" to reassure the speaker that he or she has their attention.

Passive listening is appropriate only when you are listening for pleasure, rest, or relaxation, and it doesn't matter whether or not you retain what you hear. Imagine yourself in a comfortable chair reading a magazine and listen-ing to one of your favorite albums or to a funny talk show. In such situations, you are listening passively because you don't need to hear and absorb every note of the music or every word that is said. Often, you use the music or talk as background and listen attentively only when you hear something, such as a news bulletin, that catches your interest.

In business or in school, however, passive listening is inappropriate. You must listen actively, with a higher level of concentration, because you are listening for information. You need to listen carefully to an instructor's expla-nation of an assignment or to your supervisor's directions about the proce-dure to follow in a particular project. Business conversations are filled with names, dates, places, prices, requests, and suggestions—and each is impor-tant. Active listeners concentrate on what is being said and they participate mentally. The salesclerk must hear the customer's requests and preferences; the bank teller must hear the correct amounts and denominations; the travel agent must hear the correct times, dates, and destinations. To be successful in any area of business, therefore, you will need to know how to listen actively.

Listening is also the main way of finding out what is going on around you. Active listening provides you with vital information and signals. If you are prepared to listen, you are more likely to receive the information you need from friends, teachers, coworkers, and supervisors. Listening is one of the primary means of gathering the information that is necessary in your life and your work.

IMPROVING YOUR LISTENING SKILLS

When you read, you may sometimes let your attention wander from the writer's message because you know that you can return later to read the words you missed. Spoken words, however, do not wait for the listener. They disappear. In most listening situations you have only one chance to absorb and comprehend a speaker's words, so you cannot let your attention wander.

One reason that listeners stop paying attention is that they can hear faster than the speaker can speak. The average person can say about 125 to 150 words a minute, but a good listener can take in about 300 words a minute. Because of this ability to understand faster than people speak, listeners tend to relax and listen to only part of what is being said. Missing a sentence, however, or even a single word could change the speaker's message. If you don't want to run the risk of misunderstanding the message or missing an important part of it, you have to listen *actively* to everything that is said.

Evaluate Your Skills

Everyone has listening weaknesses. Before you can improve your listening skills, you need to understand where your skills fall short — in other words, to identify your weaknesses. Begin by answering the following questions.

Listening Checklist

1. Have you had your hearing tested recently?
2. Do you try to screen out distracting sights and sounds when you are listening to someone speak?
3. Do you make it a point never to interrupt speakers before they have finished expressing their thoughts?
4. Do you avoid doing something else — such as reading a newspaper — while trying to listen?
5. Do you always look at the person who is talking to you?
6. When people talk to you, do you try to concentrate on what they are saying?
7. Do you listen for people's ideas and feelings as well as for factual information?
8. Do you believe that you can learn something from other people?
9. If something is unclear, do you always ask the speaker to repeat or explain a point or a set of directions?
10. Do you ever refuse to listen because you do not agree with what the speaker is saying?
11. Do you ever stop listening because you do not like a speaker's appearance or mannerisms?
12. In a conversation or discussion, do you think about what you will say next while another person is talking?
13. Do you ever have to ask the speaker to repeat some important information because you cannot remember what was said?

14. Do you ever let your mind wander because you believe that what the speaker is saying will not interest you?
15. Do you sometimes stop listening because you feel that too much time and effort would be required to understand what the speaker is saying?

You should have answered yes to the first nine questions and no to the last six. However, even if you had a perfect score, the following suggestions may still help you improve your listening skills.

Prepare Yourself Physically

REINFORCEMENT

To improve listening skills, prepare yourself both physically and mentally, set listening priorities, listen positively, and concentrate on listening.

CRITICAL THINKING

Ask students to suggest other techniques for effective listening.

Listening is a combination of physical and mental activities. Although the mental part of listening is more complex, you must also remember to deal with the physical part. The following suggestions will help you prepare yourself physically for effective listening.

1. Make sure you have no hearing problems. (The public health service in your community may have information about local agencies that give free hearing tests.)
2. Try to sit or stand in a place that has no distracting sights or sounds.
3. Keep your eyes on the speaker from start to finish. The sense of sight reinforces the sense of hearing.
4. If possible, choose a comfortable, well-ventilated, and well-lit place; physical discomforts are great distractions.
5. Always have paper and pencil available for taking notes on important personal or business information.

Prepare Yourself Mentally

The most important factor in effective listening is being mentally prepared. Mental preparation involves a receptive frame of mind and certain communication tools. Good listeners try to clear their minds of extraneous thoughts — meeting car payments, making a dentist appointment, deciding where to eat lunch, making plans for the weekend — so that their minds are open to receive the speaker's message. The communication tools for effective listening include the listening skills outlined in this section and an extensive vocabulary. Well-developed listening skills help the listener hear the information; a well-developed vocabulary helps the listener comprehend what he or she hears.

The general vocabulary you acquired in high school and college, however, may not be adequate for effective listening. Almost every field has its own special vocabulary, and the listener must master this vocabulary to understand the material under discussion. If you work in a computerized office, for example, you will probably need to be familiar with such terms as *default drive*, *double density*, *on-line*, and *window*. To master the special vocabulary of the field you work in, ask people in your company to recommend appropriate books. Then, as you read, write down any unfamiliar words and look them up in the dictionary. Follow the same procedure when you talk (and listen) to people.

Set Listening Priorities

Because you are often bombarded with several messages at once, you have to set listening priorities. For example, while your instructor is discussing the format of business letters, the person behind you might be talking about weekend plans, and in the background you may be aware of an ambulance siren or a honking horn.

First you must determine why you are listening. If you are listening for information on business correspondence, you must concentrate on the primary message (the lecture) and try to block out the other messages (the conversation) and noises (siren and horn), which are distractions. You must also keep another factor in mind: when you are talking, you cannot be listening. You cannot be a sender and a receiver at the same time. You can become your own distraction.

Listening With a Positive Attitude

To be a good listener, you must want to hear what the speaker has to say. Usually it is easy to see how adopting a good listening attitude is in your best interest. For example, the main purpose of a lecture or a class discussion is to learn; therefore, if students want to learn, they will also want to listen. In the business world, the employee who wants to do a good job will listen carefully to the supervisor's explanations and directions. To be productive, supervisors also need to listen carefully to the workers' problems and needs.

Listening with a positive attitude and open mind is also important when you have to listen to a speaker whose ideas or opinions clash with your own. In the first place, you cannot know for sure what someone is going to say until you actually hear it. Second, you may know the speaker's views but not the reasons for those views; passing judgment without hearing the speaker's arguments would be premature. Third, even if the speaker advocates ideas or supports a course of action that you oppose, you still should listen carefully. By listening you will learn about the opposing view and be able to argue against it more effectively.

Finally, a good listener should never judge a speaker solely on the basis of personal characteristics such as mannerisms, voice, speech patterns, or appearance. Ignoring such features may be impossible, but good listeners must not confuse the message of the speaker with the manner of speaking.

Concentrate on Listening

As you read earlier, people can comprehend words at least twice as fast as most people can speak. To some listeners, this extra time is a problem because they allow their thoughts to wander from the subject. Active listeners, however, use this free time to concentrate on the speaker's words so that they can better understand what is being said. Specifically, good listeners use their free time to accomplish the following tasks.

☑ **REINFORCEMENT**

Stress these four tasks as ways to anchor a wandering mind.

1. Identify the speaker's ideas and their relationships.
2. Summarize the main points of the message.
3. Evaluate the correctness or validity of the message.
4. Take notes to assist in better recall.

Identify Ideas. As you begin to grasp the speaker's ideas, look for relationships among them. For example, which idea is most important? Do the other ideas support the main one? What is the speaker leading up to? Can you anticipate what the speaker is going to say next? What cues is the speaker giving you to show the relationships among the ideas? Imagine that you are listening to the following excerpt from a speech.

> *Two major costs in operating a modern business are absenteeism and tardiness.* For instance, if a company with 1,000 employees averages 50 absences a month, and the average daily rate of pay is $100, the company loses $5,000 a month or $60,000 a year. Such a loss takes a big bite out of company profits.

Notice that the first sentence (the italicized words) contains the main idea. The word *major* is a cue to the importance of that first sentence. The speaker also uses the phrase *for instance* as a cue to indicate that what follows will support the main idea. Speakers often use other verbal cues, such as the following.

Verbal Cues
_____

first
second
third
another consideration
on the other hand
the most important thing
finally
in summary

Speakers also use many nonverbal cues, such as pauses and changes in volume or tone of voice. Speakers reinforce certain points by gesturing, counting on their fingers, and nodding or shaking the head. All these cues can help the listener identify the speaker's ideas and see the interrelationships among them.

Summarize. As you listen, you should rephrase the speaker's ideas in your own mind. Try to put the speaker's ideas into the simplest, clearest, and most direct words possible without changing the intended meaning. By reducing the speaker's message to its most basic terms, you will be able to understand and remember the message better. The following example shows what you might be thinking while the speaker is talking.

I have read many books on selling. There are books that bring up every possible selling situation and give you ways and means to meet those situations—several hundred of them perhaps. But when you are in the presence of a prospect, you cannot recall any of them. However, you *can* remember this formula: ask yourself the simple question, "Just what does this prospect *want*?" If you cannot find out any other way, ask the person. It is often that simple. Too many salespeople think they must do *all* the talking. Avoid it. Listen at least half the time and ask questions. It is only in this way you can uncover unsatisfied wants.[1]

You can't memorize ways of meeting every selling situation presented in books. You should find out what the prospect wants. Ask, if necessary. You don't need to do all the talking—listen half the time, and ask questions.

Evaluate. As you summarize the speaker's message and see the organization and relationship structure of the speaker's ideas, you probably will find your-self beginning to agree or disagree with the speaker. When this happens, try to trace your response to the speaker's reasons or arguments. Ask yourself if the arguments and ideas of the speaker really lead to his or her conclusions. Also determine if the speaker is trying to convince you with reason or to persuade you by pleading, coaxing, or insisting. Make sure that you are not in favor of the speaker's views simply because they are presented with humor, enthusiasm, or charm. Also make sure that you are not against a speaker's view because you dislike some of the speaker's personal characteristics.

Take Notes. Taking notes is an excellent way of keeping information for future reference. Notes, however, should be more than just aids to memory. They should also be tools that help the listener concentrate on the speaker's message.

When you take notes, you should not try to write down everything you hear. If you do, you may actually miss the major points of the message. Instead, use summarizing to help decide what you want to include and what you want to omit. Also, do not overlook such devices as underscoring, indent-ing, and drawing arrows and brackets to show the relative importance of the ideas as you write them down. Following are some additional suggestions.

1. Have available enough paper and an extra pen or pencil.
2. Listen for cues as to what is most important and then number each of the supporting ideas.

---

[1]William Phillips Sandford and Willard Hayes Yeager, *Effective Business Speech*, McGraw-Hill Book Company, New York, 1960, p. 176.

3. Abbreviate whenever possible. For example, you could use "1" for *first* and "e.g." instead of *for instance*. Even if you know shorthand, write only key words and expressions, not everything the speaker says.

4. Use devices like underscoring to highlight key points. You might underscore all main ideas, indent supporting ideas, and put brackets around examples.

5. After the speaker has finished, read over your notes as quickly as possible so that you can include any necessary explanations or additions while the speech is still fresh in your mind.

6. Label, date, and organize notes so that you can identify them later.

7. Compare your notes with those of another person who heard the same speech or lecture.

TURNING GOOD LISTENING SKILLS INTO EFFECTIVE COMMUNICATION

When you listen carefully to what is being said, you will always be prepared to respond by asking questions, giving praise, or adding to what has already been said. Good listening leads to feedback, and feedback is the listener's way of participating actively in the two-way process of communication.

As you think about what you have just read, keep in mind that effective listening is a skill, and like any other skill it requires practice. Therefore, you should take every opportunity at work and at school to practice the listening techniques discussed here.

REINFORCEMENT
Stress that listening skill improves with practice and effort.

KEY
See page I-54.

KEY
Errors are underscored.

SECTION

REVIEW

Practical Application

A. What is the difference between an active and a passive listener? Explain why it is easy to become a passive listener.

B. Answer the questions on page 461 to determine your listening strengths and weaknesses. Then explain each answer.

C. Name four techniques that can help you concentrate on what a speaker is saying.

D. List pointers that would help someone become a better notetaker.

Editing Practice

Speaking Contextually. Some of the following sentences contain words that are not used correctly. On a sheet of paper, correct each sentence that contains a contextually incorrect word, or write *OK* after each correct sentence.

REVIEW cont.

1. factor
2. cooperation
3. arraigned
4. OK
5. Dissemination

1. Keyboarding skill is an important <u>fact</u> in operating a computer.
2. We need the <u>corporation</u> of everyone in the office.
3. The defendant <u>is to be arranged</u> in court next week.
4. Tom accused the company of infringing on his patent rights.
5. <u>Discrimination</u> of confidential information is prohibited.

Critical Thinking Skills

Evaluating. A good listener is able to distinguish between facts and opinions. On a sheet of paper, identify each of the following statements as a fact or an opinion.

KEY
1. opinion
2. fact
3. fact
4. fact
5. opinion
6. fact
7. opinion
8. fact
9. opinion
10. opinion

1. The article I read on energy conservation was biased.
2. Andrew was told that his car needs two new tires.
3. If you park on the street from 9:00 a.m. to 5:00 p.m., your car will be towed away.
4. Four years of English is a requirement for graduation.
5. The price of those tires is too high.
6. Not using your air conditioner will reduce your fuel bill.
7. English is a boring subject.
8. Jake's new watch has a leather band.
9. The police shouldn't tow away as many cars as they do.
10. Your new watch is very stylish.

10.3 *EFFECTIVE ORAL COMMUNICATION*

OBJECTIVES: After completing Section 10.3, you should be able to:

1. Use body language effectively in communicating with others.
2. Demonstrate good grooming and appropriate dress in various oral communication situations.
3. Use speech qualities effectively when speaking to others.

Let's eavesdrop on two executives who are discussing two candidates for a promotion to an important and well-paying position. Perhaps you are one of the candidates they are considering.

"Roseanne and Nick seem to have similar qualifications and experience, so how can we decide which one to select for this position?"

"Well, we must remember that two important aspects of this position are the ability to talk with buyers and customers, both on the telephone and in person, and the ability to lead our sales-training sessions."

"Yes, that's undoubtedly true. We shouldn't forget about the monthly community consumers' meeting either. The person in this position must give a formal presentation at the meeting and lead the group discussion that follows the presentation."

"It's obvious, then, that the person we select must have outstanding oral communication skills in a wide range of situations. Do you still feel that both candidates are equally qualified for this position?"

"Roseanne's demonstrated that she can do a superior job in making presentations and in talking on the telephone. Also, she was very effective in persuading us to change the notification procedure last week."

"She certainly is an effective speaker and group discussion leader; she uses language well; and she impresses people very favorably with her appearance. On the other hand, Nick is weak in his oral communication skills. There's no doubt in my mind that we should select Roseanne for this position."

Would you agree with the selection these executives made? In terms of the job qualifications and the qualifications of the two candidates, you would have to agree with the executives. It is unfortunate that so many candidates for good positions eliminate themselves from consideration for promotion because they are weak in their oral communication skills.

In most business positions, oral communication is used at least as often as, if not more frequently than, written communication. Furthermore, obtaining a good position and succeeding in it depend very heavily upon persuasive oral skills. That is why it is so important that you become aware of the two major factors that determine a person's effectiveness in communicating orally — physical appearance and speech qualities. These two factors will be discussed here and in Section 10.4.

CRITICAL THINKING

Ask students if they agree with these executives. Then have students tell why or why not.

APPEARANCE

Except for situations involving the use of the telephone or a dictating machine, the speaker is visible to the listener and creates a visual impression that often influences the acceptability of his or her words to that listener. This first impression is based primarily on such factors as the speaker's posture, use of hands, eye contact with the listener, body and head movement, and overall personal appearance — dress, grooming, and so on.

A speaker's physical appearance often sets the stage for the acceptance or nonacceptance of the speaker's words. A person who makes a good physical impression quickly gains the interest of listeners. Of course, a speaker must have something interesting and worthwhile to say — and must say it in an effective manner — to hold the attention of the listeners for any length of time. The first barrier to effective oral communication will be overcome if

REINFORCEMENT

Emphasize the fact that most people are influenced by first impressions. A speaker with a sloppy appearance or with poor posture biases the listener toward expecting a carelessly prepared presentation.

the person talking has good posture, is dressed appropriately, is well groomed, and knows how to use eye contact to make each listener feel that the listener is being spoken to directly.

Posture

Many people make the serious mistake of underestimating the importance of good posture to overall good physical appearance. Regardless of how short or tall you may be, always stand up to your full height. You'll find that good posture will help you develop better breath control. Good posture will also make you appear more confident and give your listeners the impression that you know what you are talking about and that your message is really important. Of course, no speaker should appear stiff or pompous; you don't want to look like a stick of wood. Instead, try to develop a natural posture, constantly reminding yourself to stand erect, with shoulders back and stomach in. Such posture helps improve your voice quality and gives you the appearance of authority.

Hands

While you are talking, do not distract your listeners by pulling at your clothing, putting your hands to your face or hair, or toying with an object such as a paper clip, rubber band, or your eyeglasses. Listeners will automatically direct their attention to your physical maneuvers and will soon lose track of what you are saying to them. If you are standing, it is probably best to place your arms and hands in a relaxed position at your sides (rather than behind your back or folded in front of you). From time to time, make natural gestures. If you are delivering a speech and there is a lectern in front of you, you may wish to place your hands on either side of it. However, remember *never* to lean on the lectern!

When you are talking from a sitting position, you will be heard better if you sit slightly forward in your chair. You may rest your arms and hands in your lap, on the arms of the chair in which you are sitting, or partially on the edge of the table or desk in front of you. However, never use the desk or table as a place to rest your elbows. Lazy-looking speakers encourage apathy on the part of their listeners.

Facial Expressions

A speaker's facial expression influences the listeners' impressions. A relaxed, pleasant, interested expression will create a better atmosphere for communicating, of course, than a wrinkled brow and turned-down mouth. As you look in a mirror from time to time, see whether you can capture your personality as others see it. Are your facial muscles relaxed? Is your smile natural, pleasant, and genuine? What characteristics in your facial expression are appealing to those around you? See if you can develop animation and show enthusiasm in your facial expression. Above all, you must be alert and interested if you expect your listeners to exhibit those characteristics.

i **INFORMATION**

Explain that it is not desirable for a speaker to stare continuously at any one member of an audience. Rather, a speaker should make brief eye contact with individuals in various parts of the audience. Ask why this is true.

Eye Contact

One of the best ways to appear interested is to look at your audience, whether that audience includes just one person or more than a hundred people. Everyone likes to feel directly addressed by the speaker. Therefore, your eyes should never leave your listeners for any extended period of time; it's hard for them to stay interested when you are looking constantly at your notes, your shoes, the ceiling, or out the window. When talking to one or two people, look them squarely in the face (without, of course, staring them down) unless you are directing their attention to an object such as a chart. When speaking to a large audience, move your eyes over the entire audience; look into the faces of your listeners and not over the tops of their heads.

Body Movement

Body movement also contributes a great deal to the physical effect a speaker creates. The effective speaker never paces back and forth, because excessive movement will distract listeners. It is permissible to move your body from the hips in order to turn from side to side or to move your body in a forward motion to add emphasis to a remark. Occasionally, you may even want to take a step toward your listeners to emphasize an important point or a step sideways to signal a transition in what you are discussing. Of course, if you are using a chart or other illustrative material, you must move from time to time to the visual device. However, when speaking, you should try to face the listeners as much as possible and to stay in one place most of the time.

Nervousness

When you are talking to a group, pretend that you are carrying on a face-to-face conversation with just one person. Remember that the audience is just as eager for you to perform well as you are to do so. Don't be upset if you are nervous — even experienced speakers and actors are. Feeling nervous is a result of anxiety about doing a good job, and most authorities believe that a little stage fright provides needed tension.

Grooming and Dress

Personal appearance — grooming, cleanliness, and attire — is also an important factor in effective communication. How a speaker looks and dresses expresses personality just as much as the person's speech and conduct. So many factors are involved in personal appearance that not all of them can be considered in depth here. If you are interested in better oral communications, you should be aware that you communicate best when you appear your best. Good appearance breeds confidence. Appearing clean and neatly dressed, avoiding extremes in personal grooming and clothing styles, and selecting clothing and accessories that are tasteful and in harmony with one another and with your personality are some of the factors of personal appearance that you should consider.

GROOMING GUIDELINES

Following these suggestions will make it easier to be an effective oral communicator.

Special advice to women speakers:

Choose jewelry that is tasteful and that will not distract the audience from what you are saying. Above all, avoid jewelry that makes a jangling noise when you move your hands and arms.

Choose makeup suitable to your appearance, and apply it skillfully.

Although a touch of bright color is appropriate — even desirable — be careful not to overwhelm your listeners with bizarre color combinations or dazzling prints or stripes. You want your listeners' attention on what you are saying, not on what you are wearing.

Special advice to men speakers:

Wear a dress shirt and appropriate tie. Make sure that the style and color are currently acceptable. However, don't be too conservative with the necktie you choose — some experts recommend bright flecks of color.

In all but the most informal situations, leave at least one button of your jacket fastened, whether or not you wear a vest.

Because you may be seated while you are talking, wear long socks that cover your shins. Make sure that your socks harmonize with your suit and tie.

SPEECH QUALITIES

Although a speaker's physical appearance creates the first impression on listeners, the quality of speech may have an even greater influence on them. The quality of speech is determined by the following factors:

Force or volume of voice	Rate or tempo of speech
Pitch or level of voice	Enunciation
Tone of voice	Pronunciation

The force of a person's voice and the pitch and the tempo of speech depend, to a great extent, on breath control. The volume of air that is taken into the lungs and breath control help determine how much force a person's voice will have; both factors also affect the voice pitch. The rate of speaking will be determined by how frequently a speaker must breathe more air into the lungs. The speaker should talk only when breathing air out—never when taking air into the lungs. Good posture can help a speaker breathe in the maximum amount of air and control the amount of air expended.

Force (Volume)

❑ SUGGESTION

Give students sufficient practice in volume control, because most likely they are not used to speaking loud enough to be heard from the front to the back of a room. If sound equipment is available, you might give them some experience using a microphone.

For oral communication to be effective, the message must be clearly heard. Sufficient volume, achieved through good breath control, is important. If your voice is too soft and you have trouble being heard, practice breathing deeply and controlling your breath with your diaphragm and abdominal muscles, just as a singer does. The large abdominal cavity should be used to store a supply of air that can be released evenly to produce a clear, sustained tone. How much force you must use is, of course, determined by such factors as how good the acoustics are in the room in which you are talking, how large your audience is, and whether or not you are using a microphone or other electronic device to amplify your voice.

Pitch (Voice Level)

A speaker's voice will be more audible if it has a pleasing pitch. *Pitch* refers to the level of a sound on a musical scale. Practice can help correct the shrillness of a voice that is pitched too high or the excessive resonance of a voice that is pitched too low. Another pitch-related problem is the constant pitch that results in a monotone. An effective speaker varies the pitch of his or her voice to help communicate the message. The rising and falling of voice pitch is called *intonation*. Intonation can indicate that a statement is being made, that a question is being asked, or that a speaker is pausing.

A drop in pitch usually signals finality or determination and is, therefore, used at the end of a declarative sentence. For example, in reading the following sentence you should close with a drop in pitch.

> I cannot *possibly* explain all the software applications, especially in ten minutes. (Emphasize the word *possibly*.)

A rise in pitch can signal a question or an expression of suspense, doubt, or hesitation. Read the following sentences, closing with a rise in pitch.

> What *more* can I do? (Emphasize *more*.)

> I'm *so* sorry I can't give you the answer today, but I will *definitely* give it to you next week. (Emphasize the words *so* and *definitely*.)

Gliding the pitch up and down or down and up usually expresses sarcasm or contempt, as in the slang expression "Oh, yeah?"

The most important aspect of pitch is variation. Variation of pitch not only helps hold listeners' attention but also helps listeners know the exact meaning intended by the speaker. A rise in pitch can stress important words. Using the same pitch for each element can stress comparisons; pitching the

□ SUGGESTION

Most inexperienced speakers have a tendency to talk too rapidly. Ask students to observe speakers, including those on television, to determine a good rate of speaking.

first element high and the second low, on the other hand, can denote contrasts.

Notice the different shades of meaning that emerge as you read the following sentences and emphasize the italicized words.

Tony gave her the special assignment. (Tony did, not someone else.)

Tony *gave* her the special assignment. (She did not earn it.)

Tony gave *her* the special assignment. (Only she was given the special assignment.)

Tony gave her the *special* assignment. (The particular assignment, or special assignment.)

Tony gave her the special *assignment.* (He gave her the special assignment, not something else special.)

Tone

The tone of your voice often reveals your attitudes and feelings. Naturally, a pleasant and cheerful tone is desirable because it will have a good effect on your listener or listeners. On the telephone, the tone of your voice must substitute for your facial expression. In addition, you can use variation in tone, as well as in volume and pitch, to add interest to your speaking voice. The kind of tone you use should be appropriate for the words and ideas you are expressing.

Speaking Rate (Tempo)

The rate at which you speak should be varied, too, to avoid extremes in either direction. Most people tend to speak too rapidly. Although you should not speak so rapidly that words are not understood, neither should you speak so slowly that your listeners lose concentration on what you are saying. Regulate your rate of speaking so that you can enunciate each word clearly. The listener will hear each word without difficulty. A good speaking rate is 125 words a minute; oral reading rates and radio speaking tend to run slightly faster — about 150 words a minute. To determine what a rate of 125 words a minute sounds like, read aloud the paragraph below in a half minute. Reread the paragraph as many times as necessary until you achieve the desired rate. At the end of a quarter minute, you should be at the diagonal line. Use this line as a guide to either increase or decrease your speaking rate.

A good speaker talks slowly enough to be understood by the listeners and speaks in a pleasant voice, articulating and pronouncing each word correctly and distinctly. To develop a good / speaking voice, you must spend sufficient time practicing the elements of good speech. An effective speaker is a definite asset to business and will usually find more opportunities for advancing in the job. (63 words)

Changing the rate contributes to variety, as well as to clarity. Important words and ideas should be spoken slowly; unimportant words or phrases, more rapidly.

Try to speak in thought units so that you can assist the listener in interpreting your words. If the sentence is short, the thought unit can be the entire sentence, as in "My job is very exciting." When there are several thought units within a sentence, pause slightly after each thought group, as in "My job is very exciting; / but I must admit, / some days are almost too exciting."

Use pauses to stress major points. By pausing between major points or after important statements, you add variety and emphasis to the points you want your listeners to remember.

Enunciation and Pronunciation

Because good enunciation and pronunciation are so important in effective business speaking, they receive separate treatment in Section 10.4.

TOWARD MORE EFFECTIVE ORAL COMMUNICATION

Almost as important as what you say is the way you say it. The manner in which the message is delivered determines how effective the communication is. As you have learned in this section, two factors—physical appearance and speech qualities—can greatly influence the impression a speaker makes on his or her audience.

SECTION

REVIEW

Practical Application

A. Reread the first page of this section. Assume that you are also a candidate for the position discussed. How would you compare your oral communication skills with those of the other two candidates? List your strengths and weaknesses, including such factors as your personality, the first impression you make on others, your personal appearance, your facial expressions, and your mannerisms. Briefly comment on each of these factors. Would you be a likely candidate for this position? Why or why not? Would it be possible for you to overcome any handicaps?

B. Read each of the following sentences three times. Each time, emphasize a different word in the sentence, which will change the meaning of the sentence.

1. Marty mailed the letter yesterday morning.
2. I liked San Francisco more than any other city I visited on my trip.

3. Did you see Ethel at the banquet this week?
4. If possible, please arrive earlier on Saturday.
5. I really didn't expect to arrive so late; please forgive me.

C. Read the following sentences silently once or twice. Then, standing in front of the class, read them through from beginning to end. Try to keep your eyes on the audience as much as possible while reading them.

1. Barry is never late for work, if he can avoid it.
2. I doubt very much that I will be able to attend the booksellers convention next week.
3. No, in my opinion, the new computer does not perform so efficiently as the old one.
4. What difference does it make whether or not I attend your cousin's graduation next Tuesday?
5. Do you really think that he will deliver the main speech at the awards banquet?

D. Read the following paragraphs silently twice. Then, standing in front of the class, read them aloud, keeping your eyes on the audience as much as possible.

1. When you are communicating face to face on a one-to-one basis, don't do all the talking. Give the other person a chance to talk while *you* listen attentively. Watch for signs that the other person wants to say something or is becoming bored and not listening carefully. No matter how interesting you think the conversation is or how well informed and articulate you think you are, you must give your listener a chance to speak. Otherwise, you will not keep his or her attention and respect.

2. Most people take telephone usage for granted—and this is one of the reasons so many office workers are ineffective telephone communicators. Too many employees assume that a business telephone conversation is the same as a personal telephone call. Actually, the telephone is one of the most important communication media in business, and it must be used with great skill, especially when talking with outside callers and with superiors in the office.

3. Nearly every speech of any length is brightened considerably by touches of humor and by human interest narratives. Of course, such stories should not dominate the speech. Observe the following rules: Use stories and jokes that add interest to the subject or illustrate a particular point. Before telling a joke to an audience, test it on friends to make sure it has a punch line. Make sure that stories and jokes do not offend or embarrass the audience. And time your stories to make sure that they are not too long.

KEY
The underlined parts of the sentences should have a change of pitch as indicated.
1. Lower
2. Lower
3. Lower
4. Higher
5. Higher

KEY
Observe each student's eye contact with the audience. Also determine whether the volume is sufficient to enable those in the back of the room to hear.

SECTION

E. Present a three-minute (approximately) talk to the class on a topic of your choice. Try to make each person in your audience feel as though you are talking individually to that person.

Editing Practice

Synonyms or Antonyms? In each numbered item below, two words are synonyms or antonyms. For each item, identify the pair by letter and indicate whether the words are synonyms or antonyms. Use a dictionary if necessary.

1. (a) excellence (b) disparity (c) slander (d) reference (e) equality
2. (a) contract (b) report (c) letter (d) model (e) agreement
3. (a) sagacity (b) hypocrisy (c) opener (d) glamour (e) candor
4. (a) contingent (b) erudite (c) new (d) erratic (e) consistent
5. (a) affable (b) garrulous (c) gracious (d) precious (e) joyous
6. (a) busy (b) boisterous (c) happy (d) quiet (e) clever
7. (a) phlegmatic (b) stolid (c) involuntary (d) sordid (e) respiratory
8. (a) faultless (b) modest (c) serious (d) pretentious (e) extraneous
9. (a) apathy (b) hope (c) enthusiasm (d) vision (e) thoughtfulness
10. (a) demise (b) undershirt (c) death (d) contrive (e) expire

Editor's Alert. Thoroughly examine the following sentences for needed corrections. Make those corrections, rewriting any poorly worded sentences. Write *OK* for any sentence that has no error.

1. The messengers bicycles should not be parked in this area.
2. Ther're no reason for you to be sent on assignment to the Riviera.
3. Will you and him please go to Peoria instead.
4. Carl bought three airline tickets to Peoria at $150 each, making a total of $450.
5. Please continue on as though nothing were said.
6. Complete your questionaire and hand in your asignment before you leave.
7. You should follow-up on your *Road and Driver* peice while you're in Peoria.
8. This company has always in the past—and always will—be noted for its fair treatment of all employees.
9. The new assignment schedule was only given to Morgan and I last week.
10. 10 writers begged to be sent to Peoria.

Critical Thinking

Analysis. Select three prominent people (in politics, sports, or the arts) who frequently appear before the public in some type of speaking role. List the factors—pro and con—that affect their speaking effectiveness.

KEY
Particularly observe eye contact and the use of a conversational tone. The presentation should not be stilted or overly formal.

KEY
1. b, e antonyms
2. a, e synonyms
3. b, e antonyms
4. d, e antonyms
5. a, c synonyms
6. b, d antonyms
7. a, b synonyms
8. b, d antonyms
9. a, c antonyms
10. a, c synonyms

KEY
1. messengers'
2. There is *or* There's
3. he
4. OK
5. Omit *on*
6. questionnaire, assignment
7. follow up, piece
8. in the past been— and always will be—noted
9. was given to Morgan and me only last week.
10. Ten

KEY
Answers will vary.

10.4 *ENUNCIATION AND PRONUNCIATION*

OBJECTIVES: After completing Section 10.4, you should be able to:

1. Distinguish between *enunciation* and *pronunciation*.
2. List four steps for improving enunciation and pronunciation.

Chris Nagy, a secretary for the Sunrise Furniture Company, handed her supervisor a letter she transcribed from a dictation disk and then returned to her desk. In a few minutes, her supervisor came rushing out of his office, a frown on his face, obviously disturbed about something.

"Chris, you're gonna havta do this letter over. Ya made a terrible error that wudda cost us a lotta money if I hadna caught it—and, darn it, I was in a hurry to get this letter in the mail."

"What did I do wrong?" asked the distressed Chris.

Her supervisor explained, "See here, where you have 'forty wall units for $14,000'? It's supposta be *fourteen* wall units for $14,000."

"I'm sorry," apologized Chris, "but that's what you said on the dictation disk, *forty*."

"I cudna said that. Play that part again."

When the disk reached the word in question, it became apparent that Chris's boss so poorly enunciated the word *fourteen* that anyone would have mistaken the word for *forty*.

The boss apologized, but regardless of who was at fault, Chris had to take the time—and additional stationery—to revise the letter. Fortunately, the error was caught before the letter was mailed. The error could have resulted in a large monetary loss to the company.

One could cite many other instances in business—and even in social situations—where poor enunciation has led to costly delays, unnecessary expense, and the loss of goodwill. That is why it is so important for all business employees, particularly those who have face-to-face or telephone contact with customers and vendors and those who use dictation equipment, to both enunciate and pronounce words clearly and correctly.

> **STUDY TIP**
>
> The knowledge of words is the gate of scholarship.
>
> —John Wilson

ENUNCIATION VERSUS PRONUNCIATION

Although the terms *enunciation* and *pronunciation* are closely related, they do have slightly different meanings. Understanding the difference between the two terms and making a strong effort to eliminate the barriers to effective enunciation and pronunciation will contribute greatly to improved speech.

Enunciation

Enunciation refers to the distinctness or clarity with which you articulate or sound each part of a word. For instance, saying "walkin" for *walking* or "gonna" for *going to* are examples of careless enunciation. Careless enunciation often occurs in *ing* words, such as "willin" for *willing* and "askin" for *asking*. Also, whenever we speak rapidly, most of us have a tendency to run our words together, dropping some of the sounds. Saying "dijago" for *did you go* and "meetcha" for *meet you* are examples. A person who slurs too many words is likely to be misunderstood or not heard at all, particularly over the telephone or on transcribing equipment. It is annoying for both the listener and the speaker if the listener must ask the speaker to repeat something several times. With transcribing equipment, errors may result if the speaker cannot be reached for verification. Such difficulties can often be avoided if we simply speak more slowly and more carefully.

Pronunciation

Pronunciation refers either to the sound that the speaker gives to the various letters or combinations of letters that make up a word or to the way in which the speaker accents the word. A person who says "pro*noun*ciation" instead of "pro*nun*ciation" is guilty of a pronunciation error. Should you say "libary" or "library," "com′ · par · able" or "com · par′ · able"? The dictionary indicates that the pronunciations are *library* and *com′ · par · able*, and these are the pronunciations used by careful speakers.

Of course, there are regional differences in pronunciation; and, in addition, a number of words have more than one acceptable pronunciation. In the latter case, the dictionary lists the preferred pronunciation first.

Many difficulties in pronunciation arise because some letters or combinations of letters are pronounced one way in some words and another way in others. For example, the combination *ow* is given a long "o" sound in *know* but an "ow" sound (as in *ouch*) in *now*. Other difficulties in pronunciation arise because a letter may be sounded in some words while in other words the same letter is silent; for example, *k* is sounded in the word *kick*, but it is not sounded in such words as *know* and *knee*. Because of these inconsistencies in our language, it is essential to consult the dictionary whenever you are in doubt about the pronunciation of a word.

Though errors in pronunciation are less likely to cause misunderstandings than errors in enunciation — you would know what was meant if someone said "com · par′ · able" instead of "com′ · par · able" — such errors tend to distract the listener and may even cause the listener to consider the speaker careless or uneducated. The business employee who is eager to succeed does not wish to be marked with either of these labels.

Furthermore, since so many words are written according to the way they sound, you can improve your spelling ability by carefully and correctly pronouncing and enunciating each word you use. Many words are misspelled because letters that should be sounded are overlooked. Those who repeatedly say "goverment" instead of "government" probably overlooked the *n* in this word. Some words, on the other hand, are misspelled because extra sounds are inserted where they do not belong; for example, pronouncing "ath*a*letic" instead of "athletic." In still other instances of mispronunciation, the sequence of letters in the word may be rearranged. How many people do you know who say "ir*reve*lant" when they really mean "ir*rele*vant" or "nuc*u*lar" when they mean "nuc*lear*"? You can easily see how taking sufficient care in pronunciation can help prevent other errors, such as "quite" for *quiet* and "praps" for *perhaps.*

Most business employees have to give and to receive information and instructions over the telephone or in face-to-face conversation. To prevent the costly misunderstandings that may be caused by improper or careless pronunciation and enunciation, you should make every effort to develop and practice intelligible speech.

IMPROVING ENUNCIATION AND PRONUNCIATION

Follow this four-step plan to help you improve your enunciation and pronunciation:

1. Use the dictionary to determine the preferred pronunciation of words about which you are uncertain.
2. Speak slowly enough, and with sufficient care, so that each letter in a word is sounded as it is supposed to be sounded and so that words are not run together.
3. Learn to use your jaw, your lips, and your tongue (the physical organs of speech) properly.
4. Practice frequently the correct enunciation and pronunciation of words that are often mispronounced or poorly enunciated.

You have already learned how to use the dictionary to determine the preferred pronunciation of words, and you have also learned how to control your speaking rate. Now you will learn how to use effectively the speech organs that assist in correct enunciation and pronunciation. Also, you will practice enunciating and pronouncing words that frequently cause difficulty.

Develop a Flexible Jaw

A rigid jaw results in muffled speech. Many sounds need to be vocalized and should, therefore, be made by movement of the mouth. If such sounds are forced through a locked jaw, a jaw that does not move up and down on its hinges, these sounds are certain to be muffled and indistinguishable.

Keeping your jaws locked tight, try to pronounce these words — *neither, capable, try.* Can you understand what you are saying? Obviously you cannot, and you could not expect any listener to understand words that are pronounced in this manner.

To be an intelligible speaker, you must move your jaw freely between an open and a closed position. Say each of the vowels and notice the different positions of your jaw as you say *a, e, i, o, u*. Compare your jaw positions as you say first the sound "ow," as in *how*, and then the sound "oo," as in *room*. When you say "ow," your jaw is dropped. However, when you say "oo," you move your jaw only slightly if at all.

Practice will help you achieve the free-moving feeling of a flexible jaw. First, stand before a mirror and practice the following words to be certain that your jaw is unlocked.

only	winning	about	seventy-five
try	capable	arrive	nine eight one
fine	evening	idea	reporting

Practicing the phrases below will exercise your jaw and help make it flexible.

going to go	down and out	up and around
around and away	sky high	down, up, and out
I've been	you've been	I've seen

Finally, practice saying these sentences to prove that your jaw is flexible enough so that each word is clearly enunciated and pronounced.

1. Shirley-Ann placed the parcel on the table today.
2. Many men and women strive to attain power, prestige, and financial security.
3. Please telephone (805) 555-8867 this morning.
4. Your flexible jaw will contribute to better speech through clearer enunciation.

Develop Mobile Lips

As you were practicing the preceding words, phrases, and sentences, you probably noticed that in addition to the up-and-down movement of your jaw, your lips were assuming many different positions. Six consonant sounds are made by action of the lips. The lips are closed for the sounds of "m," "b," and "p." The lower lip touches the edges of the upper front teeth for the sounds of "v" and "f." The lips are rounded for the sound made by *w*, as in *woman*.

Poor enunciators do not move their lips very much; as a result, their speech is often unintelligible. The good speaker, on the other hand, uses a variety of lip positions. In addition to the lip movements for the six consonants previously mentioned, the "oo" sound in *who, lose, shoe,* and *do* requires rounded lips. The lips are widely stretched for the "e" sound in *me, we, key,* and *see*. In words like *few, boys, use,* and *how*, the speaker is required to use two different lip positions. The sound of "ow," as in *how* and *now*, requires that the jaw be dropped and the lips be rounded to form a circle.

While using proper lip positions, practice these words. First read across and then read down the columns.

wasting	mine	voice	very	wonder	pension
vocal	very	wary	file	victory	violent
winter	when	why	food	cost	careful
cool	mister	many	time	meaning	forceful

Now practice the following phrases, making certain that you avoid lazy lip movements.

office manager	readily available	answer the telephone
lose the money	when we go	empty the basket now
many men may	very fine work	what we wear

Make sure your lips are sufficiently mobile to enunciate clearly each word in the sentences given below. Practice the sentences until every sound is clear.

1. Peter Piper picked a peck of pickled peppers.
2. She sells seashells by the seashore.
3. How now, brown cow?
4. The rain in Spain falls mainly on the plain.
5. Which witch was the wickedest witch?
6. Hickory dickory dock, the mouse ran up the clock.
7. The whistling west wind whipped the whispering trees.
8. Who picked up the bale of mail this morning?

Develop a Lively Tongue

Repeat several times: *The tip of my tongue moves lively in my mouth.* Do you feel the lively movement of your tongue as you say these words? Try saying the same sentence with your tongue held loosely in your mouth, using a minimum of movement. Do you notice the lack of clarity? In order to enunciate precisely, to make your speech clear, you must move your tongue to several positions — the front of your mouth, the back of your mouth, the roof of your mouth, and even between the top and bottom rows of teeth for the "th" sound heard in *either*, *this*, and *that*.

Now that you know how a lively tongue feels, stand in front of a mirror as you practice the following words.

feel	forward	seal	sadly	saw	suit
main	many	some	sight	peace	mail
twine	train	later	legal	poster	port

Did you feel the lively movement of your tongue? Now practice these words that require your tongue to be placed between your teeth.

think	thought	either	neither	loath	thorough
then	the	with	whether	through	wrath

Using the lively tongue that you have learned to develop, practice the following phrases and sentences until each sound is clearly enunciated.

1. Health, wealth, and happiness
2. Actually colder than yesterday
3. The attempted assault and battery
4. Through thick and thin
5. This, that, those, them, and these
6. A thaw at three thirty-three
7. Linger a little longer, lovely lady.
8. The thirty-three discounts are listed on page three.
9. There were thirty thousand thermos bottles sold there.
10. Nothing gained, nothing lost, and nothing accomplished either.
11. Their number over there is 333-1237, but there is no one there now.

You have practiced the several suggestions for improving your enunciation and pronunciation that have been presented in this section. However, it is important that you continue to be conscious of the way in which you enunciate and pronounce words, to use your dictionary to determine the correct pronunciation of words about which you are in doubt, and to practice good speech habits. If you follow these suggestions, you will find that your speaking will improve and that improved speech will quickly become easy and natural for you.

SECTION REVIEW

Practical Application

A. The following phrases are frequently run together even though each word should be enunciated separately and distinctly. Practice saying these phrases properly, first in isolation and then in an original sentence that you create for each phrase.

give me	did you	going to	do you	got to
being there	want to	kind of	come here	will you
have been	didn't you	don't know	going to go	have to

B. From one of your textbooks, select a paragraph that you think will be of interest to the class. Read the paragraph aloud to the class, and be careful to enunciate words clearly and to pronounce them correctly. Each member of the class will list every word you enunciate poorly or mispronounce.

C. You want your assistant to place a number of long-distance telephone calls for you. Dictate the following names and telephone numbers, making certain that the names and numbers are intelligible. Spell the difficult or unusual names; for example, "Irvine (I-r-

KEY
For good listening practice, students who are not reciting should be asked to list those words that they hear enunciated poorly or that are mispronounced. Everyone in the classroom should be participating in these activities, not only those who are actually reciting.

v-i-n-e) Insurance Company of Nashua (N-a-s-h-u-a), Minnesota. I want to talk with Mrs. Orlando. The number is (612) 555-7814."

Person to Be Called	*Telephone Number*
1. Carmine Rizzo Westchester Employment Service Worcester, Massachusetts	(617) 555-9876
2. Personnel Manager Poughkeepsie Manufacturing Co. 101 Smith Street Poughkeepsie, New York	(914) 555-6389
3. Will speak with anyone Marcy & Yates Associates Oxnard, California	(805) 555-3770
4. Ms. Caroline Lehr Lehr Advertising Agency New York, New York	Don't know the number
5. Dr. Rosemarie Balducci Riverside Hospital Albuquerque, New Mexico	(505) 555-8347, Extension 183

D. As office manager, you find it necessary to order a number of items from a local stationer. Since you need the items in a hurry, you telephone the information to the stationer. Assume that you have dialed the number and that the person at the other end says, "Torrance Stationers; may I help you?" Pick up the conversation from this point, and place the order for the following items:

1. Six boxes of standard copier paper, No. 880, 8½ by 11½, Stock No. 2-105-19

2. Four boxes 20-lb white continuous-form paper, 9½ by 11, Stock No. 13-1276

3. One dozen No. 2 pencils, Stock No. 54-927

Editing Practice

States, Capitals, Principal Cities. In each item below, there are two states, capitals, or principal cities that are misspelled. Spell them correctly.

1. Lincoln Colombus Cheyanne Pierre Jefferson City
2. Racine Laramie Pittsburg (Pa.) Bethlahem Portsmouth
3. Michigen Idaho Arizona Montanna New Jersey
4. Honalulu Albany Richmond Charleston Indiannapelis
5. Seattle Spokane Hoboken Scenectady Cincinatti
6. Wichita Clevland Agusta Duluth Butte
7. Olympia Providence Topeka Frankfourt (Ky.) Helana

KEY
1. Columbus; Cheyenne
2. Pittsburgh; Bethlehem
3. Michigan; Montana
4. Honolulu; Indianapolis
5. Schenectady; Cincinnati
6. Cleveland; Augusta
7. Frankfort; Helena

8. Colorado; Pennsyl-
   vania
9. Minneapolis; Jef-
   ferson City
10. Pasadena; Tucson

KEY
See page I-55.

KEY
See page I-55.

REVIEW cont.

8. Minnesota <u>Colarado</u> Pensylvania Virginia Rhode Island
9. Minnapolis Juneau Trenton Charleston <u>Jeferson City</u>
10. Brooklyn <u>Pasedena</u> Brockton <u>Tuscon</u> Lowell

Editors' Alert. In each of the following sentences, make any changes that will correct or improve the sentence. Carefully check *every* detail.

1. This <u>portible</u> computer is <u>to</u> heavy to move.
2. The number of visitors in <u>attendence</u> was <u>quiet</u> large.
3. We will <u>male</u> the package <u>tomorow, however,</u> we cannot do so until the afternoon.
4. All <u>there</u> <u>employees'</u> are covered by insurance.
5. David likes filing, <u>to type,</u> and <u>being given</u> dictation.
6. <u>7</u> men and women worked from <u>six</u> to 7 P.M. for <u>over-time</u> pay.

Critical Thinking

Application. Give examples of jobs in which correct pronunciation and enunciation are particularly important.

10.5 COMMUNICATING ONE TO ONE

OBJECTIVES: After completing Section 10.5, you should be able to:

1. List guidelines for establishing effective communications on a one-to-one basis.
2. Discuss basic procedures for meeting the public.
3. Describe proper techniques for originating and receiving telephone calls.
4. Explain how to handle telephone callers who have complaints.

High on the list of communication activities for most business employees — if not at the very top of the list — is communicating orally on a one-to-one basis. Business employees talk with colleagues in their own departments, with their supervisors, with top management, and with such service workers as messengers and custodians many times during the working day.

KEY POINT

Every business worker who has contact with the public plays an important role in developing and promoting the company image.

In addition, many employees talk either on the telephone or in person with individuals outside the company — customers, sales representatives, suppliers, visitors, radio and TV reporters, and various people soliciting or giving information. As a matter of fact, many business employees depend heavily on their oral communication skill to earn their living — sales representatives, personnel interviewers, and receptionists are just a few examples.

Every business worker who has contact with the public plays an important role in developing and promoting the company image. When the agent of an insurance company speaks to customers, it is not as an individual but as a representative of the company. The same is true of a receptionist, a telephone order clerk, or a salesperson in a store. In one sense, those who speak for the company *are* the company to the people who do business with that firm.

GUIDELINES FOR ONE-TO-ONE COMMUNICATION

The following suggestions should serve as guidelines for communicating effectively on a one-to-one basis, whether communicating in person or over the telephone.

Listen Attentively

CROSS REFERENCE

Listening is covered more thoroughly in Section 10.2.

The ability to listen attentively is one of the most important skills connected with effective oral communication. Being attentive and showing interest in the other person are just two attributes of the good listener that lead to more effective communication. For example, if you are attacked verbally by an irate customer for something over which you have no control, you can go a long way toward soothing the customer by merely listening attentively. Often, you need not say anything, because what the customer most wants is an attentive and sympathetic listener.

Use the Person's Name

Be certain that you clearly hear the name of the person whom you have met or talked with on the telephone for the first time. Repeat the name right after it is given to you: "I'm happy to meet you, Mr. Zolnerzak." If you aren't absolutely sure of the person's name, ask that it be repeated; you can say, "I didn't hear your name clearly," or "How do you pronounce (or spell) your name?" Then, after hearing the name, pronounce it aloud in order to fix it in your mind. Whenever appropriate, use the name once or twice during the conversation. "Yes, I understand, Mr. Zolnerzak." Finally, always be sure that you say the person's name in your good-bye: "Good-bye, Mr. Zolnerzak; I enjoyed talking with you."

Permit Others to Talk

LANGUAGE TIP

"That which we are capable of feeling, we are capable of saying."

—Miguel de Cervantes

Don't do all the talking. Give the other person a chance to talk, while you listen attentively. Watch for signs that the other person wants to say something or is becoming bored and not listening carefully. No matter how interesting you think the conversation is or how well informed or articulate you think you are, you must give your listener a chance to speak. Otherwise, you will not keep your listener's attention and respect.

Encourage Others to Talk

Sometimes the other person seems to prefer listening to talking. Remember, however, that a good conversationalist is one who not only talks well but also encourages the listener to contribute to the conversation. Ask frequent questions to let the other party know that you are interested in listening too. And prove your interest by listening attentively.

Look at the Speaker

▼ **REINFORCEMENT**
Discuss the importance of routine business conversations and how their importance is not always realized. Employees often have deadlines that cause them to feel pressured. This tension in turn causes them to respond in a haphazard or careless way rather than giving the seemingly insignificant conversation the attention it deserves.

Of course, this guideline applies only to face-to-face conversation. A speaker likes to have the listener's complete attention. When you speak, you like to feel that your listeners are focusing on what you are saying and not being distracted by objects or sounds coming from other directions — conversations in another part of the office or something that is happening outside the building, for example. So when you listen, make eye contact with the speaker; look at the person who is talking.

Compliment When Suitable

Many people with whom we come in contact are seeking approval. Compliments are always welcome, so compliment whenever the occasion is suitable. Paying a compliment is especially effective during tense situations. If a valued employee or a customer has a complaint that you cannot justify or remedy, you can put that person in a better frame of mind for a no answer by paying a compliment. Compliment the employee for work well done or for loyalty. Compliment the customer for paying promptly or for his or her good taste. In all conversations, be generous with praise when it is timely and when it is deserved. However, never pay a compliment unless you can do so honestly and convincingly. Insincerity is easily detected.

Keep Conversations Concise

Since you should not prolong conversations, you should keep your conversation to the point. If you are asked for opinions, give them quickly and clearly. Being concise, however, does not mean you must be brusque. Try to sense what the situation calls for and act accordingly. Most people do not want to hear unnecessary details or to listen to prolonged excuses for your inability to do something they have requested. Tell them enough to satisfy them; and if you are in doubt, the best rule to follow is to keep your conversations short.

Establish the Best Atmosphere

It is said that Napoleon had his desk raised so that he could look down on everyone who came to see him. Some executives sit behind a huge desk when they talk to visitors for the same reason. These executives believe that they seem more important, more powerful, and more dominating.

The trend today for good relations with colleagues and customers is to create a conversational atmosphere that is more relaxed. Executives who are effective communicators move from behind their desks and face their visitors without a barrier between them. A barrier-free atmosphere makes possible a better give-and-take situation and, therefore, more effective communication.

RECEIVING THE PUBLIC

ℹ INFORMATION

Positive first impressions are critical when receiving the public as an official or unofficial representative of a business or an organization.

Although in most companies the receptionist greets all visitors, many employees also have contact with the public. In small offices and in most retail establishments, this situation applies to every employee. You should, therefore, be familiar with the basic procedures for meeting the public.

Give Prompt Attention to Visitors

Recognize a visitor's presence immediately. Even if you are busy, you can interrupt your work for as long as it takes to smile and say to the new arrival, "I'll be with you in a moment. Won't you sit down?"

Greet Visitors Pleasantly

Greet visitors with a pleasant smile and voice, and show friendliness by using their names in your greeting whenever possible. Add a personal touch to your greeting, such as "Good morning, Mr. Stern. It's a pleasure to see you again." Such friendly greetings make callers feel that they are getting special treatment and put them in a better frame of mind to do business with your company.

Be Courteous to All Visitors

√ REINFORCEMENT

Point out the need for courtesy in dealing with the public, both in person and on the telephone. Many successful businesses have been built upon the simple principle of being courteous.

Every visitor should receive friendly and courteous treatment, regardless of the purpose of the visit. Even if the visitor is obviously upset about something and acts accordingly, you must overlook any discourtesy and show that you are understanding. It may be that your visitor is annoyed about what he or she feels is "unfair treatment" from your company. There may be some justification for this feeling, so you now have an opportunity to mend a business problem. Even if you can do nothing about the situation, you can listen understandingly to the complaint. Treating an annoyed customer discourteously will only tend to make the situation worse. Usually a person responds well to pleasant treatment, and your courteous attitude likely will help to calm the visitor and give your company a chance to make amends.

Apologize for Delays

If an appointment cannot be kept promptly by the person who is to receive the visitor, you should explain the delay ("I'm sorry, Mr. Kravis, Ms. Wong has been delayed at a meeting with the president"), and you should tell the visitor about how long the wait will be ("Ms. Wong should be back in about 20 minutes"). Make the visitor comfortable (a selection of current magazines and today's newspaper should be available, or offer a cup of coffee if it is available). You might ask, "Would you like to use the phone to tell your office about the delay?"

You may have some visitors whose undistinguished appearance leads you to believe they could not possibly have business of interest to one of the company executives. Don't be too sure! A person who is indifferent to personal appearance may be a VIP — perhaps even the most important stockholder in the company. Everyone is entitled to your most courteous treatment.

Find Out the Purpose of the Visit

WORLD VIEW

A knowledge of geography can be useful in international communication. For example, 2 p.m. Central Standard Time is 10 p.m. in Egypt— a bit late for a business call. Many almanacs and appointment books have information about time zones that will enable you to determine what time it is around the world.

Almost every caller will have an appointment with an executive or other member of the company. For example, a visitor may say to you, "I am Mary O'Neill; I have an appointment with Paul Morgan," and you will usher her to the appropriate office or telephone the executive that his visitor has arrived. If you do not know, however, whether the visitor has an appointment, you must ask, "May I help you?" or "Whom do you wish to see?" If the visitor has no appointment, take his or her name, the name of the company he or she represents (if any), and the purpose of the call. Relay this information to the person who you think can be of most help to the caller. After getting permission to show the visitor in, invite the person to follow you to the appropriate office. Then present the visitor like this: "Mr. Morgan (host), this is Mary O'Neill (visitor)."

Be Discreet and Tactful

Protect both your employer's and the company's interests by being discreet in your comments to visitors. For example, if your employer is late coming to the office in the morning or returning from lunch, it is not necessary to supply all these details to the visitor. Instead of saying, "Mrs. Stein is late getting in this morning," say, "I expect Mrs. Stein about 9:15." If she is late returning from lunch, you might say, "Mrs. Stein had an important luncheon meeting and should return shortly." Avoid making conversation about company business or personnel. If the subject comes up, be noncommittal and change the topic of conversation as quickly as you can. Never engage in negative statements, such as "Business has really been slow lately" or "We have a terrible time getting good word processors."

Be discreet in giving any opinions solicited by the visitor. The person the visitor has come to see may have a different opinion from your own. For example, the visitor may want to show you certain products and ask whether you think your company might be interested in buying them. Unless you are responsible for company purchases, however, you should not give an opinion about the company's possible interest in buying the products. Of course, you should not be rude even though you are pressured for comment. Simply say pleasantly, "I am sorry, but I do not purchase our company's supplies."

COMMUNICATING BY TELEPHONE

Communicating by telephone requires techniques that are quite different from those used in one-to-one conversation. Since those engaged in telephone conversations are unable to see one another, they must depend entirely upon their voices to communicate friendliness, interest, and a willingness to be helpful.

Since most people assume they know how to use the telephone properly, when as a matter of fact they do not, many office workers are ineffective telephone communicators. Furthermore, too many employees assume that a business telephone conversation requires the same treatment as a personal telephone call. Actually, the telephone is one of the most important communication media in business, so it must be used with great skill, especially in conversations with callers from the outside and with superiors in the office.

The following suggestions may seem elementary to you. Nevertheless, you should read them carefully and follow them whenever you use the telephone for either personal or business use:

Talk directly into the mouthpiece.

Talk slowly and naturally. Exaggerate your enunciation slightly. Shouting is never necessary.

If a caller must be transferred to someone else in the company, say, "If you will hold on just a moment, I will have your call transferred." Then depress the hang-up button twice, very slowly, and repeat until the operator returns to the line. Then say, for example, "Please transfer this call to Kate Emerson on extension 4103." If your telephone system permits you to transfer the call yourself, enter the extension carefully.

If, while talking, you must put down the receiver and you cannot put the call on hold, place it on a book or magazine rather than drop it on a hard surface. In this way, you will protect the caller's ear from irritating noises.

Place the receiver gently in the cradle when you hang up.

Guidelines for Effective Telephone Communication

Courtesy is the key to effective telephone communication. Greet all callers pleasantly. This pleasantness is achieved both by the words you use and by the tone of your voice. If you know who the caller is, you might say something like this: "Good morning, Mrs. Sanchez," or "Hello, Bill." If you do not know who the caller is, identify yourself first — "Mrs. Rossi speaking" or

"Karen White." When answering the telephone for a department, be certain to identify both the department and yourself—"Accounting Department, Ms. Park" or "Word Processing Center, Jerry Asher." A secretary or administrative assistant usually answers the executive's telephone like this: "Miss Bertrand's office" or "Miss Bertrand's office, Linda Jordan speaking."

Your voice should be friendly and your manner courteous, regardless of who is calling. This manner is *especially* important when talking to outside callers. Remember that the impression created by your voice should be that of a friendly smile. Show the caller that you want to be helpful; always listen attentively, and don't interrupt. So that the caller will know you are listening, occasionally acknowledge comments with a "Yes" or with some other simple oral response. Use the caller's name at least once before hanging up, and conclude the call with a remark like "Thank you for calling us, Dr. Turner," or "We will look into the matter for you right away, Ms. Koch."

Originating Calls

To make the best use of your telephone time, follow these suggestions for originating calls:

1. Plan the conversation before you call. A little preparation will save both time and money. If your conversation will be an involved one, jot down notes in advance.
2. Place your own calls. Not only is it faster and easier to do so, but it is also more courteous. No busy executive likes to be greeted with "Hold on, Mr. Gomez, I have Mr. Shipton on the line." Mr. Gomez then has to wait until Mr. Shipton gets on the line. Since Mr. Gomez is the person being called, it is discourteous to keep him waiting.
3. To avoid delays, identify yourself promptly and state the purpose of your call. For example, say, "This is Walter Chen of Litton and Warren. I would like to speak to the person in charge of adjustments."

Receiving Calls

To ensure efficient use of the telephone when you receive a call, follow these suggested procedures:

1. Answer promptly and identify yourself immediately. You should answer at the first ring, if possible, and not later than the second ring.
2. Respond to inquiries graciously, take notes, and verify important details. "Yes, we will be glad to send you a duplicate copy of last month's statement. You want the December, 19—, statement; is that correct?"
3. At the close of the conversation, take the required action. Be certain that you keep all promises you make to the caller.
4. Allow the caller to hang up first.
5. If you are going to be away from your telephone, let someone know, and indicate how you would like calls handled that are directed to you during your absence.

Answering for Others

When you are answering telephone calls for other people in your firm, follow these suggestions:

1. If the person called is not available, offer to be of help or to transfer the call to someone who can help.
2. If the caller wishes to speak to only one individual and that person is not available, obtain the caller's name and telephone number and record the caller's message, if any.

Handling Complaints

The true test of your ability to handle telephone calls effectively will be revealed when you must deal with an annoyed caller who has a complaint. You must remember that you represent your company and that little or nothing is to be gained by allowing yourself to become angry. Your task will be made much easier if you follow these suggestions:

1. Listen carefully to the caller's complaint. Take careful notes of all important details.
2. Express interest in and an understanding of the caller's problem. "Yes, I can see why you were annoyed by the mistake in your bill, Mr. Hayakawa, but I am sure we can correct it right away."
3. Tell the caller what action you will take. If you cannot make the adjustment yourself, refer the caller to someone who can. Don't make the caller repeat the entire story to someone else; each time the message must be repeated to another person, the caller becomes angrier.

Radio and TV Interviews

Techniques used in one-to-one communication have another application. Business executives are frequently asked to give radio and TV interviews. You probably have listened to or watched interviews with prominent people in the business world on public radio stations or on television news or talk shows. What has made these interviews successful and productive? The host and the person interviewed have followed the techniques you learned for effective communication on a one-to-one basis.

COMMUNICATION SKILLS: A DAILY NEED

Most employees in business spend a large part of their day in one-to-one communication. Activities may range from discussing an assignment with a coworker through greeting a supplier to handling a telephone inquiry. In this section, you have learned some guidelines for one-to-one communication, basic procedures for meeting the public, and telephone techniques. Remember that in all one-to-one communications, human relations skills such as tact and courtesy are just as important as oral communication skills.

REVIEW

Practical Application

KEY
See page I-56 for examples that will show how the assistant might reply to each of the callers.

A. You are the administrative assistant to Wilfred Jaeger, president of Jaeger Chemical Products Inc. Mr. Jaeger will be holding a very important conference in his office for the next two hours and has told you that he does not want to be disturbed under any circumstances. The following situations occur during the hours Mr. Jaeger does not want to be disturbed. What would you say to each of the people involved in the following situations?

1. The plant manager, Fred Parrish, telephones and says that it is urgent that he speak with Mr. Jaeger.
2. Mrs. Jaeger, the president's wife, telephones and asks to speak with her husband.
3. Ms. Cunningham, an important customer from out of town, arrives an hour early for an appointment she has with Mr. Jaeger.
4. The chairman of the board of directors, Y. C. Potts, telephones and asks to speak with Mr. Jaeger.

KEY
See page I-56.

B. The administrative services manager, Margot Novotna, has requested that you prepare a one-page memorandum on "Improving Telephone Usage." Prepare the memo.

KEY
See page I-56 for examples of how the receptionist might respond to each of the visitors.

C. How should a receptionist respond to the following visitors who approach the reception desk and say:

1. "Good morning."
2. "I would like to see Mr. Nakama."
3. "Is there someone who can help me get this stupid error on my bill straightened out?"
4. "My name is Greg Harris. I am a sales representative from Lincoln Drapery Cleaners and would like to demonstrate our high-quality service to the person in your company who takes care of drapery cleaning." (The building superintendent is the person responsible.)
5. "I have a nine o'clock appointment with Mr. Hart." (Mr. Hart has not yet arrived at the office, and it is just 9 a.m. now.)

KEY
See page I-56.

D. List the qualities of a good listener.

KEY
See page I-56.

E. Suggest three greetings a receptionist might use to find out the purpose of a visit by a customer.

Editing Practice

Editing to Improve Writing Techniques. Rewrite the following sentences, and correct all evidence of poor writing techniques.

KEY
1. it's
2. assistant

1. The jury reached their decision, and <u>its</u> not a majority vote.
2. Her <u>assistent</u> was persistent in finding the error.

REVIEW cont.

3. omit *on*
4. an hour
5. better
6. Looking up from the desk, the receptionist
7. lose, briefcase
8. Karl (*or* Erik)
9. Chip"?
10. as well as, if not better than, I.

3. Mary Lou will continue <u>on</u> in the same position.
4. Bruce arrived <u>a hour</u> early.
5. The group agreed that it was the <u>best</u> choice of the two possibilities.
6. The receptionist recognized the caller <u>looking up from the desk.</u>
7. Where did you <u>loose</u> your <u>breif case</u>?
8. Karl told Erik that <u>he</u> would be promoted.
9. Is this stock one that is considered a "Blue <u>Chip?</u>"
10. I know that you can handle this problem <u>as well, if not better, than me.</u>

Critical Thinking

Application. How would you handle a telephone caller with whom your boss does not wish to talk because this person has an unwarranted complaint that your boss has spoken to him about several times previously?

KEY
See page I-56.

SECTION

10.6 *COMMUNICATING IN GROUPS*

OBJECTIVES: After completing Section 10.6, you should be able to:

1. Discuss the steps to take to prepare for effective group discussions.
2. Discuss the steps to take to lead effective group discussions.
3. Describe the interaction method of conducting meetings.
4. Name the six basic rules for effective participation in meetings.

If one were to ask most business executives how many meetings they attend weekly, a typical answer is likely to be "Too many!" Such responses are based on the fact that many executives spend a large part of each working day attending some kind of meeting, either as a participant or as a leader of that meeting. Often, it becomes necessary for these executives to take work home to complete because there is insufficient time during the normal work day. Although group conferences are among the most important ways to exchange ideas and report information within business, the time spent at meetings is a

REINFORCEMENT

Emphasize that learning to be a contributing, cooperating member of a group is extremely important if one wishes to succeed in business.

frequent complaint in many businesses. Reducing the time spent at meetings is possible if meetings are organized and conducted more efficiently.

As a responsible business employee, you are likely to have frequent opportunities to participate in a variety of capacities in many types of group conferences. You might be selected as a member of a *standing* (permanent) committee that meets regularly, such as a planning committee or a finance committee. You may also be called upon to serve on a committee formed for a particular purpose only, such as a committee appointed to study employee grievances or to plan the company's 25th anniversary celebration. These temporary committees, formed for a special purpose and then disbanded after the purpose has been achieved, are called *ad hoc* (pronounced *ad hock*) committees. You may even be selected as chairperson of one of these committees, with the responsibility for planning and conducting the meetings.

Because meetings consume so much time and talent in the typical business organization, they should be organized and conducted efficiently. The time spent on meetings adds up to many thousands of dollars every year for the typical business organization. After attending meetings during business hours, many business workers often go to meetings and serve on other committees outside the company — for example, in professional, cultural, social, religious, political, and civic groups.

Long-Distance Meetings by Teleconference

KEY POINT

Teleconferencing gives group members who are not located in the same place the opportunity to communicate by text, audio, and video. Group members may be widely dispersed in other cities, states, or countries.

In addition to the amount of time employees spend at meetings held at the office, many executives spend a lot of time — and company money — traveling to and from meetings held in different locations. Teleconferencing offers a solution to this problem by enabling a group of people in different locations to meet and confer electronically. A major advance in the electronic office, teleconferencing gives group members the opportunity to communicate by text, audio, and video. However, the same rules that help make office meetings effective apply to meetings by teleconference. Group members need to prepare for the meeting, express opinions tactfully, make positive contributions, be courteous, keep remarks concise and pertinent, and take notes.

PLANNING GROUP DISCUSSIONS

The success or failure of a group meeting is very often determined by preparation. Skillful planning can turn an ordinary meeting into an extremely profitable experience for each participant. Without careful advance work, the most promising meeting can result in a waste of time for everyone. To become an effective meeting planner, follow the suggestions outlined here.

Prepare Thoroughly

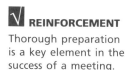

REINFORCEMENT

Thorough preparation is a key element in the success of a meeting.

A successful meeting or conference requires that the leader or leaders prepare far enough in advance to make all the necessary arrangements and to contend with any problems that may arise. Preparations should include the starting time, the length, and the site of the meeting; the names of those who are to attend; and the objectives that should be accomplished at the meeting.

Notification of a meeting usually takes the form of an agenda (a list of the topics to be discussed and the names of the persons who are to lead the discussion). The agenda should be sent as far in advance of the meeting as possible to allow the participants ample time to prepare for their roles in the meeting. For a monthly meeting, the agenda should be sent at least a week ahead of the meeting date. For a weekly meeting, the agenda should be received a day or two before the meeting. The sample agenda on page 496 shows the topics in the order in which they will be discussed. Under new items, those that are most important should be listed first in the event that there is not sufficient time to discuss them all. Some agendas include suggested time limits for discussion to encourage completion of agendas.

Prepare the Meeting Facilities

Arrangements for the meeting facilities must be planned so that the room, the furniture, and the equipment to be used are available and set up in time for the meeting. Otherwise, there may be an insufficient number of chairs, the room may be poorly ventilated, needed audiovisual or display facilities or other special equipment may not be available, refreshments may not arrive in time for the break, and so on. Any training or practice with unfamiliar equipment should be part of the preparation.

REINFORCEMENT
Prior checking of and practice with audiovisual equipment and presentation materials is essential. One should make certain that the equipment functions properly and that when it is switched on, the program or materials to be shown begin immediately.

In order to start the meeting promptly, it is best to check at least 45 minutes before the meeting that everything in the meeting room is in order. This prior checking, such as making sure that audiovisual equipment is on hand and in working order, makes it possible to take care of any problems before the meeting begins. If an operator for special equipment is required, the meeting date should be scheduled and then confirmed before the day of the meeting. Also, if electrical power is needed, make certain that there is an electrical outlet and that the extension cord is long enough. Problems can be more easily resolved if they are discovered early.

Arrive Early

The leader or leaders of the meeting should arrive a few minutes early to check the facilities and to set an example for the others. Arriving early also gives the leader or leaders a chance to distribute the agenda. (Even though everyone has received an advance copy of the agenda, not everyone will remember to bring it to the meeting.) Extra copies of reports or other papers to be discussed should also be available, even though copies may have been distributed in advance.

Establish a Businesslike Atmosphere

The chairperson or facilitator sets the tone of the meeting. If the leader begins late or is apathetic about getting the proceedings under way, the

```
        RELIABLE MEDICAL UNDERWRITERS, INC.

            Meeting of Regional Agents

            April 23, 19--, 1:30 p.m.
              at Hartford Home Office


                     AGENDA


     1.  Call to order by Chairperson Billington.

     2.  Approval of the minutes of the March meeting.

     3.  Approval of and additions to agenda.

     4.  Announcements.

     5.  Unfinished Business:

          a.  Report of employee welfare committee.

          b.  Continuation of discussion of hiring procedures.

     6.  New Business:

          a.  Recommendations for additional office locations.

          b.  Changes in advertising media.

          c.  Proposals for collection procedures.

          d.  Additional items.

     7.  Adjournment.

     8.  Coffee Hour.
```

An agenda lists the topics to be discussed at a forthcoming meeting. Under "New Business," an agenda usually lists the items in order of importance.

participants are likely to lose whatever enthusiasm they may have had when they entered the room. Generally it is best to start a meeting precisely at the hour for which it is scheduled, even though there may be latecomers. If the members of a group realize that the meeting will start without them, they are likely to make an effort to be punctual.

Guide the Discussion

The good leader talks as little as possible and draws out the opinions of the participants. Unfortunately, some people think that *leader* and *talker* are synonymous terms when it comes to running a meeting. The skillful leader brings out each participant's best thinking. The leader's function is not to show how much he or she knows but to steer the discussion in the proper direction. The experienced leader knows that the greater the participation — that is, the more minds at work on a problem — the better the chances are of accomplishing the objective of the meeting.

Encourage Participation

Everyone invited to a meeting should be able to make some contribution to the discussion. Sometimes, ground rules are needed to encourage the members of the group to participate. The leader of the meeting should make it clear that individuals are not allowed to interrupt the person who is speaking. Speakers should know that they will be able to express their ideas without being criticized or attacked.

Some people are shy and will not say anything unless they are encouraged to speak. The leader should call on these people in a manner that will offer them encouragement; for example, "Marcia, you have had a lot of experience in advertising. What do you think of José's layout for next week's ad?" or "Ken, we would be interested in having the benefit of your experience in the word processing center. Do you think we need to change the facilities if we want to create a more pleasant environment?"

A leader encourages positive participation by saying something complimentary after a speaker has made a worthwhile contribution; for example, "Thank you, Isaac, for that timesaving suggestion," or "That's an excellent idea, Ms. Kraft. Could you tell us a little more about how you think that plan might function?" Comments of this type are effective when they are obviously sincere. Negative comments, on the other hand, discourage participation and should, therefore, be kept to a minimum and be presented so tactfully that they do not discourage others from making suggestions. "That idea would work beautifully if . . . "

Discourage Excessive Talkers

In any group there will always be one or two people who want to do all the talking. Certainly they have a right to be heard, but unless they are listed on the agenda as the principal contributors, they should not be permitted to monopolize the discussion. A leader should be firm in preventing a loudmouth from taking over the meeting. "That's very interesting, Joe, but I think we ought to hear from Carla," or "Let's get back to you a little later, Eileen. I think we would all be interested in having as many points of view as we can get."

Keep the Discussion Pertinent

CRITICAL THINKING

Discuss tactful ways to discourage excessive talkers and group members who repeatedly stray from the topic.

Meetings sometimes tend to get off the track, and if the leader or facilitator permits the discussion to wander for too long, the principal problems to be resolved at the meeting will be bypassed entirely. All too often, a subject comes up that is of genuine personal interest to all those present at the meeting but has little or no bearing on the main topic. People just naturally like to tell about their personal experiences, likes and dislikes, and amusing anecdotes. However, when side issues begin to waste valuable time, they must be cut off tactfully by the leader and the discussion must be brought back on track. "That certainly was an interesting experience, Robin, but let's get back to our discussion of the employees' handbook. Yolanda, what changes do you think are necessary in the section on retirement?" Usually you can keep the discussion on track without being rude to anyone, but bluntness is sometimes necessary as a last resort. "Sandy, time is getting away from us, and we want to avoid having to call another meeting to settle this problem. Do you have any specific solutions?"

Summarize Periodically

It is neither necessary nor desirable for the chairperson of a group discussion to evaluate remarks as soon as they are presented. The group leader should always listen attentively but does not need to comment except, perhaps, to stimulate further discussion. "Excellent — that's an interesting point. I gather that you think this plan will be more effective than the one we have been following. Is that a correct assumption?" Above all, the leader does not tear down ideas or argue with participants; doing so will only discourage others in the group from expressing themselves. Since the leader of the meeting is only one member of the group, it is usually poor practice to judge every idea expressed instead of letting other members of the group participate.

From time to time, the chairperson should summarize the major points that have been presented. "We all seem to agree that we should not add more branch stores at the present time. Instead, you feel we should enlarge the existing branches and increase our advertising budget. Is that correct? Well, let's discuss which branches should be enlarged and how we should make use of an increased advertising budget. Brian, do you have any suggestions regarding which branch stores should be enlarged?"

✔ REINFORCEMENT

Stress the importance of a timely distribution of meeting minutes.

Know How and When to Conclude

If the chairperson has prepared the agenda carefully and has conducted the meeting efficiently, the meeting should end fairly close to the time scheduled for adjournment. If the discussion seems likely to extend beyond the closing hour and it is important to continue, get the approval of the group; for example, "Ladies and gentlemen, it is five minutes of twelve, and it looks as though we won't get out of here by noon. Shall we continue the discussion, or would you rather schedule another meeting for this afternoon?"

After the meeting, the secretary should prepare the minutes and distribute them as soon as possible. Memorandums should be written to those who are assigned special responsibilities at the meeting. Such a memorandum is illustrated below.

Know How to Conduct Formal Meetings

Many groups conduct their meetings on a formal basis, following parliamentary rules. If you are elected to office in such a group, you should read *Robert's Rules of Order*, the standard guide to parliamentary procedure.

The Interaction Method

The interaction method, which encourages participation by group members, is another way of conducting meetings.[2] There are four key roles: the

After a meeting, the chairperson should remind each participant of his or her assignment.

INTEROFFICE MEMORANDUM

To: Mrs. Beth Connolly   From: Karl Seltzer

Subject: Retirement Section of   Date: June 13, 19--
          Employees' Handbook

This memorandum is to remind you that at the meeting yesterday of the Handbook Revision Committee you volunteered to conduct a survey of all retired employees to determine their suggestions for improving the retirement section of the handbook.

You also indicated you would set up a subcommittee to work on this revision and would report to the parent body at its September meeting any suggestions for changes that result from your survey and the discussion at your subcommittee meetings.

Thank you, Beth, for agreeing to assist in this most worthwhile project.

KS

---

[2]Michael Doyle and David Strauss, *How to Make Meetings Work*, Wyden Books, 1976, pp. 84–87.

The *interaction method*, a different kind of approach to conducting meetings, encourages group members to share responsibility for preparation and to participate during meetings. Ideas generated are compiled in a document called the *group memory*.

facilitator, the recorder, the group member, and the manager/chairperson. The interaction method has a built-in system of balances that keeps each of the key roles in check.

1. The job of the facilitator is to propose procedural guidelines and to make sure that everyone has a chance to participate.
2. The recorder stands in front of the group and writes down the main ideas of the speakers in their own words. The group members can watch the creation of this group memory and can make any needed corrections immediately.
3. The group members must make sure that the facilitator and the recorder perform their functions properly and that the ideas of the speakers are recorded accurately.
4. The manager/chairperson is an active participant in the meeting but does not run it. In the end, however, the manager makes the decisions and can accept or reject the ideas of group members. The manager/chairperson has the role of group member during the meeting.

Silence can be an effective form of communication—one often ignored in the United States. Someone has said that Americans will agree to almost anything if the opposite negotiating party is silent long enough.

PARTICIPATING IN MEETINGS

Everyone invited to participate in a group discussion has an obligation to contribute his or her best thinking and suggestions. Here is an opportunity to exhibit your interest in the business that employs you, as well as your knowledge about the work you are doing. Too often, time and money are wasted because so many employees take meetings for granted and do not contribute their maximum efforts to the discussion. They often come to a meeting unprepared, uninterested, and uninspired. The six basic rules for participating effectively in a meeting are:

Prepare for the meeting.
Express opinions tactfully.
Make positive contributions.
Be courteous.
Keep remarks concise and pertinent.
Take notes.

Prepare for the Meeting

The first rule for effective participation in a meeting is to come prepared. Learn all that you can about the topics to be discussed at the meeting. If there is an agenda (see page 496), study each item carefully and learn more about those topics you are not familiar with. For example, if the subject of personnel evaluation is to be discussed, be sure that you know what the current company procedures are for evaluating personnel and the advantages and disadvantages of these procedures. You may wish to refer to books or articles dealing with this topic or to examine company forms that are currently in use. In addition, it may be useful to get the opinions of knowledgeable people who will not be present at the meeting. If there is to be a discussion of a revision of the evaluation form, study the form thoughtfully, try it out yourself, and ask various people who use the form to tell you what they like and do not like about it.

Being prepared also means coming to a meeting with a set of well-founded opinions. Opinions that are worth listening to in a business meeting are the ones backed up by facts. People are often opposed to a new idea merely because they don't know enough about it. Make certain that you can supply facts that will support your opinions and that will help convince others of the validity of your position.

Express Opinions Tactfully

When someone asks you for your opinion or when you volunteer an opinion, be tactful in expressing yourself. Often, opposing points of view can cause strong disagreement. No matter how strongly you may feel, your chances of winning that person's support are better if you are tactful in presenting your views. For example, don't say, "You're wrong, and here's why." Instead, you might say, "Your point of view certainly has merit, Henry, but I have doubts because . . . " Never tell someone that he or she is wrong—*wrong* is a strong term, and your right to use it requires indisputable evidence. In selling your point of view, the "Yes, but . . . " technique is effective; in other words, acknowledge the other person's point of view and show your respect for it. Then present your own ideas. For example, "Yes, I agree that the solution seems simple and that your idea represents one way to approach the problem, but . . . "

In expressing yourself, separate facts from opinions. Label as facts only those statements for which you have solid evidence. Opinions should be signaled by such words as "it seems to me," "as I understand it," or "in my opinion."

Make Positive Contributions

KEY POINT

Group members should convey a cooperative attitude by making positive contributions to discussions.

One of the most unwelcome participants in a group meeting is the person who thinks "No." This person's primary mission seems to be that of killing the ideas and proposals that others voice. Such a participant seldom presents a positive idea but is always quick to say of someone else's idea, "That won't work."

Most meetings are held for the purpose of solving problems, and problems cannot be solved in a negative atmosphere. Participants must be willing to approach a problem with the attitude that the only way to solve it is to present as many ideas as possible. No one should immediately veto an idea; instead, each person should try to see the idea's merits and to enlarge upon the idea's possibilities, no matter how weak the idea may seem at first. To smother ideas before they are fully aired is not only rude but also extremely disheartening to those who are genuinely trying to reach intelligent decisions.

Be Courteous

The ideal meeting is one in which everyone participates freely. The over-aggressive speaker who monopolizes the discussion will discourage the participation of others. Even though you may be more knowledgeable about the topic than anyone else in the group, you should never display your knowledge in an offensive, overbearing manner. You may win the skirmish and lose the battle—the too-sure, know-it-all person often does.

More victories have been won in group discussion by modesty and tact than will ever be achieved by overaggressiveness. Don't jump in while others are speaking; wait your turn patiently. Show interest in what others are saying. You will win more friends by listening and taking notes on remarks by others than by interrupting their remarks—regardless of how inane the remarks may seem to you. Acknowledge that others may have as much information or insight as you have or perhaps even more than you have.

Courteous group members do not (1) resort to sarcasm when they disagree with someone, (2) interrupt the person who is talking, (3) fidget, (4) gaze into space, or (5) carry on side conversations with other members of the group while someone else has the floor.

Keep Remarks Concise and Pertinent

Some participants in a meeting take a roundabout route to reach the point they want to make. They ramble endlessly. If you have something to say, get to your point quickly. Meetings become boring and unproductive mainly because some participants insist on relating personal preferences, experiences, and opinions that have little or no bearing on the discussion at hand.

Take Notes

It is a good idea to develop the habit of taking notes at meetings, because the act of taking careful notes (1) keeps you alert, (2) tells speakers that you consider their remarks worth remembering, and (3) provides a valuable reference source both during and after the meeting. Take notes not only on what the speaker is saying but also on what *you* want to say when it is your turn to speak. Jot down your key remarks in advance so that your comments are well organized and complete.

SECTION REVIEW

Practical Application

KEY
See page I-57.

KEY
See page I-57.

A. Make a list of the steps you would take to prepare a meeting room for an all-day discussion.

B. Prepare an interoffice memorandum to all supervisors, calling a meeting at which you and they will discuss the orientation program for all new employees. You want the supervisors to evaluate the present program, to talk with new employees hired since January 1 of this year, and to do some research regarding orientation programs used in other local businesses. These aspects will be discussed at the meeting, and the supervisors will draw up a revised program that will be put into effect September 1. Supply any other information you feel would be helpful.

C. Evaluate your ability to conduct a meeting, using as guidelines your previous experience, if any, and the qualities you consider necessary in an effective leader of group discussions.

D. How does one establish a businesslike atmosphere at a meeting?

E. Prepare an agenda for an ad hoc committee for which you are to act as chairperson. Select a discussion topic of your own choice. Then develop a list of topics concerned with phases of this subject and assign them to individuals in your class.

F. At a meeting of the Employee Retirement Planning Committee, Marietta Hart was assigned the responsibility of gathering information about the facilities for the retirement banquet and dance. Write a follow-up memorandum to Ms. Hart reminding her of the assignment. Supply all the details for the memorandum.

Editing Practice

Applied Psychology. The wording of the following letter excerpts does nothing to cement good human relations. Revise the sentences.

1. You made an error of $25 in totaling our last statement.
2. We fail to understand why you claim that the two lamp bases do not match.
3. We are unable to grant you credit because you are a poor payer.
4. You claim that your check was sent last week, but we have not yet received it.
5. You have put us through a great deal of trouble getting the merchandise to you on the date you requested.

Critical Thinking

Evaluate. Read the following statements made by group discussion leaders. If the statement is not an appropriate one, what should have been said?

1. "I don't think that idea would work."
2. "We'd like to hear more about the plan."
3. "What has been your experience with this problem?"

KEY
Answers will vary. See page I-57 for an example.

KEY
Answers will vary.

KEY
See page I-57.

KEY
Answers will vary.

KEY
See page I-58.

KEY
See page I-58.

10.7 *PREPARING AND DELIVERING A SPEECH*

OBJECTIVES: **After completing Section 10.7, you should be able to:**

1. Identify the steps to take in previewing a speaking assignment.
2. Explain how to gather and organize the information for a speech.
3. Describe how to practice giving a speech.
4. Discuss three characteristics that contribute to the effective delivery of a speech.
5. List the key points to observe in introducing a speaker.

☑ **REINFORCEMENT**

Speaking is often a requirement of a specific position. Speakers represent their companies; and they should strive to create, maintain, and enhance a positive image of themselves and their companies.

LANGUAGE **TIP**

To keep an audience's attention, make sure your speech is full of visual images. Examples are an excellent means of creating pictures.

—Phyllis Martin in *A Word Watcher's Handbook*

For many business executives, the ability to speak effectively before groups is an important requirement of their position. How much speech making they are likely to do depends upon many factors: the kind of position they hold, the degree of responsibility that comes with their position, and the effectiveness of their speech making.

A business executive may be expected to represent the company before professional organizations and many different cultural, civic, religious, and educational groups. These outside speaking duties are beyond those duties involved in speaking to members of one's own organization at employee meetings or at board meetings or at stockholders' meetings.

However, even those who are not top executives often are called upon to participate in activities involving speeches before either large or small groups — instructing subordinates, reporting to an executive committee, introducing a speaker, explaining a new company policy to a group of employees, or greeting a group of visitors.

A speech, like a letter, reflects an image of the organization that employs the speaker. An effective speech, like an effective letter, should convey a message clearly and convincingly and, at the same time, build an image of goodwill. Since nearly everyone is called upon at one time or another to "say a few words" to an audience, every business employee should be prepared to represent his or her company in a way that will reflect favorably on the company.

In order to deliver an effective speech — whether it be a two-minute introduction, a five-minute commentary, or an hour-long presentation — the first step the speaker should take is to plan the speech carefully. Planning involves four main steps: previewing the speaking assignment, gathering and organizing the material, outlining the speech, and rehearsing the presentation.

REINFORCEMENT

Previewing is an extremely important step in making a speech effective, but previewing is often overlooked.

REINFORCEMENT

Students should be taught to determine the purpose of their speech before making other decisions and preparations.

PREVIEWING THE SPEAKING ASSIGNMENT

Regardless of whether the speech topic has been selected for the speaker or the topic is the speaker's own choice, every speaker must answer three basic questions before gathering and organizing material: (1) What is the purpose of the speech? (2) To whom is the speech to be given? (3) How much time is allowed for the speech?

What Is the Purpose of the Speech?

Every speech should have a very specific purpose — to *explain* something, such as a new company policy; to *describe* something, such as the features of a new product or the steps in a new procedure; or to *report* on something, such as the results of a market survey. The primary goal of a speech may be to present a point of view, to inspire, to inform, or to win support for a new proposal. Whatever the purpose may be, every speech must be planned and organized to fit its purpose.

Assume that you have been asked to tell the company sales representatives about a sales promotion plan for your new electronic file cabinet. If your speech is entitled "Sales Promotion for the Tyler Electronic File Cabinet," obviously you are not expected to talk about how the product is made or how much it costs to produce. The purpose of your talk is to tell the sales representatives how the company plans to promote the sale of this product through advertising and any other promotional efforts the company plans to make — and how these sales representatives fit into this promotional program. Your remarks should concentrate on these promotional activities and convince the sales representatives that they will receive sufficient support to help make the selling job more efficient.

To Whom Is the Speech to Be Given?

The effective speaker finds out as much as possible about the audience before gathering material for the speech. If you are to discuss applications of robotics before a group of production supervisors, your emphasis will be quite different from the one you would use in discussing the same topic at, say, a meeting of company stockholders. If your speech is one of several that are to be given at the same meeting, you should inquire about the rest of the program so that you can put your topic in perspective with the others. You should find out as much as you can about the knowledge, interests, occupations, and age levels of the audience. In addition, it is helpful to know the expected audience size and the general background of the people. The program chairperson can supply this and other useful information. With this help, you can find out what the audience already knows about the subject and what the audience expects to learn from the presentation. With such knowledge at hand, you can avoid repeating facts already known and can give particular emphasis to areas of greatest interest to the audience.

INFORMATION

Usually, the choice is not between no knowledge and abundant knowledge. Audience members usually have varying degrees of knowledge.

INFORMATION

Nothing can be more destructive to the effectiveness of a speech than talking too long. It is better to leave the audience wanting more than to bore them with excessive length.

How Much Time Is Allowed for the Speech?

The speaker must know precisely how much time is planned for the speech. Obviously, you should not try to crowd into 30 minutes a topic that requires an hour. Therefore, once you know the amount of time you have been allotted, you should plan your speech so that you can present it adequately in this time period.

The smart speaker, when assigned 45 minutes, takes only 35 or 40 minutes. This leeway makes certain that the speech will not run overtime. If there are 5 or 10 minutes left, the time may be used to answer questions.

If you have been assigned a very broad topic like "Word Processing," you should select the aspect of the subject that best fits the audience. For example, your speech may deal with "A Voice-Input Word Processor" for an audience composed of executives, or it may deal with "How to Proofread Efficiently" for an audience composed of operators who work in word processing centers.

Tips on Preparing a Speech

1. Remember that preparing a speech is much like preparing a research paper.
2. After you have chosen or been assigned a speech topic, determine your purpose — to inform or persuade.
3. After you have analyzed your audience, narrow your topic to meet their needs and interests.
4. You probably already know a good deal about the topic of your speech. Think about your firsthand experience and your training.
5. If you wish to speak with experts on your topic, arrange meetings with them well in advance.
6. Use visual aids to illustrate or support an idea, or clarify a more complicated idea.

GATHERING AND ORGANIZING DATA

There is no substitute for preparation. Even the most gifted speakers always prepare carefully beforehand, whether they are to speak for only a few minutes or for an hour. If your topic is one that you can prepare for by reading, read as widely as possible. Find a good library that has up-to-date bulletins, periodicals, and books on your topic, and get as many points of view as you can. Check and double-check facts — especially statistical information. Take notes — more than you can possibly use in your speech. Put the notes on cards and start a new card for each new subtopic or source. Identify on each card the source of your information in case you want to refer to it later.

The advantage of writing notes on cards is that it is easy to discard unwanted material and to arrange and rearrange the remaining material in the best order for the preparation of your speech outline. In fact, if you prepare your notes well, the final arrangement of the cards will represent an outline.

For many topics, you can obtain valuable information by talking with people who are involved in the subject of your speech. For example, if you are going to speak on "Requirements for Success in Desktop Publishing," you might talk with a number of successful desktop publishers. Take notes on your findings, and use this information in preparing your speech.

OUTLINING AND ORGANIZING THE SPEECH

✓ **REINFORCEMENT**
The value of outlining should not be overlooked in planning a well-organized, effective speech.

After selecting the topic and gathering and organizing the data, the speaker is ready to begin outlining the speech. The following is a guide to preparing an outline:

1. Speech Title —   Time Allotted —
2. Purpose of Speech —
3. Introduction (arouse interest and give purpose) —
4. Body of Speech — Principal ideas to support purpose
   a. Principal idea no.1
      Supporting information and material
   b. Principal idea no. 2
      Supporting information and material
   c. Principal idea no. 3
      Supporting information and material
5. Conclusion
   a. Summary of principal ideas
   b. Plea for action (if applicable)

The Introduction

The introductory remarks should be brief and should arouse the interest of the audience in the speaker and in the subject. Various methods of introducing the talk may be used; for example:

1. A direct statement of the subject and its importance to each member of the audience.

   The title of my presentation is "Pen-Based Computers: What They Can Do for the Busy Executive." Each of you can accomplish more with one of these simple-to-use devices.

2. An indirect opening that is of vital interest to the audience, with a statement connecting the subject with this interest.

   Each day you probably waste untold minutes just waiting — waiting for the subway, the elevator, the waiter or waitress. Well, you no longer need to waste those precious minutes.

3. A striking example or comparison that leads up to the purpose or subject of the speech.

   While standing in line for an airline boarding pass, a well-known CEO filled out a form and faxed it to her operations manager.

4. A strong quotation relating to the subject of the speech.

   According to Dwight O'Hare, editor of the *New Economy Journal*, "Pen-based computers are not some vision of the future; they are here today, complete with numerous pen-based programs, and they are receiving rave reviews."

5. Relevant statistics regarding the subject.

   A recent survey revealed that more than 800 "computer-illiterate" business executives around the country are already using pen-based computers in their offices.

6. A brief anecdote.

   Last week my assistant handed me a clipping from a local newspaper. It was about the many applications of pen-based computers. My assistant never once thought about being replaced by such a device but was interested only in whether it could shorten his workday to a mere eight hours!

The Body of the Speech

Once audience interest is aroused, you are ready to provide the principal ideas that will support the purpose you have established for your speech. How many ideas you will present and develop will depend wholly upon the amount of time you have been allotted for the speech. It is better to develop each idea fully enough to be convincing than to present many ideas that are weakly developed and therefore not fully accepted or understood by the audience.

How is an idea communicated? First, it must be stated in a brief but clear and interesting way. Then the idea should be developed by explanation and illustration. Finally, the idea should be summarized.

Among the techniques available to the speaker for developing ideas are those in the following list. Which techniques the speaker selects will depend upon the nature of the data to be presented.

Giving examples.
Making comparisons.
Quoting statistics.
Quoting testimony of a recognized authority.
Repeating the idea in different words.
Defining terms used in stating the idea.
Using descriptive language that makes the listener "see" the situation.
Using narration to relate a story connected with the idea.
Using audio and visual aids.

Here is an example of how one idea used in a speech might be communicated, following several of the suggestions that have been presented. Suppose a speech is intended to convince an audience of business executives that their companies should purchase their own small airplanes for business use.

Principal Idea

A business saves both time and money by owning its own airplane.

Development

1. Tell the story of two business firms in the same city whose executives frequently travel by air from their place of business to cities about 200 to 300 miles away. One executive used the local airline service and had to spend two nights in a hotel away from home to complete the business transaction. The other executive had his own plane and was able to return home the same day as he left.
2. Show on a comparative chart the cost of using public air transportation over a one-year period as compared with the cost of using one's own plane for the same period of time and covering about the same total mileage.
3. Give several examples of travel time between your city and another heavily visited city nearby, making comparisons in time using public airline service and one's own private plane.
4. Quote executives of leading companies in your area who own their own planes and who are convinced that the convenience, as well as the saving of time and money, makes it essential that every company conducting business hundreds of miles away have its own plane.

Many speakers use such audiovisual materials as chalkboards and chalk, charts, slides, filmstrips, overhead projections (of transparencies), videotapes, and motion pictures to enrich their presentations. Before deciding to use a visual aid, be certain that you have determined whether or not the material will be visible to the entire audience. The size of the audience and the type of room in which you make your presentation will be the principal determinants. Good visual aids can make your presentation more interesting by providing a change of pace. Talks dealing with figures can be made clearer and much more effective by using well-prepared charts and diagrams. If the situation is such, however, that mechanical means would prove ineffective, then consider the possibility of using duplicated handout materials.

Motion pictures and videotapes should be previewed to determine whether they are appropriate. Above all, facilities and equipment should be checked before the presentation so that there will be no delays after the talk has started.

 **INFORMATION**

When writing a conclusion, a good thought to keep in mind is "What one idea do I want the members of my audience to take away with them?"

The Conclusion

The conclusion of a speech should be brief and to the point. A summary of the major points made in the speech and a plea for action, if applicable, are all that are needed. The summary may repeat key words or expressions already used or may restate the principal ideas in different words. Sometimes an example, a comparison, or an effective quotation serves as an appropriate summary. In any case, the final statement should tell the listeners very specifically what they should do, believe, or understand as a result of the presentation.

PRACTICING THE SPEECH

The inexperienced speaker should write the entire speech from the outline developed, *not* for the purpose of reading the speech but for refining expressions, improving the choice of words, and timing the presentation. By recording this preliminary speech and then playing it back, the speaker can determine how the words will sound to the audience. Then the speaker can make the appropriate changes.

After you have refined your speech, have read it through several times, and have timed the reading, you should prepare an outline on index cards. This outline should include phrases, quotations, and statistics. If possible, it should be prepared in large, clear handwriting or in jumbo typewriter type so that you can refer to the notes casually from a distance of two or three feet. Supplementary materials should be keyed into the outline in some way (underlining, solid capitals, or color) that will make them stand out.

Using the final outline, you should practice delivering your speech and should try to anticipate the conditions of the actual talk. A beginning speaker often finds the following practice suggestions helpful. Stand erect — before a mirror if possible — and imagine your audience before you. Watch your posture, facial expressions, and gestures as you deliver the speech. If you can practice before an audience of family or friends who will be sympathetic but frank in their analysis, so much the better. If you can record your presentation on audiotape or videotape, you will be able to hear how clearly you speak and to judge the overall effectiveness of your presentation.

DELIVERING THE SPEECH

Though *what* you say in your speech is extremely important, *how* you say it is equally important. The best talk ever written can put an audience to sleep if it is poorly delivered. On the other hand, an average speech can bring an audience to its feet if the speaker is poised, dynamic, and persuasive. To deliver a speech effectively, you must possess the following important characteristics: confidence in your ability to deliver an effective message, a pleasing personal appearance, and good stage presence and delivery.

Confidence

Surveys have consistently revealed that most people's greatest fear is the fear of having to give a formal speech. "I don't have a knack for public speaking." "Speakers are born, not made." "I'll make a fool of myself if I try

□SUGGESTION

Practicing your speech before a mirror, family, or friends can help you build confidence. If equipment is available, videotape a practice session. The videotape will help you detect detracting mannerisms and "rough" spots in your content.

√ REINFORCEMENT

Adequate preparation is the key to building confidence.

to give a speech." "I'll get stage fright and forget everything I'm supposed to say." These are typical reactions of a novice speaker. If you believe any of these statements, then you, like so many other people, underestimate yourself. You're better than you think!

When you are talking to an audience, pretend that you are carrying on a face-to-face conversation with just one person. Remember that the audience is just as eager for you to perform well as you are to do your best. Don't be upset if you are nervous — even experienced speakers and actors are. Feeling nervous is a result of anxiety about doing a good job, and most authorities feel that a little stage fright provides needed tension. Some experts even suggest that speakers mention their nervousness as a way of eliminating it and also of putting the audience at ease.

One way to develop confidence is to make sure that the conditions under which you are going to speak are as favorable as you can make them. Try to arrive 15 or 20 minutes before you are scheduled to speak. If you speak best standing behind a lectern — and most people do — ask your host to provide one. Even an improvised lectern, such as a cardboard box covered with a cloth and set on a table, is better than no lectern at all. If possible, get the feel beforehand of the space you are going to occupy when you do address the group. Know in advance how you will approach the podium. If you think your approach will be awkward for you or for others on the stage or distracting to the audience, ask your host to change the arrangement. Check the ventilation, the lighting, the public address system, and the seating arrangement. In short, make all the advance preparations you can to assure a feeling of familiarity with your surroundings. This is another big step in building confidence.

Appearance

As you learned in Section 10.3, one of the most important elements that will contribute to your confidence as a speaker in any situation is your appearance. If you can eliminate any concern about how you look to the audience, then you can concentrate on other aspects of your presentation. In preparing for your speech, spend a little extra time on personal grooming and the selection of clothing to assure yourself that your appearance will be as good as it can be. Clothing should be freshly cleaned and pressed, and shoes should be polished and in good repair.

Knowing that you are immaculately and tastefully groomed builds confidence in yourself and establishes the audience's confidence in you.

Good Stage Presence and Delivery

Speak Out. You have a responsibility to make sure that you are heard by each person in the audience. Any person who can't hear will become uninterested, bored, and annoyed. If possible, before you deliver a speech, check the volume of your voice in the room where you will speak.

Keep your chin up when speaking so that your words will be directed out to the audience rather than down to the floor. Vary the pitch of your voice so that the audience is not lulled to sleep by a monotone. When you want to emphasize a point, raise your voice; when you wish to stir emotions, drop your voice so that it is barely audible to the audience. Either extreme of tone, of course, will lose its desired effect if prolonged.

Be Poised. If you have stage fright, take a deep breath before you begin to speak; this will relax your vocal cords. Stand with your weight distributed evenly on both feet, and don't shift from one foot to the other excessively. Don't stand too stiffly or too casually—appear at ease but alert. Begin by smiling at your audience. If your listeners think that *you* are comfortable, then they are more likely to be comfortable.

Reveal Awareness of the Audience. An effective speaker must be aware of the audience at all times, not only in selecting and preparing the topic but also in giving the speech. This audience awareness must be transmitted in some way to the listeners. They respond much more favorably when the speaker talks directly to them.

As you speak, look slowly back and forth over the entire audience, and pause here and there to "take in" a particular segment of the crowd. Smile frequently. Train yourself to watch the audience carefully and to be sensitive to its changing moods. If, as you are talking, you see blank or uninterested expressions on the faces of your listeners, you will know that your talk is dragging and that the audience has tuned you out. This situation may call for an amusing story, a personal anecdote, or merely a change in the pitch of your voice. If you are using visual aids, you might direct the audience's attention to a chart or other illustration when the talk seems to pall.

If your audience seems tired because the hour is late or too many speakers have preceded you, be quick to sense its boredom. If you aren't sure you can reawaken its interest with a sparkling performance, cut your talk to the bare essentials. Usually it is better to omit a portion of your speech than to run the risk of boring an already weary audience. The audience will be grateful to you.

Avoid Objectionable Mannerisms. As noted in Section 10.3, a good speaker avoids objectionable mannerisms such as toying with an object. However, there are other kinds of objectionable mannerisms that good speakers avoid. Do you clear your throat or wet your lips frequently? Do you punctuate your remarks with an "uh," "ya know," "okay," or "anda"? Do you overuse pet expressions or slang? If you are not aware that you have any such mannerisms, ask some of your friends to listen to a rehearsal and to criticize. A speaker who has even one annoying habit cannot give a completely successful talk, for mannerisms distract an audience.

Don't Read or Memorize. Never recite your speech from memory or read it to the audience. Only a gifted actor or actress can make a memorized speech sound natural, and nothing is more boring to an audience than a singsong recitation. In addition, if you memorize your speech, you may become so flustered when you forget a line that you will find it difficult to continue. A memorized speech often does not follow a logical order because a speaker has omitted something important or has mixed up the parts.

Reading a speech so that the ideas sound convincing is also difficult. If you try to read your speech, you will lose eye contact with your audience every time you refer to your notes.

Instead of reciting or reading your speech, become sufficiently familiar with your material so that all you need is a brief outline with key words and phrases to make your speech flow in logical sequence. Use a conversational tone. Imagine that you are conversing with your audience, not giving an oration. Your voice should reflect the warm, easy tone that you would use if you were talking to a group of good friends.

Use Notes. Most speakers—even the most experienced—rely on outline notes to guide them in their presentations. There is nothing wrong with using notes. It is a greater crime for a speaker to dispense with notes and to give a rambling, disorganized speech than to use notes and to present an organized speech. Even if the notes are not actually used, having them on hand gives you confidence because you know you have something to fall back on if you should have a temporary lapse of memory.

Look at your notes only when absolutely necessary, and return your attention quickly to your audience after each glance at your notes. Keep your notes out of sight as much as possible while you are giving your talk, and turn the pages or cards as inconspicuously as you can. An audience is quickly discouraged by a large, slowly dwindling stack of notes.

Plan Use of Audiovisuals and Distribution of Material. If you plan to use audio or visual aids with your speech, key them into your outline notes so that you will not forget precisely where you want to present them. Of course, be sure that these aids are at hand and in correct order before you begin to speak. As soon as you have finished using a visual aid, remove it from sight and immediately redirect your attention to the audience.

Often the speaker will have duplicated material to distribute to the audience. As a general rule, such material should not be distributed at the beginning of a speech. If it is, the audience will be too busy examining the "giveaway" to pay attention to the speaker. The important points of a speech should be made before any material is distributed to the audience. Remember to plan the method of distribution just as carefully as you plan the rest of your presentation.

Use Stories and Anecdotes Discreetly. Nearly every speech of any length is brightened considerably by touches of humor and by human interest narratives. Such stories, however, should not dominate the speech. Observe the following rules in using humor and human interest stories:

1. Make sure they are relevant. Use stories and jokes that are related to the topic, that add interest to the subject, or that illustrate a particular point.
2. Make sure they have a punch line. The story you tell should have a point. Before telling a joke to an audience, test it first on friends. Many stories

and jokes fall flat because they are too subtle for a mass audience, because they are told poorly, or because they have weak punch lines.

3. Make sure they are in good taste. You should make certain that any story or joke you tell will not offend or embarrass the audience. Avoid risqué stories or jokes that make fun of physical handicaps, religious convictions, or ethnic groups.

4. Make sure they are short. A story or joke that lasts more than a minute or two is likely to fall flat because the audience loses interest or forgets the details that lead up to the punch line. Only the most skillful storyteller can get by with longer tales. Rehearse stories carefully before delivering them, and time them to make sure that they are not too long.

INTRODUCING A SPEAKER

One of the most important speaking assignments is introducing a speaker. A good introduction sets the stage for the main address. If the introducer does an outstanding job, the main speaker's task is greatly simplified. In introducing a speaker, observe the following points.

Use an Appropriate, Brief Introduction

The audience has come to hear the speaker, not the person who is introducing the speaker. Therefore, keep the introduction short — not more than two or three minutes in length.

When you are introducing a speaker, avoid such trite expressions as "The speaker for this evening needs no introduction," "I give you Professor Christine Gibbs," or "Without further ado, I present Dr. Adam Clay Kingsley."

Set the Stage for the Speaker

Do some research on the speaker. Find out from the speaker's friends, associates, or secretary some personal traits or achievements that do not appear in the usual sources. A human interest story about the speaker's hobby, family, or generosity will warm the audience. Although you should have complete details about the speaker's experience, education, and attainments, you do not need to use them all. An audience is quickly bored, and sometimes a speaker is embarrassed, by a straight biographical presentation, no matter how impressive the speaker's background is. Give only the most significant dates, positions, and accomplishments. You need only to convince the audience that the speaker is qualified to speak on the topic assigned, is worth knowing, and has something important to say.

Keep Your Eyes on the Audience

Do not turn from the audience to face the speaker you are introducing — always keep your eyes on the audience. After you have made the introduction, wait until the speaker has reached the lectern before seating yourself.

End With the Name

Many successful toastmasters recommend that you not mention the speaker's name until the very end of the introduction. During the introduction refer only to "our speaker." Then, at the end of the introduction, say something like: "It is my pleasure to present General Manuel Ortega."

Make Closing Remarks Brief and Appropriate

At the end of the speaker's remarks, someone on the platform or at the speaker's table should assume the responsibility for closing the meeting. If the speech was a particularly effective one, you may say with sincerity, "Thank you, General Ortega, for your most enlightening and inspiring message. We are most appreciative. Members of the audience, the meeting is adjourned." On the other hand, if the speech has been average or even disappointing, as indicated by the audience reaction, you may close by merely saying, "Thank you, Dr. Kingsley, for giving us your ideas on how to manage a multinational sales force. Members of the audience, thank you for coming to our meeting, and good night."

Under no circumstances should you prolong the closing remarks. If the speech was a good one, there is nothing more you can contribute to its effectiveness. If the speech was a poor one, the audience is probably tired and anxious to leave.

SECTION

REVIEW

Practical Application

KEY
See page I-59.

A. List three topics about which you feel qualified to speak. For each topic, give two reasons why you feel qualified to speak on this topic. Indicate one audiovisual aid that you might use in presenting each topic before a group. For each topic, suggest one attention-getting title for a 20-minute speech.

KEY
Answers will vary.

B. Select one of the topics you listed in Application A for a five- or six-minute presentation before the class. Prepare an outline for this speech, following the format suggested on page 507.

KEY
Answers will vary.

C. After the instructor has approved your outline, write your speech in full. Then read, refine, and time the speech. Finally, following the suggestions made in the text, make an outline of the speech on no more than four 5- by 3-inch index cards.

KEY
Answers will vary.

D. Suggest two ways that a beginning public speaker can overcome the common problems enumerated below:

1. Excessive verbalizing (using "uh," "ya know," "okay," "anda," and so on).

2. Nervousness.

E. You will be the master of ceremonies at your college convocation. The principal speaker will be the dean of the School of Business, and you will introduce him or her. Gather as much information as you can about the dean's background and compose an appropriate introduction. You may supply any additional details about the speaker that you feel will add interest to the introduction. The topic of the presentation will be "Making the Most of Your Business Education."

F. Compose two different closing statements that would be appropriate at the conclusion of the dean's presentation.

Editing Practice

The Editorial Supervisor.   Edit and rewrite the following paragraph.

Enclosed please find a copy of the treasurers report. I am enclosing along with this report a check herewith in the amount of $75. Kindly acknowledge receipt of the same due to the fact that a previous check transmitted through the mails was lost. Please advise at an early date if their will be any changes necessary in the report herewith submitted.

Critical Thinking

Application.   Based on your ultimate career goal, prepare an outline for a five-minute talk on "Why Choosing a Career in the Field of _____ Is a Must for the Nineties." Be prepared to give this talk to the class.

COMMUNICATING FOR JOB RESULTS

11.1 COMMUNICATING IN THE JOB SEARCH

OBJECTIVES: After completing Section 11.1, you should be able to:

1. Explain how reading, writing, listening, and speaking skills are used to achieve job results.
2. Analyze yourself and your qualifications.
3. List methods for assessing the job market.
4. Explain how you can market yourself in a résumé, an application letter, and an application form.

☐ **SUGGESTION**

Emphasize the integration of communication skills.

You are in college because you are preparing for employment or because you want to enhance your knowledge and skills so that you can advance your career status. Throughout this text, you have studied, applied, and polished your business communication skills. Chapter 11 helps you see how all these skills — reading, writing, listening, and speaking — can be combined to achieve job results.

Reading   Reading to locate sources of jobs and learn about potential employers.
Writing   Writing an application letter, a résumé, and other job-related correspondence.
Listening   Listening to questions asked in an interview.
Speaking   Speaking in response to questions asked at an interview.

Finding the position you want is similar to taking a comprehensive final exam. You must put together everything you have learned and make it work for you. The information and related assignments in this chapter will prepare you for your job search. The process will be easier if you approach it systematically in separate steps. You need to:

1. Analyze yourself and your qualifications.
2. Assess the job market.
3. Market yourself.

CRITICAL THINKING

Discuss each of these four areas thoroughly: Career Goals, Education, Experience, and Personal Characteristics.

ANALYZING YOURSELF AND YOUR QUALIFICATIONS

The first step in the job search process is to analyze yourself and your qualifications. You need to think about what kind of work interests you and what qualifications you have that would help you perform the work.

Consider the questions below:

Career Goals. What position do I have now? What position do I want when I graduate? What position do I want two years from now? What position do I want five years from now?

Education. What courses, degrees, or vocational training have prepared me for my career goals? Can I achieve my career goals with the education I now have? Do I need additional courses to qualify me for the position I want? Will I need additional education and training for the position I want two to five years from now?

Experience. What experience do I have that is related to the position I want? How is this experience specifically related to my career goals? If I have no related experience, how can I get related experience before graduation? Do I have additional — though unrelated — experience that will demonstrate a successful work history?

Personal Characteristics. What do I enjoy? Do I like working with numbers, computers, people, or a combination of these? Do I like variety? Would I like a desk job, or would I be happier with a position that involved traveling? Do I want responsibility? Do I like challenge and problem solving? Do I want to limit myself to a 40-hour workweek, or would I accept a position that offers advancement but frequently requires 50 to 60 hours a week? Would I be happy in a high-stress position? What are my major strengths and weaknesses?

❏ **SUGGESTION**

Ask students to describe their ideal employer and position by responding to questions listed for consideration. Answering these questions will help them determine what they want in a job.

Now, you should become very specific. Begin by describing your "ideal" potential employer and the position you desire with that firm. It is okay to dream a little when writing this description; it helps you determine exactly what you want. Here are some questions you will want to consider when writing the description:

- *What products am I interested in?* (for example, textiles, pharmaceuticals, construction equipment) or *What services do I want to provide?* (for example, real estate, health care, accounting)
- *Where do I want to work?* (a small community in the southern United States; Seattle or Tacoma, Washington; northern New Jersey)
- *What size company do I want to work for?* (small, medium, or large)
- *What position do I want?* (accountant, computer operator, administrative assistant, medical technologist)
- *What salary range am I looking for?* ($15,000–$20,000, $20,000–$25,000)
- *What benefits are important to me?* (flexible schedule, child care, vacation, health insurance, retirement package)
- *Am I prepared to travel on my job?* (local, overnight, moderate, or extensive)
- *What kind of career opportunity am I looking for?* (promotions, transfer, additional education, and training)

After you have described your "ideal" company and position, go back to the previous section. See if your goals, education, experience, and personal characteristics fit your ideal company and position. If everything is in agreement, proceed to the next step. If they do not agree, work through the first two sections again to decide where you should make changes.

Earlier, we said it was okay to dream when describing your ideal company and position. Now, you must face reality by finding out if such a position exists. If it does, apply for it. If it does not exist, then consider possible compromises. For example, you may find that the type of job you want as a computer programmer exists but that the available positions are in Southern California, and you were hoping to work in Seattle, Washington. Should you reconsider, or should you stick to your original plan? If you reconsider, should you change the type of job you want, or should you change the location? You must consider your choices and establish your priorities. This leads to the second step in the job search process: assessing the job market.

ASSESSING THE JOB MARKET

After you have analyzed yourself and your qualifications and know what kind of employment you want, you should begin looking for positions that meet your specifications. Many sources for information about job opportunities are readily available. Depending on the size and geographic region of your desired location, some sources may be more accessible than others. However, here are some general suggestions for locating employment opportunities.

Your Personal Contact Network

Your personal contact network, consisting of your friends, relatives, and college instructors, can be an effective source, particularly in a small community. Instructors frequently are contacted by alumni or other local business executives requesting recommendations for filling vacancies. Employees of a company often know when positions will become available because of transfers, promotions, resignations, and retirement and when new positions have been created. You should let your contact network know what kind of job you are seeking, when you expect to finish school, and when you will be available to accept a position. Even if your personal contacts do not know of an available position, they may know other people who do.

College Placement Centers

Most educational institutions have placement offices whose career counselors are eager to assist you in finding a position. Visit your school's placement center to see what services are available. Besides listing employment requests from area businesses, career counselors also promote placement by

LIVING LANGUAGE

We must open the doors of opportunity. But we must also equip our people to walk through those doors.

—Lyndon B. Johnson

SUGGESTION
Ask the career counselors from your school to speak to your class. They should outline their services and specify the procedures students should follow to obtain their assistance.

arranging job fairs that bring potential employers to the campus to interview students. Some centers offer software programs that help you make career decisions. Others offer workshops on résumé preparation and interviewing techniques. Often, career counselors can help you get a part-time job while you are in school.

Newspaper Advertisements

The classified advertisement section of newspapers carries announcements of job openings in many types of business positions. Generally, the Sunday edition of a newspaper has the most extensive listing. If you want to apply for a position in a distant city, you should start checking the classified advertisements several months in advance for available positions in that location. Your college library or community newsstand may have the newspaper for the city you have chosen. If not, you may need to take out a short-term subscription to the newspaper.

Specialized Journals

Another place to look for employment opportunities is in specialized journals, such as those for accountants, nurses, secretaries, teachers, and other professionals. *The College Placement Annual*, which offers information on a variety of employment opportunities, is available through college placement centers. This publication lists employers alphabetically and geographically. It also gives general information about the company and lists anticipated position openings.

Placement Agencies and Employment Contractors

Private employment agencies exist in most metropolitan areas. Some of these agencies fill job openings in a wide range of occupations, while others focus on one area of employment such as management, construction, or office personnel. These agencies charge a fee, which is usually a percentage of the annual salary for the position. Sometimes the fee is paid by the company seeking to fill a vacancy; other times, it must be paid by the person getting the job. Find out which agencies specialize in your field of interest and determine who pays the fee.

Employment contractors, frequently known as temporary, or "temp," agencies, employ personnel in a variety of occupations in response to specific industry requests. They "lease" these employees to industry on a temporary basis. By accepting a temporary assignment, you gain valuable workplace experience and establish a positive relationship with the industry. A temporary assignment may also result in an offer of permanent employment.

As you can see, you need all your communication skills in seeking a position. You will find that these skills will become even more important when you actually start applying for jobs.

i INFORMATION

Students can gain much information from reading newspapers from the town or city they have selected for possible employment. They can find out about such things as housing costs and availability as well as entertainment, cultural opportunities, shopping, and religious organizations.

☐ SUGGESTION

Invite a guest speaker from a placement agency or an employment contractor to address the class.

MARKETING YOURSELF

After deciding what position you want and are qualified for, you must begin the application process. This is the first step in marketing yourself to potential employers. You can answer advertisements or you can apply to companies that seem to fit your needs. The résumé, the application letter, and the application form are the usual written communications involved in getting the position you want. These three forms of communication tell a prospective employer about your qualifications and the assets you would bring to the company.

Résumé

The résumé is an outline or summary of your background and qualifications for the kind of position you want. You may think that writing a résumé is easy. It's not a difficult task, but it's definitely worth your while to devote some time and effort to doing it well. A sloppy, poorly written, or incomplete résumé is likely to be tossed aside by a potential employer and with it your chance for a job. Here are some guidelines to help you prepare your résumé.

1. Your résumé, unless you have extensive job-related experience, should be only one page long. This one page should be filled with useful information about you.
2. Choose a format that is easy to read. Use headings, underlining, columns, and capital letters to make your qualifications easily identifiable. Place your résumé attractively on the page.
3. Select a good quality paper with matching envelopes. White stationery is used most often, but you can select a professional-looking color such as cream, gray, or light blue.
4. Use brief statements rather than complete sentences. Say "President, Phi Beta Lambda" rather than "I was president of Phi Beta Lambda."
5. Choose a typewriter or word processor that has a clear, crisp print. After printing one good copy, you can photostat additional copies. Use a good quality copier and stationery so that each copy looks as good as the original. You might consider having a typesetter or professional résumé service complete your résumé. Charges for these services vary, but if the employment market is tight, the extra cost may be justified because it may give you a competitive edge.

As you prepare your résumé, remember that the care with which it is prepared and the information that it supplies often determine whether you will be invited for a personal interview. The résumé is your personal introduction to an employer. You must proofread and edit it carefully to make sure that the spelling, grammar, and facts are correct and that the wording is clear. These two steps are essential in creating a résumé that will make the all-important first impression a favorable one.

The following major sections should be included in your résumé in the order presented. As you read the descriptions of the résumé parts, refer to the sample résumé on page 524.

Identification. Begin with your name, address, and phone number. If you have a temporary address while you are in college, be sure to include your college address as well as your permanent (home) address.

Career Objective. Your career objective should express your employment goal. If you are preparing your résumé for an advertised job, you may want to be very specific. If you are preparing your résumé to send to many companies, you need to be somewhat general. A specific objective might express interest in a bank auditing position; a general objective might express interest in an accounting position for a financial, manufacturing, or service-oriented company. You can change this career objective when applying to different employers.

Education. If you have attended several colleges, list your most recent education first. Include your degree, college, and major. If you have not yet received a degree, you can include that information easily: Associate of Arts in Accounting to be awarded in May 1993, from Isothermal Community College, in Spindale, Indiana. As a prospective college graduate, your education can be your strongest selling point. Expand this section by listing some of your major and related courses. Be specific about course titles: Accounting 3206 is almost meaningless; "Managerial Accounting" is quite descriptive.

Experience. You should list work experience, even though it may be unrelated. Knowing that you have worked demonstrates that you are industrious, have initiative, and are dependable.

List your current or most recent work experience first and continue backward. Be sure to give inclusive dates of employment; for example, May 1990–June 1992. Additionally, include some of your responsibilities. Statements such as "In charge of closing cash registers and locking the restaurant" could send a signal that you are honest. If you have had many jobs, you may want to entitle this section "Selected Experience" or "Related Experience." Using one of these titles would let potential employers know that your list does not include your entire employment history.

Activities. This section should include your participation in clubs, volunteer work, team sports, and other extracurricular activities. You should specify any offices you held in organizations.

References. "References will be supplied on request" is the statement suggested to relay to a prospective employer that you will provide this information when it is needed. In most cases, you will not be asked for references until you make an appointment for an interview. As part of the résumé preparation process, you should prepare this list as a companion document. The stationery and the style of print should be the same on both documents.

ANDREA G. KOCH

<u>Present Address</u>
Post Office Box 247
Shelby, NC 28150
704-555-0862

<u>Permanent Address</u>
250 West Central Street
Marion, NC 28752
704-555-4721

<u>Career Objective</u>: To obtain a general accounting position with an opportunity for advancement.

<u>Education</u>:

1990-Present   Gardner-Webb College, Boiling Springs, NC
               Bachelor of Science to be awarded May 19--.
               Double Major: Accounting and
                                    Business Administration
               QPR: 4.0

               Representative Major Courses:
               Cost Accounting   Quantitative Methods
               Financial Accounting   Small Business Operation
               Managerial Accounting Human Resource Management
               Auditing   Management Principles
               Tax Preparation   Financial Management

               Representative Related Courses:
               Business Communication   Calculus
               Computer Applications   Decision Support Systems

1988-1990   Cleveland Community College, Shelby, NC
               Associate of Arts, May 1990.

<u>Experience</u>:

Weekends,   Snipes Landscaping, Shelby, NC
June 1990   Duties: Planting and trimming trees.
to present

Summer 1988   Furniture Retail Outlet, Marion, NC
Summer 1989   Duties: Worked with accounts receivable and
                        payable. Balanced cash registers for
                        sales clerks.

Summer 1987   Mountain Lake Resort, Hickory, NC
               Duties: Worked as lifeguard and gave private
                        swimming lessons.

<u>Activities</u>   Presidential Scholar
<u>and Honors</u>:   Dean's List
               Member, National Association of Accountants
               Historian, Phi Beta Lambda
               Member, Alpha Chi Honor Society

<u>References</u>:   Available on Request

The format of a résumé helps make it more effective. Note how underscoring is used to emphasize various aspects of this résumé.

LANGUAGE TIP

Alternatives to sexist terms:
chairman—chair, moderator, head, presiding officer, chairperson
craftsman—artisan, craftsworker, skilled worker
girl Friday— assistant, office assistant, aide
manmade— artificial, handmade, machine-made, synthetic, manufactured
manpower—staff, personnel, labor supply, available workers, work force, employees, human resources

—from Rosalie Maggio, *The Nonsexist Word Finder*

You should choose three references, usually an academic, a work, and a character reference. You could choose an instructor in your major field, a former employer or supervisor, and someone who knows you personally. You should give the name, job title, telephone number, and complete address. Answering inquiries for prospective employers is a time-consuming task; thus, courtesy demands that you ask each person before you give his or her name as a reference. Although permission may be requested by telephone or in person, it is often requested in writing.

> As you may know, I was recently graduated from Colorado Springs Community College, and I am applying at several firms in the Denver area for a position as medical technologist. May I list your name as a reference?
> Please indicate your answer at the bottom of this letter and return this letter to me in the enclosed envelope.

You should supply your references (see sample on page 526) with a copy of your résumé so that they will be prepared to answer questions about you. You should also let your references know when you accept a position.

Your résumé should be individualized to make you look your best. If you have had a lot of related work experience, you might want to note your experience before listing your education. This order is especially suited to someone applying for a second or third job. You can expand the section on activities to include special recognitions such as dean's list, academic scholarships, honor fraternities, and so on. You should list military experience if appropriate. You might also insert a section on "Special Skills," listing distinctive competencies such as proficiency in another language, ability to use popular software programs, or CPR certification. Including a section on hobbies and special activities can show that you have a wide range of interests and can give a prospective employer a beginning topic of conversation for an interview.

Federal law prohibits employers from asking the age, sex, marital status, religion, or race of applicants. Therefore, supplying such information is optional. If you consider any of this data an asset, you can provide the information on your résumé.

The Application Letter

After you have prepared your résumé and can see how your qualifications fit the job you seek, you are ready to organize your application letter, often called a cover letter (see sample on page 527). This is a sales letter that should be designed to market your qualifications to a prospective employer. The application letter is a companion document to your résumé and list of references; to show this connection, all three documents should have the same stationery and style of print. The function of the letter is to highlight your most important qualifications and persuade the employer to grant you a personal interview. Your résumé will help the employer determine whether you have the education and skills required for the job; the application letter should convince the employer that you will be an asset to the firm. The

☑ REINFORCEMENT

The purpose of the résumé and the application letter is to get an interview. The purpose of the interview is to get a job.

```
                          References For

                          ANDREA  G.  KOCH

        Present Address                        Permanent Address
        Post Office Box 247                    250 West Central Street
        Shelby, NC 28150                       Marion, NC 28752
        704-555-0862                           704-555-4721



        Dr. Gordon P. Werner, Professor of Accounting, Gardner-Webb
             College, Boiling Springs, NC 28017

        Mrs. Susan P. Snipes, Proprietor, Snipes Landscaping,
             Shelby, NC 28150

        Mr. Sam Davidson, CPA, Accountant, Harrison Freight Lines,
             Shelby, NC 28150
```

A list of references is a companion document to a résumé.

```
                              Post Office Box 247
                              Shelby, North Carolina 28150
                              April 3, 19--



Mr. Steve Stratton
1292 O'Henry Avenue
Asheville, NC 28801

Dear Mr. Stratton:

     Please consider me for the general accounting position as
advertised in the April 2 issue of The Asheville Citizen Times.

     As you can see from my enclosed résumé, I have a double
major in accounting and business administration.  In addition to
my required major courses, I have taken courses that will give me
a firm background in accounting application of microcomputers.  I
have also completed two courses in business communication.

     As a sophomore, I became a charter member of our college's
student chapter of the National Association of Accountants.
Active membership will further my learning and keep me abreast of
changes in the accounting profession.  My work experience is
extensive and varied.

     As a general accountant, I will welcome hard work and will
be willing to learn new skills and stay current on accounting
practices and procedures.  I pride myself on accuracy, neatness,
reliability, and the ability to work with others.

     After you have had an opportunity to review my résumé, I
will telephone you to request an appointment to discuss my
employment potential with your firm.  I am eager to put my
classroom knowledge into practical application.

                         Sincerely,

                         Andrea G. Koch

                         Andrea G. Koch


Enclosure
```

The letter of application is a personalized sales message.

purpose of the résumé and the application letter is to get you an interview. The purpose of the interview is to get you the job.

Get to the Point Immediately. The first paragraph of the application letter should state the following:

Your intent to apply for the position.
The position for which you are applying.
How you learned about the position (if it is not a "blind" application).

There is no one "best" opening for an application letter. The following opening sentences are suggestions that have been used successfully. You can adapt them to suit your needs.

For newspaper ads:

Please consider me an applicant for the position of management trainee, as advertised in the June 25 issue of the *Times*.

I am applying for the position of staff accountant that was advertised in *The Philadelphia Inquirer* on Sunday, May 15.

The position of assistant buyer, which you advertised in the April 1 issue of the *Examiner*, is one for which I feel well qualified. Please consider me an applicant for this position.

I am interested in the position of word processing supervisor advertised in the Help Wanted section of the June 12 *New Orleans Times-Picayune*. I should like to apply for that position.

For referrals:

A mutual friend, Marvin Klein, has suggested that I write you concerning a position as administrative assistant in your company.

Your company has been recommended to me by Mrs. Ana Perez, the placement director of OCLA College, as one with exceptional opportunities for those interested in advertising. I should like to inquire about a possible opening in the copy department.

Mr. Thomas Rooney, a family friend, has told me of an opening as editorial assistant on your company magazine. I would like to be considered for this position. (Mr. Rooney is a member of the accounting firm used by the employer.)

For general applications (applications are also made directly to a company, whether or not a position is open):

I believe my qualifications for a position as insurance adjuster will interest you.

I have chosen your company's personnel department as one in which I would like to work. Therefore, I hope you will be interested in my qualifications.

Here are five reasons why I think you will be interested in interviewing me for a sales position in your company.

■ KEY POINT

Guidelines for an application letter: (1) Get to the point immediately. (2) Tell why you should be considered. (3) Show willingness to work and learn. (4) Make it easy for the employer to ask you for an interview.

Tell Why You Should Be Considered. The second paragraph of your letter should convince the employer that you are a desirable candidate for the position referred to in the first paragraph. Don't be afraid to brag about your accomplishments. For example:

> A summary of my qualifications is enclosed. As you will see, my training at Slater Business College was very comprehensive. In addition to completing all the accounting courses offered by the college, I also studied personnel management, economics, business psychology, office procedures and management, word processing, and statistics. In all my courses, I consistently ranked in the top 10 percent of the class.

Of course, the nature of the second paragraph will depend on what you have to sell. If your business experience is limited and unlikely to impress the employer, you will have to emphasize your educational background. In such a case, you might follow the above paragraph with a statement such as this:

> Of particular interest to me in the accounting courses I took were the applications of accounting theory to computerized procedures and equipment. I am especially eager to work in a large organization, such as yours, where data processing is used on a wide scale.

Here is another example that shows how you can capitalize on your achievements in school:

> You will notice from my résumé that economics and business communication were among my best courses. In addition, I was a member of the debating team and the school newspaper staff. You will find my written and oral communication skills well above average.

The writer of the following paragraph lacks business experience but compensates for this lack by showing interest and enthusiasm.

> I am very interested in your bank and in the work your tellers do. Several times during the past year, I have talked with Harry Morgan, who started his teller training with you a year ago, about the varied duties he performs and the pleasant working conditions. He is very enthusiastic about the opportunities for advancement. These discussions make me even more certain that banking is the kind of work I want to do and that your bank is the one in which I would like to work. I know that within a short period of time, I can learn to perform effectively as one of your tellers.

If you have had business experience that is related to the position for which you are applying, make the most of it.

> I am particularly interested in accounting systems in which automated equipment and procedures are used. Last summer I was a temporary employee in the systems department of J. C. McKay Company, where I had an opportunity to observe information processing techniques. This experience was valuable, and I have decided to do further study in this field in evening school after I have obtained a position.

Show Willingness to Work and Learn. The employer who hires you is taking a risk — a risk that you may not be fitted for the position. One of the best ways to convince the employer of your suitability is by showing your willingness to learn and your genuine interest in the job. The following are examples of ways you can express your enthusiasm:

> Obviously, there will be many routines and procedures that will be new to me. You will find me eager to learn and to improve.

> I shall bring to the job a willingness to work and an eagerness to improve. Let me prove this to you.

> I am not afraid of hard work; in fact, I enjoy it.

> I pride myself on my punctuality, accuracy, and dependability.

> I learn quickly and I remember what I learn.

Make It Easy for the Employer to Ask You for an Interview. The last paragraph of your application letter should be aimed at obtaining an invitation for an interview. Make it easy for the employer to contact you.

> I can come to your office for an interview between 9 a.m. and 5 p.m. on any weekday. My telephone number is 555-7613. If you would prefer to write, please use the address at the top of this letter.

Some job hunters are more direct; they prefer to follow up on the letter rather than wait for the employer to contact them. For example:

> I can come to your office for an interview between 9 a.m. and 5 p.m. any weekday. After you have had a chance to review my qualifications, I shall call your secretary to request an appointment.

The Application Form

☐ **SUGGESTION**

If the application form is completed at home, recommend that students make a photocopy of the application form before completing it. Complete the photocopy as a rough draft and transfer the information to the original form.

Most companies require prospective employees to fill out some kind of application form for their files. In some cases, you will be asked to complete the form at the company office; in others, you will take the form home to complete. In either case, the application form requires accurate information regarding your education background, work experience, and references. Be sure to take a copy of your résumé whenever you go to a company to apply for a job. Most of the information needed for the application form will be on your résumé.

As part of the application process, many companies may also ask you to take tests evaluating your skills and aptitudes. These might include tests of your typing and computer skills, spelling and grammar, or basic math. If you apply for a government job, you will need to take a civil service test.

A typical application form is shown on the following two pages. Notice that it asks the applicant to account for all time spent from the first year of high school to the present. Notice, also, that it asks about extracurricular activities.

ALLIED INSURANCE COMPANY, INC.

an equal opportunity employer

APPLICATION FOR EMPLOYMENT

(Please Print)

<table>
<tr>
<td rowspan="3">COMPANY USE ONLY</td>
<td colspan="2">DATE APPOINTED
Month   Day   Year</td>
<td colspan="2">REAPPOINTMENT:
☐ With continuous service
☐ Without continuous service</td>
<td>DIVISION</td>
<td>SALARY</td>
<td>INITIALS</td>
</tr>
</table>

<table>
<tr>
<td>☐ HO
☐ HO Fld.
☐ Corp.
☐ Service</td>
<td>☐ Reg.
☐ Temp.</td>
<td>☐ Day
☐ Night
_____ Hours Per Week</td>
<td>TITLE OR DESIGNATION</td>
<td>JOB NO.</td>
<td>JOB LEVEL</td>
<td>VACANCY</td>
<td>TITLE CODE</td>
</tr>
<tr>
<td></td><td></td><td></td><td></td>
<td colspan="2">HOURS PER DAY:</td>
<td></td><td></td>
</tr>
</table>

DO NOT WRITE ABOVE THIS LINE

NAME	(First)	(Middle)	(Last)	DO YOU		DATE OF APPLICATION (Month)(Day)(Year)
	Celia	Elise	Jackson	☒ Live with parents / ☐ Live with other relatives	☐ Board / ☐ Own your home / ☐ Rent	9 4 9–

RESIDENCE ADDRESS (Street)	(City or Town)	(State)	(Zip Code)	DATE OF RESIDENCE FROM MO. YR. — TO MO. YR.
173 Auburn Avenue,	Cincinnati,	OH	45201	
PREVIOUS RESIDENCE (Street)	(City or Town)	(State)	(Zip Code)	2 71 Present
N/A				
PREVIOUS RESIDENCE (Street)	(City or Town)	(State)	(Zip Code)	

TELEPHONE NUMBER	SOCIAL SECURITY NUMBER	ARE YOU A CITIZEN OF THE U.S.A.?
(419) 555-9845	723-52-9076	☒ YES ☐ NO

ACCOUNT COMPLETELY FOR YOUR TIME FROM THE FIRST YEAR OF HIGH SCHOOL TO THE PRESENT IN THE BOXES BELOW.

NAMES OF SCHOOLS ATTENDED	CITY & STATE	NO. OF YRS (Day) Eve.	MAJOR SUBJECTS	GRAD. Mo. Yr.	GRADE AVERAGE	DEGREE
Millard High School	Cincinnati, Ohio	4 Yrs.	General Business	6 89	B–	
			Business Law			
Slater College	Cincinnati, Ohio	2 Yrs.	Business		B+	
			Accounting			

EXTRACURRICULAR ACTIVITIES (ATHLETICS, CLUBS, FRATERNITIES, ETC.)

ACTIVITY — HIGH SCHOOL	OFFICES HELD	ACTIVITY — COLLEGE	OFFICES HELD
Senior Class	Treasurer		
Future Business Leaders of America	Vice President		

SCHOLASTIC HONORS (SOCIETIES, AWARDS, SCHOLARSHIPS, ETC.)

Having a résumé on hand makes filling out an application form easier.

ACTIVE SERVICE WITH UNITED STATES ARMED FORCES

BRANCH OF SERVICE	SERIAL NO.	RANK OR RATE AT DISCHARGE
N/A	N/A	N/A

DATE (Mo.) (Day) (Yr.) OF ENTRY N/A	DATE (Mo.) (Day) (Yr.) OF SEPARATION N/A	TYPE OF SEPARATION (i.e., Expiration of Enlistment, Medical, etc.) N/A

PREVIOUS WORK EXPERIENCE—PART TIME AND FULL TIME (List in order, last employer first)

NAME OF COMPANY	CITY & STATE	TITLE	PERIOD OF EMPLOYMENT FROM Mo.	Yr.	TO Mo.	Yr.
Clayton's (Depart-ment Store)	Cincinnati, Ohio	Accounting Clerk	7	89	present	
		Sales Clerk	6	88	7	89

FOR WHAT SPECIAL KIND OF WORK HAVE YOU A PREFERENCE? Claim Adjuster	ARE YOU WILLING TO BE TRANS-FERRED TO ANOTHER LOCATION ☐ Yes ☒ No

WERE YOU REFERRED BY AN EMPLOYEE? ☐ YES ☒ NO	IF YES, STATE NAME	DEPARTMENT

HAVE YOU ANY RELATIVES, FRIENDS OR ACQUAINTANCES NOW EMPLOYED BY US? ☒ YES ☐ NO	IF YES, STATE NAME Peter Martinez	RELATIONSHIP Friend	DEPARTMENT Sales

CHARACTER REFERENCES (Do not use the names of relatives or former employers).

NAMES	ADDRESSES
Dr. John Kniss, Principal	Millard High School, 50 Delta St., Cincinnati, OH 45201
Ms. Elisabeth Lomax, Director	Slater College, 2000 Central Ave., Cincinnati, Ohio 45201
Mrs. Ruth Sanchez, Credit Manager	

I authorize investigation of all statements contained in this application blank if I am considered for employment and hereby authorize previous employers, personal references named, or any other person or persons to whom the Company may refer to give any and all information regarding my employment or scholastic standing together with any other information, personal or otherwise, than may or may not be on their records.

I understand that misrepresentation or omission of any fact called for hereon, or on any other statements made in connection with my request for employment, or receipt by the Company of unsatisfactory references, will be sufficient cause for dismissal from the Company's service if I shall have been employed.

Applicant's Signature *Celia* (First) *Elise* (Middle) *Jackson* (Last)

NOT TO BE COMPLETED BY APPLICANT	TO BE COMPLETED AFTER EMPLOYMENT
DATE OF INTERVIEW / COMMENTS	I have seen _____ and am satisfied that _____ Month Day Yr. is employee's correct date of birth. INITIALS

REVIEW

Practical Application

KEY
See page I-59 for Applications A, B, C.

A. List the best sources of information regarding job openings for the career field of your choice.

B. From the "Help Wanted" advertisements in your local newspaper, select a position that appeals to you and for which you are qualified (or will be upon graduation). Write a letter of application answering the ad, and attach a résumé you have prepared specifically for this job and a list of references.

C. Write a letter to one of the people listed as a reference on your résumé (Application B) to ask permission to use his or her name.

Editing Practice

KEY
1. Which, two, better
2. Whose, theirs
3. It's (*or* It is), judgment
4. to develop, procedure, he (*or* she) called a meeting, February
5. well known, personnel

KEY
Correct answers are underscored.

Editors' Alert. Here are more sentences on which you can sharpen your editing skills. Try to develop an all-seeing eye that doesn't miss a detail. If necessary, rewrite the sentences.

1. <u>Witch</u> of the <u>2</u> candidates was the <u>best</u>?
2. <u>Who's</u> book did you use, <u>there's</u> or mine?
3. <u>Its</u> my <u>judgement</u> that you should expedite the order.
4. Having planned <u>the develope</u> a new <u>proceedure</u>, the meeting was called for <u>Febuary</u> 1.
5. It's <u>well-known</u> that the <u>personal</u> department is very efficient.

Sound-Alikes. Choose the sound-alike word that correctly completes each of the following sentences.

1. We use this storeroom for (<u>excess</u>, access) supplies.
2. Because the account is now two months (<u>past</u>, passed) due, we must impose an interest charge.
3. The manager asked the members of her staff for (they're, <u>their</u>, there) views on the new procedure.
4. One of the (<u>principal</u>, principle) reasons for buying at this time is the low mortgage rates.
5. We expect the survey to show (weather, <u>whether</u>) there is a market for this product.
6. Mr. Peebles told the distributor that we would not (except, <u>accept</u>) any new orders because we had decided to discontinue the product.

Critical Thinking

KEY
See page I-60.

Analyze. Why is it important to analyze yourself and your qualifications before you begin your job search?

11.2 THE EFFECTIVE EMPLOYMENT INTERVIEW

OBJECTIVES: After completing Section 11.2, you should be able to:

1. Name two goals of an interview.
2. Prepare questions for your interviewer.
3. Anticipate questions you will be asked at the interview.
4. List the steps you can take to follow up an interview.

ℹ INFORMATION

By now, students are probably realizing the complexity of a serious approach to the job search process. Stress to them that preparing to find a job will take much time and effort.

Your job interview may be the critical factor in determining whether or not you are hired. For that reason, it is essential that you be well prepared for the interview. No matter how impressive your background, your résumé, and your application letter, you may fail to be hired if you cannot "sell" yourself when you meet a prospective employer face to face. In the last section, we spoke of your résumé and application letters as the first steps in marketing yourself to potential employers. The interview is the second phase of the marketing process.

In an interview, you have an opportunity to sell yourself every time you speak. Your response to questions, your description of experiences and situations, your explanation of procedures and methods, all contribute to the interviewer's impression of you. Therefore, you must make plans well ahead of time and prepare for the interview. The way you prepare may determine whether the interview has a positive or a negative outcome for you.

HOW TO PLAN FOR THE INTERVIEW

👤 KEY POINT

Prepare for the job interview: (1) Know the goal of your interview. (2) Do your homework in researching the company. (3) Prepare intelligent questions. (4) Plan what items to take with you. (5) Know what you have to offer. (6) Make a positive first impression.

Although you were not conscious of it at the time, preparation for the interview actually began quite some time ago. A number of years ago you had to choose the type of work you wanted to do. Then you had to obtain the necessary education and training required in this type of work. You have selected the type of company for which you want to work, compiled a résumé, written an application letter, and obtained the interview. Such long-range planning was necessary. The following discussion will be helpful in preparing for the job interview itself.

Know the Goal of Your Interview

As you begin preparing for your interview, you must realize that your goal is twofold: to sell yourself and to find out if the job fits your qualifications and career plans.

Do Your Homework

Do some research on your prospective employer. Find out about the company's products, services, and history. There are two main reasons for finding out all you can about the company. First, knowing something about the organization will help you decide whether it is a place you would like to work. Second, you should have a strong answer to the often-asked question, "Why did you choose our company?" Too many applicants have no ready answer to that question beyond "I just heard it is a nice place to work," or "It's near my home." To be effective, your answer should demonstrate that you know something about the company. "I have always been interested in investments, and I know that your company is one of the leading investment firms in this area."

How should you research facts about a company? Here are some ways for getting started:

- You might talk to the person who referred you to the organization or to someone who works there.
- If the company is a national or international company, you can find published data in the library.
- The Chamber of Commerce of a particular community can give you information on both small and large companies.

Prepare Questions

Researching a company will help you prepare to ask intelligent questions of your interviewer. Here are some examples:

I read that your company exports products to Europe. What percentage of your product is shipped abroad?

I know that your company has ten branches. Are they all located in this state?

You should also prepare questions related to your employment. These might include some of the following:

What are the opportunities for advancement?

Do you provide training and additional education for those employees who want to develop their skills?

What benefits do you provide for your employees?

Would I be called upon to travel in this position?

More often than not, a job applicant knows the salary offered for a position—at least the general range—before the interview. If the salary is not known, however, and the interviewer has not mentioned it, you should ask about it near the end of the interview. If a figure was mentioned in the job advertisement or by an employment agency, you should confirm the amount. You might say: "I understand that the starting salary for this position is $_____ a week. Is that correct?"

Plan What to Take

Each applicant should take the following items to an interview:

1. Two good pens. You should have an extra pen in case your first pen stops working.
2. Three copies of your résumé and list of references, placed in a professional-looking folder. Often you will have an interview with more than one person. Each interviewer may or may not have your résumé. Bringing copies of it makes you look prepared. Also, your résumé will help you provide details about work history and references when completing an application form.
3. The list of questions you want to ask the interviewer. This list should be in the folder with your résumé. You should not read the list to the interviewer, but it is good to have the list available to refresh your memory. You might review the list while waiting for your appointment, or if your interviewer gets a telephone call, you can use the opportunity to glance at your questions.
4. A small pad on which to take notes.

Know What You Have to Offer

Good sales representatives know their products thoroughly—better than anyone else does. They have analyzed their products from every conceivable angle; they know their strengths and their weaknesses. Because they know which features of their products are likely to appeal to prospective buyers, they emphasize these features in their sales presentations.

As a job applicant, you are a sales representative, and the product you are selling is yourself. Preparing a résumé gives you an excellent opportunity to put on paper what you have to sell—to see your strong points and compare them with those that your competitors for the position may have. The items that you want to emphasize on the résumé are those every employer is interested in—education, experience, and special interests and skills. You should know these qualifications so well that you can communicate them orally without hesitation.

Anticipate Questions

❏SUGGESTION

Ask students to respond orally to these potential interview questions.

Anticipate questions that the interviewer may ask about your education, experience, and personal qualities. Here are examples of some of these questions:

What courses did you concentrate on while attending college?

Which of these courses did you like best? Why?

Tell me something about your course in _____ (personnel administration, business communications, office management, or other subjects).

I see by your application that you worked at Gregson's for two summers. What kind of work did you do? What did you like most about your job? What did you like least?

What do you most enjoy doing outside of working hours — hobbies and other activities?

Were you active in school organizations? Which ones?

Do you like to write? Do you consider yourself strong in English?

Tell me about yourself. (This request will give you a chance to emphasize your most salable features. The interviewer doesn't want to know about your childhood but wants you to answer such questions as these: What do you do best? What do you like best?)

Review your college work and your experience. (Here you will emphasize the college courses that will best implement your qualifications for this particular job. The same is true of your experience.)

What do you think your strongest points are? your weakest?

Tell me why you think you should be hired for this position.

What job would you like to have five years from now?

What do you enjoy doing in your leisure time?

Why do you want to work for this company?

Why did you leave your last position?

Would you be willing to work overtime if necessary?

Answers to such probing questions will tell the interviewer a great deal about you and about how well you would fit the position, how quickly you would adjust to the job and to the people around you, and what your potential is for growth.

Make a Positive First Impression

What can you do to create a positive first impression with a prospective employer? Here are some suggestions:

1. Be on time for your appointment. You should allow extra travel time to allow for unexpected problems. Last-minute traffic delays can cause you to feel frustrated and apprehensive.
2. Dress in a businesslike way. On no other occasion is it more important to look your best than at an employment interview.
3. Demonstrate your self-confidence. The impression you make when you first walk into the room will very likely influence the interviewer's attitude toward you throughout the entire interview. Preparing yourself, as outlined in this chapter, is the key to building self-confidence.

□ **SUGGESTION**

Invite a human re-
source manager to
class to conduct mock
interviews. Videotape
these for later review.

THE INTERVIEW

When you arrive at the office, you will probably be greeted by a receptionist. Give your name and the purpose of your visit. "I'm (your name). I have an
appointment at nine with Mr. Higashi." If you have to wait a few minutes,
review your résumé, check the completed application form, read the literature that will probably be available in the reception office, or otherwise occupy yourself. Don't engage in conversation with the receptionist unless you
are invited to do so.

When you are ushered into the interviewer's office, try to be relaxed
(though not casual or arrogant) and to look pleasant. Greet your interviewer
with a firm handshake, a smile, and good eye contact. Introduce yourself and
express your interest in employment with the company.

Seat yourself only when you are invited to do so. Keep with you the
materials you have brought. Don't place anything on the interviewer's desk
unless you are invited to do so. The interviewer may or may not ask to see the
application form and the résumé. The moment will come, however, when
you are asked about your education and experience. This is the time to give
the interviewer your résumé if you haven't already done so. Say something
like this: "Here is my résumé, on which that information is summarized. I
also have completed the application form." (Hand both to the interviewer.)
Wait for the interviewer to make the first move. You will know at once how
the interview will be conducted—whether the interviewer is going to ask
most of the questions or prefers that you take the initiative. Usually the
interviewer will direct the proceedings.

Don't smoke. Even if you are a smoker, it is best to refuse a cigarette if it
is offered to you. Say simply, "No, thank you, not just now." If you are a
nonsmoker, you merely decline with "No, thank you."

Face and speak directly to the interviewer. Don't stare at the floor or out
the window while either of you is talking. Of course, you should take your
eyes from the interviewer's occasionally, but leave no doubt that you are
talking and listening to him or her. Speak slowly and enunciate carefully.
Give your answers and statements in a straightforward manner; show that
you have thought them through and that you can speak with precision. Give
short answers; the interviewer doesn't want your life story or your complete
personal philosophy in answer to every question. At the same time, a mere
"Yes" or "No" is not sufficient. For example, if you are asked this question "I
see you have had one course in accounting. Did you like it?" it is not enough
simply to say "Yes" (assuming that is how you actually feel). You might add,
"I enjoyed the course very much, and I plan to take more accounting in
evening school."

Be specific about your qualifications. "My accounting courses consisted of
principles, cost, and tax. In the tax course we were introduced to data processing as it relates to accounting, and I especially enjoyed that." Or "I consistently received high grades in communication courses, and I particularly
liked writing letters." Or "One of the most interesting things I did during my
summers at Laverty's was to verify the cash balance each day. It wasn't easy to

make everything balance, since we had so many people handling the cash, but I was successful and learned a lot from the experience."

On the other hand, be noncommittal about controversial matters. If you are asked what you thought of Laverty's as a place to work and your opinion isn't especially favorable, say something like this: "My work there gave me some valuable experience, and I enjoyed much of it." If you are asked for your opinions about people for whom you have worked and for whom you feel no special fondness, say something like this: "Ms. Davis was often helpful to me; I believe I profited from working with her."

The interviewer often will be interested in why you left other positions. If you complain about the people or the company policies of former employers, however, you may give the impression that you are a chronic complainer. Try to be objective and to say something like this: "I found it difficult to adjust to some of the procedures and to the unusual hours at Laverty's." The inter-viewer will appreciate your frankness as well as your discretion.

Try to be at ease; smile occasionally. Remember that the interviewer needs someone to fill an open position and is just as eager to make a decision in your favor as you are to get the job. Most interviewers are pleasant, friendly, and understanding. Try to display an air of confidence. Above all, don't fidget. Nervousness often shows up in such habits as brushing imaginary lint off clothing, straightening and restraightening a tie, fussing with hair, toying with an object such as a purse or a paper clip, and putting hands to the face. Avoid such habits; give your full attention to the interviewer.

The interviewer generally will let you know when the interview is over. The usual sign is to rise. As soon as the interviewer rises, you should also do so. The exchange that takes place might be something like the following conversation.

Interviewer (rising): I enjoyed meeting and talking with you.

You (rising): Thank you, Mr. Higashi. I appreciate the time you have given me.

Interviewer: We have your telephone number, and we will call you just as soon as we have reached a decision.

You: Thank you. I shall look forward to hearing from you.

Interviewer: Good-bye.

You: Good-bye.

Leave quickly and thank the receptionist as you depart.

FOLLOWING UP THE INTERVIEW

As soon as possible after the interview, make a written summary from notes and memory of the facts you learned in the interview and the opinions you have formed about the company and about the job for which you were interviewed. If you are being interviewed for jobs in several different companies, this written summary will prove an excellent way to refresh your memory about the interview when you are trying later to make your final job choice.

Interview Follow-Up Letters

KEY POINT

Having a follow-up letter on the interviewer's desk the day after the interview is quite impressive. This thoughtful yet aggressive act may give you the competitive edge needed to influence the job decision in your direction.

After you have been interviewed, it is good strategy to write the interviewer. Having the follow-up letter on the interviewer's desk the day after the interview is extremely impressive. The follow-up letter gets your name before the interviewer again, and it gives you a second opportunity to sell yourself by mentioning pertinent qualifications. A basic follow-up letter might follow this form:

> Thank you for your time and the many courtesies you extended to me during my interview yesterday. I came away with a much clearer picture of the work a computer operator would do in your manufacturing firm. My summer internship with Bernham Manufacturing gave me related experience and the opportunity to apply what I learned in my software applications courses.
>
> After visiting your company, I am convinced that I would like the opportunity to be part of your growing business. I look forward to hearing from you soon.

If you have not heard from the company in a reasonable amount of time, you may want to write a follow-up inquiry.

> About three weeks ago, I interviewed with you for the position of computer operator. At the interview, you indicated that you would make a decision within two to three weeks.
>
> I wanted you to know that I am still very interested in the position. Please let me know if you need additional information about my qualifications. I look forward to hearing from you soon.

REINFORCEMENT

A follow-up inquiry gets your name before a prospective employer in a favorable way.

KEY

The students can refer to the text for some of the answers to these questions. The instructor should see page I-60 for points that should be checked in each of the answers.

SECTION

REVIEW

Practical Application

A. Prepare written answers to each of the following questions and statements likely to come up in an employment interview.

1. Why do you wish to work for our company?
2. What kind of work do you enjoy doing most?
3. What kind of work do you enjoy doing least?
4. What are your job goals for the next five-year period?
5. Why have you selected this type of work?
6. Tell me about yourself.
7. Why did you leave your last position?
8. How do you spend your spare time?

REVIEW cont.

KEY
See page I-60.

KEY
See page I-61.

KEY
See page I-61.

KEY
See page I-61.

B. List eight suggestions (in the form of "Dos" and "Don'ts") for *preparing* for a job interview. Then list eight suggestions to be observed *during* the interview.

C. Make a list of the questions you might like to ask the interviewer about the position for which you are applying or the company for which you will be working.

D. Assume you are being interviewed for a position at Alexander's, a department store. Your interviewer says, "I notice that your department supervisor at Murphy's was Fred Gustafson. I've heard that Gustafson is a tough person to get along with. Did you like working with him?" Compose the answer you would give your interviewer. (Assume that what he had heard about Fred Gustafson is true, insofar as you are concerned.)

E. Assume that you have been interviewed for a position with the Williams Investment Company (for which you are well qualified and in which you are very much interested). The interviewer, Ms. Grace Peebles, was very pleasant and was favorably impressed with your qualifications. However, she told you that she plans to interview several other applicants before making a decision regarding who should be hired. Write a letter to Ms. Peebles to thank her for the interview. In the letter, emphasize special qualifications you possess or present any additional facts that may improve your chances for being hired for the position.

Editing Practice

KEY
February
too
The Tax Journal.
occurred
calendar

The Rewrite Desk.   Edit and rewrite the following paragraph to correct any errors.

Your cashier's check dated <u>Febuary</u> 10 arrived <u>to</u> late for you to take advantage of our offer advertised in "The Tax Journal." It <u>occured</u> to us that you might wish to mark your <u>calander</u> now for our forthcoming sale on April 6 and 7.

Critical Thinking

KEY
See page I-61.

1. Analyze.   In most large companies and even in some small companies, the applicant for a position is interviewed at least twice. The first interview is usually given by a personnel specialist. The second interview is given by the person for whom the applicant will actually work. What do you think is the main purpose of the first interview? How might the two interviews differ?

KEY
See page I-62.

2. Evaluate.   Why is it important to choose carefully the company for which you would like to work?

11.3 *COMMUNICATING AND YOUR CAREER*

OBJECTIVES: After completing Section 11.3, you should be able to:

1. Write letters accepting or declining a position.
2. List guidelines for resigning a position.
3. Explain why communication is a key to successful employment.

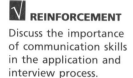

REINFORCEMENT
Discuss the importance of communication skills in the application and interview process.

As you have seen, written and oral communication skills play a critical role in the application and interview process. Preparing an attractive and informative résumé and writing persuasive application letters are the first steps in creating a favorable impression. Expressing yourself clearly and coherently in the all-important interview is the next step. Once you have been offered a position, of course, your communication skills will be called on again and again; and when you are on the job, you will have the opportunity to polish your skills through daily use. In other words, the written and oral communication skills you learn in school form the base for the skills you will use throughout your career. With constant practice and new applications, these skills should expand and improve as you advance in your career.

ACCEPTING OR DECLINING A POSITION

Suppose that you receive a letter offering you a position in a company to which you applied. You decide to take the job. Should you telephone or should you write to accept the position? If you are to start work almost immediately or if a reply has been requested by a certain date, you should probably telephone to tell the employer of your decision. Writing a letter is appropriate if your reporting date is two or more weeks away or if the firm is out of town. You might use the style illustrated in the following letter.

I am pleased to accept the position as editorial assistant with Charities International. I know that I shall enjoy working with you in the field of public relations and communications.

As you requested, I shall report to work on Monday, May 1. Thank you for the confidence you have expressed in me by giving me this opportunity.

You may, however, decide not to take the position. Declining a job offer should be done tactfully because you may be interested in working for that firm later in your career. Here is a sample letter.

Thank you for offering me the position of office manager for your legal firm. Since we last talked, I have been offered and have accepted a position as office manager in a real estate company. Working in a real estate office will help me achieve my long-term goal of becoming a commercial real estate broker.

Thank you, Ms. Harris, for your time and effort in interviewing me. I appreciate your considering me for the position in your office.

Occasionally, it may be necessary to inform an employer that you will not be taking a job that you have already accepted. You should avoid this situation if at all possible. If, however, you find yourself in this awkward position, you need to give the firm offering the first job some solid reasons justifying your change of heart. Here is a sample.

This morning, I received an offer from another firm of a position that closely matches my qualifications and career plans. The person who will be my supervisor in this firm considered my experience and education sufficient to place me well above entry-level status. In addition, he has arranged for me to take several advanced training courses in my field of interest.

I feel that I must accept this opportunity, which means declining the position you offered me. I apologize for any inconvenience my decision may cause you.

After you have accepted a job, you should personally thank each person who helped you get the job. You should write a brief note or letter to the people who provided job leads, introductions to potential employers, or personal references.

You will be pleased to learn that I have accepted a position as medical technologist with Speciality Laboratories in San Diego. Specialty Laboratories perform diagnostic tests for eight large hospitals. I start work next week, and I am eager to begin my new position. The job is exactly what I was looking for.

Thank you very much for letting me use your name as a reference. I am sure that your recommendation was instrumental in my being hired.

LEAVING A POSITION

REINFORCEMENT

Ask students to explain why resigning from a job requires almost as much tact, diplomacy, and care as applying for a job.

Most people change jobs several times in the course of their careers. You may leave a position for another job or for personal reasons. Resigning from a job requires almost as much tact, diplomacy, and care as applying for a job. You should leave on good terms with your employer. You may want to work for this company again someday or you may need to use your supervisors as references. Follow these guidelines when you resign from a job:

1. Make an appointment with your immediate supervisor and hand your letter of resignation to him or her.
2. In your letter and in the comments you make during the appointment, indicate that you enjoyed working for the organization and with the other employees. You might mention that the experience gained with the company has helped you develop in your career.
3. Give a two-week advance notice that you are leaving, unless your company handbook or employment agreement specifies a longer time period.

4. If you are leaving under unpleasant circumstances, express your reasons in a positive way: "I feel that City Realty will offer me some new challenges and a greater opportunity for advancement."
5. Make certain that all your work is up to date and that your papers and files are clearly marked and well organized.
6. Leave a list of instructions or suggestions that may be helpful for your successor.

Here is a sample letter of resignation.

Last week, I received an offer from Computer Consultants Unlimited of Lincoln, Nebraska. They have offered me a position as senior systems analyst, which represents a major career advancement for me. I have accepted the position.

Please accept my resignation effective April 1. I would be happy to help you find and train a replacement for my position.

Working with you, Ben, has been a pleasure. You gave me my first job after college, and you helped me grow and develop my skills in computer programming. I have learned a great deal and enjoyed the work and my contact with you and the other programmers in our department. I appreciate the company's investment in my career development.

ADVANCING IN YOUR CAREER

In Chapter 1, we discussed the four main communication skills and how they related to your social, academic, and work life. The chapters that followed helped you polish your communication skills. Chapters 2 and 4 focused on nouns, verbs, and other parts of speech, reviewed punctuation, and suggested how to use words more effectively. Chapters 5 and 6 were devoted to developing your writing, editing, and proofreading skills. Chapters 7 through 10 discussed major forms of written and oral communication in business. In this chapter, we have emphasized the importance of communication skills in the job search process.

We have already discussed the value of communication skills in getting a job. Communication is also a vital tool when you are on the job. You must exchange information with the people who work with you. You must explain assignments to the people who work for you and deal with conflicts and other delicate issues. Good communication skills will greatly enhance your performance on the job and your ability to communicate your ideas effectively to management. You may have expert knowledge and training in a technical area, but without effective communication skills your chances of advancement will be limited.

You will find that good communication skills and human relations techniques will pay great dividends throughout your career. When you use your communication skills to achieve company goals, you confirm to management that you have earned the opportunity for additional responsibility and pay increases. Promotions are the means by which employers recognize and reward good performance.

 **REINFORCEMENT**

Discuss the importance of effective communications in everyday job situations and in career advancement.

At this point, it should be clear that communication skills are crucial in all phases of your career:

Good communication skills will help you get a job.
Good communication skills will help you keep a job.
Good communication skills will help you get a better job.

It is true that communication skills are never perfect. What you have learned in this course will provide the base for good skills; experience will help you improve these skills.

KEY
See page I-62.

KEY
See page I-62.

KEY
See page I-62.

KEY
See page I-62.

REVIEW

SECTION

Practical Application

A. Assume that you have accepted a position as office assistant with Worldwide Travel Agency, 1400 Springfield Avenue, Lansing, Michigan 48901. Write a letter of acceptance to Patricia C. Smith, the director of the agency. In addition, write a letter to William Mazur, your communications teacher at Salem Community College, who served as a reference for you.

B. Although you accepted the position with Worldwide Travel and are scheduled to start work next week, yesterday you were offered a better position with Worldwide's main competitor. This position has greater potential for advancement, a higher starting salary, and better fringe benefits. You have decided to accept the better offer. Write another letter to Worldwide, explaining why you have changed your mind and must decline the position.

Editing Practice

The Supervising Editor. The following sentences lack writing polish. Edit and rewrite them.

1. Nothing should be done to change the procedure. You must see to it that it doesn't.
2. The ruling which takes affect today is the one concerning tardiness.
3. The reason Mel was late is because he had to pick up a report from another branch.
4. I have difficulty in distinguishing one to the other.
5. Under the last line in the return address on the envelope is to be printed his name and title.

Critical Thinking

Explain. Write a memo to new employees explaining why communication is the key to successful employment in your company.

Chapter 2
Expanding Language Skills

Section 2.1

Checkup 1
1. They (P), product (N), Atlanta, (N)
2. You (P), I (P), our (P), plant (N), March (N)
3. Indianapolis (N), site (N), our (P), division (N)
4. we (P), car (N), Des Moines (N), plant (N)
5. I (P), Joe Kettle (N), us (P), map (N), directions (N), we (P), him (P)
6. Sol (N), Chris (N), me (P), Midwest (N), their (P), part (N), country (N)

Checkup 2
1. is
2. was planning
3. hired, promoted
4. has been
5. completed, finished, met; started, began (action)
6. studies, reads, prepares (action)
7. was, is (being)
8. hope; passes (action)

Checkup 3
1. adjective (large), adverb (here)
2. adverb (immediately), adjective (new)
3. adjective (experienced), adverb (eagerly)

4. adjective (planned), adverb (surely), adjective (several)
5. adjective (original), adverb (more), adjective (large)

Checkup 4
1. preposition (from), preposition (for)
2. conjunction (and), preposition (to), preposition (in), preposition (with)
3. preposition (on), conjunction (but), preposition (on)
4. preposition (of), conjunction (nor), preposition (through)
5. preposition (with), preposition (on), conjunction (or)

Checkup 5
1. things spoken about
2. person spoken about
3. person speaking
4. thing spoken about
5. persons spoken about

Checkup 6
Student answers will vary.
1. sentence
2. sentence
3. dependent (Before the nurses meet to discuss their patients, they write brief reports on each one.)
4. dependent (If Claire does not hire another nursing assistant by May 1, she will lose the funding for that slot.)

5. dependent (When Florence meets with the nursing staff in her hospital, she first checks on any new rules.)

Checkup 7
1. VP, VP, PP, PP
2. IP, PP, PP
3. IP, PP, VP, PP
4. VP, PP
5. IP, VP, IP, PP

Checkup 8
Student answers will vary.
1. fragment (If Mr. Bartoli decides to change the policy, he will announce it at the meeting.)
2. fragment (Because both approvals are required for all checks over $5,000, we must get Ms. Hampton's signature.)
3. sentence
4. fragment (Although her reasons were valid at that time, those rules are no longer appropriate.)
5. sentence

Checkup 9
1. Scot (simple)
2. companies and agency (compound)
3. résumés (simple)
4. woman (simple)
5. files (simple)

Section 2.2

Checkup 1
1. asked
2. wants
3. are
4. has accepted
5. seemed
6. were; discussed

Checkup 2
1. keyboarded, keyboarded, keyboarding
2. elect, elected, electing
3. order, ordered, ordering
4. indicate, indicated, indicated
5. remembered, remembered, remembering
6. respond, responded, responding
7. trusted, trusted, trusting
8. use, used, using

Checkup 3
1. will be checking; checking
2. can complete; complete
3. will enter; enter
4. have approved; approved
5. have been hoping; hoping
6. does want; want

Checkup 4
Sample sentences:
1. If I had remembered to set my alarm clock, I wouldn't have been late.
2. Maria and Roberto are listening to the radio.
3. By tonight, my sister will have noticed that I borrowed her jacket.
4. Everyone will be ready to leave in an hour.
5. Two of my friends have asked me to tutor them.
6. Rita wanted to buy a new car.
7. The bank has rejected Mr. Smith's loan application.
8. Peter reviews his class notes every night.

Checkup 5
1. change known to has known (or knew)
2. change had began to had begun
3. change come to came
4. change has took to has taken (or took)

5. OK
6. change <u>have grew</u> to <u>have grown</u>

Checkup 6
1. has been evaluating
2. was (B)
3. have been (B)
4. is (B)
5. is (B)
6. have been siding

Checkup 7
1. OK
2. change <u>was</u> to <u>were</u>
3. change <u>was</u> to <u>were</u>
4. change <u>was</u> to <u>were</u>
5. OK

Checkup 8
1. had been appointed (T)
2. will be (B)
3. will be televised (T)
4. has told (T)
5. have left (I)
6. has been (B)

Checkup 9
1. raise
2. sits
3. raised
4. set
5. set
6. lay
7. laid
8. rise

Section 2.3

Checkup 1
1. change <u>editor in chiefs</u> to <u>editors in chief</u>

2. change <u>son-in-laws</u> to <u>sons-in-law</u>
3. change <u>Larries</u> to <u>Larrys</u>
4. change <u>supplys</u> to <u>supplies</u>
5. change <u>lenss</u> to <u>lenses</u> . . . <u>lenss</u> to <u>lenses</u>
6. change <u>communitys</u> to <u>communities</u> . . . <u>countys</u> to <u>counties</u>
7. change <u>district attornies</u> to <u>district attorneys</u>
8. OK
9. change <u>Averies</u> to <u>Averys</u>
10. OK

Checkup 2
1. change <u>Misses Smiths</u> to <u>Miss Smiths</u> (or <u>Misses Smith</u>)
2. change <u>30's</u> to <u>30s</u>
3. change <u>Is</u> to <u>I's</u>
4. OK
5. change <u>Everett's</u> to <u>Everetts</u>
6. OK
7. change <u>mans</u> to <u>men</u>
8. change <u>Mr.</u> to <u>Messrs.</u>

Checkup 3
1. tomatoes, mosquitos
2. logos, dittos
3. leaves, thieves
4. loaves, staffs
5. strifes, gulfs
6. bailiffs, handkerchiefs
7. volcanoes, concertos
8. radios, trios

Checkup 4
1. change <u>stimuluses</u> to <u>stimuli</u>
2. change <u>was</u> to <u>were</u>
3. OK
4. OK
5. change <u>were</u> to <u>was</u>
6. change <u>hundreds</u> to <u>hundred</u>
7. change <u>parenthesis</u> to <u>parentheses</u>
8. OK

Section 2.4

Checkup 1
1. change Rileys' to Riley's
2. OK
3. change fathers to father's
4. change womens to women's
5. change applicants to applicants'
6. change representatives to representatives'
7. change mans to man's
8. change supervisor's to supervisors'

Checkup 2
1. OK
2. change someone else to someone else's
3. change vice president's to vice presidents'
4. change us to our
5. change Neil's and Anne's to Neil and Anne's
6. change him to his
7. change Mr. Clark to Mr. Clark's
8. change Ella and Bert's to Ella's and Bert's

Checkup 3
1. change Whose to Who's (or Who is)
2. change theirs to there's
3. change its to it's
4. change there's to theirs
5. change whose to who's (or who is)
6. change they're to there
7. change its to it's
8. OK

Section 2.5

Checkup 1
1. change I to me (Exception to rule: to be has the pronoun him before it.)
2. OK
3. change me to I

4. OK
5. change him to he

Checkup 2
1. whom
2. who
3. whoever
4. whom
5. Whoever
6. who
7. OK
8. OK
9. change whomever to whoever
10. OK

Checkup 3
1. change we to us
2. change I to me
3. change he to him
4. change her to she
5. change me to I
6. change we to us
7. OK
8. change him to he
9. OK
10. change we to us
11. change her to she
12. OK

Checkup 4
1. OK
2. change myself to I
3. Ms. Romero specifically said that she herself wants to join.
4. When they reviewed the estimates, they themselves decided to cancel.
5. OK
6. change himself to he

Section 2.6

Checkup 1
1. does, its
2. are, their, them

3. wants, her
4. has, its, its
5. is, its
6. is, her, she

Checkup 2

1. change is to are (stores)
2. change there's to there are (stores)
3. change are to is (building)
4. change are to is (city)
5. change is to are (reasons)
6. change there's to there are (individuals)

Checkup 3

1. change have to has . . . their to his or her (Nobody)
2. change want to wants . . . their to his or her (Each)
3. OK (Anyone)
4. OK (or he or she . . . his or her) (executive)
5. change have to has . . . their to its (Neither)
6. OK (or his or her) (officer)

Checkup 4

1. change was to were . . . its to their
2. change is to are
3. change is to are
4. change has to have
5. change is to are
6. change is to are
7. change meet to meets
8. OK

Checkup 5

1. change have to has
2. change were to was
3. OK
4. change is to are
5. change was to were
6. OK

Checkup 6

1. change is to are
2. change are to is
3. OK
4. change have to has . . . their to his or her
5. change are to is
6. change are to is . . . their to his or her

Checkup 7

1. likes, his
2. have
3. have, their
4. are, their
5. is

Checkup 8

1. change calls his to call their
2. change has to have . . . its to their
3. change is to are
4. OK
5. change has to have . . . it to them
6. OK

Section 2.7

Checkup 1

1. first (L), realty (D), major (D), our (P)
2. special (D), new (D), these (DM), important (D)
3. two (L), well-known (C), this (DM), large (D), Brian's (P & PR)
4. two (L), her (P), older (D), this (DM), Atlanta (PR)
5. our (P), two-year (C), accurate (D), Harry's (P & PR)
6. Los Angeles (C & PR), that (DM), our (P), additional (D), Henderson's (P & PR)
7. Kelly's (P & PR), critical (D), new (D), East Coast (C & PR)
8. these (DM), tax-free (C), their (P), new (D)

Checkup 2

1. omit very
2. change the most to more
3. omit more
4. change largest to larger
5. omit very
6. change fuller to more nearly full
7. change more quiet to quieter . . . more big to bigger
8. OK

Checkup 3

1. change three time to three-time
2. change any to any other
3. change court appointed to court-appointed
4. change any to any other
5. change anyone to anyone else
6. change 15 minute question and answer to 15-minute question-and-answer
7. change word of mouth to word-of-mouth
8. OK
9. change any one to either
10. change one another to each other

Section 2.8

Checkup 1

1. CA
2. SC
3. SA, SA, CA
4. SA, SC
5. SC, SA
6. SC
7. SC, SA
8. SA, SA, SA, SA
9. SC, SA, SA
10. SA, CA, SA

Checkup 2

1. change some to somewhat
2. change real to really

3. OK
4. change sure to surely
5. change good to well
6. change angrily to angry
7. OK
8. change real to really
9. change badly to bad
10. OK

Section 2.9

Checkup 1

Prepositions are in *italics.*

1. *for* the delay; *on* the telephone
2. *of* the invoices; *on* my desk; *to* the Accounting Department
3. *of* the women; *with* the new schedule
4. *in* a rush; *to* the airport
5. *On* my desk
6. *Between* you and me; *in* that stock
7. *into* the conference room; *with* her assistant
8. *on* the site; *of* the midtown helicopter landing pad; *by* the planning board

Checkup 2

1. change at to with
2. change plans on opening to plans to open
3. OK
4. change in regards to to in regard to
5. OK
6. change than to from
7. change in to between
8. OK
9. change from to to
10. change to to with

Checkup 3

1. Omit at
2. Omit from
3. Omit to
4. OK
5. change in to into

6. Omit of
7. change between to among
8. change in to into
9. change besides to beside
10. Omit of
11. Omit of
12. Omit for

Section 2.10

Checkup 1

1. as soon as (subordinating)
2. While (subordinating)
3. both, and (correlative)
4. and (coordinating)
5. if (subordinating)
6. unless (subordinating)
7. whether, or (correlative)
8. that (subordinating)
9. either, or (correlative)
10. or (coordinating)

Checkup 2

1. change like to as if or as though
2. change without to unless or without signing
3. change and to but
4. change because to that
5. change which to who or that
6. change like to as if or as though
7. change without to unless
8. OK
9. change like to as if or as though
10. change except to unless

Checkup 3

1. change applying to apply
2. change to exercise to exercising
3. change have courtesy to courteous
4. change you can come in person to in person
5. change even immersible in water to even immersed in water
6. change a person who helps everyone to helpful to everyone

Checkup 4

1. change to either to either to
2. change either by to by either
3. change to ski to skiing
4. change neither went to to went neither to
5. change either given to given either
6. change has colored illustrations to colorfully illustrated

Chapter 3
Applying the Mechanics of Style

Section 3.1

Checkup 1

1. ?
2. .
3. .
4. .
5. .
6. .
7. .
8. ?

Checkup 2

1. change $125. to $125
2. change Inc.. to Inc.
3. change III. to III
4. OK
5. change $39.00 to $39
6. OK

Checkup 3

1. change strategies. We to strategies, we
2. change exhausted. He to exhausted, he
3. change opportunities, he to opportunities. He
4. change Tuesday, she to Tuesday. She

5. change <u>month, our</u> to <u>month. Our</u>
6. change <u>afternoon. When</u> to <u>afternoon when</u>
7. change <u>safe. Because</u> to <u>safe because</u>
8. change <u>workstations. Since</u> to <u>workstations since</u>

Checkup 4
1. change <u>ready?</u> to <u>ready.</u>
2. OK
3. change <u>he.</u> to <u>he?</u>
4. change <u>quickly?</u> to <u>quickly.</u>
5. change <u>they.</u> to <u>they?</u>
6. OK
7. change <u>report?</u> to <u>report.</u>
8. OK

Section 3.2

Checkup 1
1. change <u>week,</u> to <u>week;</u>
2. change <u>line,</u> to <u>line;</u>
3. change <u>projects,</u> to <u>projects;</u>
4. OK
5. change <u>informative,</u> to <u>informative;</u>
6. change <u>factory,</u> to <u>factory;</u>
7. change <u>month,</u> to <u>month;</u>
8. change <u>Printers,</u> to <u>Printers;</u>

Checkup 2
1. change <u>areas,</u> to <u>areas:</u>
2. change <u>follows:</u> to <u>follows.</u>
3. OK
4. OK
5. change <u>My</u> to <u>my</u>
6. change <u>use</u> to <u>Use</u>

Checkup 3
1. <u>galleries—</u>
2. <u>offer—</u>
3. <u>sample—</u>

4. <u>shape—</u>
5. <u>booklet—</u>

Checkup 4
1. change <u>isn't she—</u> to <u>isn't she?—</u>
2. OK
3. change <u>agree—</u> to <u>agree?—</u>
4. change <u>prices,—</u> to <u>prices—</u>
5. change <u>prize.—</u> to <u>prize—</u>
6. OK

Section 3.3

Checkup 1
1. omit comma after <u>offer</u>
2. change <u>Samantha,</u> to <u>Samantha;</u>
3. change <u>team</u> to <u>team,</u>
4. change <u>month</u> to <u>month,</u>
5. omit comma after <u>committee</u>
6. omit comma after <u>morning</u>
7. OK
8. OK

Checkup 2
1. omit <u>and</u> before <u>etc.</u>
2. omit comma between <u>Starr</u> and <u>&</u>
3. add comma after <u>etc.</u>
4. add comma after <u>agendas</u>
5. add semicolon after <u>messenger</u>
6. add comma after <u>Andrea</u>
7. change <u>advertising,</u> to <u>advertising;</u>
8. add comma after <u>train</u>

Checkup 3
1. add comma after <u>tomorrow</u>
2. add comma after <u>received</u>
3. omit comma after <u>printouts</u>
4. OK
5. add comma after <u>therefore</u>
6. add comma after <u>plan</u>
7. add comma after <u>cafeteria</u>
8. add comma after <u>days</u>

9. omit comma after <u>business</u>
10. change <u>approved moreover</u> to <u>approved, moreover,</u>

Checkup 4

1. omit commas after <u>recruiter</u> . . . <u>position</u>
2. add commas after <u>Anna</u> . . . <u>office</u>
3. add commas after <u>alternative</u> . . . <u>yesterday</u>
4. OK
5. omit commas after <u>attorney</u> . . . <u>consult</u>
6. add commas after <u>received</u> . . . <u>returned</u>
7. omit commas after <u>staff</u> . . . <u>CPA</u>
8. omit comma after <u>supplies</u>
9. add commas after <u>alternative</u> . . . <u>think</u>
10. OK

Checkup 5

1. add comma after <u>Salinger</u>
2. add commas after <u>Boise</u> and <u>Idaho</u>
3. change to <u>Preston Jr.</u> or <u>Preston, Jr.,</u>
4. change to <u>Givens, Inc.,</u> or <u>Givens Inc.</u>
5. add comma after <u>Barnes</u>
6. add comma after <u>1998</u>
7. add comma after <u>divisions</u> and <u>Chemicals</u>
8. add comma after <u>Texas</u>
9. change to <u>Blackstone, Inc.,</u> or <u>Blackstone Inc.</u>
10. OK

Checkup 6

1. add commas after <u>outlet</u> . . . <u>South</u>
2. omit comma after <u>products</u>
3. omit commas after <u>supplies</u> . . . <u>catalog</u>
4. add commas after <u>catalog</u> . . . <u>form</u>
5. omit comma after <u>office</u>
6. OK

Checkup 7

1. add commas after <u>brilliant</u> and <u>reliable</u>
2. OK
3. OK
4. add comma after <u>solid</u>
5. OK
6. add comma after <u>creative</u>

Checkup 8

1. add comma after <u>Doyle</u>
2. add comma after first <u>long</u>
3. add commas after <u>office</u> . . . <u>office</u>
4. add comma after first <u>risky</u>
5. OK
6. add comma after first <u>correct</u>

Checkup 9

1. add comma after <u>1995</u>
2. omit comma after <u>hours</u>
3. change <u>1,232</u> to <u>1232</u> and <u>1,336</u> to <u>1336</u>
4. omit comma in <u>4840</u>
5. OK
6. omit comma in <u>80876</u>
7. omit comma after <u>feet</u>
8. OK

Section 3.4

Checkup 1

1. change <u>11"</u> to <u>11,"</u>
2. change to <u>catalog,"</u> said Victor, "will
3. change to <u>session,"</u> announced Mr. Caruso, "because
4. change to <u>announced,</u> . . . <u>afternoon."</u>
5. omit quotation marks around <u>window of opportunity</u>
6. add quotation marks around "Fragile,"
7. add single quotation marks around 'Fragile.'"

8. add quotation marks around "Barbara Myers,"

Checkup 2
1. change to overstated";
2. change to models"?
3. change to Taken."
4. add quotation marks around "Waste not, want not"
5. OK
6. change to performers":
7. change to messenger!"
8. OK

Checkup 3
1. change to memorandum),
2. omit commas after Industries . . . Services")
3. change to 15.)
4. change to move)?
5. OK
6. change (We . . . so.) to (we . . . so)
7. add comma after photocopies)
8. OK

Section 3.5

Checkup 1
1. change to "Respectfully
2. change to Substantially
3. change to Always
4. change to Labor-Management Problems and How to
5. OK
6. change to Hard . . . Laser . . . Modems
7. change to Yes,
8. change to "Tips for Men and Women in . . . and

Checkup 2
1. change to Mexican
2. change to City

3. change to Von Spielmann . . . Serenity Inn . . . Lake George
4. change to "Women in Business: A Guide for
5. change to National Education Association . . . Building
6. change to Fourth of July . . . Hans von Hoffman
7. change to in Japan—An Up-to-Date
8. change to Monday . . . October . . . autumn

Checkup 3
1. change to Data-Processing Department
2. change to west
3. change to president
4. change to cars
5. change to Federal
6. change to supervisor . . . auditorium
7. OK
8. change to president
9. change to crackers
10. change to agency and coffee

Section 3.6

Checkup 1
1. omit Jr. after Mr. Bradley
2. change to Senator
3. OK
4. omit Dr. or M.D. (and commas before and after M.D.)
5. change to Mr.
6. omit Ms. or substitute Dr. and omit Ph.D. (along with the commas)

Checkup 2
1. change to UAW
2. change to a.m.
3. change to Tuesday, March 7,
4. change to centimeters
5. change to Minnesota,
6. change to pounds,

7. change to <u>New York</u> . . . <u>New Jersey</u>
   . . . <u>Rhode Island</u>
8. change to <u>Fort Myers, Florida,</u>

Section 3.7

Checkup 1
1. change to <u>eight</u>
2. change to <u>1970s,</u>
3. change to <u>one-third</u>
4. change to <u>Forty-seven</u> percent or
   <u>According to this survey, 47 percent</u>
5. OK
6. change to <u>3½</u> or <u>3.5</u>
7. change to <u>Sixteen</u> or <u>This morning, 16</u>
   applicants
8. change to <u>thousand</u>
9. OK
10. change to <u>seventeenth</u>-century

Checkup 2
1. OK [significant statistics]
2. change to <u>270</u>
3. change to <u>14</u>
4. change to <u>12th</u>
5. change to <u>$4 million</u>
6. change to <u>$495,</u>
7. OK
8. change to <u>8</u> and <u>9</u>

Checkup 3
1. change to <u>1</u>
2. change to <u>3</u> (for emphasis)
3. add comma after <u>15</u>
4. change to <u>5½</u> or <u>5.5</u> and <u>2</u>
5. OK
6. OK or 5th
7. OK
8. change to <u>10</u> and <u>12</u>

Chapter 4
Using Words Effectively

Section 4.3

Checkup 1
1. scraping
2. referring
3. OK
4. momentous
5. monkeys
6. filing
7. receipt
8. envious

Checkup 2
1. purpose
2. defendant
3. returnable
4. persuaded
5. OK
6. permanent

Checkup 3
1. conscientious
2. OK
3. beneficial
4. complexion
5. ambitious
6. anxious

Checkup 4
1. calendar
2. realtor
3. preceding
4. particles
5. realize
6. merchandise

APPENDIX

Abbreviations of States and Territories
of the United States

AL	Alabama	Ala.	MT	Montana	Mont.
AK	Alaska	. . .	NE	Nebraska	Nebr.
AZ	Arizona	Ariz.	NV	Nevada	Nev.
AR	Arkansas	Ark.	NH	New Hampshire	N.H.
CA	California	Calif.	NJ	New Jersey	N.J.
CO	Colorado	Colo.	NM	New Mexico	N. Mex.
CT	Connecticut	Conn.	NY	New York	N.Y.
DE	Delaware	Del.	NC	North Carolina	N.C.
DC	District of Columbia	D.C.	ND	North Dakota	N. Dak.
FM	Federated States of Micronesia	. . .	MP	Northern Mariana Islands	. . .
FL	Florida	Fla.	OH	Ohio	. . .
GA	Georgia	Ga.	OK	Oklahoma	Okla.
GU	Guam	. . .	OR	Oregon	Oreg.
HI	Hawaii	. . .	PW	Palau	. . .
ID	Idaho	. . .	PA	Pennsylvania	Pa.
IL	Illinois	Ill.	PR	Puerto Rico	P.R.
IN	Indiana	Ind.	RI	Rhode Island	R.I.
IA	Iowa	. . .	SC	South Carolina	S.C.
KS	Kansas	Kans.	SD	South Dakota	S. Dak.
KY	Kentucky	Ky.	TN	Tennessee	Tenn.
LA	Louisiana	La.	TX	Texas	Tex.
ME	Maine	. . .	UT	Utah	. . .
MH	Marshall Islands	. . .	VT	Vermont	Vt.
MD	Maryland	Md.	VI	Virgin Islands	V.I.
MA	Massachusetts	Mass.	VA	Virginia	Va.
MI	Michigan	Mich.	WA	Washington	Wash.
MN	Minnesota	Minn.	WV	West Virginia	W. Va.
MS	Mississippi	Miss.	WI	Wisconsin	Wis.
MO	Missouri	Mo.	WY	Wyoming	Wyo.

Use the two-letter abbreviations on the left when abbreviating state names in addresses. In any other situation that calls for abbreviations of state names, use the abbreviations on the right. Note that names of some states and territories have only the two-letter unpunctuated abbreviations.

CAPITALIZATION	Capitalize a letter	texas	Texas
	Lowercase a letter	This	this
	Capitalize all letters	Cobol	COBOL
	Lowercase a word	PROGRAM	program
	Use initial capital only	PROGRAM	Program
CHANGES AND TRANSPOSITIONS	Change a word	price is only $10.98 $12.99	price is only $12.99
	Change a letter	deductable	deductible
	Stet (do not make the change)	are price is only $10.98	price is only $10.98
	Spell out	2 cars on Washburn Rd.	two cars on Washburn Road
	Move as shown	on May 1 write him	write him on May 1
	Transpose letters or words	hte time the of meeting	the time of the meeting
DELETIONS	Delete a letter and close up	strooke or strooke	stroke or stroke
	Delete a word	wrote two two checks	wrote two checks
	Delete punctuation	report was up|to|date	report was up to date
	Delete one space*	good #day #	good day
	Delete space	see ing	seeing
INSERTIONS	Insert a word or letter	the in office buildng	in the office building
	Insert a comma	may leave early . . .	may leave early, . . .
	Insert a period	Dr Maria Rodriguez	Dr. Maria Rodriguez
	Insert an apostrophe	all the boys hats	all the boys' hats
	Insert quotation marks	Move on she said.	"Move on," she said.
	Insert hyphens	up to date report	up-to-date report
	Insert a dash	They were surprised – – even shocked!	They were surprised —even shocked!
	Insert parentheses	pay fifty dollars $50)	pay fifty dollars ($50)
	Insert one space	# mayleave	may leave
	Insert two spaces*	# 1.The new machine 2 #	1. The new machine

*Use marginal notes for clarification.

FORMAT SYMBOLS: BOLDFACE AND UNDERSCORE	Print boldface	<u>Bulletin</u>
	Remove boldface	<u>Bulletin</u>
	Underscore	<u>Title</u>
	Remove underscore	<u>Title</u>
FORMAT SYMBOLS: CENTERING	Center line horizontally	] TITLE [
FORMAT SYMBOLS: PAGE AND PARAGRAPH	Begin a new page	*pg* . . . order was delivered today by common carrier. We have all the . . .
	Begin a new paragraph	. . . order was delivered today by common carrier. We have all the . . .
	Do not begin new paragraph (run in)	. . . order was delivered today by common carrier. *No ¶* We have all the materials . . .
	Indent five spaces	*5* We have the raw materials in our warehouse. Production will . . .
FORMAT SYMBOLS: SPACING	Single-space	*ss* ⎡ XXXXXXXXXX ⎣ XXXXXXXXXX
	Double-space	*ds* ⎡ XXXXXXXXXX ⎣ XXXXXXXXXX
	Triple—space	*ts* ⎡ XXXXXXXXXX ⎣ XXXXXXXXXX

References

If you wish to keep up to date on the subject of business communication, you should consult professional journals both in business and in communication. In addition, some of the following books may be of interest:

Flower, Linda, *Problem-Solving Strategies for Writing*, 3d ed., Harcourt Brace Jovanovich, Orlando, Fla., 1989.

Hildebrandt, Herbert W. (ed.), *International Business Communication: Theory, Practice, Teaching Throughout the World*, Univ. of Michigan Press, Ann Arbor, 1984.

Pfaffenberger, Bryan, *Business Communication in the Personal Computer Age*, Irwin, Homewood, Ill., 1987.

Sides, Charles H. (ed.), *Technical and Business Communication: Bibliographic Essays for Teachers and Corporate Trainers*, National Council of Teachers of English, Urbana, Ill., 1989.

Tebeaux, Elizabeth, *Design of Business Communications: The Process and the Product*, Macmillan, New York, 1990.

One of the most frequent errors beginning office workers make is not consulting reference sources when in doubt about facts, spelling, or usage. Often, beginning workers have not been exposed to the many types of reference books available. Many of the following books will be available in the school library or, better yet, in the classroom.

The American Heritage Dictionary of the English Language, Houghton Mifflin, Boston.

Amy Vanderbilt's Complete Book of Etiquette, Doubleday, Garden City, N.Y.

Bartlett, John, *Bartlett's Familiar Quotations*, Little, Brown, Boston.

Bernstein, Theodore, *The Careful Writer: A Modern Guide to English Usage*, Atheneum, New York.

Camp, Sue C., *Developing Editing Skill*, Glencoe Division of Macmillan/McGraw-Hill, Columbus, Ohio.

Camp, Sue C., *Developing Proofreading Skill*, Glencoe Division of Macmillan/McGraw-Hill, Columbus, Ohio.

Fowler, H. W., *A Dictionary of Modern English Usage*, Oxford Univ. Press, New York.

Nicholson, Margaret, *A Dictionary of American-English Usage*, Oxford Univ. Press, New York.

Robert's Rules of Order, Jove Publications, New York.

Roget's International Thesaurus, Thomas Y. Crowell, New York.

Sabin, William A., *The Gregg Reference Manual*, Glencoe Division of Macmillan/McGraw-Hill, Columbus, Ohio.

Strunk, William, Jr., and E. B. White, *The Elements of Style*, Macmillan, New York.

Webster's Ninth New Collegiate Dictionary, Merriam-Webster, Springfield, Mass.

Webster's Third New International Dictionary, Merriam-Webster, Springfield, Mass.

The World Almanac & Book of Facts, Doubleday, New York. (Annual Publication.)

Zoubek, Charles E., and Mary Margaret Hosler, *20,000+ Words*, Glencoe Division of Macmillan/McGraw-Hill, Columbus, Ohio.

Note: Since these books are revised frequently, the edition numbers and dates of publication have not been given. Ask for the latest edition.

INDEX

College placement centers, 520–21
Colon, 144–46, 172
    capitalizing first word after, 180
    dashes vs., 145–46
    at end of quotation, 173
Color coding, 307
Columns, using, 307
Comma-for-period fault, 136
Commas, 151–67
    before abbreviations after personal names, 190
    with appositives, 160–61
    with calendar dates, 162
    in compound sentences, 152–53
    between consecutive numbers, 203
    with degrees, titles, and other explanatory terms, 161
    in direct address, 165
    at end of quotation, 172, 173
    with explanatory elements, 159–60
    following introductory words, phrases, and clauses, 156–58
    with interrupting elements, 159
    with modifying adjectives, 164
    in numbers and between unrelated numbers, 166
    for omissions, 165
    with parenthetic elements, 159
    pitfalls with, 163, 166
    with repeated expressions, 165
    separating subject from predicate, 163
    separating verb from object, 163
    in series, 154–55
    with state names, 162
    with subordinate clause following main clause, 158–59
    in weights, capacities, and measurements, 166
    in *which* and *that* clauses, 162–63
Common-gender nouns, 84
Communication
    business, 14–19
    components of, 3–4
    defined, 2
    factors influencing, 4–6
    interpersonal skills, developing, 6–8
    means of, 4
    purposes of, 2
    types of, 3, 17
Communication breakdowns, avoiding, 4
Communication skills, 9–13
    business, 16–19
    career advancement and, 544–45
    combining, for effectiveness, 11–13

Communication skills (*continued*)
    roles of, 9–11
    of sender and receiver, 5–6
Communications networks, 449
Company letterhead, 320, 387; *illus.*, 321
Company names, 155, 161, 191–92
Company recognition, congratulations letters for, 393
Company signature, 322
Comparative degree, 96, 97, 104
Comparison(s)
    balancing, 268
    double, 97
    as introduction in speech, 508
Comparison adjectives, 96–99
Comparison adverbs, 104
Complaints, handling telephone, 491
Complete message, 295
Compliment, paying a, 486
Complimentary closing, 248–49, 322
Compound adjectives, 95, 99
Compound nouns, 55–56, 65
Compound objects, pronouns in, 76, 77
Compound sentence, punctuating, 142–43, 152–53
Compound subject, 33–34
    predicate agreement with, 88–90
    pronouns in, 76, 77
Comprehension, reading, 240–41
Computers
    editing on, 296–98
    electronic office, communicating in, 445–51
    proofreading on, 289–90
    See also Word processing
Conciseness, 295, 332–33, 412, 486, 502
Conclusion
    to formal report, 427–28
    of speech, 509–10
Condensed expressions, punctuating, 136
Condolence letters, 395–96
Conferences. *See* Meeting(s)
Confidence in giving speeches, 510–11
Congratulations letters, 387–93
Conjunctions, 26, 122–29
    balancing, 270
    coordinating, 123, 127
    correlative, 123–24, 128
    omission of, semicolon to indicate, 142
    parallel structure and, 127–28
    pitfalls with, 125–26
    repeated, in series, 155
    so and *and so* faults, 266–67

Punctuation (*continued*)
    semicolons, 142–43, 144, 145–46, 153, 154, 173
    in social-business letter format, 387
Purchasing, oral communications in, 455

Question marks, 137–38, 173
Questions
    direct, 137
    in employment interview, 535, 536–37
    indirect, 134
    punctuating, 137–38
    requests phrased as, 133–34
    verb phrase in, 41
    who, whom in, 74
Quotation(s)
    direct, 170, 180
    indirect, 170
    as introduction in speech, 508
    punctuation at end of, 172–73
    within quotations, 170–71
Quotation marks, 169, 170–74

Radio and TV interviews, 491
raise, rise, 49–52
Reading of speech, avoiding, 512–13
Reading skill, 10, 11, 12, 13, 238–41
    adjustment to material and purpose, 239
    assessing one's, 238–39
    in business, 18
    comprehension, 240–41
    improving, 239–41
    speed, 239–40
real, really, 108
Reasonableness, 338–41, 357–58
Receiver, 3, 5–6, 7, 9. *See also* Audience
Receiving the public, 487–89
Recommendations
    on formal reports, 427–28
    thank-you letters for, 395
Recorder of meeting, 500
Records, meeting, 434–39
Redundancy, eliminating, 332
Reference initials, 322
Reference materials, 208–15, 225
    dictionary, 208–12, 215, 225–26, 284; *illus.,* 207, 211
    electronic reference tools, 212–13
    thesaurus, 213–15, 226, 284; *illus.,* 214
    for writing reports, 420

References (directions), parentheses for enclosing, 174
References with résumé, 523–25, 536; *illus.,* 526
Referrals, application letter following up on, 528
Reflexive use of pronouns ending in *self,* 78–79
regard, regards, 116
Relative-pronoun clauses, 90, 125, 162–63, 256–57
Repetition(s)
    avoiding unnecessary, 284, 295
    of modifier, 98–99
    planned, 264–65
    punctuating, 146, 165
Reply copy, 250
Reports
    choosing title of, 282–83
    formal, 418–34
    informal, 409–17
    minutes of meeting, 434–38; *illus.,* 436–37
    oral, 409
    purpose of, 281
    technical, 419
Requests, 336–51
    answering, 341–51, 413; *illus.,* 344, 348, 349
    phrased as questions, 133–34
    writing, 336–41; *illus.,* 337, 339, 340
    See also Letter(s)
Resigning from job, 543–44
Résumé, 522–25, 536; *illus.,* 524, 526
Retirement, congratulation letters for, 393
Return slip or card, 250; *illus.,* 251
Revisions, 280–85
    editing, 294–99
rise, raise, 49–52
Robert's Rules of Order, 499
Roget's International Thesaurus, 213
Roman numerals, punctuating, 134
Routing slips, 313; *illus.,* 314

Sales, role of oral communication in, 454
Sales appeals, 370
Sales letters, 365–71
    application letter as, 525–30
Sales techniques, indirect, 345–46
Salutation, 180, 322, 387
Security needs, 7
self, pronouns ending in, 78–80
Self-actualization needs, 7
Semicolons, 142–43, 173
    colons vs., 144
    in compound sentence, 153